D0085132

Food Around the World

A Cultural Perspective

Second Edition

Margaret McWilliams, PhD.
Professor Emerita
California State University, Los Angeles

Upper Saddle River, New Jersey 07458

Library of Congress Cataloging-in-Publication Data

McWilliams, Margaret.
Food around the world : a cultural perspective / Margaret McWilliams.—2nd ed.
p. cm.
Includes bibliographical references and index.
ISBN 0-13-193639-5 (alk. paper)
1. Food. 2. Cookery, International. I. Title.
TX353.M396 2003
641.3—dc22

2006016923

Editor-in-Chief: Vernon R. Anthony
Assistant Editor: Maria Rego
Editorial Assistant: ReeAnne Davies
Director of Manufacturing and Production: Bruce Johnson
Managing Editor: Mary Carnis
Production Liaison: Janice Stangel
Production Management: Pine Tree Composition, Inc.
Production Editor: Bruce Hobart
Manufacturing Manager: Ilene Sanford
Manufacturing Buyer: Cathleen Petersen
Senior Design Coordinator: Miguel Ortiz
Interior Design: Pine Tree Composition, Inc.
Printer/Binder: Von Hoffmann
Cover Designer: Marianne Frasco
Cover Image: Aurora & Quanta Productions, Inc./
Photographer: Chris Anderson
Executive Marketing Manager: Ryan DeGrote
Senior Marketing Coordinator: Elizabeth Farrell
Marketing Assistant: Les Roberts

Credits and acknowledgments borrowed from other sources and reproduced, with permission in this textbook, appear on the appropriate pages. All photos are by Margaret McWilliams unless otherwise noted.

Pearson Education LTD.
Pearson Education Australia PTY, Limited
Pearson Education Singapore, Pte. Ltd
Pearson Education North Asia Ltd
Pearson Education Canada, Ltd.
Pearson Educación de Mexico, S.A. de C.V.
Pearson Education — Japan
Pearson Education Malaysia, Pte. Ltd

10 9 8 7 6 5 4 3 2 1
ISBN 0-13-193639-5

Brief Contents

Contents

Preface

The world is a very different place than it was pre 9/11 when the first edition of this book was written, yet the traditions of eating and the pleasures of family and friends continue to provide a center in each of our lives. Perhaps these traditions and pleasures are even more important to us today than in years past. Certainly, the cultural mix we have in the United States is becoming ever more varied and exciting with the arrival of new immigrants.

No matter where we grow up and live, eating is one of the most personal experiences of life. We all find pleasure and comfort in eating foods associated with our childhood and heritage, but personal perspectives on eating and what is good to eat are only part of the global picture. With the remarkable increase in diversity within the U.S. population, we all need to learn more about the cultural backgrounds, geographic parameters, and social and economic factors that have shaped other nations and the people who have emigrated from them to the United States. Better relationships between individuals, within schools, and throughout communities and the nation begin with people learning about each other, what they value, and what they seek. Food preferences and eating habits provide a fascinating and very approachable avenue for promoting understanding between all of us.

Each of us is a member of (or soon will become a part of) a minority in the United States, but most of us have much to learn about the foods preferred by people in different subgroups within our increasingly polycultural nation. This book will help you gain a broader knowledge of what people eat around the world; the text is based on the assumption that what people eat is shaped over the centuries by geographic, historical, cultural, and economic factors. The reader will develop a broader understanding and appreciation of the cultural uniqueness as well as the food patterns in nations around the world. Numerous photographs, maps, and recipes will help you visualize and sample the actual heritage of new immigrants and other people whose ancestors came from abroad.

In recognition of the several religions discussed in this book and the influences they have imparted to food patterns, the dating system used is BCE (before the common era) and CE (common era) rather than the traditional BC. Also, some of the recipes have been slightly modified to simplify the problems of finding particularly exotic ingredients without sacrificing the character of the dishes. Changes have not been made to accommodate the typical palate of U.S. diners.

As you explore the world and its foods in these chapters, new images and a spirit of adventure about the world of food will develop. Knowledge of cultural food preferences is particularly important for dietitians, nutritionists, and food technologists so they will succeed in meeting the challenges of helping people from cultures other than their own achieve healthy and satisfying food patterns in this country. Regardless of your professional goals, you will perhaps find that you are willing to experience a broader range of foods by the time you finish this book. You may picture the romantic days of the Mughals the next time you dine at an Indian restaurant, or perhaps have images of the Ming Dynasty as you feast on Chinese food. The possibilities could go on and on. When you finish this book, you will be acquainted with the many cultures around the world and their foods.

This edition has been changed to include definitions in the margins; selected Web sites; extensive revisions of Chapters 1, 2, and 23; increased emphasis on regional foods in some countries, and an expanded examination of food patterns and influences in the United States.

Now it is time to grab your imaginary passport and journey around the world through the pages of this book. Bon voyage!

Acknowledgments

A special thank you goes to Dr. Antoinette Empringham for her perceptive comments and careful attention to detail that have been so helpful to me throughout the preparation and production of this edition. Patricia Chavez has also contributed a good many hours to help catch the inevitable errors that would have dropped into this book during production if her sharp eyes had not been reading the proofs.

It has been a real pleasure working with Vernon Anthony over the years that he has been my editor; "thank you" is barely adequate to say how much I have appreciated his patience, support, and encouragement.

I want to thank Adele Kupchik, my e-mail friend from Prentice Hall, for her recipes (pierogi, stuffed cabbage, barscz, and kapusta) and helpful information about Polish cooking. Elsa Ramirez Brisson also merits special thanks for her insight and suggestions on Mexican and Mexican-American foods.

A grateful note of appreciation must surely include my friends who traveled with me on various trips to get pictures and information for this book: Doris Riehm (who has suffered through countless photo sessions in exotic food markets and meals on many of the trips pictured in this edition), Ruth MacFarlane (who contributed some of her pictures from our travels together), Holly Heller, Diane Packard, and Esther Blackburn—who cheerfully endured picture taking before eating their meals and watched out for me while I wandered in search of pictures in questionable spots.

I am particularly appreciative of my very helpful reviewers: Jonathan Deutsch, Kingsborough Community College; Charles A. Baker-Clark, Grand Valley State University; Jane Masse, Elizabethtown Community & Technical College; Suzy Weems, Stephen F. Austin State University; and Jeffrey Yourdon, Lenoir Community College.

Margaret McWilliams
Redondo Beach, California

Food Around the World

Margaret McWilliams, PhD.

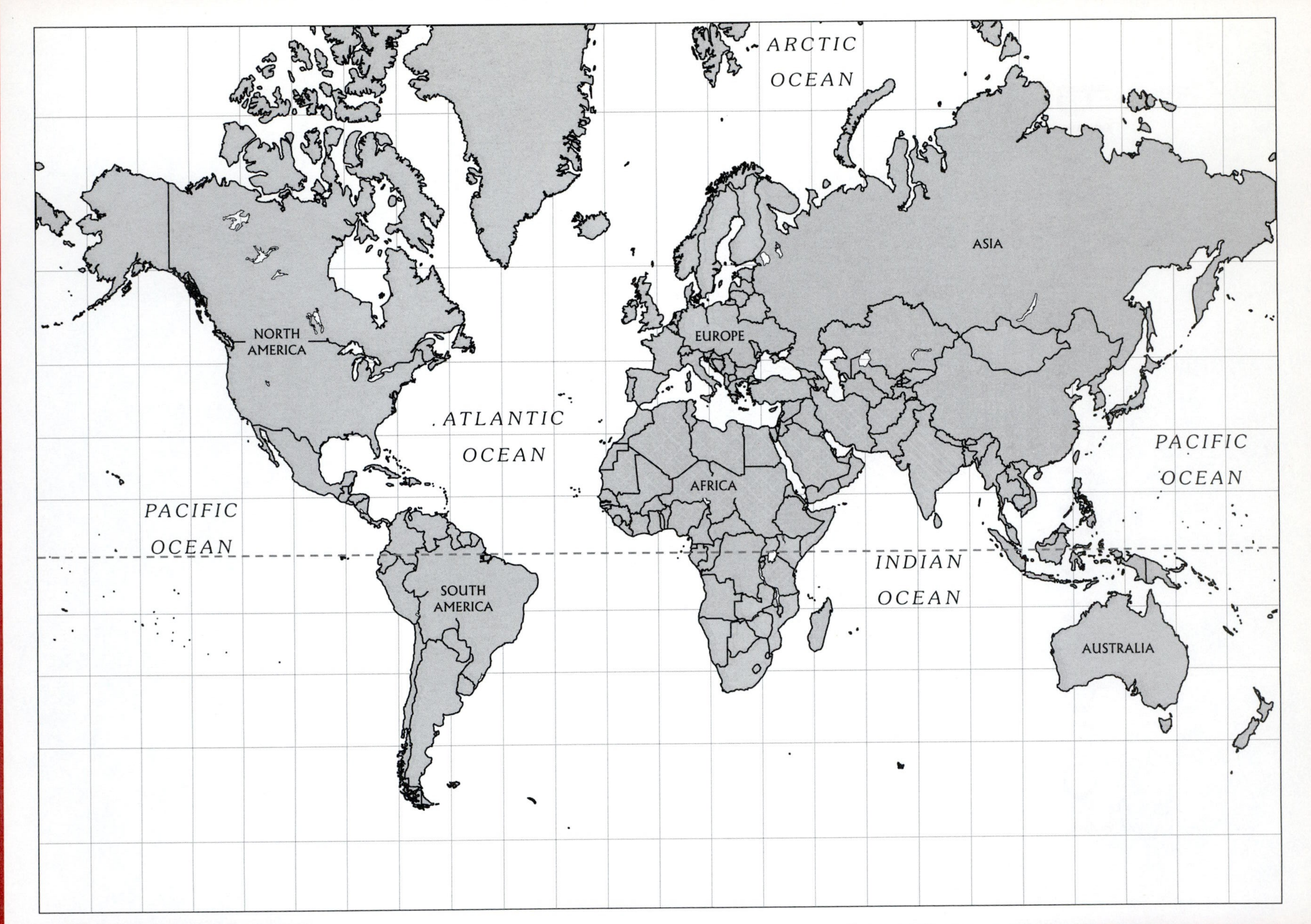
ARCTIC OCEAN
NORTH AMERICA
EUROPE
ASIA
ATLANTIC OCEAN
PACIFIC OCEAN
AFRICA
PACIFIC OCEAN
INDIAN OCEAN
SOUTH AMERICA
AUSTRALIA

Part I

Influences on Food Around the World

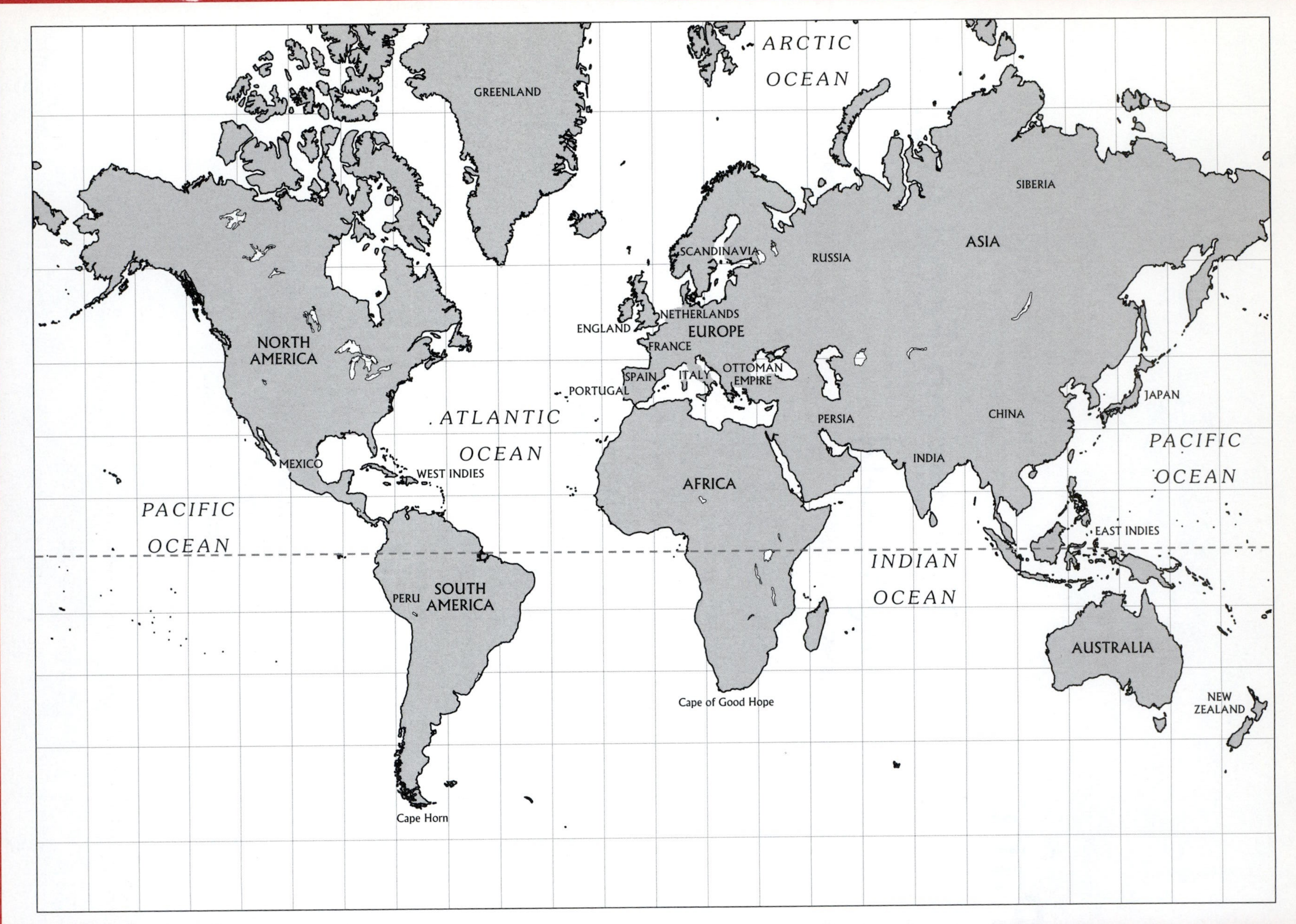
ARCTIC OCEAN
GREENLAND
NORTH AMERICA
MEXICO
WEST INDIES
ATLANTIC OCEAN
PACIFIC OCEAN
SOUTH AMERICA
PERU
Cape Horn
ENGLAND
NETHERLANDS
EUROPE
FRANCE
PORTUGAL
SPAIN
ITALY
OTTOMAN EMPIRE
SCANDINAVIA
RUSSIA
AFRICA
Cape of Good Hope
PERSIA
ASIA
SIBERIA
CHINA
INDIA
JAPAN
PACIFIC OCEAN
EAST INDIES
INDIAN OCEAN
AUSTRALIA
NEW ZEALAND

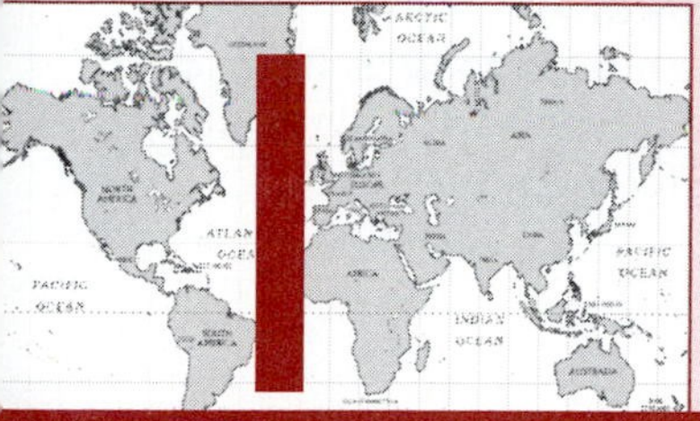

Introduction

Have you ever wondered why you eat the foods you do or why certain foods are your favorites? If you compare your food choices and preferences with those of other students, you may find some major differences. Most people enjoy eating, but what they choose varies widely, whether they are living in this country or some other part of the world. The reasons for these differences can be traced to many factors including place of birth, cultural heritage, individual preferences, and income.

This book examines cuisines in countries and regions around the world and focuses on the geographic, cultural, and historic influences that shaped these food patterns. The geographic origins of foods determined the diets of early people because they had to survive on whatever they could find to eat in their immediate environment. Development of farming practices (crops and domesticated animals) over many centuries resulted in a more reliable food supply. As foods became cultivated and plentiful, various cultures evolved in distant places, and special food patterns and preferences began to play an important role in celebrations and religions, as well as in daily living.

Travel, conquests, and migrations gradually expanded human knowledge and experiences. Exciting tales of such travelers as Marco Polo introduced ideas and evidence of different cultures from distant places. Discoveries included new foods, some of which could be traded and transported to other people and places. Even today, the global economy is continuing to expand knowledge of food from other cultures as new foods from afar appear in our markets and on menus.

Food Origins

Early Food Habits

Early people's food habits derived strictly from what was available in the near environment. Hunter-gatherers were restricted to the particular plants and prey indigenous to where they lived. Survival was the driving force that determined what was eaten. Archaeologists have been able to identify some of the foods eaten by the people who lived at the sites being studied, although many food samples have been destroyed by time (Figure 1.1).

Geographic features of their immediate environment determined significantly what foods were available to early people. If they were living in an area next to an ocean, the possibility of food from the sea was a nourishing, if challenging, prospect. Similarly, some people were fortunate enough to live near a lake or a stream where they could catch fish to eat. Civilizations with access to either fresh or salt water fishing developed dietary patterns in which fish played a very prominent role. Evidence of shellfish being used as human food as far back as 127,000 years ago has been found in southern Africa. Some early cave paintings indicate that hunting was another way of acquiring food (Figure 1.2).

In Leviticus, Chapter 11, permission for eating some insects is stated: "Even these of them ye may eat; the locust after his kind, and the beetle after his kind, and the grasshopper after his kind." Even today, various insects are popular as food among people in some parts of the world, sometimes being fried or roasted to add flavor.

Agricultural Developments

Civilizations that flourished in temperate river valleys were able to grow wheat or other cereal and vegetable crops. They also were able to domesticate animals, which were allowed to graze or were fed portions of the crops reserved for that purpose. Central Europeans developed this type of agriculture, and their dietary patterns took on quite a different character from the Japanese and others around the world living near the sea.

Around 12,000 BCE, people in Upper Egypt and Nubia were using grindstones to make flour from wild grasses (Chart 1). In Palestine, wild **emmer** (wheat) was being harvested by 10,000 BCE, and **einkorn** (a type of wheat) was eaten in Syria by 9000 BCE. Wheat, barley, and pulses (legumes) were cultivated around Jericho and in the favorable locales from Syria to Mesopotamia and Egypt by 8000 BCE. Sheep were domesticated to add to the diet in this region (Table 1.1). Before 7000 BCE, goats and pigs were domesticated as sources of meat from Anatolia (now southern Turkey) as far east as Pakistan.

Emmer—An early type of wheat farmed in Palestine by 10,000 BCE.

Einkorn—A type of wheat grown in Syria around 9000 BCE.

Barley became a food crop in India, and farming was developing in the region between the Indus River and the Baluchistan Hills around 7000 BCE. **Taro**

Barley—Cereal grain suitable for human and animal diets.

Taro—Starchy root vegetable that thrives in tropical climates.

Figure 1.1 The immediate environment was early man's only source of food.

Figure 1.2 Painting from the wall of a cave in southern Libya depicts scenes of hunting.

Table 1.1 Foods by Hemisphere of Origin

Eastern Hemisphere	*Western Hemisphere*
	Cereals
Barley	Amaranth
Buckwheat	Corn
Rice	Quinoa
Rye	Wild rice
Wheat	
	Vegetables
Beet	Peppers
Broccoli	Pumpkin
Cabbage	Squashes
Carrot	Tomato
Cauliflower	Beans
Onion	Dry legumes
Pea	Peanuts
Soybean	Potato
	Fruits
Banana	Avocado
Breadfruit	Blue-, straw-, raspberries
Cherry	Cherimoya
Kiwi	Grapefruit
Citrus	Papaya
Mango	Passion fruit
Pear	Pineapple
	Plum
	Other
Almond	Arrowroot
Cashew	Chocolate
Dairy	Tea
Eggs	Macadamia nuts
Mushrooms	Pecans
Spices	
Sugarcane	

Chart 1 Time Line—Food

12,000 BCE	Flour from wild grasses—Egypt
10,000 BCE	Emmer (type of wheat)—Palestine
9000 BCE	Einkhorn (type of wheat)—Syria
8000 BCE	Wheat, barley, pulses (legumes)—Syria, Mesopotamia, Egypt Sheep domesticated—Middle East
7000 BCE	Goats and pigs domesticated—Turkey to Pakistan Barley—India Taro—New Guinea Fermented beverage—China
6500 BCE	Goats and sheep domesticated, cereals—Balkans
6200 BCE	Farming—Western Europe, Mediterranean lands
6000 BCE	Farming—Mesopotamia, China Potatoes—Peru
5000 BCE	Wet rice farming—Eastern China Maize—Mexico Irrigation—Mesopotamia
4500 BCE	Cattle used for plowing—lower Danube
3500 BCE	Cattle used for plowing and milk, sheep for wool—Europe
3000 BCE	Millet—Korea
500 BCE	Wet rice farming—Japan
300 BCE	Rice traded from China to Mediterranean and North Africa
200 BCE	Water buffalo used as draft animals—Southeast Asia
1493 CE	Maize transported to Spain from Mexico
1500 CE	Tomatoes and sweet potatoes traded from Central America
1520 CE	Chocolate from New World to Europe
1522 CE	Spices from Southeast Asia brought to Europe (Magellan's ship)
1600 CE	Potatoes traded from South America to Europe, Africa, and India
1850 CE	Palm oil traded from Africa to North and South America and Southeast Asia

Manioc—Inclusive name for group of related tropical plants native to the Western Hemisphere that had fleshy roots rich in starch.

was a cultivated crop in New Guinea by 7000 BCE, approximately the same time **manioc** was being grown in the upper region of the Amazon in South America.

Domestication of goats and sheep and the raising of cereal crops had spread into the Balkans from Anatolia by approximately 6500 BCE. By 6000 BCE, farming was established in central Mesopotamia and China, and Peruvians in South America were raising potatoes. Around 6200 BCE, farming was extending into Western Europe and along the Mediterranean Sea, but use of cattle for plowing did not begin until around 4500 BCE near the lower Danube. Use of animals for milk and wool did not occur in Europe until about 3500 BCE, at which time the plow was introduced in western and northern areas of Europe.

Around 5000 BCE, wet rice farming was being carried on in eastern China, maize was being cultivated in Mexico, and irrigation was being developed as an aid to farming in Mesopotamia. Millet began to be cultivated in Korea about 3000 BCE. Wet rice farming was not begun in Japan until 500 BCE. Water buffalo began to be used as draft animals in Southeast Asia in approximately 200 BCE.

Influences Determining Diets

Geography

Topography was a geographic dimension that influenced agricultural land use. Mountainous regions were inhospitable settings for early people. The rugged terrain made agriculture virtually impossible, and the extreme cold due to the high elevations added to the hazards of attempting to live in the upper elevations of the Alps, the Hindu Kush, and the Himalayas.

Lower valleys in the mountains could be used for grazing animals in the summer, but the mountains were not the regions where early civilizations developed. Extremely steep slopes were appropriate only for raising goats or perhaps sheep. On the other hand, gently rolling or flat lands were well suited to growing a variety of crops. Some regions required labor-intensive terracing for crops or animal husbandry efforts to produce food.

The land available for habitation by people on the earth was limited. About 80 percent of the world was covered by oceans. Mountain ranges restricted use of large parts of Asia and South America plus many regions in Europe and North America.

Civilizations based on farming in early times were established where the land was fertile enough for good crops to be raised. The region in Mesopotamia where early civilization and agriculture flourished in the valleys of the Tigris and Euphrates rivers was dubbed the "Fertile Crescent" by historians, a name clearly reflecting the importance of rich farmland with water and weather suited to raising crops to eat.

Environmental Factors

Water Several environmental factors determined the feasibility of early farmers growing a crop in a particular location. Adequate moisture, but not too much, was vital to a crop. In contrast to Mesopotamia's favorable weather, the climate of approximately the northern half of Asia was not only dry and arid, but also severely cold in winter due to its northern latitude and some high elevations. Northern China was dry, but southern China had a wet, tropical climate. Northern Africa had a very hot, dry climate, with the Sahara Desert occupying a huge area where crops could not be grown (Figure 1.3). Western Asia was rather desert-like, especially the Arabian Peninsula and portions of the western interior. Europe and the eastern half of North America had moderate climates more amenable to a wider variety of agricultural products than could be produced in desert lands.

Figure 1.3 The Sahara Desert that covers a large area of North Africa is unsuited for growing crops because of the intense heat and lack of water.

Farmers today are still battling the problems of drought and temperatures that kill their crops. Africa has regions (e.g., Niger, Malawi, Zambia, and Zimbabwe) that are affected particularly hard by weather problems. Millions have died and many more will die in famines caused by crop failures. Natural disasters (earthquakes and floods) create serious food shortages that lead to many deaths unless food aid reaches survivors. Political corruption and problems with food distribution in times of famine are other factors that compound the deaths.

Natural rainfall has been adequate for growing many crops around the world, and this reliance on nature influenced the early crops that were raised in various regions. For instance, rice was the staple grain for centuries in the monsoonal areas of the world, from India to Japan, while wheat was the favored grain crop in farm areas that received moderate amounts of rain.

Early people living in rice-growing areas did not eat wheat because it did not grow well in such wet conditions. It did thrive in Europe, Asia, and the northern part of China, where it was the staple cereal in the diet. These contrasts illustrate how rainfall influenced the diets of people long ago in different regions, particularly before trade developed between regions.

In some parts of the world, rainfall was adequate most seasons for early people to raise a crop while in more arid regions, irrigation was required for crops to flourish. This necessitated building a functional irrigation system with an adequate supply of water if farmers were to be successful (Figure 1.4). In other regions of the world, early farmers faced failure of crops when they were inundated with rainfall to the point where fields were flooded and crops were washed away.

The need to control water for crops has been addressed for centuries in various parts of the world. Long ago, farmers terraced the steep hillsides of Bali to create rice paddies that have been maintained and utilized for centuries (Figure 1.5). In much of Southeast Asia, water is directed into and out of rice paddies as is necessary to plant and eventually harvest rice in the paddies throughout the year.

Irrigation systems were developed in Mesopotamia around 5000 BCE so crops could be watered using water from the Tigris and Euphrates as necessary, regardless of droughts. Much later in Europe, the Romans engineered and constructed aqueducts to transport water long distances to meet the needs of people and agriculture in parts of the Roman Empire where the local water supply was inadequate.

Growing Conditions Temperature was a key determinant of crop successes. An early illustration of this geographic factor is that oranges and dates (Figure 1.6) were successful crops in the warm climates at the eastern end of the Mediter-

Figure 1.4 Although Egypt is situated in the Sahara Desert, irrigation using waters from the Nile River has made it possible for farmers to raise crops in the Nile Valley for thousands of years. (Photo courtesy of Ruth MacFarlane.)

Figure 1.5 People have built and maintained elaborate terraces so they could control the water needed to raise rice successfully on the steep hills of Bali.

ranean Sea, but they were unknown to the Norsemen, whose climate was far too severe for citrus and dates to survive. Similarly, the tropical fruits of Southeast Asia could not withstand the cold winters in Beijing, China.

The length of the growing season (the number of days at temperatures warm enough for active growth) also determined whether or not a crop could be grown in a particular location. For example, corn requires a growing season of at least 140 days to mature. Countries at very high or very low latitudes did not have enough warm days for corn to mature. Vegetables requiring a comparatively short growing season to reach maturity could be grown in such northern latitudes as Alaska with surprising results because of almost continuous daylight in the height of summer.

Successes in raising livestock and crops supported earth's early population growth in places where climate and terrain were favorable (Figure 1.7a, b). Lives of these early people were gradually evolving beyond the basic pursuit of food for mere survival. In fact, evidence suggests that a fermented beverage was produced in northern China around 7000 BCE, which is far earlier than a similar drink from 5400 BCE that was found in Iran.

Trade At several points around the world, pockets of rather sophisticated cultures emerged. These civilizations began to create riches that sometimes resulted in the exchange of goods. Trade routes such as the Silk Route across Asia were developed over land; sea captains ventured around Africa to destinations in the Indian Ocean. As a result, food and other goods were carried to and from new

Figure 1.6 Date palms thrive at oases in North Africa, providing a food that can easily be dried and stored safely in the hot climate there.

Figure 1.7a Nomads on the plains in Iran still herd goats, a heritage that began many centuries ago.

Figure 1.7b Rainfall in Baja, California barely supports enough plant growth to feed a few cattle. (Photo courtesy of Jim Bull.)

markets, thus adding some variety to foods and flavors enjoyed by people over vast distances.

Sometimes envious and aggressive leaders mounted military attacks to plunder such territories and to build empires at the expense of the conquered. Selected illustrations of these developments that ultimately led to today's expanded food experiences are presented in the next section.

A Capsule of Cultures and Conquests

Early Cultural Sites

Egypt is likely to be the first early culture that comes to mind (Figure 1.8), for the dramatic temples and pyramids built by early Egyptians more than 4,000 years ago remain as testimonials to these people (Chart 2). They controlled land along the eastern end of the Mediterranean Sea and the northeastern corner of Africa as far south as the Sudan before they began to be conquered by various invaders.

The lands to the north of the Persian Gulf also fostered the development of cultures. Sumerians came south from Persia around 2000 BCE. Their contemporaries, the Hittites, who were flourishing in the Anatolian region that is now Asian Turkey, conquered Sumeria's Babylon and ruled Syria as well for four centuries, until 1200 BCE. Assyrians, the next group to conquer the region, ruled until the Persians took Nineveh in 612 BCE.

Meanwhile, Chinese culture was developing and flourishing on the eastern edge of Asia as early as 1800 BCE during the Shang dynasty. In contrast to the history of many other parts of the world, China has continued over many centuries as its own political unit, except for the Mongol incursion from 1280 CE to about 1350 CE. The ruling sequence after the Shang period included the Chou, Ch'in, Han, Sung, Ming, and Ch'ing dynasties.

In the western hemisphere, enduring evidence of the early culture of the Olmecs, who lived along the Gulf of Mexico in what is now Mexico and in Central America, dates from 1200 BCE for almost 1,000 years. They peacefully coexisted near Oaxaca with the Zapotecs, who also left enduring ruins as evidence of their culture around 500 BCE.

Figure 1.8 This giant stone sculpture of Rameses II is but one of several statues in his honor that can still be seen today at Luxor Temple on the east bank of the Nile in Luxor, Egypt.

Conquests and Empires

Achaemenid Empire—Empire that extended from the eastern end of the Mediterranean eastward to central Asia, then southward to northern India and the Persian Gulf (also called the Persian Empire); conquered in 331 BCE by Alexander the Great.

Cultural centers developed at various points around the world during the two millennia prior to the birth of Christ, but these tended to be isolated from each other. However, geographical barriers eventually began to be breeched, and knowledge of other groups led to the desire for conquest and possible riches. When conquerors established themselves by settling among the conquered for extended periods, considerable sharing of such aspects as foods and arts of both cultures resulted in lasting changes, many of which are still evident today.

The Achaemenid Empire The Persians conquered a vast empire by the 6th century BCE. The **Achaemenid Empire,** also called the Persian Empire, included

Chart 2 Time Line—Cultures

3000 BCE	Egypt
2000 BCE	Sumerians (Persia)
2000 BCE–1200 BCE	Hittites (Turkey, Babylon, Syria)
1800 BCE–1280 CE	Chinese dynasties (China)
?–1625 BCE	Minoan (Crete in Mediterranean Sea)
1500 BCE–1100 BCE	Myceneans (Greek Peloponnesus, Crete, Sicily, Troy)
1200 BCE–612 BCE	Assyrians (Turkey, Babylon, Syria)
700 BCE–300 BCE	Greeks (Greece, Mediterranean lands to Spain, Asia to India)
612 BCE–331 BCE	Achaemenid Empire (Persians)—Middle East
350 BCE–1200 CE	Mayan Empire (Yucatan to Guatemala)
?BCE–284 CE	Roman Empire (Rome, Tunisia, Levant, Europe, England)
284 CE–493 CE	Western Roman Empire (Rome and Europe)
284 CE–1453 CE	Eastern Roman Empire (Constantinople to the Adriatic)
1206 CE–1405 CE	Mongols (Middle East, Central Asia, China, Eastern Europe)
1300 CE–1533 CE	Incas (Peru and bordering regions)
1345 CE–1519 CE	Aztecs (Mexico to Guatemala)

present-day Turkey, the Levant (eastern end of the Mediterranean Sea), Armenia, eastward in Asia beyond the Caspian Sea and Samarkand, southward over the Hindu Kush Mountains of Afghanistan to the Indus River in India, then westward to the Persian Gulf and Mesopotamia. Particularly prominent among the various rulers of the Achaemenid Empire were Cyrus, Darius, and Xerxes. The ruins of the great palace at Persepolis in Iran still reveal some of the artistic glory of the Persian Empire, which finally was ended by Alexander the Great in 331 BCE (Figure 1.9 and Figure C50, p. C17).

Minoans—Mediterranean people who developed a prosperous, artistic civilization on Crete that was ended by a tidal wave in 1625 BCE.

Early Mediterranean Cultures The **Minoan** civilization on the island of Crete flourished in its Mediterranean location because of the favorable environment for farming and safety from attacks of other peoples. Art was developed and appreciated, as can be seen in the frescoes from the ruins of King Knossus' palace (Figure 1.10, Figures C59 and C60, p. C20). The bounty of their food supply is evident from the huge amphorae for storing olive oil and wine that were found at the palace. This culturally advanced early civilization was destroyed dramatically by the enormous tidal wave in the eastern end of the Mediterranean Sea that was generated following the gigantic volcanic eruption on Thera (today's Greek island of Santorini) in 1625 BCE.

Myceneans—Civilization centered on the Greek Peloponnesus that controlled Crete and other Mediterranean islands.

As a result of the abrupt end to the Minoan civilization, the **Myceneans** on the Greek Peloponnesus were able to establish control over Crete, and they extended their control to Sicily, Sardinia, and Troy at the eastern end of the Mediterranean. They even ranged as far north as the Baltic Sea and westward to Britain. Mycenean control of the region lasted four centuries (from about 1500 BCE to 1100 BCE). Agamemnon was the most prominent ruler of this vast trading empire (Figure 1.11). A period of strife dominated the region that is now Greece for almost 800 years after the fall of the Myceneans.

Hellenistic Greece—Ancient Greek civilization that reached its peak of political dominance and cultural influence from about 323 BCE to 27 BCE.

Hellenistic Greece (Classical Greece) began to emerge by 323 BCE as a civilization characterized by remarkable achievements in philosophy, mathematics, and the arts. The artistic creations of the Greeks of this era are among the leading cultural gifts to the world that are still prized today. These include the Acropolis in Athens (with its dramatic Parthenon [Figure C.34, p. C12], Erechtheum, and the Theatre of Dionysus) and Ephesus and Priene in Turkey, as well as numerous beautiful marble sculptures and vases.

Dining was an important aspect of life for wealthier Greeks of this era. Servants prepared and served meals to masters and their male guests who reclined on couches in the male dining room. Women ate separately from the men. Meals

Figure 1.9 Persians created lovely bas reliefs that decorated the palace at Persepolis in Iran.

Figure 1.10 King Knossus's palace (partially reconstructed) and a colorful mosaic illustrate the highly developed Minoan culture that once developed on Crete in the Mediterranean Sea.

featured breads and cake (made with wheat and barley), local fruits such as figs and grapes, vegetables, and perhaps seafood and cheese prepared from goat's milk, as well as wine from local grapes. Olives were important in Greek meals served as an accompaniment or used as an ingredient in various recipes. They also were pressed for their oil, which was used extensively in preparing foods.

Greeks extended their influence westward over the entire northern shores of the Mediterranean Sea to the eastern part of Spain and eastward along the Turkish shores of the Black Sea. The Macedonian military leader Alexander the Great was able to extend the conquests to central Asia by such feats as defeating the Persians at Persepolis (Figure C.50, p. C17) and then marching to Afghanistan and on southward to northern India before his death in 323 BCE at the age of 33.

Roman Empire—Vast empire based in Rome that gradually was formed to cover much of the areas along the Mediterranean coast into Turkey, France, and England.

The **Roman Empire** began in Italy but gained immense dimensions as its leaders sent legions to various points, starting with lands bordering the Mediterranean Sea. Romans fought three Punic Wars against Carthage in Tunisia from 264 BCE to 146 BCE to gain control not only of Carthage itself (Figure C.86, p. C29), but also of its territories (Sicily, Corsica, Sardinia, the Balearics, and Spain). Later conquests included the Dalmatian coast of the Adriatic Sea, the western part of Anatolia (part of Turkey in Asia Minor), land along the Black Sea, the Levant (from Syria almost to the Red Sea), and finally France and England.

Figure 1.11 The Lions' Gate decorates the entrance to the crumbled remains of Agamemnon's Palace on the Peloponnesus south of Athens, Greece.

Among the significant contributions of the Romans to their provinces were law and government, roads, aqueducts, and baths. Romans also brought their food patterns with them as their empire extended across Europe and into Africa and Asia. Greek foods and dining practices had been assimilated and further elaborated by the Roman aristocracy. When the Roman legions conquered and occupied new lands, they also introduced their cuisine featuring heavy spices, thick sauces, and wine. Such fare could be enjoyed in the provinces because the roads built by the Romans and their subjects made it possible to transport spices and some food from great distances.

The enormity of the Roman Empire made it difficult to defend from the warlike tribes threatening the borders. Emperor Diocletian (Figure 1.12) split the territories in 284 CE to establish the Eastern Roman Empire with its headquarters in Byzantium (subsequently renamed Constantinople by its emperor Constantine). This part of the Roman Empire lasted until 1453 CE when the Ottoman Turks conquered it. The Western Roman Empire was overrun by northern barbarians, thus ending that part of the Roman Empire in 493 CE. Over the course of the centuries that Rome dominated its vast empire, it was ruled by many different emperors; Julius Caesar is perhaps the best known.

Mongol Empire—Barbaric, short-lived empire ranging southward from central Asia and westward to threaten even Vienna in Europe.

The **Mongol Empire** presents a sharp contrast to the ways of the Roman Empire. It lasted for only 200 years (1206 to 1405 CE), beginning under Genghis Khan. He united very fierce warriors from the various tribes of Mongolia and central Asia, who breeched the Great Wall (Figure C.161, p. C54) and invaded China in 1211 CE. He also sent troops westward toward northern Tibet and on to encircle the Caspian Sea and penetrate Kashmir and northern India. One of the consequences of the westward push beyond the Caspian Sea was the acquisition of many Turkish-speaking people, which ultimately led to the demise of the Seljuk sultanate in Turkey and the establishment of the Ottoman Empire there.

The food habits of the Mongols were drastically different from those of the Greeks and Romans. The harsh climate and living conditions of the Mongol's native lands fostered a diet based heavily on meats from both wild and domesticated animals. Meat might be dried for later use, but much of it was consumed fresh after either being fried or boiled. Grain was also available and frequently was made into noodles. Vegetables and fruits were rare. Meals were far less elaborate in the Mongol than in the Roman Empire and were a means of survival rather than an entertainment.

One of the consequences of the Mongol Empire was a weakening of Christianity, which had been fairly strong in Constantinople, and tremendous gain in support of Islam, as well as some strengthening of Buddhism (in the Far East only). Even after Genghis Khan died in 1227 CE, Mongol hordes attacked Russia

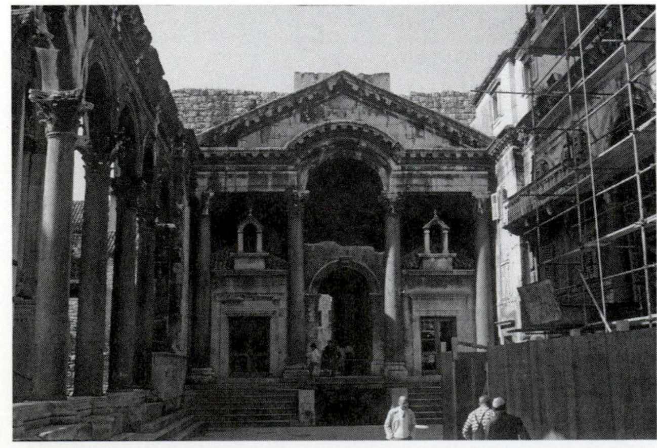

Figure 1.12 Diocletian, an Emperor of the Roman Empire, built his palace on the Dalmatian Coast in Split, Croatia, during his reign and retired there in 295 CE.

Figure 1.13 Shah Jahan built the Taj Mahal near Agra, India, but later his son imprisoned him in the Red Fort in a chamber where he could see the Taj in the distance above the river.

in 1237 CE and then went on to conquer Poland and Hungary in 1241 CE. Fortunately for Europe, the Great Khan Ogedei, the Mongol leader, died, and so did the Mongol threat to Europe. However, Mongols held control in Russia until the last ruler, Tamerlane, died in 1405 CE.

Babur, a descendant of Tamerlane, provided an interesting footnote to the Mongol Empire. He invaded India in 1526 CE to begin the Mughal Empire, which extended eastward from the Arabian Sea well into Afghanistan and included all of Kashmir, southward along the Indian side of the Himalayas, and a long coastline of the Bay of Bengal before turning westward to the Arabian Sea just north of Bombay. Akbar, the grandson of Babur, fostered the unique artistic style that blended Persian and Indian influences. The Taj Mahal (Figure 1.13. and Figures C.111 and C.112, pp. C37 and 38), built by Shah Jahan, is the architectural masterpiece of the Mughal Empire, which ended in 1707 CE.

Western Empires Three empires (Mayan, Incan, and Aztec) were dominant in different areas of the Americas, the earliest of these being the Mayan Empire (350 BCE to about 1200 CE). Remains of this culture still stand on the Yucatan Peninsula of Mexico (Figure C.191, p. C64) and in the jungle lowlands of Guatemala. The Incan Empire was the leading civilization in the mountains of Peru (Figure C.177, p. C59) and beyond in South America from about 1300 CE until Pizarro arrived from Spain, conquering the Incas and seizing Cuzco in 1533. The Aztecs gained control of land near today's Mexico City when they arrived in 1345 CE and built their capital, Teochitlan. By the time Spain's Cortez arrived in 1519, they ruled the land from the Gulf of Mexico to the Pacific and from central Mexico to Guatemala, land that immediately became Spain's.

Emerging Trade Routes

The growth of trade was a natural result of the conquests mentioned above, as well as many others around the world (Table 1.2). Wheat was one of the early items traded from the Fertile Crescent of Mesopotamia, for this was a crop that could be transported long distances to such places as Europe, Scandinavia, and the British Isles without spoiling. By the end of the 15th and beginning of the 16th centuries, wheat had even been carried to the Caribbean and Argentina. Spanish conquerors and friars aided in the introduction of wheat to North America.

Maize was developed in Central and South America, and then it was introduced to Europe when the Spanish expedition returned to Spain in 1493, carrying some maize from Mexico. A century later, maize from South America was

Table 1.2 Food Origins and Trade

Food	*Origin*	*Trade Destinations*
Cabbage	Europe	North America
Cacao	Latin America	Europe
Coffee	East Africa	Europe, Africa, SE Asia
Maize	Latin America	Europe, Africa, India
Onions	Europe	North America
Palm oil	West Africa	Americas, SE Asia
Potato	South America	Europe, Africa, India
Rice	China	India, SE Asia, Mediterranean
Spices	SE Asia	Europe
Sweet potato	Central America	Europe
Sunflower	Central America	Europe
Tea	Northern China	Westward to Europe
Tomato	Central America	Europe, North America
Wheat	Mesopotamia	Europe, North America

introduced to West Africa. European voyagers in the 16th century not only transported maize to Europe, but also carried Mexican maize to eastern South America and on to part of India and northeastern China. Rice originated in China, spread to India, and then was carried by traders to the Fertile Crescent and throughout the Mediterranean and North Africa by about 300 BCE.

Central America was the origin of the tomato and sweet potato. From there, they were introduced to Europe in the very late 15th and early 16th centuries. South America and Central America added chiles to the world's larder.

Europe provided not only onions and cabbage, but also tomatoes to North America in the 19th century (long after tomatoes had ventured to Europe from Central America). Potatoes went from western South America throughout Europe and to eastern Africa and India by the 17th century.

Coffee appears to have originated in eastern Africa. Its acceptance spread rapidly to Amsterdam and all along the routes of the Dutch traders around Africa and to Southeast Asia. Tea originated in northern China and then spread rapidly all along the trade routes back to Europe. Cocoa is the only popular beverage that originated in the New World. The wonderful discovery of chocolate was carried in about 1520 CE to a very appreciative audience in Europe.

Actions of traders in centuries past are still influencing trade practices today. Early entrepreneurs who bought cloves in Indonesia in the early days devised a plan to shorten the length of the voyage. Their solution was to carry clove seedlings to Madagascar and grow clove trees there off the eastern coast of Africa, a point much closer to Europe and with a climate that suited the trees. Cloves from Madagascar have held a strong position in the spice trade for many years, although governmental regulations and trade barriers impact the current rivalry between Indonesia and Madagascar.

Another gift of the New World to Europe was the sunflower with its excellent oil. Palm oil had its origins in the western part of Africa around the Niger River. From there, its use spread to both Americas and Southeast Asia in the 19th century. Much of the production of palm oil for the world is centered now in Malaysia, where it is an agricultural commodity of considerable importance.

Spices offered very early traders two particularly outstanding characteristics that spurred the spice trade: long shelf life and high market value per volume. Various spices were known and highly prized from China all the way to Rome and beyond long before the time of Christ. Traders carried their valuable cargoes thousands of miles, often under extremely difficult conditions. Despite these long ocean voyages, the spices from Southeast Asia brought such high prices when they finally reached their markets that many traders became very wealthy. It is said that the spices carried back in the hold of Magellan's only ship that returned from his three-year voyage of 1519 to 1522 returned sufficient money to pay for the entire expedition.

Traders from various European nations plied the seas between Indonesia and Europe, bringing home fortunes in spices. The exciting flavors were appreciated not only for their uniquely pleasing variety, but also for their ability to help disguise off flavors in the era when refrigeration was not available to extend the useful life of foods. A further subtle message conveyed by the use of spices was that the household was wealthy and could afford such luxuries.

Changes in food habits and diets occurred gradually as a consequence of conquests and trade, but improvements in transportation since the time of the early empires have accelerated this trend. Over the centuries since these early days of exploration, trading has expanded greatly. Food from all over the world is shipped to distant ports to add variety to people's meals. Thanks to refrigerated and frozen containers, perishable foods can be transported by air, sea, and land so that they arrive at markets in excellent condition. Although some of the food may be grown locally, people choose diets today that are only partially determined by climate, geography, and growing conditions. A very broad array of foods is available if people can afford and wish to buy products from other parts of the country and the world.

Summary

The diets of people very long ago were determined by food they could obtain by fishing, hunting, or gathering plant foods. Early foods native to different parts of the world included emmer, einkorn, barley, pulses, taro, and manioc. Agriculture developed gradually in temperate areas near rivers; animals also were domesticated. Factors influencing the foods that were being produced in various regions included geography and such environmental factors as water and growing conditions.

As food production became adequate to meet the needs of groups of people living fairly close together, some groups developed cultures that were so advanced that they created some buildings and art that can still be seen today. Among the early cultures were those found in Egypt, Persia (Hittite, Sumerians, and Assyrians), China, and Central America (Olmec and Zapotec). Conquests by warring on other people resulted in the establishment of the Achaemenid (Persian) Empire. Early Mediterranean cultures included the Minoans on Crete (ended when the volcano on Thera [Santorini] erupted) and the Myceneans and the Greeks, whose best-known conqueror was Alexander the Great. The Roman Empire extended over much of Europe, the north of Africa, and into the Middle East. Mongols followed briefly toward Europe but remained a comparatively short time, and little of their presence remains today. In the western hemisphere, the three key empires were the Mayan, Incan, and Aztec.

Food patterns were influenced significantly by trade routes that developed as conquests and exploration increased knowledge of other parts of the world. Foods that had originated in the western hemisphere sometimes were carried to very distant places, including the eastern hemisphere. Similarly, foods originally found in the eastern hemisphere were transported to the west.

Today shipping has evolved so that food can be marketed anywhere in the world, depending on demand and people's ability to purchase food from other regions. Diets no longer are dependent on only the local food supply.

Selected Sites

www.foodhistorynews.com—Magazine about food history.

www.arts.adelaide.edu.au/centrefooddrink/html—Australian site with articles on food and drink by members of the Research Centre for the History of Food and Drink.

http://dmoz.org/Home/Cooking/World_Cuisines/Historic/—Many different articles on food history.

www.cliffordawright.com/history/—Articles on food history in various regions of Europe, Middle East, and Africa.

www.kitchenproject.com/history/—Breadth of material on food history.

www.foodmuseum.com—Articles on food origins.

http://www.foodtimeline.org/foodfaq3.html—Timelines on food history and recipe development.

Study Questions

1. What geographic characteristics were found in the Fertile Crescent that were favorable to the development of an agrarian society?
2. Why is development of a culture dependent on the food supply?
3. Identify 10 of your favorite foods and the part of the world where each probably originated.
4. Where did the food that you ate yesterday come from? As much as possible, indicate where each ingredient probably was produced.
5. Why was rice the staple cereal in Japan? Why was wheat the traditional grain in Central Europe?
6. Briefly describe each of the following empires: Western Roman, Mughal, Persian, Mycenean.
7. Why were food patterns influenced by empire builders?
8. Compare the food patterns of citizens of the Roman Empire with those of the Mongol Empire and discuss the reasons for the differences.

Bibliography

Barraclough, G., ed. 1998. *Harper Collins Atlas of World History.* 2nd rev. ed. Border Press. Ann Arbor, MI.

Batmanglij, N.K. 2000. *New Food of Life: Ancient Persian and Modern Iranian Cooking and Ceremonies.* Mage. Washington, DC.

Billings, J. and P.W. Sherman. 1998. Antimicrobial functions of spices. Why some like it hot. *Quarterly Review of Biology 73:* 3–49.

Brander, B. 1966. *River Nile.* National Geographic Society. Washington, DC.

Civitello, L. 2003. *Cuisine and Culture: History, Food, and People.* Wiley. New York.

Davidson, A. 1999. *Oxford Companion to Food.* Oxford University Press. Oxford, U.K.

Dunn, R.E. 1986. *Adventures of Ibn Battuta, a Muslim Traveler of the Fourteenth Century.* University of California Press. Berkeley.

Fletcher, N. 2004. *Charlemagne's Tablecloth.* St. Martin's Press. London, England.

Grew, R. 1999. *Food in Global History.* Westview Press. Boulder, CO.

Grun, B. 1991. *Timetables of History.* 3rd ed. Simon and Schuster/Touchstone Books. New York.

Harper Collins. 1997. *Past Worlds: Atlas of Archaeology.* Border Press. Ann Arbor, MI.

Huot, J.L. 1965. *Archaeology Mundi: Persia I.* World Publishing. Cleveland, OH.

Kiple, K.F., ed. 2000. *Cambridge World History of Food.* Cambridge, U.K.

Lapidus, I.M. 2002. *History of Islamic Societies.* Cambridge University Press. Cambridge, UK.

Pan American. 1978. *World Guide.* McGraw-Hill. New York.

Pearcy, G.E. 1980. *World Food Scene.* Plycon Press. Redondo Beach, CA.

Pomeranz, K. and S. Topik, eds. 1999. *World That Trade Created: Culture, Society and the World Economy 1400 to Present.* M.E. Sharpe. Armonk, New York.

Shahbazi, A.S. 1976. *Persepolis Illustrated.* Institute of Achaemenid Research. Persepolis, Iran.
Tannahill, R.T. 1995. *Food in History.* Three Rivers Press. New York.
Toussaint-Samat, M.T. 1994. *History of Food.* Blackwell Publishing Ltd. Oxford, U.K.
Ward, S., C. Clifton, and J. Stacey. 1997. *Gourmet Atlas.* Macmillan. New York.

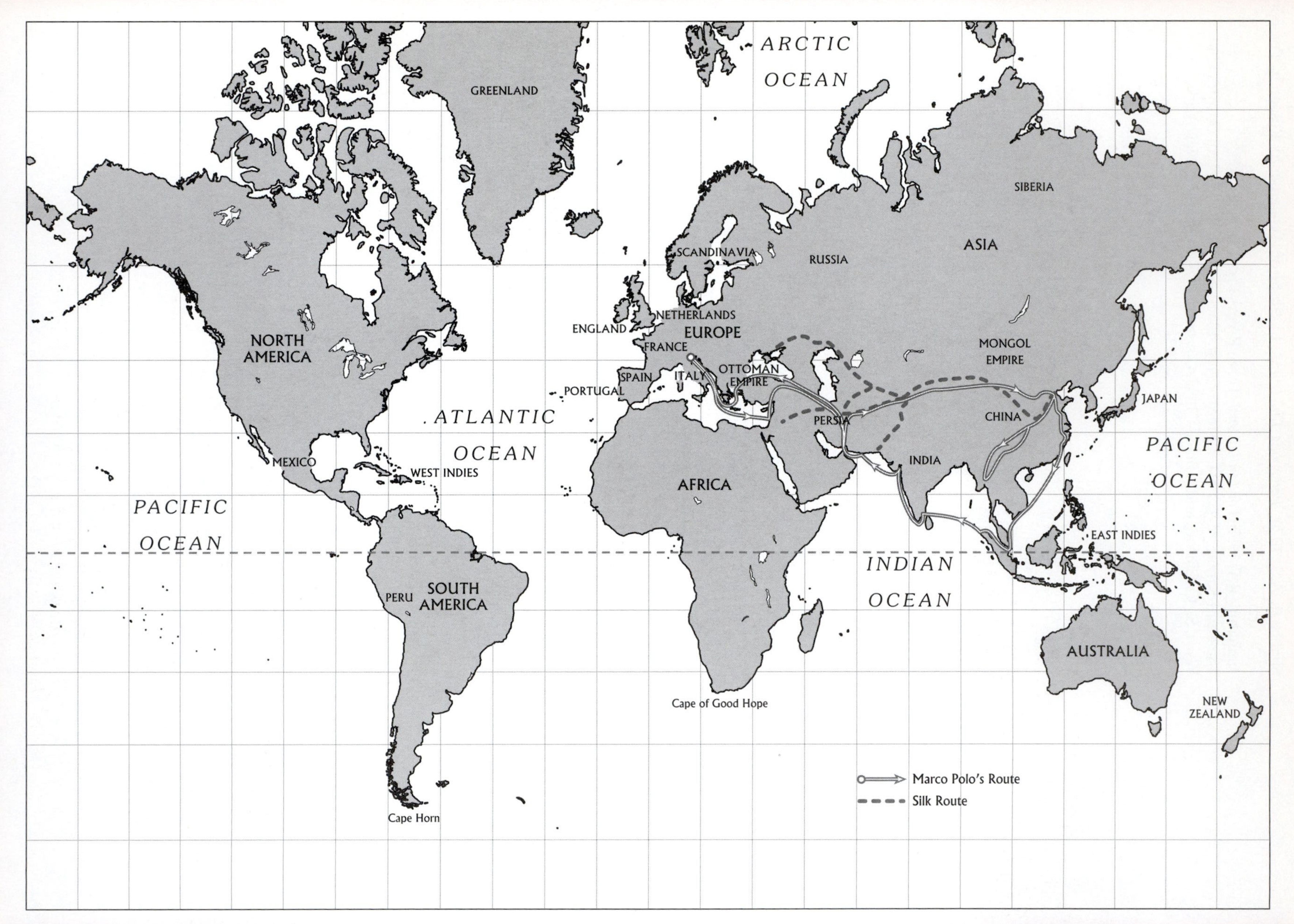
ARCTIC OCEAN
GREENLAND
SIBERIA
ASIA
RUSSIA
SCANDINAVIA
NORTH AMERICA
ENGLAND
NETHERLANDS
EUROPE
FRANCE
SPAIN
ITALY
OTTOMAN EMPIRE
PORTUGAL
MONGOL EMPIRE
JAPAN
CHINA
PERSIA
ATLANTIC OCEAN
PACIFIC OCEAN
MEXICO
WEST INDIES
INDIA
AFRICA
PACIFIC OCEAN
EAST INDIES
INDIAN OCEAN
PERU
SOUTH AMERICA
AUSTRALIA
Cape of Good Hope
NEW ZEALAND
Marco Polo's Route
Silk Route
Cape Horn

2 Cultural Parameters

Culture refers to the way of life of a people. Customs, habits, language, knowledge, housing, tools, and the arts all contribute to the uniqueness of a culture.

Five words—"You eat what you are" and "You are what you eat"—placed in two different sequences provide an intriguing introduction to this chapter. The first statement shows an appreciation of some of the cultural factors that shape food choices and preferences. The second is a pragmatic way of relating physical outcome to a lifetime of eating (nutrition). If food is thought of only as the means of getting the nutrients needed for life, the important subtleties that influence what people actually eat will be missed.

Take a moment to think about the way you eat: how many meals, foods you usually like to eat at each meal during a day, dishes served at family gatherings on special holidays, and your favorite foods. Then consider why you have these food preferences and dietary pattern. In other words, describe what influenced what you eat. These thoughts set the stage for reading this chapter.

Components of Culture

Culture—Way of life of a group of people (what they create, do, and think).

Culture is a somewhat nebulous concept because a wide variety of characteristics may all contribute to a complex picture. Customary beliefs, social forms, and material traits of a racial, religious, or social group are some of the characteristics contributing to the description of a culture. *Ethnicity* is the affiliation with a race, people, or cultural group. Culture and ethnicity are essential foundations of the study of food and people. Knowledge of the major cultures around the world and appreciation of the cultural richness that is a part of their food patterns not only add pleasure to our lives, but also strengthen the ability of food professionals to work effectively with people from cultures other than their own.

Country of Birth

To an extent, the country where a person is born and resides shapes the food patterns of the individual and families. The geographic realities of climate and terrain suitable for productive agriculture define the local foods that may be available (Figure 2.1). Other resources of the country will influence whether or not manufacturing and business and other commercial endeavors generate a vigorous economy. In countries where all is favorable, an abundant and varied food supply can be obtained by virtually all people in that country. In less favored locales, food may be in very short supply and unavailable in adequate amounts. In other words, the economy and the agricultural conditions combine within a country to define one of the parameters of the nation's food culture.

Housing

Housing is another dimension of a person's culture. People in some cultural groups live in elegant, single-family dwellings; some live in cottages; others live in apartments or condominiums. The roof may be anything from a leaky thatch (Figure 2.2) to an orderly fireproof tile. Some people have a bedroom for each person, while others live in a one-room house in which the entire family must eat and sleep. The kitchens range from spotless and completely equipped with every appliance to those in which refrigeration is unavailable or extremely limited in space, a situation that imposes serious problems of food safety and necessitates daily shopping. A family of a cultural group often lives in housing that is similar to the others in the group.

Language

Language is a key component of culture because it provides a means of sharing thoughts, ideas, and information (Figure 2.3). Accurate, meaningful communication is important in families, communities, nations, and the world. The fact that many international airports around the world require pilots to use English to communicate with the tower illustrates the importance of language as a common denominator in business. Even with the same language, word definitions may differ by country (e.g., *biscuit* in England means a different food than in the United States). Similarly, people in the same cultural group need to be able to understand what is being said in personal conversations.

Figure 2.1 Several different fruits and vegetables grown locally are brought to the outdoor market in Mandalay, Myanmar (Burma).

Figure 2.2 This thatched house is on the bank of the River Kwai in rural Kanchanaburi, Thailand.

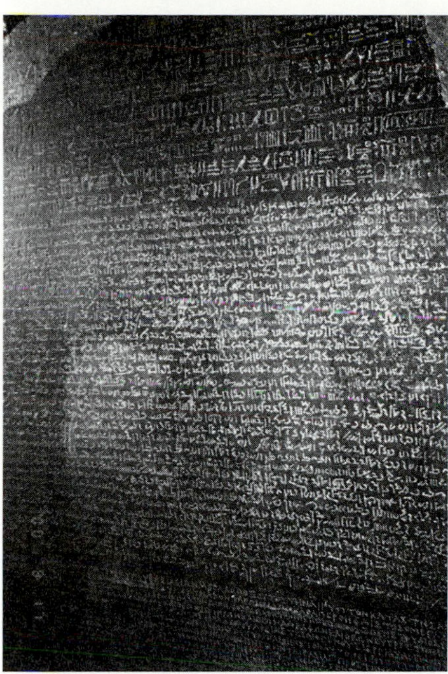

Figure 2.3 The Rosetta Stone, dating from 196 BCE, provided a communication key to ancient Egypt once the three scripts and two languages were translated by Champollion in 1822.

A national language helps to define what a nation is culturally. Even within a country speaking the same language, confusion may exist due to differences in dialects and accents. An illustration of such communication difficulties can be found in China with its numerous dialects. Mandarin is the dialect that often serves as the communication interface for people who use different dialects in their daily lives.

Lifestyle

Lifestyle adds to a cultural identification. Certain national habits of living help to define a culture. An example of this is the very late dinner hour (10 P.M. or later) in Spain and in countries that were former Spanish colonies. This tradition developed because the intense heat of mid-day was made more tolerable by taking a siesta and then continuing business in the late afternoon, thus pushing dinner to a late hour. In contrast, Americans tend to try to push as much work into the day as possible. Although these examples are generalizations, many people can relate to such cultural influences.

Food habits are shaped, at least in part, by lifestyle. For example, families with children make decisions about where their young children are cared for, and by whom. Are parents with their children most of the day, or are they away from home for long hours while working many miles away? Mode of transportation—trishaws, buses, bicycles, cars, trains, or foot—shapes lifestyle. Other aspects of lifestyle are food habits. Do families eat all meals together at home, or do they eat in some other setting for one or more meals daily? Who prepares these meals? These are some of the practical questions regarding lifestyle that help to develop some understanding of a specific cultural group.

The Arts

One of the important threads that tends to identify a culture and to continue to hold its members together as a group is that of art. Styles of art vary over the ages and around the world, yet most cultural groups have an artistic heritage that they feel to be their own (Figure 2.4). In fact, paintings, sculptures, mosaics, bas-reliefs, and other forms of art provide a somewhat historic documentation of the earlier

Figure 2.4 Lively, whimsical figures and masks are characteristic of the graceful art of Thailand.

people who helped to define the group's artistic culture. These visual works sometimes depict foods and/or dining scenes that convey a cultural message. For instance, Pieter Brueghel's *Peasant Wedding* depicts a wonderful Dutch wedding feast in the mid-16th century; Renoir's *Luncheon of the Boating Party* reveals a completely different cultural scene in France in the late 19th century.

Music and dance are other art forms that communicate directly to individuals and draw them toward the local culture. Performances of *Swan Lake* ballet (by Tschaikovsky, a famous Russian composer) and the Barong dance (traditional presentation in Bali) are representative of the cultural heritage from Russia and Bali (Figure 2.5).

Musical examples also abound. Sibelius's *Finlandia* is an orchestral work that creates pride in their heritage among Finnish people while also providing an appreciation of Finland to all people who hear this rich and very strong composition. Austria is noted for its music, which ranges from the numerous works of Salzburg's Wolfgang Amadeus Mozart to the lilting Viennese waltzes of Johan Strauss. The United States boasts such composers as Aaron Copland (works include *Appalachian Spring* and *Rodeo*), John Williams (*Star Wars*), and Stephen Foster (composer of "Swanee River" and other songs of the South). Some American

Figure 2.5 Musicians in Bali play gamelans for folk dancers and to entertain listeners.

songs such as "Rum and Coca Cola," "Short'ning Bread," and "Shoo Fly Pie and Apple Pan Dowdy" are musical reminders of some cultural foods in the South.

Literature

An enduring part of a nation's culture is the literature written by its people. William Shakespeare remains revered among British authors long after his death. Charles Dickens brought the food tradition of an English Christmas to life for all to share in his classic "A Christmas Carol." Victor Hugo, who wrote his masterpiece *Les Miserables* in the 19th century, occupies an important place among French writers. Henry Wadsworth Longfellow is the beloved American poet who wrote "Paul Revere's Ride." Carl Sandburg brought the drama of aspects of food production in early 20th-century America to life in his poetry. These are but a few examples of the contributions writers have made to the culture of their land.

Storytelling is another aspect of culture; although similar to literature, stories are embedded in the culture by being passed from person to person rather than being preserved in printed form. This is an art form in many places in Africa, particularly in the western and central regions. Legends have been told from generation to generation in many countries, and some of these have evolved into print. German fairy tales are an example of this type of literature.

Architecture

Public architecture affords additional insights into a culture. Recent excavations in Egypt have revealed two bakeries that were used to feed the workers building the pyramids more than 4000 years ago. In homes of the elite that have been unearthed in Pompeii, the *triclinium* (formal dining room) had benches for reclining around three sides of the room. In Russia, the survival of the Summer Palace and the Hermitage, as well as other grand buildings from the Tsarist era, provides mute testimony to the appreciation that the citizens of Leningrad (now St. Petersburg, once again) held for their cultural heritage even through the Revolution and eventual break up of the Soviet Union.

In the United Kingdom, the stern and imposing palaces and castles are proudly viewed as the cultural heritage of the country. The strength and independent nature of earlier citizenry were clearly expressed in the castles that were built and defended to keep invaders from their stark and windswept coastland. Cooking for all the people in the castle was done over open fires in huge fireplaces, and the privileged residents of the castle dined in the great hall.

All around the world architectural sites continue to reveal the beauty and strength of earlier cultures. The Parthenon on the Acropolis in Athens, with its open and inviting style, is an enduring reflection of the early Greeks. Karnak Temple near Luxor, Egypt, affords a glimpse of yet a different ancient culture that is an important part of a nation's culture almost five millennia later.

The famed Taj Mahal in Agra, India, is a dazzlingly lovely and graceful tribute to Shah Jahan's dead wife, its intricate inlaid designs of semiprecious stones attesting to the highly developed skills of the craftsmen and artists in India. Deeply carved bas-reliefs adorning the long walls of the huge Angkor Wat complex in Cambodia (Figure 2.6) add a different artistic dimension to the cultural context of architecture. The Forbidden City, with its temples and mazes of buildings and rooms within its encompassing walls, affords a remarkable look at the cultural heritage of both Beijing residents and all people of China.

These glimpses of the importance of the arts in creating emotions and feelings are presented to help you begin to think about similar artistic works that help to define your cultural inheritance.

Figure 2.6 Bas-reliefs at Angkor Wat reveal the remarkable artistry of the Khmer artists in northern Cambodia in the 12th century.

Additional Dimensions of Culture

Other defining aspects of cultural groups are their food traditions, national histories, and religions (see Chapter 3). When people live within a region that constitutes a nation or possibly just a portion of a nation, common experiences related to government of the land and beliefs and values can either unite people or create civil unrest and even wars. From such influences, cultural identity and groupings often result, and these groups continue for many centuries when governments are stable.

Immigration

Nations with a history that included empire building often have a mixture of cultures that is evident today. In the United Kingdom, for example, many immigrants from Pakistan or other distant parts of the realm have settled in England, thus permanently altering the homogeneity of earlier years. Similarly, France now has many residents from its earlier territory in North Africa. Even in these countries with strong national identities, the addition of significant numbers of immigrants from other cultures has altered elements of the national image permanently.

Terrible wars in past years caused many people to flee their countries to avoid persecution and probable death. These political refugees often have sought asylum and new beginnings in countries quite distant from their country of origin. An illustration is provided by the very large influx of Vietnamese, Cambodians, and Laotians (Hmong) into the United States as the Viet Nam War was ending. Their arrival in their new country brought awareness of cultures into focus, both for the new arrivals and for Americans. At first, refugees were settled all around the country in an attempt to provide community support for some individuals and families in numerous towns. Gradually, these new immigrants began to gravitate in the new country to regions where others from their own culture were already beginning to gather. The result is a few very large pockets (e.g., "Little Saigon" in Orange County, California) of residents formerly from Southeast Asia.

The hope for a better life is the reason many people choose to immigrate to the United States. Examples over the years include the Pilgrims (seeking religious freedom), the Irish in the mid-19th century (escaping the Potato Famine), students pursuing higher education, and workers looking for higher-paying jobs to support their families.

Immigrants from other cultures often tend to settle together because of strong cultural ties. Evidence of the importance of their former culture is retained in their daily lives. For example, they often speak to each other in their native language and shop where they can get food ingredients for making their native dishes. Such tangible reminders of their cultural heritage provide support and a feeling of belonging.

Thus, the cultural fabric of nations with significant immigrant populations is becoming a patchwork quilt with a piece of this culture and a piece of that one scattered in various places. However, the overall culture of a nation ties the country into a multicultural whole. The United States, a nation with a significant amount of heterogeneity since its colonial beginnings, is a living example of cultural identities being retained while being united into a single nation.

Religion is a particularly strong factor in cultural identity. Sharing common beliefs and practices that are central to a particular religion creates common threads that bind people together into a culture. By the same token, the fact that people practicing a different religion do not have the same beliefs and customs serves to separate the followers of each major religion into isolated groups or into groups who respect each other, but who are not as close between as within religious groups. Even though groups are defined, knowledge and appreciation of various religions can do much to reduce possible tensions and enrich the fabric of our American culture.

Special Messages of Food

Salt

Food sometimes carries special meanings beyond simply providing nutrients. The subtle messages conveyed by a particular food may be a nonverbal exchange between people at a meal or a social occasion. Certain foods may be absolutely essential on a particular occasion. For example, matzo (unleavened bread) must be served for Jewish Passover. Bread or wafers and wine or grape juice served at Communion are symbols of Christ's body for Christians.

Special green tea prepared in the Japanese tea ceremony conveys total welcome and hospitality to guests. Wassail is a traditional Christmas beverage in the United Kingdom that is served to welcome guests during the holidays. The specific foods and traditions vary greatly around the world. Some of these will be discussed in later chapters in this book. However, the importance of salt is sufficiently universal to all people that it warrants some attention here.

Salt, a simple yet essential part of the diet for people and animals, has been valued throughout the world for many centuries (Figure 2.7). The Romans were well aware of the importance of salt for their troops in their military conquests as they carved out their vast empire. Caesar's armies had persons responsible for making salt (by boiling down brine) for the troops. In remote Tibet during the time of Marco Polo (around 1300 CE), salt cakes served as the currency. The remains of Mayan salt-production facilities that have been excavated recently just off the coast of Belize provide evidence that salt was an important trade commodity in the Mayan Empire of Central America.

Chinese Emperor Yu, in 2200 BCE, attempted to control and tax salt in his domain. Throughout the centuries, taxes on salt have punctuated numerous political upheavals, including the French Revolution. Even in the 20th century, England's tax on salt in India and its ban on personal harvesting of salt from the sea triggered Mahatma Ghandi's famous 200-mile protest march to the sea in 1930.

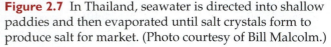

Figure 2.7 In Thailand, seawater is directed into shallow paddies and then evaporated until salt crystals form to produce salt for market. (Photo courtesy of Bill Malcolm.)

The universality of the importance attached to salt can be seen in various religious and cultural traditions of the past. Catholic priests used to place a little salt on the baby's tongue during baptismal rites so the baby would "receive the salt of wisdom." Early Jewish rites required that salt be a part of their offerings. Both Jews and Christians had a tradition of rubbing salt on infants to ensure a long life. Friendship between Arabs was sealed with the expression "There is salt between us." This meant that they would not do harm to each other when they had shared salt. The negative predictions of bad luck from spilled salt are immortalized in Leonardo's *The Last Supper* in which the salt is spilled by Judas.

Eggs

Another food that has been a symbol over many centuries and in different cultures is the egg. Since pagan times, eggs have conveyed special meaning to people. Pagans considered the egg to be a symbol of fertility and renewal of life. The shell represented earth, the membrane was air, the white was water, and the yolk was fire.

In China, eggs colored red are presented at parties announcing a baby's birth. Sometimes two hard-cooked eggs are used to symbolize birth of a girl and a single egg represents a boy. Mayans also endowed eggs with special powers, albeit very different from the symbolism of fertility. Apparently, evil spells could be broken by a medicine man with a special ceremony. He would wave an egg in front of the face of the afflicted person several times and then break the egg before burying it to break the spell.

Christians have traditionally associated eggs with Easter celebrations. Eggs are used symbolically to represent the resurrection of Christ. Hard-cooked eggs are often colored and used in Easter egg hunts in many Christian cultures. Various branches of the Eastern Orthodox Church decorate eggs very elaborately (often just the shell after the interior has been blown out). Many of the traditional symbols applied to the eggs convey particular meaning. Ukraine and other Eastern European countries are noted for their decoration of Easter eggs (Figure 2.8).

Czar Alexander III commissioned the artist Fabergé to make a very special jeweled egg for him to give to his wife, Czarina Maria, in 1884. This Easter gift was such a success that Fabergé eggs were made even after Alexander's death until 56 eggs had been made. These eggs now are admired more for their beauty than for their religious significance and sometimes are shown in special exhibits in museums.

Figure 2.8 Decorative designs are carefully painted on eggs in Romania and other countries in preparation for the celebration of Easter in Eastern Orthodox churches and homes.

Summary

Some of the key components of culture are discussed in this chapter. These include beliefs, social forms, and material traits of a racial, religious, or social group. Geography of the region where a person is born and lives is of great importance, and so is the economic strength of that nation and of the individual families. Housing has a tangible influence on lifestyles, as do the choices about working. Both of these factors certainly influence food patterns. Language, lifestyle, art, music, dance, literature, and architecture also make significant contributions to cultural identity. World history and religions are other key components defining cultural groups.

America today is made up of a kaleidoscope of immigrants from virtually all parts of the world. Regardless of how long ago immigrants first came to America, they or their descendants have stories of remembrances or at least some knowledge of their country of origin. Appreciation of this heritage helps bind people of similar backgrounds into cultural groups that reinforce the customs and traditions to maintain a richness of memories and experiences in the next generation. Often these traditions are shared with others in the community. Such sharing increases understanding and appreciation of the wonderful diversity that is becoming America.

Food conveys special symbolism in different cultures. Salt and eggs provide two examples of how food assumes significance in different cultures apart from merely serving as something to eat.

Selected Sites

www.glossika.com—Site with information on Chinese (including dialects) and other languages.

www.indo.com/culture/barong.html—Story of an important cultural dance on Bali in Indonesia.

www.tech.mit.edu/Shakespeare—Complete works of Shakespeare.

www.online-literature.com/victor_hugo—Biography and works of Victor Hugo.

http://eclecticesoterica.com/longfellow.html—Collection of Longfellow's poems.

www.timsheppard.co.uk/story/dir/traditions/Africa.html—Tradition of storytelling in Africa.

www.fln.vcu.edu./grimm/grimm_menu.html—Grimm Brothers' fairy tales in German and English.

www.touregypt.net/karnak—Information on the Temple of Karnak.

www.taj-mahal.net—Video tour of the Taj Mahal.

www.greatbuildings.com/buildings/The_Parthenon.html—Information about the Parthenon and the Acropolis.

www.angkorwat.org—Information and pictures of Angkor Wat and nearby historic sites.

www.chinavista.com/beijing/gugong/!start.html—Virtual tour of the Forbidden City in Beijing, China.

www.searac.org/vietref.html—Information on immigration program for refugees from Southeast Asia.

http://eggs-files.tripod.com/pysanky_4.html—Traditions of Ukrainian Easter eggs.

http://archive.1september.ru/eng/2003/14/2.htm—History of eggs in cultures.

www.kresy.co.uk/easter_food.html—Symbolism of eggs and other foods for Easter in Poland.

http://ourladyprairie.home.mchsi.com/Ossymbl.html—Symbolism of designs on Ukrainian Easter eggs.

http://users.vnet.net/schulman/Faberge/eggs.html—Description of the Fabergé eggs for the Czars of Russia.

Study Questions

1. What are the characteristics that describe the cultural group with which you identify most closely?
2. What are some of your food preferences and patterns? Did any of these gain this status with you because of your cultural group (or groups)? If so, explain the foods you have identified in terms of your cultural identity.
3. Using a recent newspaper, describe a current example of how some aspect of culture (as described in this chapter) is influencing the food intake of the people involved.

Bibliography

Armstrong, R.G. 1964. *Sisters Under the Sari.* Iowa State University Press. Ames, IA.

Barer-Stein, T. 1979. *You Eat What You Are.* McClelland and Stewart. Toronto, Canada.

Batmanglij, N.K. 2000. *New Food of Life: Ancient Persian and Modern Iranian Cooking and Ceremonies.* Mage. Washington, DC.

Brown, L.K. and K. Mussell. 1984. *Ethnic and Regional Foodways in the United States.* University of Tennessee Press. Knoxville, TN.

Bryant, C.A., et al. 2004. *The Cultural Feast: Introduction to Food and Society.* 2nd ed. Wadsworth. Belmont, CA.

Katz, S.H. 2003. *Encyclopedia of Food and Culture.* Charles Scribner's Sons. New York.

Geisler, E.M. 1998. *Pocket Guide to Cultural Assessment.* Mosby. St. Louis.

Kurlansky, M. 2002. *Salt.* Walker and Co. New York.

Le Couteur, P. and J. Burreson. 2004. *Napoleon's Buttons.* Jeremy P. Tarcher/Penguin. New York.

Lowenburg, M.E., et al. 1974. *Food and Man.* Wiley. New York.

McIntosh, E.N. 1995. *American Food Habits in Historical Perspective.* Praeger. Westport, CT.

Norris, R.E. and L.L. Haring. 1980. *Political Geography.* Charles E. Merrill Publishing Co. Columbus, OH.

Scarre. C. and B.M. Fagan. 2003. *Ancient Civilizations.* 2nd ed. Prentice Hall. Upper Saddle River, NJ.

Stoddard, R.H., B.W. Blouet, and D.J. Wishart. 1986. *Human Geography: People, Places, and Cultures.* Prentice Hall. Englewood Cliffs, NJ.

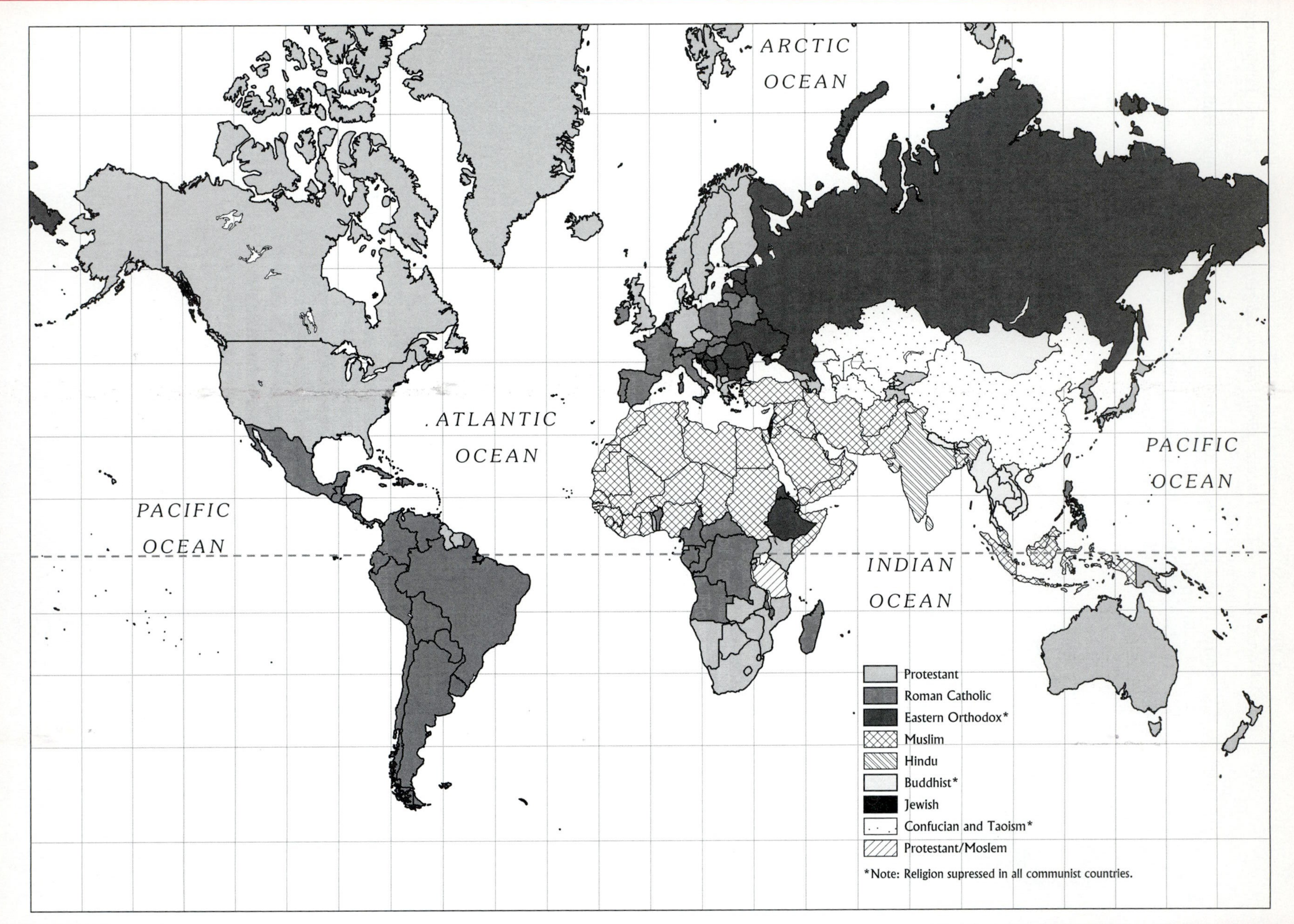
ARCTIC OCEAN
PACIFIC OCEAN
ATLANTIC OCEAN
PACIFIC OCEAN
INDIAN OCEAN
Protestant
Roman Catholic
Eastern Orthodox*
Muslim
Hindu
Buddhist*
Jewish
Confucian and Taoism*
Protestant/Moslem
*Note: Religion supressed in all communist countries.

3 Religions

Beliefs in a god (or gods) have shaped behaviors and cultural patterns of people around the world since very early times. The beliefs and the deities differed quite considerably. Sumerians worshiped Mother Goddess Innin and her son Tammuz around 3000 BCE. Isis and Osiris were important as an Egyptian goddess and god, respectively, around 2500 BCE, approximately the time when Minoans were viewing the snake and bull as religious symbols. Early Greeks had a pantheon of gods and goddesses, including Zeus, Poseidon, Athena, Aphrodite, and many more during the millennium preceding the birth of Christ.

During the intervening centuries, different religions have emerged as dominant in today's world. Christianity includes Protestant, Roman Catholic, and Eastern Orthodox, which together comprise the largest religious group. Islam is the second most numerous when the Sunni, Shiah, and other branches are counted. Hindu believers are the third in terms of numbers, although they are clustered primarily in India and Nepal. Buddhism also has many followers (somewhat more than half as many as Hinduism). Confucianism has many followers in the Far East; in the same region, Shintoism and Taoism also are found but with smaller groups of followers. Judaism is a religion with far fewer followers than the other major religions but with a very significant influence in today's world.

In the United States, significant changes in religious preferences have been taking place even since 1970, due in part to the large numbers of immigrants from many parts of the world who brought their religions with them. The practice of these religions attracted attention and heightened interest in learning about these different approaches to spirituality. Converts to these different religions and immigrants who already practiced the predominant religion of their cultures account for an increasing religious diversity, which adds to the breadth of cultures in America (Table 3.1).

All of these religions are of considerable importance in influencing not only spiritual beliefs of people, but also their value systems and their cultural behaviors,

Table 3.1 Estimates of Religious Affiliations in the United States in 1970 and 2000

Religion	*1970 (millions)*	*2000 (millions)*
Protestants	70.7	88.8
Roman Catholics	48.4	61.8
Jews	6.7	5.5
Muslims	0.8	4.0
Buddhists	0.2	2.0
Hindus	0.1	0.95
Sikhs	0.001	0.22

Adapted from *Encyclopedia Britannica Book of the Year.* 1998. Association of Statisticians of American Religious Bodies.

which may include dietary practices. This chapter provides a review of the major religions of the world. It offers background information about each of these religions but not an in-depth philosophical examination. These glimpses will add insight into the dietary patterns found in the countries and regions where each of these religions holds considerable influence.

Hinduism

Overview

Manu—Source of Hindu laws on living and ancestor of Hindus; progenitor of the human race and source of Vedas.

Vedas—Four volumes of the collective wisdom on how Hindus must live.

Hinduism probably is the oldest continuing religion in the world, with its roots going back to about 2000 BCE. India and Nepal are the primary countries where Hinduism is found. A distinctive aspect of this religion is that it is not based on the life or teachings of a single person or on the worship of a single god (Figure 3.1). Hindus believe in reincarnation and that the spirit is reborn in another form in a seemingly eternal cycle in pursuit of spiritual perfection. **Manu** was the name for the progenitor of the human race and the source of the Vedas. The **Vedas** are four volumes, which are the collective statements on how Hindus must live.

Figure 3.1 Hindu temples, such as this one in Sri Lanka, are elaborately decorated with images of the various gods.

Prominent Gods

Brahma—Creator god in Hindu religion.

Vishnu—Preserver god in Hindu religion.

Shiva—Destructive Hindu god, also called Siva.

Although there are many gods and goddesses in Hinduism, three are dominant: Vishnu and Shiva, the two of prominence today, and Brahma. The belief is that Brahma was responsible for creating the present world and that Shiva will destroy it after about 425,000 years so that **Brahma** can make the world again. In short, Brahma is the creator god of the triad of Hindu gods. In contrast, **Vishnu** is the preserver god, and **Shiva** (or Siva) is the destructive god of Hinduism.

Beliefs

Avatar—Person so saintly that he is thought to be an incarnation of a deity.

Mantra—Hindu incantation.

Om—Sound chanted repeatedly by Hindus for long periods to generate religious energy.

Hinduism is a religion with definite emphasis on mysticism and on becoming free of desires—in short, living an ascetic existence and rising above desires of the flesh. Hindus believe that some people, designated as **avatars,** are incarnations of deities here on earth. Ramakrishna, a prominent Hindu saint, is viewed as an avatar of Shiva. Hindu worship includes chanting of incantations, or **mantras.** The sound involved is **om** (pronounced with a long *o* and extended *m* sound). With extended chanting, a religious energy presumably is generated. Another prayer form is the chanting of "The Thousand Names of Sivasahastranaman (Shiva)."

Caste System

Brahmans—Highest caste in Hinduism; priests and teachers.

Untouchable—Person unworthy of belonging to a caste.

Kshatriyas—Second caste in Hinduism; warriors and rulers.

Vaisyas—Third level Hindu caste; farmers and businesspeople.

Sudras—Lowest Hindu caste; menial workers.

Talik—The colored mark (often red) that many Hindus wear on the forehead between the eyebrows.

Inherent in Hinduism is the caste system, which divides people socially into classes that are required to maintain distinct divisions and privileges (or lack of privileges) associated with each specific caste level. **Brahmans** are the highest of the castes, and the **untouchables** are the lowest. The Brahmans were the priests and teachers and were viewed as being derived from the mouth of Brahma, the universal spirit. Next is the caste called **Kshatriyas,** thought to be from the arms of Brahma and designated as the warriors and rulers.

Vaisyas, the farmers and businesspeople, were from the thighs. Brahma's feet were the caste of menial workers, the **Sudras.** Believers in Hinduism were born into the caste of their ancestors. Anybody who was not born as a Brahman, a Kshatriyas, a Vaisyas, or a Sudras was deemed unworthy and was designated as an untouchable. Indian law prohibits designation as "untouchable," but discrimination still may occur.

Hindus may wear a **talik** on the forehead between the two eyebrows. This mark may indicate caste, or it may indicate the god that is being worshiped or other special religious meaning. It is applied in this location because this is where the body is thought to emanate energy.

Reincarnation

Karma—Force generated by actions in a Hindu's life that will determine what the next life will be.

Fundamental to Hinduism is the lack of upward mobility through the good deeds one might do during life. However, such deeds are believed to be able to exert influence on the soul in which a person is reborn in the next life. The way a person lives is the responsibility of the individual. The fact that status in rebirth is the direct result of the acts in the previous life is a powerful motivation to live according to Hindu beliefs. The new form of the soul in the next life can be far lower than in the present life, or it can be better. The whole purpose is to constantly strive to reach the universal spirit during some future rebirth. The deeds performed in all previous lives determine the nature of a person's next existence; this force is called **karma.**

Respect for Life

All life, whether human or animal, is highly respected by Hindus and is believed to be sacred, because part of the spirit of Brahma is thought to be a part of any living thing. An extension of this belief is that one's ancestor might actually be the spirit of the life that is taken if something is killed. Cows occupy a particularly revered niche because they are thought by Hindus to have been created by Brahma at the same time that people were created. This reverence for **sacred cows** is still seen in India, where they are allowed to wander freely on any street, road, or land they wish.

Sacred cow—Wandering cow where Hindus live; protected from harm because of respect for life.

Holidays

Some of their numerous gods and goddess are prominent in Hindu holidays at various times throughout the year (Figure C.152, p. C51). **Krishna,** worshiped as the eighth incarnation of the god Vishnu, is a figure celebrated as Janmashtami or Gokul Ashtami on the occasion marking his birthday. This unusual celebration features pots of milk curds hung very high so that they can be reached only by boys or men forming a human pyramid topped by someone swinging a stick to break the pots.

Krishna—God celebrated as the eighth incarnation of Vishnu.

Kama, the Hindu god of love, and Krishna are honored at Holi, a lighthearted celebration in which brightly colored powdered dyes are thrown at others as men play pranks and dance around.

Kama—Hindu god of love.

On a more somber note, the festival called Dussara is a time of pageantry to honor Devi, the goddess who is Shiva's wife. This celebration continues for 10 days.

One of the more unusual gods is Ganesha, who is easily recognized because of the happy elephant head and the rotund human belly of his figure. His birthday is celebrated with the holiday Ganesha Chaturthi. Not surprisingly, quantities of food offerings (milk, fruit, and puddings) are featured at this three-day holiday.

Brahmans get new clothing and give away their old sacred clothing as a part of their celebration of Rakhi Purnima to honor Shiva (who has three eyes). The coconut, with its three eyes, is traditional for this celebration, and it is broken at a shrine as part of the festivities.

Rama Navami is another holiday featuring coconuts. In this celebration, a coconut is placed in a cradle to represent the birth of Rama, the seventh incarnation of Vishnu. Dancing and entertainment are featured at this particularly important festival.

Divali is the joyous celebration of the new year. Even fireworks are included. The greeting for the occasion is "A happy Divali and a prosperous new year!"

Hinduism has had many rituals in years past, although today some have been eliminated either by law or by practice. An example is sati, which occurred occasionally in centuries past when a widow would throw herself on her dead husband's funeral pyre and die in self-immolation. Sati was outlawed over 100 years ago. Furthermore, Hindu widows now are allowed to marry again. The class of untouchables also has been eliminated.

Underlying some rituals is the notion of purity and pollution. The ritual of bathing is dictated by the need for purity and the elimination of pollution. Since human wastes are all considered pollution, there are various rituals that are to be followed when coping with these sources of pollution. *Dharma* is a term that encompasses the rituals of daily life. These include rituals for praying, which Brahmans are to do three times daily.

When a child is born, the house must be purified, and the newborn's horoscope must be determined. On the sixth or twelfth day, the baby is named, and the occasion is marked by feeding the baby its first solid food. Ear-piercing may also be done then or at some later time. The child's head may be shaved at the age of one to thank the Deva for safeguarding the child through infancy.

Weddings are of greatest ritual importance, and every Hindu is expected to marry, because it is a religious duty. The religious debt to the couple's ancestors is paid by having children. The rituals associated with the marriage may take more than a week and involve such acts as the couple walking seven times around the sacred fire.

Funerals are needed to empower the departing spirit to leave the present world and to take care of the pollution that is associated with death. The funeral pyre is lighted by the oldest son of the departed (Figure C.115, p. C39). The mourning period, which lasts 10 or 11 days after the cremation, is marked by various rituals that restrict what the relatives can do during that time. The ending ritual involves offerings of balls of rice or barley and some milk. These offerings are also presented annually from then on. This ritual is intended to help the departed get a new spiritual body.

Worship can be done as temple worship (Figure 3.2), home worship, or in congregational worship. Priests are responsible for conducting the rituals associated with the god and goddesses of the particular temple. The ceremonies are marked by a variety of practices, including food and flower offerings, ringing of bells, prayers, music, and possibly other practices. Each household also maintains an area for worship, which may include images, yantras (geometric designs), and offerings, all of which are kept in a state of purity. Pilgrimages are undertaken to such holy sites as Banaras in the hope of achieving a spiritual experience. These efforts often are well arranged and may include religious fairs.

Food Practices

Puja—Hindu worship ritual that begins with seating, cleansing, and dressing a deity. Food is offered to the god and then some is eaten by the worshiper.

Food is offered at a shrine as a part of **puja,** a ritual that is conducted at the shrine in a home or temple (Figure 3.3). The ritual begins in front of the altar with the deity being offered a seat. Ritual washing of its feet, bathing and dressing the figure of the deity, and then adding garlands of flowers follow. Incense is burned, and a lighted lamp is waved in front of the deity. The worshiper bows and offers the deity water and then fruit and cooked food, which have been placed on the altar. Finally, the worshiper eats a bit of the food,

The high respect for life means that many Hindus are vegetarians. Since the cow is considered to be sacred, beef is not eaten by Hindus. Not surprisingly, Brahmans are the caste most likely to forgo eating meats and eggs, which potentially represent life. Castes below that of Brahman do not eat beef but do eat other meats. However, chickens and pigs, viewed as unclean because they may scavenge for food, also may be avoided. Fish seem to be more acceptable than other flesh foods. Animals that are to be killed for food can be killed by people who are in the Kshatriyas caste, for they are designated as the leaders and soldiers.

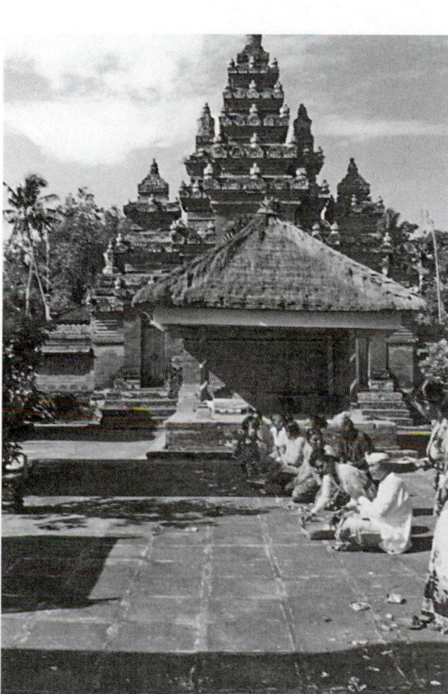

Figure 3.2 On this festival day in Bali, Indonesia, Hindus bring specially prepared food to the temple to be blessed before eating it at home.

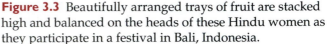

Figure 3.3 Beautifully arranged trays of fruit are stacked high and balanced on the heads of these Hindu women as they participate in a festival in Bali, Indonesia.

Pakka—Hindu word for food containing ghee; offered to gods and then high-ranking guests.

Ghee—Clarified butter made by boiling butter to evaporate the water and precipitate the milk solids before filtering to clarify it.

Kacca—Hindu term for level of food just below pakka but made without ghee.

Good sanitation underlies activities in a Brahman kitchen, for this is considered a holy place. The cook must have a ritual bath before cooking. Lower castes should not prepare the food, but they can give uncooked foods or those cooked in ghee, or clarified butter, to Brahmans. All Brahmans eating the food also need to bathe the entire body and dress in clean clothes. The foods they eat are designated as **pakka,** the foods offered to the gods and then to guests of high rank. All pakka foods contain **ghee.** The next level of food is designated as **kacca** and does not contain ghee, which makes the products, such as bread, drier. If any kacca is left over, it is designated as jutha (garbage). Jutha is suitable for animals, lower castes, or untouchables. Only wives or others of lower status are allowed to scrape kacca from plates.

Brahmans tend to avoid garlic and onions to avoid association with lesser classes. Avoidance of alcohol by Brahmans is required to avoid any possible loss of self-control. Lower Hindu castes, however, are allowed to drink alcohol.

Fasting may be done at various times of the year, particularly in the higher castes. Celestial events (e.g., summer and winter solstice, an eclipse, new and full moon) can mark a day of fasting. Special days, such as the anniversary of the death of a parent, may be fasting days to honor the memory of the person.

Recipes

Jeera Rice (Serves 3)

1 c Basmati rice
1½ tbsp ghee (or clarified butter)
1 tsp each cumin and black cumin seeds (or 2 teaspoons cumin)
1 bay leaf
1 cinnamon stick (2″)
¼ tsp ground cloves
2 tbsp cashews
2 c water
½ tsp salt (or to taste)

1. Wash rice and soak in water to cover for 30 minutes; drain.
2. Heat ghee, spices, and cashews in a 2-quart saucepan, stirring constantly until nuts are pleasingly brown.
3. Stir in the drained rice until it is coated with the ghee mixture.
4. Add water and salt; cover pan and heat to a boil before lowering heat to simmer.
5. Simmer until water is gone and holes are seen on the surface of the rice.
6. Fluff with a fork and serve.

Palak Paneer (Cottage Cheese and Spinach Curry) (Serves 3)

1 tbsp ghee or clarified butter
2 tbsp chopped onion
1 bunch spinach
2 tbsp chopped carrot
1 tbsp chopped tomato
½ tsp ground cumin
¼ tsp ground turmeric
1 tsp garam masala
1 tsp cream
1 c paneer pieces or large curd cottage cheese

1. Heat ghee and sauté onion.
2. Add spinach and carrot; stir while heating until wilted and tender.
3. Stir in tomato, spices, and cream and continue heating for 5 minutes.
4. Stir in paneer and simmer 10 minutes; stir occasionally.

Aloo Ka Bharta (Potatoes and Chilies) (Serves 3)

4 potatoes
2 onions, chopped
1 4-oz can diced green chilies
½ tsp salt
½ tsp chili powder
2 tbsp chopped coriander leaves

1. Pare and boil potatoes; drain and mash briefly.
2. Stir in remaining ingredients.

Buddhism

History

Buddha—Religious name of Siddhartha Gautama, founder of Buddhism.

Buddhism is the religion of vast numbers throughout Southeast Asia, including Taiwan, Vietnam, Cambodia, Laos, Bhutan, Nepal, Tibet, China, Japan, Myanmar (Burma), Thailand, and Sri Lanka. This far-reaching religion began in northeastern India in about 530 BCE and was based on the teachings of Siddhartha Gautama, who became known as **Buddha** (Figure 3.4).

Figure 3.4 A very tall standing Buddha quietly reminds Buddhists of their faith as they pass this statue in Colombo, Sri Lanka.

During his lifetime, Buddha renounced his worldly position and spent six years searching for the truth. His "enlightenment" occurred while he was sitting under the bodhi tree, where he reached *Nirvana* and all worldly desires disappeared. The religion that flowed from his teachings represented a departure or reformation movement from the Hindu roots of India. This was a religion that spread successfully over vast regions but did not replace Hinduism among most Indians. Asoka, the strong Mauryan ruler of India, was converted to Buddhism and did much to spread Buddhism to China, Japan, Korea, and beyond.

Although Buddha is central to the Buddhist religion and is important for his teachings, he is not worshipped as a god. Buddhism has no gods and thus is quite different from Hinduism (Figure C.158, p. C53). Also, there is no caste system. The ultimate goal of Buddhism is to reach **Nirvana,** a process that could involve countless rebirths.

Nirvana—The ultimate state in Buddhism—enlightenment; free of pain, care, and desire.

Foundations

The basic teachings, called the Four Noble Truths, are these:

1. Existence is suffering.
2. The origin of human suffering is craving pleasure, possessions, or cessation of pain.
3. Craving is cured by detachment from oneself and from all things.
4. Detachment is achieved by following the Eight-Fold Path:
   a. Right conduct
   b. Right effort
   c. Right intentions
   d. Right livelihood
   e. Right meditation
   f. Right mindfulness
   g. Right speech
   h. Right viewpoint

The code of conduct, called the dasa-sila or Ten Precepts, includes the following:

1. Thou shalt not take another's life.
2. Thou shalt not take that which is not given.
3. Thou shalt not engage in sexual misconduct. (Monks are to be celibate, and others are not to be adulterous.)
4. Thou shalt not engage in false speech.
5. Thou shalt not use intoxicants.
6. Thou shalt not eat after midday.
7. Thou shalt shun worldly amusements.
8. Thou shalt not adorn with ornaments or perfume.
9. Thou shalt not sleep on high or luxurious beds.
10. Thou shalt not accept gold or silver.

The mantra (chant) is repeated three times: "I take refuge in the Buddha. I take refuge in the teachings. I take refuge in the community."

Buddhism in Practice

Mahayana—Mystical form of Buddhism practiced in Tibet, Mongolia, and the Himalayas.

Theravada—Buddhism sect practiced in Southeast Asia in which monks carry begging bowls in the mornings.

Buddhism is broadly divided into three sects: eastern (Japan, Korea, and China) (Figure C.167 and C.168, p. C56), northern or **Mahayana** (Tibet, Mongolia, and the Himalayas), and southern or **Theravada** (Thailand, Myanmar, Sri Lanka, Cambodia, and Laos). The Theravada in Southeast Asia (Figure 3.5) developed as a monastic sect. The Mahayana (Figure 3.6) in the north developed a somewhat

Figure 3.5 This Buddhist temple in Luang Prabang, Laos, is Theravada, the sect that dominates in Southeast Asia.

Bodhisattva—Semidivine, mystical being incorporated in Mahayana Buddhism.

Kutho—Kind or generous act that brings merit to help strive toward Nirvana.

Stupa—Hemispherical mound within a central decoration, which serves as a shrine for Buddhists.

more mystical approach and included **bodhisattvas** (supernatural, semidivine beings who helped people achieve Nirvana). The Dalai Lama is considered to be the reincarnation of Bodhisattva of Mercy, Avalokitesvara.

In Thailand and the other countries where Theravada Buddhists worship, it is a common sight to see monks strolling about during the mornings with a beggar's bowl (usually brass). This enables the woman of a house to fill or add to the bowl with food she has prepared (Figure C.133, p. C45). Her generous act allows her to gain merit (**kutho**) and, of course, enables the monk to eat during the day until midday, after which he is not to eat.

All Buddhist males following the practices of the Theravada sect are expected to become monks, although their "careers" as monks may be as short as only a few days (Figure 3.7, Figure C.129, p. C43). The monasteries provide education for boys who remain in their group, and the boys provide help to the older monks and to the monastery.

Buddhism has resulted in the creation of innumerable statues of Buddha in different positions—sitting (Figure 3.8), standing, and reclining. Another feature of Buddhism is the construction of **stupas,** which are hemispherical mounds with

Figure 3.6 The Norbulinka Monastery outside Lhasa, Tibet, is Mahayana, the sect of the northern Buddhists.

Figure 3.7 This young boy who lives in Mandalay, Myanmar, is becoming a monk as family and friends join in this important ritual.

Figure 3.8 This sitting Buddha smiles at the partially reconstructed ruins of a Theravada Buddhist temple in Sukhothai, Thailand's early capital in the north.

Pagoda—Shrine of several stories where Buddhists worship.

Chorten—Tibetan (Buddhist) monument, often with some gold or silver gilding.

a central mast or decorative feature (Figure C.116, p. C39). **Pagodas** of various designs and with several stories also serve as shrines for Buddhists. Relics of religious significance may be found in these stupas (Figure 3.8) and pagodas (Figure 3.9): a tooth from Buddha, an alms bowl he used, or an object that symbolizes Buddha, for example.

In Tibet a special type of stupa called a **chorten** is built to house religious relics or to honor a special figure, such as a deceased Dalai Lama. Prayer wheels and prayer flags are other familiar aspects of Buddhist worship in Tibet, Nepal, and Bhutan. By whirling the prayer wheels, Buddhists send their prayers. Prayer flags strung along ropes and tied against the strong breezes of the Himalayas are an efficient way for Buddhists to pray (Figure 3.10).

In Tibet, China, and Japan, as well as in much of Southeast Asia, Buddhism has been influenced by wars and politics (Figure 3.11). However, Buddhism is

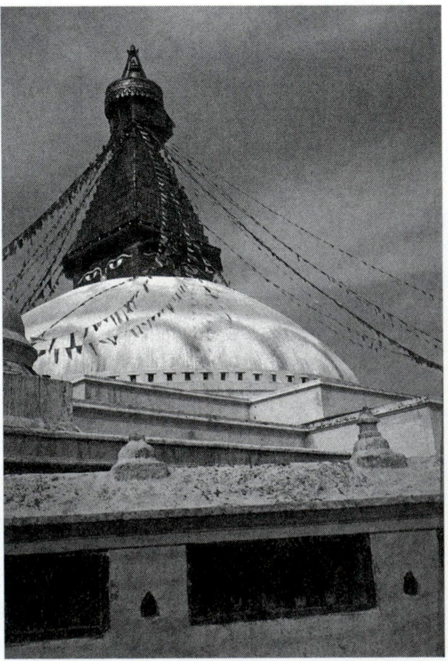

Figure 3.9 The Bodnath stupa near Katmandu, Nepal, is a destination for not only Mahayana sect Buddhists, but also for some Hindus.

Figure 3.10 Buddhist prayer flags flap prayers skyward as the wind whips them in the high Himalayas near Lhasa, Tibet.

practiced in all of these places today in whatever form it has evolved to in the various cultures. One of the enduring attributes of Buddhism over the centuries has been its flexibility to adapt to change and to the needs of its followers, regardless of the sect.

Festivals

Buddhist festivals are calculated according to lunar months, with the full moon being especially important. Festivals of agricultural significance are found in many places where Buddhism is practiced. Festivals of lights typically celebrate the full moon and Buddha's first sermon, as well as the sending out of the first Buddhist missionaries.

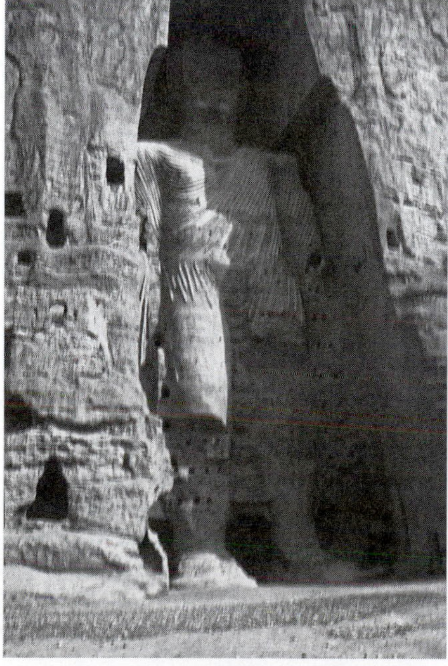

Figure 3.11 Two giant Buddhas stood recessed in their caves from the time they were created in the 3rd century CE near Bamian, Afghanistan, until the Muslim Taliban leaders ordered them destroyed in 2001.

Circumambulate—Process of prostrating and praying repeatedly while encircling a Buddhist temple once or many times.

Local pilgrimages are taken by individual Buddhists, such as can be seen in Lhasa, Tibet, as pilgrims prostrate themselves repeatedly on the road surrounding the Jogkhang Temple as they painfully **circumambulate** this most honored temple clockwise.

Food Practices

Because of the respect for life, Buddhists may abstain from eating meat and fish. However, these foods are not strictly forbidden, and many dishes do contain some meat or fish. If meat is eaten, it should not be meat from an animal that the Buddhist has killed. Rice is the staple of the diet. Moderation in eating is encouraged, and some fasting may be done occasionally.

Monks are likely to be more restricted in their dietary practices than other Buddhists. They may avoid eating meats and fish. They do not eat anything solid after noon. Fasting for the entire day is expected on the new moon and the full moon each month.

Recipes

Yoh Mari (Festival Steamed Dumplings) (Serves 5)

Dough:
- 2 c rice flour
- 1 c boiling water

Filling:
- ¾ c sesame seeds
- 3 tbsp shredded coconut
- ¾ c jaggery (or brown sugar)
- 1 tbsp water (or enough to make very thick sauce)

1. Stir rice flour while adding boiling water and moistening all of the flour. Cover and let rest.
2. Roast sesame seeds in a dry pan until slightly browned.
3. Grind seeds to a fine powder in a blender before adding coconut and grinding again.
4. Transfer to a mixing bowl and add jaggery before stirring in just enough water to make a paste.
5. Work the rice flour dough into a long log before cutting the log into 15 pieces.
6. Roll each piece between your hands to make a ball.
7. With a small spoon, shape a well in the ball, and fill it with 2 teaspoons of filling.
8. Work the filled ball so that the filling is enclosed and sealed within the ball.
9. Place on a steamer tray after shaping into a fish or other creative shape. Leave at least half an inch between dumplings because they swell during steaming.
10. Steam for 12 minutes.

Dal Bhat (Lentil Soup) (Serves 4)

- 1 c lentils
- ½ tsp salt
- 3 c water
- 2 tsp grated fresh ginger root
- 1 tbsp canned diced green chilies
- 1 tsp peanut oil
- ¼ tsp cumin seeds
- ½ tsp 5-spice powder (or curry powder)
- 4 sprigs of cilantro

1. Simmer lentils in salted water until soft (20 minutes).
2. Purée lentils with the ginger and chilies.
3. Heat oil and cumin in a frying pan until seeds pop.
4. Add lentil mixture and 5-spice powder to the frying pan and heat while stirring for 4 minutes.
5. Serve garnished with cilantro.

Potato Curry (Serves 4)

4 c potatoes (e.g., Red Triumph), cut in large cubes
1½ tbsp peanut oil
1 medium onion, chopped
1 tbsp grated ginger root
2 garlic cloves, minced
¼ tsp fenugreek
1 tsp curry powder
½ tsp powdered cumin
¼ tsp turmeric
2 c water
4 sprigs coriander

1. Boil potatoes until barely soft. Drain.
2. In a large saucepan, heat oil and sauté onion, ginger root, and garlic until barely browned.
3. Add seasonings and water to the saucepan and simmer 30 minutes, covered.
4. Add the potatoes and continue cooking until potatoes are tender. Add more water, if needed.
5. Serve garnished with coriander.

Confucianism and Taoism

Confucianism

Religion in China for the majority of the people is a blend of Confucianism, Taoism, and Buddhism. Confucianism underlies the morality and behavior of people, including rites of passage. Taoism provides for the needs and healing of the sick and is a basis for regulating festivals. Buddhism is the source of compassion in life and salvation after life. The three together provide for all aspects of life, both during and after.

Confucianism can be traced back to six centuries BCE. Confucianism evolved into a school collected into the Four Books and Five Classics. The founder of Confucianism was a 6th century BCE man named **Confucius,** or K'ung Fu-tzu (Master Kung). He taught that the way to live was by correct ethical conduct, which would allow one to achieve ideal harmony with the "way of Heaven" and make one become more than human.

Confucius—Chinese philosopher (551–479 BCE) whose teachings form the basis of Confucianism.

Actually, Confucianism presents ways to live one's life, but it is not a religion. It does not include worship of a god. Respect for parents and loyalty to the government are precepts of Confucianism. There also is emphasis on continuing in the type of social order in which a person is born and striving toward loving, kindly relationships with family and friends.

Followers of Confucianism have many guidelines for living. From Confucianism come the norms for behaviors, which embrace (1) respect, (2) family love, (3) benevolence toward strangers, and (4) loyalty to the state. However, Confucius surprisingly did not define guidelines or prohibitions on eating.

Taoism

Taoism was founded slightly later than Confucianism and was based on teachings from Chuang-Tzu and Lao-Tzu in the 6th century BCE. The goal of Taoism was to achieve a passionless oneness with the divine Absolute, a process that encouraged a passive approach to living one's life and a peaceful acceptance while awaiting death. Retreat into meditation and nature or into a life as a monk or isolated person allowed for connecting with the ways of nature. Thrift, humility, simplicity, patience, contentment, and harmony are the basic principles of Taoism.

Contributions from Taoism in current Chinese religions stem from the cosmic concept that Tao gave birth to the primordial breath (the One), which birthed yin and yang (the Two), which gave birth to water, earth, and heaven (the Three), which birthed the myriad creatures. This becomes a never-ending cycle in Taoism as the myriad creatures return to Tao. The concept of cosmos can be summarized

Yang—In taoism, the term for heaven.

Yin—In taoism, the term for the underworld and its nine stages.

in terms of yin and yang. Pure **yang** is heaven, the visible world of life is both yang and yin, and the underworld (in nine stages) is pure **yin.** The soul is believed to sink into the domain of pure yin for a period following death, where it can ultimately be freed to ascend to heaven.

Rituals and Food

Unlike Hinduism and Buddhism, Confucianism and Taoism do not provide guidelines for daily eating. However, many traditions and rituals have developed in China over the centuries during which the culture has been evolving. Several of these include food traditions that are based predominantly on a vegetarian diet. Soy products, whole grains, vegetables, nuts, seeds, herbs, (sometimes medicinal herbs), and tea are the main components, and meats, dairy, and additives are usually avoided.

Marriage Traditional marriage rituals begin with a three-day period when the characters representing the year, month, day, and hour of birth of both the prospective bride and groom are placed on the family altar in the bride's family home. If all goes well in that household during those three days, invitations are sent for the wedding. A special procession is the means for transporting the bride's vanity box and dowry to the household of the groom and his family, where he opens the vanity box (symbolizing sincere love) and the dowry is counted.

The groom matches the value of the dowry in such items as jewelry or clothing for the bride. The groom then must go to his bride's home and take her back to his home, which she enters by stepping over a cooking pot, a saddle, and an apple. At the reception following the marriage ceremony, the bride and groom make a small rice wine toast before proceeding with toasts (tea) at each of the tables of guests at their wedding dinner. The next morning the bride serves breakfast to her new in-laws, including dried dates and seeds to signify many children as a gift from the bride; then they serve her breakfast. Finally, she is a guest in her own parents' home on the third day.

Pregnancy Rituals are important in the Chinese religious culture. For example, pregnant women are excused from a variety of chores that might impose undue physical or psychological pressures. They also are expected to be fed a diet rich in protein and vitamins by other family members for one month following delivery. Gifts that might include eggs and rice or other special healthy foods to symbolize good health and prosperity are given in the first, fourth, and twelfth month after birth. The new mother's family is expected to give all of the clothing and diapers at these times too.

Death A death in the family also invokes religious rituals, beginning with wailing at the moment of death, followed by removal of jewelry and fine clothes as mourning begins. White-paper-wrapped money or other talismans are placed as a cover over the body as symbols of protection from harm and of purification for the deceased. Money gifts and condolences are given to help the family with the funeral. The burning of a paper house with its furnishings, symbolic clothes, and paper money combines appreciation of the merits of living and prayers for eternal salvation for the dead. A willow branch to represent the deceased is a part of the family's procession with the coffin to the grave, and it then is carried to the family altar at home to put the soul into the memorial tablet. Special liturgies are to be performed by the deceased's minister 7, 9, and 49 days after the burial as well as on the first and third anniversaries of the death.

Festivals Some festivals have food traditions as a part of the celebration. The Lunar New Year (festival of spring) is celebrated by a big gathering of family from all over to share a banquet. To celebrate the family's ancestors, five or seven sets of chopsticks, bowls of cooked rice, wine, and tea are placed at the family altar. The family members then share a huge banquet (16 or 24 courses): three or five kinds of cooked meat, noodles, bean curd, vegetable dishes, cake, sweets, dried fruit, and fish. The celebration includes gifts and cash in a red envelope for children. Women don flowers in their hair, and fireworks add to the festivities, which include visits to friends, to shrines, and to churches.

The third day of the third lunar month is a festival day for cleaning graves and a family picnic. Rice cakes are eaten for the festival on the fifth day of the fifth lunar month (the first day of summer), and dragon boat races are held where possible. The 15th day of the seventh month is the all souls' day festival, which is the occasion for another large family banquet. Fresh fruits and round mooncakes are the traditional fare for the harvest festival on the 15th day of the eighth lunar month.

Shintoism

Kami—The supernatural form of a deceased ancestor.

Shinto was the religion of early Japan and still is in practice today (Figure 3.12, Figure C.174, p. C58), as is Buddhism and sometimes blends of religions. Ancestors are revered in Shinto; each ancestor is assumed to become a **kami,** or supernatural being, following death, and as such remains as a life within the family. Kami can be either good or evil, depending upon the life the person led on earth.

Among the patron saints in Shinto is a dwarf named Okuninushi, or Master of the Great Land, who is the saint of rice wine brewing. The Emperor of Japan is the person who symbolically shares new rice and rice wine with Shinto deities, according to a very careful ritual, and by doing so assumes his own divinity. Some Japanese homes still maintain two altars: a kami altar for life and its activities and a Buddha altar for death and ancestral veneration. Both altars are maintained with fresh food and drink at the start of each day.

Festivals

Festivals highlight the religious calendar in Japan at various times of year. The three-day New Year celebration is marked by thoroughly cleaning house and yard and paying all debts, as well as by visits to elderly relatives, teachers, and others. If a family member has died during the year, the family does not celebrate, but it does send cards to friends, asking them not to send New Year's greetings

Figure 3.12 A Shinto shrine in Kyoto, Japan.

this time. The Bon festival is held in the summer, at which time many return to the family home to honor their ancestors who are on their ancestral tablet.

Family graves are cleaned and freshened on the occasion of the spring and autumnal equinoxes, and a family picnic is held at the graves. Children are taken to their Shinto shrine to be presented to the kami at the end of the first month of life and again at ages three and seven if a girl and at age five if a boy. These rituals are conducted to place each child under the divine care of the kami. Religious rites associated with death tend to follow Buddhist traditions.

Judaism

Torah—Five books of the Old Testament that are the foundation of Judaism.

Talmud—Authoritative body of Jewish tradition.

Maimonides—Spanish Jew who wrote the law code of Judaism in the 12th century.

Diaspora—Settling of Jews outside of Palestine.

The history of Judaism traces back to ancient Hebrews who developed their religion based on their belief in one God, who was revealed to them, the Chosen People. The **Torah** (Pentateuch, or first five books of the Old Testament of the Bible) provided the foundation to which were added the Neviim (the Prophets) and Ketuvim (writings) to ultimately compose a 24-book Hebrew Bible. The **Talmud** contains extensive oral teachings and many other important interpretations of the Jewish faith. **Maimonides,** a Spanish Jew who lived from 1135 to 1204, authored the Mishneh Torah, which provided the great law code of Judaism (Figure 3.13).

The stories of early Judaism are those of the books of Genesis, Exodus, Leviticus, Numbers, and Deuteronomy and of such powerful figures as Abraham (patriarch and founder of the Hebrews) and Moses (Hebrew prophet who led the Israelites out of Egypt). Although Judaism was centered in Judea (Figure C.53, p. C18), history has chronicled the Jewish **diaspora** to far-flung regions over a period of centuries. The conquest of Babylonia and the destruction of the First Temple in Jerusalem resulted in Jews being exiled to Babylon.

Invasion of Judea by the Romans in 63 BCE started another dark period for the Jews, a time in which the Temple was again destroyed (70 CE). The brave rebels who had fled to Masada (overlooking the Dead Sea) all died dramatically in 73 CE. Jews gained some prominence in Rome because of their cultural and economic abilities, talents that they revealed wherever they settled.

Figure 3.13 This statue of Maimonides, the noted Jewish philosopher and physician, stands in a small square in Cordoba, Spain, where he was born.

Sephardic Jews—Jews in Spain and Portugal.

Ashkenazi Jews—Jews living in northern Europe and Russia.

Rosh Hashanah—Celebration of the Jewish New Year.

Shofar—Hollowed out ram's horn blown in the synagogue during Rosh Hashanah to call man to be aware of his shortcomings and to emphasize that God is the divine king.

Yom Kippur—Day of Atonement; celebration 10 days after Rosh Hashanah.

Sukkot—Nine-day Festival of Tabernacles; celebrated five days after Yom Kippur.

Hanukkah—Feast of Lights in memory of the rededication of the Second Temple and the miracle of the oil lighting the lamp for eight days in 165 BCE; also spelled *Chanukah.*

Menorah—Jewish candelabra designed to hold four candles in a row on each side of a central holder that is slightly higher than the other eight holders; one additional candle is lighted each day of the eight days of Hanukkah.

Purim—Celebration of the rescue of Jews from under the Persian ruler Haman.

Pesach—Eight-day celebration marking the escape of the Israelites from Egypt; also called *Passover.*

Shavuot—Celebration of Moses receiving the Ten Commandments in the Sinai; Pentecost.

Shabbat—Weekly religious observance from sundown Friday until darkness falls on Saturday.

Bar Mitzvah—Celebration of maturity at which a boy reads from the Torah in the synagogue at age 13.

Bat Mitzvah—Celebration of a girl reaching maturity (age 12).

Eventually, Jews were living in much of Europe. In Spain they played very significant roles in commerce and the economy. However, the adoption of Christianity in the Roman Empire in the 4th century CE caused increasing isolation for Jews throughout the Empire. The conquest of Spain by Muslims in 711 CE gave considerable acceptance and recognition to the Jews there, but they were expelled when the Moors were driven out of Spain and the Catholic monarchs, Ferdinand and Isabella, ruled in 1492.

The Jews who lived in Spain and Portugal were identified as **Sephardic Jews,** and those who were situated in northern Europe and toward Russia were called **Ashkenazi Jews.** Sephardic Jews were treated with some degree of tolerance by people in the Muslim world, but the Ashkenazi Jews suffered extreme persecution in many cases. These two divisions have some differences, but they both believe in the foundations of Judaism.

Religious Celebrations

The Jewish ritual calendar has 12 lunar months, which requires leap months to accommodate the 11 days that would be missing to keep in step with the agricultural seasons. On this calendar, **Rosh Hashanah** (the New Year) occurs in late September or early October (2005 was 5766 on the Jewish calendar). The **shofar** (a hollowed out ram's horn) traditionally is blown in the synagogue during Rosh Hashanah (Table 3.2). Ten days later is **Yom Kippur** (the Day of Atonement). Five days after Yom Kippur is **Sukkot** (the Festival of Tabernacles), which is a nine-day event.

About two months later, **Hanukkah** (Festival of Lights) is celebrated for eight days in remembrance of the miracle that oil found in the temple after the defeat of the Greeks (who had conquered the Jewish homeland and repressed religion) continued to burn in the temple lamps for eight days. Celebration of this festival includes lighting one more candle on the **menorah** each of the eight days. Asarah Be-Tevet (the 10th of the month of Tevet) is a fast day.

The 14th day of the Jewish month of Adar is **Purim,** a festival based on the book of Esther (from the Bible). **Pesach** (Passover) is an eight-day celebration that is held in the spring. **Shavuot** (Festival of Pentecost) is held seven weeks after the second day of Passover. A three-week period of mourning begins five weeks after Shavuot with a daytime fast (Shivah Asar Be-Tammuz) and ends with a 25-hour fast (Tisha Be-Av). There also are minor festivals at the beginning of each lunar month (Rosh Codesh). **Shabbat** is celebrated each week, beginning at sunset on Friday and ending when it is dark on Saturday (Figure 3.14).

Traditions

In Judaism, traditions are very important on special occasions and in daily living. Children born of a Jewish mother are considered to be Jews; the father does not have to be Jewish, although a Jewish father is preferred. If a male baby is born, circumcision is done on the eighth day to symbolize the baby's entry into the covenant God made with Abraham and his descendants; a feast celebrates this event.

Careful and thorough instruction in Hebrew and in the translations of parts of the Torah and prayers continues for both boys and girls until they reach maturity (12 for girls and 13 for boys), at which time their maturity is celebrated by the **Bar Mitzvah** for boys and **Bat Mitzvah** for girls. At a Bar Mitzvah, a boy will read from the Torah in the synagogue, and a very elaborate family party, which also includes friends, will be held. Bat Mitzvah celebrations usually are somewhat less elaborate (and may not occur in Orthodox families).

Marriage in Judaism is extremely important, for the family occupies a central position in the religion. The ceremony is held under a canopy, sometimes in the synagogue (unless the marriage is with a non-Jewish person) and occasionally

Table 3.2 Jewish Holidays: Their Timing, Significance, and Mode of Celebration

Holiday	*Timing*	*Significance*	*Mode of Celebration*
Rosh Hashanah (New Year)	2 days; late September or October	New Year; divine judgment (fate of world for next year determined).	Shofar blown 100 times to symbolize awareness of shortcomings and repentance. Sweet foods on first day symbolize good year to come; fast on second day remembering tragic event in past.
Yom Kippur (Day of Atonement)	10 days after Rosh Hashanah	Seek atonement from God for past sins.	Fast day (25 hours beginning at dusk). Mostly spent in the synagogue in worship. No leather shoes are worn.
Sukkot (Tabernacles)	9 days; begins 5 days after Yom Kippur	Commemorates flight from Egypt.	Ritual of Tabernacles: taking of palm branch, willows, myrtle, and a citrus shaken together during prayers. No work is done on first two days or on last day. End yearly cycle of Torah readings and begin reading Genesis again. Singing, dancing, and alcohol.
Hanukkah (Chanukah, Feast of Lights)	8 days; 2 months after Sukkot	Commemorates victory of Hasmonean priests over non-Jewish and rededication of second Temple in 165 BCE; Feast of Lights recalls Talmudic tale of 1 day's oil burning in Temple for 8 days.	One candle is lighted each day on the menorah (total of 8); fruits, nuts, and sweet treats are served; children receive small gifts of wrapped money. Star of David and gifts wrapped in blue and white paper are prominent during the celebration.
Asarah Be-Tevet	10th day of Tevet	Remembers tragic event.	Fast day.
Purim	14th day of Adar	Commemorates rescue of Jews from Persia and its leader Haman (as told in book of Esther).	Elaborate, dressy day with gifts, a big feast in afternoon, and much alcohol.
Pesach (Passover)	8 days; 1 month after Purim	Commemorates the Passover and Exodus of Israelites from Egypt. Very important family holiday.	Complete cleaning of house, removal of all leaven. Seder (ritual meal) and the story of the Exodus the first night; 4 cups of wine are drunk; bitter herbs and unleavened bread are ritual foods.
Shavuot (Pentecost)	7 weeks following Passover	Festival of Pentecost; celebrates time when Moses received the Ten Commandments on Mt. Sinai.	Study the Torah all night.
Shabbat (Sabbath)	Begins every Friday at sunset; ends Saturday at dark.	Sabbath, or seventh day; day of rest and worship.	Mother lights candles before Shabbat begins, father blesses children for reciting kiddush and says blessing over two loaves of challah (special bread); hymns sung at the three Shabbat meals; Shabbat ends with prayer over wine, incense, and lighted candle.

outdoors (the preference of some Ashkenazi Jews). A ritualistic service often is presented by the rabbi and the synagogue cantor and includes the traditional breaking of a glass, symbolizing the poignancy of the great joy of the wedding with the tragedy of the destruction of Jerusalem.

Funerals for Jewish people also involve many traditions. The burial needs to be done immediately or just as soon as possible after death, and a little dirt from Israel is thrown on the coffin before it is lowered into consecrated ground in a Jewish cemetery. Official mourning is done by the next of kin for a week and in-

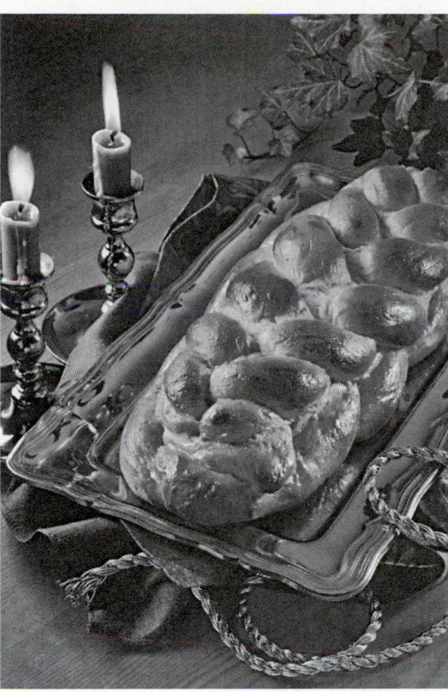

Figure 3.14 Challah is the bread traditionally served by Jews for Shabbat.

cludes sitting on low stools, not wearing leather shoes, and praying with people who come to comfort them.

Worship in the synagogue is shorter during the week than on Saturdays, but there are prayers for morning, afternoon, and evening; worshipers face Jerusalem and the Ark of the synagogue where the Torah is placed. Saturday morning services may last as long as three hours and include more reading from the Torah, prayers, and chanting.

Yarmulke—Skullcap worn by Jewish men.

Orthodox services are conducted by men, with the women attendees seated in a special gallery, whereas Reform and Conservative services, if held in a temple rather than a synagogue, have combined seating and participation in the service. Orthodox and Conservative Jewish men wear the **yarmulke** (type of skullcap) in the synagogue, and Orthodox men wear it at all times to show respect and reverence to God. Orthodox married women also cover their hair, at least in the synagogue.

In Orthodox homes, strict practices are followed. The men may choose to wear the black hats and long black coats that have so long been a traditional garment. Another traditional male garment is a four-cornered vest with strings fastened to each corner, which is a version of the prayer shawl used for morning prayers

Among Jewish people in the United States today, the differences in traditions and approaches to Judaism are creating potentially sharp divisions within the faith. A 1997 survey among Jewish households throughout metropolitan Los Angeles found that 4.3 percent of those surveyed were Orthodox, 28.2 percent were Conservative, 39.9 percent were Reform, and 2 percent were Reconstructionist. A 2001 census of U.S. synagogues reported 3,727 synagogues, of which 40 percent were Orthodox, 26 percent were Reform, and 23 percent were Conservative. The number of members was not included in the study. The trend since 1979 has been a reduction in the numbers of both Orthodox and Conservative with an increase in Reform and Reconstructionists.

Kashruth—Requirements outlining the preparation and types of food that Orthodox and other Jews may eat.

Kosher—Ritually prepared and approved for consumption.

Food Practices

Kashruth spells out kosher requirements for Orthodox Jews and others wishing to have the purity connoted by selecting foods designated officially as **kosher.** In the Orthodox kitchen, separate utensils and dishes must be used for meat and for dairy foods, and strict dietary laws (kashruth) are practiced. Kosher products in the market are designated with such markings as K.U. or COR, signs that indicate rabbinical approval.

Meats that can be eaten include only those from animals that chew their cud and have a cloven (split) hoof, and these must be slaughtered and bled according to kosher requirements, which includes slaughter by a butcher (shochet) who uses a very sharp knife (challef) following the prescribed kosher method. The meat is soaked in cold water and then salted with kosher (coarse) salt for an hour and allowed to drain on a slanted board to remove the blood. Finally, the meat is washed before it is considered fit for consumption.

The types of meat that can be eaten by people following kashruth include beef, sheep, goat, and deer. Fish with scales and fins are also approved, but mollusks and crustaceans are prohibited. Chickens and turkeys are approved, but ostrich is not.

These and other dietary laws are contained in Leviticus and Deuteronomy. The quote in Deuteronomy and in Exodus suggests that a kid should not be cooked in its mother's milk, which is the basis for waiting between one and six hours between eating meat and dairy products, the timing being quite variable among rabbis.

Hasidic Jews who trace their sect to 18th century Poland follow particularly strict kashruth rules, even requiring that such egg-containing products as egg noodles be prepared by a Hasidic because there is a very remote possibility that the egg might have a blood spot.

Food Traditions

Seder—Traditional celebration held on the second night of Passover.

Special foods are important in Jewish traditions. Although each family has special favorites, certain dishes are familiar in most homes, especially for holidays and feasts. Some of these are listed in Table 3.3. **Seder** is the traditional celebration that is held on the second night of Passover. The Seder plate (Figure 3.15) is featured before the meal and includes these symbols: maror (bitter herbs); karpas

Table 3.3 Selected Traditional Jewish Favorite Dishes

Dish	*Description*	*Holiday*
Latke	Fried potato pancake.	Hanukkah
Gefilte fish	Baked or stewed fish balls containing egg, bread, and seasonings.	Sabbath eve dinner
Matzo[a]	Unleavened flat bread made of flour and water and baked in a very hot oven.	Passover
Matzo meal	Coarsely ground matzo used in place of flour or bread crumbs during all of Passover.	Passover
Matzo farfel	Coarse pieces of matzo similar to flaked cereals; replaces noodles and pasta during Passover.	Passover
Matzo cereal	Used in place of cream of wheat and as a thickener in place of flour.	Passover
Hamantashen	Prune and poppy-seed-filled three-cornered cookies (eat Haman's hat).	Purim
Challah	Two circles or loaves baked for Sabbath, symbolizing double portion of manna provided by God on Fridays for Sabbath during 40 years in the wilderness.	Sabbath eve
Challah	Bread with birds or ladders to carry Rosh Hashanah prayers to heaven. With slice of apple and honey, gives wish for sweet new year.	Rosh Hashanah
Kreplach	Pasta-wrapped meat morsels (Jewish tortellini).	Meal before Yom Kippur fast
Honey cake	Spicy, sweet cake made with honey and perhaps dried fruit.	Rosh Hashanah or to break fast of Yom Kippur

[a] Matzo in various forms is used in preparing foods during Passover. Flour is not to be used (actually, no flour is in the house nor are any products made with regular flour in the house at that holiday).

Figure 3.15 The seder plate is arranged with maror (bitter herbs); karpas (vegetable); chazeret (bitter vegetable); charoset (apple, nut, wine, and spice mixture); zeroa (shank bone); and beitzah (egg).

(vegetable); chazeret (bitter vegetable); charoset (apple, nut, wine, and spice mixture); zeroa (shank bone); and beitzah (egg). Family and guests participate in the readings and ceremony preceding the Seder dinner.

Recipes

Gefilte Fish (Serves 4)

Balls:
- 1 lb boneless white fish, ground
- 1 onion, chopped
- 2 carrots, grated
- 2 eggs, beaten
- 1 tsp salt
- 1 tbsp sugar
- ½ tsp pepper
- ⅔ c matzo meal

Broth:
- 1 carrot, sliced
- 1 onion, chopped
- 1 tbsp salt
- 3 tbsp sugar
- ½ tsp pepper
- 1 qt water

1. Combine ingredients for the balls and shape into balls, squeezing tightly.
2. Place ingredients for the broth in a large pan and heat to boiling.
3. Carefully add the balls; simmer for 2 hours, adding more water as needed to keep the balls immersed.
4. Cool before removing balls and refrigerating. Serve cold with horseradish.

Brisket for Hanukkah (Serves 8)

- 1 beef brisket (about 4 lbs)
- ½ tsp salt
- 1 tsp pepper
- 1½ tsp paprika
- 1 tbsp corn oil
- 1 onion, chopped
- ½ c sun-dried tomatoes
- 2 tbsp lemon juice
- ⅓ c catsup
- ⅓ c brown sugar

1. Sprinkle brisket with salt, pepper, and paprika before browning all sides in a Dutch oven.
2. Scatter onion and tomato over the meat.
3. Stir lemon juice, catsup, and brown sugar together before pouring over meat.
4. Cover and simmer for 3 hours until fork tender.

Chicken for Purim (Serves 4)

2 chicken breasts, split in half
1 onion, chopped
1 garlic clove, minced
½ c chopped prunes
½ c chopped apple
⅓ c chopped raisins
⅓ c chopped dried apricots
¾ tsp cinnamon
½ tsp pepper
¼ tsp salt
¼ tsp saffron
¼ tsp curry powder
1 lemon, thinly sliced

1. Mix the ingredients except the chicken and lemon.
2. Spread fruit-spice mixture over chicken, and garnish with the lemon slices.
3. Bake in 400°F oven for 40 minutes.

Borekas (Vegetable-Filled Pastries) (15 Pieces)

Dough:
- 1½ c flour
- ¼ tsp salt
- ½ c shortening
- ¼ c water

Filling:
- 1 tbsp oil
- 1 onion, finely chopped
- 1 10-oz package frozen spinach, thawed and drained very dry
- ¼ c chopped parsley

Glaze:
- 1 egg
- 1 tbsp water
- 1 tbsp sesame seeds

1. Mix the flour and salt together.
2. Add the shortening and cut into pieces the size of rice grains.
3. Toss flour mixture with a fork while adding water by drops.
4. Stir flour mixture until it holds together. Cover and set aside while preparing filling.
5. Heat oil and sauté onion until golden.
6. In a blender, purée the onion and spinach.
7. Roll the dough into a thin sheet.
8. Cut dough into 15 circles 3 inches in diameter.
9. Place spoonful of filling on each round.
10. Fold dough over to make semicircles and seal by pressing edges continuously with a fork.
11. Transfer to a baking sheet before brushing surface with the egg and water glaze and sprinkling with sesame seeds.
12. Bake in a preheated oven at 400°F until golden brown (about 10 minutes).

Matzo Balls (12 balls)

1 c matzo meal
½ c water
1 c minced onion
1 tbsp corn oil
4 eggs
¼ tsp salt
¼ tsp pepper
¼ c chopped parsley
1 qt chicken broth

1. Soak matzo in water in a mixing bowl.
2. Sauté onion in oil until golden.
3. Beat eggs with seasonings and parsley.
4. Add the soaked matzo meal and onions; mix thoroughly.
5. Chill mixture at least an hour.
6. Roll into balls about an inch in diameter while heating a pan of chicken broth to boiling.
7. Add matzo balls and simmer until balls rise to the top (about 10 minutes). No peeking is allowed.

Carrots for Seder (Serves 4)

1 lb baby carrots
1 tbsp honey
¼ tsp salt
½ tsp grated ginger

1. Boil carrots in water to barely cover for 6 minutes. Drain.
2. Stir in the remaining ingredients.

Christianity

Christianity as a religion separate from Judaism developed in the early centuries following the death of Jesus. The Old Testament was accepted as a record of early important events, which is not surprising, since Jesus and his disciples were born as Jews and lived in that context during at least a part of their lives. However, the interpretation of Jesus on earth and thereafter provides the schism between Judaism and Christianity.

The name *Christian*, derived from the Greek *Cristos* (translation from the Hebrew word *Messiah*), was coined in about 35 CE in Syria to describe a group worshiping there. The New Testament, with its first four chapters attributed to the apostles Matthew, Mark, Luke, and John, and other books added later, provided the written foundation for the period that included Christ, and the combination of the Old and New Testaments became the Bible for Christians.

Although early believers in Christianity had been born as Jews, the religion fanned out from Jerusalem and attracted many converts who had never been Jews. Eventually, Christianity became widespread among Gentiles, and new traditions gradually evolved.

Hellenistic influences contributed to the developing religion, with a large role being played by the apostle Paul. Roman Emperor Constantine became a Christian, which led to a strong Christian influence in the Roman Empire for centuries, especially in the Eastern Roman Empire.

Eastern Orthodox Church—Church resulting when the Roman Catholic Church was split and the eastern part was no longer controlled from Rome.

The Roman Catholic Church was split permanently when the branch in Constantinople officially broke away in 1054 CE. The **Eastern Orthodox Church** (Figure 3.16), which also is referred to as the *Greek Orthodox* and the *Russian Orthodox Church*, is a version of Christianity in which icons are the tradition, and

Figure 3.16 This statue of a patriarch stands in front of a Greek Orthodox Church in Athens, Greece.

Jesus, the Divine Son, is the icon or image of what humans can aspire to be. The four patriarchates (Jerusalem, Antioch, Alexandria, and Constantinople) of Eastern Orthodoxy exist even today, although they are diminished in numbers of followers. Eastern Christianity also had an ancient group of churches that were termed *Oriental* and that remain today as the Coptic Orthodox Church (Egypt) and as the Church of Ethiopia and the Church of Armenia.

Roman Catholic Church—Western branch of the Christian faith that remained after the Eastern Orthodox Church split away.

The **Roman Catholic Church** was the branch of Christianity that developed in Roman times and remains today, with its headquarters at the Vatican and the Pope as its head. The sacraments of the Roman Catholic Church included the rites of baptism, confirmation, marriage, Eucharist, penance, anointing of the sick before death, and ordination. Latin became the language of the Roman Catholic Church and was spread throughout the western part of Europe (Figure 3.17, Figure C.22, p. C8) from Scandinavia to the Danube region despite the confusion of the Middle Ages. However, discontent with the religion was festering in the northern region of the European continent.

Martin Luther—German priest credited with creating the rift in the Roman Catholic Church that resulted in the Protestant movement.

October 31, 1517, was a historic day in Wittenberg, Germany, for it was there that **Martin Luther** (an ordained Roman Catholic priest) nailed to the cathedral doors his 95 theses enumerating objections to practices within the Roman Catholic Church. This posting sparked the break with Rome that resulted in the Protestant branch of Christianity and eventually its several independent groups around the western world, including Methodists, Presbyterians, Congregationalists, and many others (Figure 3.18).

Protestant churches used the language of the regions where they were practiced rather than the Latin of the Roman Catholic Church. The freedom of religious thought generated by the Protestant movement engendered the start of the rather wide range of church groups that are considered Christian now but are clearly neither Roman Catholic nor Orthodox. Despite the many differences among Christian groups, there is agreement that God is the Holy Father, the Spirit, and the Holy Ghost; that He made Heaven and Earth; that Jesus was God's only son and that Jesus rose from the dead. Baptism and communion (the ingestion of wine and bread, symbolizing the blood and body of Christ) are unifying rituals in Christianity.

Figure 3.17 The cathedral in Cologne, Germany, was built over a period of 600 years, starting in 1248 CE.

Figure 3.18 Protestant churches, such as this one on Cape Cod in Massachusetts, are divided into several denominations.

Sunday was the holy day in the Christian calendar because it was the first day of the week (Mark 16:2, which states that the resurrection occurred early in the morning of the first day of the week). This designation had the advantage of distinguishing the Christian holy day from the Jewish Sabbath, which was on Saturday.

Religious Holidays

Religious holidays for Christians focus particularly around Christ's death and birth. Christians dwelt more on the event of death and the hereafter than did Jews, so it is not surprising that the events around Christ's death were honored before traditions arose around his birth. Easter was established as the Sunday following the first full moon after the vernal equinox, falling between March 22 and April 25. The Eastern Orthodox Church observes its Easter only after the Jewish Passover, which can represent a delay of a month from the Easter celebration of other Christian churches.

Coincidental with the selection of the date for Easter was the pagan celebration of Eastre, the fertility goddess of spring. The tradition of the Easter bunny for Christian children may have sprung from the acknowledged fertility of hares. Another Easter pagan ritual was the sacrificing of a horned bull, which led to the practice of tracing the pattern of the crossed horns into the top of bread, probably the forerunner of Easter's traditional fare of hot cross buns.

The observance of Lent for 40 days prior to Easter evolved as a time to contemplate and consider one's life and behaviors. The precedent for the 40-day period may have been Jesus' fast for 40 days after he was baptized, or it may refer to the time Moses and Elias spent wandering in the wilderness, or it may even symbolize the 40 years the Jews wandered in search of the Promised Land. The first day of Lent is Ash Wednesday, a time when a smudge of ash in the shape of a cross is marked on the forehead, the ash preferably being from the palm leaves kept from the previous Easter's Palm Sunday celebration.

The actual week of Easter is a seven-day event, beginning with Palm Sunday, commemorating Christ's triumphant entry into Jerusalem. Holy Monday of that week is in recognition of Jesus' chasing the money lenders from the Temple. Holy Tuesday honors Christ's speaking to his disciples on the Mount of Olives outside Jerusalem, and it recognizes the plotting of the Pharisees to trap Jesus. Holy Wednesday is in recognition of Judas' agreeing to betray Christ for 30 pieces of silver. Maundy Thursday is marked as the Last Supper, at which Christ washed his disciples' feet, emphasized brotherly love, and initiated the sacrament of the Eucharist (communion). On Good Friday the march to the cross and the Crucifixion are remembered. The especially sober period is the three hours from noon until 3 P.M. when Christ was on the cross. Holy Saturday is the eve of Christ's Ascension into Heaven, which is celebrated with Easter sunrise services by many Christian churches today.

December 25 is celebrated as the birth of Christ by all Christians, despite the fact that his real birth date is far from certain. In the 4th century, this date was picked because it coincided with a pagan celebration, which allowed Christians to celebrate without too much attention. Christmas became a firm tradition on December 25 in 337 when Emperor Constantine was baptized, an act that symbolized that Christianity was the state religion.

The period from November 30 until Christmas Eve has been designated as Advent, a time for spiritually preparing for the wondrous gift of Christ to all Christians. January 6 is celebrated as the Epiphany because three major events in Christ's life occurred on that date: the visit of the Magi at his manger in Bethlehem following his birth, his baptism at the River Jordan, and the miracle at Cana when Christ changed water to wine at a marriage feast.

Food Practices

Eucharist—Religious service in which a wafer represents the body of Jesus and wine his blood; also called *communion.*

Eucharist (communion) uses food symbolically for Christians. In this most religious ceremony, a wafer or bread is placed on the tongue (or in the hand) to represent the body of Jesus, and wine is drunk symbolizing his blood. Communion is held only at religious services and is not a part of worship in the home.

The apostle Paul is credited with freeing Christians from the dietary laws practiced by the Jews, which thus served as a means of distancing the new Christian religion from its Jewish origins. In fact, the symbolic drinking of wine as a representation of the blood of Christ clearly was a great departure from the strong avoidance of blood proscribed in the Jewish dietary laws.

The prohibition of meat on Fridays apparently was an economic measure that derived from shortages in England during the reign of King Edward VI. The practice not only relieved shortages of meat a bit, but also bolstered the sale of fish, an industry that needed a boost. Meat has been returned to the tables of Roman Catholics since the 1960s by the decree of then Pope John XXIII.

Lent is the 40-day period from Ash Wednesday to Easter. During Lent, some Christians decide to forgo eating some specific food as a personal sacrifice during this most significant period. Part of the Easter celebration for many Christians includes a big meal, which often features lamb, symbolic of the Lamb of God.

Paska—Easter bread traditional in Eastern celebrations; usually dough is braided and decorated before baking in round pan.

Paska is a special Easter bread that is prominent in the Eastern Orthodox Church celebration. The name of this bread reflects the fact that Jesus was crucified during the Jewish Passover, but Paska is a sweet, yeast-leavened bread quite different from the unleavened matzo eaten during the Jewish Passover that symbolizes the exodus from Egypt.

Eggs, considered to be a symbol of the Resurrection of Christ, usually are decorated and featured by Christians throughout North America and northern Europe; Eastern Orthodox Christians transform egg shells with particularly elaborate decorations after they blow out the interior. Another tradition in eastern Europe is to have women bring their baskets containing food for the Easter dinner to church so that the priest can bless them.

Recipe

Paska (Eastern European Easter Bread) (2 loaves)

1 package active dry yeast
¼ c lukewarm water
¼ c sugar
1 tsp salt
¼ c melted butter
¾ c scalded milk
2 eggs
about 5 c flour

1. Soften yeast in lukewarm water.
2. Meanwhile, scald milk and pour over sugar, salt, and butter in a large mixing bowl.
3. Beat eggs before stirring into the milk mixture.
4. Check that milk mixture has cooled to lukewarm and then stir in about ¼ cup of the flour before stirring in the softened yeast/water mixture.
5. Add another cup of the flour and beat.
6. Gradually stir in enough flour to make a dough firm enough that it can be kneaded easily.
7. Knead the dough on a floured board until blisters start to develop under the surface.
8. Lightly coat the dough with a few drops of oil, cover, and let rest in a warm place until doubled in volume.
9. Punch the dough down. Divide into 6 pieces and roll each into long dough ropes.
10. Braid 3 of the ropes in a greased deep round pan to make a circular loaf. Repeat with the 3 remaining ropes in a second pan. (An optional technique is to braid 2 ropes and reserve the third one to shape into a crucifix on top of the loaf.)
11. Brush surface of the loaf with egg yolk and then let dough double in volume in a warm place.
12. Bake loaves at 350°F for 40 minutes until done and the crust is a pleasing brown.
13. Remove from pans immediately.

Islam (Muslim)

Prophet Muhammad—Arab man who founded Islam in the 7th century.

The youngest of the major religions of the world is Islam, the religion spawned on the Arabian Peninsula by the **Prophet Muhammad** in about 622 CE. Muhammad apparently led a somewhat unremarkable life from his birth in around 570 CE until he was 40, the time when he began seeing visions and revelations and started preaching about them in Mecca, the town where he lived.

Muhammad's protests against worshiping various gods at the stone shrine (Ka'ba) in the center of Mecca resulted in his being banished from Mecca, and he lost the protection of his clan, the Hashim. He and his followers were allowed to settle a little less than 300 miles north of Mecca in a town now called Medina, meaning the city of the Prophet. Muhammad and his group gained such strength and support between 622 and 630 that Mecca surrendered to them in 630 without a fight, and he continued to lead his movement until his death in 632 CE.

Islam spread very rapidly into many parts of the known world. The Arabs conquered the Fertile Crescent, Iran, and Egypt by the end of the 7th century and built the Dome of the Rock in Jerusalem starting in 691 CE on the site where Muhammad is said to have ascended to heaven. In 711 they invaded Spain and went to the Indus River in India. People quickly converted to Islam, and large portions of this vast region remain in the Muslim realm to this day.

Foundations of Islam

Koran—Writings from Allah given to Muhammad by Angel Gabriel to define the spiritual life for Muslims.

The **Koran** is the book containing the writings that Muhammad is believed to have received from Allah through the Angel Gabriel. Muslims are guided by the Koran with its 114 writings (some brief, some long) that are called *suras.* Considerable study and debate have been carried on over the centuries involving the interpretation and the contradictions that occur between the Koran and the hadith, which discusses the Prophet and daily life (in many volumes). The combination defines not only the spiritual life but also the practical daily life for all practicing Muslims.

Five Pillars of Islam—Requirements of Islam: Shahada (creed), Salat (prayers), Saum (fasting), Zukat (purifying tax), and Hajj (pilgrimage to Mecca).

Shahada—One of Five Pillars; chanting of creed, "There is no god but God; Muhamad is the messenger of God."

Salat—Muslim daily prayer according to the Five Pillars.

The religion's basis is the **Five Pillars of Islam,** consisting of the Shahada (creed), Salat (prayers), Saum (fasting), Zukat (purifying tax), and Hajj (pilgrimage to Mecca).

Shahada (creed) The **Shahada** or confession consists of two statements from different places in the Koran: "There is no god but God (Allah)"; and "Muhammad is the Messenger of God."

Salat (prayers) Performance of the **Salat** has evolved over the centuries from the two times indicated in the Koran to the present practice of five times daily: at sunrise, midday, mid-afternoon, sunset, and evening, the times when the muezzin (usually now a recording of the crier) chants out the call to prayer from the minaret of the mosque (Figure 3.19).

Mosque—Place of worship for Muslims; contains a mihrab pointing to Mecca, a minbar atop a staircase for delivering the Friday sermon and daily prayers, and at least one minaret.

Mihrab—Niche in an interior wall of a mosque indicating the direction of Mecca for worshipers during Salat.

Minbar—Staircase topped with a pulpit in a mosque.

Before going into the mosque, Muslims are required to achieve purity by washing according to a defined ritual in the place provided for this in the courtyard of the mosque. Inside the mosque, worshipers pray facing Mecca with all of the other worshipers and are led by the imam in a carefully structured communal prayer service that involves changes in position, including prostration, semi-kneeling, prostration again, standing, kneeling, and sitting at various points in the prayer.

Fridays are the holy day in Islam, and the noon Salat on Friday is extended into a special worship service. The original selection of Friday as the holy day apparently was made because that was the day for the weekly market in Muhammad's town of Medina, which made it possible for many people to attend. It also had the advantage of distinguishing the Muslim holy day from the Jewish choice of Saturday and the Christian selection of Sunday. The service, like the Salat during the week, is held in a mosque.

Mosques have a niche (**mihrab**) in the interior wall, indicating the direction of Mecca (Figure 3.20). The **minbar,** an ornate pulpit atop a straight staircase, is

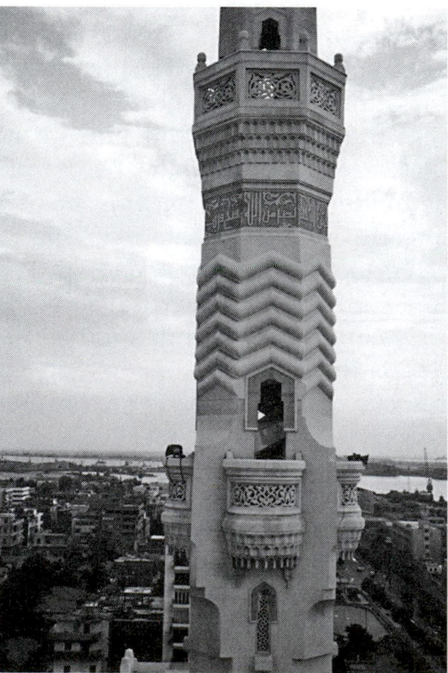

Figure 3.19 Muslims are called to prayer by a summons coming from the minaret of a mosque, such as this one in Port Said, Egypt.

Figure 3.20 The mihrab is the niche in a mosque indicating the direction of Mecca so worshipers can direct their prayers there.

Khatib—Person who reads the Friday sermon.

Minaret—Tower of a mosque from which people are called to prayer.

Muezzin—Person who calls Muslims to prayers five times daily.

Saum—Ritual of fasting.

Ramadan—One-month period of fasting from sunrise to sunset each year; one of the Pillars of Islam.

the place where the Friday sermon is read by the **khatib** and daily prayers are led by the imam in the mosque (Figure 3.21). The floor of the large interior room of a mosque is carpeted, and no seats are placed anywhere, which leaves all of the floor available for the many men praying together. Women are allowed in galleries around the side of the main room. Distinctive features of the exterior of a mosque include one or more **minarets,** or towers, for the **muezzin** to call people to prayer and the fountain or pool in the courtyard for ablutions.

Saum **Saum** is the Pillar that is observed during the ninth month of the Muslim lunar calendar, when the 30-day fast of **Ramadan** takes place. At this time, adult Muslims are expected to fast from just before sunrise until sunset. The fast requires abstaining from all food and drink during that period, as well as from smoking, intentional vomiting, and sex.

Figure 3.21 The minbar is the pulpit atop the staircase that is used for Friday worship in Muslim mosques.

Travelers, sick people, and women who are menstruating are excused from fasting but are required to make up the day(s) immediately following the celebration that ends Ramadan. Children are not expected to participate in fasting.

Since the lunar calendar causes Ramadan to occur at different times of year, the temperatures in the very hot climates may make the fast of Ramadan extremely difficult when it falls in summer. Even when the weather cooperates, this long period of fasting places considerable physical strain on many people, although a few seem to welcome the opportunity to lose a few pounds while pondering religious truths. The end of Ramadan brings the very joyous celebration of **Id al-Fitr** (Feast of the Breaking of the Fast), a three-day holiday highlighting wonderful food, new clothes, and family visits.

Id al-Fitr—Three-day holiday celebrating the end of Ramadan, the month of fasting.

Zukat—Purifying tax; one of Five Pillars.

Zukat The giving of alms, the **Zukat,** was originally a means of sharing one's blessings with the less fortunate. It evolved into taxes collected by the nations in which the Muslims lived and eliminated the voluntary aspect of giving. Now Zukat is sometimes provided as an optional giving in addition to the required governmental taxes.

Hajj—Pilgrimage to Mecca; one of Five Pillars.

Hajj The **Hajj** is the last of the Five Pillars and often is the event of a lifetime for a Muslim if the trip is financially and physically possible. The final parts of the Hajj can be done only on certain days in the 12th lunar month. The two parts of the pilgrimage can be completed in two segments or in a continuous effort. The pilgrim is to wear a white garment, and visit the mosque in Mecca as soon as ablutions are finished.

Ka'ba—Black stone cube with a meteorite in its wall; shrine in the center of Mecca that pilgrims circumambulate as part of the hajj.

Pilgrims must circumambulate around the **Ka'ba,** and hair is either shaved off or trimmed. Official ceremonies are held on the seventh and eighth days, and a sermon is given on the ninth day while the pilgrims stand on the hillside in the hot sun, listening for many hours. The tenth day there is a ritual throwing of stones at a pillar representing Satan, followed by ritual slaughtering of many animals in preparation for the Feast of the Sacrifice, which remembers Abraham's willingness to sacrifice for God. Three more days of celebration are held in Mecca before pilgrims begin to disperse for a visit to Medina and the long journey home.

In recent years there have been such crowds making the Hajj that people have been killed when stampedelike situations erupted. The small area around the sacred Ka'ba and the mosque in Mecca creates what sometimes can become fatal congestion.

Purdah—Seclusion of women in some Islamic regions.

Hijab—Dress code for Muslim women; varies somewhat in various countries and regions.

Burqa—Loose, long robe covering the body to the toes and a head covering with a thick veil and a narrow slit; form of hijab worn by Muslim women in Afghanistan.

Chador—Long, loose cloak and head covering (sometimes veiled) worn by Muslim women in Muslim countries (e.g., Iraq and Iran).

Abaya—Long, loose cloak worn by many Muslim women.

Roles of Islamic Men

In the Islamic world, men are to provide for their wives and children and to protect them, a traditional situation that has tended to curtail opportunities for women that are assumed to be their rights in other countries. Theoretically, Muslim men are able to have four wives as long as they treat them all equally. However, this is not the general practice today.

Women's Roles

Islamic women often have lived in **purdah** (isolated from public view) and spent much of their days at home caring for their families. They have traditionally dressed according to the **hijab** (dress code for Muslim women designed to create a curtain of modesty) generally followed in their country. In Afghanistan, the Taliban required women to wear the **burqa** (head to toe covering consisting of a loose, long robe and a head covering with a thick veil and only a rather narrow slit to look outward. In Iraq, Iran, and some other Muslim countries, women wear a **chador** composed of an **abaya** (loose, long cloak) and a head scarf or covering that may or may not veil the face. Usually these garments are black, although exceptions are seen in some areas.

In the 1980s, many Muslim women were no longer wearing garments that covered their faces and hid their bodies, and they were often found in the workplace alongside men who were not their relatives. This situation caused sufficient consternation that a more fundamental approach toward Muslim women is being put into play in many places throughout the Muslim world now. In fact, some young women are actively seeking to resume the more traditional Muslim lifestyle.

Architectural Heritage

Among the remarkable buildings constructed by the Muslims are the great Mosque of Damascus (705 CE), the Great Mosque at Cordova in Spain (785–987 CE), the Alhambra (Figure C.25, p. C9) in Granada, Spain (1333–1391 CE), the Mosque of Suleyman the Magnificent in Istanbul (1550–1560 CE), and the Taj Mahal in Agra, India (built by the Mughal Emperor Shah Jahan from 1632 to 1652 CE).

Historical Perspectives

European Crusaders mounted vigorous attacks on the Muslims in the Levant (Figure C.47, p. C16) and captured Jerusalem from them in 1099 CE only to lose the city to Saladin (who had been ruling from Cairo while Jerusalem was in Christian hands) in 1187. The Mamluks, who ruled in Egypt from 1254 to 1517, captured Tripoli from the Crusaders in 1289.

The Moors (Muslims from North Africa) were forced out of Spain in 1492. Istanbul was controlled by the Ottomans from 1453 until Ataturk's successful overthrow in 1922. Pakistan was formed as a Muslim country in 1947 at the time of the British partition of India. Muslim is the principal religion in many nations in the Middle East, North Africa, Central Asia, and some areas in Southeast Asia.

Muslim calligraphy is done using a pen made from a reed that has been buried in manure for four years to achieve the desired red color, ink made from ground soot, and paper dyed with tea and coated with egg white to make it easier to correct mistakes. These practices stem from the 7th century.

Muslim Calendar

The Muslim calendar is a lunar calendar with only 354 days in a year, and it starts at a different year in history than the Gregorian calendar that is used by most countries. Year 1 was 622 CE. The year 2006 on the Gregorian calendar corresponds approximately to the Muslim year 1427. Since the Islamic calendar has 12 lunar months and no extra days, the seasonal timing for various Muslim holidays shifts over time.

Dietary Laws

The dietary laws for Muslims were developed by Muhammad and served partly to differentiate Muslims from those who practiced other religions, particularly Jews and Christians. The rules were quite simple:

1. Do not eat the flesh of carrion (animals found dead).
2. Do not consume blood in any form.
3. Stay away from all swine.
4. Do not eat food that has been given as an offering to idols.
5. Do not drink anything that has the power to inebriate.

Shiite—Muslim sect that comprises a majority in Iran, Iraq, Bahrain, and Azerbaijan.

Sunni—Muslim sect that comprises a majority in some Middle Eastern countries.

Islamic Sects

Within Islam there are different groups, including the **Shiite,** the **Sunni,** and the Sufis, with each of these plus others being split into still more clusters. Shiite is a large majority sect of Islam with much of its religious activities centered in Iran.

In addition to Iran, other countries with a Shiite majority include Iraq, Bahrain, and Azerbaijan. Sunni is the majority sect in Jordan, Saudi Arabia, Egypt, Afghanistan, Turkey, United Arab Emirates, Pakistan, Syria, Yemen, and Kuwait. Sufi, another sect of Muslims, are noted for their use of music and dance in their religious observances; the Whirling Dervishes of Kona, Turkey, are examples.

Seventh Day Adventist

Seventh Day Adventist—Religious sect rooted in Protestantism and with a carefully defined behavior code.

Seventh Day Adventist is a group that had its origin in the United States in the mid-1800s when one of its founders, Ellen Harmon White, reported having visions and wrote about these visions and dreams for 70 years. Basically, this religion has roots in Protestantism, but it adds to this foundation the expectation of a second coming of Christ. The lifestyle espoused by Seventh Day Adventists included establishing the seventh day of the week, Saturday, as the holy day, with meal preparation and dish-washing chores being done either on the day before or the day following, thus leaving Saturday entirely free for dedication to their religion. The behavior code is based strongly on the Ten Commandments.

The dietary code of the Seventh Day Adventists is of particular interest in this chapter because of its thoroughness and its dedication to consuming a totally healthful vegetarian diet. This specific interest has led to considerable research that has added to the knowledge regarding this type of diet.

Simplicity of foods is one of the basic premises on which Adventists have based their lacto-ovo-vegetarian diets. However, some followers have been more restrictive and have opted to eliminate eggs or milk (or both) from their diets, changes that greatly complicate the achievement of an adequate diet for people. Emphasis for protein sources is placed heavily on a variety of legumes, with nuts, cereals, eggs, and milk rounding out the protein requirement.

Olive oil is recommended in place of animal fats, and whole-grain cereals are preferred over refined products. Alcohol, tobacco, tea, and coffee are prohibited because of their negative effects on health.

Summary

Major religions have shaped the cultures and food practices of people around the world for many, many centuries (Table 3.4). These include Hinduism, Buddhism, Confucianism, Taoism, Shintoism, Judaism, Christianity, and Islam.

Hinduism is the oldest religion and includes the worship of several gods, notably Vishnu, Shiva, and Brahma, as well as the concept of castes. Hindus believe in repeated reincarnation. They frequently are vegetarians, a reflection of their reverence for life, and they also avoid alcohol. India is home to the majority of Hindus, although followers can be found in the United States and other parts of the world, too.

Buddhism is a religion based on the Four Noble Truths and a carefully defined code of conduct. Among the directions for living are the avoidance of alcohol and, if a monk, not eating after midday. Animals are not to be killed to become a source of food, although eating meat is approved if the animal was not killed specifically to feed the person who might eat it. Buddhism is the major religion in the Himalayan countries and other places in Southeast Asia. In China, Confucianism and Taoism are blended with Buddhism, while in Japan Shintoism is blended with Buddhism.

Table 3.4 Food Guidelines in Selected Religions

Religion	*Restricted Foods*	*Other Food Practices*
Hinduism	Beef because sacred; may avoid pigs and chickens because not clean Brahmans avoid alcohol	Ritual bath before cooking in Brahman kitchen Brahman food contains ghee; no ghee for lower castes Brahmans avoid garlic, onions Food offerings at temples
Buddhism	Meats, but can eat if killed by non-Buddhist	May eat fish Monks beg and eat only until noon Avoid overeating
Confucianism, Taoism		Diet rich in protein, vitamins in pregnancy until 30 days after birth Eggs and rice for health and wealth Rice wine wedding toasts Food for ancestors on family altar
Shintoism		Altars in home with daily food, drink
Judaism	Pork, ostrich, mollusks, crustaceans	May eat beef, sheep, goat chicken, turkey, fish Separate dishes for meat/dairy (Orthodox) Kosher products for Orthodox
Christianity		Wafer and wine for Communion
Islam	Pork, alcohol	Fasting during Ramadan
Seventh Day Adventist	Meat, alcohol	Most are ovo-lacto-vegetarians Usually avoid animal fats

Judaism is a religion based on the Torah (particularly Genesis, Exodus, Leviticus, Numbers, and Deuteronomy) and the Talmud. This religion spread widely and contributed to the cultures of many different people scattered throughout Europe, Asia, and Africa prior to and after Christ. There are varying traditions, depending on the particular Jewish sect. However, the key holy traditions for all sects include Rosh Hashanah, Yom Kippur, and Passover. Kosher food is required among Orthodox Jews with the added stipulation that separate utensils and dishes must be maintained for meat dishes and dairy products. Pork is not a part of Jewish menus because it is from an animal that has a cloven hoof but does not chew its cud.

Christianity also utilizes the Old Testament, but it adds to this the New Testament and a belief that Jesus was the son of God, which is in direct contrast to the Jewish interpretation of Jesus. The Roman Catholic Church was prominent in Europe, and the Eastern Orthodox Church represented Christianity in Greece and farther east. Protestantism split from the Roman Catholic Church. Catholics in years past have avoided eating meat on Fridays, but this is no longer required.

Islam is the youngest of the major religions, the product of the teachings of Muhammad, an Arabian prophet who lived in the 7th century. This religion is prominent among Arab populations but also is the religion of many other people around the world today. Its foundation is the Five Pillars of Islam: Shahada, Salat, Saum, Zukat, and Hajj. Saum requires fasting, and Ramadan, the ninth lunar month, is a 30-day fasting period, which places strong demands on followers, particularly when this fast occurs in the heat of summer. The Five Pillars and all aspects of the lives of Muslims are described in the Koran and the hadith. Food prohibitions include avoiding eating swine, the flesh of carrion, blood in any form, food previously offered to gods, and alcohol.

The Seventh Day Adventist religion is included in this chapter because of its dietary dictates, which are based on vegetarianism (usually lacto-ovo), whole-grain cereals, and legumes. Alcohol, tea, coffee, and tobacco are prohibited.

Selected Sites

http://www.gadnet.com/fooodx.html—Many Indian recipes.

www.penzeys.com—Source of Indian spices.

www.food-india.com—Information on Indian ingredients and recipes.

www.asiarecipe.com—Glossary of terms and recipes.

www.everythingjewish.com—Extensive information about Judaism.

www.holidays.net/passover/seder2.htm—Discussion of the celebration of Passover and the Seder.

www.jewish-food.org—Web site for numerous Jewish foods.

http://islam.about.com/blintroc.htm—Information about Five Pillars of Islam.

www.religioustolerance.org/var_rel.htm—Background information on several different religions.

www.adherents.com/Religions_By_Adherents.html—Census data on religions around the world.

Study Questions

1. Give a brief description of each of the following religions: (a) Hinduism, (b) Buddhism, (c) Judaism, (d) Christianity, and (e) Islam.
2. Which three major religions view Jerusalem as a very important city for their faith, and why does each religion attach this importance?
3. Compare the dietary laws and food practices of the religions discussed in this chapter.

Bibliography

Barer-Stein, T. 1999. *You Eat What You Are.* 2nd ed. Firefly Books, Ltd. Ontario, Canada.

Confucius. 1960. *Four Books and Five Classics.* Hong Kong University Press.

Cousins, L.S. 1997. Buddhism. In J.R. Hinnells, ed. *A New Handbook of Living Religions.* Penguin. London, England.

Goldman, A.L. 2000. *Being Jewish.* Simon and Schuster. New York.

Hinnells, J.R., ed. 1997. *A New Handbook of Living Religions.* Penguin. London, England.

Hussaini, M.M. 1993. *Islamic Dietary Concepts and Practices.* Islamic Food and Nutrition Council of America. Bedford Park, IL.

Jackson, M.A. 2000. Getting religion—For your products, that is. *Food Tech. 54*(7): 60.

Kilara, A. and K.K. Iya. 1992. Food Practices of the Hindu. *Food Technol. 46:* 94-104.

Lowenberg, M., E.N. Todhunter, E.D. Wilson, J.R. Savage, and J.L. Lubawski. 1974. *Food and Man.* 2nd ed. Wiley. New York.

Marcus, A.D. 2000. *The View from Nebo: How Archaeology Is Rewriting the Bible and Reshaping the Middle East.* Little, Brown. Boston.

Mbiti, J.S. 1970. *African Religions and Philosophy.* Doubleday Anchor. Garden City, NY.

Morgan, K.W. 1953. *Religion of the Hindus.* Ronald. New York.

Panati, C. 1996. *Sacred Origins of Profound Things.* Penguin. London, England.

Regenstein, J.M. and C.E. Regenstein. 1992. Kosher food market in the 1990s—Legal view. *Food Technol. 46:* 122–124.

Simoons, F.F. 1994. *Eat Not This Flesh.* 2nd ed. University of Wisconsin Press. Madison.

Unterman, A. 1997. Judaism. In J.R. Hinnells, ed. *A New Handbook of Living Religions.* Penguin. London, England.

Walls, A. 1997. Christianity. In J.R. Hinnells, ed. *A New Handbook of Living Religions.* Penguin. London, England.

Weightman, S. 1997. Hinduism. In J.R. Hinnells, ed. *A New Handbook of Living Religions.* Penguin. London, England.

Welch, A.T. 1997. Islam. In J.R. Hinnells, ed. *A New Handbook of Living Religions.* Penguin. London, England.

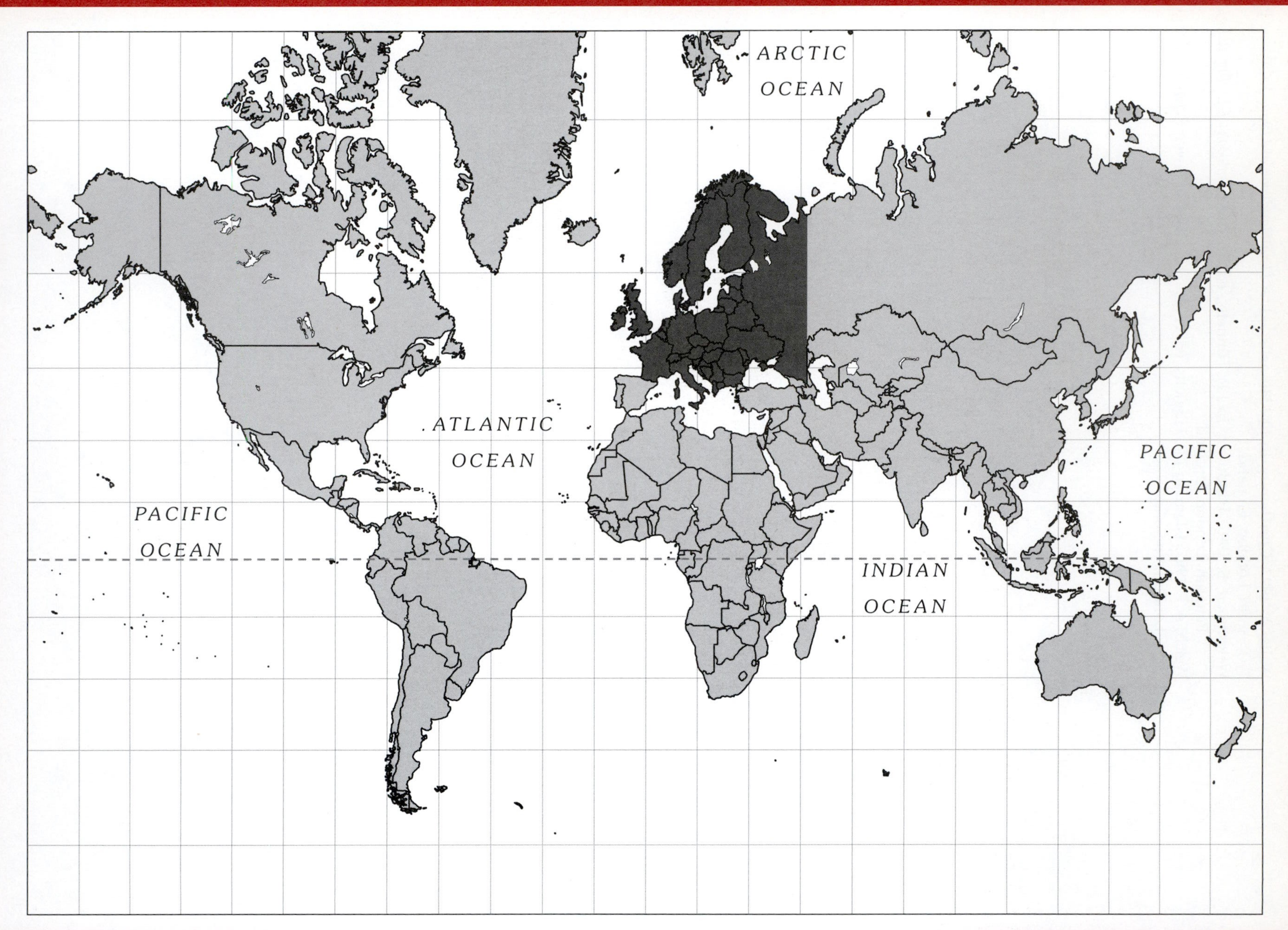

ARCTIC OCEAN
ATLANTIC OCEAN
PACIFIC OCEAN
PACIFIC OCEAN
INDIAN OCEAN

Part II

Europe: Roots of Our American Cuisine

ATLANTIC
OCEAN
SCOTLAND
North
Sea
Edinburgh
NORTHERN
IRELAND
ENGLAND
Irish
Sea
IRELAND
WALES
London
Thames River
English
Channel
ATLANTIC
OCEAN
FRANCE

4 British Isles

A Geographic Overview

The British Isles consist primarily of a very large island containing Scotland, England, and Wales, plus a somewhat smaller island, which is divided into Northern Ireland and Ireland. Although not actually a part of the European continent, the proximity to Europe and the long associations with it historically justify the inclusion of the British Isles here.

This also is a very suitable spot for beginning our closer look at the various nations of the world, because many of the early settlers in the American colonies were from these islands, including the Pilgrims who sailed from Plymouth in southern England. Certainly, we are all aware that the United States was a British colonial region before declaring independence in 1776 and subsequently winning freedom after the Revolutionary War.

The United Kingdom (consisting of England, Scotland, Wales, and Ireland) is actually not even as big as the state of Oregon, yet at one time it ruled over a vast empire that reached around the world, leading to the claim that "the sun never sets on the British Empire." From a food perspective, crops (especially wheat, barley, potatoes, fruits, and vegetables) can do well there because there is ample rain and the climate tends to be temperate, if a bit chilly.

The land is generally suited to agriculture of various types, but the fields are rather small, probably due to centuries of a gradually increasing population that resulted in many villages situated fairly closely together, thus limiting farming areas. Even the mountains are on a rather small scale, with the highest in the United Kingdom being Ben Nevis (4,406 feet); the highest point in Ireland is only 3,800 feet.

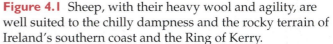

Figure 4.1 Sheep, with their heavy wool and agility, are well suited to the chilly dampness and the rocky terrain of Ireland's southern coast and the Ring of Kerry.

Livestock production has been a part of the rural scene in the British Isles for centuries. Cattle are the dominant species in England, whereas sheep graze in large numbers in the highlands of Scotland and the rugged areas of Wales and Ireland. The importance of beef in the British diet is highlighted by the famous Beefeaters, who guard the Tower of London to this day. Cheddar, Stilton, and Cheshire cheeses are justifiably famous, and so is their cream. Lovely sweaters and other apparel produced from the wool of all the sheep are valued in cold climates around the world. At home, the people of the British Isles have made mutton a major meat in their diet for centuries (Figure 4.1).

Perhaps as famous as Britons' love of beef and mutton is the widespread consumption of fish. This certainly is not surprising in view of the convenient access to the surrounding ocean and the adequate supply of haddock, sole, mackerel, and other saltwater fish. Certain areas are especially noted for the fish caught there; salmon in Scotland, shrimp from the North Sea near the coast of Yorkshire, Dover sole, sea trout, and lobster around Dublin are just some examples of specialties.

History and Culture

Various sights around England serve as enduring reminders of the long history of the British Isles. Stonehenge, the remarkable circle of huge stones constructed in the era around 1700 BCE, apparently for some form of worship, still stands to the south of London (Figure C.1, p. C1). Romans occupying England in the 1st and 2nd centuries built various structures that are still in evidence today: the baths at Bath, for example (Figures 4.2 and C.2, p. C1). Remnants of Hadrian's wall, built to separate England's Brigantes from the lowland Novantae and Selgovae, can be seen around Chester and on to York today.

After the Romans, invasions of the British Isles by tribes from northern Europe and Scandinavia slowed the development of the region as a nation. However, a monarchy was in place by the 11th century, a tradition that still continues. Under William the Conqueror, who reigned for 20 years until his death in 1087, butchers, bakers, and grocers enjoyed some recognition in Britain, although the traditions were not refined then. People from the British Isles participated in the Crusades that were waged to attempt to free Jerusalem from the "Infidel." Perhaps the most renowned leader from England was Richard Lionheart, King of England, who led his forces on a 16-month expedition that ended in failure in Palestine in 1192.

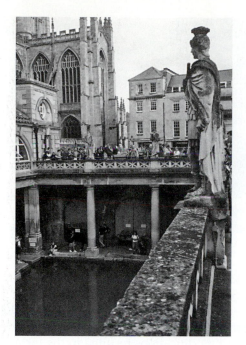

Figure 4.2 The contemporary world of Bath swirls around the public baths the Romans constructed and enjoyed to warm themselves when they were the rulers of this province so distant from sunny Rome.

Feasts of food, fancy clothes, music, and dances were all parts of life in "Merry England." The shopping list for the installation of Bishop Neville at York in 1467 included 104 oxen, 6 wild bulls, 1,000 sheep, 304 calves, 304 suckling pigs, 400 swans, 2,000 geese, 1,000 capons, 2,000 pigs, plus plenty of tarts and custards, all of which was to be washed down with bounteous amounts of ale and wine.

A little over 400 years later, a religious contribution was made by England in 1611 when King James I published the King James version of the Bible, a version still held in great repute. For almost 100 years considerable turmoil existed between Parliament and the Crown (monarch), but both parts of the government survived. Scotland became united with England in 1707 during the reign of Queen Anne.

Great Britain's success in establishing the British Empire as a means of extending its trade throughout the world did much to add interest to the foods available for common folk in the British Isles. The British East India Company performed a major role in bringing India into the Empire (Figures 4.3, 4.4, and C.112. p. C38). This dominance began about 1690 and continued until independence was granted to India and Pakistan in 1947.

In Africa, Kenya was under British dominance from 1888 to 1963. Cecil Rhodes was instrumental in gaining the rights for the British South Africa

Figure 4.3 India, including its fabled "Pink City" of Jaipur, was considered to be the "jewel in the crown" of the British Empire, but gained independence in the mid-20th century.

Figure 4.4 Tea from plantations, such as this one in Sri Lanka (formerly Ceylon) and in India, helped to establish it as a favorite beverage in the British Isles.

Company to remove minerals from Rhodesia in 1889, and Britain was basically in control of Southern Rhodesia until 1923. Several changes of government led to the eventual formation of Zimbabwe in 1980, and Britain was no longer involved in its governance. The tip of Africa came under British control in 1806; gradual acquisitions and modifications resulted in the formation of South Africa, which still is a part of the British Commonwealth. Apartheid, the particularly contentious aspect of South Africa as a nation, ended in 1993.

The Dominions of the British Empire today include Canada, Newfoundland, New Zealand, Australia, South Africa, and Ireland/Eire. Hong Kong reverted to China in 1997, 146 years after it came under British occupation.

As a result of the far-flung reaches of the British Empire, traders brought foods to the local British markets from all parts of the world. Exotic produce and spices were introduced. The introduction of tea, first from China and then from India, changed the beverage habits of not only Londoners, but also people throughout the British Empire.

The traditions of afternoon tea and high tea can be found wherever the British ruled during the heyday of the Empire (Figure 4.5). The reverse trend also can be noted, because many people from the various Dominions have emigrated to the British Isles today, bringing with them their curries, chutneys, and other food traditions to enliven the typical British table.

Figure 4.5 Afternoon tea is a favorite tradition in the United Kingdom, its tasty treats providing a welcome bridge to the evening meal.

Food Patterns

Class influences

Breakfast The food patterns of the British are somewhat different, depending upon whether they are from the upper or the working class, for there is a class distinction that has persisted over the centuries. Time pressures have begun to erode the breakfast pattern that was the solid start for the day typically consumed by upper-class gentlemen.

For countless years, the tradition for the upper class breakfast began with oatmeal porridge, followed by either bacon or kippers (or other small fish) and eggs, accompanied by fried bread and perhaps a grilled tomato. Dundee orange marmalade always was available for topping the fried bread. Working-class men usually had a sturdy bit of bread and a hefty slice of meat or cheese. For both classes, plenty of strong, hot tea diluted with milk was the beverage.

Upper-class ladies used to eat a leisurely breakfast in the middle of the morning, a light meal of cake and tea. Now everyone is likely to eat lighter (and probably faster) at breakfast, with the trend moving toward the typical continental breakfast of a baked bread of some type and either tea or strong coffee.

Lunch Class distinctions may still persist for Sunday lunch (the noon meal that is the heaviest of the day). A large beef roast or perhaps mutton is likely to be featured in an upper-class home. Typically, the beef roast (usually cooked rare) is accompanied by **Yorkshire pudding,** oven-roasted potatoes, and a horseradish sauce to add excitement to the roast (Figure 4.6). Overcooked vegetables seem too often to be an item served more as a duty than an enhancement to the fare.

Fish and chips is a favorite of the working class and is bought away from home, wrapped snugly in newspaper, and finally eaten with a generous sprinkle of vinegar. Incidentally, the chips are deep-fat fried potatoes cut in strips half an inch wide, and the fish is haddock, cod, or other white fish dipped in a batter of flour, egg, and beer, and then fried.

Yorkshire pudding—Puffy, crusty pudding baked on meat drippings in a very hot oven; batter is a thin egg, milk, and flour mixture similar to popover batter.

Fish and chips—Batter-dipped pieces of cod or other fish that are deep-fat fried; served with deep-fat fried thick strips of potato.

Afternoon Tea Perhaps the most appealing tradition in British dietary patterns is afternoon tea. The long time that typically occurred between lunch and the very late dinners that were eaten in upper-class families made it almost imperative to have a snack of some type in the late afternoon, and teatime became the answer to this problem.

Tea preparation requires that the teapot be preheated with boiling water, emptied, and then prepared with tea leaves (a teaspoon per cup plus one for the

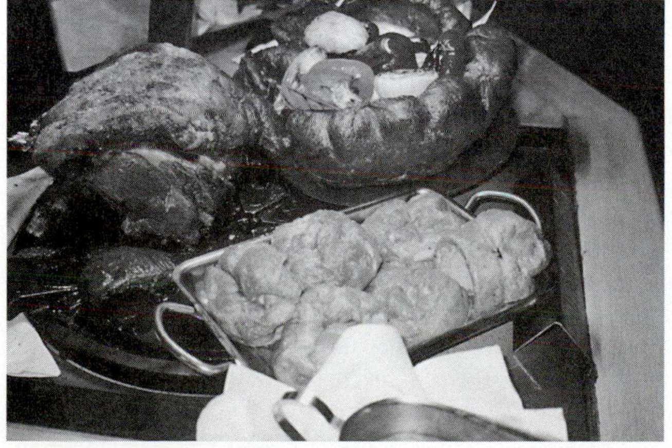

Figure 4.6 Beef rib roast with horseradish sauce and a puffy Yorkshire pudding are the highlights of a traditional British dinner.

pot) over which boiling water is poured to fill the pot before the lid is replaced and a tea cozy (heavy cloth cover) is added to keep the tea hot. This ritual requires 5 minutes of patient waiting to allow the tea to brew in its cozy before it is ready to be poured and enjoyed.

Scone—Quick bread made from a dough that is rolled and cut into triangles or circles, and then baked in a very hot oven; popular for teatime.

Trifle—Elaborate dessert made in a pretty glass bowl, which has been lined with lady fingers or slices of pound cake and then filled with layers of stirred custard, whipped cream, slivered almonds, and raspberries, and generously laced with sherry.

Other menu items vary considerably, from perhaps **scones** or cakes to some sherry, small sandwiches, and fancy cakes or even a **trifle** with a generous dollop of whipped cream garnished with berries.

Dinner After such generous fare earlier in the day, the British typically do not place much importance on the evening meal. Although tradition may be somewhat lacking regarding the menu for evening dining, there is a reasonable consistency to the pattern of young adults spending some time in the evening in a local pub, playing darts, quaffing ale, stout, or beer, and chatting with friends.

Country Distinctions

England England's geographic isolation from the European continent led to a pattern of eating in medieval times that relied heavily on meat. Vegetables and several kinds of fruit were grown locally; some could be preserved or held in cold storage well into the winter to help augment the meat. As England developed its empire, imported foods became available to those with sufficient money to afford them.

Jugged—Slow, moist heat cooking of meat in a covered clay pot.

Even today the earlier diet pattern relying heavily on meat and some vegetables and fruits is the typical choice, all washed down with ale, stout, or other national brews. Sometimes hare or other wild game would be **jugged** (meat and vegetables cooked for a very long time in a clay pot or covered casserole) to give a hearty meal. Fish from the surrounding sea and mutton remain particularly popular items on the menu. Cabbage, potatoes, root vegetables, onions, and apples are among the produce items from earlier times that are still favorites today in England.

In years past, England's food sometimes was described as plain and rather bland. That description no longer applies, at least in many commercial and home kitchens around the country. The changes can be traced primarily to influences from the French, whose cuisine set the standard for fine food for many years, and to the many immigrants from India, Pakistan, and other former parts of the British Empire, who brought with them many different seasonings, spices, and recipes that broadened British menus.

Cornish pasties—Turnovers filled with meat and vegetables; pronounced 'pas·tē (rhymes with nasty).

Bubble and squeak—Dish of leftover beef, potatoes, and vegetables that makes these noises while being fried together.

Steak and kidney pie—Hearty, savory pie containing pieces of beef steak and kidneys in the filling.

Shepherd's pie—Deep-dish meat pie made with cooked meat, gravy, and onions, and topped with a crust of mashed potatoes before baking.

Mulligatawny—Curry-flavored rich soup made with a chicken or lamb base; reflects British period in India.

Among typical favorites are **Cornish pasties,** which originated in Cornwall in southwestern England. These hearty pastry turnovers are filled with generous quantities of meat and vegetables. Their popularity stems from the ease of packing them for a lunch as well as from their flavorful heartiness at lunchtime.

Bubble and squeak is another favorite lunch dish. Its imaginative name reflects the noises that are heard when its ingredients (beef leftovers, potatoes, and other vegetables) are frying.

Two hearty pies often found on British menus are **steak and kidney pie** and **shepherd's pie.** Steak and kidney pie is a delectable pastry with a flavorful filling of beef steak (round or other less tender steak), kidneys, and seasoned gravy. Shepherd's pie usually is made with lamb (hence its name), although other meats may be substituted. This pie is made in a deep pie dish although it is not made with pastry. It is created by arranging a layer of leftover cooked meat, onions, and gravy in the bottom of the dish and then topping it with mashed potatoes. Shepherd's pie is then baked until the mashed potatoes are pleasingly browned.

England's chilly, damp climate is very compatible with an imported favorite, **mulligatawny.** This nourishing soup, with its curry seasonings, evokes images of India and the days of the Raj.

Toad-in-the-hole sounds rather like a fanciful dish from *Alice in Wonderland,* but it is actually quite a simple dish. Sausages are covered with a quick-bread batter before they are baked in a hot oven about 30 minutes to cook the sausages and bake the batter covering them. This and many other recipes are garnished generously by many British diners with **Worcestershire sauce.**

Baked goods are popular in England. For breakfast or teatime, **crumpets,** similar to English muffins, are popular. **Sally Lunn** is yeast bread that originated in the English town of Bath centuries after Romans left the area (Figure 4.7). It is baked in a tube pan and served warm with butter or whipped cream. **Hot cross buns** are a specialty baked at Easter. The shape of the cross is pressed into the dough before baking and often decorated with white icing before being served. **Biscuits** in England are crackers or cookies, not the light quick bread that we call biscuits.

Among sweets enjoyed by the British are lemon curd, treacle, and fool. **Lemon curd** is a lemon filling thickened with egg yolk that frequently is used to add a somewhat sharp, but sweet, accent to cookies, tarts, and cakes. **Treacle** is a hearty, sweet molassses that is used like syrup. **Fool** is a simple chilled dessert made by blending custard with a sweetened pureé of fruit.

Scotland Food in Scotland generally is rather simple and bland. It is recognized for some foods, however. Probably the item that is best known and appreciated the least by foreigners is Haggis. Following closely in this dubious list is blood pudding. **Haggis** is made using toasted oatmeal, suet (beef fat), variety meats (e.g., liver, heart), chopped onions, and seasonings that have been mixed together carefully before being packed into a sheep's stomach and boiled. **Blood pudding,** also called black pudding although it is not a dessert, is a related dish that is popular in Scotland. It is made by using blood from a freshly slaughtered animal in place of the variety meats in haggis, and the mixture is packed into sausage casings before boiling. Its usual place would be on the breakfast table after being sliced and fried. This dish clearly illustrates the importance the Scots place on not wasting any part of the animal.

Figure 4.7 Sally Lunn is a tasty yeast bread served warm with whipped cream or butter that originated in Bath, England.

Toad-in-the-hole—Sausages cooked in a quick-bread batter.

Worcestershire sauce—Pungent sauce made of soy sauce, vinegar, and garlic, and used quite universally at British tables; originated in Worcestershire, England (pronounced 'wús-.ta(r)-shir).

Crumpet—Similar to an English muffin but somewhat thinner and more springy.

Sally Lunn—Light yeast bread baked in a tubular pan, sliced in half, and then topped with whipped cream or melted butter; originated in Bath, England.

Hot cross buns—Yeast buns containing cinnamon, allspice, and raisins and topped with a cross of candied orange peel or a strip of dough to represent the cross of Christ; traditional for Easter.

Biscuit—Flat cracker or cookie.

Lemon curd—Egg yolk-thickened sweet filling flavored with lemon juice and rind; often used as filling for tarts and pies.

Treacle—Very thick, sweet molasses.

Fool—Sweetened fruit puree blended with custard or cream; served cold.

Haggis—Scottish traditional pudding of oatmeal, variety meats, suet, onions, and seasonings boiled in a sheep's stomach; often served at dinners honoring Robert Burns, Scotland's famous poet.

Blood (black) pudding—Sausage made of toasted oatmeal, blood, onions, and seasonings.

Finnan haddie—Smoked haddock poached in milk served on a bed of onions.

Kippers—Herring prepared in the traditional Scottish way of splitting them and then salting, drying, and smoking them to preserve them.

Colcannon—Scottish dish of boiled potatoes, cabbage, turnips, and onions that are sautéed in butter.

Cockaleekie soup—Hearty soup containing chicken, barley, and leeks.

Scotch broth—Thick soup made of vegetables and a meat broth.

Bannocks—Pancakes made with oat instead of wheat flour.

Shortbread—Very rich, buttery cookie (biscuit) often rolled into a circle and cut into wedges before baking.

Cawl—Welsh name for soup or one-dish meal, usually containing cabbage, leeks, and bacon, as well as other ingredients that may be available.

Laverbread—Jellylike mass resulting from boiling a special seaweed harvested along the coast of Wales.

Scots also eat fish caught off their many miles of sea coast. Finnan haddie and kippers are two of the fish dishes you can expect to eat in Scotland. **Finnan haddie** is made by poaching smoked haddock in milk and then serving it with cooked onions. **Kippers** are preserved herring that have been salted, dried, and smoked.

Vegetables, including turnips, cabbage, potatoes, onions, carrots, and cauliflower, are cooked in various combinations, often for a very long time. **Colcannon** is a popular vegetable recipe in Scotland. It is made by boiling a mixture of potatoes, turnips, cabbage, and onions until very soft before sautéing the drained vegetable gently in butter for about 20 more minutes.

A lunch favorite at home is **cockaleekie soup,** a Scottish soup made with stewed chicken, barley, and plenty of leeks. Its unique name reflects the ingredients: cock (chicken) and leek (leeks). The penetrating cold of Scotland makes soup a particularly important type of food for residents and visitors alike. **Scotch broth** (a.k.a. hotch-potch) is a thick soup made with a base of rich stock prepared by boiling mutton, beef, or chicken. Diced vegetables and some barley are added to the boiling stock and then simmered until the vegetables are tender.

Cereals used in Scotland include oats, barley, and wheat. **Bannocks** can be described as pancakes made of oat rather than wheat flour. *Porridge* in Scotland is defined as boiled oatmeal, a favorite breakfast item. Baked products from wheat flour are key parts of the Scottish diet. Pies with savory meat and onion fillings are served frequently at lunch or later in the day. **Shortbread** is the most famous of Scottish desserts made with wheat, but tarts and cakes are also popular.

Wales Many of the common ingredients in Welsh food are the same as in other parts of the United Kingdom, but the dishes are identified by distinctive names. An example is **cawl,** which basically is a name for a soup or one-dish meal. The ingredients may vary widely, depending on what food happens to be available in the kitchen that day. Cabbage, leeks, and bacon are basic ingredients for most cooks when making cawl.

Laverbread is a unique favorite in Wales. Surprisingly, this ingredient is not a bread at all but a special seaweed harvested along the coast of Wales (Figure 4.8), which is washed thoroughly and then boiled to make a jellylike food. It can be sliced and fried to be served at breakfast, and it can also be an ingredient in a variety of dishes to which it adds a flavorful hint of the sea.

The Welsh, like other residents of the United Kingdom, are fond of the cheeses produced locally. The abundance of sheep and goats in the rugged countryside accounts for the use of milk from these animals in Welsh cheese making. Restrictions by the European Union regarding soft cheeses made from unpasteurized milk have had a negative impact on the production of these cheeses for export.

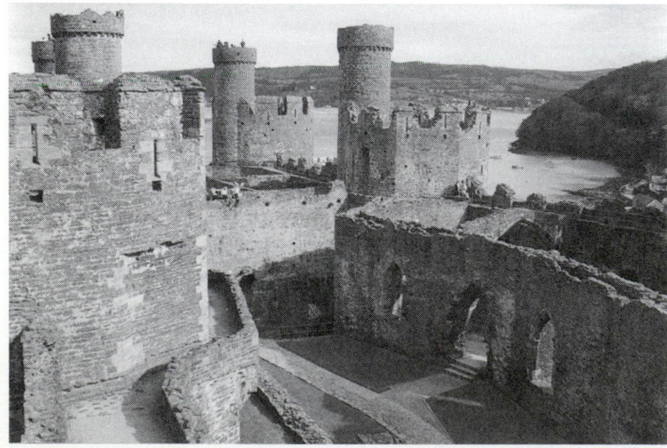

Figure 4.8 Massive castles were built along the coast in Wales to protect against invaders from the sea.

Pikelets—Small pancakes served at tea in Wales and Scotland.

Welsh rarebit—Sauce usually made of cheddar cheese and beer that is served over toast or other bread as a main dish.

Teatime is a familiar tradition in Wales. A variety of cakes and breads includes **pikelets** (little pancakes similar to crumpets). Of course, the featured beverage is hot tea, which is a welcome drink in this chilly country.

Last but far from least in the list of Welsh foods is **Welsh rarebit.** This simple sauce containing cheddar cheese and beer (or similar basic ingredients) is served over toast or other bread. Its use as an inexpensive replacement for rabbit or other meat in Wales explains the name Welsh "rabbit." However, Welsh rarebit (a title with no social stigma attached) is the preferred name for those wishing to be politically correct.

Ireland The food that immediately comes to mind when thinking about Irish meals is the potato. Surprisingly, potatoes were brought to Ireland by Sir Walter Raleigh from America, yet they grew so well in Ireland that they became the principal subsistence food of many living there in the 19th century. The potato famine that swept through Ireland from 1846 to 1850 killed many people and prompted many others to escape to America for a fresh start. However, potatoes are once again part—but far from all—of the diet of the Irish.

Irish stew—Stew featuring lamb cubes or other meat, potatoes, onions, leeks, cabbage, and/or other vegetables, frequently served with red cabbage in Ireland.

Irish soda bread—Round loaf of bread leavened by carbon dioxide produced from buttermilk and soda, ingredients in the dough.

Corned beef and cabbage—Cured (corned) beef simmered with cabbage wedges.

The climate and rocky terrain of Ireland are suitable for raising sheep, cattle, and pigs, which explains the generous use of meats and dairy products in meals. Added to the ingredients for the Irish kitchen are seafood and freshwater fish, a variety of vegetables, and apples grown locally.

In Ireland, **Irish stew** and **Irish soda bread** are specialties. Today these foods are also popular in various forms in the United States, a gift of the many Irish immigrants who have enriched the American scene, particularly in New England. Another Irish dish is **corned beef and cabbage.** It got its name from the "corns" or pellets of salt in which the meat was cured and preserved for later use. Cabbage was boiled near the end of cooking the corned meat because cabbage also was able to be stored in a cool place for a reasonable period of time.

The British Isles are noted for their pubs and their production of various alcoholic beverages. Beers, ales, stout, and whiskeys are brewed for local consumption and export (Figure 4.9).

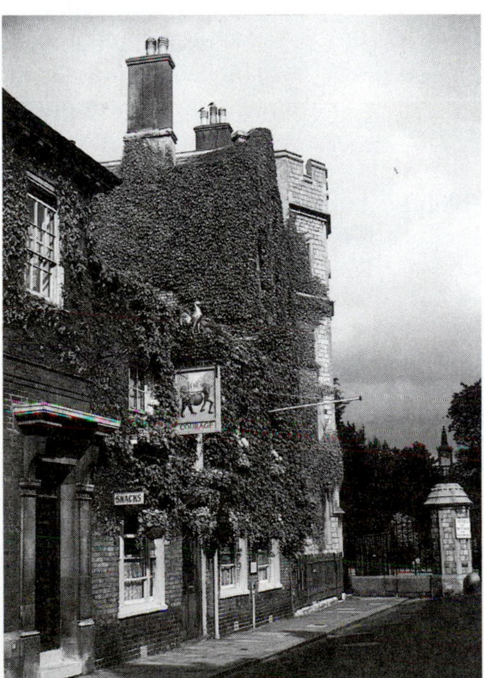

Figure 4.9 Pubs are the center of the social scene for drinking and dining for many people living anywhere in the United Kingdom.

Wassail—Traditional spiced wine or ale drink served at Christmas in the United Kingdom.

Plum pudding—Dense, steamed pudding containing some suet and a generous amount of dried and candied fruits that is served warm, usually with hard sauce and often flamed with brandy.

Holidays

Christmas is the big holiday of the year in the United Kingdom, and a big holiday dinner is the tradition. Frequently, the dinner may feature turkey, but goose or a joint of beef (a large beef roast) is often preferred. **Wassail** (an alcoholic wine or ale beverage containing spices and perhaps baked apples) is a traditional beverage for toasting the holiday season. Accompanying the main course of Christmas dinner are such items as dressing, potatoes, (usually roasted, mashed, or simply boiled), and a vegetable (peas and brussels sprouts or other traditional favorites).

To conclude the dinner, a **plum pudding** flamed with a brandy or served with another sauce is likely to be presented. The beauty of such a meal is that there are usually sufficient leftovers to feed the family on Boxing Day, the legal holiday that follows Christmas and that honors service workers, such as the postman.

Recipes

Roast Beef (England) (Serves 10)

Standing rib roast, 6 lb, approximately

1. Preheat oven to 500°F.
2. Place roast in a shallow pan so that the ribs serve as the rack.
3. Roast 20 minutes at 500°F.
4. Reduce heat to 350°F and continue roasting until meat reaches desired interior temperature (145°F for rare, 160°F for medium, or 170°F for well done). Check doneness with thermometer. The time required is about 20 minutes per pound for rare, 25 for medium, and 30 for well done.
5. Remove from oven and reset oven to 400°F. Place meat on warm platter, and cover loosely with tent of foil.

Yorkshire Pudding (England) (Serves 6–8)

1 c all-purpose flour
½ tsp salt
1 c milk
2 tbsp roast drippings
2 eggs

1. Place eggs, flour, salt, and milk in blender and blend for 45 seconds, stopping twice to scrape sides with spatula.
2. Remove all but 2 tablespoons drippings from roasting pan.
3. When oven is 400°F, heat drippings in pan over direct heat until spattering.
4. Immediately pour batter over hot drippings and bake in 400°F oven for 15 minutes, and then turn oven down to 375°F.
5. Bake 15 minutes more so that pudding is crisp and brown on surface. Cut into 6 or 8 portions and serve with roast beef.

Horseradish Sauce (England) (Makes 1¼ cups)

3 tbsp prepared horseradish (squeezed in towel)
1 tsp white vinegar
½ tsp sugar
¼ tsp dry mustard
½ tsp salt
½ tsp white pepper
½ c chilled whipping cream

1. Blend everything but the cream together in a bowl.
2. Beat cream until it will pull up into a peak.
3. Fold whipped cream with mixture completely. Refrigerate until ready to serve with roast beef.

Plum Pudding (England) (Serves 12–16)

2 c sugar
2 c flour
2 c fine bread crumbs
2 tsp cinnamon
1 tsp nutmeg
1 tsp allspice
2 c ground suet
1 lb chopped raisins
1 lb chopped dates
1 lb chopped English walnuts
1 tsp baking soda
2 c milk

1. Mix sugar, flour, bread crumbs, spices, and suet in a bowl.
2. Stir in fruit and nuts.
3. Add milk and soda (dissolved in milk).
4. Place in metal molds and cover.
5. Steam 3 hours in covered steamer, adding water to steamer if necessary.
6. Pudding can be stored in freezer for up to a year or for a somewhat shorter time in refrigerator.
7. Reheat pudding thoroughly by steaming in mold until hot in middle. Serve with sauce (see next recipe) or hard sauce.

Sauce for Plum Pudding (Makes 1 cup)

½ c sugar
2 tbsp flour
1 c boiling water
1 tsp vanilla
1 tbsp butter

1. Mix sugar and flour.
2. Add boiling water, stirring constantly.
3. Heat to boiling and until sauce is clear, stirring constantly.
4. Add butter and vanilla.
5. Serve hot over plum pudding.

Crumpets (England) (Makes 8)

½ oz dried yeast
1 c lukewarm water
3 c flour
½ tsp salt
1 c milk

1. Soften yeast in lukewarm water.
2. Stir in half the flour and beat until smooth.
3. Cover and set in a warm place about 20 minutes until batter is frothy.
4. Add the milk, salt, and enough of the remaining flour to make a pour batter.
5. Mix until smooth.
6. Arrange greased crumpet rings on greased griddle or frying pan and heat.
7. When griddle is hot, pour batter to half fill the rings.
8. Cook on medium heat until structure sets.
9. Remove rings and turn crumpets over to brown the second side.
10. Serve hot with butter and honey or jam.

Bannock (Scotland) (Serves 6)

½ c rolled oats
¾ c flour
¾ c whole wheat flour
¼ tsp salt
1 tbsp sugar
2 tsp baking powder
2 tbsp butter, melted
¾ c water
5 tbsp raisins

1. Mix the dry ingredients together thoroughly.
2. Make a well in the dry ingredients and add the butter, water, and raisins.
3. Transfer to a greased pie pan and bake at 400°F for 20 minutes or until golden brown. Cut into wedges to serve.

Colcannon (Scotland) (Serves 4)

4 russet potatoes
Water to cover
1 tsp salt
1 bunch kale
2 tbsp butter
¼ c milk
1½ tbsp minced onion

1. Boil potatoes in water and salt until very soft.
2. In a covered saucepan, cook kale (after throughly washing) until wilted and tender. Drain thoroughly and chop. Set aside.
3. Drain potatoes, mash and then add butter and milk. Mash until fluffy.
4. Stir chopped kale and onion into the mashed potatoes and serve hot.

Cockaleekie Soup (Scotland) (Serves 4)

4 c chicken broth
1 c slivers of stewed chicken meat (optional)
4 leeks, sliced
1 tbsp butter
½ c half and half
Salt and pepper to taste

1. Heat broth to boiling before adding slivered chicken (if desired) and leeks and simmering for 7 minutes.
2. Stir in the butter and cream.
3. Season with salt and pepper to taste.
4. Serve immediately to avoid curdling.

Shortbread (Scotland) (24 Wedges)

1 c butter
½ c sugar
1 tsp vanilla
2 c flour
⅓ c cornstarch

1. Cream butter and sugar until fluffy; stir in vanilla.
2. Sift flour and cornstarch before gradually stirring into the creamed mixture.
3. Press the dough evenly into two 8-inch cake pans, and prick entire surface with a fork.
4. Bake at 250°F for 35 minutes, but do not brown the surface.
5. Cut each into 12 wedges while still hot.

Welsh Rarebit (Wales) (Serves 4)

1 tbsp butter
1 tbsp flour
½ c beer
½ lb sharp cheddar cheese, grated
½ tsp dry mustard
¼ tsp salt
Dash Tabasco sauce
1 tsp Worcestershire sauce
1 egg
4 slices toast or toasted English muffins

1. Melt butter and stir in flour thoroughly before stirring in the beer.
2. Heat to boiling while stirring constantly.
3. Remove from heat and stir in the cheese and seasonings.
4. Melt cheese while stirring over medium heat.
5. Beat egg and stir into sauce.
6. Serve over toast or English muffins.

Corned Beef and Cabbage (Ireland) (Serves 8)

2 lbs corned beef
1 onion
5 whole cloves
5 peppercorns
2 tsp dried parsley
1 head cabbage
½ c sour cream
2 tsp prepared horseradish

1. Place corned beef in a Dutch oven or deep pot and cover with water.
2. Add seasonings; cover and simmer until tender (about 3 hours).
3. Add wedges of cabbage to the pot; cover and simmer about 20 minutes until tender.
4. Mix sour cream and horseradish together and serve as an accompaniment.

Irish Stew (Ireland) (Serves 4)

1¼ lb lamb stew meat
1 tbsp oil
1 onion, chopped
4 potatoes, pared and cubed
1 c diced celery
½ tsp salt
¼ tsp pepper
¼ tsp thyme
Water
1 c chopped cabbage

1. Brown lamb in oil in a Dutch oven.
2. Add onion and potatoes; sprinkle with seasonings.
3. Add water to just cover the vegetables.
4. Cover and heat to boiling; reduce heat and simmer 1 hour.
5. Add cabbage and simmer 30 minutes more. Serve hot.

Summary

The British Isles were the source of some of the early American colonists who brought their food traditions to the United States and laid the cornerstone of American food preferences. The land and climate of England, Scotland, Wales, and Ireland shaped the agricultural products that formed the basic diets of the early Britishers—wheat, barley, potatoes, fruits, vegetables, livestock, and fish (Figure 4.10).

Such items as Stonehenge, Hadrian's Wall, the St. James version of the Bible, and many castles represent the long history of Britain. The government has been a monarchy with a Parliament since the 11th century.

Figure 4.10 The Lake District of England combines fields for growing food with craggy hills better suited to grazing sheep.

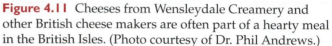

Figure 4.11 Cheeses from Wensleydale Creamery and other British cheese makers are often part of a hearty meal in the British Isles. (Photo courtesy of Dr. Phil Andrews.)

The British Empire extended all around the world at one time, but now is considerably reduced. The trade resulting from this extensive empire brought a wide range of food and other products to markets in the British Isles. Now immigrants from India, South Africa, and other Commonwealth members add to the diversity, particularly in England.

Britons tend to eat according to whether they are members of the upper class or the working class. The upper class eat a hearty breakfast, and all usually eat a filling lunch (Figure 4.11). Teatime is an important tradition with a fairly elaborate variety of savory items and sweets served for high tea. The evening meal is rather light. Hearty meat dishes and fish and chips, as well as tempting sweets and plenty of ale, stout, or beer, are familiar items. Many other dishes favored in Scotland, Wales, Ireland, and England are identified in this chapter.

Selected Sites

www.britainexpress.com/articles/Food—Information on food and recipes in England.

www.geo.ed.ac.uk/home/scotland/fooddrink.html—Food and drink in Scotland.

www.greatbritishkitchen.co.uk/—Background information on Welsh food.

www.foodireland.com/recipes—Recipes of some Irish dishes.

Study Questions

1. Identify the location of the British Isles and name the countries that are found on the two major islands.
2. What two grains are grown in Great Britain in comparatively large quantities?
3. Describe the influence of countries in the British Empire on the food patterns of people living in the British Isles.
4. Why are meat and fish so prominent in the British diet?
5. Identify three different desserts that could be considered to be British fare.
6. Plan a day's meals using ingredients and recipes that are part of the cultural food heritage of Great Britain.

Bibliography

Ashley, B. and J. Hollows. 2003. *Food and Cultural Studies.* Routledge. New York.
Bailey, A. 1969. *Cooking of the British Isles.* Time-Life Books. New York.
Bober, P.P. 1999. *Art, Culture, and Cuisine: Ancient and Medieval Gastronomy.* University of Chicago Press. Chicago.
Davidson, A. 1999. *Oxford Companion to Food.* Oxford University Press. Oxford, England.
Freeman, B. 1997. *Traditional Food from Wales.* Hippocrene Books. New York.
Mason, L. 2004. *Food Culture in Great Britain.* Greenwood Publishing Group. Portsmouth, NH.
Mason, L. and C. Brown. 2004. *Traditional Foods of Britain: An Inventory.* Prospect Books. Devon, U.K.
Mercer, D. 1996. *Chronicle of the World.* D. K. Publishing. New York.
Palmowski, J. 1997. *Dictionary of Twentieth Century World History.* Oxford University Press. New York.
Pearcy, G.E. 1980. *World Food Scene.* Plycon Press. Redondo Beach, CA.
Spencer, C. 2002. *British Food: Extraordinary Thousand Years of History.* Columbia University Press. New York.
Viault, B.S. 1990. *Western Civilization Since 1600.* McGraw-Hill. New York.
Woolgar, C.M. 1999. *Great Household in Late Medieval England.* Yale University Press. New Haven, CT.

Barents Sea
Norwegian Sea
Arctic Circle
SWEDEN
FINLAND
Gulf of Bosnia
NORWAY
Helsinki
Oslo
Stockholm
ESTONIA
RUSSIA
North Sea
LATVIA
DENMARK
Baltic Sea
Copenhagen
LITHUANIA
NETHERLANDS
BELARUS
POLAND
GERMANY

5 Scandinavia

Geographic Overview

The Midnight Sun

When you think of Scandinavia, images of sunlit fjords and strains of Grieg's *Peer Gynt Suite* come to mind, but it also is realistic to add the somber, piercing paintings of Munch (particularly *The Scream*) to round out the picture. The sharp contrasts found in the culture of Norway and its Scandinavian neighbors of Sweden and Finland are consistent with the extreme climatic shifts that result from the far-northern location of these countries.

The length of days and nights changes significantly between midsummer and midwinter because parts of Norway, Sweden, and Finland extend several degrees north of the Arctic Circle (Figures C.5 and C.6, p. C2). The dramatic change in light over the seasons exerts a significant influence on life in Scandinavia. This region, romantically called "Land of the Midnight Sun," is famous for the frantic, night-long celebrations of Midsummer's Night at Rovaniemi, Finland, and other towns above the Arctic Circle in Norway and Sweden (Figures 5.1 and C.4, p. C2). Even as far south as Denmark, the long hours of daylight in summer are effective in fostering rapid growth of crops. Fortunately, the long days help to offset the comparatively short growing season for farmers.

The opposite end of the extended daylight in summer is represented by the very long nights and very brief hours of light during the winter, a situation that appears to present a psychological challenge to some people in the northern climes.

Figure 5.1 Midsummer's Night is celebrated joyously in Rovaniemi, a town north of the Arctic Circle in Finland.

Influenced by the Sea

The four countries of European Scandinavia (Denmark, Finland, Sweden, and Norway) have long coastlines, which have focused the lives of many Scandinavians over the centuries on the sea. Denmark consists of a peninsula (Jutland) that extends northward with the North Sea on the west and the Baltic Sea and islands to the east. Finland is separated from the Scandinavian Peninsula by the Gulf of Bothnia, with the Baltic Sea lapping its southern coast.

Fjord—Narrow, steep-sided inlet from the sea.

Sweden has a much longer coastline than Finland, for it extends considerably farther south to its tip before its northwesterly reach toward Norway. By far the longest coastline (especially if the deep indentations of the **fjords** are included) is that of Norway, which is touched by the North Sea, Atlantic Ocean, and the Norwegian and Barents Seas.

Norway's physical geography is dominated by mountains, which has led most residents to live within a distance of little more than 10 miles from the coast. The steepness and ruggedness of these mountains have fostered a life dominated by the sea and small settlements since early days.

Although Sweden also contains some mountains, its terrain generally is far less precipitous than that of Norway. However, many lakes and forests are dominant features of much of Sweden. Similarly, Finland has innumerable lakes and

Figure 5.2 The gently rolling terrain in Sweden is well suited to thriving forests that feed the lumber industry; long rafts of logs are floated to the lumber mills.

vast reaches of forest (Figure 5.2), but only limited farming is done in the southern portion, which also is the region where most of the population lives.

History and Culture

The Vikings

Evidence of inhabitants in Scandinavia dates back at least to the Bronze Age, but it is the period from around the era of the Vikings that is of particular interest in examining the various cultures of the world. The limited space for settlements and the inescapable presence of the sea combined to spur early Scandinavians to set forth in their small but seaworthy boats to explore and conquer other lands.

As was noted in Chapter 4, the Scandinavians found the British Isles very tempting targets. Britain was within a reasonable sailing distance, and the resistance presented by the local people was unequal to the strength and ruthlessness of these tall plunderers from the north, who began to arrive near the end of the 8th century. Danes and Norwegians directed their conquests toward Britain, while the Swedes turned eastward to overrun Finland and venture into Russia and even conducted trade along the Black Sea and in Constantinople.

Without doubt the most dramatic evidence of Viking seafaring was provided by Leif Ericsson near the beginning of the 11th century. Remains of the small settlement he built near the tip of Newfoundland around 1000 CE attest to the fact that the Vikings arrived in North America well ahead of Columbus. However, the Vikings did not establish enduring colonies.

The final invasion of England from the north occurred in 1066, but King Harold was able to repel the Vikings. Immediately, he was drawn to Hastings to protect England against William of Normandy, who invaded with his Norman soldiers (primarily Norsemen who had settled in Normandy and adopted the ways of the French). The death of Harold in the Battle of Hastings and the superior equipment and fighting techniques of the Normans established the Normans in England, and William became known as William the Conqueror. This event is the capstone of the Vikings in Europe.

Political history

Considerable intertwining of governance has occurred between the Scandinavian countries since the time of the Vikings. From time to time, alliances through war or marriage have resulted in such combinations as Denmark and Norway, Norway and Sweden, and even the Kalmar Union (which united all three countries from 1397 to 1523). Sweden dominated Finland for much of the time from 1200 until the early 1700s, at which time Russia began to occupy Finland. Russian control was relinquished following the Russian Revolution of 1917. Finland's constitution was ratified in 1919.

Religion

One word basically summarizes religion in the Scandinavian countries: Lutheran. Although Catholicism predominated in this sphere prior to the Reformation, Martin Luther's message in the mid-16th century (particularly at the Diet of Worms in 1521 in Germany) quickly spread among Christians in Scandinavia. Eventually, Protestantism predominated, and the denomination selected was Lutheran (Figure 5.3).

Figure 5.3 The simple decor in this Lutheran church in Finland subtly underlines the split that occurred between Protestants and Catholics at the time of the Reformation.

Despite the uniformity of the basic religion, church attendance among the majority of people is reserved for such special times as Christmas and Easter. The exception to the Lutheran choice is a small group of Russian Orthodox worshipers in Finland, the result of the extended relationship that Finland had with Russia in past centuries.

Holidays

Christmas Holidays in the Scandinavian countries have seemingly as close a tie to the environment as to religion. Celebration of St. Lucia Day on December 13 in Sweden and Finland illustrates this point, for it marks the beginning of the Christmas season and brings considerable light and festivity to people who are already enduring the gloom of long winter nights. A young relative or daughter in the household wears a long white robe tied with a red sash and a metal crown of seven lighted candles with lingonberry sprigs entwined in it as she serves coffee and Lucia buns (lussekatter) to her family members while they are still in bed. This brightly lighted celebration is a welcome prelude to the enthusiastic celebration of Christmas. This entire season serves as a warm, happy antidote to the darkness of the Arctic winter.

In Finland, the celebration of Christmas has been superimposed on an ancient celebration of the end of the harvest season and the start of the long, hard winter on the darkest day of the year (December 23). Food and fellowship were always the tradition at this celebration, but the Christmas tree became part of the scene about a century ago. Soon thereafter, the idea of Santa bringing gifts in his sleigh pulled by reindeer in Lapland also captured the nation's children.

The Christmas tree is brought indoors on Christmas Eve in Sweden, and the tradition of decorating it then follows in many homes, a pleasant and social time following weeks of intensive baking and making of gifts. A big, festive dinner is a prelude to the exciting opening of gifts (often brought by Santa). A light meal is topped by a rice porridge (risgrynsgröt) and lutefisk (a very strong fish dish). The person who gets the whole almond that is hidden in the risgrynsgröt is the lucky one who will have a year of prosperity or will marry (if single). On Christmas Day a special service, the julotta, is held to celebrate the birth of Christ and to remember departed loved ones (Figure 5.4). Several days of parties and hearty eating typically close the season's festivities in Sweden.

The day to decorate homes for Christmas in Denmark is December 23, when the tree is bedecked with lights and colorful decorations, including small Danish

Figure 5.4 Lutheran churches throughout Scandinavia are the setting for celebrations, particularly at Easter and Christmas.

flags. The following evening, Christmas Eve, is the special time when Santa distributes gifts to the children in the family and a festive holiday dinner is served. Similar to the Swedish tradition, Danes serve ris al'amande (rice pudding complete with one almond that entitles the finder to a special gift). Christmas Day may include attendance at a Christmas church service, dinner, and time with family, friends, and new gifts.

Christmas extends over a prolonged period in Norway with all preparations needing to be done by December 21, St. Thomas' Day. Christmas Eve dinner is identified with "twig meat," so called because lamb ribs are steamed on a rack made of twigs. Gløgg, a derivative of Vikings' mead, is a mulled, spicy beverage that traditionally is served. Singing carols and exchanging gifts around the Christmas tree are key parts of the festivities. An almond ring cake occupies a prominent place on Norwegian Christmas tables, samples of which are given to all guests throughout the season until Epiphany on January 6. Final vestiges of Christmas continue until January 13 (St. Knut's Day), which marks the end of the 20-day holiday.

Easter Easter also is a time of celebration that is linked to the changing of seasons, for it is recognized as the celebration of the beginning of spring and the close of the long, dark winter. For those living at the Arctic Circle or farther north, this marks the return (if very briefly) of the long-departed sun and is surely a time of great rejoicing. Family holidays as well as celebrations of solitude mark this holiday time. Attendance at a church service also is part of the celebration for many.

The Arts

Arts and crafts are an important part of the culture in Scandinavia (Figure 5.5) Although the folk art and contemporary arts and music today differ somewhat from country to country, they have certain commonalities. The simplicity of the designs, whether in such table appointments as silverware and china or in crystal, incorporates a feeling of quiet strength and elegance that is distinctive. Similarly,

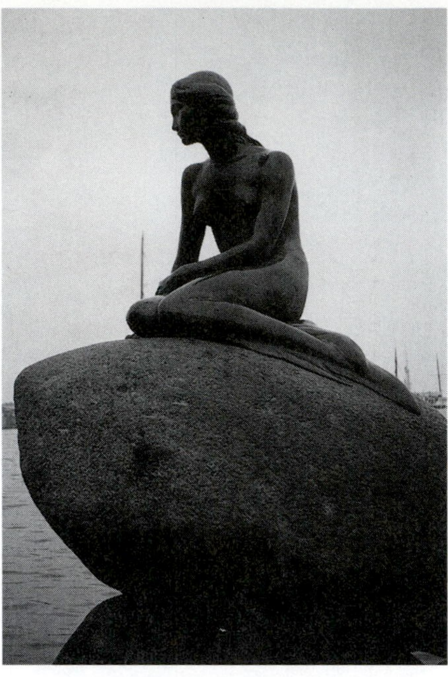

Figure 5.5 The signature sculpture that signifies Copenhagen and Denmark is the statue of *The Little Mermaid.*

the folk art demonstrated in wood carvings painted in joyous colors and in tastefully and carefully crafted textiles expresses the appreciation of color and design by Scandinavian people. Famous music composers from Scandinavia include Grieg (Norway) and Sibelius (Finland).

The sauna is so vital to the Finns that it may be built before the rest of the house. Steam for the sauna rises from water tossed on hot stones in a cozy, tightly closed room.

The sauna is a distinctive part of Finnish culture. Its origins go back to early days when families living in the forests would have a log cabin where they could keep a fire going to have a warm place to gather and to bathe themselves. It was even used as a birthing room. The practice evolved into either keeping a special room in the home or a small cabin at a family vacation spot. The ritual involves making the room very hot by burning wood in the chimneyless room and then expelling the smoke before entering to bathe. An antidote to the extreme heat is available in winter when people race from the sauna to roll in snow or to jump in an icy lake.

The Food Larder

Fish of various types play a significant role in the diets of people in all of the Scandinavian countries, which is not surprising in view of the easy access to the sea. Norwegians rely more heavily on fish than do other Scandinavians, perhaps because of their more rugged countryside and difficult farming conditions.

Agricultural crops are limited in Scandinavia by the climate and terrain (Figure 5.6). Denmark, the most southerly of these countries, has well over half of its land under cultivation, but only about 9 percent of the land in Sweden and Finland and less than 3 percent in Norway are dedicated to raising crops. Much of the farmed lands must be used to grow crops to feed to livestock. The remaining space is used to grow potatoes, sugar beets, turnips, and barley. Vegetables and fruits are grown in the southern areas adjacent to the cities (Figure 5.7).

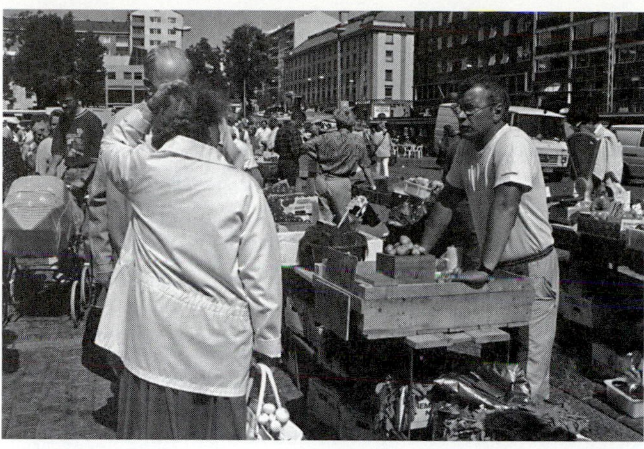

Figure 5.6 Shoppers can buy local produce at outdoor markets in Scandinavia throughout the long days of summer.

Figure 5.7 Peaceful, tranquil scenes, such as this town in Sweden, abound in the Scandinavian countries.

Sami—Nomadic reindeer herders (Laplanders) living in the arctic reaches of Scandinavia; shorter in stature and darker in coloring than the Scandinavians from the lower parts of this region.

Cloudberries—Orange-yellow, plump berries that are similar in shape to blackberries; primarily available briefly from the far north in summer.

Lingonberries—Mountain cranberrylike fruit particularly popular in Sweden.

The Danes are particularly noted for their animal products, including bacon, milk, cheese, eggs, and pork. Norwegians make some cheese, and they may raise sheep or goats on their precariously steep hillsides. Limited numbers of livestock also are raised in Sweden and Finland. The small amount of good pasture for animals is reflected in the comparatively limited production of farm animals.

Sami (also called *Laplanders*) live somewhat nomadic lives in the northernmost reaches of Norway, Sweden, and Finland. They still rely heavily on their reindeer herds for their food, shelter, and even some clothing.

Cloudberries and **lingonberries** are two special types of berries that may be found on Scandinavian menus. Cloudberries, so named because of their resemblance to a puffy cloud at sunrise, are available briefly in summer. Lingonberries resemble a cranberry. They are used fresh, or they are preserved for use throughout the year. They are particularly popular in Sweden.

Food Patterns

Rømmegrøt—Norwegian porridge of milk and sour cream thickened with flour and flavored with cinnamon and coarse sugar granules.

Although there are subtle differences between the cuisines of the various Scandinavian countries, there are far more similarities. For breakfast, Norwegians often choose **rømmegrøt**, a porridge of thickened milk and sour cream with added sugar and cinnamon. Coffee is the beverage of choice for breakfast and frequently throughout the day in all Scandinavian countries. Generally, it is brewed to be quite strong, but sometimes it is combined with another ingredient, such as a liqueur.

Gravet—Smoked salmon, a Norwegian delicacy.

Lutefisk—Unique cod dish.

Crayfish—Freshwater crustacean; apparently introduced to Scandinavia via ships from Britain.

Lefse—Norwegian flatbread.

Smørrebrød—Scandinavian open-faced sandwiches, usually with a base of rye bread and butter and artfully arranged toppings.

Another pervasive part of the Scandinavian diet is fish. Herring and other sea fish are consumed in many different preparations, including pickling and smoking. Salmon appears in Scandinavian menus, often as **gravet** or lox. Cod also is found on many menus. Perhaps the most familiar cod preparation is as **lutefisk,** a unique dish in which cod is soaked in lye for two or three days, then washed in running water for a similar length of time, and finally boiled. **Crayfish** provide a special treat.

Bread is the backbone of the diets, with special preference given to rye bread. **Lefse** is a flat bread often served at Norwegian meals. Particularly in Finland, but also in Sweden and Norway, rye bread is sliced carefully to serve as the base for open-faced sandwiches called **smørrebrød.** These are particularly popular for lunch, and they may actually be served almost any time of day. However, breakfast likely will find rye or other breads or rolls being served with butter and cheese or jam. Porridge, cold meats, fish, and pastries are other possible breakfast items.

Lapskaus—Chunky and thick meat and potato stew.

Fårikål—Thick lamb stew with cabbage; popular in Norway.

Fiskebeller—Norwegian fishballs.

Frikadeller—Danish meatballs.

The main meal generally is quite hardy. Potatoes are common in Norwegian meals and are prepared in various forms. Often, they are a part of fish or meat stews. They also appear on tables throughout Scandinavia. **Lapskaus** is a hearty stew made of chunks of meat and potatoes; **fårikål** is a Norwegian lamb stew that features cabbage. Norwegians like to eat **fiskebeller** (fishballs), while Danes are famous for their **frikadeller** (meatballs).

Root vegetables, notably turnips and rutabagas, are well suited to the rigors of life in Scandinavia and are particularly appreciated by the Finns. Fresh fruits and vegetables are far more plentiful and utilized in the summer than in the winter when they are difficult to obtain.

Smørgasbørd—Very elaborate Scandinavian buffet with ample arrays of cold foods and hot dishes, as well as dessert choices.

Koldt bord—Literally, cold table; bread, butter, and cold dishes that are the beginning part of a smørgasbørd.

Probably the first image that comes to mind when thinking of Scandinavian foods is the **smørgasbørd.** Although this tremendous buffet originally was spread by Swedes, smørgasbørds are popular in all four countries. The actual menu for a smørgasbørd can be quite varied.

The first part of the smørgasbørd is the **koldt bord,** which consists of cold foods. Round balls of butter (smør) piled into a small pyramid are one of the many small plates of food arranged on a smørgasbørd in Sweden. In fact, their name supplies the first part of the term *smørgasbørd.* Although dark breads and knäckebröd (hardtack) accompany the plate of butter, they are only the beginning of the spread.

Herring in many forms is featured prominently along with cold cuts, salads, an omelet (perhaps with mushrooms), other meats (usually pork or lamb) and fish, potatoes, and dessert. Nobody goes away from a smørgasbørd hungry.

(Akvavit) aquavit—Scandinavian liquor distilled from potato mash and flavored with caraway; possibly considered the national Scandinavian drink.

Aebleskiver—Small Danish doughnuts prepared in a special pan.

Kringle—Nut-filled coffee cake from Denmark.

Spritsar—Swedish ring-shaped cookie often made at Christmastime.

The history of alcoholic beverages in Scandinavia goes back at least as far as the Vikings, who apparently drank plenty of mead to chase away the cold. **Akvavit** is a Scandinavian liquor brewed from potatoes and flavored with caraway. It originally was used as medicine in the 16th century. Today it is often chilled in the freezer until being poured into a small glass to be consumed in one gulp.

Beers are especially popular today. Scandinavian beers are respected and enjoyed on other continents too. Finland is noted for its production of vodka. Regardless of the type of spirit being consumed, a cheerful and hearty "Skal" is said by all to toast the convivial occasion.

In the dessert department, Danish pastry and cookies from these countries stand out. Apples may be featured in a cake, **aebleskiver** (Figures 5.8 and 5.9), or pastry. **Kringle** (a Danish coffee cake filled with nuts) and **spritsar** (Swedish cookies piped into a ring shape before baking) are traditional favorites with cof-

Figure 5.8 Aebleskivers are puffy little cakes somewhat like doughnut holes; these are being turned over to brown the other side.

fee or as dessert. Berries from the Scandinavian Peninsula are extremely popular, particularly when cloudberries from the far northern areas are available fresh. Lingonberries appear in several different forms in meals throughout the year, adding a bright touch of color and heightening flavor in various dishes. The tradition of **fruit soup** evolved because fruits were dried in the summer for use throughout the winter; this dessert dish added a warm, sweet finish to a winter meal.

Fruit soup—Dessert soup popular in Scandinavia; often made with various dried fruits that are readily available through long winters.

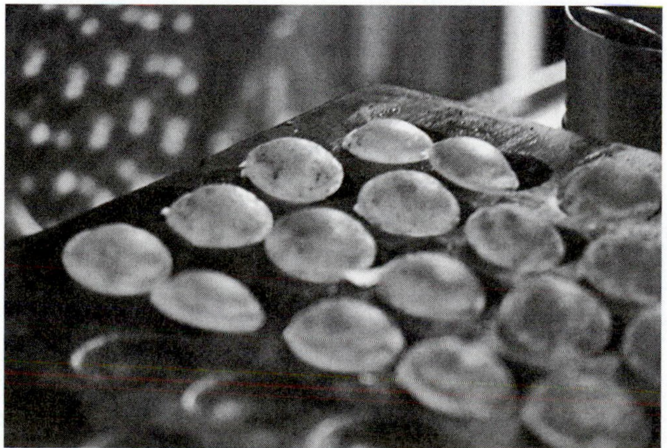

Figure 5.9 The special pan for baking aebleskivers is of cast iron with several small sunken hemispheres to hold the dough.

Recipes

Fiskesuppe (Fish Soup) (Norway) (Serves 6–8)

½ c sliced carrots
¼ c finely chopped parsnips
1 medium onion, chopped
1 potato, peeled and chopped
¾ lb boneless halibut or cod
1 bay leaf
¼ tsp coarsely ground black pepper
¾ tsp salt
4 c water
¼ c finely sliced leeks
1 egg yolk, beaten
2 tbsp chopped parsley
4 tbsp sour cream (garnish)

1. Place water and all preceding ingredients in a 6-qt saucepan, cover, and heat just to boiling.
2. Simmer, covered, 10 minutes.
3. Add leeks and simmer 2 more minutes.
4. Remove pan from heat; remove fish from pan and flake it.
5. Whisk a tablespoon of hot soup into beaten egg yolk and repeat until 4 tbsp soup have been blended smoothly with yolk.
6. Slowly pour yolk mixture into soup, stirring constantly.
7. Add parsley and flaked fish.
8. Reheat soup to serving temperature and adjust seasonings.

Smørrebrød (Open-Faced Sandwiches) (Denmark)

Rye bread, thin or medium slices
Butter
Toppings (any or all of the following, or others to add flavor and beauty): thinly sliced roast beef or cooked ham, shrimp, roast pork, paté, pickled herring, chopped or sliced hard-cooked egg, salami, gherkins or other pickles, bacon, sliced boiled new potatoes, sliced tomatoes, onions, cheeses.

1. Spread butter evenly to the edges of slices of rye (or bread of choice).
2. Decorate each slice of buttered bread with topping of choice, being careful to make each as beautiful and tempting as possible.
3. Serve. (Heat those that need to be served hot.)

Karelian Stew (Mixed Meat Stew) (Finland) (Serves 4–6)

½ lb beef
1 onion, coarsely chopped
⅛ tsp allspice
1 tsp salt
¼ lb mutton (or lamb)
¼ lb pork
¼ lb liver
Water to cover meat

1. Trim fat from meat and cut into chunks.
2. Arrange beef to cover bottom of oven-proof casserole dish.
3. Spread a third of onion and seasonings over beef.
4. Similarly, arrange a layer of mutton and liver topped with more onion and seasonings.
5. Top with a layer of pork, onion, and seasonings.
6. Brown the meat in a 475°F oven (uncovered).
7. Add water to cover meat.
8. Cover the casserole and continue braising the meat by reducing the temperature to 350°F for 2 to 3 more hours until meat is tender.

Ärter med Fläsk (Pea Soup with Pork) (Sweden) (Serves 6–8)

2 c dried yellow split peas
4 c water
2 medium onions, chopped
1 carrot, chopped
¼ lb chopped ham
¼ tsp thyme
¼ tsp marjoram
Salt to taste

1. Heat peas and water to boiling in covered pan.
2. Reduce heat, and simmer for 30 minutes.
3. Add vegetables, ham, and seasonings.
4. Continue simmering until peas and added vegetables are tender.
5. Adjust seasonings (if necessary) before serving.

Sillgratin (Herring and Potato Bake) (Sweden) (Serves 4–6)

1 tbsp butter
1 large onion, sliced thinly
3 large potatoes
2 herring fillets (in ½″ diagonal slices)
black pepper
1 tbsp fine bread crumbs
⅓ c light cream
1 tbsp butter

1. Saute onion in butter over medium heat until transparent.
2. Peel potatoes and slice thinly.
3. Beginning with a layer of potatoes, arrange layers of onion, fish, and end with a layer of potatoes in a 1½-qt casserole.
4. Sprinkle black pepper and bread crumbs on top and pour cream over the surface. Dot with butter.
5. Microwave casserole on high for 1 minute.
6. Bake in preheated oven at 400°F for 1 hour (until potatoes are tender).

Lökdolmar (Baked Onion Roll Ups) (Sweden) (Serves 4)

3 large onions
1 tbsp butter
2 tbsp chopped onion
½ c mashed potato
1½ tbsp fine bread crumbs
½ lb ground sirloin
2 tbsp cream
½ tsp salt
½ egg
3 tbsp butter, melted
2 tbsp fine bread crumbs

1. In a saucepan, cover peeled onions with water.
2. Bring to a boil and then simmer for 40 minutes; drain and cool.
3. Sauté chopped onion in butter.
4. Combine sautéed onion, potato, crumbs, meat, cream, salt, and egg. (Note: Mixture may be sautéed to make Swedish meatballs.)
5. Pull off outer layers of cooled onion, cutting in half if very large.
6. Place heaping teaspoon of meat mixture on each piece of onion (excluding inner area).
7. Roll each onion leaf to encase meat.
8. Place seam down in a casserole containing melted butter after first rolling over to coat the top surface.
9. Bake in 400°F oven for 15 minutes.
10. Sprinkle with bread crumbs and bake 15 minutes more.

Frikadeller (Meatballs) (Denmark) (Serves 4)

½ lb cooked ground meat
¼ lb chopped bacon
1 onion, chopped
2 slices white bread soaked in water
2 eggs, beaten
½ tsp salt
¼ tsp black pepper

1. Place meats and onion in a mixing bowl.
2. Squeeze water from bread, cut into cubes, and add to bowl.
3. Combine all ingredients and shape meat into small balls.
4. Fry slowly, turning frequently to brown on all sides. Cook until done in the center.

Länttulaatikko (Rutabaga Casserole) (Finland) (Serves 4)

1 medium rutabaga, peeled and cut into very small cubes
½ tsp salt
½ c fine bread crumbs
2 tbsp cream
¼ tsp nutmeg
1 egg, beaten
½ tsp salt

1. In a saucepan, heat rutabaga (covered with salted water) to boiling. Boil gently until tender (15 to 20 minutes).
2. Drain and puree.
3. Soak bread crumbs in cream, and then mix with remaining ingredients.
4. Stir in pureed rutabaga and place in buttered 1½-quart casserole.
5. Bake at 350°F for 1 hour.

Fruit Soup (Sweden) (Serves 4–6)

½ c dried apricots
½ c dried prunes
4 c water
2 tbsp cornstarch
⅔ c sugar
2″ cinnamon stick
2 slices lemon
2 tbsp raisins
2 tbsp golden raisins
1 tbsp dried currants

1. Soak apricots and prunes in water for 30 minutes.
2. In a small bowl, mix sugar and cornstarch thoroughly.
3. Add this mixture and cinnamon and lemon to fruit.
4. Heat to simmering while stirring.
5. Simmer, covered, for 10 minutes, stirring occasionally.
6. Add raisins and currants, and simmer another 5 minutes.

Ris al'Amande (Rice/Almond Pudding) (Denmark) (Serves 4–6)

½ c uncooked long grain rice
1½ c milk
½ c sugar
2 tbsp sherry
1 c whipping cream
½ c chopped, toasted almonds
Berries (optional)

1. Combine rice, milk, and sugar in saucepan and heat to boiling while stirring.
2. Reduce heat to simmer until milk is absorbed, stirring constantly.
3. Remove from heat, stir in sherry, and chill.
4. Beat cream, and then blend with rice and almonds.
5. Chill until served. Garnish with berries, if desired.

Spritsar (Cookies) (Sweden) (Makes 2 dozen)

¼ lb butter
¼ c sugar
2 egg yolks
1 tsp almond extract
2½ c all-purpose flour
¼ tsp salt

1. Cream butter and sugar thoroughly until fluffy.
2. Beat in egg yolks and extract.
3. Add flour and salt gradually and stir until well mixed.
4. Use a pastry bag or tube with a star tip to pipe desired shape (*S*-shape about 2" high is typical) onto baking sheet.
5. Bake in oven preheated to 400°F until barely brown (10 to 12 minutes). Cool on paper towel.

Summary

The Scandinavian countries, their history, and their food patterns have been shaped significantly by their extreme northern location. Norway and Sweden form the Scandinavian Peninsula, which extends far north of the Arctic Circle. Neighboring Finland also has an extensive region into the Arctic. Denmark consists of a peninsula extending northward from Germany and of islands in the Baltic Sea. The seas (Baltic, Atlantic, Norwegian, and Barents) influence the climate of the region and are a rich source of food. They also provided the pathway for Viking expeditions. The short growing season and very long winters fostered a diet not only of fish, but also of pork, mutton, dairy products, and hardy vegetables that could be kept for several months.

Vikings influenced world culture by their forays into Britain and France. Leif Ericsson is credited with establishing an early 11th-century temporary settlement in Newfoundland on the North American coast.

Holidays also tend to reflect the northern influence. The celebrations around Christmas start with St. Lucia Day in Sweden on December 13 and extend through St. Knut's Day in Denmark on January 13, thus providing many warm, bright memories in the long period of winter darkness that follows. Easter celebrations mark the return of the sun and herald the growing season that will follow a bit later. Celebration of Midsummer's Night, the longest day of the year, is a time of tremendous revelry, with huge bonfires and Maypole dances often extending throughout the bright night (the sun never sets in all parts of Scandinavia north of the Arctic Circle).

Folk art, clean and beautifully simple contemporary designs, and music are strong cultural contributions from Scandinavia. Food contributions are also noteworthy: smørgasbørds, smørrebrød, Danish pastries, and herring in innumerable preparations are some examples.

Selected Sites

http://www.norway.org.uk/culture/food/—Background information on Norwegian food and recipes.

www.sofn.com/norwegianculture/recipes—Recipes of many traditional Norwegian foods.

www.smorgasbord.sb/smorgasbord/index.html—Recipes and some background on celebrations and culture in Sweden.

www.world-recipes.info/denmark-danish—Some recipes typical of Denmark.

www.cbel.com/european_recipes—Large collection of recipes from Scandinavian countries, as well as other European nations.

http://virtual.finland.fi/netcomm/news/showarticle.asp?intNWSAID=26068—Recipes and information about Finland.

Study Questions

1. What parts of North America are at the same latitude as the northernmost and southernmost parts of Scandinavia?
2. Describe the influence of the Vikings on the world just before the end of the first millennium.
3. How has geography influenced the culture of Scandinavia over the past 11 centuries?
4. How has Finland's location affected its culture as contrasted with Norway?
5. Why is livestock more important in Denmark's agricultural scene than in Norway's?
6. Plan a day's meals using ingredients and recipes that are part of the cultural food heritage of Scandinavians.

Bibliography

Barer-Stein, T. 1999. *You Eat What You Are.* 2nd ed. Firefly Books, Ltd. Ontario, Canada.

Brown, D. 1968. *The Cooking of Scandinavia.* Time-Life Books. New York.

Butler, E. 1973. *Horizon Concise History of Scandinavia.* American Heritage Publishing, New York.

Davidson A. 2002. *Penguin Companion to Food.* Penguin Books. London, England.

Flandrin, J.L. 1999. *Food: Cultural History from Antiquity to the Present (European Perspectives).* Columbia University Press. New York.

Heldke, L. 2003. *Exotic Appetites. Ruminations of a Food Adventurer.* Routledge. London, England.

Jones, G. 1984. *A History of the Vikings.* (Rev.). Oxford University Press. Oxford, England.

Kagda, S. 1995. *Cultures of the World: Norway.* Marshall Cavendish. New York.

Kurlansky, M. 1997. *Cod: Biography of Fish That Changed the World.* Walker and Co. New York.

Lee, T.C. 1996. *Cultures of the World: Finland.* Marshall Cavendish. New York.

Lorenzen, L. 1986. *Of Swedish Ways.* Gramercy Publishing, New York.
Pateman, R. 1995. *Cultures of the World: Denmark.* Marshall Cavendish. New York.
Pearcy, G.E. 1980. *World Food Scene.* Plycon Press. Redondo Beach, CA
Tannahill, R. 1988. *Food in History.* 2nd ed. Three Rivers Press. New York.
Toussaint-Samat, A.B. 1994. *History of Food.* Blackwell Publishing. Malden, MA.

ATLANTIC
OCEAN
SWEDEN
FINLAND
NORWAY
ESTONIA
LATVIA
DENMARK
LITHUANIA
RUSSIA
IRELAND
NETHERLANDS
BELARUS
UNITED
KINGDOM
POLAND
GERMANY
BELGIUM
CZECH
REPUBLIC
UKRAINE
SLOVAKIA
AUSTRIA
FRANCE
HUNGARY
SWITZERLAND
ROMANIA
SLOVENIA
CROATIA
ITALY
BOSNIA &
HERZE-
GOVINA
YUGOSLAVIA
BULGARIA
PORTUGAL
MACEDONIA
ALBANIA
SPAIN
GREECE
Mediterranean Sea
TURKEY
TUNISIA
ALGERIA

6 Central Europe

Geographic Overview

Central Europe is not a precisely defined term, but in this chapter it includes Germany, Austria, Switzerland, and the Benelux countries of Belgium, the Netherlands, and Luxembourg.

The Benelux lowlands hugging the northern shore of the European continent are quite small and rather densely populated. Luxembourg, the smallest, is a tiny country tucked between France, Germany, and Belgium. Belgium, with its French speakers in the south and Flemish speakers in the north, is a somewhat larger country that shares its borders with France, Germany, and the Netherlands. Like Belgium, the Netherlands is bordered by the North Sea. The Netherlands is unique in that 3,000 square miles of its land—some as low as 22 feet below sea level—have been reclaimed from the sea (Figures 6.1 and C.8, p. C3). This immense engineering effort is testimony to the work ethic and perseverance of the Dutch people.

A gradual rise in elevation occurs in the European continent as it is viewed from the north toward the south. Much of the land in Germany, the Netherlands, and Belgium is well suited to growing crops. This region has considerable population, which limits the amount of land actually available for farming. This situation has led to intensive farming to maximize the yields from the land that is being farmed (Figure 6.2). The latitudes of Central Europe are suitable for raising rye, barley, wheat, oats, fruits, vegetables, and such root crops as potatoes and sugar beets.

Progressing southward, the terrain rapidly becomes rougher, and soon the Alps become dominant, particularly in Switzerland and parts of Austria. Some livestock can be raised in the Alps, which has led to outstanding cheese production in Switzerland (Figure 6.3).

Figure 6.1 Windmills historically were used as sources of power to pump water as the land was reclaimed from the sea to create and maintain the Netherlands.

Figure 6.2 Cattle are raised for dairy and also for some meat in Central Europe.

Figure 6.3 The mural painted on the wall of this dairy in Switzerland artistically summarizes life with the fabled dairy cattle of Switzerland.

Figure C.1 Stonehenge, a circle of huge stones built by the Druids in southern England around 1700 BCE, is the remarkable legacy of these early people.

Figure C.2 Although the facade of the baths has been altered significantly since the Romans built them over 2000 years ago, the baths remain an enduring reminder of the Roman occupation of Britain.

Figure C.3 Conwy Castle in Wales, built by King Edward I beginning in 1283, was one of the castles built to guard against invaders from the sea. It presents a protective aura even today.

Figure C.4 The colorful costumes of Samis (Lapplanders) are still worn on such festive occasions as Midsummer's Night north of the Arctic Circle in Finland and along the North Cape of the Scandinavian Peninsula.

Figure C.5 The long daylight hours in summer are ideal for this outdoor vegetable market in Helsinki, Finland, but the darkness and harsh cold of winter drive sales indoors at that time.

Figure C.6 The joy of the outdoor life of summer is reflected in the al fresco seating provided by this restaurant in Turku, Finland.

Figure C.7 Vineyards, the source of Germany's popular Rhine wines, and fortified castles are familiar sights along the Rhine River, a major artery for commerce in Central Europe.

Figure C.8 Drawbridges across canals that interlace Amsterdam not only have inspired painters such as Van Gogh, but also continue to serve motorists and boaters.

Figure C.9 The castle of Chillon on the shores of Lac Leman near Vevey, Switzerland, inspired Lord Byron's poem "The Prisoner of Chillon."

Figure C.10 Bold statues in Heroes' Square in Budapest commemorate the fierce Magyars who conquered and developed the region that included what is now Hungary.

Figure C.11 Paprikas are a vital ingredient in many Hungarian dishes, a fact emphasized by this banner outside a store in Szent Endre, Hungary.

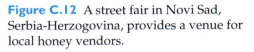

Figure C.12 A street fair in Novi Sad, Serbia-Herzogovina, provides a venue for local honey vendors.

Figure C.13 The kitchen in this home in Arbanassi, Bulgaria, is a cheerful, convenient room in which to cook and eat.

Figure C.14 This original bridge in Mostar, Bosnia-Herzeovina, was destroyed during the war in the Balkans in the 1990s but now has been rebuilt.

Figure C.15 The European focus that Catherine the Great brought to St. Petersburg, Russia is evident in the public buildings and churches that remain today, more than 200 years after her death.

Figure C.16 Romans go about their daily lives often oblivious to such familiar reminders of their heritage as the ruins of the Roman forum, just across the street.

Figure C.17 Egg noodles are the form of pasta that this Italian cook is separating after rolling out the dough and cutting it into strips the desired width.

Figure C.18 Brightly painted carts are a familiar sight in Sicily, particularly around Corleone at festivals.

Figure C.19 Despite its proximity to Rome, Sicily's early occupation by Greece is revealed at the Valley of Temples near Agrigento on the south shore of the island.

Figure C.20 The Ponte Vecchio, which was constructed starting in 1345 to span the Arno River in the Tuscan city of Florence, Italy, still unites the city.

Figure C.21 The hill town of Assisi in Italy's Apennine Mountains, with its dominant, lovely cathedral, is best known as the home of St. Francis.

Figure C.22 The cathedral in Strausbourg, France, is a classic Gothic structure with a lovely rose window above the main entrance.

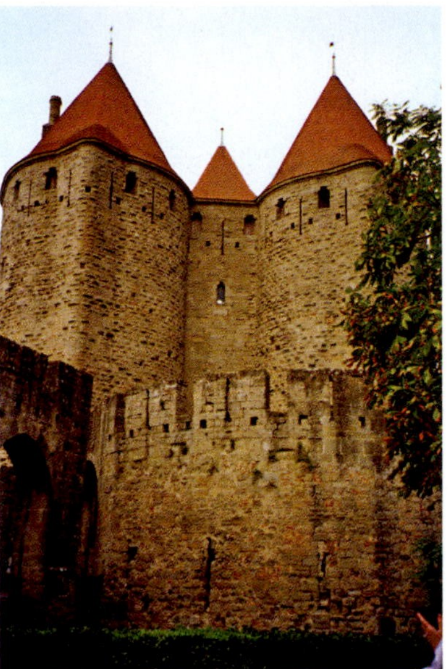

Figure C.23 Carcassonne has been attacked by many different invaders over the centuries and was heavily fortified with thick walls in the 13th century. Its restoration has made it a popular tourist spot in southwestern France.

Figure C.24 Chenonceaux is a unique, lovely chateau featuring a long gallery extending across the Loire River in France.

Figure C.25 The Alhambra, the palace built on the hills above Granada by the Moors in the 13th century during their occupation of Spain, is an outstanding example of graceful Moorish architecture.

Figure C.26 Spain is famous for its lovely painted tiles used effectively in decorating such structures as the Plaza of the Americas at the park where Seville hosted a world exposition in 1929.

Figure C.27 This view of Toledo, Spain, across the Tagus River still closely resembles the scene painted by El Greco in 1609.

Figure C.28 Spain is noted for its wines. This winery and its vineyards are in southeastern Spain near Barcelona.

Figure C.29 Paella, which features various seafoods, saffron, rice, and other flavorful ingredients, is considered by many to be the national dish of Spain.

Figure C.30 Bullfighting is a tradition in Spain; the running of the bulls in Pamplona is an annual event in which bulls are released to run down the city streets, scattering and even goring running thrill seekers.

Figure C.31 The Monument to the Discoverers near the port of Lisbon, Portugal, depicts many different people and the caravels in which they sailed on voyages of discovery under the sponsorship of Prince Henry the Navigator, who ruled Portugal in the first part of the 15th century.

Figure C.32 Pots are ready to be loaded onto a boat and carried to an area for trapping lobsters and other crustaceans off the coast of Cascais, Portugal.

Figure C.33 The elaborately decorated entrance to Geronimo cathedral and monastery in Lisbon, Portugal, presages the elaborate decor within.

Figure C.34 The Parthenon atop the Acropolis dominates the city of Athens, serving as a reminder of the glory that was classical Greece.

Figure C.35 Moussaka is an eggplant (aubergine) casserole that may be made with various other ingredients added, but it still is one of the favorite Greek dishes.

Figure C.36 Baklava, a sweet pastry made with layers of phyllo, finely chopped nuts, and a sweet syrup or honey, is a popular dessert throughout Greece and the Levant.

Figure C.37 The 17th century Blue Mosque, with its six delicate minarets, is considered one of the most beautiful mosques in Istanbul, Turkey.

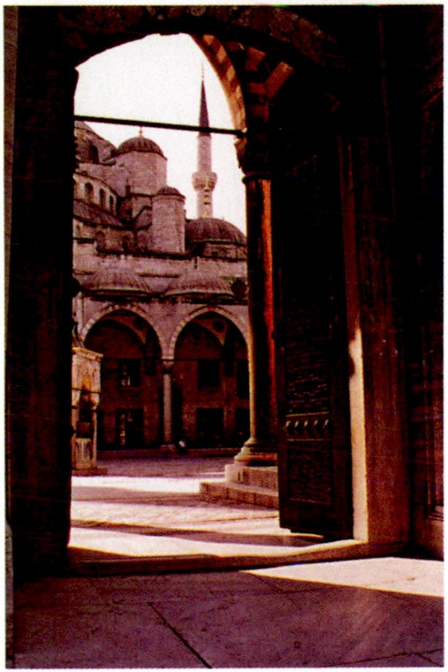

Figure C.38 The inner courtyard of the Blue Mosque includes a fountain in the center for Muslims to wash before entering the mosque for prayers.

Figure C.39 The Hagia Sophia was first built in 415 to be a Christian church and was rebuilt following a fire more than 100 years later; subsequently, the Turks converted it to a mosque, but it is now a museum.

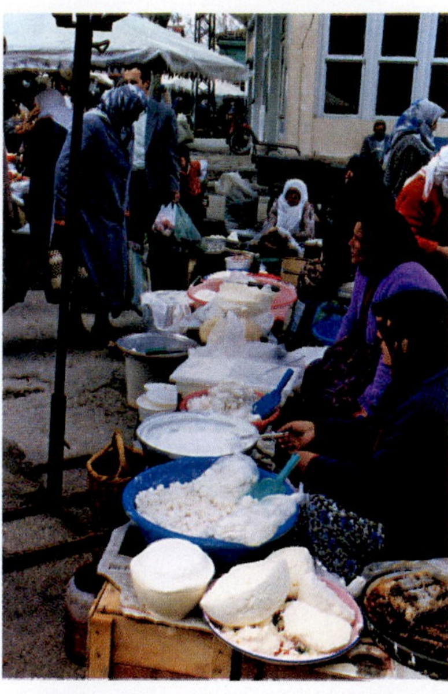

Figure C.40 Women sell their homemade soft cheeses at an outdoor market in a Turkish village.

Figure C.41 Women card and spin wool in preparation for weaving Turkish carpets.

Figure C.42 A veiled Turkish woman sits outside her unique cave apartment in Cappadocia near Goreme in Central Turkey.

Figure C.43 Ionians established Ephesus on the Turkish shore of the Mediterranean before 1,000 BCE, but the Romans are credited with rebuilding it after an earthquake destroyed it in 17 CE. The library is the tall facade in the center.

Figure C.44 Although evidence of Greek architecture still can be seen in Priene (near the central western coast of Turkey), the town became a part of the Roman Empire in 129 BCE.

Figure C.45 This colorfully garbed Muslim woman crochets busily at Aspendos, Turkey, to create belts for sale.

Figure C.46 Sheep can graze on the relatively barren land of Syria, providing not only wool, but also milk and meat for herders.

Figure C.47 Krak des Chevaliers was built on a peak in northwestern Syria by Kurds in the 11th century and became a Christian fortress when the Crusader Order of the Hospitallers captured it in 1142; eventually it fell to the Muslims.

Figure C.48 The ruins of Palmyra in the eastern Syrian desert reveal still the glory of this Roman-controlled city on the Silk Route.

Figure 6.4 The Rhine is a working river with many barges and ships sailing along it carrying coal, freight, and passengers all along its length.

Figure 6.5 The Burg Katz (Cat's Castle) still stands guard over vineyards and the town from high above the Rhine River in Germany.

Austria has an important geographic feature, the Danube River, which flows basically from west to east across the northern region. The other major river in Central Europe is the Rhine, which originates in Switzerland and flows northward to enter the North Sea in the Netherlands (Figures 6.4, 6.5, and C.7, p. C3). Both of these rivers have been important through the ages for transportation of goods and communication among people along their routes.

History

Strife pretty much typified the relationships among various parts of Central Europe as the people in the Middle Ages and later sorted out their political allegiance and dominance. In what is now Germany, Saxons ruled in the 10th century, followed by the Salian Dynasty, and then by the Hohenstaufen Dynasty until the middle of the 13th century. The Hapsburg Dynasty was in charge when the Protestant Reformation, spurred by Martin Luther in 1517, swept through this region. The result was that both Catholicism and Lutheranism could be practiced, depending on the decision of the current ruler.

Trading Powers

Dutch traders set the stage for gaining wealth from other parts of the world beginning in the 17th century. The Dutch East India Company began developing trade in Southeast Asia, and subsequently Belgium traded with some African nations. Both Belgium and the Netherlands, despite their small size, were able to gain control over regions far from Europe. The Netherlands established itself in Indonesia by acquiring it from Portugal, the earlier trading power. The Netherlands also established a presence in the western hemisphere in Brazil briefly and on the northern shoulder of South America.

The lengthy involvement that the Netherlands had with the Dutch East Indies has had a lasting impact on Dutch food. The exotic spices from Indonesia add a strong cosmopolitan flair to the Dutch cuisine. Belgium claimed the Congo in Africa in the late 1800s and proceeded to capitalize on its abundance of minerals, rubber, and ivory, but this acquisition had little influence on Flemish food.

Powerful Families

Hohenzollern—Family that ruled Prussia and neighboring regions for three centuries, ending with the end of World War I.

Hapsburg—Family that ruled Austria and its neighbors for about seven centuries until World War I.

Early in the 15th century in the regions east of the Netherlands, powerful families started to control considerable land and wealth. In northern Germany, the Hohenzollerns began to amass an empire that was rivaled only by the vast Hapsburg Empire (Figure 6.6). Frederick William, the Great Elector, began his rule in 1640 and established a tolerant yet militaristic and well-governed regime. Somewhat later, Frederick the Great extended and strengthened his Prussian domain, a move that resulted in the **Hohenzollern** family's ruling there until the end of World War I in 1918.

To the south, the Hapsburg Empire encompassed not only Austria, but also Bohemia (Czechoslovakia), Hungary, and the northern part of the Balkan states. This meant that the Hapsburgs were governing not only Germanic peoples, but also Slovaks, Magyars, Slovenes, Romanians, Italians, and Croatians—a truly formidable challenge! Gradually, increasing freedoms were granted to the people by the rulers, particularly by Joseph II late in the 18th century. However, Francis I, the first emperor of Austria, undid much of the work accomplished by Joseph II. Hapsburg rule continued over the Empire until 1848, when the revolutionary spirit that was sweeping France and much of the rest of Europe fomented the unrest needed to overthrow the control of the Hapsburgs.

The World Wars

Although foreign trade was especially important economically for the Netherlands and Belgium, political power within Europe remained the most significant factor shaping European history. In the mid-19th century, King Wilhelm I of Prussia appointed Otto von Bismark as minister-president, and he proved to be so strong militarily and politically that he was able to force Austria out of the German Confederacy and form the German Empire in 1871. Austria and Hungary then formed Austria-Hungary.

The murder of the heir to this throne, Franz Ferdinand, and his wife in Sarajevo in 1914 plunged the world into what is now referred to as *World War I.* Germany agreed to back Austria in its Balkan crisis in 1914, which meant going against Russia and its support of the Serbs. Thus, Germany was quickly and deeply involved in World War I. Austria was created as a nation following the end of that war.

The Weimar Republic that was established at the conclusion of World War I experienced the problems that other nations were undergoing as a result of the Depression, setting the stage for the rise of Hitler and the Third Reich. World War II encompassed Europe, finally ending with the fall of Berlin and Hitler's suicide.

Figure 6.6 St. Stephen's Cathedral's construction was started in 1147 in the center of old Vienna where the Hapsburg Empire rivaled the Hohenzollerns.

Figure 6.7 The Matterhorn that looms above Zermatt, Switzerland, is in the Alps Mountains in Central Europe.

The division of Germany that followed the close of World War II was erased at last when the Berlin Wall was torn down in 1989.

The scene in Switzerland stands in sharp contrast to the destruction that swept the rest of Europe in both World Wars I and II. Switzerland declared neutrality, which was unique among European nations. Its location in the center of the continent ensured that it would serve as the crossroads for the continent, yet its size and political interests contributed to its ability to maintain a neutral stance during the 20th century wars (Figure 6.7).

Culture

The Arts

The disastrous impact of the two world wars of the 20th century may tend to overshadow some cultural developments that occurred at various times in Central Europe. It is important to recognize the musical geniuses from Germany and Austria who contributed so much to classical music literature: Bach, Handel, Beethoven, Brahms, and Wagner are among the German composers who are best known. Mozart, and Johann Strauss are recognized as outstanding composers from Austria.

Pieter Brueghel the Elder and sons Jan and Pieter, Rubens, and Van Dyck are famous Flemish painters. The Netherlands also made significant contributions to the art world through the works of Rembrandt, van Gogh, Vermeer, and others.

Although Lord Byron was an English poet, one of his most famous poems (The Prisoner of Chillon) is set in a castle near Vevey, Switzerland (Figure C.9, p. C3).

Holidays and Celebrations

The Netherlands The Netherlands celebrates the Queen's birthday with the Queen riding through the streets of Amsterdam in a golden carriage drawn by fine horses while multitudes of her subjects joyously cheer (Figure 6.8). The surprising

Figure 6.8 The canals and tall, narrow homes (with their pulleys high above the middle windows to hoist furniture to the upper floors) are the setting for celebrating the Queen's birthday and other holidays in Amsterdam, Holland.

Figure 6.9 Hops are grown in Germany to provide an important ingredient for the famous German beers.

part of this tradition is that the celebration occurs on the birthday of the Queen's mother in April, a time when the weather is far more suitable for this outdoor event.

Celebration of the Christmas season is another time for festivities, beginning on December 5 with the arrival of Sinterklaas and his helpers in a boat. Gifts are brought by **Sinterklaas** and left by the fireplace. Householders leave carrots by the fireplace to help Sinterklaas feed the horses that help him on that special night.

Sinterklaas—Name for Saint Nicholas in the Netherlands.

Another part of the Dutch Christmas is the Christmas tree. Each of these trees is decorated imaginatively and then taken into a designated area in the streets on New Year's Eve for a huge midnight bonfire and fireworks to usher in the new year.

Germany The celebration of Christmas in Germany has some similarities as well as some differences when compared with the celebration in the Netherlands. Saint Nicholas Day celebration begins the evening before December 5. During that night, Saint Nicholas or a helper leaves nuts, candies, and apples in the stockings good children have hung, but bad children are greeted the next morning with a switch in their stockings! Another feature of Christmas is the Advent wreath, which has four candles; one is lit each week to mark the four weeks before Christmas. Also, an Advent calendar is a special treat as children open a window in it each day, with the last window opened on Christmas Eve featuring a picture of a Christmas tree. Fragrant evergreen boughs, considerable Christmas baking, and a lovely Christmas tree are other traditions of a German Christmas.

Germany has a special celebration in honor of the harvest each fall. This Oktoberfest is celebrated in Munich for more than two weeks in September and early October. Originally, the event was held to celebrate a wedding (of Crown Prince Ludwig to Princess Therese in 1810), but the revelry, abundant beer (Figure 6.9), and plentiful food became a tradition. Today crowds from all over the world converge on Munich and its beer tents every fall to carry on the tradition. Enthusiastic musicians in German "Oompah" bands add to the merriment.

Food Patterns

A continental breakfast is a basic, light breakfast favored by many Europeans. This usually consists of coffee (or a variation, such as coffee with milk) and a bread or roll of some type. For many people, this is the means of getting through the first part of the day until more substantial food can be fitted into the day's activities.

Meals in this region of Europe generally are hearty, featuring generous portions of meat and potatoes, plus vegetables. Bread usually accompanies a meal, and beer or wine often is the beverage served.

Muesli—Breakfast cereal of toasted oats, nuts, and dried apples developed by a Swiss doctor.

Fondue—Swiss dish prepared by melting cheese with wine in a chafing dish and using long-handled forks to dip cubes of bread into the cheese mixture.

Raclette—Swiss favorite consisting of melted cheese served with a sliced, boiled potato, sweet gherkin, and pickled pearl onions.

Rösti—Swiss dish of parboiled, grated potatoes sautéed in sizzling butter to make a pancakelike disk that is browned well on both sides.

Switzerland

Switzerland presents a surprising variety of foods for such a small country, doubtless the result of its much larger neighbors whose influences have spilled over the borders. Overtones of Germany are found in the northeast, of Italy along the southern region, and of France in the west and northwest.

Switzerland has its own special dishes. A popular breakfast treat is **muesli,** a mixture of toasted oats, dried apples, and nuts that a Zurich doctor developed.

The cheeses of Switzerland (Figure 6.10) are notable and have served as the basis of two specialties: **fondue** and **raclette.** The original fondue was made by melting cheese diluted with wine in a chafing dish. Then long forks were used to dip bite-sized cubes of bread into the hot cheese mixture. Fondue is still very popular, but variations on it, including dipping pieces of fresh fruit in melted chocolate, also may be found. Raclette also is based on melted cheese, which is placed on a special plate with a sliced, boiled potato, a sweet gherkin, and pickled pearl onions.

Potatoes gain prominence in Switzerland's menus when they are parboiled, coarsely grated, and then fried like a pancake in sizzling butter until well browned on both sides. This traditional potato dish is called **rösti.**

Switzerland also is known for its excellent chocolate candies.

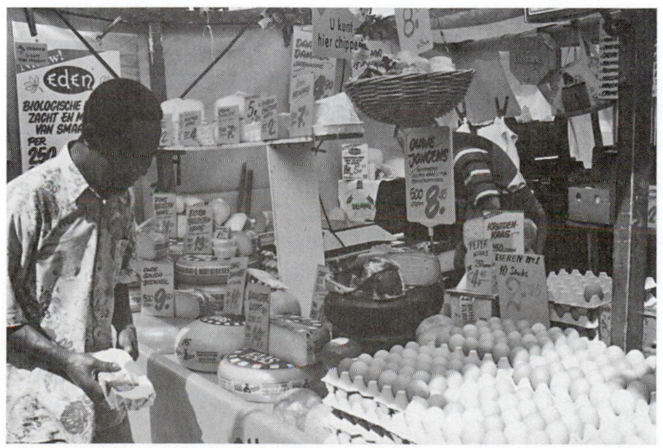

Figure 6.10 Cheeses of various types are popular in Switzerland and other countries of Central Europe.

The Netherlands

In the Netherlands, menus are hearty, often featuring potatoes, soups, pork or other meats, fish, cabbage and other vegetables, and apples or other fruit for the one hot meal of the day. The other meals are considered to be "bread-and-butter" meals. These simpler meals may contain a variety of other items, such as an egg dish or other casserole, perhaps with meat or fish, and some fruit, along with milk, buttermilk, or coffee.

Tea is a popular beverage for breakfast and at teatime around 4 P.M. Coffee with milk or cream is the preference at "elevenses," the break accompanied by a sweet touch at 11 A.M. After the evening hot meal, coffee may be served. **Borrel** (Dutch gin) or sherry and bitterballen (savory meatball appetizer) are favorites around 5 P.M.

Borrel—Dutch gin.

Appelflappen—Fried, batter-dipped slices of apple sprinkled with confectioner's sugar.

Rijsttafel—Rice table originating in Indonesia and brought to the Netherlands by the Dutch East Indies Company; consists of some highly spiced dishes and many other somewhat bland dishes, which are prepared at the table (usually in restaurants).

Hutspot—Hearty stewlike dish made in the Netherlands by simmering a large cut of meat with vegetables and then mashing the cooked vegetables before serving them with the sliced meat.

Special holiday treats include pepernoten (very hard Christmas cookies traditionally prepared for December 5 to be tossed mysteriously by the gloved hand of Black Peter, Sinterklaas's helper), spekulaas (rolled cookies flavored with cinnamon, nutmeg, cloves, and almonds and cut into doll or other shapes), borstplaat (fudgelike candy), **appelflappen** (fried, batter-dipped apple slices favored for New Year's celebration), and oliebollen (balls of yeast dough containing apples, currants, and raisins that are fried in deep fat and then sprinkled with powdered sugar to celebrate New Year's Eve).

At any time of year, especially when dining out, a favorite meal in Holland is **rijsttafel** (rice table), a multicourse meal of many hot and spicy foods as well as other milder items (usually prepared and served at the table by an Indonesian). This dining ritual is a result of the long association the Dutch traders of the Dutch East India Company had with the Spice Islands (today's Indonesia). Another special dish favored by people in the Netherlands is **hutspot,** a stewlike mixture of meat and vegetables in which the vegetables are mashed together and then served with the sliced meat.

Belgium

Belgian waffle—Oblong, crisp waffle with deep indentations.

Belgian endive—Oblong, small head vegetable consisting of very pale leaves around a central core; grown in the dark to prevent greening and displayed in light only when being sold in the market.

Stoemp—Mashed potatoes made with plenty of butter, cream, and seasonings in Belgium.

Waterzooi—Belgian fish stew.

Lapin—Rabbit, a popular meat in Belgium.

Belgian waffle is a specialty that springs to mind when people think about the foods of Belgium. Many different versions of the recipe exist; baking powder leavens some, and yeast leavens the more elaborate ones. However, regardless of the ingredients, Belgian waffles are baked until they are quite crisp and dry in a distinctive waffle iron that bakes the batter into an oblong rectangle with indentations about twice as deep as those of regular waffles.

Another unique food is **Belgian endive,** which is exported to many markets around the world. This vegetable may be served raw as svelte leaves topped with shrimp or other tempting salad ingredients. It also may be cooked whole and featured in casseroles with ham or other meat.

Stoemp is a flavorful Belgian dish. It features potatoes mashed with plenty of butter and cream, served with onion sauce and carrots. **Waterzooi** is a popular stew containing seafood or freshwater fish, leeks, butter, herbs, eggs, and cream; sometimes it is made with chicken in place of fish. **Lapin** (rabbit) is served in a variety of dishes. The popular beverage with these hearty dishes is a Belgian beer.

Germany

Sauerkraut—Fermented shredded cabbage, a German specialty.

Frederick the Great is credited with establishing the potato as a central part of the German diet when he required all peasants to grow potatoes in 1744. This ubiquitous vegetable has found its way into all parts of the German menu, even as an ingredient in schnapps, a distilled liquor. Cabbage is another cornerstone of German food, most commonly in the form of **sauerkraut,** which is shredded cabbage with salt that is fermented. This tasty means of extending the useful food life of cabbage has been incorporated in a wide range of recipes; it is often served with plump sausages or a hearty roast.

Pork, beef, and veal are served in generous portions and in various preparations throughout the day. Thin cutlets (often veal) are termed **schnitzel.** Schnitzel may be prepared breaded or plain, stuffed, in sauces, or even topped with an item such as a fried egg.

Hearty stews of vegetables and meat plus barley or other cereal or dumplings are popularly called **eintopf.** The practice of mixing a sour taste with somewhat sweet flavors is represented by **sauerbraten,** which is a roast that has been marinated in a seasoned vinegar and wine with bay leaves and other herbs, simmered until very tender, and then served with a gingersnap-containing gravy and boiled red cabbage with tart apples.

Baked favorites include **springerle** (popular picture cookies with anise flavoring), **lebkuchen** (gingerbread cookies baked in picture molds), stollen (Christmas bread), and hearty dark breads such as **pumpernickel** and rye.

Beers and Rhine wines are dear to the hearts of most Germans (and many other people as well).

Schnitzel—German term for thin cutlets of veal or other meat that is dipped in a batter prior to being fried.

Eintopf—Hearty German stew of meat, vegetables, and a cereal or dumplings.

Sauerbraten—German dish; roast marinated in vinegar and wine and simmered with seasonings until very tender, and then served with a gingersnap-containing gravy and red cabbage cooked with tart apples.

Springerle—Anise-flavored German picture cookie popular at Christmas.

Lebkuchen—German gingerbread cookies baked in picture molds.

Pumpernickel—German dark, coarse bread made with unsifted rye flour.

Sachertorte—Austrian dessert; layered chocolate cake spread with apricot jam and topped with a chocolate glaze.

Austria

Austrian cuisine is similar to that of Germany. However, there is a special fondness for coffee and something tempting to eat with it. **Sachertorte** (Figure 6.11) is a lovely, layered chocolate cake with apricot jam spread between the layers and a chocolate glaze gracing the top and sides.

Apfel strudel is another popular pastry. This treat is made by stretching a dough to cover a tablecloth (4 feet by 6 feet) so that it is almost thin enough to see through, brushing the dough with melted butter, and then spreading cinnamon-flavored chopped apples onto it before rolling the dough into a log and cutting it into 3-inch lengths for baking.

Meats, including veal, are prominent on Austrian menus. In fact, **Wiener Schnitzel** is named for the city that made it famous, Vienna. This dish is prepared by pounding thin slices of veal even thinner before dipping in flour, egg, and bread crumbs and frying them in butter (Figure 6.12). Roasted potatoes are usually served with the cutlets.

Vienna is noted for its elaborate desserts and pastries. Near the end of the 18th century, the court of Emperor Franz Joseph (known also for hiring Mozart as court composer) had a vast and well-stocked kitchen that included even small metal molds for shaping ice cream into individual servings.

Apfel strudel—Austrian pastry made with extremely thin dough spread with melted butter and an apple filling, rolled into a log, sliced into 3-inch lengths, and then baked.

Wiener Schnitzel—Traditional Viennese dish consisting of thin veal cutlets dipped in flour, egg, and bread crumbs before being fried in butter.

Figure 6.11 Sachertorte as it is served in the Sacher Hotel in Vienna where this delicacy (chocolate cake with thick chocolate icing and apricot jam filling) was created.

Figure 6.12 Wiener schnitzel is a popular veal dish often served in Vienna, Austria, its hometown.

Recipes

Belgian Waffles (Belgium) (Serves 4)

3 eggs, separated
3 tbsp melted butter
1 c milk
1 c flour
1 tsp baking powder

1. Beat yolks until light.
2. Stir in the butter and milk.
3. Blend flour with baking powder before stirring into the liquid mixture.
4. Beat egg whites until peaks fold over and then fold gently into the batter.
5. Spoon one-fourth of the batter into a preheated Belgian waffle iron and bake to golden brown.

Bitterballen (The Netherlands Appetizer) (Serves 4–6)

2 tbsp butter
2 tbsp flour
¼ tsp salt
½ c milk
1 c chopped, cooked meat
1¼ tsp minced parsley
1 tsp Worcestershire sauce
1 egg
Fine bread crumbs
Oil for deep-fat frying

1. Melt butter, stir in flour and salt, and then gradually stir in milk.
2. Heat, stirring constantly, until sauce boils. Chill.
3. Stir together sauce and remaining ingredients except for the bread crumbs and oil.
4. Roll mixture into 1″ balls and coat each with bread crumbs.
5. Preheat oil to 400°F and fry balls until done (1 to 2 minutes). Serve hot with mustard, if desired.

Swiss Fondue (Switzerland) (Serves 4–6)

12 oz grated Swiss cheese
2 tbsp flour
⅛ tsp white pepper
1¼ c dry sauterne
2 tsp kirsch
½ loaf French bread, cut into cubes

1. Toss the cheese and dry ingredients together.
2. Heat sauterne in a fondue pot or chafing dish.
3. Stir in cheese gradually until all has been added and melts.
4. Stir in the kirsch.
5. Diners place a bread cube on long-handled forks and dip to coat them in fondue.

Sauerbraten (Germany) (Serves 6–8)

Medium rump roast
2 c vinegar
2 c water
2 medium onions, sliced
20 whole cloves
4 bay leaves
20 peppercorns
½ green pepper, sliced
½ c gingersnap crumbs

1. Marinate the meat with the other ingredients (except gingersnaps) for two days in the refrigerator.
2. Remove meat from marinade and brown in oil in a Dutch oven.
3. Add marinade to cover pan about ½″ deep.
4. Cover pan and simmer meat until it is fork tender (2+ hours).
5. Remove meat and thicken drippings with gingersnaps.

Rotkohl mit Äpfeln (Red Cabbage with Apples—Germany) (Serves 4)

1 medium onion, chopped
1 tbsp bacon drippings
1 head red cabbage, shredded
2 tart apples, pared and cubed
¼ c vinegar
2 tbsp brown sugar

1. Saute onion in drippings.
2. Add other ingredients to skillet and cover.
3. Simmer 20 minutes, stirring occasionally and adding water as needed.

Pepernoten (Cookies—The Netherlands) (Makes 4 dozen)

1¼ c flour
1¼ c self-rising flour
½ c brown sugar
2 tbsp water
1 egg yolk
¼ tsp cinnamon
¼ tsp nutmeg
¼ tsp ground cloves
¼ tsp anise or cardamom

1. Mix all ingredients to make a dough.
2. Make dough into 1″ marbles and place 2″ apart on cookie sheet.
3. Flatten balls slightly.
4. Bake in oven preheated to 350°F for 20 minutes (until hard).

Springerle (Germany) (Makes 4–5 dozen)

4 egg whites
5 egg yolks
2 c sugar
4 c flour
1 tsp baking powder
¾ tsp anise oil

1. Beat egg whites until stiff.
2. Beat in yolks, one at a time.
3. Stir in sugar followed by flour and baking powder.
4. Stir in anise oil.
5. Roll on floured board ¼″ thick.
6. Carefully roll springerle (picture-carved) rolling pin over dough firmly enough to print the pattern clearly and deeply.
7. Cut cookies apart and place on cookie sheets 1″ apart. Store on counter uncovered for 24 hours.
8. Bake in oven preheated to 250°F for 20 to 30 minutes until firm but not browned.
9. With spatula, put cookies on a cooling rack. Store in tight jars.

Appelflappen (The Netherlands) (Serves 4–6)

1 c flour
Beer to make thick batter
2 Pippin apples
Oil for deep-fat frying
Confectioner's sugar (optional)

1. Stir enough beer into the flour to make a batter thick enough to coat apple rings.
2. Core and pare apples, then slice into rings ¼″ thick.
3. Heat oil to 375°F, dip each apple slice into batter to coat thoroughly.
4. Fry until browned on bottom, turn, and brown other side. Drain on absorbent paper towel.
5. Repeat until all slices are fried.
6. Sprinkle with confectioner's sugar.

Oliebollen (The Netherlands) (Serves 8–10)

1 loaf frozen bread dough
¼ c dried currants
¼ c raisins
¼ c golden seedless raisins
¼ c candied orange peel
2 tbsp lemon zest
Oil for deep-fat frying
Confectioner's sugar, optional

1. Thaw bread dough completely.
2. Knead fruits evenly into the bread dough.
3. Let dough almost double before punching down and squeezing off about ¼ c dough for each ball.
4. Meanwhile, preheat oil to 375°F fry the balls (a few at a time), turning as they brown.
5. Drain on absorbent paper towel.
6. Dust with confectioner's sugar.

Summary

Central Europe includes the Benelux countries of Belgium, the Netherlands, and Luxembourg, as well as Germany, Austria, and Switzerland. The northern part of this section of Europe is generally good for agriculture, but the rugged Alps toward the south present farming challenges. Particularly good crops in Central Europe include rye, barley, oats, potatoes and other root vegetables, and fruits; livestock is raised successfully in this region too.

Numerous wars have raged over this region, except for Switzerland, which was able to maintain neutrality in both world wars of the 20th century. The resulting interchange of people has blurred cultural distinctions, but each of these countries still maintains some cultural uniqueness. The Netherlands in particular has introduced overtones of culture from its world trading dating back to the 16th century and its involvement with Indonesia. Traditionally Catholic Europe was rocked by the Protestant movement led by Martin Luther in 1517. Still today, many Lutherans and Catholics practice the religions followed by their ancestors in Central Europe.

Central Europe set the stage for such prominent musical composers and artists as Bach, Beethoven, Brahms, Mozart, Rembrandt, and van Gogh. Appreciation and support for these cultural pursuits were apparent in the period of the Hapsburgs and under other political regimes over the centuries. Musical contributions range from the very dramatic music of Wagner to the lighthearted joy of Johann Strauss.

Christmas celebrations vary a bit from one country to another but usually include some version of Santa Claus and a Christmas tree. Often, the Christmas holiday extends for a month, which adds considerable brightness to a fairly long winter. Oktoberfest is a particularly uninhibited celebration centered in Munich, Germany, for two weeks, starting in late September.

Each of these countries is known for special dishes. Tiny Switzerland boasts such treats as fondue, raclette, and chocolate candies. A restaurant meal favored in the Netherlands is rijsttafel (rice table). Holiday treats in the Netherlands include oliebollen, appelflappen, and spekulaas. Hutspot, a stewed dish in which vegetables are mashed at the end and served with sliced meat is another favorite throughout the year.

Germany's menus often feature potatoes, sauerkraut, and some hearty meat dish. Beer is a favorite beverage, as are the Rhine wines produced from the grapes grown along this prime waterway of Europe. Austria adds some special dishes to the list of European favorites including strudel and Sachertorte.

Selected Sites

www.germany-info/relaunch/culture/life/recipes.html—Variety of German recipes for all parts of a meal.

http://bitsyskitchen.com/dutch.html—Recipes from Holland.

http://www.about.ch/culture/food/index.html—Information about culture and food of Switzerland.

http://www.aboutaustria.org/recipes/recipes—Information about Austrian culture, food, and recipes.

http://www.archaeolink.com/belgium_cooking_archeology_of_.html—Archeological perspective on Belgian food and recipes.

http://www.luxembourg.co.uk/recipes—Information on Luxembourg and some recipes.

Study Questions

1. Describe the key event that significantly altered religion in Central Europe in the 16th century.
2. Identify at least five musicians and artists from nations in Central Europe and briefly describe the cultural contributions each made.
3. Name at least five food crops that are particularly prominent in the food patterns found in Central Europe; explain why each type of food is part of the diet.
4. Define the following: hutspot, rösti, schnitzel, muesli, and rijsttafel.
5. Name and describe two Swiss dishes featuring cheese made in Switzerland.
6. Plan a day's meals using ingredients and recipes that are part of the cultural food heritage of a country in Central Europe.

Bibliography

Barer-Stein, T. 1999. *You Eat What You Are.* 2nd ed. Firefly Books, Ltd. Ontario, Canada.

Field, M. and F. Field. 1970. *A Quintet of Cuisines.* Time-Life Books. New York.

Flandrin J.L. and M. Montanari, eds., 1999. *Food: A Culinary History.* Columbia University Press. New York.

Halverbout, H.A.M. 1987. *The Netherlands Cookbook.* De Driehoek Publishers. Amsterdam.

Hazelton, N.S. 1969. *The Cooking of Germany.* Time-Life Books. New York.

Palmowski, J. 1997. *A Dictionary of Twentieth Century World History.* Oxford University Press. Oxford, England.

Pearcy, G.E. 1980. *The World Food Scene.* Plycon Press. Redondo Beach, CA.

Solsten, E. and D.E. McClave, eds. 1995. *Austria: A Country Study.* Office of Federal Register, National Archives and Records Administration. Lanham, MD.

Solsten, E., ed. 1996. *Germany: A Country Study.* Department of the Army. Washington, DC.

Viault, B.S. 1990. *Western Civilization since 1600.* McGraw-Hill. New York.

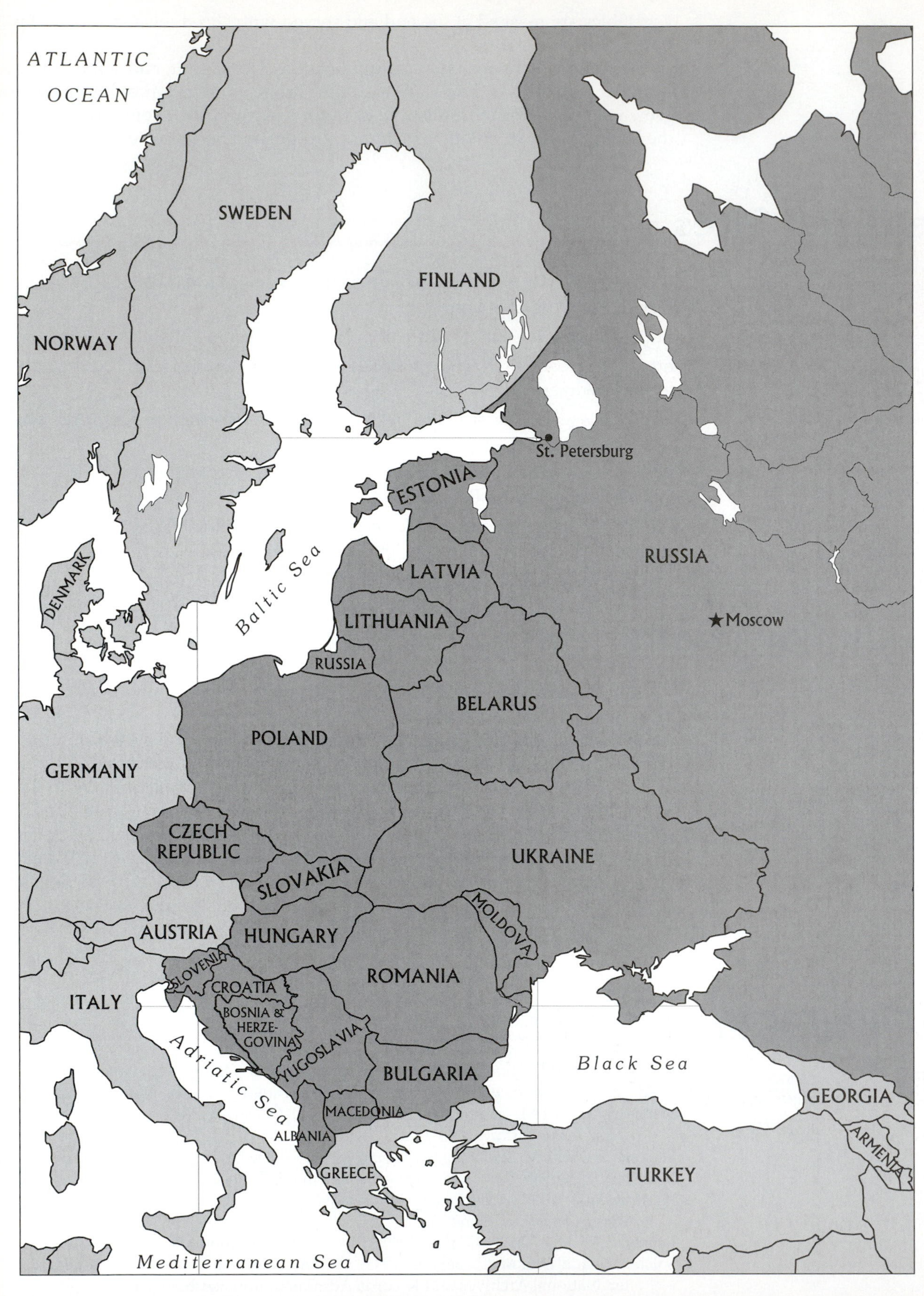

ATLANTIC
OCEAN
SWEDEN
FINLAND
NORWAY
St. Petersburg
ESTONIA
DENMARK
Baltic Sea
LATVIA
RUSSIA
Moscow
LITHUANIA
RUSSIA
BELARUS
POLAND
GERMANY
CZECH
REPUBLIC
UKRAINE
SLOVAKIA
MOLDOVA
AUSTRIA
HUNGARY
SLOVENIA
CROATIA
ROMANIA
ITALY
BOSNIA &
HERZE-
GOVINA
YUGOSLAVIA
Adriatic Sea
BULGARIA
Black Sea
GEORGIA
MACEDONIA
ALBANIA
ARMENIA
GREECE
TURKEY
Mediterranean Sea

7 Eastern Europe

Geographic Overview

Eastern Europe is surprisingly difficult to define geographically because it has no specific defining barrier, such as a river or sea, to distinguish this part of Europe from Asia. The result is some ambiguity about what countries Eastern Europe comprises. For our purposes, the region covered in this chapter ranges from countries bordering on the Baltic Sea south to the Adriatic and Black Seas, as far west as the Czech Republic, and as far east as Russia. This means that the Baltic states of Lithuania, Latvia, and Estonia in the far north, Poland, Belarus, Russia (Figure C.15, p. C5), Ukraine (Figure 7.1), Moldova, Romania, Slovakia, the Czech Republic, Hungary, and the Balkan countries of Slovenia, Croatia, Yugoslavia, Bosnia-Herzegovina, Albania, Macedonia, and Bulgaria are included in this chapter.

If you look on a globe, you will discover that the northern end of the Adriatic Sea is slightly north of the latitude of Montreal, Canada. This latitude limits agricultural production because of the dramatic shifts in daylight that occur between winter and summer in many countries in Eastern Europe. However, the Ukraine is quite a productive agricultural region despite the fact that the area is at approximately the same latitude as Duluth, Minnesota.

The actual terrain is a positive characteristic of the area. Much of the northern region has land that is flat enough to make crop farming an excellent agricultural choice. In particular, cereal and root crops can thrive in the soil and climate of Poland, Hungary, Belarus, and most of the plains regions of Eastern Europe.

The mountains that extend down the Balkan Peninsula significantly impact the agricultural opportunities. The rough terrain makes raising livestock more appropriate than growing crops in many areas of the Balkans. The countries of Slovenia, Croatia, Yugoslavia, Bosnia-Herzegovina, Macedonia, and Albania are especially rugged in terms of raising crops because of their mountains.

Figure 7.1 Yalta (the site of the historic meeting of Roosevelt, Churchill, and Stalin in 1945 near the end of World War II in the European theater) hugs the eastern shore of the Black Sea in the southern region of the Ukraine.

History and Culture

Invasions

Illyrians—Group of people settling the Balkans prior to the Romans.

Prior to 700 BCE, **Illyrians** settled on the Balkan Peninsula, and Greeks extended their influence into Albania beginning in the 7th century BCE. Rome came into conflict with the Illyrians and conquered the Balkans in 167 BCE. Under the Romans, this region flourished; one of the Roman emperors (Diocletian) was Illyrian and had his palace built in Split (what is now Croatia) on the Adriatic coast. Subsequently, the division of the Roman Empire resulted in some of the Balkans being a part of the Eastern Roman Empire (later known as the *Byzantine Empire*).

Eastern Europe experienced invasions for many centuries. The Slavic tribes had originally been located north of the Carpathian Mountains, the range that runs between Poland, the Czech Republic, Slovakia, and into Romania. Between the 6th and 9th centuries, the Slavic tribes moved into the lands of Eastern Europe, westward from Berlin, and south all the way down to Greece, mingling with the Illyrians, who were already in the Balkans. Beginning at the end of the 9th century, the **Magyars** (Hungarians now) took over the central basin region (Figure C.10, p. C4) that included land as far south as Belgrade and **Transylvania** (now Romania).

Magyars—Ancestors of today's Hungarians.

Transylvania—Region in western Romania bounded by the Carpathian Mountains.

The Turks attacked Eastern Europe from the southeasterly region, actually driving as far as Vienna and capturing much of Hungary. By 1479, Albania and the other Balkan regions had fallen to the Turks and become part of the Ottoman Empire, a situation that persisted until the early 20th century. The Hapsburgs then defeated the Turks and claimed Bohemia (now the Czech Republic), Hungary, and Croatia, slowly following the Turks as the Ottoman Empire withdrew from the Balkan countries (Figure 7.2). Austria and Hungary shared control of a large domain in this region by 1867.

Throughout the 20th century, various occupations and conflicts raked the Balkans (Figure C.14, p. C5), which led to significant immigration to various other parts of the world, including the United States and Canada. The Balkan nations (most of which were joined in the Yugoslav Federation under Tito) were behind the Iron Curtain from the end of World War II until near the end of the 20th century.

Poland has been carved up repeatedly by the nations that have waged their wars across its land. By 1795, Prussia and Russia claimed most of Poland, giving the remaining tidbit to Austria. This situation explains why the Poles supported Napoleon prior to his defeat at Waterloo in 1815. Poland once again became a nation at the end of World War II but ended up behind the Iron Curtain until almost the end of the 20th century (Figure 7.3).

Figure 7.2 The Danube River served as the route of attack and retreat for the Turks in their attempt to conquer the region between the Black Sea and the Hapsburg Empire seated in Vienna. The small church is Eastern Orthodox.

Tatars—Mongol invaders who originally gathered military might under Genghis Khan and who conquered Russia under his grandson's leadership.

The Eastern Slavs lived in Russia from early times, successfully defending themselves from the Vikings and establishing agrarian lands and villages. They also ranged on forays as far away as Constantinople (today's Istanbul). Unfortunately for the Russian Slavs, Genghis Khan, the extremely powerful and ruthless leader of the Mongols (also called **Tatars**), began to attack. Russia was able to hold out against the Tatars until near the end of the 1250s, but Genghis Khan's grandson eventually defeated them. Russia finally freed itself from the Tatars early in the 16th century, and the reigns of the Ivans began.

The next dynasty, the Romanovs, began in 1613 and continued until the Russian Revolution in 1917. Peter the Great made considerable progress toward developing Russia. Subsequently, Catherine the Great (Catherine II) exerted her strong influence in shaping the nation toward a more European focus (Figure C.15, p. C5) and extended the boundaries of Russia significantly during her reign (1762 to 1796). Later efforts by Nicholas I to gain more territory resulted in the Crimean War (1853 to 1856). Russia and Turkey were the original opponents, but French and English troops later assisted Turkey to victory.

The oppressive conditions under which peasants had lived for centuries in Russia and the stress of World War I set the stage for Tsar Nicholas II's overthrow and subsequent murder during the Russian Revolution. The remainder of the 20th century was characterized as a period of considerable Russian communist power and tentative steps toward change.

Figure 7.3 The central square in Warsaw, Poland, has been restored following its destruction by the Nazis in World War II and once again is a popular gathering place in the summer.

Cultural Components

Cyrillic alphabet—Alphabet developed by Cyril and Methodius, Byzantine monks who lived in the 9th century; used in Russia and many Slavic regions.

Roma—Nomadic group originating from India but particularly numerous in Romania that has spread into most parts of Europe.

The Slavic languages are based on the **Cyrillic alphabet** that was developed by two monks, Cyril and Methodius, of the Byzantine church (Figure 7.4) in the 9th century. The literature from Russia and the various Balkan nations is written with this alphabet even now, which makes reading signs and travel information quite a challenge for visitors in these countries. The use of the Cyrillic alphabet in the Slavic regions stands in direct contrast to the use of the Roman alphabet by most of the northern and central parts of Eastern Europe.

One rather nomadic group that transcends national boundaries is the **Roma** (also called *Romany* and *gypsies*) who originated in India but are scattered from Romania to Russia and indeed throughout Europe. Romania probably has the largest population of gypsies, but any attempt to get an accurate count appears to be impossible because of their nomadic lifestyle and ability to mingle and disappear.

A particularly appealing contribution of the gypsies is their music, which ranges from haunting folk melodies to spirited, very exciting dances. Their fiercely independent spirit has enabled many of them to continue their wanderings all around Europe and even to other distant parts of the world despite the concerted efforts that various European countries have exerted to integrate the gypsies into the rest of their society and mores.

Very gifted musicians, artists, and writers from Eastern Europe have given the world some outstanding cultural contributions. Among the famous musicians and composers are Chopin and Rubinstein from Poland, Dvorak and Smetana from the Czech Republic, and Liszt and Bartok from Hungary. This list must also include such renowned names as Tschaikovsky, Mussorgsky, and Rimsky-Korsakoff. Tolstoy and Dostoyevsky were great Russian writers.

Bohemia, now the Czech Republic (Figure 7.5), gets the credit for originating the lively dance called the polka. The mazurka comes to us from Poland. However, dances of all types, ranging from folk dancing (Figure 7.6) to the formality of the wonderful Russian ballet, are very important parts of the cultural heritage of this entire region.

The many waves of conquest throughout Eastern Europe have resulted in a complex overlay of religions. The Byzantine influence established the Orthodox

Figure 7.4 This Byzantine cathedral in Varna, Bulgaria, is a testament to the dominance of the Eastern Orthodox faith in the Balkans.

Figure 7.5 The Charles Bridge, which dates from 1357 when King Charles IV ordered its construction in Prague, Czech Republic, is decorated with statues of various heroes.

Church in this region, but its specifics vary a bit from one country to another. The Russian Orthodox Church is regaining strength after many years of repression under the Soviet regimes that ruled following the Revolution. The preponderant religion in Bulgaria, Romania, and among the Serbs in the region formerly called the Yugoslavia Federation is the Eastern Orthodox Church (Figure 7.7).

However, Roman Catholicism predominates in Hungary, Slovakia, the Czech Republic, and Poland. In fact, Pope John Paul II, elected in 1978, was Polish. Albania has a large Muslim population, approximately 70 percent of whom are Sunni. Bosnia-Herzegovina also has a significant Muslim following. Protestantism and Judaism can be found in Eastern Europe, but the numbers of these followers are much smaller than those that either the Eastern Orthodox or Islamic religions claim.

Although religious activities were repressed in Eastern Europe during a significant portion of the latter half of the 20th century, the various faiths are rebuilding strength in this sphere. Religious holidays are the basis of some of the more important festive celebrations in the various countries of Eastern Europe.

Figure 7.6 Dancers in native costumes energetically perform folk dances of Bulgaria.

Figure 7.7 This church is the place of worship for followers of the Eastern Orthodox faith in Belgrade, the capital of Serbia and Montenegro.

Christmas is a high point of the year for many people in the Christian religions, as is Easter (Figure 7.8).

Russian Orthodox Easter celebrations used to begin with Maslenitas a week before the start of Lent, but that week has evolved in many Orthodox homes until it is a single meal that features **bliny** (small, thin Russian pancakes) served with a wide array of festive toppings. Particularly colorful and artistic features of the Easter celebration in Russia and the Ukraine are elaborately decorated hard-cooked eggs that often feature intricate geometric designs. This practice apparently preceded the coming of Christianity in the Ukraine. The epitome of this art is the Fabergé eggs made for Russian royalty each year, beginning in 1884.

Bliny—Small, thin Russian pancake.

Two food traditions of Easter in Russia are **kulich** (a special yeast-leavened Easter cake containing candied and dried fruits, nuts, and liqueur) and **paskha** (pyramid-shaped cake containing pot cheese, eggs, cream, sugar, candied fruits, and nuts). Midnight services preceding Easter Sunday are the tradition in Orthodox celebrations. Incidentally, the use of two different calendars (the older Julian calendar to calculate the Orthodox Easter and the Gregorian calendar for Catholic and other western churches to determine Easter) may place the two celebrations in different months.

Kulich—Russian traditional yeast-leavened Easter bread containing candied and dried fruits, nuts, and liqueur.

Paskha—Pyramid-shaped Russian Easter cake.

Figure 7.8 This Bulgarian kitty naively tries to hatch some brightly colored Easter eggs.

Christmas is a holiday in much of Eastern Europe, although the celebrations are somewhat simpler in nature than in other parts of Europe. However, religious holidays are only part of the scene in Eastern Europe. Most of the countries have a celebration of their founding, and many have other traditional holidays as well.

Food Patterns

Baltic Countries

The Baltic countries have a food supply very similar to that of their neighbors, which translates into similarities in food patterns. Popular dairy products include soured milk, sour cream, buttermilk, and soft cheeses. Root vegetables and cabbage (particularly in the form of sauerkraut) are standbys that are augmented in the summer by berries and other fresh fruits that can be grown in the cold climate of the Baltic region. A favorite dish in Lithuania is kugelis, which is a potato pudding.

Russia

Russian food maintains its distinctive foundation based on its climatic influence on available foods, but it also has overtones introduced from the west as a result of Peter the Great's interest in European ways. **Shchi** (vegetable soup containing cabbage) surprisingly is baked in the oven and then given a dollop of sour cream (Figure 7.9). Other popular soups include ukha, which is made of fish and vegetables, and **borsch,** featuring beets and cabbage and served frequently, always topped with sour cream.

Kasha (often buckwheat groats cooked in water until light and fluffy, but which could be another cereal grain) may have such added flavor as onions or mushrooms to make it a tasty starch in a meal. **Shashlyk** (the Russian version of Turkish shish kebabs), caviar, the elaborate dish kulebiaka (seasoned salmon loaf encased in a rich and artfully decorated pastry before baking), **pirozhki** (small, meat-filled pastries), and chicken Kiev (chicken breast with bits of butter implanted under the skin before frying) are other highlights of the foods found in Russia, Ukraine, and Belarus (Figure 7.10).

Mention also needs to be made not only of vodka, but also of the **samovar,** the ubiquitous tea-making device introduced to Russia by the Mongols centuries ago. The tea essence contained in the teapot at the top of the chimney is poured into a cup and then diluted with the boiling water drawn from a spigot near the bottom of the samovar.

Shchi—Cabbage-based soup made in Russia.

Borsch—Russian soup featuring beets and cabbage and topped with sour cream.

Kasha—Buckwheat groats (or sometimes other cereals) boiled in liquid until light and fluffy; popular in Russia and its environs.

Shashlyk—Russian version of shish kebabs.

Pirozhki—Small Russian pastry filled with meat.

Samovar—Elaborate Russian device equipped with a chimney, a teapot for the essence of the tea, and a large area where the water is boiled for dispensing from the spigot.

Figure 7.9 Cabbage is a ubiquitous vegetable in Russian and other Eastern European kitchens; it often is an ingredient in soups.

Figure 7.10 Visions of borsch, caviar, chicken Kiev, and shashlyk leap to mind when looking at an onion-domed Eastern Orthodox Church in Odessa, Ukraine.

Poland

Polish cuisine reflects the Italian influence brought by an Italian queen who married the king of Poland in the 16th century and by a son of Catherine de Medici who had a brief reign in Poland late in that century. Russia, Germany, Austria, and Hungary added cosmopolitan touches to the Polish diet too. The result is abundant use of pork and beef, sour cream, bland cheeses, potatoes, beets, sauerkraut, honey, a variety of cereal grains (especially rye), butter, lard, and tea.

A light breakfast in the morning is usually followed by a light lunch; dinner is usually heavier and served in the late afternoon. Hearty soups, such as a vegetable and barley soup called *krupnik,* are popular and well suited to the Polish climate. Polish sausages called **kielbasa** are popular not only in Poland, but also in the United States, and they find their way into many Polish dishes. Bigos is a favorite dish made of cabbage, sauerkraut, onions, pimiento, pork, beef, sausage, and mushrooms, and seasoned with bay leaves, garlic, and tomato paste. It often is served on New Year's Day along with generous amounts of vodka. Beet soups (chlodnik) and other soups, often served with pierogi, are popular menu items. **Pierogi** is a dish consisting of small pockets of dough that contain a filling such as mushroom, cheesy potato, or a sweet jam or fruit.

Kielbasa—Polish sausage made of ground beef and pork, well seasoned with garlic.

Pierogi—Polish dish consisting of small pockets of dough containing a filling (vegetable or sweet).

Czech Republic and Slovakia

Czechs and Slovaks usually have a light continental breakfast with coffee as the beverage, a potato and meat casserole lunch, and maybe a meat (perhaps sausage) and potato supper or a sandwich. In general, the fare is rather simple but hearty. The Czechs are fond of their beers for which they are noted. The Slovaks generally choose wine, and **slivovitz** (potent plum brandy) is enjoyed by all. The basic diet in both countries includes dairy products, particularly sour ones; wheat and rye breads and other baked products; potatoes and other vegetables, including kohlrabi and cabbage, and meats with plenty of gravy. Carp is traditionally served at Christmas when herring also is eaten. **Knedliky,** flat circular dumplings made with potatoes or bread, are popular accompaniments to meat dishes. These dumplings are a popular dessert when made with fruit.

Slivovitz—Plum brandy liqueur drunk by Czechs and Slovaks.

Knedliky—Flat, circular potato or bread dumplings popular in the Czech Republic and Slovakia.

Hungary

Paprika and goulash (**gulyás**) are culinary terms that immediately say Hungary, although how paprika got from the Americas to Hungary is a mystery (Figures 7.11 and C.11, p. C4). Goulash varies widely but basically is stew featuring braised meat seasoned with onion and paprika and cooked with varying amounts of liquid. The wine industry today is the result of the Roman occupation

Gulyás—Hungarian stew made with chunks of braised meat, seasoned with onion and paprika, and cooked with varying amounts of liquid.

Figure 7.11 Chicken paprika and gnocchi are the main course of lunch in this home in Holloko, Hungary.

Szent-Györgyi, a Hungarian biochemist from Szeged, had been conducting research on hexuronic acid but needed more of the compound. He needed a cheap source and thought that perhaps paprikas, which were an inexpensive staple of Hungarian cuisine, would provide the needed chemical. The rest is history. Paprikas are rich in hexuronic acid (vitamin C), and Szent-Györgyi received a Nobel prize in 1937 for his research.

Mamaliga—Romanian cornmeal mush similar to Italian polenta.

Ghiveciu—Romanian casserole consisting of browned chunks of pork or veal and vegetables combined with tomato paste, red wine, and green grapes.

Dulceata—Romanian dish of simmered fruits in very heavy syrup.

Slatko—Sweet Serbian dish made of fruit simmered with blossoms in a thick sugar syrup.

In Bulgaria, ethnographers have recorded more than 500 different shapes, sizes, and kinds of bread used to observe different customs. Custom even suggests that bran placed under the threshold of a home will prevent evil from entering.

of Hungary centuries ago, and other conquerors have left their marks on the Hungarian menu.

Among the most common ingredients in the Hungarian kitchen are pork, sour cream, cabbage, potatoes, onions, green and red peppers, tomatoes, tea, coffee, wine, and paprika. Strudels and tortes with coffee are popular at a break during the day or as dessert at dinner. Whipped cream is a favorite means of adding flavor—and calories—to the already rich, sweet, and abundant desserts.

Romania

The cuisine of Romania, like that of Hungary, has been drawn from the various conquerors who have passed through the country during the past ages. An example of this is the seemingly pervasive **mamaliga,** a very thick cornmeal mush that can be cut into slices when cooled; mamaliga is closely related to the Italian dish polenta. **Ghiveciu** is a multi-ingredient dish: chunks of veal or pork and then about eight different vegetables are browned separately; the ingredients are then combined with some stock, tomato paste, and red wine plus green grapes in a pot (güvec) and then baked. This dish is from the reign of the Turks. Turkish coffee may be the choice of many Romanians.

The ingredients frequently used in preparing Romanian meals include yogurt, sweet and sour cream, sheep's and goat's milk cheeses, cabbage and sauerkraut, eggplant, pork, veal, onions, leeks, black olives, and olive oil. **Dulceata,** a dish in which fruits are preserved in a heavy syrup, is popular, as are pastries and cakes reflective of Austria and Turkey.

The Balkans

The food in the remaining regions of the Balkan Peninsula is similar to that of neighboring countries, with considerable Turkish and Greek overtones. Dairy products generally are in clabbered forms and include local cheeses. Plums, apples, pears, peaches, and cherries are among the fruits that are grown there. The wide array of vegetables includes seasonal items like string beans, zucchini, tomatoes, eggplant, onions, and potatoes.

Breads are very popular, especially those made with wheat and rye; other cereals available include corn, oats, and rice. Honey is enjoyed with bread and as a sweetener (Figure C.12, p. C4). The usual meats are lamb and pork. Garlic, paprika, and caraway seeds are used generously in recipes. **Slatko,** a sweet fruit dish made by simmering selected fruits and sometimes blossoms in a thick syrup, is often an accompaniment to thick and very sweet Turkish coffee; both are popular with the Serbs.

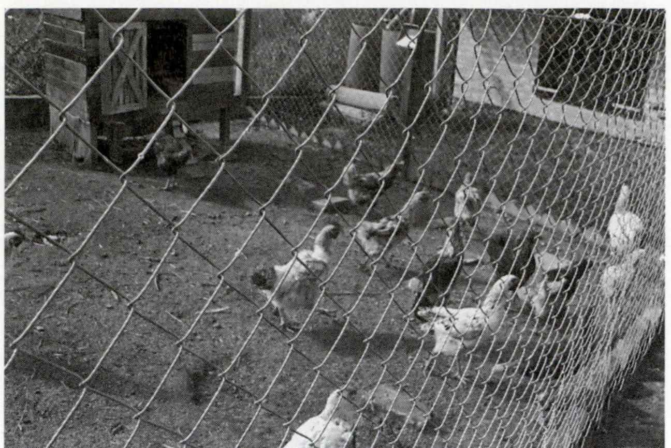

Figure 7.12 In the villages in northern Croatia, vegetable gardens and chicken coops reflect the close connection people feel to their land.

Figure 7.13 Lunch is just about ready to be served in this contemporary home in Osijek, Croatia (near the scene of some very intense fighting close to the Danube during the Croatian-Serbian war of 1991–1995).

Gnocchi—Yugoslavian small dumplings of wheat or cornmeal, or both.

Zeljanica—Yugoslavian cheese and spinach pie.

Gibanica—Yugoslavian layered cheese pie.

Slivova—Bulgarian plum brandy.

Croatians eat dishes that are similar to those originating in Austria and Hungary (Figures 7.12, 7.13, and 7.14). **Gnocchi** (small dumplings made from wheat or cornmeal, or both) reflect the proximity to northern Italy. Potika is a Slovenian coffee cake filled between the many layers with nuts. Srpska salata (Serbian salad composed of raw peppers, onions, tomatoes, oil, vinegar, and chili) is a popular salad in Yugoslavia. Main dish pies include **zeljanica** (spinach and cheese pie) and **gibanica** (layered cheese pie).

The food in Bulgaria draws heavily from its propinquity to Greece and its occupation at one time by the Turks. Musaka, sarma (stuffed grape leaves), yogurt, fetalike cheeses, and gyuvech are examples of the Greek and Turkish influences. Also prominent are some of the hearty dishes from Hungary, although meat is used less abundantly. Shopska salata is a uniquely Bulgarian salad featuring tomatoes, unpeeled cucumbers, and a goat cheese called *sirene.* Hot red peppers are a product of the region that are included in many main dishes. **Slivova** is a popular plum brandy dear to Bulgarians. Sausages and Bulgarian red wine are also favorites (Figures 7.15, 7.16, and C.13, p. C5).

Figure 7.14 Soup is followed by a main course that includes cole slaw made with home-grown cabbage and chicken, also raised by the host in Osijek, Croatia.

Figure 7.15 This cozy room with its ceramic fireplace is the perfect setting for residents of this home in Arbanassi, Bulgaria, to enjoy sipping slivova on a cold winter evening.

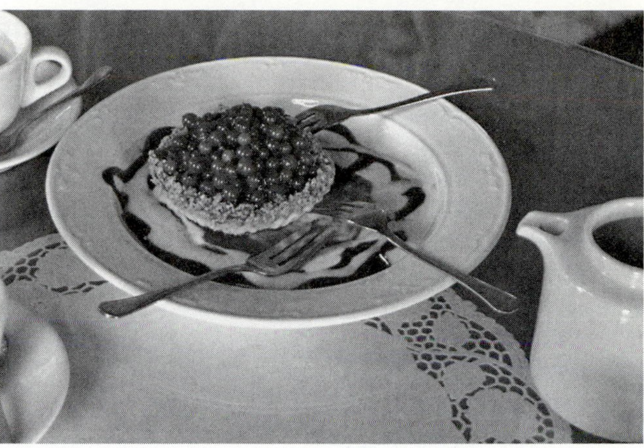

Figure 7.16 A currant tart is ready to be shared as an accompaniment to slivova or hot tea.

Recipes

Barscz (pronounced "barsht")—Polish Mushroom Soup (Serves 8)

1 c dried shitake or Polish mushrooms
2 lb kielbasa (Polish sausage)
8 c stock (kielbasa water with fat skimmed off)
2 beef bouillon cubes
½ tsp salt
½ c flour
½ c water
½ pt sour cream
Optional:
  Cooked kielbasa, sliced
  Baked smoked ham, cubed
  Hard-cooked egg, chopped
  Rye bread, torn into bits
  Horseradish, white or with beets

Day 1 preparations:

1. Rinse dry mushrooms lightly, cover with water, and soak overnight in the refrigerator.
2. In a large pot, simmer kielbasa covered with water for 45 minutes. Remove sausage before refrigerating it and the broth overnight.

Day 2 preparations:

1. Skim fat off the kielbasa broth; slice the kielbasa and refrigerate until near serving time.
2. Heat kielbasa broth and add soaked mushrooms after they have been carefully removed from the mushroom liquid.
3. Strain the mushroom liquid through doubled cheesecloth a few times (being careful to avoid any sand in the bottom), add salt, and add to the broth.
4. Simmer about an hour and a half in a large stockpot.
5. Blend flour and water until smooth before whisking the mixture into the broth; stir while heating the broth for about 10 minutes to thicken.
6. Stir sour cream into the soup and heat quickly until very hot but without curdling the cream.
7. Place desired optional ingredients in a soup tureen or bowls before adding the soup.

Kapusta (Polish Sauerkraut Soup) (Serves 8)

1½ lb pork spareribs, slab cut to fit into pot, but not in single ribs
1 large onion, sliced
1 large can of sauerkraut, rinsed (well for semisour, very well for mild)
Water to fill a large (6 qt) pot about ⅔ full
2 tbsp flour
½ c water
Salt and pepper to taste
4 boiled potatoes

1. Wash spareribs and trim off any excess fat before placing in a large pot and adding water to cover.
2. Bring to a boil, skim off any scum, cover, and reduce heat; simmer 1 hour.
3. Add sliced onions, sauerkraut, salt, and pepper to taste. Cover and continue cooking another hour.
4. Mix flour and water until smooth before stirring into the soup, and continue stirring while heating another 5 minutes.
5. To serve, put some cooked potatoes in soup plate and ladle in kapusta. Fried onions may be added over potatoes to give a slightly different flavor.

Golumpki (Polish Stuffed Cabbage) (Serves 6)

1 large head regular cabbage
1 to 1½ lb very lean ground beef
½ lb ground pork
1 c cooked white rice (salt added with its cooking)
2 eggs
1 medium to large chopped onion, sautéed to light golden color
Salt and pepper
1 tsp of salt
¼ tsp pepper
Large can (8 oz) tomato sauce or purée

1. Rinse cabbage and cut out the core. Place cabbage head in large pot of boiling or near-boiling water and allow to soften leaves just enough so they can begin to be peeled off.
2. Use wooden spoons to separate the leaves while the head is still in the water, thus continuing to soften the inner leaves while the outer leaves are being removed.
3. When leaves are cool enough to handle, slit them along the ribs so that the leaves lie flat.
4. To make the filling, thoroughly mix the meats and all remaining ingredients except tomato sauce.
5. Assemble the golumpki by placing about ½ cup filling in the center of a leaf. Fold the bottom end (the side with the rib) over the mixture first; then fold in the side flaps before folding over the remaining flap to make a bundle.
6. Line the bottom of a large pot with some of the extra cabbage leaves before placing the golumpki on them (flaps down).
7. Add tomato sauce and enough water to cover.
8. Tightly cover the pot and simmer on low heat for about 1½ to 2 hours.

Bigos (Polish New Year's Day Main Dish) (Serves 8–10)

1 onion, chopped
2 tbsp butter
1 small head cabbage, finely shredded
3 c sauerkraut
6 mushrooms, sliced
2 c kielbasa (Polish sausage), diced
2 c cooked pork or beef, diced
2 bouillon cubes in 1 c water
2 Pippin apples, pared and diced
4 pitted prunes
1 c tomato paste
1 bay leaf
¾ c red wine
1 clove garlic, crushed
Salt and pepper

1. Sauté onion in butter.
2. Place all ingredients through the bay leaf in a 3-qt casserole.
3. Cover and bake for two hours at 300°F.
4. Add remaining ingredients and bake 30 minutes more.
5. Cool, and then refrigerate for at least two days.
6. Reheat and serve.

Chlodnik (Polish Beet Soup) (Serves 6–8)

1 lb cooked or canned beets, drained
1 cucumber, diced
1 pickle, diced
½ c diced radishes
1 garlic clove, crushed
1 qt yogurt
1 beef bouillon cube dissolved in 1 c beet juice
1 c cooked veal, cubed
2 hard-cooked eggs, sliced
1 tbsp chopped onion
Salt and pepper
1 tbsp chopped parsley
2 tbsp chopped dill

1. Cut beets in slivers.
2. Combine all ingredients except dill and parsley.
3. Chill.
4. Serve garnished with dill and parsley.

Ovocné Knedliky (Czech/Slovak Flat Dumplings) (Makes 12 dumplings)

1½ tbsp butter
½ c cottage cheese
1 egg yolk
½ tsp salt
¼ c milk
1¾ c flour
3 apples, chopped
Boiling salted water
3 tbsp melted butter
3 tbsp sugar

1. Cream first five ingredients.
2. Stir in flour until dough pulls away from bowl and is not sticky.
3. Roll dough on floured board into 9″ × 12″ rectangle and cut into 3″ squares.
4. Place spoonful of apple in center of each square and wrap into a ball.
5. Drop dumplings into 6-qt saucepan of boiling water.
6. Cook for eight minutes; remove and drain thoroughly.
7. Pour a bit of melted butter and sugar over each dumpling.

Pierogi (Polish Stuffed Pockets) (Serves 8)

Potato/cheese filling:
- ½ onion, chopped
- 1 tbsp butter
- 3 potatoes
- ⅓ c milk
- 1 c grated cheddar cheese

Sauerkraut filling:
- 1 8-oz can sauerkraut
- ½ onion, chopped
- 2 tbsp butter
- Salt and pepper to taste

Dough:
- 4 c flour
- 1½ tsp salt
- 3 eggs
- about ¾ c lukewarm water

1. Make potato/cheese filling the day before. Boil potatoes in salted water. Sauté onion in butter. Mash potatoes, add milk, onion, and cheese. Beat with electric mixer until smooth. Chill overnight.
2. Make sauerkraut filling the day before, if desired. Thoroughly drain and rinse sauerkraut before parboiling 10 minutes. Drain, rinse, and squeeze out extra water. Sauté onion in butter; add sauerkraut, salt, and pepper and fry gently 10 minutes without browning. When cool enough to handle, shape into balls an inch in diameter.
3. Mix the flour and salt before making a well and adding the eggs. Stir briefly and mix in enough water to make a soft dough. Knead 5 minutes on a floured board.
4. Roll dough into a rectangle ¼ inch thick.
5. Place heaping tablespoons of filling at 4″ intervals about 2½″ from the edge of the dough.
6. Fold the edge of the dough over the filling. Use a large biscuit cutter or cup to cut half circles with the filling in the center of each pierogi.
7. Press the edge and then fold small tucks to form little pleats and seal in the filling.
8. Place in simmering water for 10 minutes. Drain.
9. Fry until a light brown color.
10. Serve with fried onions and sour cream.

Szekely Gulyás (Hungarian) (Serves 3)

½ lb pork shoulder
½ lb pork ribs
½ tbsp lard
2 onions, chopped
1 garlic clove, crushed
¼ tsp caraway seeds
½ tsp paprika
½ c water
1 tsp salt
1 qt sauerkraut
Water to cover
1 tsp flour
1 c sour cream

1. Brown meat (cut into 2″ pieces) in lard. Add onions and cook until golden.
2. Add all ingredients through the salt and simmer for 1 hour.
3. Add sauerkraut and enough water to cover. Simmer for 45 minutes.
4. Stir flour into sour cream, and then stir mixture into the other ingredients.
5. Stir slowly while heating for 5 minutes to a simmer.
6. Serve with noodles and ½ medium onion, chopped.

Borsch (Russian Beet Soup) (Serves 4–6)

1 tbsp fat
½ c diced potatoes
¼ c diced carrots
½ c finely shredded cabbage
¼ c chopped celery
1 qt beef bouillon
½ c canned tomatoes, puréed
1½ tsp lemon juice
Salt and pepper
1 c diced beets with juice
¼ c sour cream

1. Sauté onion in the fat.
2. Add all ingredients except beets and sour cream.
3. Simmer until vegetables are done.
4. Add beets and heat to serving.
5. Serve hot with a dollop of sour cream.

Bliny (Russian Pancakes) (Serves 6)

1 pkg dry yeast
½ c lukewarm water
½ c buckwheat flour
2 c flour
2 c lukewarm milk
½ tsp salt
1 tsp sugar
¼ c melted butter
1½ c sour cream
3 eggs, beaten
Caviar or thinly sliced smoked salmon

1. Dissolve yeast in lukewarm water and let stand 5 minutes.
2. Meanwhile, mix flours and 2 cups of lukewarm milk.
3. Add yeast mixture, salt, sugar, and 3 tablespoons each of melted butter and sour cream; add eggs. Beat vigorously until smooth.
4. Cover and let rise until light.
5. Preheat oven to 300°F and heat a nonstick skillet on the range until water sprinkled on it dances.
6. Pour three pancakes (about 3 tbsp each) on the skillet and fry for 2½ minutes; brush top with melted butter and fry the second side.
7. Keep baked bliny in a dish in the oven until ready to serve topped with sour cream and caviar or salmon.

Nockerl (Hungarian Dessert) (Serves 4–6)

7 tbsp sugar
2 tbsp butter
1 tbsp milk
2 tbsp flour
½ tsp lemon zest
Powdered sugar

1. Preheat oven to 450°F.
2. Beat egg whites with electric mixer while gradually adding 6 tablespoons of sugar, and continue beating until stiff.
3. Meanwhile, heat 1 tablespoon of sugar with butter and milk until this browns slightly. Pour into soufflé dish and set in oven.
4. Beat egg yolks; stir in flour and lemon zest to blend.
5. Gently but thoroughly fold yolk mixture into whites.
6. Place four large dollops of mixture vertically in baking dish to fill the dish. Lightly sprinkle with powdered sugar.
7. Bake at 450°F for 4 to 5 minutes to lightly brown peaks.

Soft Custard Sauce for Nockerl (Makes 1½ cups)

3 egg yolks, beaten
¼ c sugar
1 c scalded milk
2 tsp kirsch
Berries for garnish (optional)

1. Combine yolks, sugar, and milk, and heat in top of double boiler.
2. Stir continuously until thick enough to coat a metal spoon.
3. Cool slightly. Stir in kirsch. Pour a spoonful onto each dessert plate, and then spoon a large dollop of nockerl on top. Garnish with berries.

Mamaliga (Romanian Cornmeal Mush) (Serves 4–6)

1 qt water
1 tbsp salt
2⅔ c cornmeal
4 tbsp butter, melted

1. Bring water and salt to a boil.
2. Stir while slowly adding cornmeal and keep stirring until the mixture is smooth and beginning to thicken.
3. Cover and simmer for 10 to 12 minutes until water is absorbed.
4. Serve on a platter with melted butter, or let it cool and serve with dill, sour cream, black olives, and sliced hard-cooked eggs.

Summary

The countries of Eastern Europe include Lithuania, Latvia, Estonia, Poland, Belarus, Russia, Ukraine, Moldova, Romania, Slovakia, the Czech Republic, Hungary, Slovenia, Croatia, Yugoslavia, Bosnia-Herzegovina, Albania, Macedonia, and Bulgaria. These countries have undergone numerous invasions by soldiers and marauders from many distant regions. The Illyrians preceded the Romans in the Balkans. Part of the region was in the Byzantine Empire after the division of the Roman Empire, and part was retained with the western part of the Roman Empire. Later a large area came under the rule of the Ottoman Empire.

Slavic tribes have been actively involved in the conflicts and the settling of the eastern part of Eastern Europe. The Magyars became the main group in the region of Hungary. The Tatars took over the eastern region, particularly in Russia. The Russian Revolution in 1917 and the two world wars greatly altered this region during much of the 20th century.

The variety of religions, which include Orthodox, Muslim, Protestant, Jewish, and Roman Catholic faiths, can be cited as significant reasons for some of the unrest that still prevails, particularly in the Balkans. Use of both the Cyrillic and Roman alphabets adds to the difficulties in communication. The nomadic group that is concentrated in Romania but roams a good bit of Europe is the Roma, who came centuries ago from India.

The cultural richness of this diverse and large region of Europe can be seen in the large numbers of musicians, composers, and artists who have made their homes in Eastern Europe, particularly in the countries of Russia, Poland, Czechoslovakia, and Hungary. Great literary works and a wide range of political ideologies and philosophies have also been created there.

The food patterns in Eastern Europe are influenced by the limited growing season for farm crops, although there are many excellent farming areas where wheat, rye, and other cereals, vegetables, and a variety of fruits can be grown. Great reliance in most of the countries is placed on hearty, relatively simple foods, with cereals, potatoes, cabbage, pork, and lamb or mutton being particularly common. In the areas where the Turks ruled for a time, various dishes reflect their influence. The same is true where Romans ruled.

Selected Sites

http://www.thenagain.info/WebChron/EastEurope/EastEurope.html—Chronology of the history of Eastern Europe.

http://www.fordham.edu/halsall/mod/modsbook50.html—History of Eastern Europe since 1945.

http://www.osi.hu/exhibition/bauerd/rbm.html—Photo essay of gypsies in Eastern Europe.

http://www.bulgaria.com/art/index—General information about Bulgaria.

Study Questions

1. Where are the following countries located: (a) Estonia, (b) Croatia, (c) Bulgaria, (d) Poland, (e) Slovakia, (f) Ukraine, (g) Russia, (h) Latvia, (i) Albania, (j) Hungary, (k) Bosnia-Herzegovina, (l) Lithuania, (m) Belarus, (n) Slovenia, (o) Moldova, (p) Macedonia, and (q) Yugoslavia?
2. Where do each of the following or their descendants live in the greatest concentrations in Eastern Europe: (a) Magyars, (b) Tatars, (c) Illyrians, and (d) Romas?
3. Why are both Orthodox and Roman Catholic believers living in various parts of Eastern Europe?
4. What was the avenue for spreading Islam to Eastern Europe?
5. What alphabet is used primarily in (a) Russia and (b) the Czech Republic?
6. Generalize about the differences in the typical foods in Poland and in Bulgaria. Explain some causes of these differences.
7. Plan a day's meals using ingredients and recipes that are part of the cultural food heritage of a country in Eastern Europe.

Bibliography

Barer-Stein, T. 1999. *You Eat What You Are.* 2nd ed. Firefly Books, Ltd. Ontario, Canada.

Chamberlain, L. 1990. *Food and Cookery of Eastern Europe.* Penguin Books. New York.

Chamberlain, L. 2003. *Food of Eastern Europe.* Anness Publishing. London, England.

Chamberlain, L. 2004. *Russian, Polish, and German Cooking.* Anness Publishing. London, England.

Cook, T. 1994. *Illustrated Guide to Prague.* Passport Books. Lincolnwood, IL.

Dydynski, K., S. Fallon, K. Galbraith, P. Hellander, and R. Klaskin. 1999. *Eastern Europe.* Lonely Planet. Oakland, CA.

Farley, M.P. 1990. *Festive Ukrainian Cooking.* University of Pittsburgh Press. Pittsburgh, PA.

Field, M. and F. Field. 1970. *A Quintet of Cuisines.* Time-Life Books. New York.

Heale, J. 1994. *Cultures of the World: Poland.* Marshall Cavendish. New York.

Millstone, E. et al. 2003. *Penguin Atlas of Food: Who Eats What, Where, and Why.* Penguin Books. New York.

Palmowski, J. 1997. *Dictionary of Twentieth Century World History.* Oxford University Press. New York.

Papashvily, H. and G. Papashvily. 1969. *Russian Cooking.* Time-Life Books. New York.

Pearcy, G.E. 1980. *The World Food Scene.* Plycon Press. Redondo Beach, CA.

Pettifer, J. 1994. *Blue Guide Albania.* W.W. Norton. New York.

Sheehan, S. 1994. *Cultures of the World: Romania.* Marshall Cavendish. New York.

Torchinsky, O. 1994. *Cultures of the World: Russia.* Marshall Cavendish. New York.

Viault, B.S. 1990. *Western Civilization since 1600.* McGraw-Hill. New York.

Ward, P. 1991. *Bulgaria: A Travel Guide.* Pelican Publishing. Gretna, LA.

FRANCE
GERMANY
SLOVAKIA
AUSTRIA
HUNGARY
SWITZERLAND
SLOVENIA
CROATIA
Venice
Po River
BOSNIA
Florence
ITALY
Appenine Mountains
Adriatic Sea
CORSICA
Rome
SARDINIA
Mediterranean Sea
SICILY
TUNISIA

8 Italy

Geographic Overview

Italy extends from the southern side of the Alps in Europe all the way down the boot-shaped Italian Peninsula to its very toe in the Mediterranean Sea. It includes Sicily, the large island across the Straits of Messina, and Sardinia. The northern region begins in the southern Alps and the Dolomites, and the Po River wends its way east more than 400 miles to empty into the Adriatic Sea. The Po Valley in the northern part of Italy is the major agricultural region, but there also is a good bit of farming done throughout Italy.

Olives, the source of Italy's famed olive oil, grow in abundance on the trees climbing the sides of the Apennine Mountains that form the backbone of the entire peninsula. The eruption of Mt. Vesuvius, which destroyed Pompeii in 79 CE (Figure 8.1), and the ongoing rumbling and spewing of Mt. Etna on Sicily are evidence of the volcanic nature of southern Italy.

Most of Italy is either on the coast or very close to the sea; the Tyrrhenian Sea lies on the west, the Mediterranean and Ionian seas to the south, and the Adriatic Sea to the east. This large amount of water has a somewhat moderating effect on the climate, but the southerly location of much of Italy results in summers that can get uncomfortably hot (Figure 8.2). The winters are fairly mild except in the mountainous northern area.

The land in the Po Valley provides the space for about one-sixth of Italy's agriculture; its flat fields are well suited to growing cereal crops, notably wheat, corn, and rice. Fruits and vegetables are grown in abundance in Italy, too. Its vineyards are the source of a wide array of wines. Animals are a very limited part of the farm scene, and even fishing is not a very large industry in Italy. However, meats of various kinds, fish, and dairy products (particularly cheese) are important in the diet, even if they have to be imported.

Figure 8.1 In the distance, Mt. Vesuvius provides a constant reminder of the volcanic nature of southern Italy.

Figure 8.2 Fountains in Rome and its environs provide a welcome spray to cool passersby on hot summer days.

History and Culture

Early Societies

Etruscans—Group who settled in Tuscany and moved south, ultimately taking over Rome and contributing their alphabet, speech, and ability to wage war.

The land that presently is Italy has seen a seemingly endless parade of people from other regions since human history began. The earliest group that developed a society and left its imprint was the **Etruscans,** who probably settled in the region now known as Tuscany sometime shortly after 1000 BCE. Within 300 years, they began moving south until they encountered Greek settlements near Naples (Figures 8.3 and C.19, p. C7). A different (Latin) group founded Rome on the Tiber River in 753 BCE (according to legend), but the Etruscans seized Rome about 550 BCE and proceeded to instill their ways of speaking and writing (alphabet), as well as their skills in waging wars (Figures 8.4 and C.16, p. C6).

Empire Building

Dreams of expansion beyond the Italian Peninsula led to Rome's attempts to acquire land in North Africa and to the Punic Wars with Carthage (modern Tunisia) between 246 and 146 BCE. Roman expansion also is evidenced by the baths Romans constructed in Bath, England, and by Hadrian's Wall, which Hadrian built to keep out invaders from Scotland and the north in the 1st century CE. Rome's re-

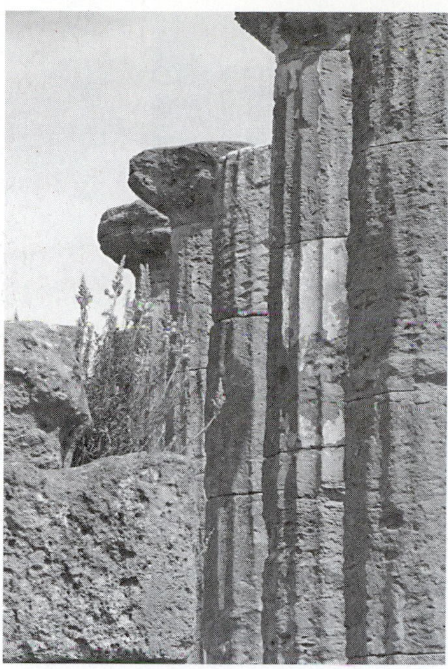

Figure 8.3 Although deeply pitted from wind and salty ocean air, columns of Greek temples outside Agrigento on the south coast of Sicily still stand, mute evidence of the once dominant presence of the Greeks.

markable engineering achievements can still be seen at the Pont du Gard, an amazing aqueduct built in 19 CE in southern France near Nimes.

At the zenith of the Roman Empire, Rome controlled vast reaches of the western world, but the power slowly eroded as the lifestyle began to focus on revelry and pleasures, which unfortunately included gladiatorial events at the expense of Christians and animals. In 330 CE, the governmental control was moved to Byzantium (renamed Constantinople), and the realm was split in two. By the late 3rd century, tribes from the north (Visigoths, Ostrogoths, Vandals, and Huns) caused chaos in the Roman Empire, but Diocletian and subsequent rulers restored order by the 4th century.

Medici—Powerful Florentine banking family; Cosimo, Lorenzo, and Caterina (who carried the excellence of Florentine cuisine to France when she married future King Henri II) are credited with influencing the artistic and culinary renaissance, particularly in the 15th and 16th centuries.

Between the 11th and 14th centuries, an extended contest between the land-owning popes and the emperors kept Rome in turmoil. This allowed the rise of such city-states as Venice. Eventually, the papacy was transferred from Rome to Avignon in France, where the popes lived from 1309 to 1377.

In the 14th century, Florence became the golden city in Italy as a result of the tremendous strength of banking interests and cultural achievements fostered by the powerful **Medici** family (Figure 8.5). The center of enlightenment moved from Florence to Rome at the beginning of the 16th century.

Figure 8.4 Ruins of the Roman Forum are only slightly removed from Rome's chaotic traffic, but they still give a sense of the political and social order of Rome in its glory days.

Figure 8.5 The Duomo (Cathedral) of Florence, Italy, was begun in the 13th century, and the campanile (bell tower) designed by Giotto was built in the 14th century.

Various European powers, including Spain, France, and Austria, held sway in parts of Italy until the mid-19th century. Finally, Italy was united and Victor Emmanuel II was crowned king. Subsequent political events added to the problems Italy has faced, probably the most difficult being the period of Mussolini's dictatorship prior to and during World War II.

Artistic Achievements

Despite the seemingly endless conflicts that have occurred during Italy's history, some remarkable cultural achievements mark the creativity that appears to be almost inherent to Italians (Figure C.18, p. C6). In art, the giants Leonardo da Vinci, Michelangelo, and Botticelli are but a few of the many gifted painters and sculptors from Italy. Well-known musicians from Italy over the centuries have included such well-known composers as Palestrina, Scarlatti, Paganini, Rossini, Verdi, and Puccini. Literary lights have included Ovid, Dante, Machiavelli, and the adventurer Marco Polo.

Architecture has been the forte of the citizens of the Italian Peninsula. Innumerable ruins are in evidence in Rome and various parts of the country. The Pantheon, Forum (Figure C.16, p. C6), Constantine's Arch, St. Peter's Basilica (Figure 8.6), and the Colosseum serve as magnets for tourists visiting Rome. Florence has the Ponte Vecchio (Figure C.20, p. C7), Giotto's bell tower, the Baptistry, and the Pitti Palace, to name just a few of the structures of architectural interest there. Of course, the city of Pisa is perhaps best known for its structural difficulties in the Leaning Tower. Venice presents another side of Italian architecture with many palaces built along its canals as well as the Palace of the Doges and St. Mark's Cathedral, which serve as centerpieces for its central piazza.

Religion

The numerous large and beautiful cathedrals, such as the remarkable ones in Milan (Figure 8.7) and at the Vatican, are impressive reminders of the power and wealth of the Catholic Church, which clearly is Italy's dominant religion. In fact, the Vatican actually is a city-state set within the city of Rome. The Vatican has

Figure 8.6 St. Peter's Basilica and the surrounding buildings are actually in a sovereign state, the Vatican, which issues its own postal stamps, although Rome surrounds it.

St. Peter's Basilica—Very large cathedral in the Vatican in Rome.

been the Pope's residence for more than 600 years. Not only is the huge **St. Peter's Basilica** located in the Vatican, but so are the famous Sistine Chapel, with its ceiling painted by Michelangelo, and the remarkable art collection of the Vatican Museum. Huge throngs gather in the square designed by Bernini in front of the Pope's apartment adjacent to St. Peter's Basilica to receive the Pope's blessing. Swiss Guards are the traditional protectors of the Pope and the Vatican. The policies and statements emanating from the Catholic pope play an important and continuing role in the everyday lives of Italian Catholics.

The ubiquity of the Catholic Church in Italy is reflected in the large number of holidays that are celebrated in honor of religious figures. Of course, Christmas and Easter are celebrated throughout Italy, as are All Saint's Day, the Feast of the Immaculate Conception, and St. Stefan's Day. Various cities also celebrate their special saints on other days. Among the important features surrounding Christmas is the display of carefully carved and painted crèches depicting the story of the Christ child's birth. Processions in many cities mark the Good Friday observances around Italy.

Figure 8.7 The Cathedral in Milan, begun in the 17th century and completed 200 years later, is clad in Carrera marble and decorated with 3,400 statues, imparting a quality of ethereal beauty blended with an enduring spirit for the ages.

Food Patterns

Part of the love of the good life for Italians seems to include romance. For example, Baci candy boxes in Perugia reportedly began to include romantic expressions when a girl working in the candy kitchen wrapped love notes to the store's owner in candies. He responded to this novel idea by ultimately marrying her and carrying on this romantic tradition of wrapping his candies with these notes.

Pesto—Flavorful thick sauce made by pulverizing fresh basil and adding such ingredients as piñon nuts, parmesan cheese, garlic, and olive oil.

Gelato—Italian ice cream.

Risotto—Rice dish from northern Italy made by sautéing Arborio or other short-grain rice before slowly adding a bit of white wine and other liquid as needed (2 tablespoons at a time) while cooking and stirring until grains are tender and the texture is creamy.

Polenta—Traditional northern Italian dish; cornmeal cooked in milk or other liquid with frequent stirring until it forms a mushy, soft paste, at which time butter and sometimes other ingredients are added.

Gnocchi—Miniature dumplings made by adding just enough flour to riced boiled potatoes to make a soft dough that is rolled and cut into pieces and then boiled.

"Love of the good life" seems to be the creed of many Italians, although the bursts of song from Venetian gondoliers and the cheers from operagoers may be just a bit more muted today than in earlier years. Still, the highlight of Italian daily life has to be the food! Food and family are firmly implanted in the hearts of Italians (Figure 8.8). In contrast to the rushed pace of eating seen so often in northern countries, a meal in Italy is meant to be treasured and savored. Worldly concerns should not interfere with the concentration on the senses that good food requires. The result of this dedication to good food is a cuisine that has captured diners around the world (Figure C.17, p. C6).

The tantalizing aromas that waft from dishes created with wonderful olive oil, garlic, tomato, balsamic vinegar, mushrooms, and perhaps a bit of **pesto** (a flavorful thick sauce) simply entice the lucky diner (Figure 8.9). Don't forget the wonderful Italian breads, often washed down with a hearty red wine. Then, if there is still a bit of room for it, a **gelato** (ice cream) may be the perfect ending to a leisurely and sensually gratifying dining experience.

Regional Cuisines

Northern Italian Meals that might be served elegantly in northern Italy in such cities as Milan and Venice traditionally feature generous servings of meat (e.g., veal, pork, game, or lamb). Rich sauces often accompany them. Meat plays a less prominent role in households with limited income.

Butter, lard, and olive oil are used generously in cooking. **Risotto,** prepared with Arborio or other specialty short-grain rice, and **polenta,** a simple dish made with cornmeal, are traditional cereal dishes that feature crops grown in the region. **Gnocchi,** small potato and flour dumplings, make up another popular form of starch. Fresh vegetables and fruits appear in a variety of dishes on the menu. Wine is an essential accompaniment to meals except breakfast.

Central Italian Meals in central Italy (from Tuscany and Umbria south to Rome) include pasta, vegetables, meat (often veal, pork, or seafood if the area is close to the ocean), bread, cheese, and wine (Figure 8.10). Olive oil is an essential in a Tuscan kitchen. Generally, the food in this region is light and seldom includes the richer sauces of the Northern Italian cuisine. Beans frequently occur in menus,

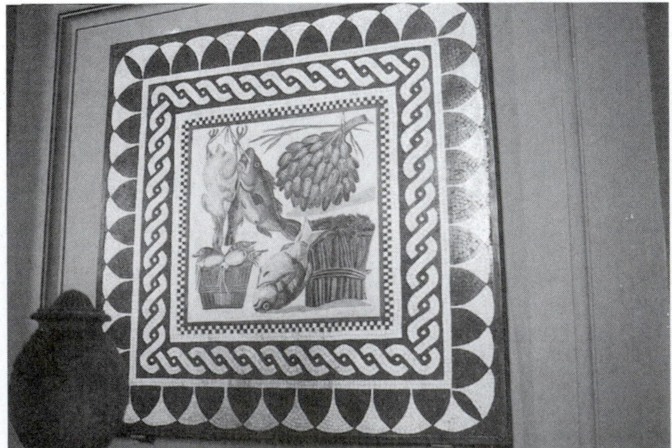

Figure 8.8 The importance that Romans attach to food is reflected in this mosaic that features beautiful food ingredients.

Figure 8.9 Outdoor vegetable and fruit markets attract Italians so they can get the freshest, most flavorful produce for creating dinner on the same day.

Chianti—Hearty red wine originating in Tuscany.

Caterina de' Medici, a member of the powerful Medici family of medieval Florence, moved to France from Florence and married Prince Henri in 1533 when she was 14. The Tuscan cooks, bakers, servants, and friends who accompanied her to France brought many tempting dishes and pastries, as well as elegant table settings and manners that were incorporated into gracious dining at the French court.

Porchetta—Whole, suckling pig flavored with fennel, peppercorns, and garlic and roasted; popular entrée in Tuscany.

Pecorino—Italian cheeses made from ewe's milk; the texture of specific types ranges from soft to very hard.

Ricotta—Soft cheese made from the whey of cow's milk that is popular in central Italy.

and favored cooking herbs include sage, rosemary, thyme, and marjoram. **Chianti,** an inexpensive red wine, once marketed in a unique basket-encased bottle, is a product of central Italy.

Porchetta, whole suckling pig stuffed with fennel, peppercorns, garlic, and rock salt for flavor and then roasted tenderly over a wood fire, is a particularly spectacular dish from this part of Italy. **Pecorino** cheeses, made in central Italy from sheep's milk, range in texture from soft to hard enough to grate; in contrast, **ricotta** is a soft cheese made from whey of cow's milk and is often used in Tuscany.

Southern Italian Southern Italy, including the islands of Sardinia and Sicily, is noted particularly for its Mediterranean diet that features olive oil, pasta, breads, some meat and cheese, vegetables (particularly tomatoes and eggplant), and wine. Pork is the usual meat; the craggy, rocky terrain of the region is more compatible with raising pigs than cows. The food in southern Italy reflects the rural scene and availability of seafood, vegetables, and cheeses. Pizza, breads, and pastas play a very significant role in the diet. The dishes reflect the waves of Greeks, Arabs, and other groups who traded with and/or conquered Sicily and southern Italy many centuries ago.

Figure 8.10 Tuscany is fabled for its fine cuisine, which utilizes artichokes and other produce grown in its sunny fields near Florence, often barely yards from the kitchen.

Specialties

The food choices available throughout Italy are truly amazing. Creative ways of using the various flavorful ingredients from the local farms have fostered this broad menu. Underlying much of the diet is wheat, the basic ingredient for the breads and pastas featured in Italian meals.

Pastas Pastas may be made at home and used fresh, or they may be purchased from local shops, which feature a dazzling array of shapes, dimensions, and even a choice of color (for example, spinach may be added to the dough to make it green). Fresh pasta is often the choice in the northern part of the country while dried pasta is used more often in the south. Ribbon-shaped pastas are used frequently in regions north of Rome, while tubular pastas may be the popular choice south of the city. The names of some of the pastas are spaghetti, ziti, **penne, capellini, fusilli** (Figure 8.11), **lasagne,** tortellini, **cannelloni, ravioli, lumache, manicotti, tagliatelle,** and macaroni. However, there really is not a strong regional preference; the choice depends on the chef and the dish being prepared.

Penne—Tubular pasta cut on the diagonal into pieces about an inch long.

Capellini—Angel hair (very thin, spaghetti-like pasta).

Fusilli—Wavy, spaghetti-like pasta.

Lasagne—Broad, ribbonlike pasta used in casserole dishes.

Cannelloni—Ridged tubes of pasta that are designed to be filled with various stuffings for entrées or desserts.

Ravioli—Rectangular pasta pouches stuffed with ground meat or cheese.

Lumache—Large, conch shell–shaped pasta suitable for stuffing.

Manicotti—Long, plain tube of pasta appropriate for stuffing.

Tortiglioni—Spiral-shaped pasta.

Cheeses Cheeses are a mainstay of Italian menus and cooking. Hundreds of small cheese-making operations lovingly produce a vast array of cheeses, ranging from soft, fresh cheesses to very hard ones requiring considerable aging. Italian cooks are careful to select just the right cheese for the dishes they are making.

Parmigiano (**parmesan**) doubtless is the best-known of Italian cheese, but others are noteworthy and used widely. **Romano,** a sharp cheese made with sheep's milk, is very hard cheese for grating. **Fontina** is popular for use in fondue, and provolone and **gorgonzola** (a blue-veined, sharp flavor) are considered table cheeses.

Pizza seems to call for **mozzarella,** while ricotta (unsalted cottage cheese) is used in preparing blintzes and in recipes as a substitute for cottage cheese. Mozzarella originally was made with water buffalo milk, but the scarcity of this milk has caused most of this type of cheese to be made using cow's milk. **Mascarpone** is an unripened cheese that can be blended readily with liqueurs or a bit of honey and served along with fresh or candied fruit.

Parmesan—Hard cheese often aged for more than two years; frequently grated over Italian dishes.

Romano—Sharp, sheep's milk cheese; very hard cheese, ideal for grating.

Fontina—Cheese well suited for making fondue; originally from Valle d'Aosta in northern Italy near Great St. Bernard Pass.

Gorgonzola—Blue-veined cheese that originated in Gorgonzola near Milan in northern Italy and is now produced in the Po Valley.

Mozzarella—Cheese used on pizzas, originally made from buffalo milk, but now often made from cow's milk.

Mascarpone—Unripened Italian dessert cheese made from fresh cream; may be flavored with honey, liqueurs, or candied fruit.

Oil and Vinegar Olive oils of excellent quality come from Tuscany, the south, the Piedmont and Emilia-Romagna near the coast, and the northern Apennine Mountains. Although cooking in the south uses olive oil extensively, butter is the more common fat in northern Italy. Nevertheless, northerners also use plenty of olive oil.

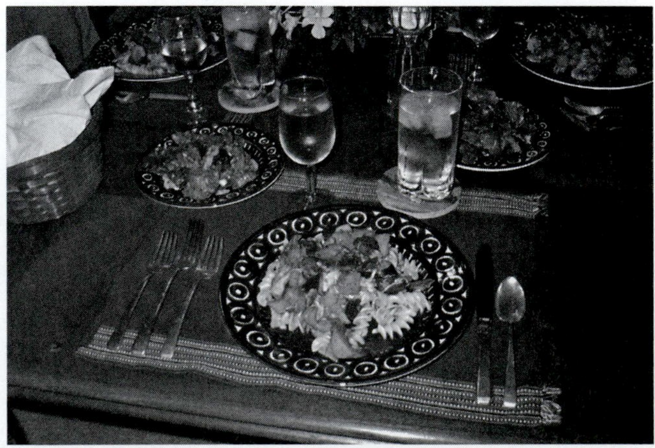

Figure 8.11 Fusilli is the pasta featured in this Italian dinner.

Extra virgin olive oil produced from the first cold pressing is the highest quality and has low acidity. Olive oil sometimes is made at the farm where the olives are grown, and its color may vary from a shady olive green to a rather golden color. These oils should be used before they are a year old.

Balsamic vinegar—Special vinegar made by aging a thick syrup boiled from sweet white grapes; acidified with the addition of some aged balsamic vinegar; the best is made in the vacinity of Modena and Reggio Emilia in northern Italy.

Northern Italy also contributes **balsamic vinegar,** a special vinegar that has been adopted by gourmets in other countries as well. This vinegar is made by boiling special sweet white grapes in a copper pot to eliminate more than half of the water and make a thick syrup. In preparation for aging, the syrup is transferred to wooden barrels and some aged balsamic vinegar is added. Aging may range from a period of only 3 years to more than 150; longer aging continues to enhance the flavor, but also raises the price. The prized balsamic vinegars are from the area of Modena and Reggio Emilia in northern Italy.

Like most foods, some balsamic vinegars are much more flavorful than others; the fact that a vinegar is made in Modena or Reggio Emilia does not guarantee the exciting flavors possible in a truly fine balsamic vinegar. If the vinegar from these areas has been aged at least 12 years, it is labeled "tradizionale." Vinegars from either area may be labeled "condimento" balsamic vinegar, a designation that connotes a shorter aging period or other variance from the standards required for the more expensive "tradizionale" balsamic vinegars. Condimento grade balsamic vinegar is well suited to use in cooking.

It is wise to read the ingredient label before buying balsamic vinegar. Some commercial balsamic vinegar has red wine vinegar, caramel coloring, or other ingredients added to achieve the dark color. Unfortunately, this impacts the flavor characteristics of these less expensive versions of balsamic vinegar.

Prosciutto—Thinly sliced, well-cured Parma ham.

Osso bucco—Braised veal shanks simmered with herbs and wine until very tender.

Parma hams and Parmigiano-Reggiano cheese have much in common. This world-famous cheese is made from cows'milk that is produced in the Po Valley in northern Italy. Whey, a by-product of cheese making, is then fed to the pigs, a diet that is believed to help contribute to the excellent flavor of Parma hams.

Meats Among the best-known meats from Italy is **prosciutto,** the thin slices obtained from Parma hams. Parma hams, which come from the northern Italian region near Bologna, are made by salting and then drying for about six months, producing a delicate flavor and a reddish color. Sausages are—not surprisingly—made in and around Bologna. Among the varieties are toscana (a rather fatty pork sausage made in Tuscany), salami, mortadello, and pepperoni. Veal is a very popular meat and is prepared in a variety of ways, including the popular veal scaloppini, veal parmagiana, and **osso buco** (braised veal shanks).

Meals

Caffe latte—Coffee with a generous amount of milk added.

Antipasto—"Before the pasta" (hors d'oeuvre); wide variety of tidbits or appetizers, often olives, bread sticks, pickled vegetables, and other simple items.

Bruschetta—Italian bread brushed with olive oil, garlic, and sometimes tomato, and then broiled.

Espresso—Very strong Italian coffee made by brewing dark-roast, finely ground coffee with steam.

The typical meal pattern in Italy begins with a continental breakfast of **caffe latte** (coffee with milk, usually the only milk drunk during the day) and a bread, perhaps with jam. This fare is sufficient for Italians until time for lunch, which usually is the largest meal.

Lunch and dinner start with **antipasto** (before pasta). Salami or other cold-cuts, peppers or other pickled vegetables, and perhaps **bruschetta** (½-inch thick slices of Italian bread topped with olive oil, a hint of garlic, and sometimes a bit of tomato, and then broiled), and olives might be found as the appetizing start. Some type of pasta or soup ordinarily follows the antipasto.

The main course is likely to feature veal (perhaps osso buco), but it may be some other meat, perhaps in a casserole dish. Braised vegetables (or vegetables cooked by another means) may serve as an accompaniment. Risotto, often flavored with special seasonings such as saffron, is a favorite dish in northern Italy; so is polenta, the cornmeal mush preparation that apparently was the antecedent of polenta of the Balkans. Finally, fruit and cheese or some sweet may close the meal.

Espresso is a favorite Italian beverage. It is made most easily using an espresso machine. A dark-roast coffee bean, ground to a fine powder, is essential to preparing espresso. This special coffee is then brewed using steam under pressure to create espresso, which is served in a small cup (despite the fact that it may

Cappuccino—Espresso topped with frothy white milk.

Pannetone—Coarse, sweet yeast bread containing raisins and candied fruit.

seem almost strong enough to not even require the cup). A fancy version of espresso is **cappuccino,** which is espresso wearing a hat of frothy hot milk.

A special Italian coffee cake called **pannetone** is an ideal accompaniment to either espresso or cappuccino. This rather coarse-textured but delectable, sweet yeast bread is punctuated with candied fruits and raisins. The festive look of a slice of pannetone clearly explains why this is a favorite especially at Christmas.

Recipes

Manicotti with Ricotta Filling (Serves 4–8)

1½ c ricotta
¼ c chopped parsley
½ tsp salt
1 egg, slightly beaten
8 manicotti shells
1 c marinara sauce
½ c shredded mozzarella cheese
¼ c grated parmesan cheese

1. Combine ricotta, parsley, salt, and egg; refrigerate.
2. Boil manicotti according to package directions.
3. Drain and cool in cold water.
4. Pour half of marinara sauce into 9″ × 9″ baking dish.
5. Stuff drained manicotti with filling and place on sauce in dish.
6. Moisten with remaining marinara sauce.
7. Scatter mozzarella on manicotti and sprinkle Parmesan cheese over top.
8. Bake in preheated 350°F oven for 25 to 30 minutes.

Marinated Mushrooms (Serves 4–8)

⅔ c olive oil
½ c water
¼ c lemon juice
1 garlic clove, crushed
5 peppercorns
½ tsp salt
16 small mushrooms

1. Simmer all ingredients except mushrooms for 15 minutes.
2. Add mushrooms; simmer another 5 minutes, turning as needed.
3. Cool and then store in refrigerator.
4. Drain before serving mushrooms.

Osso Buco (Braised Veal Shanks) (Serves 4–6)

1 c onions, chopped
¼ c sliced carrot
¼ c chopped celery
1 small garlic clove, minced
2 tbsp butter
3 to 4 lb veal shank, sawed to 2½″ lengths
½ c flour
Salt and pepper
¼ c olive oil
½ c white wine, dry
2 tbsp chopped fresh basil
1 c beef bouillon
½ tsp thyme
2 c chopped tomatoes
4 sprigs of parsley
Grated rind of 1 lemon

1. Sauté vegetables in butter in Dutch oven slowly for 10 minutes, stirring a bit.
2. Tie string around each bone, and then roll in flour, salt, and pepper to coat.
3. Brown veal in oil in skillet.
4. Put browned veal on vegetables in Dutch oven.
5. Deglaze the skillet with wine, boiling briefly, then stir in the remaining ingredients, and boil for 1 minute.
6. Pour this mixture over the veal in the Dutch oven.
7. Add more bouillon if needed to bring liquid halfway up the shanks.
8. Place covered Dutch oven in oven heated to 350°F and simmer for about 1¼ hours until tender. Check liquid and add, if necessary.

Saffron Risotto (Serves 4)

¼ c minced onion
2 tbsp butter
1 c polished rice
3½ c chicken bouillon
¼ c dry white wine
Pinch of saffron, powdered
2 tbsp butter
¼ c freshly grated parmesan cheese

1. Sauté onions in butter, without browning, for 7 minutes.
2. Add rice and stir while heating until it is opaque.
3. Add 2 tablespoons bouillon and all of the wine, and boil until most liquid has been absorbed, stirring frequently.
4. Continue adding remaining liquid 2 tablespoons at a time and the saffron, and continue cooking slowly with stirring.
5. Add more bouillon as needed to soften the rice. Cook until rice is soft.
6. Use a fork to stir in the butter and parmesan cheese. (Rice should be creamy and very hot when served.)

Pesto (Makes 1½ cups)

2 c basil leaves, packed
2 garlic cloves
⅔ c grated parmesan cheese
¼ c piñon (pine) nuts
½ c olive oil
Pepper to taste

1. Place basil, garlic, cheese, and nuts in blender and blend on medium, scraping often with spatula.
2. Slowly add olive oil with blender set on medium and process until smooth.
3. Add pepper and blend in.
4. May be stored in refrigerator for up to 4 weeks or in freezer for 6 to 9 months.

Zabaglione (Serves 4)

4 eggs, slightly beaten
½ c sugar
½ c marsala or sherry

1. Combine eggs and sugar in top of double boiler set over very hot water.
2. With a whisk, beat the eggs while very slowly adding the wine.
3. Continue beating while heating the double boiler for about 10 minutes until the mixture will mound.
4. Serve hot in sherbet glasses or small dessert bowls.

Summary

Italy is the boot-shaped peninsula that extends southward from the middle of Europe and includes the island of Sicily. It is bordered on the north by the Alps. The best agricultural land is in the valley of the Po River in northern Italy, but farming also occurs throughout the rest of Italy, despite the challenges the Apennine Mountains present along the length of the peninsula. Crops include wheat, corn, rice, olives, grapes (for wine), and fruits and vegetables; the country also raises some livestock for meat and dairy products.

Italy's location and climate have beckoned many people through the ages, the earliest actual society being the Etruscans in Tuscany. They later spread to the south and took over Rome. The Romans conquered a vast empire, and left their mark in England, much of Europe, and around the Mediterranean. Northern tribes came over the Alps to finally lay waste to parts of the Roman Empire.

By the 14th century, the Medicis in Florence and other enlightened people were fostering creative efforts in thought, music, art, and literature. Finally, the city-states that had sprung up in the peninsula were united (with the exception of the Vatican), and Italy was ruled by King Victor Emmanuel II. The 20th century was difficult because of the two world wars, particularly World War II under Mussolini.

The importance of the Catholic Church is evidenced by the many large and beautiful cathedrals throughout Italy and the many holidays celebrated to honor Christ and special saints. The Vatican operates as an independent state but is situated within Rome, and the pope's actions are a dominant part of life in Italy.

Dining and excellent food are very much a part of life in Italy, and time is taken to savor the food experience. The most elaborate meals are those served in the north around Milan and Venice. Tuscany and other parts of central Italy feature lighter but delightful food; Southern Italy is famed for its pastas, olive oil, and other foods that represent a blend of cuisines contributed by traders and conquerors over the centuries. The cuisine often includes rice dishes and some corn (polenta is a favorite), but wheat in the form of pastas, pizzas, and breads dominates the menus. Olive oil and such cheeses as parmesan, Romano, ricotta, and mozzarella are essential ingredients in many recipes. Veal and pork, often in the form of flavorful hams and sausages, are the favored meats. Tomatoes, a wide array of vegetables, fresh herbs, and fruits also are eaten frequently. Antipasto usually begins every meal except breakfast. Pasta also appears at least once a day. Caffe latte is the breakfast beverage, wine accompanies other meals, and espresso or cappuccino is served in the evening and at many other times. Gelati, pastries, and pannetone or other cakes are often eaten with espresso.

Selected Sites

http://www.sicilianculture.com/food/index.htm—Information about food in various regions of Italy.

www.made-in-italy.com/winefood/food/regions—Recipes and traditions in various regions of Italy.

www.italianfoodforever.com—Extensive information about Italian cuisine, including menus and recipes.

http://www.foodsubs.com/PastaShapes.htm—Descriptions of a wide variety of pastas.

www.sicilianculture.com/food—Descriptions of regional differences throughout Italy.

www.italianmade.com—Discussions of many aspects of food and wine in Italy.

Study Questions

1. Indicate the part(s) of Italy where each of the following is the key agricultural crop: (a) corn, (b) olives, (c) rice, (d) wheat, and (e) grapes.
2. Select a famous Italian artist, musician, or writer whose work you particularly enjoy. Search references to find where this person was born, lived, and worked, and identify some of the works for which the individual is known.

3. Describe what a typical day's menu might be if you lived in Milan.
4. Plan a dinner in Florence featuring foods typical of that area.
5. Plan a dinner in Sicily featuring foods typical of that area.
6. Name 10 specific food items for which Italy is known.

Bibliography

Cronin, V. 1972. *Horizon Concise History of Italy.* American Heritage Publishing. New York.

De Blasi, M. 1999. *Regional Foods of Southern Italy.* Penguin Group. New York.

De Blasi, M. 2003. *Regional Foods of Northern Italy: Recipes and Remembrances.* Crown Publishing. New York.

De Blasi, M. 2006. *Taste of Southern Italy: Delicious Recipes and a Taste of Culture.* Crown Publishing. New York.

De Mane, E. 2004. *Flavors of Southern Italy.* John Wiley and Sons. New York.

De'Medici, L. 1996. *Tuscany: The Beautiful Cookbook.* Harper Collins. New York.

Famularo, J.J. 2003. *Cook's Tour of Italy.* HP Books. New York.

Kramer, M. 1988. *Illustrated Guide to Foreign and Fancy Food.* Plycon Press. Redondo Beach, CA.

Kubly, H. 1961. *Italy.* Time, Inc. New York.

Mayes, F. 1996. *Under the Tuscan Sun.* Broadway Books. New York.

Negrin, M. 2002. *Rustico: Regional Italian Country Cooking.* Clarkson Ponce Publishers. New York.

Parasecoli, F. 2004. *Food Culture in Italy.* Greenwood Publishing Group. Portsmouth, NH.

Pearcy, G.E. 1980. *The World Food Scene.* Plycon Press. Redondo Beach, CA.

Pinder, D. 1998. *The New Europe: Economy, Society, and Environment.* John Wiley and Sons. New York.

Porter, D. and D. Prince. 1997. *Italy.* Macmillan. New York.

Root, W. 1968. *The Cooking of Italy.* Time-Life Books. New York.

Toor, F. 1953. *Festivals and Folkways of Italy.* Crown Publishers. New York.

UNITED KINGDOM
London
NETHERLANDS
GERMANY
BELGIUM
LUXEMBOURG
English Channel
Seine River
Marne River
CHAMPAGNE
NORMANDY
Paris
ALSACE
BRITTANY
BURGUNDY
Loire River
Dijon
SWITZERLAND
FRANCE
Lyon
ATLANTIC OCEAN
ITALY
Dordogne River
Bordeaux
Garonne River
PROVENCE
BORDEAUX
Nice
Marseille
Pyrenees
CORSICA
Mediterranean Sea
SPAIN
SARDINIA

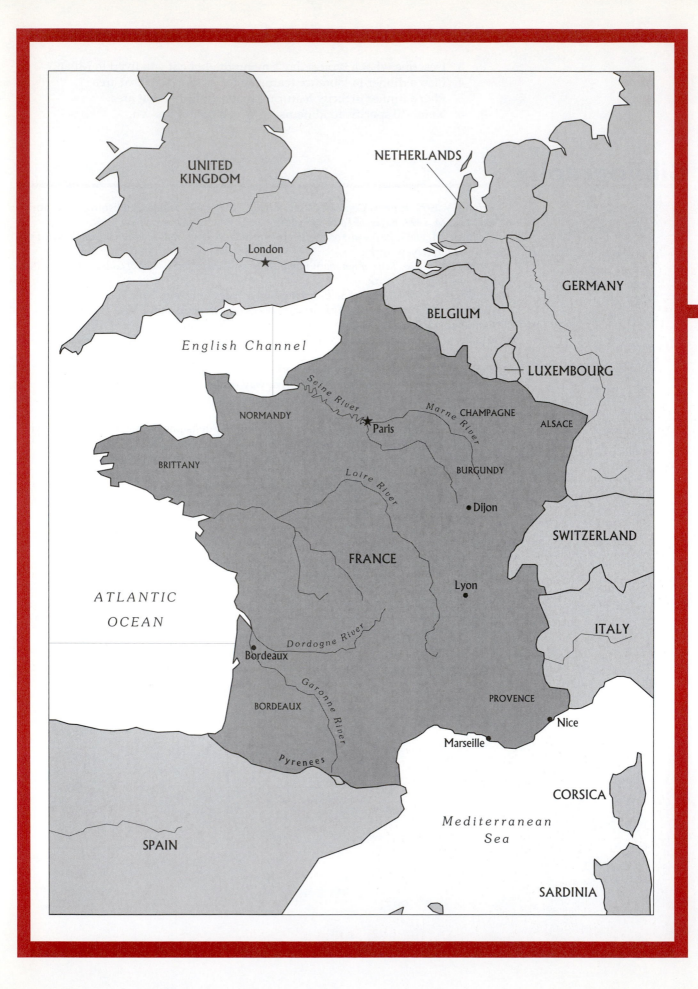

9 France

Geographic Overview

France is bordered by Spain on the south and by Italy, Switzerland, Germany, and Belgium on the east. The Atlantic Ocean lies along its west side, the English Channel forms the barrier in the north, and the Mediterranean laps the southern shores of France (Figure 9.1). Thus, France is in a key location in western Europe. The climate near the Mediterranean generally is quite mild—almost semitropical at times—certainly much less severe than it is in countries farther north. Rainfall throughout France is usually adequate for producing excellent crops.

France has parts of two mountain ranges: the Pyrenees along its border with Spain and the Alps, which loom over its borders with Switzerland and Italy.

Figure 9.1 Canals are part of the waterways providing transportation avenues in France.

Figure 9.2 Castles in the Loire Valley, such as Chenonceaux, were the grand homes to which the wealthy retreated from Paris for elegant weekends in the countryside as early as the 16th century.

However, only a small fraction of the French landscape actually is mountainous. Much of the country is a highland area known as the *Central Massif,* which is ringed by two low-lying areas: the Paris Basin and the Loire Valley (Figures 9.2 and C.24, p. C8) toward the northwest and the Rhone Valley eastward.

The Seine River, which passes through Paris on its way to the English Channel, and the Rhine River, which forms part of the border with Germany, are two other rivers that are among the geographic features of France. France also has an extensive canal system that augments trade and tourism.

Regions

Ile de France—Region within a 50-mile circle of Paris.

Ardennes—Region north of Paris to the English Channel.

Normandy—Northern region of France along the coast of the English Channel just east of Brittany.

Brittany—Peninsula jutting from the northwest corner of France.

France is surprisingly diverse in its character and in its cuisine in various parts of the country. Geographers often designate different regions as follows: The **Ile de France** is the area within a 50-mile radius of Paris. The **Ardennes** is the area north of Paris between Ile de France and the English Channel. Immediately west of Ardennes is **Normandy,** the region that includes the beaches where allies landed on D-Day in 1944 during World War II. **Brittany** is the peninsula that juts out into the Atlantic Ocean at the northwest corner of France. Just east of Brittany and south of Normandy is the Loire Valley, the region where royalty built their lovely, sumptuous estates.

Continuing down the west side of France, the Atlantic coast region is home to some of the finest vineyards and wineries that produce cognac as well as

Figure 9.3 Historic distillation equipment is on display at a cognac distillery in the Bordeaux region.

Bordeaux—Western region of France that is home to some outstanding wines including cognac.

Perigord—Area north of the Pyrenees where truffles are found.

Truffles—Dark, subterranean fruity body of a fungus; especially rare and flavorful ingredient prized in French recipes.

Languedoc-Roussillon—Region in southern France that includes the marshy delta of the Rhone River.

Carcassonne—Walled city founded by Visigoths that served as a fortress in southwest France during the Middle Ages.

Provence—Region in southern France adjacent to the French Riviera.

Burgundy—Region on the eastern side of France north of the Rhone Valley and southeast of Paris; wine is produced in the region.

Alsace-Lorraine—Eastern region of France bordering Germany.

Champagne—Region east of Paris where sparkling wine is produced.

wines. (Figure 9.3). This is the region of **Bordeaux.** The Basque Country is just south of Biarritz, a posh seaside resort on the Bay of Biscay, and the Pyrenees provide a rugged southern border. Northward and inland is **Perigord,** the home of foie gras (Figure 9.4) and **truffles.**

The region of **Languedoc-Roussillon** is a marshy locale where the Rhone River forms its delta on its way into the Mediterranean Sea in the south of France. **Carcassonne** (Figure C.23, p. C8), a famous walled city founded by Visigoths in the 5th century, served as an almost impregnable fortress until the mid-17th century for the people living in the delta area. Now the secure walls are invaded daily by throngs of tourists rather than by arrow-armed warriors.

The French Riviera is along the Mediterranean coast to the east of Marseille (Figure 9.5), and the famous region of **Provence** is just to the north. Avignon was the location of the Pope during the 14th century (Figure 9.6) when rivalry existed with the Vatican in Rome. **Burgundy** is a large region in the east of France. **Alsace-Lorraine** (just to the north and bordering Germany) and **Champagne** (lying east of Paris) are other regions of France of importance in the production of wine and other products.

Agriculture

France is one of the agricultural leaders in Europe, producing significant quantities of export commodities. The climate is very favorable for production of wheat, corn, barley, and oats. The delta of the Rhone even serves as a site for production of rice for domestic use. In addition to such root crops as potatoes and sugar beets, domestic production of vegetables and fruits contributes a wide array of high-quality produce (Figure 9.7). The range of climates from north to south enables farmers to grow almost any fruits and vegetables except those that require tropical growing conditions. One of the particularly successful crops is grapes for wine (Figure 9.8). Although the types vary from one region of France

Figure 9.4 A stuffed goose subtly reminds diners that Perigord is where paté de foie gras (paste of fatty goose liver) originated.

Figure 9.5 The French Riviera draws countless visitors to its sunny shores, some arriving in their private yachts and many wearing beach attire.

Figure 9.6 The cathedral and palace of the popes at Avignon became the seat of French Catholicism in the 14th century when a schism split the church and two popes reigned.

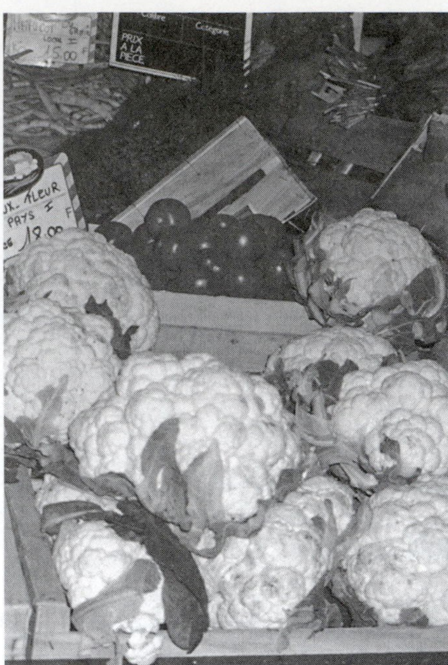

Figure 9.7 Cauliflower, tomatoes, beans, and spinach are just some of the lovely vegetables grown in France to delight chefs and diners alike.

Figure 9.8 The owner's lovely home sits amid the vineyards that provide grapes for his winery in the Burgundy region of France.

to another, many areas are recognized as the sources of some of the world's leading wines.

Livestock include pigs, poultry, cattle for meat, and dairy herds for milk, cream, and cheese. Although fishing is not a main industry, excellent fish are harvested from the surrounding waters for domestic consumption.

History and Culture

Lascaux—Area in southern France where cave paintings from prehistoric people have been found.

Evidence of early humans is found in southern France in the caves at **Lascaux** (near Perigueux). The remarkable paintings of what appear to be animals such as deer, wild boar, and bulls were apparently done by people living in the Stone Age between 15,000 and 20,000 years ago.

People continued to live in the southern part of the land that is now southern France. Eventually, the Roman armies invaded more than a century before Christ was born, and the region around the caves and northward became part of the Roman Empire. The antecedent to the city of Paris was established in 52 BCE by the Romans on an island in the Seine, and is still part of Paris today.

Along with many buildings in the region, the Romans left the Catholic Church firmly entrenched as a part of the local culture before they were defeated by the Franks and Clovis I in 511 CE. More than two centuries later, Charlemagne, who then was leader of the Franks, established his Carolingian dynasty and was even crowned Emperor of the Holy Roman Empire by the Pope in Rome in 800 CE. Although Charlemagne ruled over the areas that encompass both France and Germany today, his empire was divided after his death to define the boundaries that are basically the same today.

The next landmark event after Charlemagne's rule was the conquest of England in 1066 by William the Conqueror. This set the stage for repeated contests between England and France, including the efforts of Joan of Arc to inspire the French to drive the English out of France. Her burning at the stake in Rouen in 1431 has been the subject of numerous plays and heated discussions over the intervening centuries.

Perhaps the best known monarchs of France are those beginning with Louis XIV (the Sun King), who ruled from 1643 to 1715. He was a powerful ruler who fostered a quite luxurious court. This tradition of opulence (Figure 9.9) peaked during the reign of Louis XVI, who ruled from 1774 until the French Revolution of 1789, when he and his wife, Marie Antoinette, were imprisoned and, ultimately, submitted to the guillotine.

The bloodshed that followed the revolution finally led to the emergence of Napoleon Bonaparte, who became the First Consul and Master of France in Paris in 1799. He led subsequent military attacks that were successful in northern Italy but led to his downfall when he had to retreat from Moscow in 1812 and then was defeated at Waterloo in 1815. The Franco-Prussian War later in the 19th century and both world wars in the 20th century were fought on French soil, which has taken a toll on both the population and economy. However, France today is a vigorous and productive European nation.

Religion

As might be surmised from the many beautiful cathedrals in France and from such special places as the grotto at Lourdes, where the young Bernadette reportedly had 18 visions of the Virgin Mary. France is predominantly a Catholic country (Figure C.22, p. C8). The holidays also reflect the importance of Catholicism,

Figure 9.9 Versailles and its elaborate formal gardens remain today as evidence of the opulent lifestyle of the French royals that led to the French Revolution.

although Protestants share some of these days, such as Christmas and Easter. Ascension Day, Whit Monday, Feast of the Assumption, and All Saints Day are other religious holidays.

Not surprising, events related to wars also are holidays. These include Bastille Day on July 14, which celebrates the fall of the Bastille (jail) in 1789 at the beginning of the French Revolution, Victory in Europe Day (May 8 celebration marking liberation in World War II), and Armistice Day (November 11, the end of World War I).

The world is richer for the creativity of numerous French writers, musicians, architects, and artists. Voltaire, Balzac, Colette, and Victor Hugo are among the more prominent French writers. Composers from France include Saint Saëns, Debussy, Franck, Chausson, Fauré, Gounod, and Poulenc.

The Arts

Paris has been like a magnet for creative people from many countries, not just the French. For example, George Gershwin immortalized Paris with his *American in Paris* score, and Ernest Hemingway and other notable writers such as James Joyce gathered there to share the excitement of that unique city and its residents.

Creativity is also reflected in the architecture in France. The **Gothic** cathedrals featured pointed arches and stained glass windows; their walls were reinforced with exterior **flying buttresses,** as can be seen in Notre Dame in Paris. Numerous examples of Gothic cathedrals are found throughout France.

Gothic—Style of cathedral featuring pointed arches and high, thin walls containing stained glass and strengthened by flying buttresses on the exterior.

Flying buttress—External architectural feature to support the relatively thin windowed walls of Gothic cathedrals.

The lovely castles and homes of royalty are found in several locations; the Loire Valley has such special ones as Chenonceau, which gained a unique feature when Caterina de' Medici extended the palace by having a two-story gallery added across the river flowing beside the rest of the palace (Figure C.24, p. C8). The palace at Versailles outside Paris is particularly well known for its Hall of Mirrors; the treaty ending World War I was signed there.

In a totally different style, the Eiffel Tower was constructed in 1889 as a highlight for the Universal Exhibition; it still affords a commanding view of Paris. A less visible but nevertheless contemporary addition to Paris is the 71-foot high pyramid designed in 1989 by I.M. Pei to serve as the new entrance to France's most famous museum, the Louvre. A nearby museum, the Musée d' Orsay, is a converted train station now housing a fabulous collection of paintings by the Impressionists.

France contributed to the art world the Impressionist movement, which has continued to be extremely popular among art lovers around the world. Pissarro was among the first of the French Impressionists. This group eventually included Cézanne, Gaugin, Manet, Degas, Monet, Renoir, and others, such as van Gogh (Figure 9.10), who came to France from other countries to paint with the French Impressionists.

Figure 9.10 Van Gogh sometimes painted sunflowers, but they also are a food crop whose seeds are eaten as snacks or pressed for their oil.

Another dimension to the contributions the French have made to the world is in the realm of haute couture (high fashion). Paris has been the focal point of elegant fashions and sometimes "far-out" designs for many years, although Milan and other cities have challenged this dominance at times.

Food Patterns

Even in the Middle Ages, a great French cook enjoyed such special privileges as carrying the first dish to the banquet table and occupying the coziest seat in the kitchen by the chimney corner. The cook also had the right to carry a big wooden spoon as a symbol of importance and could use that for tasting and to wave when scolding assistants.

Brillat-Savarin—Author of *The Physiology of Taste.*

Escoffier—Chef considered to be the definitive writer about French cuisine (1846–1935).

Béchamel sauce—Basic white sauce made with cream or milk and thickened with flour.

Hollandaise sauce—Sauce made of an emulsion of butter, egg yolks, lemon juice, and seasonings.

Béarnaise sauce—Sauce similar to hollandaise but with vinegar, shallots, and seasoning used instead of lemon juice.

Velouté—Basic flour-thickened sauce made with fish or chicken stock.

Soufflé—Baked foam of egg whites combined with a yolk and chocolate (or cheese or other flavoring) sauce.

Crêpe—Thin French pancake served with a variety of fillings and sauces.

Haute Cuisine

The concept of French haute cuisine surprisingly stems from the Italian Renaissance figure Caterina de' Medici, who brought her Florentine chefs with her when she moved to France as a bride to the future King Henry II in 1553. The elegance and appreciation of fine food grew amid the splendor of King Louis XIV. A cookbook written by Françoise Pierre de la Varenne, a famous chef of that period, added further refinement to French cooking despite the emphasis on gluttony in the royal court.

Another famous French food writer is **Brillat-Savarin** (1755–1826), who wrote the classic *The Physiology of Taste.* **Escoffier,** perhaps the most famous French chef who was also a writer, wrote definitive books chronicling haute cuisine during his lifetime (1846–1935). It remained for Julia Child, in collaboration with Louisette Bertholle and Simone Beck, to bring widespread interest in French food to America in 1961 via their book *Mastering the Art of French Cooking.*

Sauces play a significant role in French cuisine. **Béchamel** (basic white sauce made with butter, milk, seasonings, and flour), **hollandaise** (emulsion of egg yolks, lemon juice, seasonings, and melted butter), **béarnaise** (similar to hollandaise except that vinegar, shallots, and seasonings are reduced and then used in place of the lemon juice), and **velouté** (similar to béchamel except that a veal or chicken stock is used instead of milk or cream) are some of the basic French sauces.

Classic French cooking is time consuming in its preparation and presentation but is deemed by many appreciative diners in fancy restaurants around the world to be well worth the effort. The range of menu items is complete, from elaborate hors d'oeuvres to the most delectable and eye-appealing desserts possible. Some dishes, such as quiches, utilize flaky pastry. **Soufflés** and **crêpes** are other French creations that may be found at just about any point in a menu.

Even the names of French creations heighten the drama of the food. Examples might be quenelles (dumplings made of puréed fish or other protein mixed into a cream dough and then poached), moûsse (molded creation given its stability by using gelatin in the recipe), paté (finely mashed and seasoned spread of some type of meat), flan (baked custard), and gâteaux (cakes).

Provincial French Cooking

Provincial French cooking is less elaborate but certainly as flavorful and delightful on the palate as is the haute cuisine. As the name implies, provincial French cooking originated in the various provinces; it features particularly fine ingredients from the immediate locale.

Brittany The provincial foods of Brittany emphasize dishes with seafood because of its peninsular setting (Figure 9.11). Crêpes, thin delicate pancakes often served in Brittany, may be part of an entrée or a dessert. Sometimes they are rolled with a filling, or they may be folded and simmered briefly in a sweet syrup.

Figure 9.11 Mt. St. Michelle is the site of a Benedictine monastery built on land that is transformed to an island by tides that contribute to its isolation on the coast of Brittany.

Brioche—Rich, uniquely shaped bread that highlights the special butter of Normandy.

Camembert—Ripened dessert cheese originating from Camembert in Normandy.

Calvados—Apple brandy from Normandy.

Tarte tatin—Apple tart made in Normandy by arranging apples neatly in a tart pan and covering with a pastry; tart is inverted after baking.

Coquilles St. Jacques—Dish made in Normandy by poaching scallops before serving in a flavored white wine sauce.

Quiche Lorraine—Tart featuring a bacon and custard filling originally made in Lorraine region of France.

Choucroute garnie—Casserole of sauerkraut, sausage, and pork that is popular in Alsace.

Coq au Riesling—Chicken cooked in Riesling, a white wine.

Normandy Dishes from Normandy frequently feature milk, cream, and apples, all of which are abundant there. **Brioche** (a yeast bread rich in butter and eggs) is a specialty of the area that is baked in a fluted, tapering pan to give its unique shape, complete with a top knot. **Camembert** from the town of that name in Normandy is a ripened cheese that may be served at the end of a meal. **Calvados** (apple brandy) and **tarte tatin** (a distinctive inverted apple tart) are two popular products using apples. **Coquilles St. Jacques,** scallops in a tasty wine sauce flavored with mushrooms, is a dish from Normandy that brings a hint of the sea to the table.

Alsace-Lorraine **Quiche Lorraine** a tart with an open face revealing its flavorful custard and bacon filling, is named for its origin in Alsace-Lorraine. **Choucroute garnie** is a casserole of sauerkraut, pork, and sausage that reflects the heritage from neighboring Germany. Wines are used in making such dishes as **coq au Riesling,** which features chicken cooked with a white wine.

Figure 9.12 Dijon is the home of Grey-Poupon and other fine mustards.

Boeuf bourguignon—French beef stew with vegetables and red wine.

Escargot—Snails usually served with butter or other sauce in Burgundy.

Coq au vin—Chicken simmered in red wine.

Ratatouille—Highly flavorful medley of vegetables and herbs from Provence.

Cassoulet—Meat and bean casserole from Toulouse in Languedoc-Roussillon (southwestern France).

Bordelaise—Dark sauce made with meat juices, bone marrow, tarragon, shallots, and red wine of Bordeaux.

Bouillabaisse—Soup made with many types of seafood; created originally in Marseilles.

Le petit déjeuner—French breakfast (typically a croissant and coffee).

Café au lait—Coffee with milk, the most common breakfast beverage.

Boulangerie—French bakery.

Le goûter—Afternoon snack.

L'apéritif—Cocktail hour preceding dinner in France.

Burgundy Burgundy boasts of **boeuf bourguignon,** its namesake beef dish utilizing beef stock, red wine from the region, onion, carrot, boiled with beef stew meat, all of which are braised together for up to four hours until the meat is extremely tender. Dijon, medieval capital of the Dukes of Burgundy, is noted for the mustards created there (Figure 9.12). Burgundy is noted also for **escargot** (snails) served in butter and other sauces as well as **coq au vin** (chicken in red wine).

Provence Dishes originating in Provence are especially flavorful creations, stemming in large measure from the judicious use of the flavorful herbs that flourish in this region of southern France. **Ratatouille** is a wonderful vegetable medley that comes from Provence.

Other Regional Specialties **Cassoulet,** a delectable casserole starring white beans, carrots, and onions, plus duck and herbs, was created in Toulouse in southwestern France. The Bordeaux region in western France contributed **bordelaise,** a dark sauce made with meat juices, bone marrow, tarragon, shallots, and a hearty Bordeaux red wine. The fish soup called **bouillabaisse** is another famous dish; it came from Marseilles on the Mediterranean coast of France.

Dining Patterns

Breakfast (**le petit déjeuner**) in France gets scant attention, usually being simply **café au lait** (coffee with milk) and a croissant (always available at the **boulangerie**) or bread, maybe with jam, eaten in time to get to work by 8 A.M. is popular. Lunch is important in the middle of the day, requiring at least an hour and a half to do it justice. This meal, preferably eaten at home, often is a three-course meal that starts with soup or an appetizer and continues with a main dish, followed by cheese and fruit or dessert.

The afternoon work schedule occasionally is broken for a snack (**le goûter**), but leaves a good appetite when people depart from the job either to go home or to a café for **l'apéritif,** a bit of spirits (Figure 9.13). Eventually a pleasing meal, but less elaborate than midday lunch, ends the day's dining pleaures.

Figure 9.13 Outdoor cafés are the setting for afternoon snacking in the summer.

Recipes

French Onion Soup (Serves 6)

1 lb onions, thinly sliced
2 tbsp butter
4 tsp flour
½ tsp salt
4 c beef stock
6 slices French bread (1″ thick)
Olive oil
Garlic clove, cut
½ c grated Swiss cheese

1. Slowly sauté onions in butter in a Dutch oven for about 20 minutes to a golden brown.
2. Sprinkle flour and salt over onions. Stir while cooking for 3 more minutes.
3. Add the stock and simmer (covered) for 30 minutes.
4. Meanwhile, brush bread lightly with olive oil on both sides and place on baking sheet.
5. Dry the bread in 325°F oven until lightly browned on both sides.
6. Rub toast with garlic.
7. Ladle soup into oven-proof soup bowls, top with toast, and then grated cheese.
8. Place bowls on baking sheet in 375°F oven and heat until cheese melts; then top-broil to brown the cheese a bit.

Sausage Soup (Serves 6–8)

¾ lb smoked sausage (¼″ thick slices)
3 slices bacon, diced
1 large onion, chopped
4½ c water
2 turnips, cubed
2 carrots, sliced
1 leek, sliced thinly
3 potatoes, diced
2 c shredded cabbage
½ tsp salt
¼ tsp pepper
1 tbsp parsley, chopped

1. Brown sausage, bacon, and onion in Dutch oven over medium heat.
2. Remove fat; add water and heat to boiling.
3. Add turnips, carrots, leek, and potatoes.
4. Simmer 35 minutes, and then add cabbage, salt, and pepper.
5. Simmer 5 minutes more; then serve garnished with parsley.

Quiche Lorraine (Serves 4–6)

1 c flour
¼ tsp salt
⅓ c shortening
8 tsp water
4 strips of bacon
½ c chopped onion
2 eggs, beaten
½ c dairy sour cream
¼ tsp salt
4 oz grated Swiss cheese (optional)

1. Stir flour and salt; then cut shortening with a pastry blender into rice-sized grains.
2. Use fork to toss flour mixture while sprinkling water slowly all over mixture.
3. Stir to moisten all flour; then turn onto foil and form into ball.
4. Roll pastry to fit quiche pan and fit in pan.
5. Microwave bacon for 3 minutes or until crisp.
6. Crumble bacon and combine all other ingredients.
7. Pour into pastry and bake in 375°F oven until set (about 30 minutes).

Cheese Soufflé (Serves 4)

¼ c butter
¼ c flour
¼ tsp salt
1 c milk
¼ lb cheddar cheese, grated
4 eggs, separated
½ tsp cream of tartar

1. Melt butter in 1-qt saucepan.
2. Stir in flour and salt completely, and then stir in milk until smooth.
3. Heat, stirring constantly, until mixture thickens and boils.
4. Add cheese, heating only if needed to melt cheese.
5. Meanwhile, beat yolks.
6. Stir spoonful of cheese mix into yolks; repeat three times.
7. Stir yolk mix into sauce; set aside to cool.
8. Beat whites with electric mixer until frothy, and then add cream of tartar.
9. Continue beating until peaks just bend over.
10. Pour sauce at the edge of the whites and use rubber spatula to gently but thoroughly fold the sauce into the whites until there are no streaks of yellow.
11. Pour into soufflé dish and bake in preheated oven at 325°F for 55 minutes (until knife inserted in center comes out clean). Serve immediately.

Chicken Normandy (Serves 4–6)

1 frying chicken (in pieces)
2 onions, chopped
3 tbsp butter
1 tsp parsley
¼ tsp thyme
6 tbsp cider
2 tbsp cream

1. Brown chicken in butter; add onions and brown.
2. Add seasonings and cider; cover Dutch oven and simmer until chicken is tender.
3. Remove chicken and keep warm while reducing juices to half and then add cream. Serve over chicken.

Ratatouille (Serves 4–6)

2 garlic cloves, minced
1 large onion, chopped
3 tbsp olive oil
1½ c diced eggplant
1½ c diced zucchini
1 green pepper, very coarsely chopped
1 red pepper, very coarsely chopped
4 Roma tomatoes
1 tsp salt
1 tsp pepper
1 tbsp fresh basil, minced

1. Sauté garlic and onions in oil until soft.
2. Add all other ingredients.
3. Simmer over moderate heat for 10 minutes while stirring.
4. Bake in a casserole in 350°F oven 30 minutes. Serve hot or cold.

Cherries Jubilee (Serves 4–6)

⅔ c red currant jelly
2 c canned dark sweet cherries (Bing) and juice
2 tsp cornstarch
¼ tsp each ground cloves, cinnamon, and allspice
½ tsp grated lemon rind
2 tsp grated orange rind
¼ c kirsch (cherry brandy)
⅔ qt vanilla ice cream

1. In chafing dish, melt jelly.
2. Drain cherry juice; blend with cornstarch until smooth.
3. Stir juice into jelly and heat to boiling while stirring vigorously.
4. Add spices, rinds, and cherries, and heat until cherries are hot.
5. Warm kirsch in very small pan; then pour onto hot cherry sauce. Immediately ignite with a long match without stirring.
6. Very carefully spoon onto each dish of vanilla ice cream.

Crêpes Suzette (Serves 6–8)

1¼ c flour
3 tbsp sugar
1¾ c milk
4 eggs
¼ c Grand Marnier (or Cointreau)
2 tbsp melted butter (cooled)
¼ lb butter
½ tsp grated lemon rind
2 tsp grated orange rind
½ c orange juice, strained
3 tbsp sugar
¼ c Grand Marnier (or Cointreau)
2 tbsp dark rum

1. In a blender, blend flour, sugar, milk, eggs, liqueur, and 2 tablespoons melted butter for about 40 seconds, stopping and scraping sides; blend until smooth.
2. Heat 5″ skillet (nonstick coating) until water drop skips and evaporates immediately.
3. Pour 2 tablespoons batter into pan and immediately tip it to coat bottom. Pour any excess batter back with remainder of batter.
4. Heat skillet until edges of crêpe brown a bit; flip and cook for 1 more minute.
5. Stack baked crêpes on plate.
6. Repeat steps 2 to 4 with rest of batter. (Freeze extras.)
7. Melt the butter in chafing dish, and then add rinds, juice, and sugar.
8. Heat to reduce to ½ cup sauce.
9. Using a serving spoon in one hand and a fork in the other, transfer a crêpe to the chafing dish and moisten both sides of it, fold it into quarters, and place it at edge of chafing dish. Repeat with all crêpes to be served.
10. Pour liqueur and rum into center of chafing dish. Ignite with a match if it has not flamed.
11. As soon as flame ceases, spoon sauce over crêpes and serve.

Summary

The geography of most regions in France is well suited to raising a wide variety of crops. Cereals, particularly wheat, thrive in the relatively level terrain of the country. Produce is grown close enough to the cities to provide an abundance of fruits and vegetables in season. Grapes for producing wines are grown in several regions, with the varieties varying according to the specific growing conditions of each locale. Livestock for meat and dairy products are important aspects of France's agriculture. Some fishing is done to add to the food supply.

The numerous unique regions in France include Ile de France (surrounding Paris for 50 miles), Ardennes, Normandy, Brittany, the Loire Valley, Bordeaux, the Basque Country, Perigord, Languedoc-Roussillon, French Riviera, Provence, Burgundy, Alsace-Lorraine, and Champagne.

France was part of the Roman Empire for more than 500 years. Romans left behind buildings and a strong Catholic Church when they were defeated by the Franks and Clovis; eventually, Charlemagne not only ruled France, but also was crowned Emperor of the Holy Roman Empire in 800 CE by the Pope in Rome.

William the Conqueror invaded England in 1066. Tempestuous relations between England and France persisted for a very long time. The splendor of court life during the reign of Louis XIV and continuing to Louis XVI was shattered with the storming of the Bastille and the French Revolution in 1789. Ten years later Napoleon became Consul and Master of France and began his military attacks that resulted in a retreat from Moscow in 1812 and defeat at Waterloo in 1815. Subsequently, France survived the Franco-Prussian War and World Wars I and II.

France has provided a setting that inspired considerable creative accomplishments in all of the arts: literature, music, painting, and sculpture. Architectural contributions include the Gothic cathedrals and their flying buttresses, as well as lovely castles and palaces. In addition to tours of these buildings, excellent museums make it possible to view many artworks.

Food has been a passion in France, particularly among royalty and the well-to-do. This has led to the development of haute cuisine, which emphasizes complex preparations and very carefully crafted presentations to please the eye as well as the palate. Provincial French cooking is less elaborate, but still exciting for diners. Sauces, soufflés, crêpes, mousse, paté, flan, and gâteaux are just some of the types of dishes created by the French. A wide vocabulary of culinary terms has been developed by the French and adopted by many serious cooks and professional chefs throughout the world.

Selected Sites

http://www.beyond/fr/food/eng_french_diet_.html—Dictionary of terms and recipes for French cuisine.

www.oxfam.org.uk/coolplanet/ontheline/explore/journey/france/foodday—Recipes and information about French food.

www.frenchwinesfood.com—Detailed descriptions of French wines from the vineyards to the table.

http://www.cuisinenet.com/glossary/france.html—Interesting comments about various aspects of French cookery.

www.understandfrance.org/France/Recipes—Practical comments about French food and recipes.

http://www.moutarde-de-meaux.com/en/moutarde-dijon.php—Background information on mustards.

Study Questions

1. Identify the region where each of the following is produced: (a) champagne, (b) Bordeaux, (c) burgundy, and (d) truffles.
2. What contribution(s) did each of the following people make: (a) Escoffier, (b) Monet, (c) Debussy, (d) Brillat-Savarin, (e) Renoir, (f) Victor Hugo, and (g) Gounod?
3. Why are flying buttresses necessary for large Gothic cathedrals?
4. How is a soufflé prepared?
5. Name five sauces used in French cooking and describe each one.
6. Write a dinner menu using foods that are available in Provence.

Bibliography

Child, J., L. Berthotte, and S. Beck. 1961. *Mastering the Art of French Cooking.* Alfred A. Knopf. New York.

Claiborne, C. et al. 1970. *Classic French Cooking.* Time-Life Books. New York.

David, E. 1999. *French Provincial Cooking.* Penguin Group. New York.

Evans, E.S. 1966. *France: An Introductory Geography.* Frederick A. Praeger. New York.

Fisher, M.F.K.1991. *Long Ago in France. Years in Dijon.* Prentice Hall. Upper Saddle River, NJ.

Kramer, M. 1988. *Illustrated Guide to Foreign and Fancy Food.* Plycon Press. Redondo Beach, CA.

LaCroix, P. 1963. *France in the Middle Ages.* Frederick Ungar Publishing Co. New York.

Mayle, P. 1989. *A Year in Provence.* Vintage Books. New York.

McKay, J.P., B.D. Hill, and J. Buckler. 1999. *History of Western Society.* Houghton Mifflin. Boston.

McWilliams, M. 2005. *Illustrated Guide to Food Preparation.* 9th ed. Prentice Hall. Upper Saddle River, NJ.

Pearcy, G.E. 1980. *World Food Scene.* Plycon Press. Redondo Beach, CA.

Porter, D. and D. Prince. 1998. *France.* Macmillan. New York.

Rothert, L.A. 2002. *Soups of France: Regional French Cooking.* Chronicle Books. San Francisco.

Schehr, L.R. and A.S. Weiss. 2001. *French Food: On the Table, on the Page, and in French Culture.* Routledge. London, England.

Viault, B.S. 1990. *Western Civilization since 1600.* McGraw-Hill. New York.

Walden, H. 1995. *Book of French Provincial Cooking.* HP Books. New York.

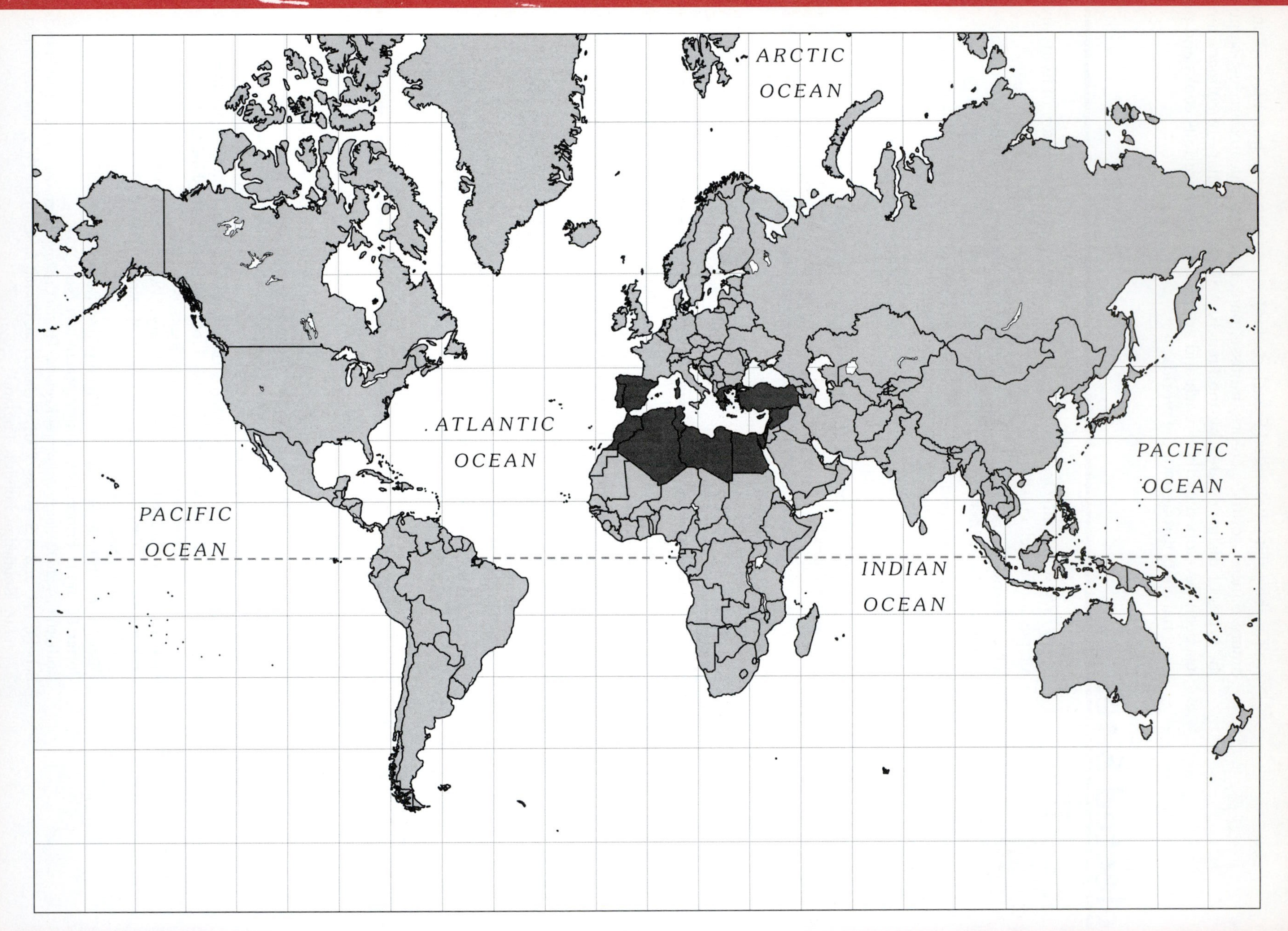
ARCTIC
OCEAN
ATLANTIC
OCEAN
PACIFIC
OCEAN
PACIFIC
OCEAN
INDIAN
OCEAN

Part III

Enriched by the Mediterranean Sphere

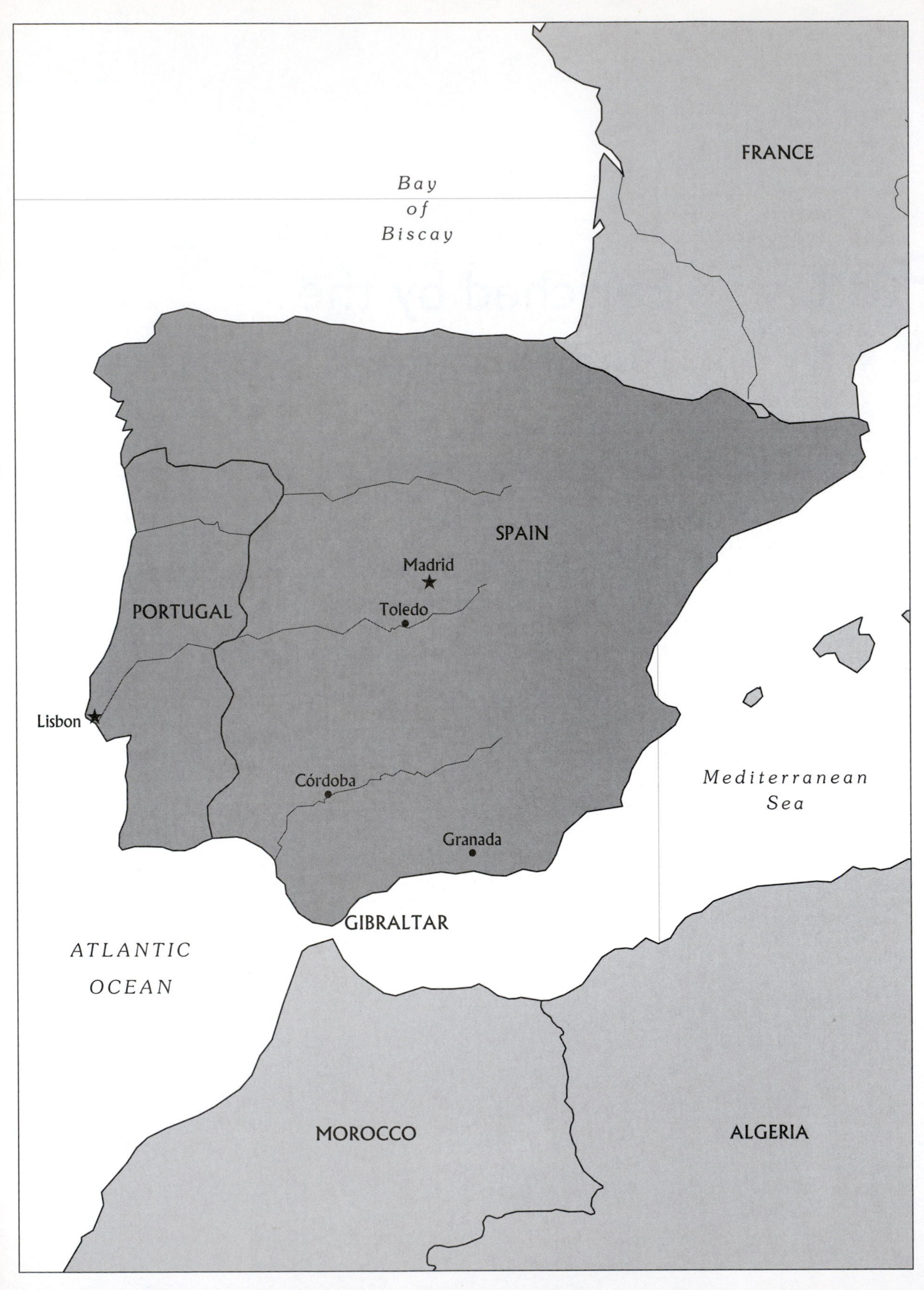
FRANCE
Bay
of
Biscay
SPAIN
Madrid
PORTUGAL
Toledo
Lisbon
Mediterranean
Sea
Córdoba
Granada
GIBRALTAR
ATLANTIC
OCEAN
MOROCCO
ALGERIA

10 The Iberian Peninsula

Geographic Overview

Features

Iberian Peninsula—Peninsula composed of Spain and Portugal forming the western part of Europe.

Although the **Iberian Peninsula** actually is a part of Europe (the southwestern corner) and has a significant amount of land bordering the Atlantic Ocean, it nevertheless shares many commonalities with the various countries surrounding the Mediterranean Sea. Another reason for including this region along with others touched by the Mediterranean is that the rugged Pyrenees Mountains (Figure 10.1) form an extremely effective geographic barrier that inhibited interactions with other European countries. This isolation promoted the development of cultures that were quite different in France and Spain, despite the shared border. In fact, the proximity of the tip of this peninsula to the continent of Africa made interactions with Africa easier than with other countries on the European continent.

Spain and Portugal are the only two countries on the Iberian Peninsula, and Spain is by far the larger (about five times). Portugal is tucked along the Atlantic Ocean shoreline from the Gulf of Cadiz northward for more than 300 miles and extends eastward about 200 miles in a rectangular shape. The south-facing shoreline of Portugal along the Gulf of Cadiz is a famous resort area known as the *Algarve.* Lisbon, the capital, is on the Atlantic about a third of the way north in the country at the mouth of the Tagus River (Figure 10.2). The Duoro is the other river emptying into the Atlantic; Oporto, at the mouth of the Duoro, is famous as the home of port wine.

Meseta—High central plain in Spain.

In the center of Spain is the **meseta,** which is a rather barren and large plateau about 2,000 feet high that is ringed by the Sierra Nevada mountains rising to more than 11,000 feet in Andalusia (southern Spain) and by the Pyrenees along the French border. "Green Spain" on the north and northwest of the peninsula

Figure 10.1 Mont Serrat (literally "serrated mountain") in the Pyrenees Mountains near Barcelona, Spain, clearly illustrates the rugged nature of this range that separates Spain and France.

has sufficient rain to keep it verdant, whereas the climate is dry and hot in summer in much of the rest of Spain. Winters can be a bit harsh on the Meseta, although snow generally is seen in Spain only in the mountains.

Agriculture

The terrain and weather hinder agricultural efforts in both Spain and Portugal. However, wheat can be grown in the northern Meseta regions, and some rice is grown where irrigation is possible. Corn, potatoes, apples, and rye are other crops.

Madeira wine—Sweet, fruity wines produced on Madeira, the Portuguese island in the North Atlantic Ocean.

In Portugal and southern Spain, wine grapes are grown, and both countries are noted for some distinctive wines (Portugal for its port and rosé and **Madeira wine,** and Spain for its sherry and many other fine wines from various parts of the country). The Mediterranean climate and the somewhat rocky soil of the southern part of Spain also are well suited to growing olives and oranges (Figure 10.3). The production of olives and olive oil is a large business.

Livestock production is limited primarily to sheep and pigs, with sheep being particularly well suited to the rugged lands tended by the Basques in the

Figure 10.2 The Monument to the Discoverers where the Tagus River flows into the North Atlantic at Lisbon is a remarkable sculpture that serves as a tribute to the adventurers who sailed caravels great distances to claim land and trade advantages for Prince Henry the Navigator and for Portugal.

Figure 10.3 Groves of olive trees cover the lower hillsides in southern Spain.

Pyrenees. Cork trees are a unique, albeit inedible, crop that generates some income in both countries despite the threat of plastic replacing cork as stoppers in wine bottles.

History and Culture

Foreign Influences

The history of Portugal and Spain, like its geography, is somewhat intertwined. Actually, the early destiny of the peninsula was shaped by the Romans, but when the Roman Empire collapsed, the peninsula gradually was invaded from different directions. Germanic tribes attacked from Europe, and the **Moors** successfully began taking over much land in 711 CE when they crossed over from North Africa (Figures 10.4 and C.25, p. C9). Christian attempts to rid the continent of the Moors and their Islamic influence began in the northern part of the Iberian Peninsula, with the result that Portugal became a nation state in 1139, according to the declaration of King Afonso Henriques.

Moors—Islamic invaders from Africa (Morocco).

Spain remained in the grip of the Moors for about 350 years, but the Christians gradually drove the Muslims from Toledo in 1085. Around this time, **El Cid** (whose actual name was Ruy Diaz de Vivar) became a Spanish hero for his military exploits despite sometimes fighting for the Moors and other times for the Catholics. He is best known for freeing Valencia from the Moors in 1094. The Catholics finally defeated the Moors at Granada in 1492 and forced them back to Africa. This defeat left the Catholic monarchs Ferdinand and Isabella in power.

El Cid—Spanish military hero who fought many battles for both the Moors and the Catholics, and freed Valencia from the Moors in 1094.

Caravels—Sturdy vessels with lateen sails (triangular sails extended on a spar and flying from a rather low mast).

Prince Henry the Navigator—Portuguese leader who sponsored voyages of exploration aboard caravels to very distant places.

Exploring and Colonizing

Portugal's numerous exploits of discovery began in the first half of the 15th century with sea voyages in **caravels** that reached the Azores and later in the century rounded the Cape of Good Hope at the southern tip of Africa. **Prince Henry the Navigator** was the first Portuguese leader to show support and interest in developing the trade possibilities along the west coast of Africa (Figure C.31, p. C11).

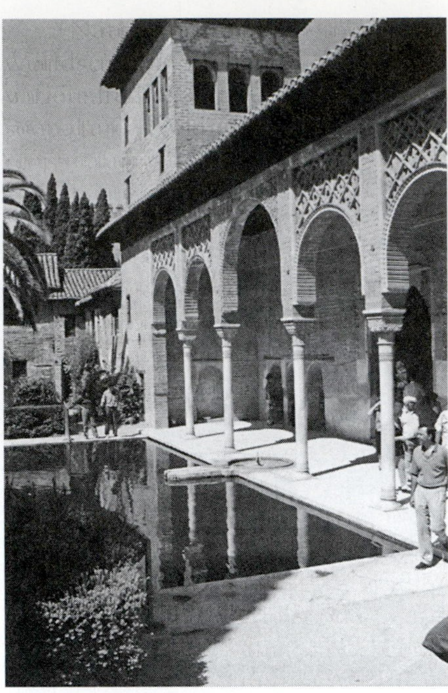

Figure 10.4 The Moors built a graceful complex (the Alhambra) with many pools and fountains in the 14th century high atop the hills above Granada, Spain.

Magellan—Portuguese navigator who led the first circumnavigation of the world from 1519 to 1522; but died in the Philippines during the trip.

Bartolomeu Diaz—Portuguese navigator who sailed around the Cape of Good Hope (southern tip of Africa) in 1488.

Vasco da Gama—Portuguese navigator who opened trade routes to India in 1498 and 1502.

Cortés—Spanish explorer in Central America, particularly Mexico, in the 16th century.

Pizarro—Spanish explorer who conquered the Incas in Peru in the 16th century and established Spanish dominance there.

Among the famous Portuguese who explored and claimed distant places for their country were **Magellan** (who led the first circumnavigation of the world from 1519 to 1522 but was killed in the Philippines), **Bartolomeu Diaz** (who sailed around the Cape of Good Hope in 1488), and **Vasco da Gama** (credited with opening trade routes to India with his voyages in 1498 and 1502).

Considerable wealth came to Portugal from colonies developed in Brazil (in 1500), Goa (next to India) (in 1510), and Macao (in 1557) for many years following the navigational exploits of the early explorers. Brazil became independent in 1822, Goa was annexed to India in 1960, and Macao reverted from trading post status to China in 1999, thus ending the imperial phase of Portugal's history.

Meanwhile in Spain, King Ferdinand and Queen Isabella, almost immediately upon ascending the throne, sponsored the voyages of Columbus. His discovery of the "New World" and subsequent voyages that he, **Cortés,** and **Pizarro** led brought great riches back to Spain, enabling it to become a powerful and wealthy nation for more than a century and a half. These voyages enriched Iberian menus because of the introduction of new foods from the newly discovered lands (see Chapter 2).

Spain had lost much of its power in Europe by the end of the 16th century. Its famed Armada of 133 ships was defeated when it tried to invade England in 1588, a financial as well as a psychological blow to Spain's image. Actually, Europe viewed Spain almost as a pawn during the 17th and 18th centuries as the Hapsburgs, the Bourbons, and later Napoleon used it to their advantage at different times.

Portugal gained its independence from Spain in 1668, and Spain gradually lost its colonies in the western hemisphere one by one over the next two centuries as they became independent nations.

The Inquisition

Inquisition—Period when Spain required non-Catholics to convert or leave the country; torture sometimes was part of the imprisonment process in Spain, Peru, and Portugal.

Upon expulsion of the Moors and the crowning of Ferdinand and Isabella, Catholicism was vigorously imposed on Spaniards. This evolved into the **Inquisition,** a sad chapter in Spain's history; Jews, Moors, and all other non-Catholics were required either to convert to Catholicism or leave the country. The penalty for failing to comply was severe torture, displacement, or both. As a result, Spain lost large numbers of bright and creative people—a tragedy for not only for its victims, but also for the nation's welfare and strength. The Inquisition extended to the Spanish-dominated regions of South America and continued on both continents well into the 18th century.

Franco—Spanish dictator for about 40 years in the 20th century.

A civil war raged within Spain from 1931 to 1939, further adding to the stresses the nation faced. During this period, **Franco** emerged as the dictator, and he continued to hold power until his death in 1975, even though a king had been named in 1969. Both Spain and Portugal were able to remain neutral in World Wars I and II, aided significantly in this position by the geography of the peninsula. This same geography, notably the Pyrenees where the Basque population lives, has enabled this group to engage in a separatist movement for an extended period to the present. Other developments have caused Spain to evolve basically into a democracy with a parliament and a king.

Language

Despite the frequent exchanges and interactions between Spain and Portugal, each nation has maintained its individual language, Portuguese in Portugal (and Brazil) and Castilian as the official language in Spain. Other major dialects are spoken in different parts of Spain, including Catálan, Galician, and Basque. A unique characteristic of Castilian is the practice of speaking with what seems to be a lisp, or *th* sound, rather than an *s* when before the letters *e* or *i*. Rumor has it that this practice was adopted when the region was ruled by a king who lisped.

What started as a Portuguese tradition to honor the country's favorite saint, St. Anthony, on Saints Day has evolved into an intense competition. Each year, ever-taller and more elaborate thrones are built and paraded through the streets to be presented to St. Anthony.

Religion

By far the dominant religion in both Portugal and Spain is Catholicism (Figure 10.5). This is not surprising in view of the early rule by Romans who were Catholic and as a continuing result of the long period of the Inquisition.

The Muslim influence spread by the conquering Moors centuries ago was expunged when the Catholic forces of Ferdinand and Isabella ultimately drove the Moors out of Spain in 1492. However, the role that the Islamic religion played during the reign of the Moors is evident from the remnants of mosques that

Figure 10.5 Elaborate Catholic cathedrals have been built in cities all across Spain, which has been a predominantly Catholic nation since the Moors were driven out in 1492.

remain in both Spain and Portugal. The occupation by the Moors in Portugal was confined largely to the southern portion and for a comparatively short time, but Arab characteristics are still seen.

The most amazing reminder of the Moslem presence in Spain is the huge mosque at Cordoba. It dates from 758 CE and has been modified many times by various builders, the most lavish of whom was al Hakam II. He added a fancy mihrab (prayer niche) and maqsura for the caliph in the 10th century. The remarkable aspect of this imposing mosque is that the Catholics, who subsequently took control of it after defeating the Moors, built their own cathedral within the inner portion of the mosque. It is a somewhat curious sight to encounter an Italianate cathedral within the depths of the 850 granite columns that serve as the supports for the roof of the mosque.

The Arts

The architectural heritage of the Moors is seen throughout southern Spain. One of the most exciting sights is the Alhambra at Granada (Figures 10.6 and C.25, p. C9). This royal complex was built atop a hill overlooking the main part of Granada and appears as a most graceful reminder of the delicacy of line and ornamentation that marked the buildings during the Moorish occupation of Spain. The only jarring note within the walled complex is the palace that King Charles had constructed later in a much heavier style in 1526. A particularly refreshing and lovely estate called the *Generalife* (Figure 10.7) is connected to the Alhambra by way of a short path and lovely gardens.

Lending distinction to many Portuguese and Spanish buildings are the tiles that add artistic touches throughout many homes and public buildings (Figures 10.8 and C.26, p. C9). These painted ceramic tiles represent one manifestation of the love of beauty shared by the people occupying the Iberian Peninsula. Styles of painting, subjects, and colors vary with the time in history and the skill and artistry of the tile painters. Decorated ceramic dishes, vases, figures, and pots are all part of the cultural heritage in these countries.

Among the names of famous Spanish artists are Velázquez, Murillo, and El Greco, painters from the 16th and 17th centuries. Actually, El Greco was born in Crete but generally is considered a Spanish painter because he painted for the rest

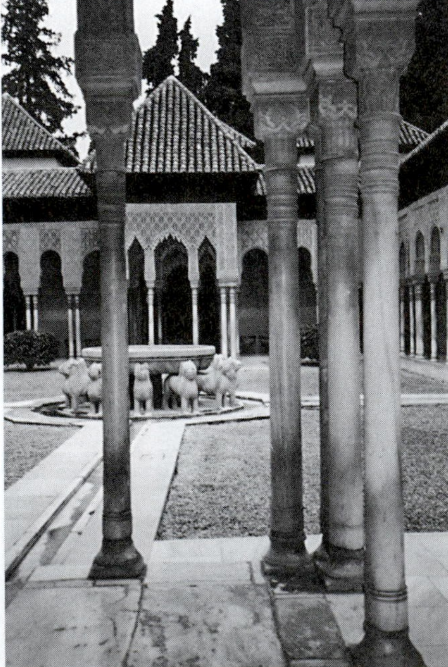

Figure 10.6 The Lions' Court built by the Moors in the last half of the 14th century is part of the Harem in the Alhambra at Granada, Spain.

Figure 10.7 Pools and fountains add beauty, sound, and cooling spray to the gardens in the Generalife, the summer garden area of the Alhambra.

of his life in Spain after he arrived in his 30s (Figures 10.9 and C.27, p. C9). Goya also was a prominent Spanish artist, but he painted during the late 18th and early 19th centuries. Picasso, Miró, and Dali are prominent among 20th century artists born in Spain but who did much of their work in France and other places because of the civil unrest in Spain during their lives.

A 20th century architect who showed a very creative style was Gaudi, who is particularly noted for his unfinished Cathedral of the Holy Family (Sagrada Familia) and numerous remarkable homes and other buildings in Barcelona (Figure 10.10). The most familiar Spanish writer is Cervantes (1562–1635), who wrote *Don Quixote* and clearly portrayed human dignity and innate goodness through this title character and his faithful companion Sancho Panza.

Music seems to be an inherent part of the Spanish soul, and some wonderful musicians have contributed particularly to the country's cultural heritage. The names of the artists Segovia and Casals were known to concertgoers around the globe during the 20th century. Other well-known performers today include Placido Domingo and Alicia de Larrocha.

Fado—Distinctive sad musical form of the blues sung to a guitar accompaniment.

A unique part of Portuguese culture is **fado,** a form of blues from Lisbon. Fado is a heartfelt vocal accompanied by a classical guitar and an acoustic guitar,

Figure 10.8 Mural depicting life on a ranch raising bulls for bullfights is painted on tiles on a wall in Seville, Spain.

Figure 10.9 Toledo, the Spanish town where El Greco painted, is dominated by the Alcazar with the Tagus River flowing around the base of the hill on which the city is built.

or both; it has also been the subject of paintings. One of the most famous Portuguese writers was Eca de Quieros, and Jose Mulhoa from Portugal was an artist of some renown.

Flamenco, thought to have been brought by the gypsies in the 1500s, is a dance that has captured the essence of Spain. Its exciting rhythms and melodies skillfully played on the guitar add high drama to the gypsylike dances. Stamping feet, clapping, and a sense of urgency or sadness add to the flavor of flamenco.

Bullfighting is a national sport in both Spain and Portugal. Some believe that this is definitely an artistic expression (Figure 10.11 and C.30, p. C10). Certainly, matadors execute almost dancelike, artistic movements as they battle the bull. The traditions surrounding the fights have considerable color including the

Figure 10.10 The highly decorated, complex structure of the Cathedral of the Holy Family envisioned by Gaudi was started in 1882 and remains unfinished in Barcelona, Spain.

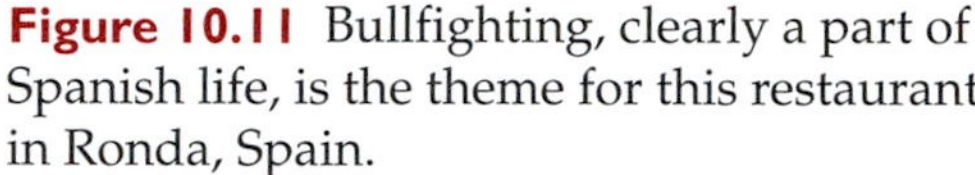

Figure 10.11 Bullfighting, clearly a part of Spanish life, is the theme for this restaurant in Ronda, Spain.

initial parade of the picadors on horseback, the banderillos and the matador marching on foot, and the bull.

A famous tradition related to bullfighting is the running of the bulls in Pamplona, a hazardous festivity featuring unfettered bulls running through the town behind people who risk their good health and sometimes their lives as they attempt to keep out of the reach of the stampeding bulls' horns.

Holidays in Spain and Portugal reflect the strong Catholic faith of the people. In addition to Christmas and Easter, many local celebrations are held honoring the various saints. Parades with elaborate floats and with penitents carrying crosses are seen at religious celebrations in Seville and other cities in Spain.

Food Patterns

The extensive trading of the Portuguese with distant parts of the world—South America, the coast of Africa from the Atlantic around the Cape of Good Hope, the Indian Ocean to Goa, India, and Macao in the Far East—meant that exotic foods became a part of the meals when the adventurers brought back their discoveries. Corn, tomatoes, pineapples, potatoes, pumpkin, squash, beans, and coffee are examples of the foods from afar that became part of the culture of Portugal.

Tea and a wide array of spices are other food items brought from the voyages the Portuguese traders made in their caravels, which Prince Henry the Navigator launched to meet the challenges of sailing along the African coast. Added to these new foods was an abundance of salted, dried cod. This preserved fish fared well for use on long sea voyages and served as a mainstay for the Portuguese at home.

Portugal

The typical food patterns of the Portuguese are generally quite simple. Breakfast is frequently a cup of coffee with milk (or hot chocolate) plus some bread and jam. Milk usually is consumed at breakfast in one of these beverages and in the form of cheese at other times of day. It is not considered a beverage to be

Bachalhau—Salted, dried cod.

Chorizo—Sausage flavored with paprikas and chilies that may be seasoned to be picante (hot) or dulce (sweeet).

Flan—Baked custard dessert, usually containing caramel in both Spain and Portugal.

Churro—Spiral-shaped fried quick-bread similar to a doughnut but extruded into a fluted, thick stick before frying.

Paella—Traditional rice dish colored and flavored by saffron and topped with cooked vegetables and meats.

Food plays a very important role in the Basque section of northeastern Spain. Gastronomic societies are a tradition; men (rarely a few women) gather together to share their love of food, cooking, and dining. These groups are also committed to cooking, dining well, and preserving their culinary heritage.

consumed by itself. Lunch and dinner are quite substantial meals that more than make up for the slim breakfast menu. Although there is plenty of hearty food, Portuguese meals are actually quite simple. This may reflect in part that many of the women work outside the home, which limits the time they are available for preparing meals.

Pork and fish are the most important sources of protein in Portuguese meals. Pork sausages of various types are popular. Smoked ham is another common form of pork. Fish are available from the sea (Figure 10.12), but perhaps the most abundant fish included in meals is the salted, dried cod mentioned earlier. **Bachalhau** recipes are abundant in Portugal; they combine salted, dried cod with greens, other vegetables, and seasonings adding an individual touch from the cook.

Peppers, onions, tomatoes, and potatoes are particularly important vegetable ingredients in many dishes. Potatoes may be served with other starch-rich foods, particularly rice. Vegetables are almost always cooked rather than served raw. Kale, which is abundant, is the main ingredient in julienne slivers in caldo verde, a soup featuring pork sausage (Figure 10.13), potatoes, and garlic (Figure 10.14). **Chorizo** is a sausage spiced with paprikas and chilies to be sweet (dulce) or hot (picante). Eggs are served in many different ways, one of the favorites being caramel **flan** for dessert. Crusty breads are available and enjoyed at meals. Portuguese wines are popular as the beverage at meals, and coffee and tea are often served.

Spain

The food in Spain tends to be more adventuresome and somewhat fancier than the dishes commonly served in Portugal. For example, Spaniards may choose to start the day with a delectable **churro** accompanied by a strong cup of coffee or hot chocolate. This fluted, straight version of a doughnut is a traditional food that was introduced into the Spanish colonies in the Caribbean and Latin America and is still popular there.

Probably the most familiar dish served in Spain is **paella,** a rice and meat concoction that is prepared in a wide, shallow pan with sloping sides (Figures 10.15 and C.29, p. C10). The meat is first browned in the paella pan and then set

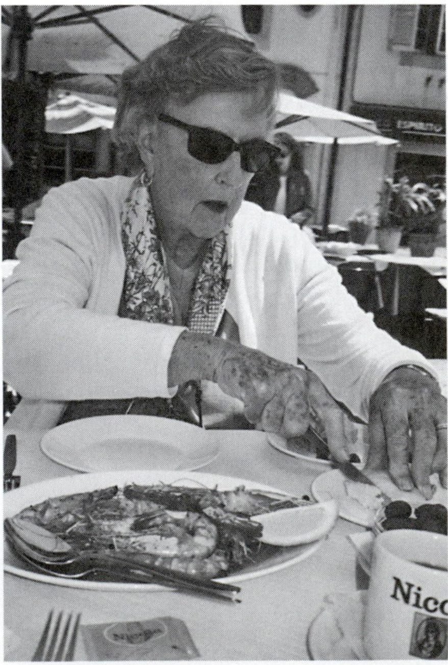

Figure 10.12 Langoustines caught in the Atlantic Ocean near Cascais, Portugal, provide a delectable lunch al fresco at a local restaurant.

Figure 10.13 Many types of sausages can be found throughout Spain and Portugal. The ones hanging on the wall in this market have a high salt and low moisture content, conditions that enable them to be stored without refrigeration.

Figure 10.14 Strings of garlic, an essential ingredient in many Spanish recipes, hang prominently on display in this market in Madrid, Spain.

Figure 10.15 Paella is a flavorful, colorful mixture of various seafood, saffron rice, and vegetables.

Saffron—Orange to yellow spice; the stigma of purple crocus; adds color and flavor to dishes.

Cocido—Meal consisting of three traditional courses (soup, cooked vegetables, and boiled meats) with the specific ingredients varying.

Tapa—Small plate of tidbits of food designed for nibbling while having a drink in the late afternoon or early evening.

Sopa de ajo—Garlic soup popular in Spain.

Gazpacho—Chilled soup traditional in Spain; made with many chopped vegetables plus beef or chicken stock, red wine vinegar, and olive oil.

Sangria—Red wine blended with fruit juices.

Basques—Group living in the Pyrenees Mountains near the Bay of Biscay in northeastern Spain; some are seeking independence from Spain.

Marmitako—Basque stew made with tuna and potatoes.

Porrusalda—Basque soup that features potatoes and leeks.

Bacalao al Pil-Pil—Basque dish made with salt cod served in a garlic sauce.

aside while the vegetable ingredients are sautéed. Rice and liquid are added before the meat is arranged on top. The assembled dish is baked on the floor of the oven for about 30 minutes so the rice absorbs the water and the flavors blend. **Saffron** is always an ingredient in paella. The orange to yellow color of the rice in paella is the result of using saffron (the orange to yellow stigmas of purple crocus). This also adds to the flavor of the dish.

Another national tradition is **cocido,** which varies greatly from place to place but consists of three courses: clear soup, a platter of cooked vegetables, and an array of boiled meats. This is often consumed for the midday meal around 2:30 P.M. Appetites for this meal generally are quite large, for the breakfast eaten around 7 A.M. probably is a cup of coffee with milk and a churro.

Spaniards typically have a long rest period for much of the hot afternoon. This siesta is followed with more work before stopping to enjoy drinks and **tapas** (little plates of food served at bars) to help control appetites until dinner is served, usually at 10 P.M. or later. The Spanish people thrive on their late dining hours and sociable evenings. Life is not meant to be rushed in this warm climate. Spanish wines usually are served at meals. Flan is a favorite dessert that has been transplanted to countries in the western hemisphere by Spain.

Sopa de ajo (garlic soup) is a specialty in the central part of Spain. Another traditional soup is **Gazpacho,** a chilled mix of chopped tomatoes, peppers, onions, cilantro, basil, cucumber, and avocado with chicken or beef stock, red wine vinegar, and olive oil. **Sangria** (a wine-fruit punch) is a favorite beverage; wines from various parts of the country are a part of all meals except breakfast in Spain.

The **Basques** in the northeast corner of Spain have created a cuisine over many centuries that clearly reflects their geography. The rugged terrain of the Pyrenees Mountains and the proximity of the Atlantic have fostered sheep herding and a bit of cattle and hog production as well as considerable fishing. The result is a cuisine that focuses on the natural flavors of their ingredients. Lamb, pork, some beef, cheeses (often made from ewe's milk), and a wide variety of local seafoods provide the protein in Basque meals. Local vegetables include haricot (dry) beans of varying colors, green beans, peas, broad beans, cabbage, cardoons, potatoes, and mushrooms. Apples, cherries, and walnuts are other foods produced in the region that appear frequently in various dishes. A typical Basque dish is **marmitako,** a stew featuring potatoes and tuna; a potato and leek soup (**porrusalda**) is also popular. Salt cod appears in several Basque dishes, such as **Bacaloa al Pil-Pil** in which the salt cod is served in a garlic sauce.

Recipes

Gazpacho (Serves 4–6)

1 c water
1 c bread crumbs (no crust)
2 c peeled, chopped tomatoes
½ medium cucumber, chopped
½ garlic clove, crushed
½ onion, coarsely chopped
½ green pepper, coarsely chopped
1 tbsp olive oil
2 tbsp red wine vinegar
Salt and pepper to taste

1. Mix all ingredients in bowl.
2. In a blender, puree about 2 cups of mixture until smooth.
3. Transfer puree to another bowl and keep repeating until all of the mixture is puréed.
4. Adjust seasonings, and then chill for 2 hours or more. Serve chilled.

Sopa de Ajo (Serves 4)

¼ c olive oil
2 garlic cloves, minced
1½ c French bread crumbs (no crust)
½ tsp paprika
Pinch cayenne pepper
½ tsp salt
3 c water
4 poached eggs (optional)
2 tsp chopped chives (optional)

1. Sauté garlic in olive oil for 2 minutes (do not brown).
2. Add bread and stir while heating to golden.
3. Stir in spices and water.
4. Poach eggs in separate pan while simmering soup.
5. Serve soup and add egg. Garnish with chives.

Caldo Verde (Serves 6–8)

1 lb potatoes, peeled and sliced
5 c water
1½ tsp salt
¼ lb chorizo (sausage with garlic)
¼ c olive oil
¼ tsp black pepper
½ lb kale leaves, julienne cut

1. Boil potatoes in salted water until tender.
2. Meanwhile, simmer chorizo in water for 15 minutes, then drain and slice ¼″ thick.
3. Place potatoes in a bowl and mash with a fork.
4. Put potatoes back in pan, stir in olive oil and pepper, and heat to boiling.
5. Add kale and boil for 4 minutes.
6. Add chorizo and simmer for 2 minutes.

Cocido Madrileno (Serves 8–12)

½ c dried chickpeas (garbanzo)
5 qt water
1 large stewing hen
1 lb beef brisket
1 lb boneless ham
2 carrots, pared
2 leeks
1 garlic clove, crushed
½ lb chorizo
Cabbage (cut in 6 cored wedges)
6 potatoes, pared

1. Soak garbanzos according to package directions for 12 hours.
2. Drain and place garbanzos in a large stock pot and add water, hen, and brisket. Simmer for 2 hours.
3. Add ham, carrots, leeks, plus seasonings, and simmer for 30 minutes.
4. Meanwhile, simmer chorizo for 15 minutes in water, then drain and slice ¼″ thick.
5. Add chorizo, cabbage, and potatoes; simmer for 30 minutes.
6. Serve broth first, followed by a platter of vegetables and then a platter of meats.

Paella (Serves 6–8)

6 pieces chicken
¼ c olive oil
16 raw shrimp, shelled (or 2 raw lobster tails and 8 shrimp)
½ lb chorizo (garlic-flavored sausage)
3 strips bacon, diced
1 large onion, finely chopped
1 tsp minced garlic
1 sweet red pepper in julienne strips
1 large tomato, finely chopped
1 8-oz can garbanzos or cooked beans
6 c water
3 c long grain rice (uncooked)
1 tsp salt
¼ tsp ground saffron
Salt and pepper to taste
6 uncooked hard-shelled, small clams
6 raw mussels
Lemon for garnish

1. Carefully brown chicken in ¼ cup of olive oil, removing from skillet when well browned.
2. Simmer seafood for 3 minutes. Meanwhile, simmer sausage for 5 minutes in water, drain, and slice ¼″ thick.
3. In a skillet, sauté sausage, bacon, onion, garlic, red pepper, tomato, and beans, stirring while heating until thick enough to pile lightly.
4. Preheat oven to 400°F while heating water to boiling. Put rice, 1 teaspoon salt, sautéed vegetables, and saffron in a two-handled ovenproof, 14″ skillet or paella pan.
5. Pour boiling water over rice and stir well. Heat again while stirring to bring mixture to boiling.
6. Remove from heat and then arrange the seafood and chicken on top.
7. Place pan very low in the oven and bake at 400°F until water is absorbed (25 to 30 minutes). Garnish with lemon and serve from pan.

Churros (Serves 4–6)

2 c water
½ tsp salt
2 c all-purpose flour
Oil for deep-fat frying
Sugar
Cinnamon (optional)

1. Boil water in 2-qt saucepan.
2. Immediately remove from heat and add flour and salt in one addition. Beat hard to form a dough mass that pulls away from the sides.
3. Cool to room temperature; begin heating the oil to 400°F.
4. Fill metal cookie press with the dough.
5. Using the star disc on the cookie press, drop 6″ lengths of dough into the hot fat.
6. Fry until pleasingly browned (5 to 7 minutes), turning occasionally.
7. Drain on paper towels and sprinkle with sugar.

Sangria (Serves 6–8)

½ c brandy
¼ c curaçao or Cointreau (orange-flavored liqueurs)
½ c lime juice
2 c orange juice
1 bottle chilled red wine (Spanish)

1. Mix everything but the wine and refrigerate in a large pitcher for at least 3 hours.
2. Add the wine. Stir before serving.

Summary

The Iberian Peninsula and its countries of Portugal and Spain form the southwestern tip of Europe, a region that is shut off from the rest of the continent by the Pyrenees Mountains. Other mountain ranges ring the central plateau of Spain, the Meseta. The climate is quite varied, which allows the production of a variety of crops ranging from cereals in the central and northern regions to oranges and olives in the southern region.

The Romans left their mark on Spain and Portugal and were followed by the Germanic tribes from the north. The Moors invaded from Morocco in 711, bringing Islamic followers to the previously Catholic peninsula.

The proximity to the sea fostered the remarkable voyages of exploration by sea that reached around the world. Prince Henry the Navigator encouraged voyages along the coasts of Africa. King Ferdinand and Queen Isabella (who reigned immediately after the defeat of the Moors in 1492) sponsored the voyages of Columbus. Both countries were able to establish colonies and trade routes that brought the countries considerable wealth as well as power to Spain. The lengthy period of the Spanish Inquisition resulted in the ouster of Jews and Moors who refused to bend under painful pressure to adopt the Catholic religion. This resulted in the loss of many bright and creative people and cost Spain dearly in human power and material goods.

Portugal became a nation when it gained independence from Spain in 1668. Franco was the dictator who ruled Spain following its civil war, fought from 1931 to 1939. He was in power until he died in 1975. Presently, Spain is ruled by a monarchy with an elected parliament.

The language in Portugal and in its former colony of Brazil is Portuguese. Spain has a number of dialects, but the formal language is Castilian Spanish. The distinctive feature of Castilian is the lisplike character that results from pronouncing the letter *s* as *th* if the *s* precedes an *e* or *i*.

The dominant religion in both Spain and Portugal is Catholicism. Most Muslims were either driven out by the war that ended in 1492 or were forced out by the Inquisition. The Inquisition also removed the Jewish believers, although some Jews were invited back when the Spaniards became aware of the importance of their abilities.

The Moors left a lasting array of highly creative and artistic buildings, including the mosque at Cordoba and the Alhambra in Granada. Portugal's contributions to the arts include the fado, a unique form of the blues. Spain brought other exciting music, flamenco dancing, plus many artists and writers, including Velázquez, Murillo, El Greco, and more recent artists including Picasso, Miró, and Dali. Cervantes, the author of *Don Quixote,* and Gaudi, the imaginative Barcelona architect, also were Spaniards.

Bullfighting and the running of the bulls in Pamplona add to the color and excitement that represent Spain today. The deeply moving religious holiday celebrations, particularly the parades with floats and the participation of penitents carrying crosses during Holy Week in Seville, are clear evidence of the importance of the Catholic church and its beliefs in Spain and in Portugal.

Foods on the Iberian Peninsula are quite imaginative because of the wide array of ingredients that are available, but Portuguese foods tend to be somewhat simpler than the fare in Spain. Breakfast in both countries is simple: coffee with milk and some bread and jam or churros. The two other meals of the day are much more substantial. The combination of a big meal in the early afternoon and the heat of the day (particularly in summer) has fostered the tradition of a long break or siesta in the afternoon, followed by more work and then some drinks and tapas with friends before finally eating a late dinner (often at 10 P.M. or even midnight in Spain). Sausages and salted, dried cod are staples in the Portuguese diet. Paella, cocido, and flan are national dishes in Spain. Soups, wines, olives and olive oil, oranges, and tapas are items that invoke the essence of Spanish food. Basque food in northeastern Spain focuses on ingredients from that region, notably seafood, lamb, cheeses, beans of many types, potatoes, cabbage, apples, cherries, and walnuts.

Selected Sites

http://www.churros.com/churros.htm—Description of churros and their preparation.

http://www.gourmetsleuth.com/flan.htm—Background information about the history of flan and suggestions for preparing it.

www.paellapans.com—Description of paella preparation techniques and recipes.

www.donquijote.org/culture/spain/food—Information about Spain, its food and recipes.

http://www.lingolex.com/spanishfood/glossayen.htm—English/Spanish and Spanish/English glossary of foods and cooking terms, and also some recipes.

www.cellartastings.com/en/food-portugal—Description of regional foods in Portugal and some recipes.

Study Questions

1. What contributed to Portugal's rise in power and wealth during the 15th through 17th centuries?
2. Briefly describe the contribution of each of the following: (a) Vasco da Gama, (b) Dali, (c) Prince Henry the Navigator, (d) Gaudi, (e) King Ferdinand and Queen Isabella, (f) Magellan, (g) Velázquez, (h) El Greco, (i) Cervantes, and (j) Picasso.
3. Name and describe at least two buildings in Spain that were built by the Moors.
4. What was Spain trying to accomplish by its Inquisition? Where did its practices occur? What were some of the results of the Inquisition?
5. Describe the meal pattern that is typical in Spain.
6. Briefly define the following: (a) cocido, (b) paella, (c) tapas, (d) saffron, and (e) churros.

Bibliography

Barer-Stein, T. 1999. *You Eat What You Are.* 2nd ed. Firefly Books, Ltd. Ontario, Canada.

Barrenechea, T. et al. 2005. *Cuisines of Spain: Exploring Regional Home Cooking.* Ten Speed Press. Berkeley, CA.

Feibleman, P.S. 1969. *The Cooking of Spain and Portugal.* Time-Life Books. New York.

Hilliard, C.B. 1998. *Intellectual Traditions of Pre-Colonial Africa.* McGraw-Hill. New York.

Inman, N., ed. 1996. *Spain.* Dorling Kindersley, Ltd. London, England.

Irving, W. 1953. *The Alhambra.* Macmillan. New York.

Kohen, E. 1992. *Spain.* Marshall Cavendish Corp. New York.

McKay, J.P., D.H. Bennett, and J. Buckler. 1999. *A History of Western Society.* Houghton Mifflin. Boston.

Medina, F.X. 2005. *Food Culture in Spain.* Greenwood Press. Westport, CT.

Michener, J.A. 1968. *Iberia*. Random House. New York.
Palmowski, J. 1997. *Dictionary of 20th Century World History*. Oxford University Press. Oxford, England.
Passmore, J. 1993. *Complete Spanish Cookbook*. Tuttle Publishers. North Clarendon, VT.
Pearcy, G.E. 1980. *The World Food Scene*. Plycon Press. Redondo Beach, CA.
Rios, A. and L.K. March. 1996. *Heritage of Spanish Cooking*. Random House. New York.
Symington, M. 1997. *Portugal with Madeira and the Azores*. Dorling Kindersley, Ltd. London, England.

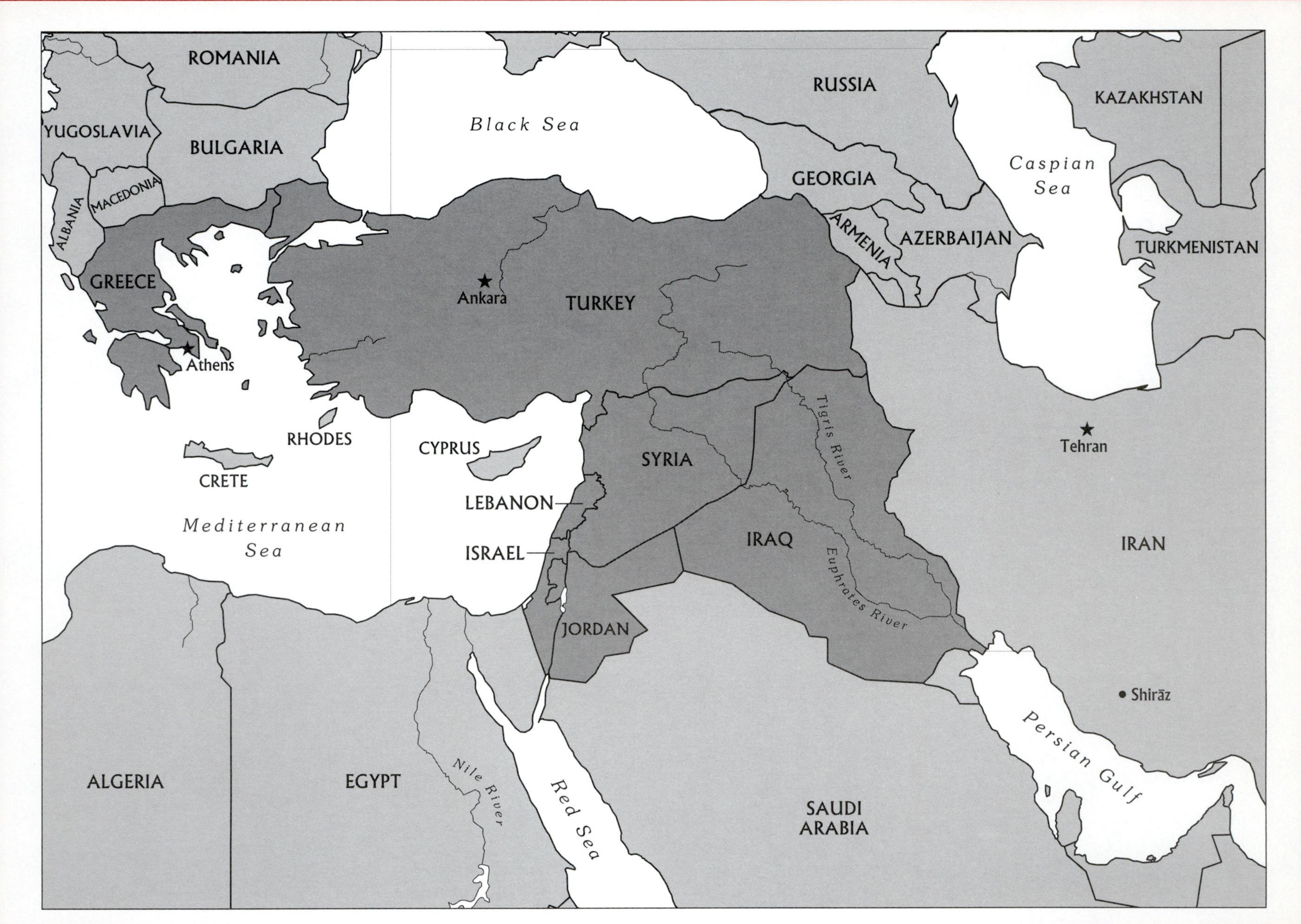
ROMANIA
YUGOSLAVIA
BULGARIA
MACEDONIA
ALBANIA
GREECE
Athens
Black Sea
RUSSIA
KAZAKHSTAN
Caspian Sea
GEORGIA
ARMENIA
AZERBAIJAN
TURKMENISTAN
Ankara
TURKEY
RHODES
CRETE
CYPRUS
Mediterranean Sea
SYRIA
LEBANON
ISRAEL
Tigris River
Tehran
IRAQ
IRAN
Euphrates River
JORDAN
Shirāz
Persian Gulf
ALGERIA
EGYPT
Nile River
Red Sea
SAUDI ARABIA

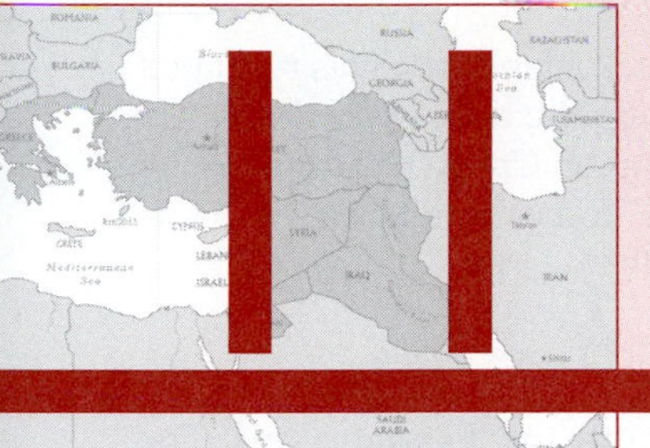

11 Greece, Turkey, and the Levant

Geographic Overview

The Mediterranean Sea provides the common denominator among Greece, Turkey, and the Levant, although some distinct differences exist, both in the terrain and in the people. Greece is part of the Balkan Peninsula but also extends to the southern tip of the **Peloponnesus** and includes numerous islands in the seas surrounding the nation (Figure 11.1). The rugged terrain has served to maintain Greece as a unique nation, one with a remarkable heritage from a time when the Greeks represented the epitome of culture and learning.

Peloponnesus—Peninsula extending off the southwestern region of Greece.

Turkey is adjacent to Greece; this proximity has fostered considerable unrest at various times in history between the two countries. Turkey is a unique country because it straddles two continents: Europe and Asia. A waterway from the Aegean (consisting of the Dardanelles, the Sea of Marmara, and the **Bosporus**) leads directly into the Black Sea, forming a division not only between the continents, but also between parts of Turkey. This pathway between Europe and Asia has placed Istanbul (formerly called *Byzantium* and *Constantinople*) on the route of armies and traders over the centuries.

Bosporus—Narrow channel that separates Europe from Asia between the Sea of Marmara and the Black Sea.

This unique country has almost 2,500 miles of shoreline, touching seas including the Aegean, Marmara, Black, and Mediterranean. It also has high mountains in the east, with Mt. Ararat rising 17,000 feet. The Taurus Mountains near the Mediterranean in southern Turkey are more than 12,000 feet high.

Turkey's neighbors in Asia include Syria, Iraq, and Iran. However, Iraq and Iran are at quite a distance east of the Mediterranean and do not share the climatic influence of that sea. Hostilities have isolated these countries for many years, but they influence the rest of the world because of their abundant supply of oil. Iraq is noteworthy as the land where the Tigris and Euphrates rivers flow

Figure 11.1 Santorini is the Greek island that was reshaped when its volcano erupted, creating the tidal wave that destroyed the Minoan civilization on Crete. The immense crater it left filled with seawater. Today people live atop the island along the edge of the crater.

together and form the Shatt-al-Arab before flowing into the Persian Gulf. The Iraq War has made the deserts there all-too-familiar.

Syria, Lebanon, and Israel have some Mediterranean seacoast, but arid conditions exist in much of their lands. Military concerns have limited agricultural development, although Israel has been able to effectively develop its agricultural potential to meet the challenge to feed its people. Mountains are a part of the landscape in these three countries and in neighboring Jordan. Israel and Jordan border the Dead Sea (Figure 11.2), which is the lowest spot on earth (1,286 feet below sea level).

Agriculture

Greece Although more than half of the land in Greece supports only stunted vegetation interspersed among many rocks and large rock formations, the country does a surprisingly good job of providing its own food, and even exports some. Wheat, corn, and rice are the favored cereal crops, although the sparse rainfall limits production. Grapes (consumed as wine, fruit, or leaves) and olives are important crops that figure prominently in the diets of the Greek people. Olive oil is used generously in cooking, and Greek olives are favorites. Citrus fruits and vegetables are other crops suited to the land and climate.

Sheep can be raised successfully in this rocky land and are important in the diet both as meat and as a source of dairy products. Feta cheese is a product of ewe's milk. Fish is available from the sea to round out the sources of protein.

Figure 11.2 Masada, site of Jewish resistance to the Romans, overlooks the Dead Sea (the lowest point on earth); the high salt content in this inland sea makes it impossible for life to exist in it.

Figure 11.3 Legumes of different types, oranges, dates, olives, and nuts are displayed in this market in Turkey.

Levant—Land at the eastern end of the Mediterranean Sea including Syria, Lebanon, Israel, and Jordan.

The Levant Although some agricultural efforts are very successful when irrigation is available, water is a very scarce commodity because of the hot and dry desert climate that dominates the **Levant.** The central Anatolian Plateau of Turkey is large and quite barren but grows wheat successfully. Corn, fruit, tobacco, and nuts are grown in abundance along the plains facing the Black Sea in the northern part of the country. Grapes, figs, olives, cotton, and tobacco in quantities adequate for exporting as well as for home use are grown along the shores of the Aegean Sea. The land along the Mediterranean in the southern part of Turkey produces citrus, sesame, bananas, oil seeds, olives, and cotton when irrigation appropriate to the particular crop is provided.

Iran is noted for its beluga caviar, which is harvested from sturgeon in the Caspian Sea on its border. Iran's high mountains limit land for agriculture, and a fairly dry climate adds to farmers' problems.

Olive trees are productive in this region of the world, and citrus, papaya, eggplant, dates, tomatoes, and various vegetables also are grown under irrigation (Figure 11.3). The primary livestock is sheep, which are well adapted to the terrain of this area, but cattle and chickens are also raised.

History and Culture

Greece

The country that is now Greece has a long and complicated history dating back beyond the early Bronze Age of 3000 BCE. Minoans and Myceneans left their marks on the region before 1200 BCE, and Homer described the Trojan War around 750 BCE. City-states, notably Sparta and Athens, were developed and protected against many invaders, sometimes successfully and sometimes not.

The defeat of the Persians under Xerxes paved the way for the Golden Age of classical culture, beginning in 475 BCE. In this period the Parthenon and other classical structures were built on the Acropolis (Figure 11.4). Unfortunately, the Peloponnesian Wars between the city-states of Athens and Sparta led to a decline in the culture.

The Macedonians took over Greece next, followed by the Romans in 146 BCE. By the 5th century, other invaders began to challenge the people living in the region of modern Greece. Goths, Franks, and Venetians all fought there at various times. The Crusaders also went through Greece.

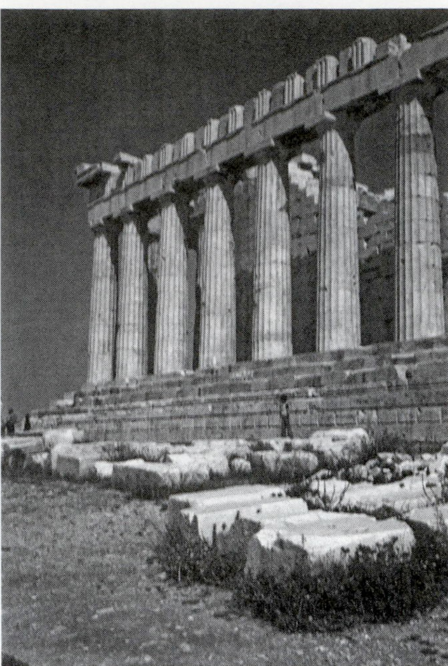

Figure 11.4 The Parthenon on the Acropolis in Athens still stands high above the city, a constant reminder of the glorious heritage Greeks have.

Finally, the Ottoman Turks gained control of Greece and ruled for almost 400 years, from the late 1400s until the 19th century. A strong surge of nationalism culminated in the Greek War of Independence, which was fought from 1821 to 1829. This laid the groundwork for the establishment of the country of Greece. However, animosity toward Turkey has not been resolved completely and remains as exemplified by the contest for control of some Aegean islands and the divided island of Cyprus.

Turkey and the Levant

Hittites—Civilization occupying parts of Turkey and Syria, to Mesopotamia for more than four centuries, ending in about 1200 BCE.

The history of Turkey and the Levant shares some common threads with Greece, but the region has a unique record of its own. The early settlers in the central part of what is now Anatolia were the **Hittites,** who lived near modern-day Ankara (capital of Turkey today). The Hittites, whose empire once spanned Turkey, Syria, and Mesopotamia, were advanced for their day (1700 to 1200 BCE), leaving behind written records, metal sculptures, and rock carvings that can be viewed today in a museum in Ankara (Figure 11.5).

Figure 11.5 Examples of Hittite art, including this bas-relief, are displayed in Ankara, Turkey.

Phoenicians—People living in Lebanon who sailed extensively to trade with many other regions by 1000 BCE.

Byzantine Empire—Eastern part of the former Roman Empire; powerful for almost a millennium (129 BCE to 1071 CE).

Byzantium—Early name for the city once called Constantinople but now called Istanbul.

Ottoman Empire—Large empire centered in Turkey that ruled for more than 600 years, ending after World War I.

Impact of Trade After the end of the Hittite occupation, smaller states were formed, the most noteworthy being Phrygia and Lydia. Greeks traded with these states. In Lebanon, **Phoenicians,** with their fleets of ships, evolved into powerful traders with other Mediterranean regions by 1000 BCE.

On land, trade routes in ancient times wended their way between Egyptian settlements in Africa, Mediterranean ports in North Africa, Antioch, Tyre, and Gaza, and on through either Petra (Figures 11.6 and C.57, p. C19) in what is now Jordan or Palmyra, now in Syria (Figures 11.7 and C.48, p. C16). The routes extended onward to reach the civilizations of Babylon on the Euphrates or Kuwait and Bahrain on the Persian Gulf. Trade was very much alive from as early as the 5th century BCE.

Farther to the east, the Persians established and expanded their empire. Under Cyrus the Great, Persia controlled much of the area of Turkey and the Levant until the conquests of Alexander the Great. His destruction of Persepolis in southern Iran in 330 BCE (Figures 11.8 and C.50, p. C17) marked the end of an era in this part of the world.

Roman rule in Turkey began in 129 BCE. Later, under Hadrian and several successive emperors, Rome gradually acquired and maintained control of much of the Middle East. Emperor Constantine split the Roman Empire and established the **Byzantine Empire.** He claimed the city of **Byzantium** for its capital in 330 CE and changed the city's name to Constantinople.

The Byzantine Empire fell to the Turkish tribes in 1071, bringing Islam into what then was predominantly a Christian realm. The rulers of this new Turkey were Seljuks. Two centuries later (in 1299), Mongols conquered the Seljuks; Osman, an Anatolian, established the **Ottoman Empire,** the seat of which was moved to Constantinople (currently Istanbul) when that city was captured in 1453.

Eventually, the Ottomans expanded their holdings westward as far as Vienna, where the Hapsburgs halted their advance in 1529 and 1683. The Ottomans maintained a powerful stance in Turkey, and the actual empire lasted until the end of World War I. Then Kemal Ataturk became the leader of Turkey and is credited with making many of the changes that form the foundation of modern Turkey.

Figure 11.6 Petra, a city carved from reddish sandstone cliffs, was on the trade route between Egypt and cities to the north in the Levant.

Figure 11.7 Palmyra, Syria, was another prominent city on the ancient northern trade route, often receiving goods transported by camel caravans from Africa.

Religious Impact on the Levant

Religion has played a significant role in shaping the history of the Middle East for many centuries. During these centuries, different religions have dominated in sequence: Judaism was significant before 1100 BCE; Christianity gained in prominence as some people became believers in Christ; and Islam spread from the Arabian Peninsula throughout the Levant after the fall of the Byzantine Empire. Each of these three major religions views Jerusalem as a focal point for its beliefs, an unfortunate convergence that has led to seemingly endless bloodshed throughout the previous two millennia and continues today.

Greek Orthodoxy Religion varies considerably in Greece, Turkey, and, as noted, the countries of the Levant. Greece is almost entirely a nation of Greek Orthodoxy, which branched centuries ago from the Roman Catholic doctrines. However, people in Greece are free to observe any religion they please.

In Turkey, most of the Muslims are Sunnis, who carefully follow the teachings of Muhammad as stated in the writings in the Hadith. However, some Turks

Figure 11.8 Despite the sacking of Persepolis by Alexander the Great, some columns and art can still be seen.

are Shiite Muslims; this group pays special attention to Ali (son-in-law of Muhammad) and believes in hidden meanings in the Koran. Sacrifice and martyrdom are part of this branch of Islam.

Turkey has been rather broadminded in its expectations for practicing Muslims. Women often are not required to cover their heads, and both sexes sometimes drink alcoholic beverages despite the prohibition of alcohol in Islam. Another sect of Muslims in Turkey is Sufism, which is a somewhat mystical interpretation of the faith. The Whirling Dervishes, such as those in Konya, are examples of this Muslim sect (Figure 11.9).

Judaism The first of the major religions practiced in the Levant was Judaism. David, the son of King Saul (who united the Israelites around 1050 BCE), began building Jerusalem to be the capital of his kingdom. Solomon, his son, built a temple where the Israelites could worship their God (Figure C.53, p. C18). Two factions developed after Solomon split Israel into a northern section, with Samaria as its capital, and a southern section called *Judah*. People who lived in Judah were the first people to be called *Jews*.

When the Romans took the land in 63 BCE, the Jews were not allowed to practice their religion in their own way. This led to the dramatic standoff at Masada, where the Jews who had fled from conquered Jerusalem gathered on a mountain plateau high above the Dead Sea in 70 CE. It took the Roman army of 15,000 almost two years to build a ramp up the most vulnerable side of the fortress and break down the wall to enter the site, where less than 1,000 Jews had held out. Apparently, the Jews committed suicide to escape being captured alive by the Romans, thus ending a particularly sad and dramatic episode in the history of Israel.

Another revolt in 132 CE caused the Romans to scatter the Jews along the shores of the Black Sea, throughout the Greek islands, and around the Mediterranean Sea, an action referred to as the *diaspora*. Many Jews fled as refugees to northern European locations of their own choosing to escape the Roman actions. Christianity increased in numbers in this region (then known as *Palestine*) after Roman rule.

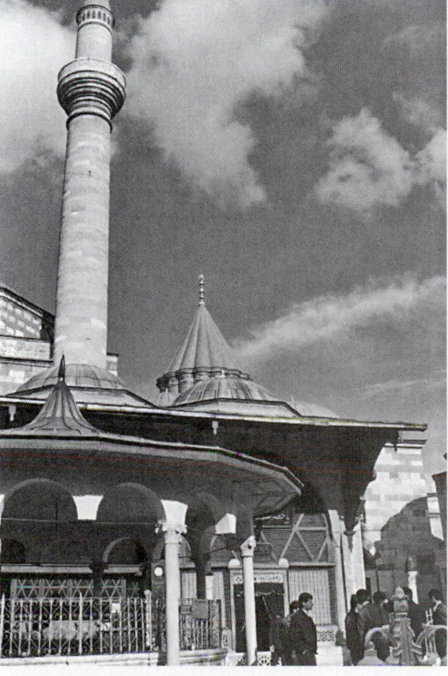

Figure 11.9 The Whirling Dervish Sect of Islam is centered in this mosque in Konya, Turkey.

Judaism is the state religion of current-day Israel, but there are different approaches to its observance. Orthodox Jews practice the faith in the traditional ways with its strong adherence to observing the Sabbath, following kashruth (Jewish dietary laws), celebrating all holy days, and separating men and women at worship (head covering and prayer shawls for men and head coverings for all married women). Hebrew is the language used in Orthodox services. Reform Jews conduct their services in the language of the particular country and are less strict in dietary and clothing practices.

Degrees to which they adhere to the law underlie the various Jewish groups in Israel. These differences sometimes lead to political problems. Israel also has Christians from different Protestant groups, Catholics, and Muslims. This diversity is not surprising in view of the history of the region and the focal point that Jerusalem and Israel represent in these religions.

Islam The Muslims ruled the Byzantine Empire, which was predominantly Christian. The dominance of Islam alarmed Pope Urban II, who in 1095 called for a Crusade (in the name of Christianity) to liberate Jerusalem from the Muslims. Eventually, other Crusades swept through the western region of Turkey and on south to Jerusalem, leaving evidence of the Christian invasions along their routes (Figures C.47, p. C16, and C.58, p. C20). Possession of Jerusalem passed back and forth between Christians and Muslims for almost two centuries.

When the powerful sultan Saladin (who ruled much of the Middle East) recaptured Jerusalem in 1187, Richard the Lionheart from England, Frederick Barbarossa of the Holy Roman Empire, and Phillip Augustus of France launched the Third Crusade which also was unsuccessful. The Fourth Crusade (1202 to 1204) was a religious disaster, for the capture of Constantinople caused a schism between the Roman Catholics and Eastern Orthodox Catholics that remains today.

When the Mamelukes (Muslims from Egypt) ruled the Ottoman Empire for about 250 years after the Crusades, they tolerated no religious differences. However, later Ottoman rulers were fairly tolerant of religions and gradually allowed Jews to return and gain more presence in Palestine.

The culmination of the gradual return of Jews was the establishment of the nation of Israel in 1948. When the British withdrew from the region and Israel declared its independence, four Muslim nations (Egypt, Jordan, Iraq, and Lebanon) attacked, only to have Israel gain more land than it originally had, including half of Jerusalem. Syria and Egypt attacked Israel in 1967, but Israel emerged six days later and added the Golan Heights, Sinai Peninsula, all of Jerusalem, and the West Bank of the Jordan to its territory.

The Syrian and Egyptian attack occurring on Yom Kippur in 1973 and numerous other skirmishes resulted from disagreements over land disputed since 1967. Peace negotiations have made gradual progress, and Palestinians finally have their own nation. Lebanon is functioning again, but tensions, both political and religious, remain high throughout the Levant.

Greek Holidays

Vassilopita—Rich sweet bread containing a good-luck coin to celebrate the New Year.

The Feast of St. Basil marks the New Year, a Byzantine holiday tradition celebrated in Greece in which a special sweet bread called **vassilopita,** containing one coin, is eaten; the person who gets the coin will have a lucky year. Greek Independence Day is celebrated March 25, a holiday that marks the struggle against the Ottomans and the religious event of the Feast of the Annunciation. Several other religious holidays are celebrated, with the Easter celebration keyed to the celebration of Orthodox Easter. The feasting for Greek Orthodox Easter includes red-dyed Easter eggs and lamb roasted on a spit.

Architecture of the Levant

The diversity of religions has inspired the building of quite different structures of worship in this part of the world, and nowhere is it more apparent than in Jerusalem. The Christian part of old Jerusalem contains the Church of the Holy Sepulchre while the Muslim Quarter contains the Temple Mount. The Temple Mount includes the Dome of the Rock, which is the most important spot in Jerusalem for Muslims because it contains the spot where Muhammad is believed to have departed from earth to enter heaven (Figure C.52, p. C18).

The Western Wall, or Wailing Wall, is a stone wall forming part of the Temple Mount; it dates back to 20 BCE when King Herod had the retaining wall for the Second Temple built (Figure C.53, p. C18). The Wailing Wall is all that remains as a result of the Roman destruction of the Second Temple in 70 CE. Because of its historical and religious significance, the Wailing Wall is a very important site for Jews to pray (men at one section and women at the adjacent part of the wall).

Evidence of the Crusades can be found throughout the Levant. At the Krak de Chevalliers (Figure C.47, p. C16) in the western part of Syria, the architectural style is clearly that of the Crusaders from England. However, within its lovely little chapel is the minbar (stairway always found in Muslim mosques), silently revealing the fact that the Crusaders ultimately lost their fortress to the Muslims. On the island of Rhodes, the Knights of St. John built protective walls around the old city that still stand today, providing mute testimony that European Crusaders once invaded and fought there (Figure C.58. p., C20).

In Istanbul, Hagia Sophia is a dominant building. This huge domed church was built by Byzantine Emperor Justinian for Christian worship, subsequently converted to a mosque, and finally changed to a museum (Figure C.39, p. C13). Both nature and man have attacked this monumental edifice over the ages; an earthquake caused the vaulted dome to fall only 20 years after the church was completed in 537. When the dome was repaired in 563, sturdy (but not very artistic) buttresses were added, providing the necessary support for the gigantic dome (rising more than 180 feet above the floor).

Catholics in the Fourth Crusade did considerable damage to the building, but they were driven out by the Byzantines, who then lost it to the Ottomans in 1453. The numerous transitions throughout its history have left some mosaics from the Byzantines as well as a minbar and other evidence of the Muslim religious observances that occurred for centuries prior to the transition to its current status of a museum.

A more beautiful mosque that remains active even today is the Blue Mosque, with its six intricate and delicate minarets standing very close to the rather awkward vastness of the Hagia Sophia (Figures C.37 and C.38, p. C13). Although the Blue Mosque may be the most beautiful of the mosques in Istanbul, it has plenty of competition for the honor (Figure 11.10).

Central Turkey offered a unique terrain for places of worship for the various religions. There, in a region called *Cappadocia* (Figure 11.11), tufa (marshes that contained volcanic ash of a consistency that was carved over the eons by wind and erosion into weird shapes, some resembling mushrooms) provided the isolation and material needed by Christians escaping from Romans. Early Christians used these almost unearthly formations to live, worship, and create paintings and altars secure from persecution (Figure 11.12).

A few palaces and public buildings, or at least their ruins, in Greece and the Levant illustrate various phases in the history of the region. The Persians, under Darius the Great in 518 BCE, built a remarkable palace at Persepolis in southern Iran. Although Alexander the Great burned it in 330 BCE, some beautiful bas-reliefs and stone carvings remain (Figures 11.13 and C.50, p. C17).

In Damascus, Syria, the Umayyad Mosque was built from 705–715 CE and remains active today (Figure 11.14). Surprisingly, the tomb of St. John the Baptist

Figure 11.10 The skyline of Istanbul, when seen from the Bosphorus, provides a panoply of mosques with their minarets and domes.

Figure 11.11 Cappadocia's weird landscape provided sanctuary for early Christians when they carved caves in the soft tufa.

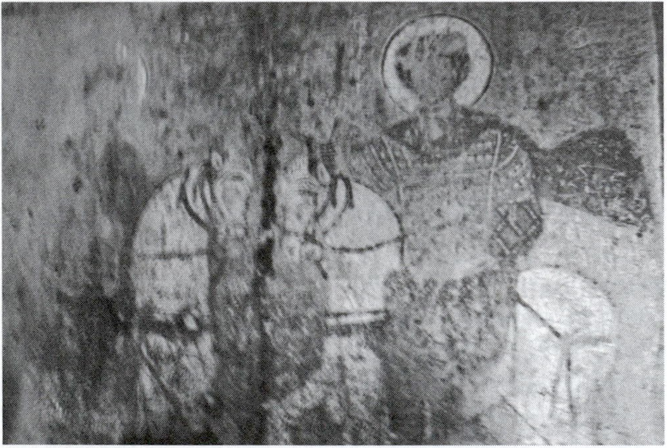

Figure 11.12 Some caves in Cappadocia in Central Turkey were decorated and used as chapels by early Christians when they lived there.

Figure 11.13 A few statues, such as this one, remain at Persepolis, Iran, clearly illustrating the highly developed art of the Persians before Alexander's conquest in 330 BCE.

Figure 11.14 The Umayyad Mosque in Damascus, Syria, has been a place of worship for Muslims since 715; the tomb of John the Baptist is inside the mosque.

is housed within the huge mosque. Another unusual feature of the Umayyad Mosque is the glazed decorative tile facade above the main entrance to the building from the courtyard.

In Greece on the Peloponnesus, the famous Lions' Gate is the centuries' weathered remnant of the art of the Myceneans around 1250 BCE. This style is totally different from that of the Persians (Figure 11.15).

In Jordan, the ruined trade city of Petra is best known for the Treasury (Khasneh), which is a rose-colored facade and rooms carved into a dramatic cliff at the end of a narrow gorge (Figure C.57, p. C19). The facade bears evidence of the influences of the Greeks and Romans, which is not surprising because the ancient artisans who carved it doubtless had contact with these cultures because of the trade that passed through this strategic point in the desert. Other interesting ruins are found in Baalbek (Figure C.51, p. C17) in Lebanon and Palmyra in Syria (Figures 11.16 and C.48, p. C16).

Greece's contributions to both art and architecture are legendary. The Parthenon probably is the world's most famous building or ruin; its simplicity and detail (e.g., the Elgin Marbles, part of the decorative frieze) have inspired many buildings and designs throughout the world.

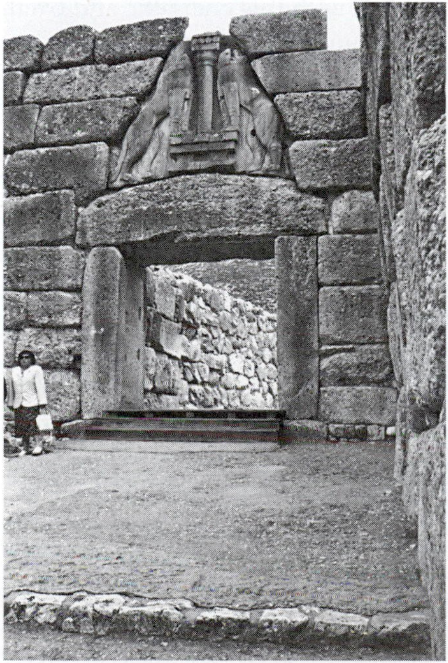

Figure 11.15 The Lions' Gate at the remains of Agamemnon's Palace on the Greek Peloponnesus is an example of Mycenean art.

Figure 11.16 The theater at Palmyra, Syria, was a lovely place for plays to be presented in this ancient trading center in the desert.

Art

Among the most famous art created by Greeks are the Elgin Marbles, which have inspired extensive and heated arguments regarding the benefits and appropriateness of allowing them to continue in their protected but expatriate address in the British Museum in London. The Caryatids (beautifully carved women's draped figures) that support the porch roof of the Erechtheum on the Acropolis are other statues cherished by the world (Figure 11.17).

Istanbul features not only mosques, but also palaces. The most famous, the Topkapi, is now a museum that provides a clear perspective on the court life of the Ottomans. Built by Mehmet the Conqueror from 1458 to 1465, the harem quarters, vast kitchen complex, and living quarters as well as administrative rooms indicate his total power. The Dolombache Palace presents a marked contrast, for it was not built until the mid-1800s when the Ottomans were influenced greatly by European, particularly French, love of the ornate. Ataturk, considered to be the founder of modern Turkey, lived in this palace, which now is a museum.

Music and art from this area are gradually becoming familiar in the western world; the intensity and compelling rhythms and haunting melodies capture the attention of listeners. Israel's klezmer music is probably the most familiar type of music from this region, although its origins may belong to Eastern Europe. Certainly, Israel is alive with this energetic and exciting music. Many famous concert soloists, such as Daniel Barenoim, Itzhak Perlman, and Pinchas Zukerman have claimed Israel as home. Love of music and the ability to pursue highly polished performances on their instruments are hallmarks of these special performing artists.

Figure 11.17 The Caryatids that support the roof of the Erectheum (built in 421–405 BCE) on the Acropolis show the grace and detail of Greek sculpture.

Alphabets

Another distinctive cultural separation within the Greek and eastern Mediterranean countries is the alphabet used. This is a factor that makes communication difficult. The Greeks still use Greek letters in their signs and some of their writing while many other countries in this region rely heavily on flowing Arabic script, and Jews in Israel use Hebrew. The dissimilarity in appearance and vocabulary makes it far more difficult to read even simple signs in this part of the world than in Europe, where the commonality of the letters and the similarities of many of the essential words in the different Romance languages facilitate at least superficial understanding.

Food Patterns

Many similarities exist in the food patterns of people in the various countries considered in this chapter. The overarching Mediterranean climate characterized by limited rainfall, high temperatures, and the generally rocky terrain results in an abundance of such foods as olives, eggplant, onions, other vegetables, legumes, wheat, lamb, and mutton (Figure 11.18). The ways in which these and other ingredients are used may vary a bit among countries, but commonalities label the food patterns throughout the region as Mediterranean.

Challah, the traditional bread served in celebration of Rosh Hashanah, represents the cycle of life and the beginning of the Jewish New Year. The dough may be shaped as ladders to help people reach great heights or hands to help people be inscribed in the book of life for the coming year. Before baking, seeds are sprinkled on top to symbolize fertility and plenty.

Pita—Pocket bread that is common throughout the Middle East.

Lavosh—Armenian cracker bread; basically a very thin version of pita without a pocket.

Perhaps the major cause of the differences is the particular religion(s) practiced in a country; Muslim and Jewish dietary laws play an important role (see Chapter 3), and this is especially evident in Israel because of the predominantly Jewish population. In the other countries except Greece, Muslim dietary laws are the foundation of the diet. Greece does have some followers of each of these religions, but the major religious group is Greek Orthodox, which allows more freedom in food preparation.

The typical dietary pattern is a light breakfast (Figure 11.19) fairly early in the morning (often just tea or coffee and a baked bread or other baked item), a rather hearty lunch (which seems to beg for a subsequent nap on hot afternoons), and a late supper. Snacking is an acceptable means of stretching the time between the day's three meals. Particularly in Greece, a very late dinner (Figure 11.20) with considerable revelry before retiring is the preferred schedule for those who have enough energy.

Pita, or pocket bread, is quite universal throughout the region, but the character of the bread may vary from fairly thick and hearty to quite thin and rather crisp. **Lavosh,** or Armenian cracker bread, is a very thin, crisp, breadlike variation

Figure 11.18 In Cappadocia, a Muslim woman is double-tasking by crocheting while tending her sheep (valuable both for meat and wool) outside her rocky home.

Figure 11.19 This street vendor in Athens offers her bread rings topped with sesame seeds as a breakfast treat to people hurrying to work.

Phyllo—Extremely thin dough that is formed into large sheets and serves as the main ingredient for desserts and some main dishes.

Baklava—Baked dessert made of multiple layers of phyllo brushed with butter, honey or rosewater (or both), and chopped nuts.

Spanakopite—Main dish consisting of many layers of phyllo, spinach, and various other ingredients according to taste.

Falafel—Dish made by creating a paste of soaked chickpeas and seasonings, shaping into balls or other forms, and frying in deep fat.

of pita that is sometimes available. These breads commonly are purchased from a local baker, or the homemade dough is carried to a special shop where it is baked for the customer. In Syria, it is not unusual to see freshly baked, unwrapped rounds of pita cooling on staircases or even on the hoods of parked cars. The basic ingredient of these breads is refined wheat flour.

Phyllo (also spelled *filo*) is a very thin pastry from this region. The thin sheets of dough usually are brushed with oil or melted butter and then stacked to the desired depth. Chopped nuts, sweetened rosewater, and honey are interspersed with the sheets of dough before baking to make the ubiquitous dessert called **baklava** (Figure 11.21). There are many different but quite similar versions of this popular dessert. In fact, some bakeries have as many as 10 or more variations, some of which resemble shredded wheat in appearance and others that are twisted or cut to add variety to the choices available.

Phyllo also is the basis of some appetizers or main dishes, such as **spanakopite,** a pastry that contains spinach.

Legumes are found in many Middle Eastern dishes. The chickpea, or garbanzo, is particularly popular. **Falafel** is a favorite dish made with chickpeas that are soaked and ground into a paste, seasoned, and then formed into balls or other shapes before being fried.

Figure 11.20 Dinner in Athens includes a wide array of dishes featuring lamb, legumes, phyllo dough (encasing the triangular spanakopite), eggplant, tomatoes, zucchini, and other vegetables; bread and wine accompany the feast.

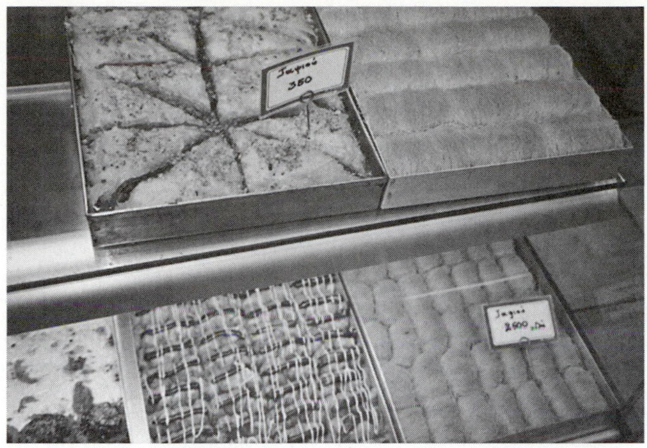

Figure 11.21 Baklava can be made in a variety of forms; this bakery is displaying the most common form at the upper left, but the other three forms displayed are also popular.

Hummus—Dip made with pureed, cooked chickpeas, tahini, lemon juice, garlic, and olive oil.

Tahini—Paste of finely ground sesame seeds, sesame oil, and lemon juice.

Foul (pronounced fool)—Mixture of cooked chickpeas and black or broad beans that have been soaked together for at least two days before being cooked; served with topping of garlic, olive oil, lemon, tomato, and cilantro.

Bulgur—Partially cooked and dried cracked wheat.

Kibbeh—Deep-fat fried, egg-shaped shell of finely minced lamb and cracked wheat paste encasing a filling of another meat.

Tabouli—Salad containing soaked bulgur, minced parsley and mint, diced tomatoes, olive oil, and lemon juice.

Dolmas—Stuffed grape leaves usually containing rice and often other ingredients; may be served hot or cold.

Shawarma—Thinly sliced chicken or lamb layered tightly with fat and formed into a solid that is grilled vertically on a rotisserie and sliced off in very thin, long slices while still on the skewer.

Kabob (kebab)—Meat grilled, sometimes with other items, on a skewer.

Moussaka—Eggplant casserole usually containing lamb, onions, tomato sauce, and eggplant slices.

Another use for garbanzos is **hummus,** a dip made by diluting a puree of cooked garbanzos with tahini, lemon juice, and garlic, and finally pouring a bit of olive oil on top before dipping bits of pita into it.

Tahini is a rather simple blend of ground sesame seeds, lemon juice, and sesame oil. It is a very common ingredient in Middle Eastern cuisine that can be made at home or purchased in finished form to save some time in preparing the array of foods that often is expected, particularly at the midday meal.

Black or broad beans often are soaked with chickpeas for several days before being cooked until tender. Then garlic, olive oil, lemon, tomato, and cilantro are added; the finished dish is called **foul.**

Cracked wheat may be used in such dishes as kibbeh and tabouli or even as the basis of pilaf. Partially cooked and dried cracked wheat is called **bulgur** (sometimes burghel). **Kibbeh** can be made by grinding lamb and finely ground cracked wheat together to make a thick paste that can be pressed into the shape of an egg shell, which then is stuffed with a filling, pressed closed, and deep-fat fried.

Tabouli (a salad) is quite a different dish, although it too is made with bulgur. The bulgur in tabouli is soaked with water and then combined with minced mint and parsley, diced tomatoes, olive oil, and lemon juice.

Whether they are called **dolmas** or dolmades, stuffed grape leaves are treasured as a dish throughout this region. Their origin is not certain; some attribute them to the Greeks, and others the Persians. Rice usually is at least part of the stuffing; it is often combined with lamb or other ground meat and various spices. Dolmas may be served either hot or cold, frequently with yogurt.

Shawarma, which is prepared by closely packing layers of chicken and fat into a solid that can be grilled vertically on a rotisserie, is available from street vendors in Greece and many other locations in the Middle East (Figure 11.22). Another popular way of preparing meat is the **kabob,** or **kebab** (marinated lamb or chicken and sometimes vegetables grilled on skewers). Turkey is thought to be the origin of this dish.

Eggplant, a very common vegetable in the region, has been elevated to prominence by the Greeks. They are credited with creating **moussaka,** a casserole featuring eggplant slices, ground or small pieces of lamb, onions, and tomato sauce. Many kinds of fruits and vegetables are important components of the diet throughout Greece and the Levant. This is evident in the markets throughout the region (Figure 11.23).

Figure 11.22 Shawarma, a tightly packed cylinder of marinated lamb or chicken and fat is grilled vertically before being sliced for a customer on Mykonos Island in Greece.

Olives also find their way onto the table, either as ingredients or as side dishes. They may be processed in various ways to alter their texture and flavor. Greek olives often are treated to develop a rather soft and somewhat wizened texture.

Feta—Soft cheese made from ewe's milk.

Lebneh—Soft cheese made by draining whey from yogurt.

Feta is a soft, crumbly cheese made from ewe's milk that is used frequently by the Greeks. Yogurt (fermented cow's milk) is another dairy food that may be eaten or used in cooking in the region. **Lebneh** is a soft cheese that is made by draining yogurt to reduce the whey content. After draining for about half a day or longer, the desired firmness can be achieved.

Tea is a ubiquitous beverage throughout the Middle East. Turkey is a convenient source of tea, which is grown near its coast along the Black Sea. Often the tea is flavored with mint leaves and sweetened with a generous amount of sugar. Traditionally, it is served in rather short glasses without handles, even though the beverage is extremely hot. A spoon in the glass helps to absorb part of the heat and prevent the glass from breaking when extremely hot tea is poured with a flourish into the glass.

Turkish coffee is quite unlike the brew in the United States. The beans intended for preparing Turkish coffee are roasted very dark and ground to an

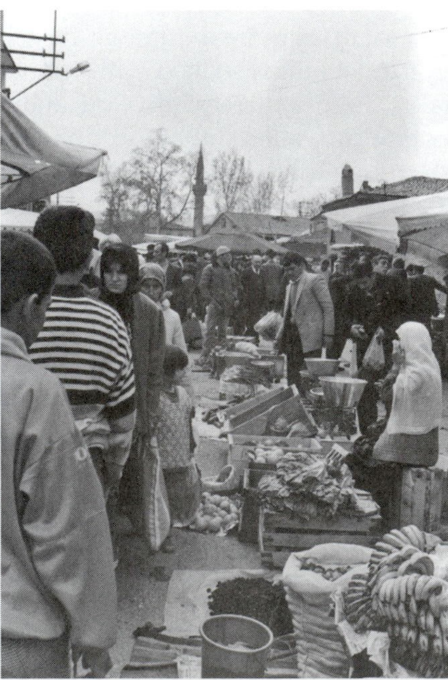

Figure 11.23 Shoppers throng this street market in Turkey to buy the produce and other ingredients needed for the daily meals.

Ibrik—Turkish coffee maker designed with a long handle and a narrow neck.

Raki—Distilled Turkish alcoholic beverage made from grape residue with anise for added flavor; turns milky if water is added.

Ouzo—Greece's distilled alcoholic drink from grape skins that are cooked with star anise and a variety of other herbs prior to distillation; turns milky if water is added.

Retsina—Greek rosé or white wine flavored with pine resin.

extremely fine, pulverized powder. Cold water and the desired amount of sugar are heated to boiling in a long-handled, narrow-necked coffee maker called an **ibrik,** which is removed from the heat long enough to pour in the pulverized coffee. This mixture is then heated again until the brewing beverage foams up toward the top of the ibrik, at which time it is removed from the heat to reduce the foaming. After reheating briefly once or twice, the foaming beverage is poured into demitasse cups. Ideally, a foamy layer tops each cup. The coffee grounds settle a bit in the cup, but they seem to make the beverage almost chewy. The coffee usually is sweet and often flavored with cardamom.

Although many people in the Middle East, particularly Muslims, do not drink alcoholic beverages, other people do. **Raki** is a particularly popular alcoholic beverage in Turkey. This unique beverage is distilled (not fermented) from grape residue and flavored with anise. If water is added to raki, it turns milky. A similar alcoholic beverage in Greece is **ouzo;** its flavor depends on the herbs included during the cooking period. **Retsina** is a rosé or white wine flavored with pine resin that is made only in Greece and is considered by many to be the perfect wine to drink with Greek food. Various other wines may be available, particularly in Greece.

Recipes

Avgolemono (Greek) (Serves 4–6)

3 c chicken broth
3 tbsp uncooked rice
2 eggs
2 tbsp lemon juice
Salt to taste

1. Simmer broth and rice for 15 minutes until al dente.
2. Beat eggs and lemon juice thoroughly, and then stir while adding ½ cup of the hot broth to the eggs.
3. Add egg mixture to broth and rice. Stir constantly while heating slowly until mixture coats spoon. Be sure not to boil it.
4. Salt to taste and serve immediately.

Baba Ghanouj (Makes 1½ cups)

1 lb eggplant
2 tbsp tahini
5 tbsp lemon juice
½ garlic clove, minced
1 tsp salt
¼ tsp black pepper
1 tbsp cold water

1. Prick eggplant skin in many places with a fork, and then broil it until skin blisters all over.
2. Cool, then peel, slice, and chop pulp.
3. Puree and mix in the rest of the ingredients.
4. Serve as dip for vegetables, lavosh, or flat bread.

Kibbe Naye (Serves 4–6)

1½ c fine bulgur
1 lb finely ground lamb
⅛ tsp allspice
⅛ tsp freshly grated nutmeg
⅛ tsp cayenne
1 tsp salt
Black pepper
Oil for deep-fat frying

1. Cover bulgur with water; soak 10 minutes.
2. Drain in sieve, squeezing out extra moisture with hands.
3. Combine bulgur, lamb, and seasonings, kneading until smooth.
4. Form into meatballs and deep-fat fry. Use a stuffing in the kibbe (meatballs), if desired.

Dolmades (Makes 30–40)

30–40 grape leaves in brine
2 qt water
2 onions, finely chopped
½ c olive oil
3 garlic cloves, minced
⅔ c cooked lentils
½ c uncooked long grain rice
½ bunch parsley, chopped
2 medium tomatoes, chopped
2 tsp dried mint
Dash ground cloves
Salt and pepper
Juice of 2 lemons

1. Rinse leaves well; soften in scalding water for 3 minutes.
2. Sauté onions gently in 3 tablespoons of olive oil in a skillet until translucent.
3. Remove from heat and stir in garlic, lentils, rice, parsley, tomato, mint, cloves, salt, pepper, and 3 tablespoons of olive oil.
4. Put a layer of grape leaves on the bottom of a saucepan containing 2 tablespoons of olive oil.
5. Using one leaf at a time, put a teaspoon of rice mixture in the center at the bottom of the leaf. Fold both sides over the filling, and roll from bottom to form a log.
6. Place log in prepared saucepan, seam side down.
7. Repeat with remainder of leaves and stuffing mixture.
8. Pour remaining olive oil, lemon juice, and enough water to cover the leaf logs by 1½ inches. Put a plate over the leaves to hold them in place.
9. Cover pot and simmer over low heat for 50 to 60 minutes until rice is done.
10. Serve either warm or cold. Yogurt is good on the side.

Moussaka (Serves 6–8)

2 lb eggplant
Salt
1 lb ground lamb or beef
2 onions, chopped
¼ tsp pepper
½ tsp oregano
¼ c red wine
1 c grated mozzarella cheese
½ c soft bread crumbs
1 lb canned plum tomatoes, drained and quartered
2 tbsp olive oil
3 tbsp flour
1½ c milk
Dash of nutmeg
1 egg, beaten
¼ c parmesan cheese

1. Pare eggplant and slice ½″ thick. Salt both sides and drain on paper towels, pressing to get water out.
2. Sauté the meat, adding onions in time to brown lightly.
3. Add pepper, oregano, and wine, and simmer to remove excess liquid.
4. Remove from heat; stir in cheese and ¼ cup crumbs.
5. Blot eggplant and sauté both sides in hot oil.
6. Scatter rest of crumbs over bottom of 9″ × 13″ greased baking pan; place alternating layers of eggplant, meat, and tomatoes, ending with eggplant.
7. Sprinkle remaining crumbs on top.
8. Stir flour into oil and then stir in milk; heat to boiling while stirring constantly.
9. Carefully blend in nutmeg and egg and pour over top of casserole; then sprinkle with parmesan cheese.
10. Bake at 350°F for 50 minutes.

Figure C.49 Nomads herd their sheep and goats on the plains in Iran.

Figure C.50 Alexander the Great burned the Persian city of Persepolis (in today's Iran) in 331 BCE, but intriguing ruins still can be seen.

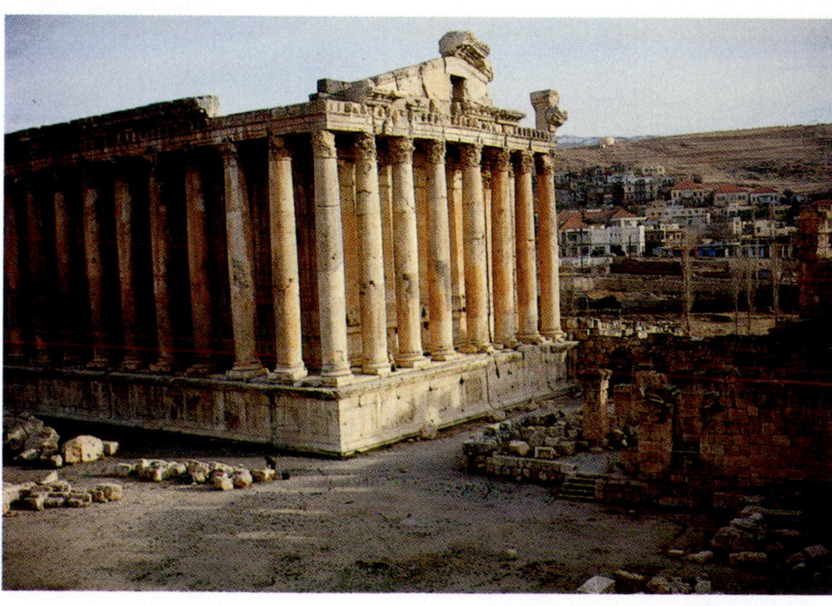

Figure C.51 The temple at Baalbek in Lebanon is an impressive reminder of the imposing architecture built by Romans in various parts of their extensive empire.

Figure C.52 The Dome of the Rock and the Al-Aksa Mosque on the Temple Mount are structures of great religious importance to Muslims in Jerusalem, Israel.

Figure C.53 The Western Wall (also called the *Wailing Wall*), the remaining part of Solomon's Temple in Jerusalem, is the holy place where Jews in Jerusalem go to pray.

Figure C.54 Arabs wear clothing consistent with their Muslim heritage.

Figure C.55 Dates thrive in the hot, dry climate of the Levant and are popular as an ingredient or a snack.

Figure C.56 Spices used extensively to season many Middle Eastern foods are displayed in basic fashion in this Levantine market.

Figure C.57 The Treasury is an ornate facade and room carved into the sandstone cliffs at Petra, Jordan, which was an important center on the trade route from Egypt to various destinations in the Middle East from around 300 BCE.

Figure C.58 The Knights of St. John, forced from Jerusalem during the Crusades, occupied and fortified the Island of Rhodes, staying from 1308–1530. The main gate still protects the City of Rhodes.

Figure C.59 The throne room in Knossos's palace on the island of Crete reveals some of the artistic decor of the Minoan frescoes.

Figure C.60 Dolphin frescoes decorated part of the palace of the Minoan King Knossos.

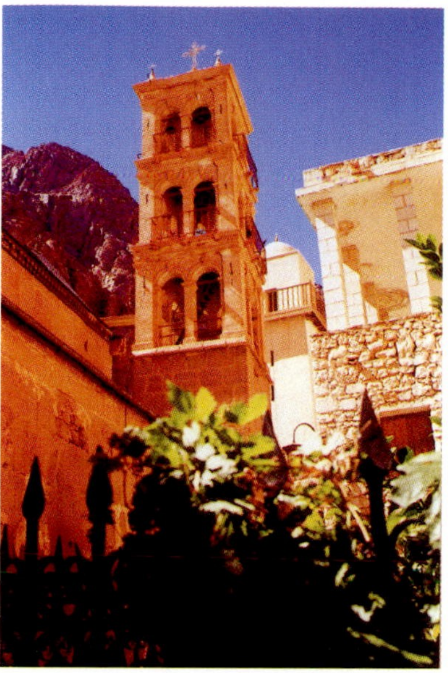

Figure C.61 St. Catherine's Monastery offers solitude in its isolated location at the base of Mt. Sinai in the Sinai Desert where Moses is said to have received the Ten Commandments. Although St. Catherine's is Eastern Orthodox, the grounds include a mosque (the white dome).

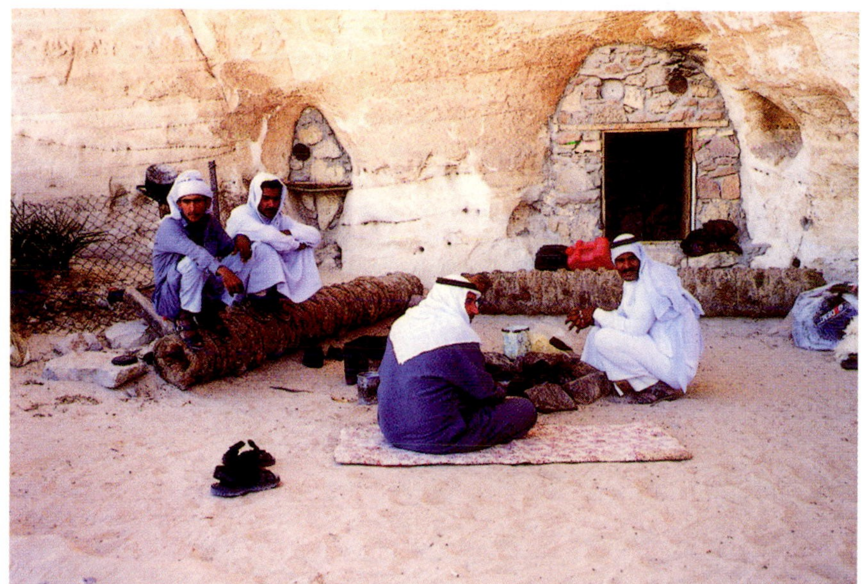

Figure C.62 Bedouins warm themselves around the fire in front of their home carved into a cliff in the Sinai Desert in western Egypt. (Photo courtesy of Ruth MacFarlane.)

Figure C.63 The pyramids of Giza outside Cairo, Egypt, were built more than 4,500 years ago yet remain as impressive reminders of Egypt's early rulers.

Figure C.64 The Sphinx was constructed near the pyramids at Giza around 2500 BCE, yet still looks out at its countless visitors today.

Figure C.65 Dovecotes in northern Egypt maintain a source of pigeons for various recipes favored in North Africa. (Photo courtesy of Ruth MacFarlane.)

Figure C.66 The Avenue of Sphinxes built by several pharaohs over many years beginning around 1300 BCE, leads into Karnak Temple, the major temple site near Luxor, Egypt.

Figure C.67 Goats are being herded near Luxor, Egypt; the hills of the Valley of Kings on the west bank of the Nile are in the background. (Photo courtesy of Ruth MacFarlane.)

Figure C.68 Interior of King Tut's tomb in the Valley of the Kings near Luxor, Egypt.

Figure C.69 Egyptian farmers work in irrigated fields near the Nile River on the west bank across from Luxor, Egypt.

Figure C.70 The Nile River at Aswan in southern Egypt still contains sufficient water below the huge dam for feluccas to sail and to sustain agriculture north toward the Mediterranean; the Aga Khan's mausoleum can be seen dimly at the top of the hills on the western side of the river.

Figure C.71 This Nubian village in southern Egypt relies on water from the Nile for irrigating farm crops and living.

Figure C.72 Shish kebabs are popular throughout North Africa as well as the Levant.

Figure C.73 In the 7th century BCE, Greeks built this Temple of Zeus at Cyrene near the Mediterranean coast in northwestern Libya near today's city of Benghazi, Libya.

Figure C.74 This triumphal arch honoring Emperor Marcus Aurelius, who ruled from 161–180 CE, is a reminder in contemporary Tripoli, Libya, of its history of Roman rule.

Figure C.75 Romans built cities on the northern shores of Libya during their reign; Sabratha declined after the Roman era, but its ruins overlooking the Mediterranean shore west of Tripoli are being restored.

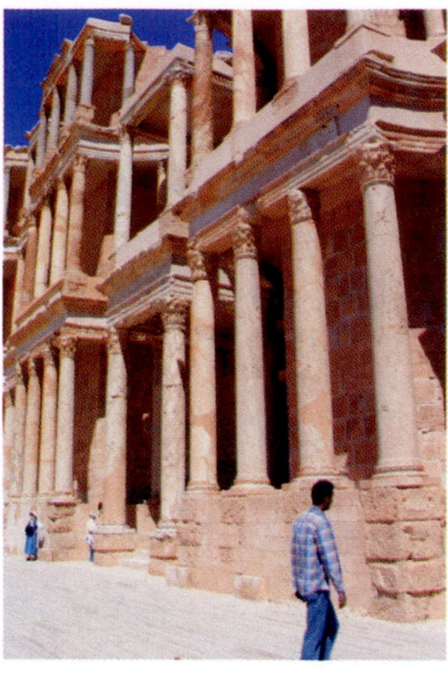

Figure C.76 The back facade of the remarkable Roman theater at Sabratha has been restored, revealing its former splendor.

Figure C.77 Mosaics that depicted various aspects of life during the Roman era (e.g., types of fish that swam in the Mediterranean waters off the shore of Sabratha) still can be seen today in the National Museum.

Figure C.78 This archway is the main entrance to Libya's largest Roman ruins, the city of Leptis Magna. (Photo courtesy of Susan Stenberg.)

Figure C.79 The theater at Leptis Magna overlooked the Mediterranean but had a more open design to the back facade than did the theater at Sabratha. (Photo courtesy of Sue Stenberg.)

Figure C.80 The stadium at Leptis Magna was the site of gladiatorial bouts in the Roman era and was the place where wild animals, captured south of the Sahara, were housed until they were shipped to the Colisseum in Rome.

Figure C.81 This mosaic of a fishing expedition displayed in the National Museum in Tripoli, Libya, displays the achievement of artists during the Roman period.

Figure C.82 Thick walls protected the old city of Sousse on the southwest coast of Tunisia against invaders from the sea many centuries ago.

Figure C.83 Colorful spices are available in large quantities in the markets of Sousse, Tunisia, to add excitement to the flavorful local cuisine.

Figure C.84 The newspaper gets a thorough reading while this entrepreneur waits for someone to buy his artichokes in the market at Sousse, Tunisia.

Figure C.85 Legumes and pumpkins are available at this stall in the market at Sousse, Tunisia.

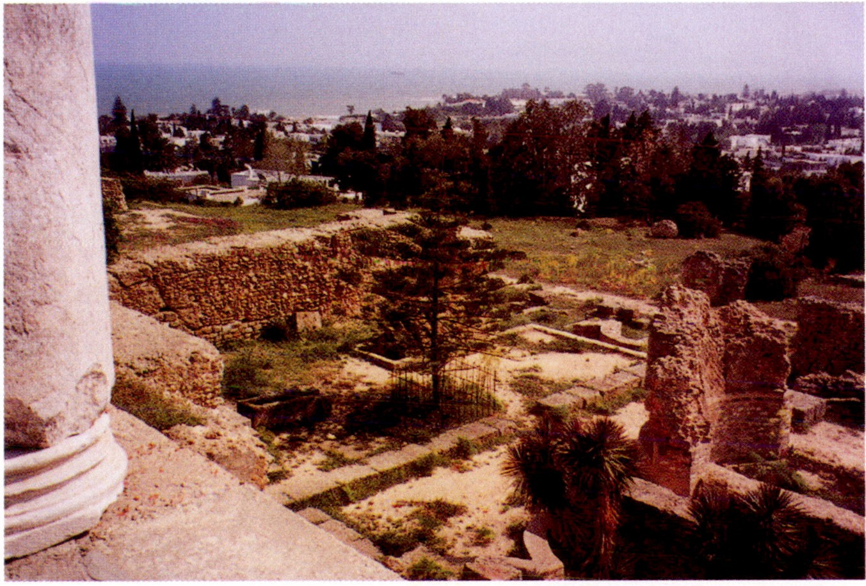

Figure C.86 Carthage was founded by Phoenicians in 814 BCE but conquered and colonized by Romans several centuries later; limited ruins remain from this early city, which is near the modern city of Tunis in Tunisia.

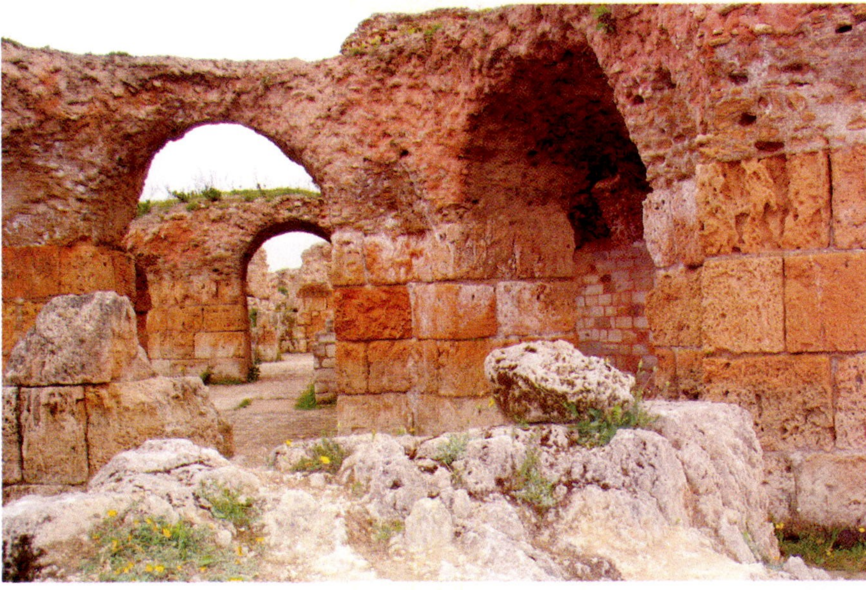

Figure C.87 The ruins of the Roman baths at Carthage provide a clear picture of the baths that the ancient Carthaginians enjoyed.

Figure C.88 Dried fruits are the specialty of this outdoor vendor in the casbah of Tunis, Tunisia.

Figure C.89 Honey-sweetened pastries provide temptation to all who wander past this vendor in Tunis, Tunisia.

Figure C.90 This Tunisian belly dancer performs to native music while balancing a jug on her head.

Figure C.91 Lamb and vegetables are the main course of this lunch in Tunis, Tunisia.

Figure C.92 Legumes and spices are displayed grandly in this shop in the souk at Tangier, Morocco.

Figure C.93 Vegetables are important ingredients in Moroccan recipes.

Figure C.94 Wearing the hat that gave Fez, Morocco, its name, this man and a heavily loaded donkey share one of the crowded streets in Fez's medina.

Figure C.95 These chickens clearly are fresh as they await a customer in the souk in Fez, Morocco.

Figure C.96 Bread dough is brought to this neighborhood baker in Morocco; each person gets the bread that is baked from the dough that he or she brought in.

Spanakopite (Greek Spinach-Cheese Pie) (Serves 6–8)

1 onion, chopped
¼ c chopped green onions
2 tbsp olive oil
1 8-oz pkg frozen chopped spinach, thawed and drained
2 tsp dry dill weed
¼ c parsley, finely chopped
¼ tsp salt
¼ tsp white pepper
2 tbsp milk
½ lb feta, finely crumbled
4 eggs, beaten
16 sheets (½ lb) phyllo
¼ lb butter, melted

1. Sauté onions in oil; add spinach, cover, and cook for 5 minutes.
2. Add dill, parsley, salt, and pepper; heat while stirring to evaporate liquid.
3. Stir in milk and cool.
4. Add cheese and eggs, beating to combine.
5. Cover 9″ × 13″ × 2″ baking pan with 8 sheets of phyllo; brush each sheet with melted butter.
6. Spread spinach mixture over sheets, cover with 8 more sheets of phyllo, and then brush with butter.
7. Bake at 300°F for 1 hour until crisp and lightly browned.
8. Cut into squares and serve warm or at room temperature.

Hummus bi Tahini (Chickpea and Garlic Dip) (Makes 2¼ cups)

2 c canned chickpeas
3 garlic cloves, minced
¼ c tahini
5 tbsp lemon juice
½ tsp salt
2 tbsp water (or enough for dip consistency)

1. Drain chickpeas; add garlic and mash to a paste.
2. Beat in remaining ingredients.

Tabouli (Serves 4–6)

¾ c bulgur
2 c cold water
2 bunches parsley, minus stems and finely chopped
½ bunch fresh mint leaves, finely chopped
4 tomatoes, diced
1 bunch green onions and tops, chopped
½ c lemon juice
2 tbsp olive oil
Salt and pepper

1. Soak bulgur for 15 minutes in water; drain and squeeze out the water. Discard water.
2. Combine drained cracked wheat and vegetables.
3. Add lemon juice and oil, and then toss the salad. Salt and pepper to taste.
4. Store overnight in refrigerator to allow flavors to blend if time permits. Stir to serve.

Turkish Delight (Makes 12 pieces)

¼ c cold water
2 tbsp unflavored gelatin
½ c rosewater
2 c sugar
½ c orange juice
¼ c lemon juice
Powdered sugar

1. Soften gelatin in cold water.
2. Boil rosewater and sugar to 255°F.
3. Stir in gelatin until dissolved; add orange and lemon juices and stir.
4. Pour into a buttered square pan and cool until firm.
5. Cut in squares and roll each square in powdered sugar.

Honey Cake (For Rosh Hashanah) (Serves 8–10)

½ c chopped dried apricots
¼ c rum
2 eggs
1 c honey
⅓ c oil
Zest and juice of 1 orange and 1 lemon
⅓ c sugar
½ tsp salt
⅓ c apricot jam
1¾ c all-purpose flour
¼ c cake flour
½ tsp baking soda
½ c slivered almonds

1. Soak apricots in rum.
2. Combine eggs, honey, oil, citrus, sugar, salt, and jam in a bowl.
3. Add flours and soda, and stir.
4. Stir in rum drained from apricots, and then fold in apricots and almonds.
5. Bake in two greased 5″ × 9″ loaf pans at 350°F for 40 minutes or until toothpick inserted in center comes out clean.

Potato Latkes (For Hanukkah) (Serves 4–6)

3 large potatoes, pared and cubed
2 tbsp nondairy margarine, melted
1 tsp kosher salt
2 tsp sugar
Oil

1. Cover potatoes with water and boil in covered saucepan for about 15 minutes until tender.
2. Rice or sieve to make 3 cups riced potatoes.
3. Add margarine, salt, and sugar.
4. Mix well and cool.
5. Make eight balls from mixture.
6. Heat waffle iron and brush with oil.
7. Place one ball in middle of iron and close lid. Bake 4 to 5 minutes.
8. Repeat to bake others.

Hamantaschen (For Purim) (Makes 5 dozen)

½ c butter
½ c sugar
3 eggs
1 tsp orange zest
2 c flour
1½ tsp baking powder
1 tbsp poppy seeds
3 cans (8 oz) poppy seed filling

1. Cream butter and sugar.
2. Beat in 2 eggs and orange zest.
3. Carefully but thoroughly stir in flour, baking powder, and poppy seeds.
4. Divide dough in quarters on floured board and roll each quarter ½″ thick.
5. Cut into 2½″ circles and put 1 tsp poppy seed filling in center of each. Fold edges toward middle to make a triangle with a bit of filling showing.
6. Pinch seams to seal and brush with last egg.
7. Bake on foil-lined sheet for 10 minutes at 375°F.

Matzo Farfel Kugel (For Passover) (Serves 6–9)

Oil
¼ c finely chopped nuts
4 matzo farfel
Boiling water
Salt and pepper
4 eggs, separated
½ c unsalted margarine, in pieces
½ c golden raisins
½ c diced apples
1 tsp cinnamon
2 tsp sugar

1. Brush 8″ × 8″ baking pan with oil and scatter nuts in it.
2. Soften farfel in colander by pouring boiling water over it.
3. Combine softened farfel, salt, pepper, egg yolks, margarine, raisins, and apples.
4. Beat egg whites until peaks just bend over and immediately fold into farfel mixture.
5. Transfer to prepared pan and sprinkle with mixture of cinnamon and sugar.
6. Bake at 350°F for about 45 minutes until golden brown.

NOTE: Matzo is unleavened bread made from flour and water that is baked at a high temperature. Matzo can be crushed finely to make matzo meal. When matzo is broken coarsely, it is *matzo farfel*.

Summary

Greece, western Turkey, Lebanon, and Israel near the coast have a climate moderated by the Mediterranean Sea, but the remainder of the Levant inland, and east as far as Iraq and Iran have very hot summers except in the mountainous regions. The rugged terrain and limited rainfall of the whole area make agriculture difficult except where irrigation water is available. Wheat, olives, grapes (in some areas), eggplants, onions, and other vegetables are produced in this region with irrigation. Sheep adapt well to this type of landscape, and some pigs, cattle, and fowl are raised. Fishing generally is somewhat limited as a source of food in most of the area.

Despite the difficulties, trade routes have extended across these several lands since long before the time of Christ. This region also was in the direct path of armies attacking from various directions over the centuries. The region that is now Greece was invaded by the Persians and later the Romans, followed by Goths, Franks, Venetians, Crusaders, and the Ottomans.

Turkey also experienced various conquests, which resulted in changes in religions from largely Christian (Eastern Orthodox) to predominantly Muslim, with others living there, too. The Seljuks (who were Muslims) captured Byzantium, which caused Pope Urban II to call for a Crusade (the first) to liberate the region from what he viewed to be infidels. Subsequently, three other Crusades passed through western Turkey.

Then came the Mongols; the Ottomans finally seized power to create the strong Ottoman Empire. The Ottomans ruled for centuries, finally being replaced at the end of World War I. Then Ataturk was able to develop the modern state of Turkey.

Palestine and Jerusalem in particular have been and still are wracked by many religious disagreements because Christianity, Judaism, and Islam all have sites of great significance in Jerusalem and the surrounding area. These places today include the Dome of the Rock, the Wailing Wall, and the Church of the Holy Sepulchre. Historical arguments over the region have involved Romans and later the Crusaders. Even today, negotiations are continuing to attempt to resolve territorial issues.

Religious problems are not a great concern in Greece; much of the population is Greek Orthodox. Turkey has many Sunni Muslims, but other religions are free to worship there, too.

Architectural structures, some standing and some in ruins, are prominent in this region of the world. Examples are the Parthenon and other structures on the Acropolis in Athens; Hagia Sophia and the Blue Mosque in Istanbul; the Treasury in Petra, Jordan; and such palaces as the ruins at Persepolis in Iran and the Topkapi Palace and the Dolmabache Palace in Istanbul.

Food patterns throughout this region have some strong similarities. The most common ingredients are wheat, lamb and mutton, eggplant, olives, various vegetables, and legumes. Muslim avoidance of pork and alcohol and the Jewish dietary laws influence food practices in families adhering firmly to these dictates. Phyllo is the key ingredient in several desserts and main dishes. Pita is the most common type of bread, although lavosh and Arab flat bread also are very popular.

Several different legumes are used, but the most common is the chickpea. Tahini is a ubiquitous paste made with sesame seeds and their oil and lemon juice added. Bulgur is used in a variety of dishes, including tabouli. Other common foods are dolmas (or dolmades), kebabs, shawarma, feta, and lebneh; beverages include tea, Turkish coffee, raki, ouzo, and retsina.

Selected Sites

http://www.cannylink.com/historyottoman.htm—Extensive information about the Ottoman Empire.

http://www.pbs.org/empires/islam/profilessuleyman.html—Profiles of various Ottoman rulers.

www.tripoli-lebanon.com/lebanesefood.html—Descriptions of some Lebanese dishes.

www.turizm.net/turkey/tips/storyfood.html—Description of food in various regions of Turkey.

http://www.farhangsara.com/iranian_food_culture.htm—Description of food patterns in Iran.

http://www.syrialive.net/food/food.htm—Some typical recipes of Syria.

http://nabataea.net/tplaza.html—Pictures and description of the facade of the Treasury in Petra, Jordan.

http://mosaic.lk.net/g-masada.html—Pictures and information about Masada near the Dead Sea in Israel.

http://oi.uchicago.edu/OI/MUS/PA/IRAN/PAAI/PAAI.html—Photos and information about Persepolis and its history.

http://www.turizm.net/turkey/tips/storyfood.html—Information about Turkish food.

http://www.ineedcoffee.com/04/turkishcoffee/—Directions for brewing Turkish coffee in an ibrik.

Study Questions

1. Identify the countries that border (a) Turkey, (b) Israel, and (c) Syria.
2. What food crops are grown in Greece and countries in the Levant?
3. How did the Crusades influence food choices in the Middle East?
4. Describe at least one dish in which the following ingredient is significant: (a) phyllo, (b) bulgur, (c) eggplant, and (d) sesame seed or sesame oil, or both.

5. Identify similarities and differences between Muslim and Jewish dietary rules.
6. Plan a menu for a Greek dinner.

Bibliography

Algar, A. and Algar, A.E. 1999. *Classical Turkish Cooking: Traditional Turkish Food for the American Kitchen.* Harper Collins. New York.

Barer-Stein, T. 1999. *You Eat What You Are.* 2nd ed. Firefly Books, Ltd. Ontario, Canada.

Batmanglij, 1992. *New Food of Life: Ancient Persian and Modern Iranian Cooking and Ceremonies.* 3rd ed. Mage Publishers. Washington, D.C.

Browning, I. 1997. *Petra.* Chatto and Windus. London, England.

Bsisu, M. 2005. *Arab Table: Recipes and Traditions.* Harper Collins. New York.

DuBois, J. 1993. *Israel.* Marshall Cavendish. New York.

Facaros, D., M. Davidson, and B. Walsh. 1993. *Greek Islands.* Cadogan Books. London, England.

Forst, B. 1993. *Laws of Kashruth.* Mesorah Publications. Brooklyn, NY.

Hassig, S.M. 1993. *Iraq.* Marshall Cavendish. New York.

Humphreys, A., P. Hellander, and N. Tilbury. 1999. *Israel and the Palestinian Territories.* 2nd ed. Lonely Planet. Oakland. CA.

Kramer, M. 1988. *Illustrated Guide to Foreign and Fancy Food.* 2nd ed. Plycon Press. Redondo Beach, CA.

Lorentzen, C.R. and P.C. Pihos, eds. 2000. *Let's Go Greece.* Let's Go Press. Cambridge, MA.

McKay, J.P., B.D. Hill, and J. Buckler. 1999. *History of Western Society.* Houghton Mifflin. Boston.

Mesulam, S. and E.S. Daniel. 2001. *Let's Go Turkey.* Let's Go Press. Cambridge, MA.

Packard, D.P. and M. McWilliams. 1993. Cultural foods heritage of Middle Eastern immigrants. Nutr. Today 28(3).

Pearcy, G.E. 1980. *The World Food Scene.* Plycon Press. Redondo Beach, CA.

Roden, C. 1996. *Book of Jewish Food: Odyssey from Sarmarkand to New York.* Knopf. New York.

Shahbazi, A.S. 1976. *Persepolis Illustrated.* 25th Shahrivar Printing House. Tehran.

Sheeban, S. 1993. *Turkey.* Marshall Cavendish. New York.

Simopoulos AP. 1995. The Mediterranean food guide. Nutrition Today 30 (2): 54–61.

Stewart, D. 1965. *Turkey.* Time, Inc. New York.

Uvezian, S. 1999. *Recipes and Remembrances from an Eastern Mediterranean Kitchen.* University of Texas Press. Austin, TX

Valent, D. et al. 2000. *World Food: Turkey.* Lonely Planet. Oakland, CA.

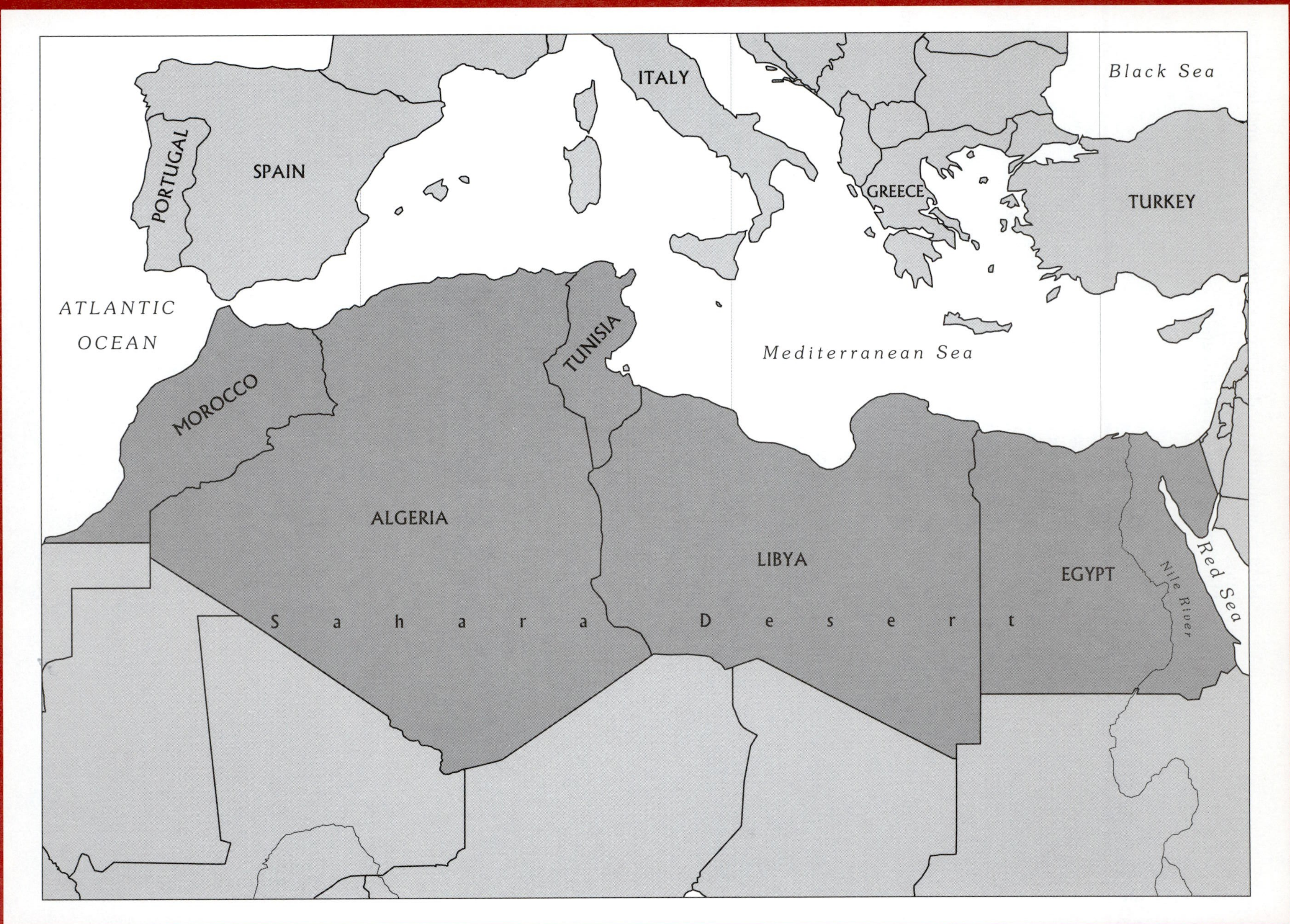
Black Sea
ITALY
PORTUGAL
SPAIN
GREECE
TURKEY
ATLANTIC OCEAN
TUNISIA
Mediterranean Sea
MOROCCO
ALGERIA
LIBYA
EGYPT
Nile River
Red Sea
Sahara Desert

12 North Africa

Geographic Overview

Maghreb—Countries in the northwestern part of Africa: Morocco, Algeria, and Tunisia.

Five countries extend across North Africa from the Sinai Peninsula east of the Suez Canal to the western shoreline of Morocco overlooking the Atlantic Ocean. They share the Mediterranean Sea's southern waters. Egypt occupies much of northeastern Africa and includes the Sinai (Figures 12.1, C.61 and C.62, p. C21)) to the east of the Suez Canal (Figure 12.2). Just to the west of Egypt is Libya, a large country with a long Mediterranean coastline. The next countries westward (Tunisia, Algeria, and Morocco) compose the **Maghreb.**

Tunisia is a small country that is sandwiched between Libya and neighboring Algeria; it has considerable shoreline as a result of the continental protrusion into the Mediterranean. Algeria is the largest country in this group. Morocco is a bit larger than Tunisia but has four mountain ranges: the Rif in the north, and the Middle Atlas, High Atlas, and Anti-Atlas mountains. The High Atlas Mountains are so high that they may have some snow in a few spots throughout the year, which is surprising in view of the intense heat of the Sahara Desert that is such a dominant feature of these countries. Mountains extend into Algeria and Tunisia, although they are considerably lower than the High Atlas of Morocco.

Immediately along the shores of the Mediterranean Sea, all of these countries derive a bit of a respite from the heat and have some arable land that is of significance in feeding their people. However, temperatures soar in large regions of these lands, particularly in summer (Figure 12.3) but are generally comfortable during the winter. The very dry conditions promote chilly nights.

Adequate water is the universal problem throughout North Africa. The only river of any significance is the Nile River in Egypt. It has long provided Egyptians with some farmland. In years past, its annual flood deposited silt to enrich fields along its course from the south of Egypt to its delta leading into the

Figure 12.1 The Sinai Peninsula to the east of the Suez Canal is a harsh land of desert and rugged mountains that isolate St. Catherine's Monastery from the world.

Mediterranean (Figures C.69, C.70, and C.71, pp. C23 and C24). The construction of the Aswan Dam in southern Egypt was completed in 1971, a feat that eliminated the annual floods and altered the environment.

Considerable controversy regarding the advantages and detrimental effects of the Aswan Dam continue to rage and may never be settled. The steadier supply of water along the Nile enables farmers to raise as many as three crops per year rather than the single crop that was possible before construction of the dam. However, the Nile Valley is very narrow (from about 2 to 14 miles wide) and provides a comparatively small amount of land for feeding the ever-increasing population of Egypt.

Agriculture

Some farmers along the arid northern coastlands of Africa maintain dovecotes that provide stylish homes for the birds and ultimately tasty fowl for family dinner tables (Figure C.65, p. C22). Bastila, a favorite specialty of Morocco, features pigeon as the main ingredient.

Agriculture in all of these North African countries is severely limited by lack of rainfall and the vast expanses of the Sahara Desert, where only a few oases afford a bit of water for the nomads of the region. Sheep, goats (Figure C.67, p. C23), and camels can be raised in some parts of this forbidding landscape, but only a small amount of beef is produced. Pigeons sometimes are housed in dovecotes along the northern coast and serve as another source of meat for the family (Figure C.65, p. C22).

Cereal crops raised in Egypt and the other countries of this region include wheat, millet, and some corn and rice as well as broad beans and vegetables (Figure C.69, p. C23). Some fruits add to the local foods. These crops are produced in the northern regions of these countries and in some of the valleys in the

Figure 12.2 The Suez Canal splits northeastern Egypt, making a path for ships from the Mediterranean to the Red Sea.

Figure 12.3 Moroccan water vendors in their unique costumes carry a tank of water on their backs and pour water into cups hanging around their necks; they wait for customers to drink the water before reclaiming the cup and selling a cupful to the next customer.

mountains of Morocco. Because of these limitations on agriculture in this region of the world, a variety of foods in the diet depends on imports.

History and Culture

Egypt

History The history of Egypt, accentuated with its dramatic remnants of the glorious structures dating from 5,000 years ago, has captured the world's interest perhaps beyond that of any other part of the world. Rulers in the Fourth Dynasty built the pyramids and the sphinx at Giza between 2650 and 2500 BCE (Figures C.63 and C.64, pp. C21 and C22). Thirty-one dynasties ruled Egypt before Alexander the Great conquered it in 332 BCE.

Then a general of Alexander, Ptolemy I Soter, assumed the role of king and established the Ptolemaic Dynasty. The Ptolemy rulers were in power until 30 BCE, when Cleopatra (the last of them) and Mark Antony committed suicide as Octavian captured Alexandria. Egypt then came under Roman rule, but its governance was shifted to Constantinople when the Roman Empire was divided. At that time, the official religion was Christianity.

However, Arabs brought the Muslim religion to Egypt when they invaded in 640 CE. Saladin established his dynasty in Egypt and then proceeded to capture Jerusalem in 1187. The Mameluke sultans ruled Egypt for 300 years before it became part of the Ottoman Empire in 1517.

The French occupied Egypt for a mere three years at the end of the 18th century, just long enough for some of Napoleon's soldiers to be accused of shooting off part of the nose of the sphinx (Figure 12.4). The British also occupied the country for half a century (1882 to 1936), and they returned to help drive out the Germans and Italians during World War II. Since then, Egypt has been ruled by its own leaders.

Culture The cultural heritage of Egypt is great. The engineering feat of building the pyramids is considered a wonder even today. The architectural features of the

Figure 12.4 The pyramids and sphinx were the hallmarks of early Egyptian civilization, but Napoleon's soldiers were rumored to have shot off part of the nose of the sphinx.

temples from ancient Egypt and the style that characterized the art of the early Egyptians are admired and sometimes serve as the stimulus for architecture and design today. The golden funeral mask of King Tutankhamen and many of the items found in his tomb have been exhibited in cities around the world, attracting huge crowds wherever they are shown.

The temples at Karnak, Luxor, and Abu Simbel are perhaps the best known of the many places of worship built by the ancient Egyptians (Figures 12.5 and C.66, p. C22). Countless artifacts found during many archaeological expeditions in Egypt are on display in museums in Cairo and other countries (Figure C.68, p. C23). In Istanbul, an obelisk from Egypt stands near the Blue Mosque and another stands in Paris in the Place de la Concorde. Architect I.M. Pei added a pyramid-shaped glass entrance to the Louvre as part of his renovation of this noted museum.

The sturdy buildings of the pharaohs, the highly decorated tombs and temples they built, and the hieroglyphics (translated by such scholars as Champollon when the Rosetta Stone was found and studied) are still viewed as objects of wonder by people today. The amazing thing is that these achievements date back more than two millennia before Christ! Such antiquity of culture not only is a matter of pride for today's Egyptians, but also is embraced by people throughout the world.

Religion occupies a prominent position in the lives of many Egyptians, with Islam being the religion of about 90 percent of the people. A small population of Jewish people is found in urban areas. Most of the remaining people are Christians, many of them Coptics. However, the dominance of the Muslim faith is evident in the myriad of mosques (Figure 12.6), the calls to prayer throughout the

Figure 12.5 Hieroglyphs were carved into the stones of Karnak and other Egyptian structures to add decoration and serve as a means of communication.

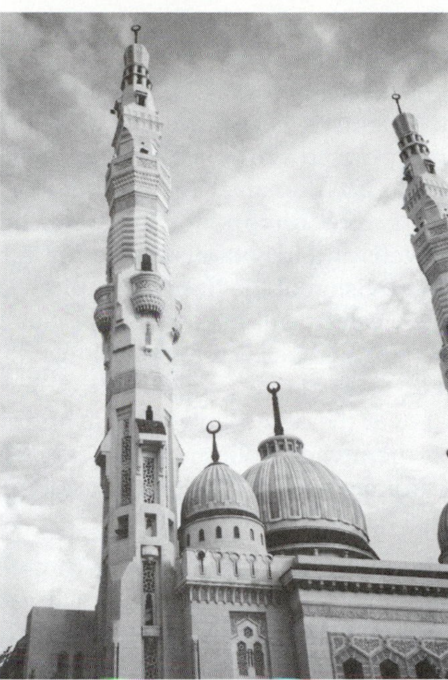

Figure 12.6 This mosque in Port Said, Egypt, is a new and important structure with two minarets from which calls to prayer are broadcast to the faithful five times each day.

day, the holidays that are celebrated, and even is represented in scenes painted on the homes of some people who have completed the Hajj (Figure 12.7).

The Coptic Christians were formed at the time that the Byzantine Empire was being overthrown, and this small group in Egypt remained rather isolated from other forms of Christianity. Monasteries along the Nile in northern Egypt provide places of retreat and meditation for Coptics, and there is a Greek Orthodox monastery (St. Catherine's) in the Sinai desert in eastern Egypt, dramatically positioned below Mt. Sinai, the mountain where Moses is reported to have received the Ten Commandments.

Libya and the Maghreb

Roman Domination For much of the period of the early civilizations around the Mediterranean Sea, all of the northern coast of Africa except Egypt was viewed as being one region, Libya. No divisions were noted for the countries (now the countries of Tunisia, Algeria, and Morocco) collectively known as the *Maghreb.* The region was known to the seafaring Phoenicians, who used the tip of the semipeninsula in the middle of the northern shore of Africa as a port for their

Figure 12.7 Some people celebrate their completion of the Hajj by painting scenes from their trip on their homes and businesses, as can be seen in this area on the west bank of the Nile near Luxor, Egypt. (Courtesy of Ruth MacFarlane.)

trading ventures. This port was Carthage, and a bit of its ruins can be seen near Tunis today (Figure C.86, p. C29).

Carthage was the point in Africa that was closest to Rome, which was of significance to the Romans as they were establishing their ever-widening domain in the millennium prior to Christ. Following their conquest of Carthage in 146 BCE (Figure C.87. p. C29), Romans began to develop the northern part of the present country of Libya as an important source of wheat and other grains, establishing the necessary wells and irrigation needed for agriculture.

When the division of the Roman Empire was made in 395, this area of Africa was part of the western empire, and Egypt was in the eastern domain. Christians and Jews lived in this western region along the coast. Inland in the desert and mountain areas were native peoples called **Berbers.** These fierce fighters maintained control over the desert and its caravan routes, ruled in the mountains, and even defeated the invading German Vandals when they ousted the Romans and took over the Roman forts and settlements along the coast in the north.

Berbers—Early inhabitants of much of Libya and the Maghreb; noted as fierce fighters.

Arabs and Islam Arab invasions began in the middle of the 7th century, bringing Islam with them. However, not all Muslims believed in belonging to a single sect, and division and fighting set the tone for the ensuing centuries in the Maghreb region (Tunisia, Algeria, and Morocco). **Shiite** Muslims (followers of the descendants of Ali, the prophet's son-in-law) from what is now northern Algeria sought to conquer Egypt to widen their religious base. The result was that they founded Cairo in 972. However, their homeland in Algeria reverted to **Sunni** (based on descendants of the fifth caliph) beliefs.

Shiite—Branch of Islam practiced by those who follow Ali, the prophet's son-in-law.

Sunni—Branch of Islam practiced by those who follow the descendants of the fifth caliph.

Then Arabs (Shiites) from the southern part of Egypt invaded the Maghreb in large numbers, ultimately remaining as settlers throughout the region and replacing the Berbers as the majority and converting them to Islam. Religion assumed considerably more importance in the region when a Berber chieftain (Abdullah ibn Tashfin) founded the Almoravid dynasty following his Hajj to Mecca. He expanded his control to include Morocco and Algeria; Marrakesh became the capital of Morocco in 1069.

The **Moors** crossed the Strait of Gibraltar to conquer much of the Christian lands (Spain and Portugal) by the end of the 11th century. Eventually, the Christians in Spain and political pressures from the east of the Maghreb resulted in the downfall of the Berber's Almoravid regime.

Moors—Inhabitants of northwestern Africa (mixture of Arabs and Berbers) who invaded Spain in the 8th century.

Pirates and Turks Morocco was under the control of successive regimes until the middle of the 19th century. The remainder of the Maghreb was the domain of Barbarossa, a Turkish pirate who raided ships plying the Mediterranean off the Barbary Coast of Algeria and Tunisia. He and his brother formed an alliance with the Turks, who supplied 6,000 troops and the assistance needed to overthrow the Spaniards in Algiers in 1529 and to regain control of Tunis a few years later.

Although Spain again took Tunis, by 1574 the Ottoman Turks and the Barbary pirates were in control of Algeria, Tunisia, Libya, and the Mediterranean in that region. Ottoman control lasted until the end of the 18th century in Algeria and Tunisia, and until the 20th century in Libya. Throughout the centuries however, the desert nomads, dubbed the *Bedouins,* pursued their wanderings relatively free of political shifts.

European Presence Control of Algeria was wrested by the French in 1830; Algeria became a French protectorate at that time and remained so until independence from France was finally accomplished by a six-year war that ended in 1962. The French held Morocco from 1881 to 1956 and Tunisia from 1912 to 1956 as protectorates.

Italy invaded Libya in 1911 when the Italians and Turks went to war. The Italian control of Libya was a period of intense cruelty by the Italians against the Arabs. Finally, Libya became an independent nation in 1951 following the end of World War II, parts of which were fought across the Libyan terrain. Subsequently, the regime of Muammar Qaddafi has resulted in serious problems of terrorism that isolated Libya from other nations for many years until he changed his policies in 2004.

Cultural Heritage

Pre-Islamic Art and Architecture The early art of Egypt and some paintings found on rocks in the desert in Tunisia and Libya provide evidence of the creative efforts of early pre-Islamic inhabitants. Romans added their artistic achievements when they controlled the North African coast. Among the architectural heritage the Romans left in North Africa are the ruins in Libya at Sabratha (Figures 12.8 and C.75–C.77, pp. C25 and C26) and Leptis Magna (Figures 12.9, 10, and C.78–C.81, pp. C26 and C27) and in Morocco at Volubilis (Figure 12.11), They created wonderful mosaics (Figures 12.12 and C.81, p. C27) and some sculptures that remain today, attesting to the artistry of their craftsmen.

Islamic Art The teachings of Islam have influenced the cultural heritage of this region, and they continue to dominate the lives of the people throughout North Africa today. Art generally is restricted to calligraphy, which utilizes the very beautiful script of Arabic writing (Figure 12.13). Intricate geometric patterns and designs are carefully inlaid on furniture, boxes, and other decorative objects, but no natural forms or pictures are used.

Exotic simplicity describes much of the architecture of North Africa. Mosques reflect the importance of tradition in their design. Towering minarets are prominent features of villages and cities throughout this part of the world. They provide architects opportunities for creative expression consonant with Islamic tradition.

A high wall with gates controlling entrance to the courtyard usually surrounds the courtyard, mosque, and minaret. The large, enclosed courtyard features a fountain or special place for washing before praying. The courtyard walls may be decorated with some artistic Arabic lettering of passages from the Koran. The mosque comprises a large room where men worship and discrete areas where women pray separately. A large chandelier with several concentric circles of lights dimly illuminates this room. Carefully crafted rugs, sometimes handwoven with geometric designs, cover the entire floor inside the mosque.

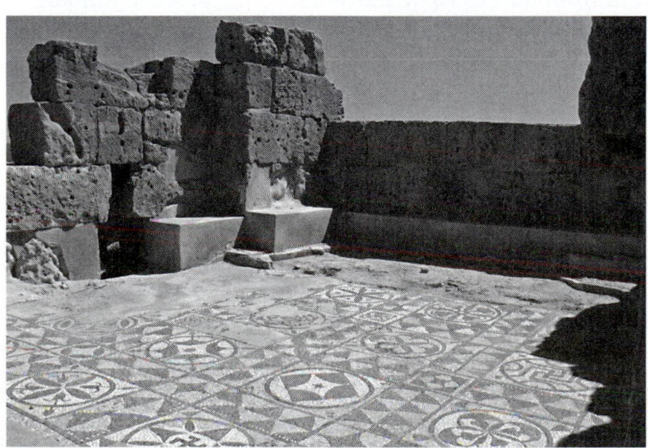

Figure 12.8 The mosaics can still be seen on the floor of this room in Sabratha, Libya.

Figure 12.9 An archway leads out of the ruins of the Roman walled city of Leptis Magna in Libya. (Photo courtesy of Susan Stenberg.)

Figure 12.10 Ruins of the marketplace are the site where residents shopped in Leptis Magna, Libya. (Photo courtesy of Susan Stenberg.)

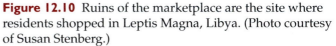

Figure 12.11 Romans built the city of Volubilis in Morocco inland from the sea early in the 1st century; some Roman mosaics can be seen there.

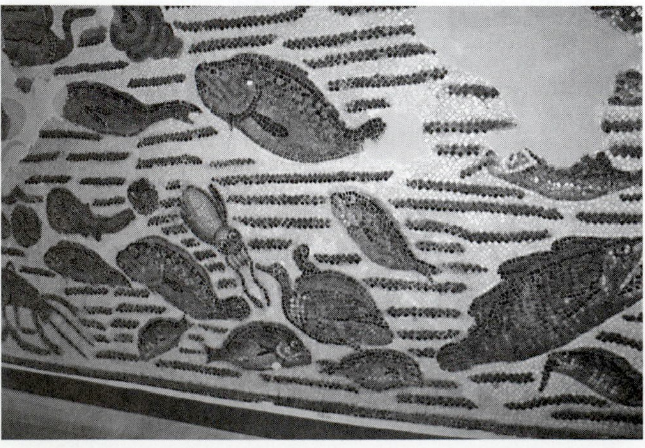

Figure 12.12 Ducks and several sea creatures (including a lobster, squid, and fish of various sizes and types) can be identified in this Roman mosaic in the Bardo Museum in Tunis, Tunisia.

Figure 12.13 The exterior of the Bardo Museum in Tunis, Tunisia, exemplifies the delicacy of Moorish design, with slim columns, archways, calligraphy (at the entrance), and wrought iron in a simple, flowing design covering the window.

Casbah—Old, walled part of Arab city in North Africa.

Medina—Old, walled, Arab quarter of a North African city.

Souk—Arab marketplace featuring specific types of shops that sell items such as spices and gold.

Safsari—Robes worn by women in North Africa to cover their bodies, including a headpiece with a veil to cover their faces except the eyes.

Daily Life Doorways and courtyards afford the aesthetic highlights of many public buildings and homes. Privacy and a certain quality of mysticism are achieved by the use of limited, high windows blended with the decorative arches that beckon visitors to enter. Interiors feature seating on huge cushions, low tables for dining, and kilims, or carefully knotted and handcrafted carpets, to adorn the floors and walls.

The **casbah** (also called **medina**) is the old, walled part of North African cities (Figure 12.14). Immersion in the culture is accomplished faster in no way other than by wandering through this realm and shopping in the various **souks** (Figure 12.15) where the countless stalls featuring spices, gold, and many other items are for sale.

Clothing choices are quite varied in this part of the world. Many women wear modest garments designed to avoid showing their bodies and even their faces if they are from families following traditional practices. In some families, adolescent girls begin to don the long, off-white robes worn in Tunisia, called **safsari,** or dark ones, such as those worn in Libya and Egypt, and a headpiece with a veil that covers all of the face except the eyes. However, traditional dress

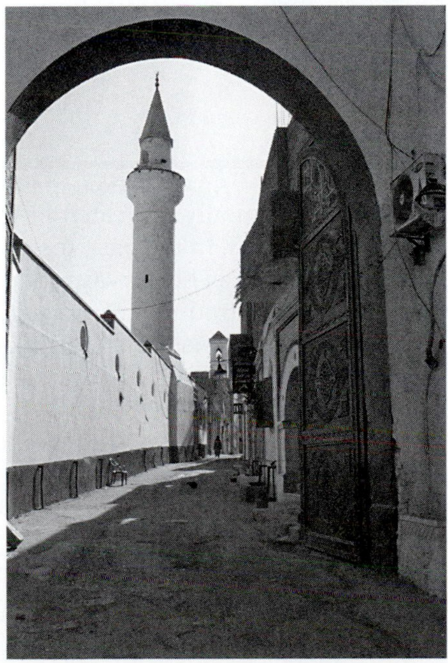

Figure 12.14 This gate leads into the old walled city of Tripoli in Libya.

Figure 12.15 The souks in North Africa are fascinating places in which to wander and bargain for food, clothing, and other desired items.

for women is not the rule for many women in this region, particularly in the cities.

Burnoose—Dark, capelike, hooded garment worn by Arab men, particularly in Morocco.

Men often wear the **burnoose** (or burnous), which is a dark, long, capelike garment with a hood. Some men may wear white robes and a cloth over the head secured by twisted rope, and a few (particularly in Morocco) choose the red fez to cover their heads. In the cities, businessmen may wear western-style clothing (Figure C.94, p. C32). The overall effect on the street is a dazzling and exotic look into a different part of the world.

Even the calendar of Islam differs from that of the western world, for it is based on 12 lunar months. The result is that the calendar is 10 days shorter each year; the timing of the religious holidays is shifted 10 days each year, bringing the fasting of Ramadan (the ninth month) at various seasons of the year. When Ramadan falls during the heat of summer, the hardship of avoiding drinking from sunrise to sunset is extremely great in these torrid regions.

Daily life is influenced by Islamic traditions throughout this region. Since Islam is almost the universal religion of the people, the holiest of days is Friday. Of course, prayer five times daily is also practiced during the entire week.

From the age of puberty onward, males and females generally tend to be separated in public and in school beyond the elementary grades. Secular entertainment is not the usual choice for leisure hours. Actually, the time devoted to religion, work, and family leaves little opportunity for other activities.

Food Patterns

Meals in North Africa commonly are eaten at low tables with diners sitting on cushions scattered on the floor. In the past, the men usually ate before the women and children, but this pattern is not always followed now because of the lack of space in city apartments. The tradition of a meal begins with hand washing (often in rose-scented water) while diners are seated at the low dining table. A small, narrow glass containing sweet green tea flavored with mint serves as the opener followed usually by two more glasses of it.

When a platter of food is placed in the middle of the table, the main part of the meal begins. Silverware is not used, but each diner has a large napkin. Eating is done using the first three fingers of the right hand. The left hand is never used, for to do so is considered bad manners. Diners remove a bite of food from the platter, dip it in any desired sauce that is provided, and then quickly put it in their mouths. This process continues until the food is gone or the diner is satisfied. Little conversation occurs while people are dining, for this is important business that is worthy of full attention. When the meal is finished, diners again rinse their hands with water.

Throughout this region, brass and copper serving trays (often with flowing designs), sturdy copper cooking pots, uniquely shaped coffee pots, pottery bowls, and skewers for shish kebabs are standard equipment in most kitchens. Emphasis is on large trays and pots because of the family-style service. Morocco has a unique type of cooking and serving container called a **tagine,** which is also the name of the stew that traditionally is prepared in it. The tagine is a round pottery bowl that has a conical-shaped pottery cover. Traditionally, individual place settings of dishes are not used.

Tagine—Stew prepared in a round pottery bowl topped with a conical lid (bowl and conical lid also called *tagine*), a unique product of Morocco.

Breakfast often is simply coffee and some bread or cereal product. Coffee (usually sweet and strong) and sweet, minted green tea appear at frequent intervals throughout the day. These are important sources of fluid needed because of the heat in these countries, whose culture does not accept its consumption of sodas and especially alcoholic beverages. However, men sell water by the cupful on the city streets, particularly in the squares and parks where people gather (Figure C.99, p. C33). Milk (goat, water buffalo, or ewe) is not widely used as a beverage, although leben (similar to buttermilk) is used a bit, as are some cheeses.

Meats are included in special meals and occasionally at other times, but the expense limits their use. Since strict Muslims need to have their meats from animals that have been sacrificed according to a prescribed ritual, markets are likely to have live chickens, lambs, and other sources of protein available for purchase so that the householder can assume the responsibility for the ritual.

Lamb, goat, and camel may be included in the diet, but pork is prohibited in both Islamic and Jewish dietary laws, which leaves too few customers for this meat. Meats may be eaten in the form of shish kebabs (Figure 12.16), but they often are included in casseroles and stews augmented with vegetables.

Vegetables and legumes occupy an important part of the diet in all of North Africa. Eggplant, onions, cabbage, spinach, potatoes, cauliflower, and okra are quite common; carrots, cucumbers, and sometimes tomatoes are also used. Fruits available include olives, dates, oranges, limes, and even some pomegranates, bananas, and grapes. Legumes are used extensively; ful (beans simmered slowly) and tamiya (fried bean patties) are favorite ways of eating legumes, but beans also are often basic ingredients in soups and stews.

Bet tai—Disc-shaped, yeast-leavened wheat flour Arab bread, usually about 14 inches in diameter.

Bet tai (or bettawa) is the name of the classic large disc of leavened wheat bread that is popular in Egypt and the other countries of North Africa. Variations in this basic staple food abound, including fenugreek to contribute the flavor of anise, and corn, millet, or sorghum as supplemental types of flour. The influence of the French in the Maghreb can be seen in the extensive use of baguettes and croissants.

Figure 12.16 Shish kebabs are a popular dish in North Africa.

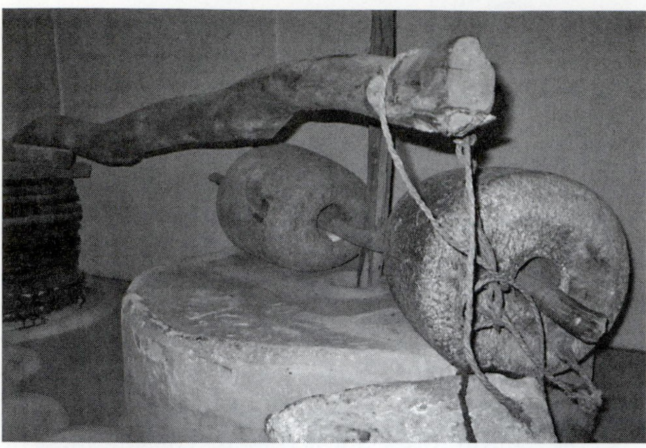

Figure 12.17 Olive oil is pressed from olives using a donkey to push the stick that forces the roller to crush the olives as the stone rolls in a circle; the oil drains into a trough and is collected in a vessel.

Burghul—Granular cereal product made by boiling and drying cracked wheat; also called *bulgur.*

Couscous—Cereal product made by drizzling water on wheat flour and rolling it into small pellets, which are then steamed until fluffy.

Bastila—Flaky-crusted pigeon pie flavored with ginger, cumin, cayenne, saffron, and cinnamon and dusted with confectioner's sugar; Moroccan specialty.

Harira—Hearty soup containing legumes, meat, and vegetables and seasoned with spices and lemon; important for suppers during Ramadan.

Burghul, the cereal product made by boiling and drying cracked wheat, is a popular food that may be used uncooked in salads after soaking or as an ingredient in a variety of casseroles and stews. Rice also is used in main dishes. However, breads and **couscous** are the dominant forms of cereal used. The Berbers are acknowledged as the originators of couscous, which commonly is made from dry wheat flour into which water is drizzled while the mixture is manipulated manually into very small pellets. These pellets then are steamed in an uncovered steamer (with a perforated bottom) placed atop a boiling pot of stew until the couscous is light and fluffy. The finished couscous sometimes is combined with stew ingredients, or it may be served as a separate dish.

Oils are used fairly extensively in North African meals. Olive oil is poured generously over various dishes (both main and side) as a type of garnish (Figure 12.17). Sesame oil also is popular for this purpose while peanut oil often is the choice for cooking. Sometimes clarified butter is used. The consumption of oils is of importance in the diets of people in this region. Sweets also are very popular, especially desserts made with honey, such as baklava.

Although much of the diet of the people in North Africa is similar to that of those living in the Levant, some dishes are uniquely characteristic to one or more of the countries in the Maghreb. Perhaps the most unique dish is **bastila** (or pastilla), which is Morocco's fabulous flaky-crusted pigeon pie.

Harira is a hearty legume-meat-vegetable soup seasoned with cinnamon, saffron, ginger, turmeric, and lemon that traditionally ends each fast day in Morocco during Ramadan. Pastries that have been boiled in honey (mahalkra or shebakia), dates, other fruit, and coffee round out this meal.

Recipes

Bastila (Morocco) (Serves 6–8)

4 Cornish hens or pigeons, 1 lb each
5 tbsp butter
1 c chopped onion
2 tbsp chopped cilantro
1 tbsp chopped parsley
1 tsp ground ginger
½ tsp ground cumin
½ tsp cayenne
¼ tsp turmeric
⅛ tsp saffron
⅛ tsp cinnamon
1 c water
1½ c blanched almonds
½ tsp cinnamon
2 tbsp sugar
6 eggs, beaten together
10 sheets phyllo (16″ × 12″)
½ c melted butter

3 tbsp oil
2 tbsp confectioner's sugar
1 tbsp cinnamon

1. Brown fowl (washed, patted dry) in butter in large skillet until browned on all sides.
2. Remove fowl; brown onions, add herbs, spices, and water, and heat to boiling.
3. Add fowl to skillet, cover, and simmer for about 1 hour until tender.
4. Brown and chop almonds, and then stir in sugar and cinnamon.
5. Skin and debone fowl and cut meat into 2″ strips.
6. Pour and reserve 1¼ cups liquid from skillet and then quickly reduce the remaining liquid to ¼ cup in the skillet.
7. Return liquid to skillet, add eggs, and heat while stirring until eggs form soft curds.
8. Overlap 6 sheets of phyllo on board, forming a circle; fold two sheets in half and put in center of phyllo circle.
9. Sprinkle almond mixture in a 9″ circle in center of phyllo; spread half of egg mixture over it.
10. Arrange all fowl in a circle to make a layer, and then cover with rest of egg and two folded sheets of phyllo.
11. Brush exposed phyllo with melted butter; fold each leaf of protruding phyllo over circle and brush each lightly with butter; fold over the next phyllo to completely enclose the pie.
12. Heat remaining butter and oil in large skillet until very hot. Carefully slide the bastila into the hot fat to brown for 2 to 3 minutes on each side or bake 15 minutes at 400°F.
13. Top with mixture of confectioner's sugar and ground cinnamon; slice into wedges.

Harira (Morocco) (Serves 4–6)

½ lb lamb stew meat
2 tbsp olive oil
½ tsp ground ginger
¼ tsp turmeric
¼ tsp ground cinnamon
½ c chopped onion
2 medium tomatoes, coarsely chopped
1 lb canned chickpeas, drained
2 tbsp cilantro, chopped
Salt and pepper
1 qt water
¼ c orzo (or rice)
2 eggs, beaten lightly
2 tsp lemon juice
Sprinkle of cinnamon

1. Brown meat in hot olive oil, and then stir in ginger, turmeric, cinnamon, onions, tomatoes, chickpeas, cilantro, water, salt, and pepper.
2. Simmer 1 hour.
3. Add orzo and simmer another 10 minutes until orzo is tender.
4. Beat in eggs, lemon juice, and cinnamon. Serve.

Brik bil Lahm (Tunisia) (Serves 4)

½ c chopped onion
½ lb ground lamb
2 tbsp chopped cilantro
⅛ tsp ground saffron
Salt and pepper
1 tbsp butter
2 tsp grated parmesan cheese
4 sheets phyllo (16″ × 12″)
4 eggs
Lemon garnish

1. Thoroughly mix onions, lamb, cilantro, saffron, salt, and pepper; brown in butter in a skillet, being sure to break into small pieces.
2. Remove from heat and stir in cheese.
3. Brush sheet of phyllo with butter; fold sheet of phyllo in half and again in half to make a rectangle 8″ × 6″, and then fold 2″ over to make a 6″ square.
4. Make a mound of ¼ of lamb so it will be in center of a triangle if the dough is folded over to make a triangle.
5. Make a well in the mound and crack egg into the well.
6. Moisten the edges of phyllo, and then fold dough over to make a triangle enclosing the filling. Be sure to press dough firmly to seal.
7. Fry in very hot olive oil for 2 to 3 minutes per side.
8. Repeat to make 4 briks.

Djedje Tagine (Morocco) (Serves 4–6)

1 chicken fryer, in pieces
3 tbsp butter
1 c water
2 medium onions, chopped
½ tsp ground ginger
⅛ tsp cumin
⅛ tsp cayenne
1 lemon, sliced (seeds removed)
¼ c chopped parsley
¼ tsp black pepper
1 7-oz jar pitted whole green olives
2 tbsp flour
2 tbsp cold water

1. Brown pieces of chicken in butter in Dutch oven; add the cup of water, onions, ginger, cumin, cayenne, lemon, parsley, and pepper.
2. Simmer, covered, for 45 minutes.
3. Meanwhile, drain olives. Cover olives with water in a saucepan and heat to boiling. Drain and boil again in water to cover.
4. Add olives to chicken and stir, then transfer to serving platter.
5. Thicken remaining liquid with flour mixed with cold water to make a smooth paste. Stir while heating slowly to thicken. Add 2 tablespoons of water if necessary to make 1½ cups.
6. Pour over chicken and olives, and serve.

Tunisian Doughnuts (Makes 12)

2 eggs
¼ c salad oil
¼ c orange juice
1 tsp orange zest
¼ c sugar
2 c flour
3 tsp baking soda
2 c water
2 c sugar
2 tbsp lemon juice
½ c honey
1 tsp orange zest
Oil for frying

1. Beat together eggs, oil, orange juice, orange zest, and sugar until smooth.
2. Stir in flour mixed with soda and continue beating until very viscous. Cover for 30 minutes.
3. Boil water, sugar, and lemon juice in small saucepan to 230°F.
4. Add honey and zest, and simmer 6 minutes.
5. Preheat deep-fat fryer oil to 360°F while shaping doughnuts.
6. Divide dough into 12 and roll each piece into a ball into which a hole is punched with a finger.
7. Fry doughnuts for 5 minutes without crowding them, turning to brown them evenly on both sides. Drain on paper towels.
8. Dip each doughnut in warm syrup and serve.

Couscous with Lamb (Algeria) (Serves 6–8)

2½ c water mixed with 2½ tsp salt
1 tbsp olive oil
2 c couscous
1½ lb lamb stew meat
1 medium onion, minced
¼ c olive oil
½ tsp ground cinnamon
⅛ tsp cumin
¼ tsp black pepper
4 c water
2 c canned chickpeas, drained
4 carrots, pared and sliced (2″ slices)
1½ lb turnips, pared and quartered

1. Pour salt water and olive oil over couscous; gently lift and rub couscous between palms of hands until water has been absorbed. Cover for 20 minutes.
2. Brown lamb and onion in olive oil, cinnamon, cumin, and black pepper in a Dutch oven or bottom of couscoussier.

3. Add 4 cups of water and chickpeas, and then place cheesecloth-lined colander or top part of couscoussier and seal the two parts with aluminum foil to trap steam upward through the couscous.
4. Boil to generate steam and slowly add couscous, a cup at a time, while rubbing pellets between hands. Steam 20 minutes after all couscous is added.
5. Add vegetables to bottom of pot; sprinkle cinnamon and salt water over couscous and fluff a bit.
6. Steam couscous and boil vegetables for 20 minutes. Serve couscous mounded on a large platter with meat, vegetables, and some of the juices over it.

Summary

North Africa comprises Egypt, Libya, Tunisia, Algeria, and Morocco; the latter three often are referred to as the *Maghreb.* All have a shoreline on the Mediterranean and large desert regions (the Sahara) as well as some mountain ranges, the best known being the Atlas ranges. The very dry climate and heat have shaped the agricultural patterns so that some crops are raised in the northern regions and along the Nile and wherever irrigation is possible. Meat sources raised in the region include sheep, goats, camel, some beef, and poultry. Wheat and some other cereals are grown with irrigation, as are some vegetables and fruits.

Egypt was the site of an advanced and artistic civilization that included hieroglyphic writing more than 2,000 years before Christ. Artifacts and architectural monuments from this period are admired around the world today. Additional historic mementos of subsequent Phoenician and Roman conquests are also in evidence all along the shores of North Africa.

Religion shifted from that of the early Egyptians to a Christian era that gave way to the dominant Islamic beliefs and practices of modern North Africa. There are still some Coptics, other Christians, and Jews scattered throughout these countries today, although they definitely are the minority in all of these countries.

In addition to the early Egyptians, other groups lived throughout this expanse of northern Africa. The Berbers in the mountains and valleys of what is now Morocco were early settlers. Bedouins managed to survive the rigors of desert life by practicing a nomadic lifestyle, and still can be found today in some regions of the Sahara and its borders.

The Moors, the name given to the mixture of Arabs and Berbers living in the region of Morocco, invaded Spain by way of the Straits of Gibraltar during the 11th century and controlled much of that peninsula until late in the 15th century. Their advanced culture and architectural designs left structures and traditions that still remain as a significant part of Spain. The similarities between southern Spain and Morocco are evident today despite the changes that have ensued in the 500 years since the days of the Moors in Spain.

Phoenicians, Greeks, and Romans interacted with people in North Africa as they traveled through the Mediterranean Sea in search of trade and conquest. Piracy based from North Africa occurred during the late 16th and 17th centuries when the Ottoman Turks were in control of much of the region. Eventually, France gained control of Algeria, Morocco, and Tunisia during the 19th and part of the 20th centuries. Italy controlled Libya for much of the first half of the 20th century.

The cultures of these countries today are largely a reflection of their Islamic heritage. Mosques are adorned with lovely calligraphy that is based on the Koran. Privacy and quiet are fostered by building designs that feature lovely doorways and interior courtyards. Clothing is modest; some women wear long robes and veils that reveal only the eyes. Some segregation of sexes occurs after the age of puberty. Dining may be separated according to gender in some families, and eating with the right hand is the accepted practice, usually while diners are seated on cushions surrounding a low table. The food patterns are quite similar to those found in the Middle East, although couscous, bastila, and tagine are particular favorites in North Africa.

Study Questions

1. Identify three distinctive geographic features that are important to North Africa and describe the influence that each of these features has had in shaping the region.
2. Describe the cultural impact of Islam on Egypt's architecture and other features.
3. Cite at least one aspect of today's life in North Africa that can be traced to the presence in the past of each of the following: (a) Phoenicians, (b) Romans, (c) Ottoman Turks, (d) Arabs, (e) Christians, (f) Italians, and (g) French.
4. Define (a) Maghreb, (b) tagine, (c) Berber, (d) Moor, (e) Bedouin, (f) couscous, and (g) bulghur.
5. Compare some of the dining traditions of Morocco with those in France, and explain why they are different.
6. Plan a dinner menu that features North African foods.

Selected Sites

http://www.foodproductdesign.com/archive/1995/0895fp.html—Article about the distinctive cuisines of North Africa.

http://www.foodproductdesign.com/archive/2001/0101ap.html—Background about influences on the foods of North Africa.

http://www.inmamaskitchen.com/FOOD_IS_ART/mideast/mainmideast.html—Brief overview of Egyptian food patterns and some recipes.

http://touregypt.net/food.htm—Information on foods and dining in Egypt.

http://ourworld.compuserve.com/homepages/dr_ibrahim_ighneiwa/food.htm—Recipes for Libyan food.

http://www.cliffordawright.com/recipes.html#morocco—Recipes for dishes typical of Morocco and other countries in North Africa and the Middle East.

http://dmoz.org/Home/Cooking/World_Cuisines/African/Tunisian/—Recipes for Tunisian foods.

http://www.world-cuisines.com/Top_Home_Cooking_World_Cuisines_African.html—Contains information about food and recipes from many different African countries.

Bibliography

Anonymous. 1995. What makes it North African? *Food Product Design* 5(8) 11.

Barer-Stein, T. 1999. *You Eat What You Are.* 2nd ed. Firefly Books, Ltd. Ontario, Canada.

Bowles, P. 1992. *Morocco.* Harry N. Abrams. New York.

Brander, B. 1966. *River Nile.* National Geographic Special Publications. Washington, DC.

Budge, E.A.W. 1979. *Tutankhamen.* Bell Publishing. New York.

Crowther, G. and H. Finlay. 1992. *Morocco, Algeria, and Tunisia.* Lonely Planet Publications. Berkeley, CA.
Desroches-Noblecourt, C. 1965. *Tutankhamen.* Doubleday. Garden City, NY.
Field, M. and F. Field. 1970. *Quintet of Cuisines.* Time-Life Books. New York.
Haag, M. 1994. *Illustrated Guide to Egypt.* Passport Books. Lincolnwood, IL.
Hanger, C. and M. Lahlou. 2000. *World Food: Morocco.* Lonely Planet Publications. Oakland, CA.
Jenkins, N.H. 2003. *Essential Mediterranean: How Regional Cooks Transform Key Ingredients into World's Favorite Cuisines.* Harper Collins. New York.
Malcolm, P. 1993. *Libya.* Marshall Cavendish. New York.
Morse, M. et al. 1998. *Cooking at the Kasbah: Recipes from My Moroccan Kitchen.* Chronicle Books. San Francisco.
Neubert, O. 1972. *Tutankhamen and the Valley of the Kings.* Mayflower Books. London, England.
Paliouras, A. 1985. *Monastery of St. Catherine of Mount Sinai.* St. Catherine's Monastery at Sinai. Sinai, Egypt.
Pearcy, G.E. 1980. *The World Food Scene.* Plycon Press. Redondo Beach, CA.
Reader, J. 1997. *Biography of the Continent of Africa.* Vintage Books. New York.
Roden, C. 2000. *New Book of Middle Eastern Food.* Knopf. New York.
Stewart, D. 1977. *Pyramids and Sphinx.* Newsweek. New York.
Tompkins, P. 1971. *Secrets of the Great Pyramid.* Harper and Row. New York.
Uhl, S. 2001. North African Cuisines. *Food Product Design* 11(1): 14.
Walden, H. 2002. *Moroccan Collection: Traditional Flavors from North Africa.* Hamlyn Books. London, England.
Walden, H. 2000. *North African Cooking: Exotic Delights from Morocco, Tunisia, Algeria, and Egypt.* Apple Press. Grants Pass, OR.
Wright, C.A. 1999. *A Mediterranean Feast.* William Morrow. New York.

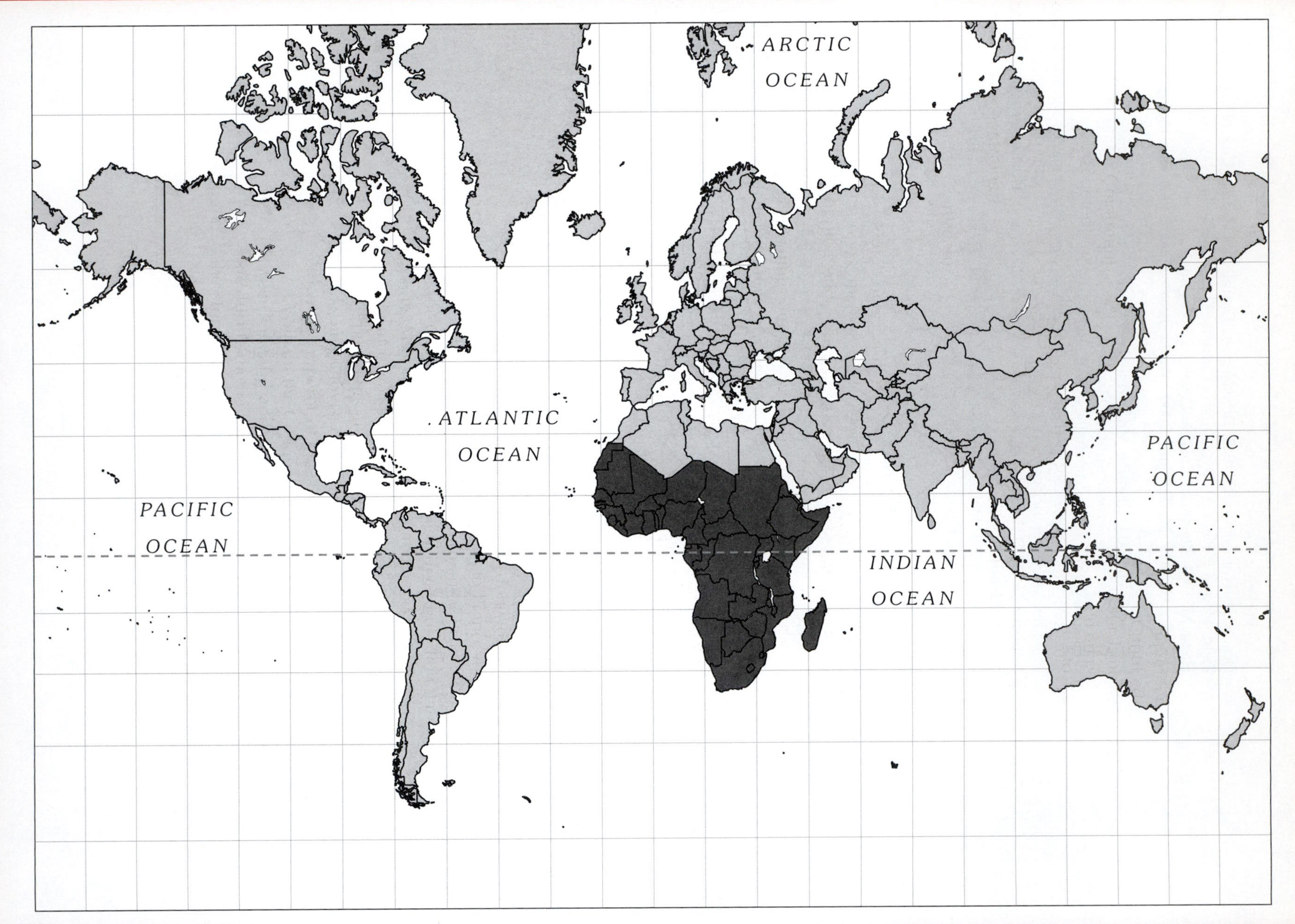
ARCTIC OCEAN
PACIFIC OCEAN
ATLANTIC OCEAN
PACIFIC OCEAN
INDIAN OCEAN

Part IV Heritage from Sub-Saharan Africa

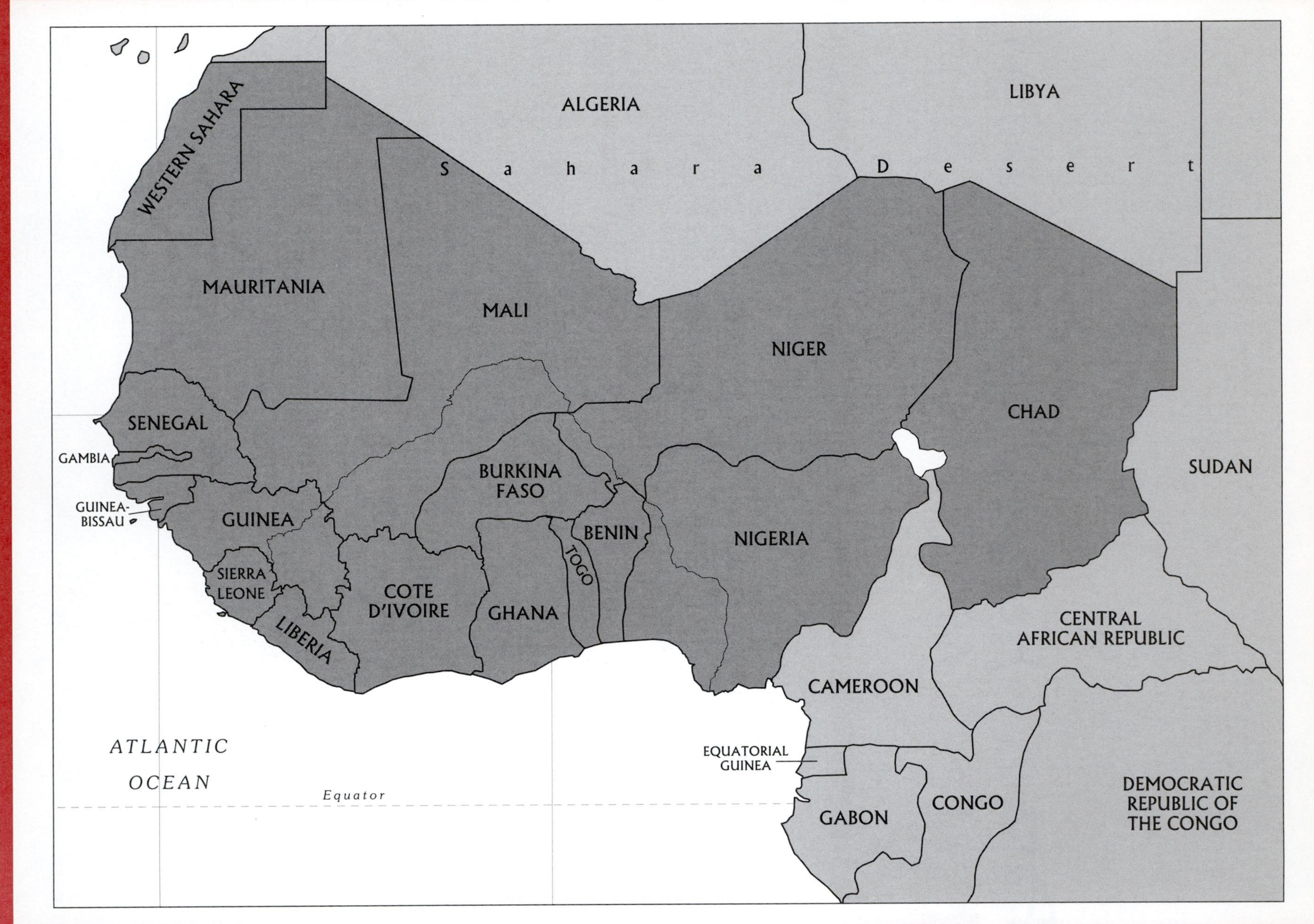
WESTERN SAHARA
ALGERIA
LIBYA
Sahara Desert
MAURITANIA
MALI
NIGER
CHAD
SUDAN
SENEGAL
GAMBIA
GUINEA-BISSAU
GUINEA
SIERRA LEONE
LIBERIA
COTE D'IVOIRE
BURKINA FASO
GHANA
TOGO
BENIN
NIGERIA
CAMEROON
CENTRAL AFRICAN REPUBLIC
EQUATORIAL GUINEA
GABON
CONGO
DEMOCRATIC REPUBLIC OF THE CONGO
ATLANTIC OCEAN
Equator

13 West Africa

Geographic Overview

Niger River—One of the longest rivers of the world; traverses much of West Africa, running north before turning east and south; has an interior delta and one at the coast.

Sahel—Broad band of land across West Africa between the Sahara and the lush vegetation along the southern coast.

Tsetse fly—Vector for sleeping sickness, a serious disease in parts of West Africa.

Geographically, West Africa is viewed as including the countries south of the Sahara that constitute the large western bump of the African continent. Most of these nations (Gambia, Guinea, Sierra-Leone, Ivory Coast, Ghana, Togo, Benin, and Nigeria) have at least some shoreline on the Atlantic Ocean, but Chad, Niger, Mali, and Burkina are isolated from the sea. The **Niger** and Volta are long, navigable rivers that provide limited transportation of some crops and goods in the various countries they traverse.

In general, the coastal strip is fairly narrow before the rise to the continental plateau that comprises much of the African continent south of the Sahara. This plateau has considerable breaks that limit the usefulness of the terrain for farming. However, subsistence farming is possible in parts of these West African countries. The rainfall in parts of West Africa creates an equatorial rainforest, although the amount of rain begins to dwindle farther north, reducing the amount and type of crops that can be grown, until the edge of the desert completely eliminates agriculture. The broad strip of land north of the rainforest and up to the southern edge of the Sahara (the **Sahel**) varies from grassy savanna to semidesert.

Although much of the agricultural effort is basically subsistence farming, food exports are a source of some national income. Among the export crops are peanuts, palm oil, cocoa, kola nuts (for cola beverages), coffee, bananas, sugar, and pineapples. Livestock can also be raised successfully in areas that are free of the **tsetse fly.**

The tsetse fly is not the only health hazard found in the difficult climatic conditions in West Africa. The intense heat of the tropics and the rainfall patterns also create unfortunate opportunities for parasites and bacteria to propagate and infect the population, sometimes with conditions that are debilitating or even life threatening. Productivity is sometimes seriously impacted by the prevalence of disease (including HIV and AIDS) while intermittent recurrences of malaria and other tropical health factors are ongoing problems that sap the population's energies. Unsafe water supplies and a high rodent population also add to health problems in many areas in West Africa.

History and Culture

Early People

Jenné-Jeno—Early town (before 500 CE) in Mali.

Empire of Ghana—Dominant power in West Africa from 5th to 11th centuries.

Empire of Mali—Empire dominating trade from Senegal to Egypt from the 13th to the 15th centuries.

Empire of Songhai—Dominant empire in West Africa (including Timbuktu) after splitting from Mali in the 14th century and into the 16th century.

The history of the African continent extends back to early humans in various regions. Evidence of farming in the Sahel goes back as far as 6,000 years ago. Relics of early farming include bones from cattle herds, hoes, scythes, pottery, and remnants of crops (yams, millet, and rice). Stone village remnants found in the Sahel of West Africa have been dated at about 1200 BCE. The early settlers centered along the Niger River and Lake Chad, both suitable regions for developing agriculture (Figure 13.1). The tools that could be made from iron began to improve farming there by about 450 BCE. Perhaps the earliest town of significance was **Jenné-Jeno** in Mali, which was flourishing before 500 CE. In fact, the Bantu (large African ethnic group) migration (about 1000 BCE) from Central Africa east and south was significant to the development of the rest of Africa.

The social history of West Africa is extremely complex because the region consisted of numerous tribes, none of which was numerically dominant enough to reign over its neighbors for long periods. The result was the development of many languages and familial traditions that tended sometimes to foster disagreements and battles. Among the established empires were the following:

- **Empire of Ghana,** from about the 5th to the 11th centuries,
- **Empire of Mali,** which dominated trade from Senegal to Egypt from the 13th to the 15th centuries,
- **Empire of Songhai,** which detached from Mali from the 14th to 16th centuries and included the fabled trading outpost of Timbuktu.

Figure 13.1 Ankle bracelet c. 1500–1600 CE Africa. (Courtesy of Pitt Rivers Museum, Oxford.)

Other smaller groups existed to the south of these empires but played less important roles in trade.

European Interactions

European nations have a long history of interchange with Africa. These interactions developed along the western coast (Figure 13.2) as a result of the interests of Prince Henry the Navigator, who sent Portuguese ships in the early 1500s to explore opportunities for shipping gold from Africa via Portuguese vessels. As a result, the Portuguese were able to ship valuable cargo from Senegal and other ports by sea, thus avoiding the costly and uncertain trade routes via camel across the Sahara.

Berlin Conference of 1884–85—Meeting at which European colonial powers divided the African continent without including Africans in their decisions.

Belgium, England, and France also quickly became interested in trading with and colonizing West Africa. This imperialistic frenzy culminated in the **Berlin Conference of 1884–85** when the concerned European powers essentially carved up Africa without any input from the affected populations. Belgium ended up with the Congo, Germany had Togo and Cameroon, Portugal received Guinea-Bissau and some islands in the Atlantic, England had a bit of the coastline of West Africa as well as much of the regions of East and South Africa, and France got the remainder of West Africa and the central part.

Germany lost its holdings as a result of World War I, and the remainder of the countries in West Africa were able to achieve independence at different times following World War II. This independence has led to considerable conflict both between and within nations, which has extracted a haunting human toll.

Slavery

The specter of slavery immediately comes to mind when examining the history of West Africa. A portion of its coastline in Benin and Nigeria was once even termed the *Slave Coast.* Natives of this area had been taken as slaves by such conquerors as Alexander the Great and various Roman leaders as part of their booty long before the use of slaves in West Africa apparently began.

In fact, prior to the arrival of the Portuguese, conquered Africans were being sold to other Africans or were taken to the victors' home territories and used to

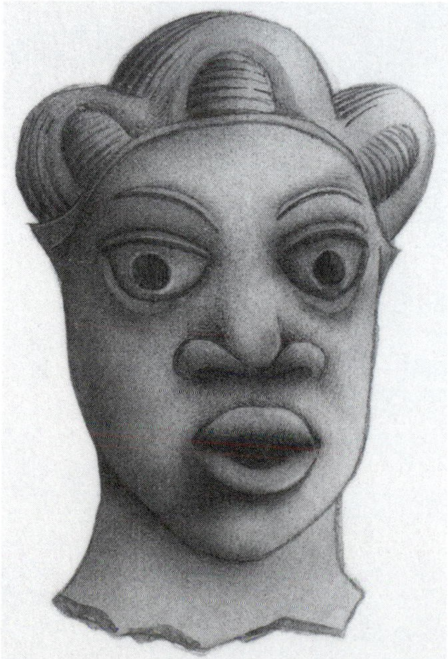

Figure 13.2 The Nok people of West Africa c. 900 BCE, a Western African Terracotta head. (Courtesy of Dorling Kindersley.)

perform heavy labor. However, slave trade increased markedly after the Portuguese traders developed their markets along the West African coast and acquired slaves to take to Brazil to provide labor for the sugar plantations.

Several European nations who were building their colonial holdings in the western hemisphere had a seemingly insatiable need for slave labor to work the sugarcane, tobacco, cotton, and other fields being farmed to the benefit of the controlling nation. During the 17th and 18th centuries, four European colonial powers (Spain, England, Holland, and France) were heavily involved in transporting West African slaves to work in regions of South America and the Caribbean as well as in their territories in Southeast Asia.

Goree—Island just off the coast of Dakar, Senegal, from which vast numbers of slaves were shipped to the Americas and Caribbean islands.

Slaves were shipped by sea from ports in the western part of Africa (most frequently from the island of **Goree** near Dakar, Senegal) and overland across the trade routes to the east. U.S. ships eventually were involved in the slave trade, too. The impact of the use of African slaves in the South is a well-known cause of the Civil War in the United States. Thus, the African slave trade has had a lasting and significant effect on both sides of the Atlantic.

Despite the fact that the trade in slaves across the Atlantic was abolished by a series of treaties in the early part of the 19th century, and did not end totally until 1830, the practice of slavery persisted well beyond that time. Abolition occurred in the United States in 1865 and in such distant places as India in 1843 and Saudi Arabia in 1962. Many, but certainly not all, of the slaves affected were the natives of West and Central Africa.

Religion

Religion in West Africa appears to have been essentially that of animism prior to the arrival of the message of Islam in the Sahel by the 14th century. Muslims in this region adapted Islam somewhat, incorporating overtones of nature and spirits to retain some of their earlier culture. Many Muslims live today in the Sahel across West Africa (Figure 13.3), the exact number being impossible to determine.

Christians from Europe brought their message to West Africa, and this faith was accepted, particularly in the southern coastal regions of West Africa. Again, converts to Christianity retained some aspects of their traditional beliefs when they accepted the faith of the Christians. Estimates of religious affiliations are that

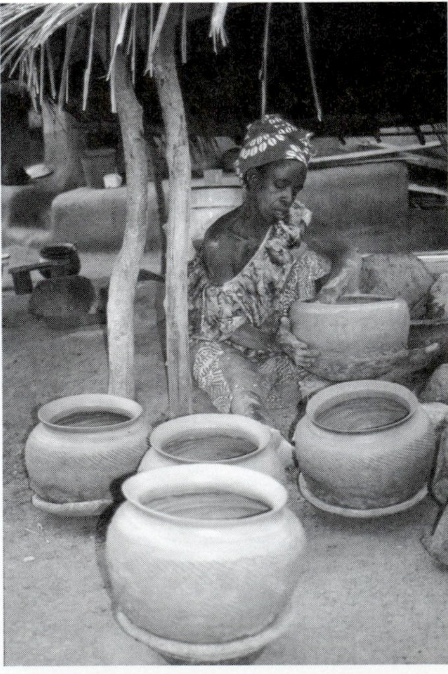

Figure 13.3 Potter in the Muslim section of Yacouba Village, Nigeria. (Courtesy of Dorling Kindersley/Gales.)

the southern region along the coast of West Africa is predominately Christian, and the northern part is mostly Muslim, for an almost equal representation in the total area.

Most of the people living in West Africa prior to the early part of the 20th century lived in rural circumstances (Figure 13.4), and many still live on land that they farm to support their families' food and living requirements—often at subsistence level.

Urbanization is developing in some places, and a trend toward a two-class system has developed. This is particularly apparent in Nigeria, where the oil boom of the late 1960s and 1970s brought sudden wealth to a limited number of people but left a trail of problems when it burst and profits were severely diminished. The problems confronting comparatively rich Nigeria and the other countries of West Africa are large and seemingly impossible to solve in the near future. Such accepted basics as safe water for drinking and enough food to provide adequate calories are not available to many people, especially when weather problems reduce the harvests from their land.

The Arts

Oral traditions have been passed from generation to generation over the centuries in West Africa. The spoken word in the form of elaborate storytelling has enriched the heritage of innumerable people for whom access to education and to libraries has often not been possible. The Yoruba living in southwestern Nigeria represent an ethnic group with a long and rich history of storytelling as a means of shaping and retaining their cultural uniqueness.

The African spirit is truly amazing. The cultural heritage is handed down from generation to generation, even though reading and writing may not be a part of many lives. This explains the great value placed on storytelling in West Africa. The history and imagination of West Africans have been captured in the stories they tell, not only to each other but also to the world. The story of Br'er Rabbit is among the stories thought to have originated in Africa.

Music is another forte of West Africans. Vocal music, which usually includes spirituals if the origin was a Christian area, provides a rich heritage and pleasure for all people, both performers and the audience. Instrumental music also is a part of West Africa's cultural traditions; drums of various pitches produce exotic and exciting rhythms that are unique and lasting.

Adornment plays a significant role of identity for the many tribes of West Africa. Various remarkable masks, often used in tribal dances, represent a key element of the artistic culture. Other artistic achievements include fabric designs and large bead and shell necklaces.

Figure 13.4 Carving and decorating gourds; the bottom of a beautifully painted gourd. (Courtesy of Powell Cotton Museum.)

Food Patterns

The foods that thrive in West Africa on family farms have formed the foundation of the diet in this part of the world. Two of the most important crops, maize and cassava, were promoted heavily by slave traders in earlier centuries because they could be fed to the slaves on long ocean voyages. Both are mainstays of diets today. In addition, sorghum, wheat, rice, millet, plantain, greens, legumes, groundnuts (peanuts), and yams are key components of meals. Eggs, milk in various forms, chicken, and small amounts of beef, goat, sheep, or wild game are sometimes included in the diet.

Fufu—Starchy paste produced by pounding and boiling manioc or other rich source of starch and then dipping each bite in a spicy sauce; popular in West Africa.

The dish that forms the backbone of the diet for many people in West Africa is **fufu.** It is made by pounding or grinding a starchy vegetable or cereal until it becomes pasty and then adding boiling water to make a very thick dish. No single recipe is used for fufu. The starch source may be manioc (cassava), yams, millet, rice, or plantain. Diners eat fufu by scooping up a bite of cooked fufu paste in the right hand (left hand is used only for toilet chores), forming it into a ball, and then dipping it in some type of spicy sauce.

Cooking likely is limited to recipes that can be boiled in a single pot or fried (Figure 13.5). Ovens are not available in many homes. Frying is popular, usually in palm oil or peanut oil. The palm oil is likely the type that is a reddish color; the higher cost of peanut oil limits its use.

Vegetable mixtures cooked in a pot are varied according to the vegetables that are available at the particular moment. Often, a bit of meat or egg is added if available, but the cost of these protein foods limits the frequency and the amount used.

To add excitement to these dishes, various seasonings and sauces are used. Preference seems to run toward hot, hotter, and hottest! Peppers and chilies are essential in West African cooking. Seeds, particularly sesame, are used generously too. Not surprising, salt is a key ingredient; it is helpful in replacing the body's salt lost in perspiration in the hot days typical of West African weather.

Yassa—Dish made with lemon-marinated chicken or meat.

Gari foto—Stew of hard-cooked eggs, onions, and tomatoes.

Jollof rice—Dish composed of layers of meat, tomatoes and other vegetables, and steamed rice.

Fruits are available in the tropical parts of West Africa. Bananas, papayas, mangoes, pineapples, melons, and citrus are among the most common. However, some more exotic tropical fruits may be eaten on special occasions.

Peanut butter (called *groundnut butter*) has many uses as a dip, spread, or ingredient in a range of dishes. Chopped peanuts also are used to add texture and nutrients to some stews. Other popular dishes are **yassa** (a dish made with meat or chicken that has been marinated in a lemon sauce), **gari foto** (a stew of hard-cooked eggs, onions, and tomatoes), and **jollof rice** (layers of meat, tomatoes and other vegetables, and steamed rice simmered together).

Figure 13.5 Meals usually are cooked in a single pot over a fire.

Recipes

Banana Fritters (Serves 4–6)

6 ripe bananas
1 c flour
¼ c sugar dissolved in ¼ c water
½ tsp ground nutmeg

1. Mash bananas with fork until smooth.
2. Stir in other ingredients, adding a little water if needed for a consistency like pancake batter.
3. Fry like pancakes, turning once.

Fish Stew and Rice (Serves 4–6)

½ onion, chopped
2 tbsp oil
3 tbsp tomato paste
2 carrots, sliced
½ lb cabbage, shredded
½ pkg (8 oz) frozen okra
2 yams, cubed
1½ lb fish, deboned and cubed
4 c water
2 tsp salt
3 c cooked rice

1. In Dutch oven, sauté onions in oil until golden.
2. Add tomato, paste, vegetables, fish, water, and salt.
3. Simmer for 1 hour, covered.
4. Meanwhile, cook rice.
5. Ladle stew over mound of rice.

Fried Chicken with Peanut Butter Sauce (Serves 4–6)

1 chicken fryer, cut in pieces
2 tbsp peanut oil
¾ c chopped onion
1 tomato, diced
2 tbsp tomato paste
1 tsp salt
1 tsp paprika
1 bay leaf
2 c water
1 c peanut butter

1. Brown chicken in oil in Dutch oven.
2. Add onions, tomato, paste, seasonings, and water. Cover and simmer for about 45 minutes until chicken is almost tender.
3. Remove chicken. Blend chicken stock into peanut butter to make a smooth sauce.
4. Return chicken to pan and pour peanut butter sauce over it; cover and simmer until chicken is very tender.

Jollof Rice (Serves 4–6)

1 small frying chicken, in pieces
2 tbsp oil
⅓ lb ham, cubed
2 onions, chopped
1 tsp salt
¼ tsp pepper
½ tsp ground allspice
2 (1-lb each) cans tomatoes
1 6-oz can tomato paste
¼ lb green beans
¾ c water
1 c rice
2 c water
1 tsp salt

1. Brown chicken in oil in Dutch oven.
2. Add ham, onions, seasonings, tomatoes, paste, beans, and water.
3. Cover and simmer for 1 hour, stirring occasionally.
4. Meanwhile, simmer rice in salted water for 15 minutes, covered.
5. Spoon rice over vegetables and chicken, cover, and simmer 10 minutes.

Lamb Gumbo (Serves 6)

2 lb cubed lamb stew meat
2 tbsp peanut oil
½ c minced onion
3 tbsp flour
1 6-oz can tomato paste
2 red peppers (seeds removed), diced
1½ tsp salt
4 c water
1 10-oz pkg frozen okra
1 c whole wheat flour
½ c water
Salted water

1. Brown lamb in oil in Dutch oven.
2. Add onion and flour, stirring and heating to brown flour.
3. Add tomato paste, peppers, salt, and water.
4. Cover and simmer for 1 hour.
5. Add okra and simmer until soft.
6. Meanwhile, make whole wheat balls: Mix flour and water together, and then cook (covered) in top of a double boiler for 30 minutes.
7. Scoop balls of dough and drop in boiling, salted water for 10 minutes.
8. Drain balls and serve with the lamb gumbo.

Bananas, Black-Eyed Peas, and Shrimp (Serves 4–6)

2 c dried black-eyed peas
1 qt boiling water
½ c chopped onion
1 tomato, chopped
1 tbsp crushed, dried red peppers
2 tbsp tomato paste
½ lb canned shrimp
3 large bananas (¼″ slices)
½ tsp salt
1 c oil

1. Rinse black-eyed peas, boil for 2 minutes, and then let them soak without heat for 2 hours.
2. Simmer peas until tender.
3. Add vegetables and boil very gently for 15 minutes.
4. Add tomato paste and shrimp, and simmer for 15 minutes.
5. Meanwhile, sprinkle bananas with salt.
6. Deep-fat fry bananas to a golden color. Drain well on paper towels.
7. Serve bananas with the peas.

Peanut Butter Soup (Serves 4)

1½ c cooked chicken, cut in ½″ chunks
½ c peanut butter
3 oz canned tomato paste
½ onion, chopped
5 c water

1. Combine ingredients and simmer 30 minutes, stirring occasionally.

Fufu (Serves 4)

1 yam
2 large baking potatoes

1. Boil yam and potatoes in salted water in a covered pot until very soft.
2. Drain and pare yam and potatoes.
3. Mash and then beat very hard until completely smooth and sticking together to form a ball.

Note: Eat fufu by tearing off a bite-sized chunk, rolling it with the fingers into a ball, and then dipping it into a meat dish and sauce or other dish in the meal.

Chicken Yassa (Serves 6)

4 onions, sliced
10 garlic cloves, minced
4 tsp Dijon mustard
½ c red wine vinegar
1 bay leaf
2 tsp chopped chili peppers
3 lemons, sliced
1 chicken
2 tbsp cooking oil
2 chicken bouillon cubes
½ c water

1. Mix all ingredients except chicken, oil, and bouillon cubes together in a mixing bowl.
2. Wash chicken, cut into pieces, and blot dry on paper towels.
3. Place chicken pieces in a bowl and stir to coat with the marinade. Marinate for at least 45 minutes.
4. Remove chicken from marinade and fry each piece in oil until brown.
5. Sauté onions in oil.
6. Put the chicken, onions, marinade, and water in a pot and simmer for at least 35 minutes.
7. Serve with boiled rice.

Summary

West Africa includes Gambia, Guinea, Sierra-Leone, Ivory Coast, Ghana, Togo, Benin, Nigeria, Chad, Niger, Mali, and Burkina. The latter four countries are without access to the sea, but the other nations have coastlines on the Atlantic. The region has rainfall heavy enough to support equatorial rainforests in the southern areas but is extremely arid in areas approaching the Sahara toward the north. Subsistence farming is found in much of the region, but only a few crops, such as peanuts, cocoa, kola nuts, and bananas, are raised in sufficient amounts to be exported. The tsetse fly is a hazard to animals and people in some regions. Tropical illnesses, parasites, and rodents add to the health hazards for people in West African countries.

Evidence of agriculture in West Africa dates from more than 6,000 years ago, and iron tools were used around 450 BCE. The Bantus appear to have gradually migrated east and south from the eastern edge of West Africa over the next 1,500 years. The empires that developed in West Africa included Ghana (5th to 11th centuries), Mali (13th to 15th centuries), and Songhai (14th to 16th centuries).

The Portuguese ships of Prince Henry the Navigator visited the coast of West Africa in the 1500s. This led to trade via the Atlantic to compete with the camel routes through the Sahara. European nations carved up Africa at the Berlin Conference of 1884–85, establishing control of various West African countries by England, France, Germany, and Belgium. This situation evolved slowly into the establishment of independent nations.

Slavery had been a fact in various nations long before the practice in the Roman Empire, but it became a tragedy for people living in West Africa during the era of colonialism. Slaves were bought in various West African ports and shipped under the flags of Spain, England, Holland, and France to their respective colonies in the Americas and the Caribbean. Those slaves who survived the terrible conditions during the ocean voyages were sold at slave markets to work in the fields or on the plantations of their masters. The slave trade was abolished in most countries by the mid-1800s, but many people continued to live in slavery for some time after that.

Religion is varied in West Africa. The people living just south of the Sahara most frequently are Muslims, but Christianity is found in the southern parts of the region. Some of the aspects of their earlier religion have been incorporated into the Muslim and Christian practices of West Africans.

Storytelling is a rich cultural tradition of West Africa. Music features exciting rhythms from drums and includes songs. Dances, often with costumes and masks, are another cultural expression of the region.

The food traditional to West Africa is based on extensive use of cassava, maize, rice, plantain, legumes, yams, sorghum, wheat, and rice. Limited amounts of meat, chicken, eggs, and milk may be consumed too. Recipes that can be cooked in a single pot over an open fire form the basis of the diets of many people. Frying is also a common means of cooking food. Root vegetables and various tropical fruits such as bananas and pineapples are served frequently.

Selected Sites

http://www.africaguide.com/cooking.htm—Information about food habits and ingredients in West Africa.

http://www.afrol.com/archive/food_staples.htm—Brief descriptions of some of the staple foods in West Africa.

http://www.globalgourmet.com/destinations/westafrica/wafrwhat.html—Overview of some foods popular in West Africa.

http://emeagwali.com/nigeria/cuisine/nigerian-jollof-rice.html—Brief report of Nigerian food written by a woman now living in America.

http://www.congocookbook.com/c0170.html—Recipes and information on African foods; avoid opening pop-ups.

Study Questions

1. Compare the typical foods in the diets of West Africans with those from North Africa. Why are these diets different?
2. Identify at least three factors that have influenced the dishes West Africans usually eat.
3. Why was Prince Henry the Navigator interested in West Africa?
4. Did slavery have its beginnings in West Africa? If not, identify some earlier domains where slavery existed.
5. What are the two most common religions in West Africa, and where is each predominant? Why does this difference exist?
6. Plan a menu using dishes popular in West Africa.

Bibliography

Appiah, K.A. and H.L. Gates, Jr., eds. 2000. *Africana.* Basic Books. New York.

Barer-Stein, T. 1999. *You Eat What You Are.* 2nd ed. Firefly Books, Ltd. Ontario, Canada.

Burenhult, G. 1994. *Traditional Peoples Today.* Harper Collins. New York.

Coetzee, R. 1982. *Funa—Food from Africa.* Butterworths. Durban, South Africa.

Devere, J. 1980. *Black Genesis: African Roots.* St. Martin's Press. New York.

Else, D. et al., eds. 1999. *West Africa.* 4th ed. Lonely Planet. Oakland, CA.

Hafner, D. 2002. *Taste of Africa: Traditional and Modern African Cooking.* Ten Speed Press. Berkeley.

Jackson, E.A. 1999. *South of the Sahara: Traditional Cooking from the Lands of West Africa.* Fantail. Hollis, NH.

Levy, P. 1993. *Nigeria.* Marshall Cavendish. New York.

National Council of Negro Women. 1998. *Mother Africa's Table.* Broadway Books. New York.

Osseo-Asare, F. and K. Albala. 2005. *Food Culture in Sub-Saharan Africa.* Greenwood Publishing Group. Westport, CT.

Page, H. and C. Alexander. 1999. *Aspects of African American Foodways.* Aspects Publishing. Tokyo.

Pearcy, G.E. 1980. *The World Food Scene.* Plycon Press. Redondo Beach, CA.

Reader, J. 1997. *Africa: A Biography of the Continent.* Vintage Books. New York.

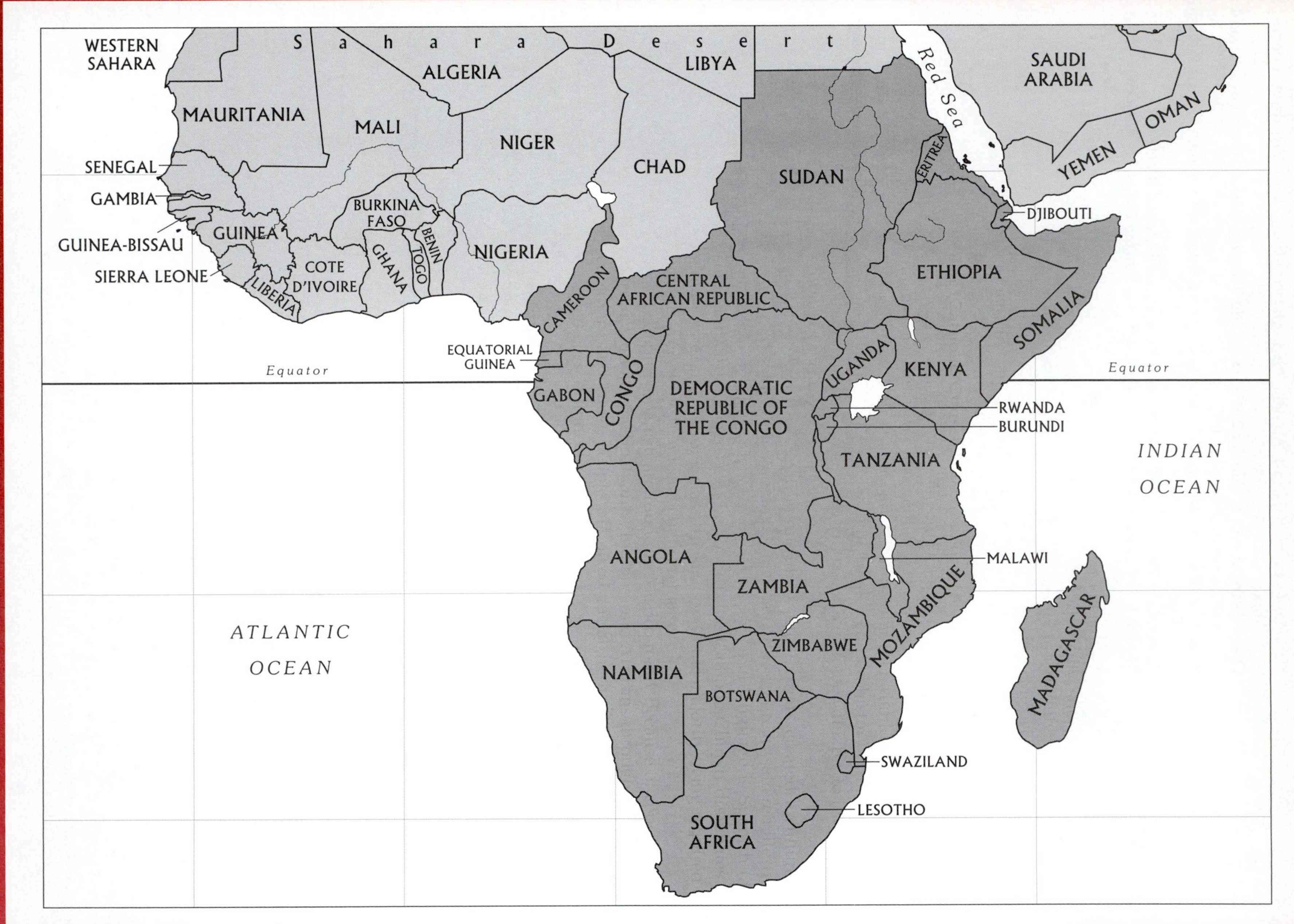
Sahara Desert
WESTERN SAHARA
MAURITANIA
MALI
ALGERIA
NIGER
LIBYA
CHAD
SUDAN
Red Sea
SAUDI ARABIA
OMAN
YEMEN
ERITREA
DJIBOUTI
SENEGAL
GAMBIA
GUINEA-BISSAU
GUINEA
SIERRA LEONE
LIBERIA
COTE D'IVOIRE
BURKINA FASO
GHANA
TOGO
BENIN
NIGERIA
CAMEROON
CENTRAL AFRICAN REPUBLIC
ETHIOPIA
SOMALIA
EQUATORIAL GUINEA
GABON
CONGO
DEMOCRATIC REPUBLIC OF THE CONGO
UGANDA
KENYA
RWANDA
BURUNDI
TANZANIA
Equator
Equator
INDIAN OCEAN
ATLANTIC OCEAN
ANGOLA
ZAMBIA
MALAWI
MOZAMBIQUE
MADAGASCAR
ZIMBABWE
NAMIBIA
BOTSWANA
SWAZILAND
LESOTHO
SOUTH AFRICA

14 East and South Africa

Geographic Overview

The whole continent of Africa is so vast that it is difficult to grasp its total extent. Perhaps the fact that its area is larger than the combined areas of the United States, China, Europe, India, New Zealand, and Argentina will help to establish a sense of its size. The total area of the United States is somewhat smaller than the part of Africa lying south of the equator.

Obviously, the geographic details of such a huge area as that encompassed in the eastern and southern parts of Africa cannot be presented; only a broadly brushed examination is feasible here. The countries included in this chapter are Sudan, Eritrea, Djibouti, Ethiopia, Somalia, Kenya, Tanzania, Uganda, Rwanda, Burundi, Gabon, Cameroon, the Democratic Republic of Congo, Angola, Zambia, Malawi, Mozambique, Zimbabwe, Botswana, Namibia, and South Africa.

Great Rift Valley—Vast depression in the earth extending from Jordan south and west to Mozambique.

These areas of Africa are mostly high plateaus, but there are some outstanding geographic features. Mt. Kilimanjaro (Figure C.105, p. C35) on the border of Kenya towers to a height of 19,340 feet. Second in height is Mt. Kenya, which rises to an impressive 17,058 feet. The **Great Rift Valley** extends from Jordan in the Middle East, south and west to its end in Mozambique (Figure 14.1). The depth of this valley varies greatly at various points but overall is a fairly deep depression in contrast with the rest of the landscape of the African continent.

Cape of Good Hope—Region at the southern tip of the African continent where the Atlantic Ocean meets the Indian Ocean.

The rivers of note in this part of Africa include the Zambezi with its remarkable Victoria Falls, the Congo, and the Limpopo. The Atlantic Ocean lies on the west, and the Indian Ocean on the east, with the two confronting each other where they meet at the **Cape of Good Hope** in South Africa.

The climate of South Africa is temperate (much like Southern California) because of its distance from the equator. However, the other countries of this region generally have considerable heat and extremes in rain or drought, depending on the time of year (Figure 14.2). The temperatures in areas of high elevations are

Figure 14.1 The Masai live in the Great Rift Valley in Kenya.

Figure 14.2 The vegetation in parts of Kenya and neighboring countries is fairly sparse in many areas due to the heat and drought conditions that often occur there.

Figure 14.3 Elephants and other wild game in eastern and some parts of southern Africa are important now as a means of bringing tourists to the region to help the economy, whereas earlier people used the animals primarily for meat.

more comfortable despite being in the Tropics. However, the low coastal regions are hot and steamy.

Agricultural efforts have been quite varied in this part of Africa. The original inhabitants basically were subsistence farmers or herders. In regions receiving enough rain, crops could be raised in quantities sufficient for farmers to feed their families. Where rainfall was inadequate, there still was sufficient vegetation available to raise livestock (cattle, goats, and sheep).

Europeans who came to East Africa as settlers introduced new crops to grow as export commodities. Coffee and tea were planted in Kenya, for example. The traditional crops of the subsistence farmers include corn, legumes, sweet potatoes, potatoes, millet, sorghum, and bananas. Wild game animals sometimes served as sources of meat in earlier times, but their primary role today is to bring in tourist dollars, which help indirectly to feed people living in parts of Africa, particularly south of the equator (Figure 14.3).

History

Early Inhabitants

Some of the very earliest traces of humans have been unearthed in the Olduvai Gorge in Tanzania, attesting to the presence of early hominids in Africa more than 1.5 million years ago. The climate in much of Africa south of the Sahara appears to have been favorable to the survival of early inhabitants with adequate food available for the picking and hunting. Petroglyphs, such as those in Botswana at the Tsodilo Hills and in Zimbabwe at Matobo, Domboshawa, and Ngomakurira National Parks, afford glimpses of the animals these people confronted in the early Stone Age. However, little else was found to provide information about the developments of early civilizations until comparatively recent discoveries.

Much later in early Egypt, Africa to the south of it was referred to as the land of *Punt*. Queen Hatshepsut was one of the Egyptian rulers who sent expeditions to Punt to bring back such goods as ivory, myrrh, and human slaves.

Aksum—Early, well-developed settlement in the highlands of Ethiopia of importance in the 4th and 5th centuries CE.

Perhaps the most successful early settlements south of Egypt were **Aksum** and Great Zimbabwe; some of their structures can still be seen today. Aksum's people worshiped in the churches they carved from stone in the highlands of northern Ethiopia. There the climate was cool and wet, making living easier during the time of year when the nearby Red Sea coast of today's Ethiopia was at its hottest and driest. The abundant crops and the energies of the people fostered a society that peaked in the 4th and 5th centuries CE. The Red Sea afforded trading opportunities with Egypt, the Arabian Peninsula, and the countries on the eastern end of the Mediterranean. Aksum residents developed a language that was spoken, not written. Their stone churches provide permanent evidence of their civilization.

Great Zimbabwe—Settlement in Zimbabwe featuring the Great Enclosure built of stone in the 14th century.

Beginning around the 11th century, people settled southwest of Aksum in what is now the country of Zimbabwe. This civilization, **Great Zimbabwe,** developed for three centuries leading to the construction of the Great Enclosure, which was constructed in the 14th century. The amazing stone structure called the *Great Enclosure* defined an ellipse that was more than 90 yards wide and about 250 yards in total length. Imagine the amount of stone that had to be placed to construct this wall, which was 5 yards thick and as many as 10 yards high. Among the artifacts that have been unearthed during the archaeological explorations of Great Zimbabwe are shards of Chinese and Persian wares, mute evidence of the trade that obviously existed during the zenith of Great Zimbabwe.

Much of the development of the eastern and southern regions of Africa stems from a combination of the climatic and trading influences. A migratory procession of Bantus slowly moved into these regions when rains and weather favored agricultural production of crops and livestock, notably cattle (Figure 14.4).

Figure 14.4 Although the vegetation is somewhat limited, cattle can graze successfully in parts of Kenya and other countries in East and South Africa.

The demands of the slave traders for slaves added to the impetus for Bantus and others to move into the new regions to avoid this threat.

Many different groups of Blacks migrated over many centuries into South Africa as well as Botswana and Zimbabwe. Some of the more predominant groups included the Zulu, Ndebele, Xhosa, Sotho, and Tsonga. Shaka, a particularly strong chief of the Zulus, ruled from 1816 until he was killed in 1828.

Foreign Involvement

Portuguese traders were at the forefront in opening trading in the southern reaches of Africa. The Cape of Good Hope was so named by Bartolomeu Diaz, leader of the first Portuguese expedition to round the southern tip of Africa. Vasco da Gama returned nine years later in 1497 and continued his voyage of exploration all the way to India. This voyage revealed the strong presence of Arabian and Indian traders already along the west coast of Africa.

Prester John—Mythical Christian leader of a domain originally rumored to be in India and then reported to be deep in Africa.

Foreign probes into Africa were triggered not only by interest in trade, but also by religion. Christians during the time of the Crusades believed that there was a Christian kingdom in India ruled by the mythical **Prester John,** who was rumored to be bringing his forces to help the Crusaders defeat the Moslems. When this failed to happen, the tales about Prester John shifted to suggest that his distant and rich Christian domain was somewhere in the depths of the African continent beyond the Sahara. The Portuguese were highly motivated to find and join forces with Prester John. They were eager to defeat Islamic forces they had encountered as a result of Vasco da Gama's voyage, and they wanted to secure the riches that could be obtained by trading along the east coast of Africa.

The Dutch and then the French and English were attracted to Africa as the slave trade and the Middle Passage (transportation of slaves by sea from Africa to the various colonial possessions) became economically significant in the 16th century. Even after the abolition of the Atlantic slave trade in the 19th century, it flourished in the eastern and southern parts of Africa and continued eastward from the east coast for much of the remainder of the century. Throughout Africa, the introduction of cassava and maize by the early European slave traders left at least the lasting benefit of these two important food crops that have provided so much sustenance for people throughout much of Africa.

The Cape of Good Hope was a logical site for establishing a provisioning post to facilitate the trading voyages the Dutch wished to make to the various ports in India and beyond. This need led to the settling of the land that is now South Africa, beginning at its southern shore, which is about as far south of the equator as Greece is north of it. Successful development of such a post required agricultural efforts by the new settlers.

North from the Cape of Good Hope

Bantus—Large group of Africans originally from west and central regions of Africa who spread east and south prior to colonial days.

Boer—South African of Dutch descent.

Dutch East India Company—Trading company that established Cape Town as a post to restock its ships plying between the East Indies and Holland.

Voortrekker—Boer who used oxen and covered wagons to make the Great Trek between 1835 and 1839; also called *trekboers*.

Trekboer—Boer who made the Great Trek to settle the interior of South Africa.

Afrikaans—Language spoken by Afrikaners (South African farmers of Dutch heritage); one of the official languages of South Africa.

The **Bantu** farmers (originally from north of the equator) had not traveled as far south as South Africa during their expansion because their major crops of millet and sorghum grew much better farther north than in the Cape region. This left the land relatively available to the Dutch settlers who arrived in Table Bay in 1652, and they worked hard to achieve good harvests. The native Khoisans raised cattle and moved them around as necessary for adequate grazing lands. This arrangement worked well at first, but the increasing need for farmland as new Dutch settlers (called **Boers**) arrived began to restrict the grazing land and inexorably moved the original inhabitants of the Cape from their land.

The **Dutch East India Company,** the trading company that started the development of what is now Cape Town, had intended only to restock ships at its new port. However, employees who left the company to settle in Cape Town and new arrivals from other countries began to crowd the surrounding farmland to the point that expansion to the east and into the interior regions had to occur These developments eventually led to the inland migration dubbed the *Great Trek,* which took place between 1835 and 1839. Participants in this migration were called **Voortrekkers** (or **Trekboers**); this movement is commemorated at a memorial built near Pretoria, one capital of South Africa (Figure 14.5).

Not surprising, conflicts were frequent between the Whites (who were usurping much of the good land previously available to the original inhabitants) and the Blacks. The Afrikaners (farmers of Dutch heritage) faced daunting times as they developed their farmlands in the interior, but the problems confronting the Blacks were also overwhelming. Nevertheless, the language of **Afrikaans** eventually gained status with English as the country's languages. The various Black languages were ignored.

Adding to the racial complexities was a group termed the *Coloreds,* which included Indians, Malays, and offspring of interracial marriages. Such marriages occurred commonly in the early days when very few White women settled in the region, causing the White settlers to reach out to other racial and cultural groups for sociability.

The final straw in this rather volatile milieu related to the diverse backgrounds of the Whites, who were Dutch Boers and British. Their inability to utilize each other's strengths and their clashes in philosophy, land, and governance resulted in the bloody Boer War at the end of the 19th century. The governmental stance that emerged from this war led to the divisive policy of *apartheid,* with its tragic treatment of Blacks and Coloreds.

Figure 14.5 The former home of South African statesman Paul Kruger in Pretoria, South Africa, is a historical museum.

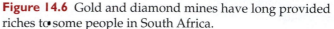

Figure 14.6 Gold and diamond mines have long provided riches to some people in South Africa.

Customs in Africa vary widely from tribe to tribe, sometimes contrasting sharply with traditions in America. An example is the custom of the Tswana, who live between the Kalahari Desert and the mountains of southern Africa. Their tradition is to marry a cousin to be certain that the children of the marriage belong to the husband's family. The groom pays a dowry (usually cattle) to the bride's family.

Finally, in the late 20th century, apartheid was abolished, and a Black president, Nelson Mandela, was elected. The situation in South Africa has undergone a significant transformation. The mineral riches of this nation, particularly diamonds and gold, should strengthen the new approach of its government in the 21st century (Figure 14.6).

Southern Africa suffered under its White rulers for a very long time, but it also gained some benefits in terms of development and organization. At the Berlin Conference of 1884–85, the rest of eastern and southern Africa was handed over to various European nations. The Congo was awarded to Leopold of Belgium with the result that huge numbers of people died while harvesting the rubber and other riches of the region that were being shipped to Belgium.

Britain received the Sudan, Kenya, Zimbabwe, Botswana, and South Africa (Figure 14.7). Germany received Tanzania, and Italy gained Somalia. The results in these countries generally were far less damaging than in the Congo, but national freedom became the goal of each. The various nations achieved independence at different times during the 20th century. However, evidence of the British remains wherever the British established their organization and administration, leaving a legacy that generally has aided countries to move forward after independence (Figure 14.8).

Figure 14.7 Cape Town, South Africa, developed as a modern city with British overtones, but also it reflected the harsh realities of the apartheid policy that was in effect so many years.

Figure 14.8 Contemporary architectural designs reflect the modern look of South Africa.

Culture

Religion

Missionaries were very active during the colonial period in Africa; they represented various Christian denominations as they brought their messages of the Bible and their faith. They also brought education to many people who had never had an opportunity to receive one. Sometimes the missionaries and their congregations melded their beliefs and practices well, but the Africans at times retained their beliefs in mysticism, the use of mediums, and magic as well their practice of polygamy in some cases. Nevertheless, the overall interaction was viewed as successful and helpful to the people the missionaries reached.

Muslims also were practicing their faith in some parts of Africa, particularly along the eastern coast, and some Hindus were worshiping the faith they brought with them from their homes in India. Although many Africans practice the Lutheran, Anglican, Dutch Reform, Methodist, Roman Catholic, and other religions brought by the missionaries, many people in this region still have a strong belief in animism. There is special veneration of ancestors and a strong interest in communicating with them, often with the assistance of a medium. Beliefs in potions and spells can also be quite strong among these people.

The Arts

Music plays a role in the various countries of Africa. For instance, the marimba and a variety of drums and rattles are utilized in music from Zimbabwe. Horns from wild animals sometimes find a role in making music. Missionaries also encouraged singing religious songs, providing a heritage that continues today.

Other creative expression in Africa includes storytelling, a particularly effective art among the populace where educational opportunities have been rather restricted. In South Africa, attention has been directed toward developing authors and poets. Zimbabwe also has some excellent sculptors who produce uniquely lovely native sculptures. Native dancing is another creative art that affords considerable pleasure and creativity to the dancers and can sometimes be seen by tourists.

Festivals

Some annual festivals illustrate the importance of the relationship between the people and their daily routines. In Zimbabwe the festival "Making the Seeds Grow" begins with the elders of the village meeting with a medium, an event that is held prior to the beginning of the rainy season. An evening bonfire forms the setting for feasting and dancing. The following day preparations are made for the growing season that will be coming, including gathering seed, which a medium then treats with special remedies to help ensure protection against pests once they are planted. The "Rainmaking" celebration is held just before the rains are to begin. It is a village event usually held in a sacred place at night with the intent of making ancestral spirits happy to help bring the desired rain.

Circumcision of both adolescent boys and girls is a ritual that is practiced to mark the passage into adolescence in some tribal groups. When this procedure is done to girls, the event is held in private. However, the ritual passage for males is celebrated in public by Masai in villages in Kenya and in many other tribal villages in Africa.

Food Patterns

Colonials who ruled in eastern and southern African countries have influenced food patterns there significantly. However, indigenous food habits and preferences still play an important role in the diets of these countries. An illustration of the influence that Europeans exerted is the extensive use of cassava and maize, introduced by slave traders, throughout much of Africa south of the Sahara.

British food patterns have influenced food habits as much as England has determined the side of the road on which drivers will proceed. Tea is clearly an example of a dietary tradition brought by the British to South Africa, Kenya, and other areas where they established colonies. However, diets still clearly reflect the crops that can be grown in the various regions and the suitability of the climate for raising livestock (Figure 14.9).

Traditionally, tribal societies in the eastern and southern parts of Africa have counted on women to grow and harvest their field crops, and children and adolescent males tend to the grazing livestock during the day. Women also are ordinarily responsible for preparing the two meals each day.

Meal Patterns

Calabash—Dried hard shell of a gourd suitable for holding liquids and foods.

Breakfast in the villages consists of a porridge made with a cereal and water that is boiled over a fire of twigs and grasses. It may be served in a communal pot or ladled into bowls or **calabashes** (dried hard shell of a gourd). The men may eat together in the tribal council, in which case a young girl delivers the porridge to her kinsmen. Women and children eat inside or outside their huts.

Figure 14.9 Outdoor markets provide a gathering place to buy local produce and other useful items for daily life in many towns in Africa.

Mealie meal—South African name for cornmeal (*mealie* means *corn*).

Sadza—Zimbabwean name for a stiff cornmeal porridge.

Ugali—Kenyan name for a stiff cornmeal porridge.

Pombe—Kenyan beer.

Nsima (pronounced en-see' ma) is the name people in Malawi use for the finely ground maize that is made into the thick porridge, which is the mainstay of most people in the country. Although maize is not a native African food but was introduced into Africa from the Americas, it has served as the main cereal staple in much of eastern and southern Africa for more than 150 years. Unfortunately, maize is particularly susceptible to drought, and much of this part of the continent has been plagued with famine triggered by the lack of or inadequate rain for growing maize. Reliance on this single grain has also caused nutritional problems because of the limited intake of essential nutrients, particularly niacin. The government of Malawi has been promoting the consumption of other cereals and vegetables to augment the nsima that people eat traditionally, but the broadened menu has received very limited acceptance. Unless they have eaten nsima, many in Malawi feel they have not eaten at all. When nsima is scarce, famine unfortunately follows.

The porridge usually is made from corn that has been ground into a meal, which accounts for the South African name **mealie meal** to designate the meal they make from mealie (their name for *corn*). Zimbabweans term their rather stiff corn porridge **sadza,** and Kenyans call it **ugali.** Despite the name, this porridge made from maize is a cornerstone of native diets, and other dishes prepared later in the day frequently rely on cornmeal or corn kernels (dried or fresh, depending on the season). Even beer is made from corn in some homes. In Kenya, this beer is called **pombe.**

The other meal of the day also includes cornmeal in some form as a significant part, but vegetables and sometimes meat are added for variety. Usually, these ingredients are cooked along with the porridge in a one-dish meal, which also is served from a large pot or from calabashes (Figure 14.10). Fingers are the preferred tools for eating. People eat together, but men commonly eat before women and children.

Some insects and small creatures are considered delicacies among various groups in these regions of Africa. Termites, for example, are a treat (either roasted or raw) to some Africans living south of the equator! Field mice provide another source of protein for some people.

Safe water is one of the significant problems for rural Africans, particularly in the tropical areas. Often, it must be carried some distance and then stored in jugs or calabashes for subsequent use. Boiling is necessary to help ensure safety. Added to the problems of food safety is the lack of refrigeration in many villages. The practice of boiling the ingredients in a common pot to make porridges and stews certainly is of great value in helping to maintain health.

Milk is not a prominent part of the diet after children are weaned, although some people do use a bit of it in cooking. The Masai in Kenya are noted for keeping cattle and for their practice of combining blood from the animals with some milk, which then is drunk promptly before it spoils. By using their cattle in this way and only occasionally using them for meat, the Masai are able to get maximum dietary benefits while generally maintaining the size of their herds.

Root vegetables are very important in the African evening meal. Cassava is used in abundance and is nutritionally valuable as a good source of starch. To avoid the potentially poisonous effect of fresh cassava, the root must be

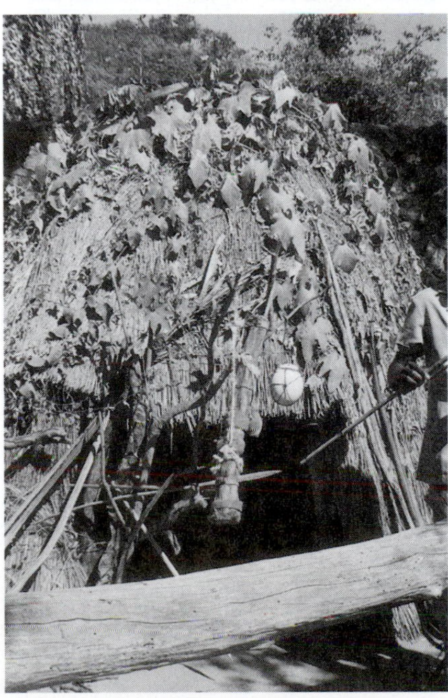

Figure 14.10 A calabash full of water hangs outside this native hut in Botswana.

Fufu—Starchy paste or dough made of cassava; popular specifically in Kenya.

Braaivleis—Barbecues in the southern countries of Africa.

Sosaties—Barbecued pieces of meat on a stick.

pretreated carefully by soaking it for a few days before boiling it for at least 10 minutes and then squeezing out the liquid. The remaining pulp of the cassava is then ready to beat or to work in a mortar with a pestle to make a soft dough. Kenyans call this cassava dish **fufu.** Pumpkins, various types of squash, sweet potatoes, and potatoes are also used extensively.

Other ingredients for meals may include various meats. Barbecues (**braaivleis**) are popular; barbecued pieces of meat are called **sosaties.** However, some people have a particular animal as a totem (family symbol), and meat from this animal must absolutely not be served to them. Otherwise, the meat may be either domestic or a wild animal (or the aforementioned small rodents). Fruits vary with the season but are popular when they are available. In the tropics there may be considerable variety. Coconut is popular; its liquid is used in cooking, and its meat is used in a variety of ways.

Recipes

African Beef Stew (Serves 4–6)

1 lb beef stew meat (1″ cubes)
1 onion, chopped
1 tbsp oil
3 plantains, cut in quarters
2 tbsp lemon juice
3 tbsp tomato sauce
½ tsp salt
¼ tsp ground sage
¼ tsp pepper
Water to cover

1. In a Dutch oven, sauté meat and onion in oil until browned.
2. Rub plantain pieces with lemon juice, and add to meat.
3. Stir while heating slowly for 5 minutes.
4. Add remaining ingredients, and then simmer (covered) for 2 hours.

Vegetable Stew (Serves 4–6)

1 c dried beans
4 c water
½ lb cubed lamb stew meat
1 onion, chopped
2 potatoes, pared and cubed
2 stalks celery, 1″ slices
3 carrots, pared and sliced
1 c corn
1 tsp curry powder
1 tsp salt
1 c boiling water

1. Boil beans in water in a Dutch oven for 2 minutes. Let stand without heat for 1 hour.
2. Simmer beans for 1 hour.
3. In frying pan, brown meat and onion in oil.
4. Add meat, onion, and other ingredients to beans and simmer for 1 hour.

Chicken in Peanut Butter Sauce (Serves 4–6)

1 frying chicken, cut in pieces
¼ c oil
1 6-oz can tomato paste
1½ c water
1 tsp salt
½ tsp pepper
¼ c peanut butter

1. Brown chicken in oil; discard oil.
2. Dilute tomato paste with water, and pour over chicken.
3. Cover and simmer 30 minutes.
4. Add seasonings and peanut butter; simmer 20 minutes.

South African Chutney (Makes 3 cups)

¼ lb dried pears, chopped
¼ lb dried apricots, chopped
¼ lb dates, chopped
¼ lb dried apples, chopped
¼ lb golden raisins
2 c water
1 c cider vinegar
1 c brown sugar
¼ tsp chili powder
¼ tsp ground nutmeg
¼ tsp ground ginger
½ clove garlic, crushed

1. Soak fruit in water in covered bowl overnight.
2. Transfer to a big pan and add the rest of the ingredients.
3. Stir while bringing to a boil, and then simmer 1½ hours to thicken, stirring occasionally.

Fufu (Serves 4)

1 lb cassava
Water to cover

1. Peel cassava and soak for 4 days.
2. Cut out the core.
3. Put in a saucepan and add water to cover.
4. Bring to a boil, turn down heat, and simmer 10 minutes.
5. Pound in a mortar using a pestle until the cassava makes a soft dough.
6. Serve with stew.

Lamb Sosaties (Serves 4–6)

1 c vinegar
1 onion, thinly sliced
12 dried apricot halves, chopped
½ tsp curry powder
2 tbsp brown sugar
2 c water
Leg of lamb or chops in 1″ slices, cut to make pieces for barbecuing
2 tbsp cornstarch
½ c cold water

1. Make marinade by boiling vinegar, onion, apricots, curry powder, sugar, and water for 3 minutes.
2. Pour cooled marinade over lamb, adding water if necessary to cover lamb.
3. Refrigerate for 2 days.
4. Thread lamb onto skewers and barbecue.
5. Stir cornstarch and water mixture into marinade and bring to boil while stirring.
6. Serve lamb with thickened marinade.

Peanut Butter Soup (Serves 4–6)

½ lb lean ground beef
1½ qt water
1 onion, chopped
2 cloves garlic, pressed
½ tsp coarse grind black pepper
1½ tsp salt
1 stick cinnamon
2 cardamom seeds, ground
2 tbsp peanut butter
2 tbsp lemon juice

1. Simmer all ingredients except peanut butter and lemon in a saucepan for 1½ hours.
2. Stir ½ cup stock into peanut butter, and then add peanut butter and lemon juice to the soup.
3. Simmer for 5 minutes.

Mashed Plantains and Chicken Stew (Serves 4–6)

1 frying chicken, cut in pieces
1 onion, sliced
¼ c oil
2 tomatoes, chopped
2 potatoes, peeled and cubed
Salt and pepper
2 c water
3 plantains, peeled and quartered
Water
Salt and pepper

1. Brown chicken and onions in oil in a Dutch oven.
2. Add tomatoes, potatoes, seasonings, and water, and then simmer (covered) for 1 hour.
3. Meanwhile, steam plantains on a rack in a steamer until tender.
4. Mash plantains and season with salt and pepper.
5. Serve chicken stew over plantains.

Summary

The countries included in this chapter are Sudan, Eritrea, Djibouti, Ethiopia, Somalia, Kenya, Tanzania, Uganda, Rwanda, Burundi, Gabon, Cameroon, the Democratic Republic of Congo, Angola, Zambia, Malawi, Mozambique, Zimbabwe, Botswana, Namibia, and South Africa. The terrain includes much of the Great Rift Valley, a high plateau, some high mountains, low tropical seacoasts, varying agricultural conditions ranging from very humid to arid, and a dramatic tip (the Cape of Good Hope) where the Atlantic and Indian Oceans meet very far south of the equator.

Some farmers can raise some commercial crops, such as tea and coffee, but many subsistence farmers are able to grow barely enough food for their families. Some livestock are raised, and wild game is occasionally eaten. The wildlife are valued more for the ability to attract tourist dollars than as a meat source for the continent.

Traces of very early humans have been found in such places in Africa as the Olduvai Gorge in Tanzania. Much more recently, evidence of the early Ethiopian city of Aksum, dating from the 4th century, and Great Zimbabwe, with its Great Enclosure, built in Zimbabwe in the 14th century, also have provided historical perspectives. Portuguese traders opened up the coasts of Africa in their quest to find a sea route to the East Indies. After rounding the Cape of Good Hope, they discovered that Arab and Indian traders were already exchanging goods with the people along the east coast of Africa.

Colonization by the Dutch with its Boer farmers at the Cape of Good Hope began the settlement by Europeans in the southern part of Africa. Bantus migrated into eastern and southern regions from their homelands in the western and central parts of Africa. Eventually, considerable conflict erupted, particularly in South Africa, where the British and the Boers (Dutch settlers) were attempting to establish authority over what is now South Africa and the neighboring regions. Belgian colonization of the Congo also resulted in considerable loss of life among the natives. Added to this situation was the ongoing problem of slavery and the slave trade for more than 200 years.

The various colonies have now gained their independence, although considerable political unrest still occurs in some of them. The end of apartheid in South Africa and the free elections that followed are beginning to bring a period of greater tranquility and productivity there.

Missionaries worked extensively in these countries to bring Christianity to the natives. This religion still is often mixed with animistic practices by many African natives. There also are other religions, particularly Muslim, the result of the Arab influence. Immigrants from India have also brought Hinduism to a limited extent.

Music, especially with drums and percussive instruments, is popular in Africa. Dancing is a traditional cultural heritage. Storytelling is another favorite way of keeping tradition alive from generation to generation.

Women traditionally prepare the two meals that are served in many families. A thick porridge, usually made of cornmeal, is commonly served for breakfast. The evening meal also is likely to feature a cornmeal or cassava dish as a source of starch. Some meat and plenty of vegetables may be cooked together to make a stew when these items are available. Fruits are also popular. Meals prepared in a single pot are well suited to regions where good water and a regular stove may not be readily available. Insects and small field animals are found in some diets. Milk is sometimes consumed when it is available, but lack of refrigeration in living quarters can make it a hazard to health.

Selected Sites

http://www.sas.upenn.edu/African_Studies/Cookbook/Ethiopia.html—Directions for preparing an authentic Ethiopian dinner.

http://www.sas.upenn.edu/African_Studies/Cookbook/Kenya.html—Information for preparing an authentic Kenyan dinner.

http://www.sas.upenn.edu/African_Studies/Cookbook/Tanzania.html—Description of food and dinner preparation in Tanzania.

http://www.globalgourmet.com/destinations/southafrica—Discussion of food in South Africa and some recipes.

http://www.trufflepig.co.za/sa_food_scene.asp—Extensive information about South African history, food, and ingredients.

http://www.africa.upenn.edu/NEH/kfood.htm—Information on food and other aspects of life in various countries in East Africa.

http://www.africaguide.com/cooking.htm—Recipes and foods in various East African nations.

http://www.recipes4us.co.uk/Cooking%20by%20Country/South%20Africa.htm—Discussion of various aspects of food patterns and recipes typical of South Africa.

Study Questions

1. Why were the Portuguese so eager and persistent in their efforts to explore the coasts of Africa?
2. Compare the problems of establishing colonial settlements in the Congo with those in South Africa.
3. What were some of the problems that Bantu farmers had to overcome in growing crops in the equatorial regions? Why did they halt their southward migration before they got to the coast of South Africa?
4. What are some vegetables commonly eaten in eastern Africa?
5. Describe the way in which a village family in Zimbabwe might eat for a day.
6. Plan a menu for dinner in Kenya and one for South Africa. What differences did you note in making your plans?

Bibliography

Abrahams, C. 1995. *Culture and Cuisine of the Cape Malays.* Metz Press. Welgemoed, South Africa.

Allison, S. and M. Robins. 1997. *South African Cape Malay Cooking.* Absolute Press. Bath, England.

Barer-Stein, T. 1999. *You Eat What You Are.* 2nd ed. Firefly Books, Ltd. Ontario, Canada.

Byars, D. 1996. Traditional African foods and African Americans. *Agriculture and Human Values 13:* 74–78.

Coetzee, R. 1982. *Funa—Food from Africa.* Butterworth. Durban, South Africa.

Duckitt, H. 1996. *Traditional South African Cooking.* Hippocrene Books. New York.

Harris, J.B. 1998. *Africa Cookbook.* Simon and Schuster. New York.

Harris, J.B. 1999. *Iron Pots and Wooden Spoons: Africa's Gifts to New World Cooking.* Simon and Schuster. New York.

Hopkinson, T. 1964. *South Africa.* Time, Inc. New York.

Hurford, E. and C. Fraser. 2000. *Simply South Africa: Culinary Journey.* Struik Book Distributors, London.
Kiley, D. 1976. *South Africa.* B. T. Batsford. London, England.
Kingsolver, B. 1998. *Poisonwood Bible.* Harper Flamingo. New York.
Mbiti, J.S. 1970. *African Religions and Philosophy.* Doubleday Anchor. Garden City, NY.
Nabwire, C. and B.V. Montgomery. *Cooking the East African Way.* Lerner Publications. Minneapolis, MN.
O'Shea, M. 2005. *Food and Cooking of Africa and Middle East.* Lorenz Books. London.
Pateman, R. 1993. *Kenya.* Marshall Cavendish. New York.
Pearcy, G.E. 1980. *The World Food Scene.* Plycon Press. Redondo Beach, CA.
Reader, J. 1997. *Africa: A Biography of the Continent.* Vintage Books. New York.
Sheehan, S. 1993. *Zimbabwe.* Marshall Cavendish. New York.
Swaney, D. 1999. *Zimbabwe, Botswana, and Namibia.* 2nd ed. Lonely Planet. Oakland, CA.
Van Wyk, M. and P. Barton. 1996. *Traditional South African Cooking.* Central News Agency, Ltd. Johannesburg, South Africa.

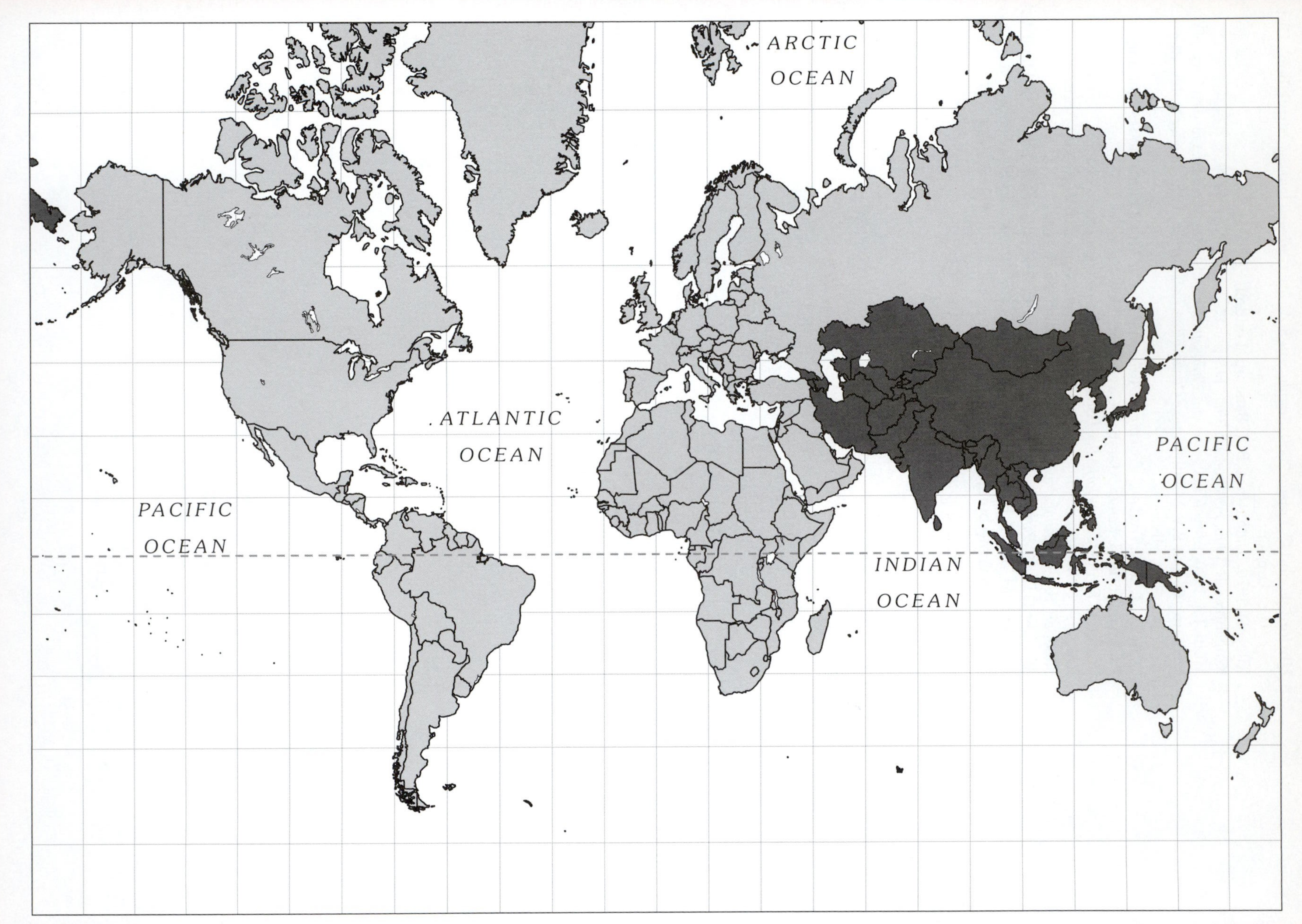
ARCTIC OCEAN
ATLANTIC OCEAN
PACIFIC OCEAN
PACIFIC OCEAN
INDIAN OCEAN

Part V

Food Treasures from the Orient and the Pacific

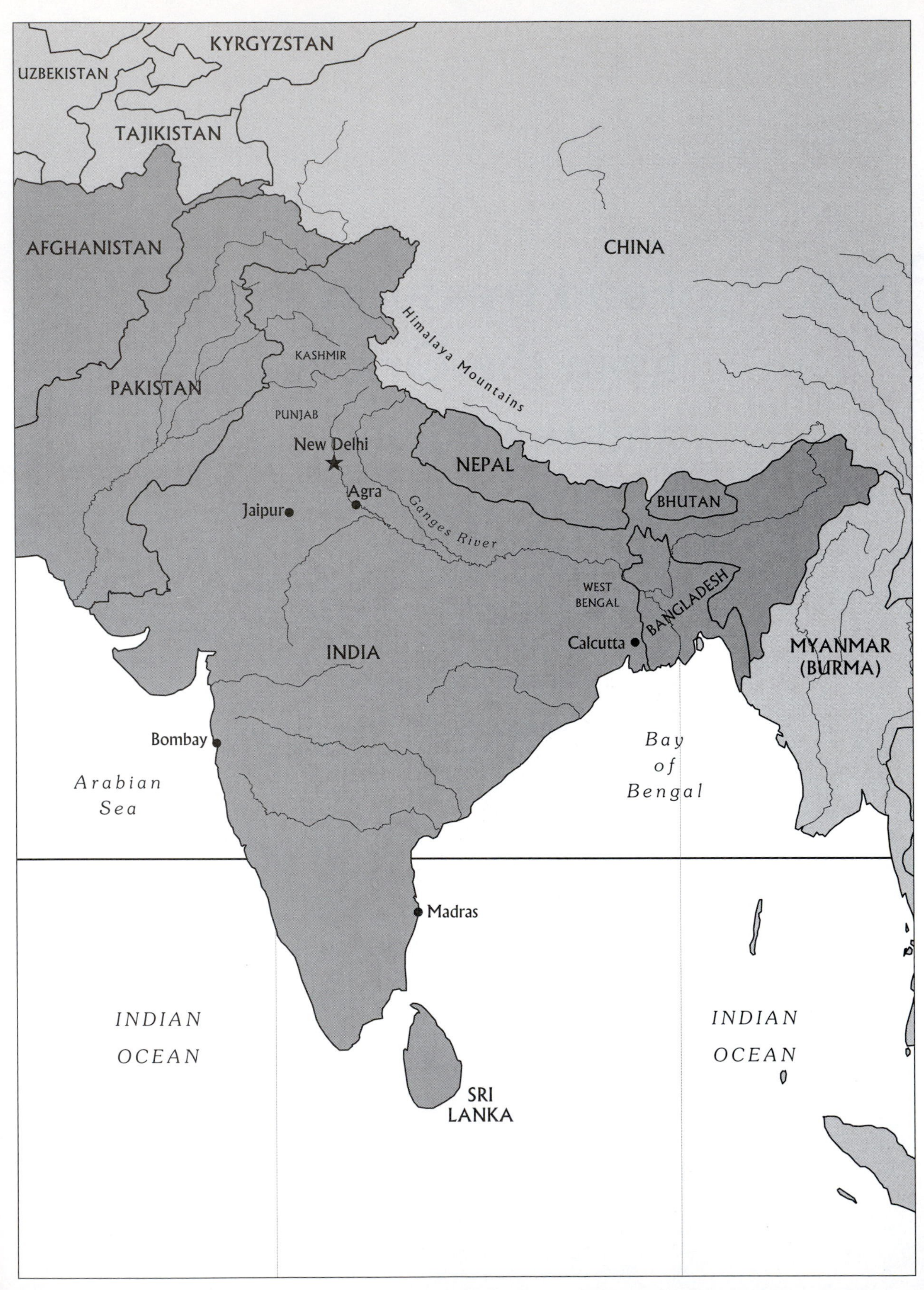

KYRGYZSTAN
UZBEKISTAN
TAJIKISTAN
AFGHANISTAN
CHINA
Himalaya Mountains
KASHMIR
PAKISTAN
PUNJAB
New Delhi
NEPAL
BHUTAN
Agra
Jaipur
Ganges River
WEST
BENGAL
BANGLADESH
Calcutta
INDIA
MYANMAR
(BURMA)
Bombay
Bay
of
Bengal
Arabian
Sea
Madras
INDIAN
OCEAN
INDIAN
OCEAN
SRI
LANKA

15 India and Its Neighbors

Geographic Overview

India is described as a subcontinent of Asia where the Himalayas are being shoved ever higher on the northern reaches of the country as its plate slides under the main plate of Asia. The result of this slowly evolving shift is a protective barrier that served in centuries past as a deterrent to invaders from the north. Mt. Everest, the highest mountain in the world, stands more than 29,000 feet and is still growing. Other Himalayan peaks of more than 20,000 feet are found all along this imposing range that touches on not only India, but also its northern neighbors: Afghanistan, Pakistan, Nepal, Bhutan, and Tibet (Figure 15.1). The other countries surrounding India are Bangladesh to the east and Sri Lanka, the island nation to the south.

Traversing between the eastern and western parts of northern India and Pakistan is the Indus River, which empties into the Arabian Sea on the west after flowing many miles through Pakistan. The Ganges, considered to be the holiest of rivers, and the Brahmaputra flow east into the Bay of Bengal soon after entering Bangladesh on the east of northern India. These rivers plus lesser ones in the north are fed by the melting snows of the Himalayas as well as the heavy rains that pelt the region during the monsoon season (Figure 15.2).

Trading via rivers in India is not generally practical, and the extensive shoreline of the peninsula that comprises southern India also presents challenges to trade because of the limited number of good ports. Nevertheless, such ports as Bombay and Madras are able to accommodate a considerable amount of freight via ships.

India has rather diverse agricultural areas. The Himalayan foothills in the north have long been the source of excellent tea, which flourishes in the relatively cool and adequately moist climate (Figure 15.3). Some of the most favorable conditions for farming are found on the Indo-Gangetic plain, for the seasonal flooding helps to bring fresh soil to support the crops that are grown there. The

Figure 15.1 The Potala (former home of the Dalai Lama and the religious center of Tibetan Buddhism) in Lhasa, Tibet, is at an elevation of about 12,000 feet in the Himalayas north of India.

Figure 15.2 Rivers in Northern India, such as the one below the Amber Fort outside Jaipur, become increasingly shallow as the melt from the Himalayas declines until the monsoon rains arrive, usually late in May.

Figure 15.3 Darjeeling, in the foothills of the Himalayas, is noted for the high-quality tea that is grown there; it also was the place where British Colonials retreated in the summers from the heat in New Delhi.

Figure 15.4 Cardamom pods containing the seeds form above the ground; the seeds are ground into powder and used as a flavoring ingredient in curries.

areas affected by the monsoon rains are well suited to raising rice, which begins with the flooding of the fields followed by the gradual drying as the crop matures. The Thar Desert, south of the Indus River, is hostile to farming.

Wheat, some barley, sorghum, and millet are other cereal crops that are grown in some parts of India. In addition to various fruits and vegetables, coconut and some spices are also grown in India south of the vast Deccan Plateau (Figure 15.4). Legumes are important crops, particularly because of the vegetarian diets of many people in India. Cooking oils are available from cottonseed, peanuts, rapeseed, and sesame grown in the country.

Buffalo milk is the dairy product commonly used; cows are sacred and thus are not generally considered a source of food, but some people do consume their milk. Some beef is consumed in India, although lamb is more popular, particularly in the north.

History and Culture

India

Dravidians—Early people of southern India.

Early in the history of southern India, a dark-skinned people called the **Dravidians** appear to have made their way beyond the Deccan Plateau into the hospitable region at the southern tip of India (Cape Comorin). There they were generally isolated from the struggles that often marked the development of northern India. Their language, Tamil, was distinctly different from the Aryan languages that evolved in northern India. The Tamil also migrated to the island of Sri Lanka, just off the tip of India.

In the Indus Valley, farming communities began to evolve as early as 4000 BCE. This led to trading and an advance in civilization that even included development of seaports and a form of writing with pictographs. Aryans invaded from north of the protective mountains and ravaged the existing civilization in the Indus Valley before they began to settle in the region around 2000 BCE.

The Aryans brought changes that eventually shaped the region. India became the spiritual home of two major religions, Hinduism and Buddhism (Figure 15.5), that are still practiced today. Aryan priests carefully created the Vedas, the four books outlining Hinduism, over the course of 10 centuries prior to 500 BCE. This religious documentation established the caste system and other significant aspects of Hinduism that are very much a part of life in India today. The Aryans are credited with bringing the language of Sanskrit to India and to Hinduism. Gautama Buddha, who was born about 567 BCE in India, developed his version of religion, which is Buddhism.

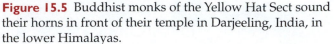

Figure 15.5 Buddhist monks of the Yellow Hat Sect sound their horns in front of their temple in Darjeeling, India, in the lower Himalayas.

Numerous small political units evolved as a result of conflicts in India, and eventually India felt the impact of Cyrus the Great when his Persian troops defeated the people in the Indus Valley and the Punjab in 531 BCE. Persian dominance contributed to the culture of the region while exacting its toll in the form of troops for wars as far away as Greece. Subsequently, Alexander the Great invaded India for several years but left in 323 BCE.

Alexander's departure led the way for the formation of the Mauryan Empire, a unifying force for India. Ashoka, the Mauryan king from 272 to 236 BCE, was a powerful convert to Buddhism who played a major role in promoting the spread of this religion.

The Gupta Empire reached across northern India during the period from 320 to 750 CE. Although this was a Hindu empire at that time, much evidence of Buddhism, such as stupas (dome-shaped religious mounds) and statues (Figure 15.6) coexisted with the art associated with Hinduism. During the reign of the Gupta monarchs, art and literature flourished. Astronomy and mathematics also were major interests.

The golden period of the Guptas ceased when the Huns invaded. Muslim invaders pushed their way into parts of western and northern India over a period

Figure 15.6 This giant Buddha carved in a sandstone cliff in Bamian, Afghanistan, looked down on the local scene (including the invasion by Genghis Khan) until 2001 when the Taliban destroyed it.

of about 200 years and stayed to become a part of the religious scene of the country. The barbarous attacks of Genghis Khan in central Asia drove many well-educated and artistic Muslims to seek refuge in India, which added to the cultural richness of the region.

A gradual decline in political leadership left the way open for the invasion of Babur, a Mongol descendant of Genghis Kahn, who created a powerful and culturally rich empire in northern India. This Mughal Empire ruled much of India from 1524 to 1707 and left such cultural richness as the Taj Mahal (Figures C.111 and C.112, pp. C37 and C38) and other artistic accomplishments (see Chapter 1). Although the religion of the Mughals was Muslim, Hinduism and Buddhism continued to flourish throughout India, gaining strength after the fall of the Mughals.

European influence began to be felt along the seacoast of India. Portugal established trading posts at Bombay, Goa, and other ports along the Arabian Sea in western India. The British, Dutch, and French also began a vigorous trade with India during the 17th century. However, it was the British who eventually controlled India. They brought their excellent administrative abilities and helped to establish the foundations of business, education, and government that are still a part of India today.

Significant changes have taken place since India achieved independence from England in 1947. A particularly dramatic change was the creation of Pakistan as a separate Muslim country and subsequently the formation of Bangladesh from what was East Pakistan. The extensive shifting of Muslims from India to Pakistan and of Hindus from Pakistan to India that occurred as a result of this cleavage of a once united land resulted in incredible bloodshed. This continues even today in the disputed region of Kashmir, the lovely northern tip of India.

India is a densely populated country that faces the challenging problems associated with feeding, educating, and governing so many people. The diversity of populations within the country complicates matters. Since becoming a nation free of the rule of the British Raj, several changes have occurred in the leadership of the government, some of which have been accomplished by violence. Despite such problems, the nation continues to develop as a significant part of the world community.

In view of the lengthy history of India and its unique background that melds influences from diverse religions and a variety of ethnic backgrounds, it is not surprising that India presents a very rich cultural heritage. Caves near Ajanta in western India still display the wall paintings done by Buddhist monks over the eight centuries prior to 600 CE. Artistic cave paintings that are a blend of Buddhist and Hindu art also exist in the same region near Ellora. Later artistic expression can be found throughout many parts of India where numerous statues of Buddha and many ornate and intricately decorated Hindu temples attest to the highly developed artistic skills of the people living in India over the centuries.

Taj Mahal—Mausoleum built by Shah Jahan in Agra, India, to honor the memory of his favorite wife, Mumtaz.

The Mughals left some intricately executed and delicate structures, such as the **Taj Mahal** as well as some sturdily built yet beautiful palaces and forts in Rajasthan in northern and northwestern India (Figures C.111–114, pp. C37 and C38). The love of detailed art is evident in many creations in this nation.

Music also is a passion for many Indians. The style of Indian music is distinctly different from western forms and is based on individual creativity as well as melodies learned by rote from gurus or teachers of music. The instruments also are quite varied and include several types of stringed instruments that can be bowed, plucked, or tapped in addition to drums and wind instruments. The sitar is an Indian stringed instrument that has gained some popularity in the United States. To the western ear, Indian music seems often to have a rather sing-song quality and a meandering style that captures the unique spirit of the Indian people.

The official languages of India are Hindi and English, but there are many different dialects. English serves as the unifying mode of communication between speakers of these many dialects. Considerable literature has been created in India over the centuries. Tamil and Sanskrit were early languages for literature, but contemporary literature usually is written in the country's official languages. Also, storytelling is an ancient art that remains a popular part of the culture today. India is a land that embraces holidays and practices elaborate traditions to celebrate them.

The calendar is quite full of religious holidays because of the many religions in India including Hindu, Buddhist, Muslim, and Christian groups. Holi is the popular festival of spring; it is celebrated by tossing purple-colored powder or water at any hapless person who comes within range on that day. The greatest celebration of the fall is Divali, which celebrates Lord Krishna's triumph over a demon and the return of Rama from his exile. Independence is also marked by a day of celebration on August 15.

Other dimensions of India's culture are mysticism, meditation, and physical tests of concentration. Levitation demonstrations, walking on hot coals, and snake charming are sights that can still be seen in India. Another exotic aspect of India is the presence of tigers, elephants, and other wild game in the northern part of the country (Figure 15.7). Clearly, this world is quite different than the one familiar to Americans.

India's neighbors have their own distinctive cultures, although each has some overtones of the culture of its large neighbor.

Nepal

Nepal lies just on the northeast shoulder of India and borders Tibet along its northern edge, thus sharing part of the Himalayan range with Tibet. Much of the country is mountainous, but the southern part of Nepal is low enough to be home to some wild tigers and elephants. Population pressures have led to deforestation and serious erosion in populated areas, but much natural beauty—spectacular mountain peaks, tree-sized rhododendrons alive with their red blooms, and wild orchids—sets this country apart from most others.

Of cultural interest are the Durbar Squares in Kathmandu, Patan, and Bhaktapur in the Kathmandu Valley (Figure 15.8). The Hindu and Buddhist religions are melded in this setting, which unites earlier centuries with life today. Two Buddhist **stupas** in the Kathmandu Valley keeping watchful eyes over the scene are Swayambhunath and Bodhnath (Figure C.116, p. C39).

Stupa—Covered mound, often containing a relic of significance for Buddhists.

A Hindu Shiva shrine, Pashupatinath (Figure C.115, p. C39) is the scene of ritual bathing, cremation, and religious devotions in Kathmandu Valley. The ghats (cremation pedestals) amid the worshipers and wild monkeys create a picture that lingers long in memories. A glimpse of the Living Goddess, a prepubertal girl considered to be an incarnation of Shiva's consort, is seldom forgotten. She lives in seclusion and comfort in the Kumari Bahal (an 18th century structure in Kathmandu) during her reign, which ends when she enters puberty. The Pokhara Valley to the west provides a look at rural life and the village agricultural scene

Figure 15.7 Asian elephants have a cooling bath in a stream in Sri Lanka, where they are used for work and transportation; they also are seen in some places in India.

Figure 15.8 Durbar Squares in Patan and Bhaktapur near Katmandu, Nepal, preserve the cultural heritage of the Katmandu Valley.

Nepal, India, and Bhutan lie along the southern side of the Himalayas and have provided refuge for many Tibetans who fled over the mountains when the Chinese invasion forced the Dalai Lama to flee in 1959. The Buddhist monasteries in these countries have been instrumental in providing safe harbors and a spiritual home for these refugees for more than 25 years.

(Figure 15.9). The towering mountains beckon mountain climbers, who are aided by local Sherpas, the mountain people in the region.

Bhutan

Bhutan is a small kingdom a bit east of Nepal that offers an even different cultural flavor. Its state religion is Mahayana Buddhism, and this sets the tone for a somewhat contemplative, unhurried lifestyle that is very much in touch with nature. The careful control of tourist traffic and the small population create an unusually tranquil setting in today's world. Even the style of the buildings, although quite massive, is pleasing and harmonious. The country's slogan, "Gross national happiness," and its alternative name of "Land of the Thunder Dragon" clearly capture Bhutan's essence.

Among the sights of Bhutan are the many dzongs (thick-walled, large and sturdy stone buildings with windows placed high from the ground), prayer flags frantically waving their messages heavenward in the winds, and the precariously perched Taksang, or Tiger's Nest, Buddhist monastery high on the cliffs of the Paro Valley (Figures 15.10 and 15.11).

Tibet

Potala—Seat of Tibetan Buddhism and former home of the Dalai Lama.

Tibet's architecture and religious features have much in common with those of Bhutan, which is not surprising, since they are very close neighbors separated more by the precipitous mountain peaks than their religious beliefs. The outstanding building in Tibet is the **Potala** in Lhasa, the home of the Dalai Lama before his flight to Dharamsala, India, in 1959.

Figure 15.9 Rural life in the Pokhara Valley in Nepal is one that involves hard work but little luxury.

Figure 15.10 Tiger's Nest, a Buddhist monastery, was built clinging precariously to the steep mountainside and is accessible only by a trail in Bhutan.

The Dalai Lama's summer palace, the Norbulingka, affords another glimpse of his early life in Tibet (Figure 15.12). The most holy place of worship in Tibet is the Jokhang Temple, which has an endless parade of pilgrims prostrating themselves as they circumambulate the holy site. All through Tibet, as well as in Bhutan and Nepal, whirling prayer wheels seem to constantly be in motion in the hands of devout Buddhists. The faithful also whirl larger prayer wheels as they pass outside the temples (Figure 15.13).

Pakistan

Pakistan is to a certain extent a country of contrasts. It clearly is a Muslim country whose traditions and clothing are conservative, following the teachings of the Koran. Another contrast exists between the rural populace who struggle to subsist and the urban dwellers who live a modern existence. Cities range from Peshawar, with its frontier (close to Afghanistan) costumes and character, to Lahore and its remaining mosques and monuments from the Mughal Empire, and on to Karachi and its bustling urban life and seaport. The country's modern technology, exemplified by its nuclear capability, is in sharp contrast to its agricultural tradition of raising camels, goats, and sheep, which graze in remote areas.

Figure 15.11 Thanka art is the form of artistic expression created in Tibet, Bhutan, and Nepal.

Figure 15.12 Norbulingka, the former summer home of the Dalai Lama in Lhasa, is set in a parklike setting a short distance below the Potala.

Afghanistan

Afghanistan, which lies along the northern border of Pakistan, is also a Muslim country. Although war resulted in ouster of the Taliban, Islam remains the dominant factor shaping daily life. Food patterns reflect Islamic traditions, just as is true in Pakistan.

Bangladesh

Bangladesh became an independent nation in 1971 when it declared itself free of West Pakistan; India sided with Bangladesh and quickly defeated West Pakistan when it sent its army against the former East Pakistan. This rather young nation has a precarious existence because of its dense population and its physical position at a low elevation at the head of the Bay of Bengal, which leaves it devastated by floods when monsoon conditions are especially vicious. Tidal waves and heavy rainfall are continuing threats to humans, animals, and crops. The problems of an adequate food supply sometimes seem insoluble.

Figure 15.13 Tibet has several monasteries, including Tashilumpo in Shigatse, where monks spend their lives in meditation and prayer. (Photo courtesy of Eileen Welsh.)

Sri Lanka

Sinhalese—Descendants of Aryans living in Sri Lanka.

Tamils—Descendants of early invaders of Sri Lanka.

Sri Lanka is India's other immediate neighbor. Its location just off the tip of southern India gives it a quite different character. Parts of the island are dry while other parts have adequate rainfall and crops that are able to thrive (Figures 15.14 a, b, and c). The culture in Sri Lanka is a mixture of ethnic groups and religions. The dominant ethnic groups are the **Sinhalese** (of Aryan heritage) and **Tamils** (descendants of Chola and other Indian invaders from many centuries ago).

Figure 15.14a A Sri Lankan lady picks tea, a crop that was started by the British. in the hill country of Sri Lanka.

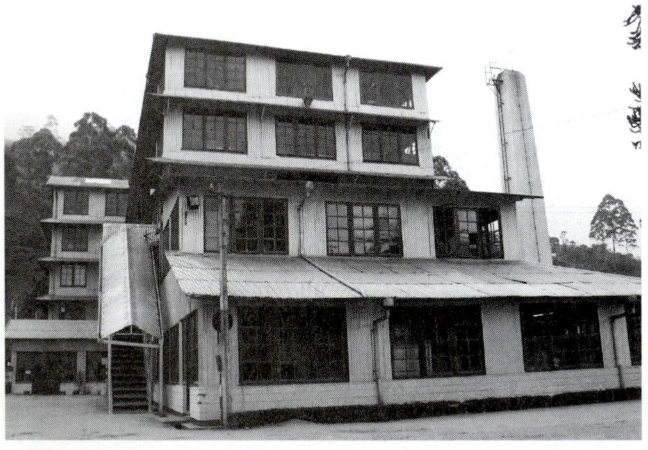

Figure 15.14b In this tea factory, tea is processed to become black tea, the form favored in Sri Lanka.

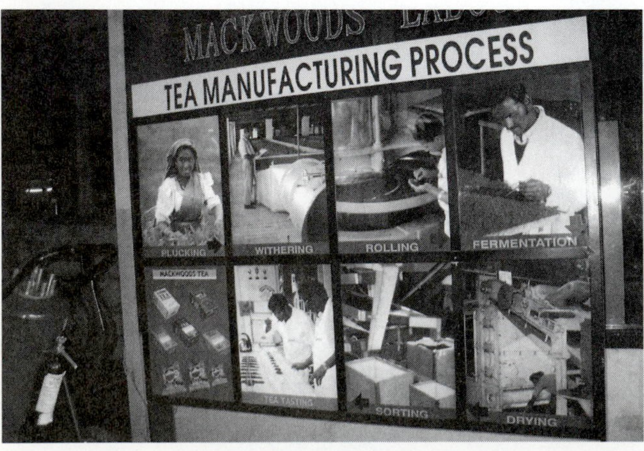

Figure 15.14c This display outlines the processing steps (withering, fermenting, and drying) that tea leaves undergo to become black tea in this Sri Lankan tea factory with a very British-sounding name.

Hindu and Buddhist followers are prominent in Sri Lanka and are often quite intertwined. Islam and Christianity also have followers here. Sri Lanka currently experiences racial problems between Sinhalese Buddhists and the Tamils in the northern part of the island. This tension was evidenced during relief efforts in the country's tsunami-stricken areas early in 2005, but cooperation now seems to have improved.

Reminders of British rule still are in evidence, although the British left in 1948. Some factories, such as those processing chocolate, started when the British were in Sri Lanka, continue to operate effectively today, thus contributing to the country's exports and to its own markets (Figures 15.15 a, b, and c).

Figure 15.15a Pods on the Theobroma cacao tree are the source of the nibs from which chocolate is produced.

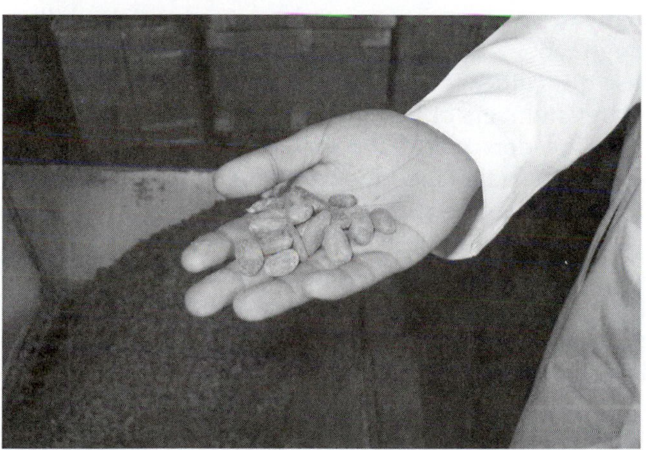

Figure 15.15b Nibs are fed into the crushing machine at a chocolate factory in Khandi, Sri Lanka.

Figure 15.15c Molds on a moving conveyor belt are filled with tempered, molten chocolate and chopped nuts as they proceed along the production line on their way to becoming bars of chocolate with nuts.

Remnants of much earlier cultures that go as far back as the third century BCE include water reservoirs as well as Buddhist and Hindu artifacts.

Food Patterns

The food patterns throughout the region of India and its neighboring countries reflect the religions that dominate the lives of the populace. Vegetarianism is quite common, partly because of economic factors and partly because of religious dictates (Figure 15.16.). Legumes and cereals are the major components of most meals. If meat is included, it is usually in small quantities. Buddhists and Hindus avoid beef and usually pork. Eggs are sometimes used. Milk in various forms, often clabbered and from different animals, may be consumed. Fruits and vegetables are eaten, although somewhat sparingly.

Perhaps the most unique and compelling part of dishes typical of this part of the world is the imaginative and pervasive use of a wide variety of spices and seasonings. These additions turn basic ingredients into an exciting dish (Figure 15.17).

Food availability and economic factors exert a significant impact on the dietary intake of many Indian families. Over the centuries, the traditionally available cereals have been rice and wheat, which are particularly well suited to the agricultural conditions in India and have therefore served as the main components of meals (Figure 15.18).

The other cornerstone of Indian diet is the legume family, which includes the ubiquitous lentils and a wide array of beans. These legumes and cereals not only conform to religious requirements, but also have the advantage of being comparatively inexpensive, with long storage lives without refrigeration. Even today, large numbers of Indian families have no way to keep foods safely chilled. They also may not have enough money to buy even the basic food needed for an adequate diet. Added to these difficulties is the often serious problem of obtaining safe drinking water. For large numbers of Indians, eating is a daily challenge.

Considering the array of invaders who have forced their way into India over the centuries, the uniqueness of Indian food is surprising. The Indian cuisine has overtones of Persian and European contributions, but the special ways in which Indians prepare and season their traditional dishes are their own ideas.

In fact, it can be argued that Indians have given more to the culinary world than they have taken from the cuisines of other cultures. Among the spicy seasonings and flavors featured generously in Indian cookery are turmeric, ginger, cinnamon, mint, dill, coriander, cumin, pepper, cardamom, saffron, poppy seeds, cloves, chilies, fennel, mace, and nutmeg. The use of this wide range of flavoring

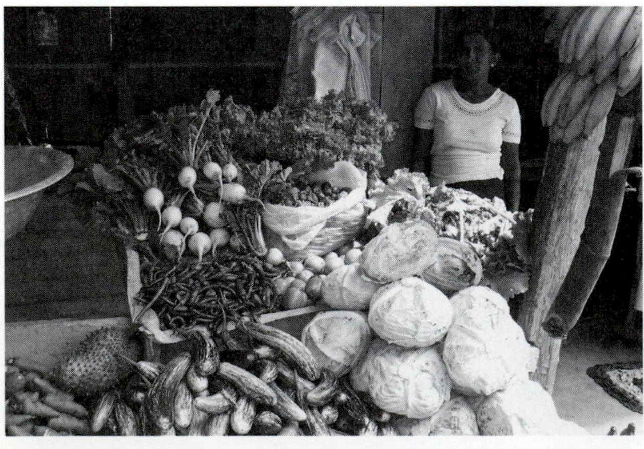

Figure 15.16 Fresh vegetables are grown in abundance in Sri Lanka, which is not surprising considering the vegetarian diet recommended for Hindus, a major religion in the region.

Figure 15.17 A mixture of spicy, hot seasonings in the bowl at left can be added to curry to suit the diner's ability and desire to experience moderate to sizzling heat in the mouth while dining. The beans and pumpkin on the tray offer calming relief to the palate. after they are cooked. The papandan (thin round dough) is broken into strips and deep-fat fried (on plate at left) to add a textural contrast to the meal.

ingredients requires judicious blending into recipes if the results are to meet the critical expectations of Indians. They rely heavily on the right seasonings to lift what could be a rather bland diet into a higher realm of excitement in eating (Figures C.125–127, pp. C42–C43).

Garam masala —Basic mixture of spices usually prepared in quantity and used as desired to season many different dishes in India.

The term Indians use to designate a blend of spices is *masala*. Many different blends are used, but a basic blend (generically dubbed **garam masala**) usually contains cardamom, cloves, cumin, cinnamon, nutmeg, saffron, and other spices that are ground together thoroughly and then stored for use in many different dishes. Sometimes spices are ground and mixed with herbs, water, and vinegar to make a wet masala that will be used immediately in preparing a particular dish. Whether a masala is composed of a skillful blend of dry spices or wet ingredients is not important to the success of a dish; the pleasure in the mouth provided by the masala is the final test.

Curry—Hearty and well-seasoned, stewlike dish featuring meat or legumes and served with several accompaniments.

The word **curry** seems almost synonymous with Indian food. Surprisingly, the curry powder that is sold in U.S. markets is not the seasoning used to make Indian curries. Instead, each recipe for curry includes a complex list of spices to achieve just the right flavor for the particular curry being prepared. Indeed, use of spices is considered to be an art in Indian kitchens, and the truly fine food of India is prepared in private homes rather than in commercial restaurants. Recipes for curry are extremely varied and may feature shrimp or other seafood, mutton or lamb, vegetables, or other imaginative ingredients.

Chutney—Chunky and flavorful sauce often served as accompaniment to curry.

At least one **chutney** accompanies curry dishes. Chutneys also afford considerable leeway for the creative cook. They may feature fruits cooked with spices to a thick, sweet product, or they may be quite spicy or even sour. Their individuality is truly amazing.

Figure 15.18 Indians share lunch away from the busy street scene outside.

Sambar—Spicy puree of lentils, which often is served with idlis.

Idlis—Rice cakes.

Dal—Puree of lentils or other legumes, usually rather blandly seasoned.

Ghee—Clarified butter that has been cooked down a little to add flavor; expensive but preferred fat for cooking in India.

Roti—Indian word for bread.

Chapati—Pancakelike grilled whole wheat bread popular in India.

Paratha—Whole wheat bread circles about 7 inches in diameter made with ghee in the dough and fried in ghee on the griddle.

Naan—Oval-shaped whole wheat bread baked by sticking it to the wall of a tandoor.

Tandoor—Thick-walled, deep jar-shaped clay oven used for roasting meats and baking naan.

Puri—Deep-fat fried rounds of whole wheat bread that puff in the middle during frying.

Samosa—Fried pastry enclosing a filling.

Betel nut—Nut from a climbing pepper with a deep red juice; chewed for its digestive qualities.

Lentils are a favored legume, and they appear in many different forms. They can be cooked and puréed with various spices or other ingredients to make **sambar,** which frequently is served with **idlis** (rice cakes) to add flavor to the meal. A usual part of the evening meal is **dal,** which is commonly a fairly bland purée of lentils of varying consistency, ranging from very thin to a bit pasty. Other legumes, including various peas called *gram,* are familiar ingredients in dishes for the evening meal.

Ghee, which is clarified butter that has been cooked down a bit and poured from the milk solids, adds a distinctive flavor when used in cooking and is the preferred fat to use if it can be afforded. Peanut and other oils also are used and are certainly less costly than ghee. Vegetable shortenings are another type of fat used in India.

The general name for breads is **roti.** There are some interesting types of roti, such as chapati, paratha, naan, and puri. **Chapati** is a whole wheat bread made by rolling a 2-inch ball of dough into a 5-inch circle and then frying it on a hot griddle, much like cooking of a pancake. **Paratha** is a bread similar to the chapati, but it is rolled into somewhat larger rounds, and more ghee is used in its preparation, both in the dough and in frying it on the griddle.

Naan is baked in a **tandoor,** a deep, jar-shaped clay oven heated by a charcoal fire. The naan dough is patted into an oval shape and then slapped against the upper wall of the tandoor for baking. (Incidentally, the chicken or other meats that may be roasted in a tandoor will be just as tasty as the delicious naan!) **Puris** are deep-fat fried, 5-inch rounds of whole wheat bread dough, which puff up in the middle during frying.

Samosas are popular in India, not only for their delicious flavors, but also for their convenience. They are pastries that tightly enclose any of a variety of fillings and then are fried. Since the fillings are sealed inside the pastry, samosas make a very portable and tasty snack or dinner item.

People in India and some of the surrounding countries enjoy concluding a meal by chewing on a betel nut or its leaf, or both. In India, paan (a **betel nut** wrapped in a betel leaf) may be seasoned with other ingredients and chewed at the close of a dinner. Betel nuts also often are chewed between meals. They have a distinctive deep red color, which quickly stains the teeth and lips a noticeable shade. The suggestion is that betel aids digestion, and some people credit it with other therapeutic qualities that have yet to be proven.

Recipes

Chapatis (Serves 2–6)

1 c whole wheat flour
4 tsp ghee (or clarified butter)
½ c warm water 110°F (more as needed)

1. With a fork, mash ghee into flour to make a mealy texture.
2. Gradually add measured amount of water, stirring hard between additions.
3. Very gradually add (while mixing) just enough more water to make a dough that will form a firm ball.
4. Knead vigorously on a floured board until dough surface is very smooth.
5. Very lightly grease the surface of the dough ball, and then let it rest at least half an hour.
6. Shape dough into balls, using about 2 tablespoons per ball, and then roll or pat each into a 5″ circle.
7. Heat griddle until a drop of water dances on it.
8. Bake first side of chapatis until the top edges begin to brown; flip and bake the second side for a minute. (Use a spatula to keep from sticking during cooking.)

Beef Biryani (Serves 4)

1 onion, sliced thinly
1½ tbsp oil
1 green chili, minced
2 garlic cloves, crushed
1″ ginger root, minced
1 c long grain rice
¼ tsp ground turmeric
1 lb beef tenderloin, cut in 1″ chunks
2 tsp curry powder
¼ tsp garam masala
3 tomatoes, thin wedges
2 bay leaves
2 cardamom seeds
¼ tsp saffron
4 cloves
Chutney, if desired to serve with this dish

1. Stir-fry onions in oil, adding chili, garlic, and ginger just as onions begin to turn golden. Continue to cook for about 2 minutes.
2. Prepare rice according to package directions, but with turmeric added.
3. Add beef to onion mixture and stir-fry for 5 minutes, stirring every minute or so.
4. Add curry, garam masala, and tomatoes to beef mixture; stir together and heat gently for 8 minutes.
5. Add bay leaves, cardamom, saffron, and cloves to rice; stir gently to mix.
6. Layer rice and beef mixtures in a baking dish, ending with rice.
7. Bake in preheated 375°F oven for 15 minutes.

Dal (Serves 4–6)

½ c lentils
2 c water
1 tsp grated ginger
1 tsp crushed garlic
¼ tsp turmeric
2 green chilies, chopped
1 tsp salt
1 tbsp oil
1 onion, thinly sliced
¼ tsp mustard seed
4 dried red chilies
1 tomato, chopped
Cilantro and mint, chopped

1. Boil lentils with water, ginger, garlic, turmeric, green chilies, and salt until very soft (about 20 minutes).
2. Purée, adding water if needed to achieve desired consistency.
3. Heat oil in frying pan, and then add onion, mustard seed, dried chilies, and tomato; sauté until onion is tender.
4. To serve, pour over lentils and garnish with coarsely chopped cilantro and mint.

Ghee (Makes about 1 cup)

1 lb unsalted butter

1. Melt butter in large saucepan, stirring to keep it from browning.
2. Heat rapidly until the surface is covered with white foam.
3. Immediately reduce heat while stirring.
4. Simmer, uncovered, for about 45 minutes without stirring. (Solids on bottom are golden brown.)
5. Very carefully pour off ghee through a filter of linen or cheesecloth. Repeat if any solids are in the filtered ghee.

Garam Masala (Makes 1 cup)

5 sticks cinnamon (3″ each)
¼ c cardamom seeds
½ c cumin seeds
½ c black peppercorns
¼ c coriander seeds

1. Spread spices on jelly roll pan and bake at 200°F for 35 minutes, stirring occasionally.
2. Crush cinnamon between layers of linen towel, using a hammer.
3. Mix spices together, and then grind together.
4. Store tightly sealed for up to 6 months. Use as needed.

Khir (Milk and Rice Pudding) (Serves 4–6)

1 qt milk
3 tbsp long grain rice
½ c sugar
¼ c blanched almonds, chopped
⅛ tsp cardamom seeds, crushed
½ tsp rosewater (optional)
2 tbsp toasted, sliced, blanched almonds

1. Bring milk quickly to a boil in a heavy saucepan and immediately reduce heat to simmering.
2. Simmer milk for 30 minutes, stirring occasionally.
3. Add rice and stir often while simmering for the next 30 minutes or until rice is completely soft.
4. Add sugar and chopped almonds; heat while stirring until pudding is thick enough to coat the stirring spoon.
5. Add rosewater and cardamom and stir, and then pour into a dish; chill for 4 or more hours. Garnish with toasted almonds.

Mango Chutney (Makes ½ cup)

1 mango
1 hot red or green chili
1 tbsp coriander, finely chopped
2 tsp salt
⅛ tsp cayenne pepper

1. Thoroughly wash mango before cutting flesh (with skin) away from its seed, and then slice fruit into very thin slices.
2. Discard chili seeds; slice into thin rings.
3. Add other ingredients and mix well; refrigerate for 1 hour (or 1 day maximum).

Mulligatawny Soup (Serves 6–8)

Stewing chicken in serving pieces
6 c water
2 tsp salt
1 c canned tomatoes
1 onion, chopped
1 garlic clove, crushed
½ tsp coriander seeds
1 tsp cumin seeds
½ tsp ground ginger
1 bay leaf
3″ cinnamon stick
12 peppercorns
2 tsp peanut oil
2 tbsp lemon juice
1 c coconut milk (or half and half)

1. Stew chicken in water and salt for 30 minutes, and then add tomatoes, half the onion, garlic, and seasonings.
2. Simmer 30 minutes more.
3. Remove chicken and strain stock.
4. In same pan, brown remaining onion in fat; return chicken and strained stock to pan. Add lemon juice and coconut milk, and heat to serving temperature.

Naan (Makes 6 ovals)

3½ c flour
1 tbsp sugar
1 tbsp baking powder
½ tsp baking soda
½ tsp salt
2 eggs, beaten
½ c plain yogurt
½ c milk
¼ c ghee

1. Combine dry ingredients in mixing bowl and stir well.
2. Beat eggs and yogurt into dry ingredients.
3. Stir while slowly pouring milk in. Mix thoroughly to combine all ingredients.
4. Knead dough vigorously, adding flour to board and hands to prevent sticking while kneading until dough is very smooth.
5. Grease dough ball surface with ghee and let rest 30 minutes.
6. Preheat oven (and baking stones, if available) to 450°F.
7. Grease palms with ghee, and then flatten one-sixth of dough into 10″ circle. Repeat with other five parts of dough.
8. Stretch each into an oval and arrange on cookie sheets to bake on the hot tiles in oven.
9. Bake for about 6 minutes until firm on surface, and then broil for a minute to brown the surface a bit.

Saag Aloo (Greens and Potatoes) (Serves 4–6)

1 lb spinach
1 tsp black mustard seeds
1 tbsp oil
1 onion, thinly sliced
2 garlic cloves, crushed
1″ ginger root, minced
1½ lb potatoes (1″ pieces)
1 tsp chili powder
1 tsp salt
½ c water

1. Wash spinach and blanch in boiling water. Pour into strainer to drain well, pressing to force water out.
2. Fry mustard seeds in oil in skillet until they pop; add onion, garlic, and ginger, and fry for 5 minutes more.
3. Add potatoes, chili powder, salt, and water to skillet; stir-fry for 5 minutes.
4. Add spinach, cover, and simmer for 15 minutes until potatoes are done.

Samosas (Serves 4–6)

2 c flour
½ tsp salt
¼ c butter
¾ c plain yogurt
Filling of choice
Vegetable oil for frying

1. Mix flour and salt, and then cut in butter to create the consistency of coarse meal.
2. Stir in yogurt until dough forms a ball.
3. Wrap tightly in foil; refrigerate for 1 hour or more.
4. Roll a fourth of dough on floured pastry cloth to 1/16″ thick.
5. Cut 4″ circles, and cut each in half.
6. Moisten edges, place teaspoon of filling in middle; fold dough edges over filling to form a triangle, pressing edges to seal.
7. Refrigerate up to a day before frying.
8. Fry in deep fat at 375°F for about 4 minutes to brown both sides and heat filling.

Shrimp Filling for Samosas (Fills 4–6 samosas)

½ c minced onion
1 garlic clove, crushed
2 tbsp oil
½ lb shrimp, deveined and chopped
¼ c tomatoes, diced
½ tsp salt
1 tsp coriander seeds, crushed
1 tsp cumin seeds, crushed
⅛ tsp red pepper, crushed

1. Stir-fry onion and garlic for 6 minutes.
2. Add remaining ingredients and continue to stir-fry for 5 minutes.
3. Store in refrigerator until needed for filling pastry.

Summary

Southern Asia includes the very large country of India, plus its neighbors: Pakistan, Afghanistan, Nepal, Bhutan, Tibet, Bangladesh, and Sri Lanka. The major rivers in this subcontinent of Asia include the Indus, Ganges, and Brahmaputra. Particularly productive farmland for India is found in the Indo-Gangetic plain, but the Thar Desert and the Deccan Plateau are quite limited in terms of agriculture. Particularly prominent crops in India are wheat, rice, peanuts, and a fairly wide assortment of fruits and vegetables; some livestock is also raised.

India's long history revealed that Dravidians settled in the south, developing their language, Tamil. Somewhat later, Aryans came from the north. Aryan priests wrote the Vedas, which laid the written foundation of Hinduism. Gautama Buddha was born in Hindu India, but he gradually developed Buddhism, a somewhat mystical religion that has incorporated some aspects of Hinduism and gathered many worshipers in many countries.

Over the centuries, many have held power in India, among them Persian invaders, Alexander the Great from Greece, Mauryans, people of the Gupta Empire, Muslim invaders, and people of the Mughal Empire. Subsequently, Europeans, spurred by desires to trade with this exotic region, established trading posts, and Great Britain eventually governed India before granting it independence in 1947.

Indian love of art is reflected in its architecture, which shows the style in favor during the various ruling periods. Music is another aspect of Indian culture that is distinctly different from western music. The instruments, meandering compositions, and rhythms evoke feelings of mysticism and nature. Storytelling and dancing are other expressive cultural outlets that are popular in India.

Religion plays a major role in the year's holiday calendar and in the dietary patterns of the people. The various religions practiced in India contribute many holidays that are celebrated. Similarly, the avoidance of meat on the part of some religions accounts in part for the vegetarian diet that is followed broadly in this region. Economic considerations and available commodities reinforce vegetarian food choices.

India's neighbors differ from each other and from India. Pakistan was created as a Muslim nation when India was partitioned, and the Hindus were concentrated in India. Muslim traditions present a contrast, both in traditions and attitudes (see Chapter 4). Nepal melds Buddhism and Hindu traditions. In contrast, Tibet has remained strongly Buddhist even though its Dalai Lama had to flee from the Potala to Dharamsala in India when the Chinese took over in 1959. Bhutan is an idyllic Buddhist kingdom. Bangladesh, in sharp contrast, experiences severe problems of poverty and food shortages. Sri Lanka is maintaining a fragile peace with Tamil rebels who are striving to have their own separate state on the island.

The foods of India concentrate on legumes and cereals, which are the basis of the vegetarian diet (Figure 15.18). Wheat and rice are the favored cereals, and lentils of various types as well as dried beans and peas are used in many different ways. Creative use of spices has made the flavors of Indian cuisine exciting and different from those of western food. This unique Indian food preparation has been altered only a little by the various invaders who dominated the country at different times. Among the dishes in Indian menus are ghee, naan, samosas, curry, chutney, paratha, roti, and puri.

Selected Sites

http://www.indianfoodsco.com/Recipes/Home.html—Variety of Indian recipes and pictures.

http://asiarecipe.com/indfoodtour.html—Extensive information on Indian food and culture.

http://www.food-india.com/—Broad coverage of recipes, ingredients, and regional Indian foods.

http://www.india-tourism.net/cuisine.htm—Information on regional foods of India.

http://www.food-india.com/—Considerable information about Indian foods and India.

http://www.indiaforvisitors.com/food/bread/naan.htm—Extensive site with many recipes and pictures of Indian food.

http://www.contactpakistan.com/pakfood/—Pakistani recipes.

http://www.indianfoodsco.com/Newsletter/Afghanistan/afghanistan.html—Information on food in Afghan menus and recipes.

http://www.infolanka.com/org/srilanka/food.html—Recipes and articles about food in Sri Lanka.

http://www.food-nepal.com/—Recipes and pictures of Nepalese foods.

http://thinley.tripod.com/recipe/—Some recipes for Bhutanese food.

http://www.mapsofworld.com/country-profile/india1.html—Brief overview of many aspects of India, its geography, culture, economy, and other topics.

Study Questions

1. Where is each of these countries located, and what geographic features influence the lives of people living in each: (a) India, (b) Bangladesh, (c) Sri Lanka, (d) Bhutan, (e) Tibet, (f) Nepal, and (g) Pakistan?
2. Select one of the empires or reigns in India's history and describe it by discussing its (a) time period, (b) rise to power and fall, (c) influence on the region at its introduction and/or subsequently its end.
3. Describe an Indian work of art, literature, dance, or music performance. Visit art galleries, libraries, music stores, or live performances, if possible, to experience or observe the work you are describing.
4. Define (a) ghee, (b) naan, (c) masala, (d) tandoor, (e) chapati, and (f) curry.
5. Identify 10 spices used in Indian cooking. Why do you think spices are so important in Indian cooking?
6. Plan a dinner menu featuring foods from India.

Bibliography

Achaya, K.T. 1994. *Indian Food: A Historical Companion.* Oxford University Press. Delhi, India.

Ang, C. 2000. Tibetan food and beverages. *Flavor & Fortune* 6(3): 21.

Barer-Stein, T. 1999. *You Eat What You Are.* 2nd ed. Firefly Books, Ltd. Ontario, Canada.

Collingham, L. and E.M. Collingham. 2006. *Curry: Tale of Cooks and Conquerors.* Oxford University Press. Oxford, England.

Ellerbee, L. 2005. *Take Big Bites: Adventures Around the World and Across the Table.* Penguin Books. New York.

Hoefer, H. 1990. *Insight Guide: Asia.* APA Publications. Singapore.

Lonely Planet et al. 2001. *World Food: India.* Lonely Planet. Oakland, CA.

Macmillan, M.K.K. et al. 2000. *Curried Favors: Family Recipes from South India.* Abbeville Press. New York.

Moxham, R. 2004. *Tea: Addiction, Exploitation, and Empire.* Avalon Publishing Group. Emeryville, CA.

Neal, W.C. and J. Adams. 1976. *India.* 2nd ed. Van Nostrand. New York.

Nicholson, L. 1994. *Festive Foods of India and Pakistan.* Trafalgar Square. London, England.

Pearcy, G.E. 1980. *The World Food Scene.* Plycon Press. Redondo Beach, CA.

Rau, S.R. 1969. *Cooking of India.* Time-Life Books. New York.

Saran, S. and S. Lyness. 2004. *Indian Home Cooking.* Crown Publishing Group. San Francisco.

Schulberg, L. 1968. *Historic India.* Time-Life Books. New York.

Sheehan, S. 1994. *Pakistan.* Marshall Cavendish. New York.

Sinclair, T. 1995. *India.* Guidebook Co. Hong Kong, China.
Srinivasan, R. 1992. *India.* Marshall Cavendish. New York.
Taylor, C. et al. 2004. *Food Culture in India.* Greenwood Publishing Group. Westport, CT.
Wanasundera, N.P. 1991. *Sri Lanka.* Marshall Cavendish. New York.
Wickramasinghe, P. et al. 2006. *Food of India: Journey for Food Lovers.* Whitecap Books. Toronto.
Wickramasinghe, P. et al. 2002. *Food of India.* Whitecap Books. Toronto.

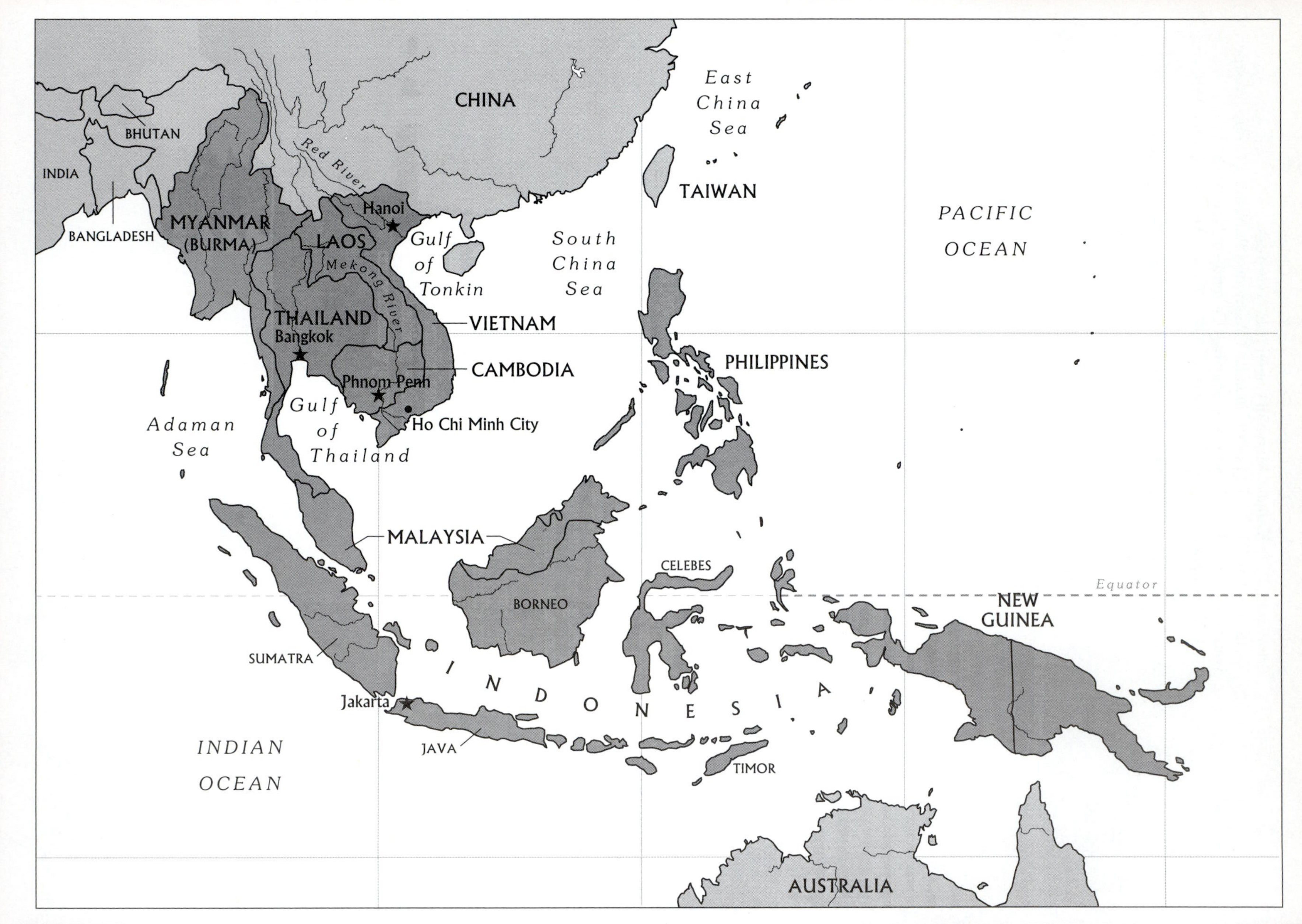

CHINA
East China Sea
TAIWAN
PACIFIC OCEAN
BHUTAN
INDIA
BANGLADESH
Red River
Hanoi
MYANMAR (BURMA)
LAOS
Gulf of Tonkin
South China Sea
Mekong River
THAILAND
Bangkok
VIETNAM
PHILIPPINES
CAMBODIA
Phnom Penh
Ho Chi Minh City
Adaman Sea
Gulf of Thailand
MALAYSIA
CELEBES
Equator
BORNEO
NEW GUINEA
SUMATRA
INDONESIA
Jakarta
JAVA
TIMOR
INDIAN OCEAN
AUSTRALIA

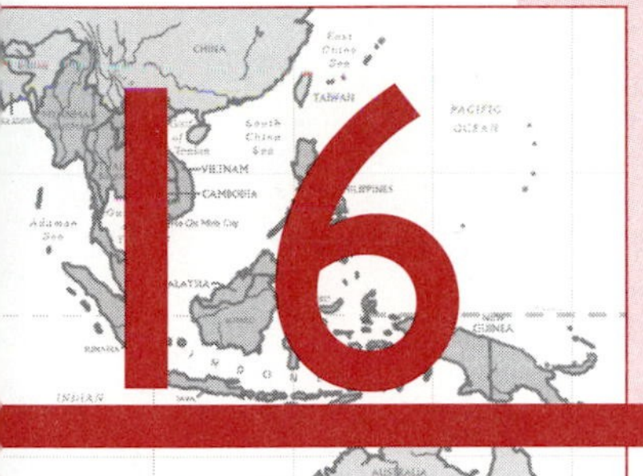

16 Southeast Asia and Its Islands

Geographic Overview

The discussion of the southeastern part of the Asian continent and the related islands considered in this chapter includes Myanmar (formerly Burma, which lies to the east of India and Bangladesh and extends southward along the eastern shores of the Bay of Bengal), Thailand, the three countries of the Indochina Peninsula (Cambodia, Laos, and Vietnam), and the western part of Malaysia (Figure 16.1). These countries are part of the Asian continent. Singapore actually is an island connected to the Malay Peninsula by a causeway. The eastern part of the nation of Malaysia encompasses part of the northern edge of Borneo, a large island lying to the east of Sumatra.

Indonesia is a very scattered country consisting of many islands, some large and others quite small. Sumatra, Java, Bali (Figure 16.2), Borneo, and Sulawesi are some of the larger and more familiar islands in this nation. To the north of Sulawesi and east of Vietnam is the group of islands composing the nation of the Philippines.

Actually, many other islands are scattered in clusters in the Pacific and at various distances east of Indonesia. Among these are the Solomon, Gilbert, Fiji, Samoa, Society (Figure 16.3), and Marquesa island groups, the latter two lying east of the international dateline. These various islands appear to have been settled over many centuries as adventurous seafaring people set their courses into unknown seas and eventually even brought their culture to the Hawaiian Islands. Although this chapter encompasses a vast amount of ocean, the dietary patterns and the foods available in this extensive geographic area are closely related.

The northern areas of the countries on the Southeastern Asian continent have highland and somewhat mountainous terrain that give rise to rivers serving as important links to the marketplaces within each country. The Irrawaddy in

Figure 16.1 Pedicabs and street vendors are common sights in Myanmar, formerly called *Burma*.

Figure 16.2 Bali and other islands in Indonesia have a very hot, humid climate that is ideal for growing rice, the staple cereal crop of Southeast Asia.

Figure 16.3 The vanilla beans this Polynesian lady is holding are part of the vanilla that is a commercial crop grown on the island of Tahaa, one of the Society Islands that compose French Polynesia in the South Pacific.

Figure 16.4 The Irrawaddy River is a very shallow river in Myanmar that meanders lazily between very wide banks during the dry season.

Myanmar (Figure 16.4), the Chao Phyra in Thailand, and the Mekong in the Indochina Peninsula are major rivers that have important seaports at their mouths, enabling these countries to participate in international trade in their cities of Yangon, Bangkok, and Ho Chi Minh City, respectively.

This region experiences monsoons, which bring the rain needed for growing rice and other crops. The hottest part of the year is the dry season, particularly the spring months; the monsoons begin in the summer and help to alleviate the intense heat. However, these countries are sufficiently close to the equator that they are never really cold except at the high elevations. Myanmar has mountains in its west and north, the highest of which is more than 19,000 feet.

Much of the land in the central part of these countries is sufficiently flat to make farming quite successful. In fact, farming is the primary way of life in many regions of these nations. The crops in addition to rice (Figure 16.5) include a wide array of fruits and vegetables. Tropical fruits, such as mangoes, coconuts (Figure 16.6), papayas, durian, bananas, rambutan, breadfruit, and pineapple, are available throughout this region. Cattle, poultry, and fish also are raised for food.

Similarly, inhabitants of the islands are generally able to grow reasonable crops. The sea provides fish for the catching in the various island groups but complicates the food situation because those not raised on the island must be brought in. This added cost of air or sea importation limits what may be available to people with limited incomes. The various islands raise coconuts, bananas, and some other fruits (Figure 16.7), as well as a wide range of spices in quantities sufficient to generate good income for some people. The proximity of the islands to the equator promotes crop production throughout the year, thus providing food for the islanders and export goods.

Figure 16.5 A Cambodian farmer, with the aid of his two bullocks, plows his rice paddy in preparation for planting.

Figure 16.6 This man in Luang Prabang, Laos, has split a locally grown coconut with his machete before holding half of the coconut against the rotating grater in the bowl; the freshly grated coconut meat is put into a plastic bag ready for sale.

Figure 16.7 Breadfruit thrives on the Society Islands and many other tropical islands in the South Pacific.

History and Culture

Myanmar (Burma)

Mons—People native to Burma.

Some evidence of early cave dwellers has been found in the hills on the eastern edge of the northern region in Myanmar. Later settlers came from southern Tibet and developed a civilization in the 8th century, only to be defeated by the Shans and the **Mons.** The region around Pagan eventually became the First Burmese Empire and was ruled for a time by King Anawrahta, who brought Buddhism to his kingdom. The First Burmese Empire came to an end in 1287 when Kublai Khan and his forces destroyed it, causing the Mons to shift south and the Shans to move to the west (Figures 16.8 and C.132, p. C44).

Almost 300 years later, the Second Burmese Empire governed from 1551 to 1752 and took territory from what is now Thailand to increase its holding. Traders from Europe and Arabia were active in the country during the latter part of this period. In fact, France supported the Mons in overthrowing the government in 1752.

The Third Burmese Empire lasted until 1885, during which time Siam (the earlier name for *Thailand*) brought much of its highly developed culture to Burma; this influence is still evident today. The British cast a greedy eye (backed by military force) on Burma and finally gained control of it in 1886, after three wars between the two nations. The imperialism of British rule was unacceptable to Burmese nationalists, who wanted independence. Their struggle was led by

Figure 16.8 Thousands of pagodas were built near Pagan, Myanmar, during the 11th to 13th centuries at the height of the First Burmese Empire, but Kublai Khan conquered the region in 1287.

Aung Sun, but the Japanese took over the country during World War II, and the British regained control briefly after the war until independence finally was achieved in 1948.

This story still does not have a happy ending because a very repressive and backward-thinking regime has hung onto its power despite the efforts of Aung Sun's daughter, Aung San Suu Kyi (who has been under house arrest for many years following her return to Burma in 1988) and others who want democracy. Education is nearly nonexistent; universities are closed except when examinations are given. The isolation achieved by the current regime has trapped Myanmar in a time warp remote from the rest of the nations of the world (Figure 16.9).

Thailand

The history of Thailand involves interactions among people in neighboring countries and shifts of power back and forth, depending on who emerged victorious from the battles. Among the early settlers were the Yunnan immigrants from southern China, who arrived in the northern part of Thailand and established a kingdom in 1238. Even earlier, the Mons had been pressing in from their base in

Figure 16.9 Government repression has stifled development of Myanmar, causing most people to work very hard but for very little money.

Khmers—People native to Cambodia.

Burma and made contact with the **Khmers,** who came in from their domain in Cambodia to the east.

The Khmers built the city Sukhotai in northern Thailand, which operated as the capital of the region (Figure 16.10). Hinduism was the first religion, but Buddhism soon became dominant. The result is that the ruins of Sukhotai include a Hindu temple (Wat Phra Phai Luang) at the city's edge as well as numerous Buddhist temples and chedis (lotus bud-shaped stupas). Wat Mahathat, a particularly lovely temple ruin, and Wat Sra Sri (the temple on two islands in a lake) are remains of the old Sukhotai that have been restored.

After Sukhotai lost its power in the 14th century, Rama Tibodi I established Ayutthaya farther south on the Chao Phyra River. This center was the capital of Thailand for more than 400 years until Burmese invaders destroyed it in 1767.

Subsequently, the capital of Thailand was established in Bangkok, where its exotic Grand Palace eventually was built and remains the most remarkable sight in the city (Figures 16.11 and C.135, p. C45). Although Siam had contact with European traders and other foreigners, it did not actually become a part of any other nation's colonial empire. Instead, it remained comparatively free of cultural influences from others and retained its unique and complex cultural styles.

Cambodia

Cambodia had a culturally distinguished past that culminated in the building of the vast complex at Angkor Wat (Figures 16.12 and C.139, p. C47) between the 9th and 11th centuries in the northern part of the country near Siem Reap. Somewhat later, Jayavarman VIII, a strong Buddhist king, built Angkor Thom and many other wats quite close to Angkor Wat, resulting in an amazing collection of ruins from this fruitful period of Khmer rule (Figure 16.13).

After invaders from Thailand defeated the Khmers in 1594, an extended period of weak rule followed, and the capital was moved south to Phnom Penh. Thailand and Vietnam basically were in control of the region until the French arrived in the latter part of the 19th century. The French controlled Cambodia from the 1870s until 1954, except for a period of Japanese occupation during World War II.

Finally, the country achieved independence but not stability. Traumatic years were to follow as the regime of Lon Nol and the Khmer Rouge jousted for control. The Pol Pot regime exacted a terrible human toll, which led to the Vietnamese invasion to liberate Phnom Penh in 1979. Landmines were planted extensively during that war, causing extensive damage even today as minefields are still being cleared. Maimed people throughout the country bear physical testimony to the damage these explosives have caused. The country is moving toward

Figure 16.10 Pagodas and Buddhas are numerous in Sukothai, the first capital of Thailand.

Figure 16.11 The Grand Palace in Bangkok was built in 1783 and remains today a remarkable complex encrusted with much gold and dramatic folk art.

Figure 16.12 Steep steps, well-worn by weather and tourists, challenge the hardy and the religious to reach the highest temple of Angkor Wat in Cambodia.

Figure 16.13 An aged monk uses his twig broom to tidy the courtyard inside Ta Phrom, the aging temple near Angkor Wat that is being strangled by tree roots crawling over the ancient stone walls.

normalcy, but the terrors of the past have left its people with haunting memories. It is difficult to reconcile today's Cambodia with the glories of the Khmer domain at the time of Angkor Wat.

Laos

Laos, like the rest of the countries in the southeastern region of the Asian continent, was home to early settlers from China to the north. Fa Ngum became the ruler of Lan Xang (now Laos) in 1353. The capital of his Buddhist kingdom was established at Luang Prabang in northern Laos (Figures C.145 and C.146, p. C49). Two centuries later, the king moved the capital to Vientiane toward the south, where it still remains. By the 18th century, Thailand had control of parts of Laos, and Burma controlled the northern part around Luang Prabang briefly before losing this region to Thailand.

During the 19th century, many Laotians were moved to Thailand, and the French were beginning their move to obtain regions of what was to become French Indochina. The French, in concert with Britain and China, geographically defined the country that now is Laos. The Japanese occupation of Laos in 1941 actually provided a small opportunity for more local control, but France quickly returned after the war in 1945, only to be driven eventually from French Indochina as resistance to it and the desire for freedom set war in motion.

Events during this period were stormy. The ultimate result was that communism infiltrated into Laos, heavy bombing and loss of life occurred during the Vietnam War, and thousands of Hmong from northern Laos lived in refugee camps in Thailand for many years. Many of the **Hmong,** who were mostly from the northern hill region of Laos, have emigrated to the United States.

Hmongs—People native to the northern hill regions of Laos.

Vietnam

With its long seacoast, Vietnam attracted Chinese settlers many centuries ago. The excellent farming available in the deltas of the Red and Mekong rivers and the opportunity for trade at prospective seaports were driving forces for these settlers. Even today all aspects of life in Vietnam bear the imprint of the early and later Chinese immigrants and the results of the rule of China for more than a millennium. One of the particularly important contributions of the Chinese was the development of dikes and canals to control floods and assist farmers. They also brought a panoply of religions: Taoism, Mahayana Buddhism, and Confucianism.

After 900 CE, Vietnam began to exert its strength against its neighbors in the Indochina Peninsula. However, France became involved in this peninsula and its governance when the French East India Company and French missionaries arrived in the 18th century. Cochin China was the name applied to the Mekong Delta area that the French shaped politically (Figure 16.14). The peninsula became a French protectorate in the mid-19th century. French influences could be seen in the major cities of Cambodia, Laos, and Vietnam until World War II.

After the war, the division of Vietnam into North Vietnam and South Vietnam set the stage for what was to evolve into the Vietnam War that created a tragic situation for the people living in both parts of that country and for many other nations that fought on both sides. Today, unification of Vietnam seems to have improved relations between people from both the former North and South Vietnams; strengthening economic factors finally are beginning to improve the lives of people living in Vietnam (Figure 16.15).

Malaysia

Malaysia occupies the Malay Peninsula's southern half and shares a border with Thailand on the north. Its western shoreline borders the Indian Ocean. A particularly significant geographic factor in Malaysia's history was the Strait of Melaka,

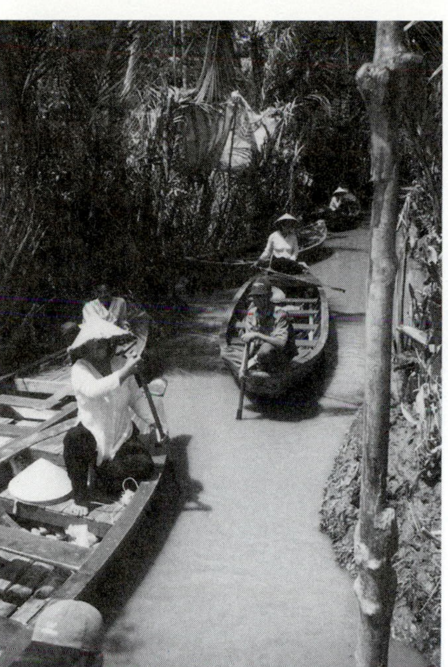

Figure 16.14 Vietnamese use the waterway of the Mekong Delta to take their wares to market.

which not only separated the island of Sumatra from the Malay Peninsula, but also afforded a place for early trading vessels from Europe, India, and China to be protected from bad weather and provided opportunities for trading. Indian traders brought religions with them to Melaka (now spelled *Malacca*) along with their trading goods (Figure 16.16). The trading activity caused some friction with Thailand (then Siam) even before European trade arrived.

Portugal claimed the Straits of Melaka in 1511, bringing Christianity in the form of Roman Catholicism to the region. However, the Dutch soon were sailing on the western side of Sumatra, using a route that precluded the need to land at a Portuguese port on the way to Java, an important island south of Sumatra and the Asian mainland. Nevertheless, the Dutch wrested Melaka from the Portuguese in 1641. By the time the British claimed the island of Penang just off the northern coast of Malaysia in 1786, no other significant trading was taking place along western Malaysia.

Politically, there were several Malay states, all basically protected by Britain until the Japanese invasion in 1943 during World War II. After the war, Malaysia was organized to include the peninsular region and Sarawak and Sabah, two former British colonies on the island of Borneo. This final arrangement was

Figure 16.15 A threshing machine used to harvest rice near Ho Chi Minh City (formerly Saigon) eases the work for both water buffalo and men in Vietnam.

Figure 16.16 Hinduism was brought to Malaysia by Indian traders centuries ago, and this temple provides a place of worship for Hindus in Kuala Lumpur today.

completed in 1963. Singapore, which arguably should be part of Malaysia, opted to become its own republic in 1965.

This federation of 13 states not surprisingly has an extremely varied population. A few of the original peoples of the Malay Peninsula and Borneo can still be found, but modern Malays plus Chinese and Indians, who are permanent residents, represent the largest part of the population today. Britain has continued to maintain commercial ties with Malaysia, which results in a detectable British overtone in the country. This cultural milieu is evident in the clothing worn by people in the city and in the mosques, temples, and churches. Although the official language is Bahasa Malaysia, many languages are spoken on the street, and newspapers in several languages are available.

Indonesia

The islands of Indonesia are geographically even more far flung than the Malay states. Its more than 13,000 islands spread for more than 3,000 miles from the Pacific Ocean on the east to the Indian Ocean on the west and for more than 1,000 miles from Asia on the north to Australia. This reality inevitably causes more significance to be placed on some of the larger islands while smaller (sometimes uninhabited) islands are pretty much ignored.

The islands were the destination of Arabian and Chinese traders for more than 1,000 years before the Europeans began to explore possible routes to reach the exotic spices available there. Marco Polo was aware of the trading riches that were to be found in Java in the 13th century. Europeans paid huge prices to Arab traders, which clearly provided them the incentive to find another way to the source that bypassed the Arab profiteers.

The Portuguese did sail beyond Melaka as far as Macao on the edge of the Chinese mainland, but they left the Indonesian islands to the Dutch. In fact, the Dutch settled in Java and many other islands as they established control of this valuable source of spices in the 16th century and held Java as well as Bali, Sumatra, Borneo, Sulawesi (Celebes), and others. The Dutch extracted a considerable amount of wealth from these ports during the almost 300 years they controlled them. However, the Japanese seized the region during World War II, bringing an end to Dutch power in the region.

The focus on the role that trade played during the colonial era misses the fact that Bali and some of the other islands had been inhabited for many centuries and had developed cultures that built lovely temples and created beautiful sculptures that are still enjoyed today. This focus also minimizes the warlike behaviors that often existed between islands (Java and Bali, for example) and even between groups living on one island. Difficulties between islands and groups persist today in serious conflicts between Timor and the Indonesian government in Jakarta and in the riots against the Chinese businesses in Jakarta. Nevertheless, this federation of islands remains as Indonesia.

Secret societies play an important role in communities on such Pacific islands as the Solomons, Fiji, New Caledonia, New Hebrides, and Vanuatu. Wealth is a requirement for belonging to one of these societies. Belonging to a secret society is considered a distinct honor, but the inner workings of these groups remain totally secret and are known only to members. The best known is the Dukduk Society of the Tolai people.

French Islands

Various other Pacific island groups also contribute to the cultural richness of this region. An example of these island groups are the Society Islands in which such familiar island states as Tahiti, Moorea, and Bora Bora are found. The original islanders had developed their own culture long before the arrival of the Europeans, and a few petroglyphs remain, as do some of the dances and food patterns (Figure 16.17). Captain James Cook, the British explorer, visited Tahiti in 1769, but France's Bougainville had been there the previous year.

The French were the Europeans who eventually controlled these islands, and French influence is evident in French Polynesia today, the result of being a French protectorate in 1842, a French colony in 1880, and now an overseas territory of France (Figure 16.18). The language is French, financial matters are under French supervision, and France has the ultimate legal authority, although many governmental affairs are handled by the islanders.

French Polynesia includes 14 islands, some of volcanic origin; others are atolls composed of coral reefs and motus barely above sea level. The beauty of the region and easy availability of food and simple housing create an idyllic setting for an unpressured lifestyle, one that has resisted change. Pareus (wrap-around one-size-fits-all garments) are the favored garment, because they are both convenient and easy to market.

Philippines

People from the Philippines had contact with other groups perhaps as early as 5000 BCE when people from what is now Vietnam arrived by sea. Arrivals from the Malay Peninsula as early as 300 BCE added to the mix of people living on some of the islands in the Philippines. Trade with Arabia, India, and China clearly flourished by the 7th century CE. Islam arrived with some of the Arab, Islamic Malaysian, and Sumatran traders in the southern islands of the Philippines

Figure 16.17 Fish traps have been maintained for centuries in this bay on Huahine in the Society Islands.

Figure 16.18 Bread boxes long enough for the delivery of French baguettes along a bakery route on Moorea in French Polynesia are a whimsical reminder of the island's relationship with France.

during the 15th century, but the situation changed when Europeans began to arrive in 1521.

Ferdinand Magellan, the Portuguese explorer, was the first European in the Philippines, an honor that led to the loss of his life at the hands of some natives less than two months after his first landfall. However, Magellan's ship finally returned to Europe in 1522. Information about the Philippines and other islands motivated the Spanish to send more ships there. The purposes of these expeditions were twofold: to convert the natives to Catholicism and to gain wealth through trade.

The Spanish influence served to halt the spread of Islam. Plans for development of the Philippines as a Spanish possession included creating Manila as the capital. Over the centuries, Spain did little to develop the Philippines after it accomplished the Catholic conversion in the north. However, the Islamic regions in the south generally did not convert to Catholicism.

Spain's dominance of the Philippines was not accepted without protest from other European powers, for the Portuguese, Dutch, and British attacked at various times. In fact, the British actually were in charge of the Philippines for a little less than two years in the 18th century.

The Spanish-American War that was fought halfway around the world from the Philippines caused the United States to send Admiral Dewey and his ships to attack the Spanish fleet at Manila. As a result, the United States, showing little respect for the local people, took over the Philippines.

A strong desire for independence eventually led to an agreement that would have resulted in independence in 1945, which was delayed by the Japanese invasion and occupation during World War II, but the Philippines became independent in 1946. Since that time, efforts to establish a truly effective government have tended to veer in various directions but finally seem to be coalescing to begin to meet the needs of the citizens despite Muslim unrest on the southern islands (Mindanao and some neighboring smaller islands).

Religion

The religions practiced in Southeast Asia and the Pacific Islands reflect the various waves of traders and the missionaries who brought their messages to the people of the region. Buddhism is the dominant religion in Myanmar, Thailand, Laos, Cambodia, Vietnam, and Singapore. Hinduism is practiced by most people on Bali and by some in Malaysia and Singapore. Islam was embraced in Malaysia, Indonesia, the southern Philippines, and to an extent in Singapore. Catholicism found some followers where the French were involved, notably in Vietnam; Spain's Catholic priests were very effective in converting many in the Philippines. In the Pacific, islanders have often been receptive to the efforts of missionaries, whether protestant, Catholic, or Mormon. The dominant religion in these various countries has a strong influence on many aspects of their cultures, particularly on the holidays and how they are celebrated. Singapore and Malaysia have a range of religious holidays throughout the year because of the importance of more than one religion to significant numbers of citizens. Christian holidays are celebrated in the Philippines.

Malaysia and most of Indonesia plus the southern region of the Philippines celebrate Islamic holidays. The practices of fasting during Ramadan and breaking the fast are events of tremendous religious importance. In contrast, Bali's predominantly Hindu population has elaborate celebrations that feature food displays arranged artistically, if somewhat precariously, atop the heads of lovely young Balinese women, young men carrying religious images, and villagers in festive attire wending their way to the temples for blessings. Thaipusam, the Hindu day of penance, is marked by parades.

Buddhist holidays are celebrated in the many Buddhist countries of this region. Festival of Lights is a joyous celebration of the end of the three months of Buddhist Lent, which fortuitously occurs at about the end of the rainy season. This celebration is especially elaborate at the Shwedagon Temple in Yangon (formerly Rangoon), Myanmar, where its lights add to the splendor of the amazing number of shrines encircling its central pagoda.

Lunar New Year celebrations are traditional throughout most of the countries in Southeast Asia. Because of their tie to the lunar calendars of the area, these events occur in January or February, but not on January 1. The celebrations differ in various countries, but they often involve intensive cleaning in preparation for the new year and wearing new clothes on the actual holiday. Fireworks are likely to be a noisy and bright feature of the night. Harvest festivals also are held in many of these nations, with the colorful rituals varying somewhat from country to country. Independence is cause for celebration in this region, which is not at all surprising considering the countries' relatively recent emergence from colonial subservient status.

The Arts

Throughout Southeast Asia, the artistry and creativity of the people can be seen in the beautiful and imaginative crafts they make. Artistic abilities are evident in Thailand in the carvings, statues, and architecture as well as the amazing array of silks in many colors and dazzling jewelry featuring precious and semiprecious stones set in gold and silver in original designs (Figure 16.19). Myanmar has

Figure 16.19 Craftsmen in Mandalay, Myanmar, sculpt Buddhas in a variety of poses and sizes.

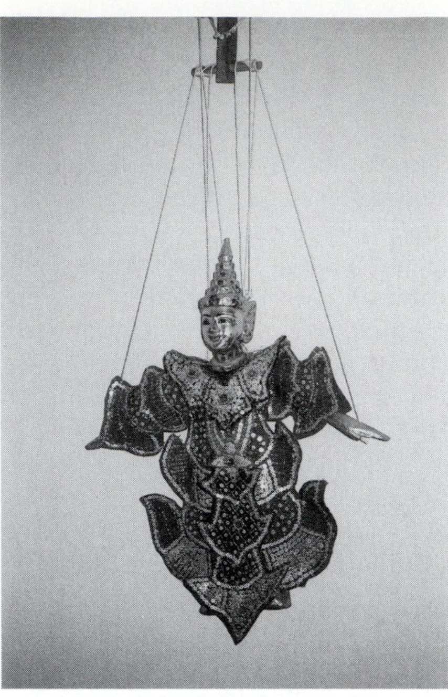

Figure 16.20 This traditional Burmese puppet is intricately decorated with metallic borders and patterns; the head is painted with gold leaf.

patterned its artistic styles after those of the Thais, a deliberate move when Burma brought some of the Thai craftsmen to Rangoon as captives after its incursion into Siam.

The elaborate use of gold leaf and many Thai designs are evident in Myanmar in temple decorations and in unique puppets (Figure 16.20). Puppet shows feature wonderfully imaginative characters that bring the tales of Rama and other familiar personalities to their audiences. Water puppets (Figure 16.21) are used to dramatize folk tales in Hanoi, Vietnam.

The carvings and art predominant in Cambodia and Laos are clearly similar to those in Thailand, yet they have a bit stronger, more primitive character than the graceful quality of Thai art. The wood carvings and other arts found in Bali are often very intricate, revealing qualities similar to Thai art, yet even more fanciful in their execution.

The work in these countries is distinctively different from the carvings seen in the Pacific islands of Polynesia, where the work is less detailed, yet conveys the spirit of the artist or carver. Of course, Paul Gauguin painted his interpretations

Figure 16.21 Water puppets are a unique way of dramatizing folk stories in Hanoi, Vietnam.

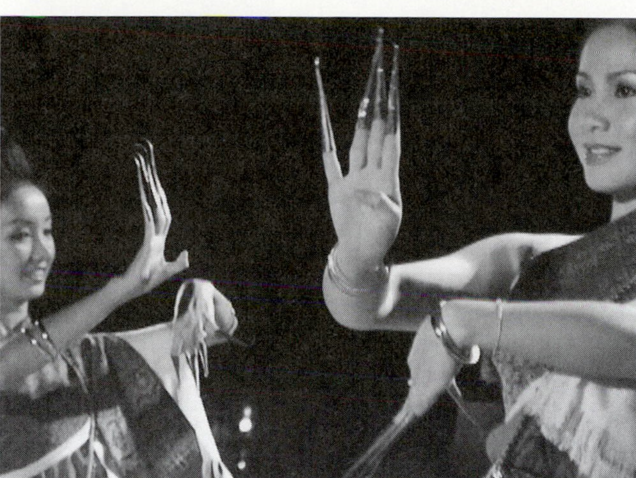

Figure 16.22 Hands are used to convey much meaning in Thai dancing. (Photo courtesy of Bill Malcolm.)

of Polynesia, which have been admired around the world, but his paintings are by a European, and therefore do not represent local art. Nevertheless, he immortalized lovely scenes of Polynesia and its people.

Dance is a form of art found throughout this region, expressing many folk tales transmitted from one generation to another throughout Southeast Asia. This is a very effective way of preserving stories and passing on the culture. The costumes worn by the dancers are often elaborate to create a feeling of mysticism and fantasy befitting the myths that are conveyed through the dances and their musical accompaniments. A particularly amazing part of Thai and Cambodian dancing is the graceful backward bending of fingers to which incredibly long curved nails are added. The hands are used to convey part of the story's message (Figure 16.22).

Hands are an important part of Polynesian dancing too, but the whole hand rather than fingers extended with artificial nails is featured. Another component is the seemingly impossible hip movement in Polynesian dancing.

Music for the dances and for its own sake can be heard throughout the nations of this region. The groups usually have drums, flutes, or similar instruments, variations of strings, and unique percussion (Figure 16.23). Gamelan groups play many folk melodies on their various gongs, providing lovely music for the dancers.

Figure 16.23 A Cambodian combo plays traditional instruments under a tree while villagers listen and enjoy the holiday celebration.

Figure 16.24 Thanaka wood bark is ground and mixed with water to make a yellowish paste, which women and children rub on their faces as a combination beauty aid and sun screen.

Longyi—Long, saronglike cloth worn in Burma, tucked in at the waist; can be hiked up in the very hot weather.

Certain garments and customs set some of the people in the various countries of Southeast Asia a bit apart from people who live in cities around the world. The creamy yellow paste that is smeared generously on the cheeks of Burmese children and women, a cosmetic called *thanaka* (Figure 16.24), immediately tells the traveler that this is Myanmar. Presumably, this paste will help prevent burning under the scorching Burmese sun. The **longyi,** which is a length of cloth like a sarong, is wrapped around the lower torso and legs by both men and women in Myanmar and tucked in at the waist, but it can be hiked up as needed for walking or for cooler comfort on the legs. Monks throughout Southeast Asia are wrapped in saffron-colored robes.

Most of the rural people in the rest of the region dress quite simply to accommodate the demands of working in flooded rice paddies, threshing rice, and herding water buffalo or oxen. Simple, widely flaring straw hats provide shade for field workers. Filipino men wear beautifully embroidered, tailored shirts over pants for dressy occasions while the women wear rather elaborate dresses with uniquely puffed sleeves. Thai, Malay, and Indonesian women are likely to wear garments of colorful silks, often rather tailored and with a fairly long skirt.

Food Patterns

The style of eating also varies a bit by country. The tradition in Myanmar, Thailand, Malaysia, Indonesia, Cambodia, Laos, and southern Vietnam is to eat using the fingers of the right hand while northern Vietnamese prefer chopsticks. The difference indicates the strong Chinese influence in northern Vietnam. However, many people opt for using silverware today.

Foods

Cereals Rice is the cereal grain used universally in the nations of Southeast Asia, the type varying from north to south within the various countries. Long grain, fluffy rice is popular in Vietnam and Malaysia. Sticky rice, often used to make sweet desserts, is preferred in the north of Thailand and among its neighbors. An appetizing example of this use is the Thai dessert featuring glutinous rice cooked in coconut milk accompanied by slices of fresh mango.

Rice in these countries is likely to be included in at least two meals a day, served either in a mixed dish or separately with various sauces or other accompaniments to round out the meal, depending on the country or the available food.

Rice may be the basis of the dramatic cone (nasi tumpeng) that is prepared in Java for religious ceremonies and decorated colorfully with strips of such foods as shredded beef, peanuts, slivers of red chilies, and chopped hard-cooked egg arranged to lead to the tip of the cone and its topping of green coriander. Fried rice is also popular.

The versatility of rice and its suitability as an agricultural crop have made it a staple used in numerous dishes and in various applications. For example, rice can be made into a vinegar, and it can be fermented to make wine (Figure 16.25). It can be made into delicate, edible rice paper in which fillings can be wrapped and then fried noodles. It may appear at breakfast as a rice gruel called **congee.**

Congee—Rice gruel often served at breakfast in Southeast Asia.

The other predominant cereal in these countries is wheat, which is used to make a variety of breads and noodles. The shapes of bread in the area may be round and flat, reminiscent of India, or baguettes and loaves that reflect the influence of France and other countries formerly under French control.

Meats and Soy Although, chicken, duck, fish, pork, beef, and eggs are popular, the meats served in these countries are influenced greatly by religious dictates of the dominant religions (see Chapter 3). Pork is avoided in Malaysia and most of Indonesia because of the dominance of Islam, whereas beef is shunned in Bali with its dominant Hindu population. Many Buddhists throughout Southeast Asia generally avoid all meats as well as fish.

This practice of avoiding some or all meats has fostered extensive use of soy products as a source of protein. Tofu and tempeh (fermented soybean curd) appear in many dishes throughout these countries. Mung beans and other legumes also are used extensively as meat substitutes, either totally replacing meats and fish or reducing the quantities served. Peanut oil is the preferred cooking oil in much of this region. Its flavor adds to the dishes.

Produce Fruits and vegetables are used generously throughout the region. In addition to the fruits and vegetables familiar in the United States, there are exotic tropical fruits such as rambutan, mangosteen, carambola (star fruit), jackfruit, breadfruit, durian, and coconut. Vegetable greens and various peppers are traditional ingredients. Thai cookery is noted for its generous use of chilies and peppercorns, making some dishes among the most fiery experiences you can find.

Spices and Sauces Creative use of spices and herbs can be found not only in Thailand, but also in Malaysia, Indonesia, and pretty much throughout Southeast Asia. Curry variations are popular, and they are prepared using such spices as turmeric, peppers, ginger, and saffron. Other flavoring ingredients used in the

Figure 16.25 Rice wine is being produced in this primitive winery near Luang Prabang, Laos.

region include lemon grass, coconut milk, mint, coriander, garlic, green onions, and chives.

Nuoc mam—Fermented, salted fish sauce popular in Vietnam.

Nuoc cham—Vietnamese condiment made with chili peppers, citrus juice, garlic, onions, and vinegar.

Nam pla—Fermented fish sauce popular in Thailand.

Kapi—Thai salty, dried shrimp paste.

Bagoong—Filipino fermented, salted shrimp paste.

Patis—Fermented, salty fish sauce popular in the Philippines.

Various sauces are characteristic of the region. Vietnam features **nuoc mam** (fermented, salted fish sauce) and **nuoc cham** (chili peppers, lime or other citrus juice, garlic, onions, and vinegar condiment), both of which are virtually used as staples (Figure 16.26). **Nam pla** (a fermented fish sauce) and a dried shrimp paste called **kapi** are popular ways of adding some salt to the diet in Thailand. Soy sauces are used throughout the area and are particularly popular among people of Chinese descent. Filipinos are fond of **bagoong** (salty, fermented shrimp paste) and other sauces featuring soy or salty anchovy paste (**patis,** toyo, and hipon sauces).

Foreign Influences

Adobo—Filipino stew using meats marinated in vinegar seasoned with bagoong, fried with onions and garlic, and then stewed.

Cocido—Hearty Filipino stew containing a variety of meats, Spanish sausage, chickpeas, saba (sweet cooking bananas), tomato sauce, and lard.

Coconut cream—Puréed and strained creamy liquid prepared from freshly grated white meat of mature pared coconut and some hot water.

Coconut milk—Coconut liquid similar to coconut cream but with more liquid.

The various conquerors and traders who played significant roles in the history of Southeast Asia have left their marks on the foods that are favored in the different countries. For example, Myanmar, Malaysia, and Indonesia often feature curries and satays (Indian version of shish kebab), which is not surprising considering the proximity of India and the trade that existed. The Philippines reflect their involvement with Spain in such dishes as flan and **adobo** (featuring chicken and pork in mingling Spanish seasonings with vinegar and soy sauce) and **cocido** (hearty stew combining various meats and starchy ingredients) which are characteristic of the area. French breads are familiar fare in Cambodia, Laos, and Vietnam, where the French ruled before the war.

Thailand, which really never was conquered by countries other than its immediate neighbors, has developed its own somewhat unique cuisine. Thai dishes are noted for unique combinations of seasonings, which frequently include very hot peppers. Careful attention also is given to beautiful presentations to ensure that the food delights both the eye and the mouth (Figure C.137, p. C46).

The foods that dominate the diets of the Pacific Islanders are somewhat different from those in Southeast Asia. The islands are excellent sources of breadfruit, taro, coconut, pineapple, banana, papaya, yams, and cassava. The meats include pork, chicken, and seafood (Figures 16.27 and C.156. p. C52). Coconut is crucial to preparing many Polynesian dishes. The young coconut (one forming for six months on the tree) can be scraped out with a spoon and eaten; it is sometimes fed to babies. Usually, coconuts remain on the tree for a year so that they ripen and develop the familiar hard brown shell.

Coconut cream and **coconut milk** can be made using grated fresh coconut and are included in many recipes. The liquid that can be drained by puncturing

Figure 16.26 Nam pla and kapi are Thai sauces used to add salt and flavor to fried fish.

Figure C.97 Volubilis is an inland city in Morocco that was built by the Romans. Some mosaics can be seen in the ruins.

Figure C.98 Bastila (pigeon pie) is a traditional dish of Morocco that originated in Fez but is served throughout North Africa.

Figure C.99 "Water men" wearing their traditional lampshade hats peddle water to thirsty customers in Jemaa El Fna Square in Marrakech, Morocco.

Figure C.100 Agriculture is difficult in many parts of West Africa because of the climate that often challenges people, crops, and animals.

Figure C.101 In Africa, living in houses built on high platforms and with retractable ladders, can keep wild animals at bay.

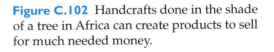

Figure C.102 Handcrafts done in the shade of a tree in Africa can create products to sell for much needed money.

Figure C.103 Houses in villages in many parts of Africa are quite basic, and usually are fairly close to the fields.

Figure C.104 Market day in Kenya and other countries in Africa draws local people to sell their wares and bargain for goods they need.

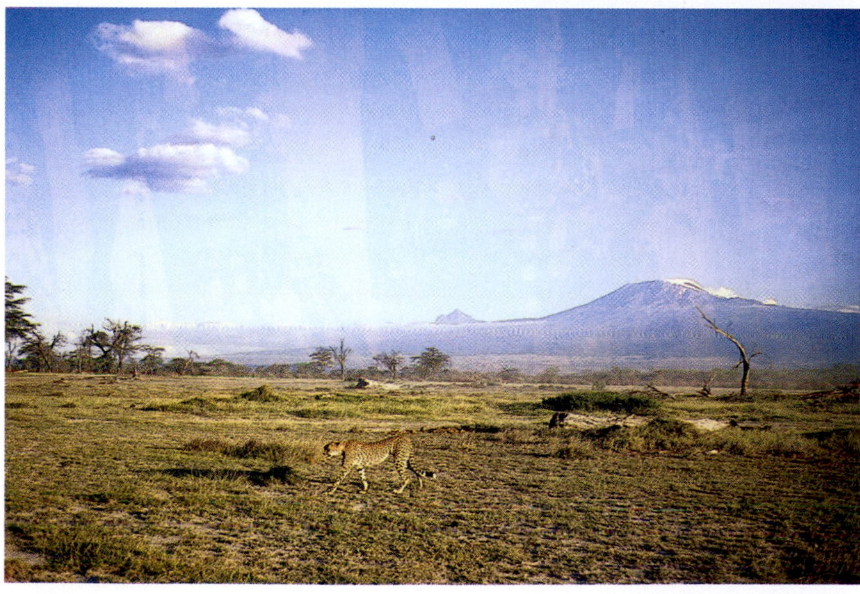

Figure C.105 Cheetahs are among the wild game roaming the Serengeti Plain, with Mt. Kilimanjaro as a backdrop.

Figure C.106 This Botswana mother cooks for her young family in a single pot over an open fire outdoors.

Figure C.107 Chickens can scratch for food and lay eggs until the time is right to become the family meal.

Figure C.108 In Djibouti, Djibouti, this beautiful Muslim woman sits in a stall selling wild animal pelts, butterflies, and other items available on the Horn of Africa.

Figure C.109 The Qutb Minar, constructed to celebrate the Moslem victory in 1193, soars 240 feet into the sky of Delhi.

Figure C.110 Paratha, used as a wrap for various fillings, highlights this vendor's wares in New Delhi, India.

Figure C.111 Started in 1630, the Taj Mahal near Agra, India, was built by Shah Jahan to honor the memory of his wife Mumtaz.

Figure C.112 At close range, graceful designs of semiprecious stones inlaid in the white marble of the Taj Mahal can be seen.

Figure C.113 The Amber Fort atop the distant hill can be seen from the Maharajah's palace in Jaipur, India.

Figure C.114 The Amber Fort and its palace were built over two centuries starting in 1592 during the reign of the Moghul Emperor Akbar.

Figure C.115 Cremation pyres appear outside a Hindu temple at Katmandu, Nepal.

Figure C.116 Boudanath, the largest Buddhist stupa in Nepal, casts watchful eyes in four directions in the Katmandu Valley.

Figure C.117 Prayer wheels turn at a small temple across the valley from the Potala, the original seat of Tibetan Buddhism in Lhasa, Tibet.

Figure C.118 Yaks are used in Tibet to plow fields and haul crops; their milk is used for drinking and making butter. (Photo courtesy of Eileen Welsh.)

Figure C.119 Creative arts in Sri Lanka include making batiks.

Figure C.120 The vendor of this colorful fruit stand along a road in Sri Lanka is wearing a sarong, a garment worn by many men on that island.

Figure C.121 Tending this roadside fruit stand in Sri Lanka is a family affair.

Figure C.122 Vegetables play a major role in the diets of Sri Lankans, and a wide array of fresh produce is readily available at stands along the road.

Figure C.123 Colorful, remarkably fresh fruits and vegetables are the cornerstone of the healthful meals traditionally served in Sri Lanka.

Figure C.124 Planting rice seedlings in flooded paddies is physically challenging even when many people work together.

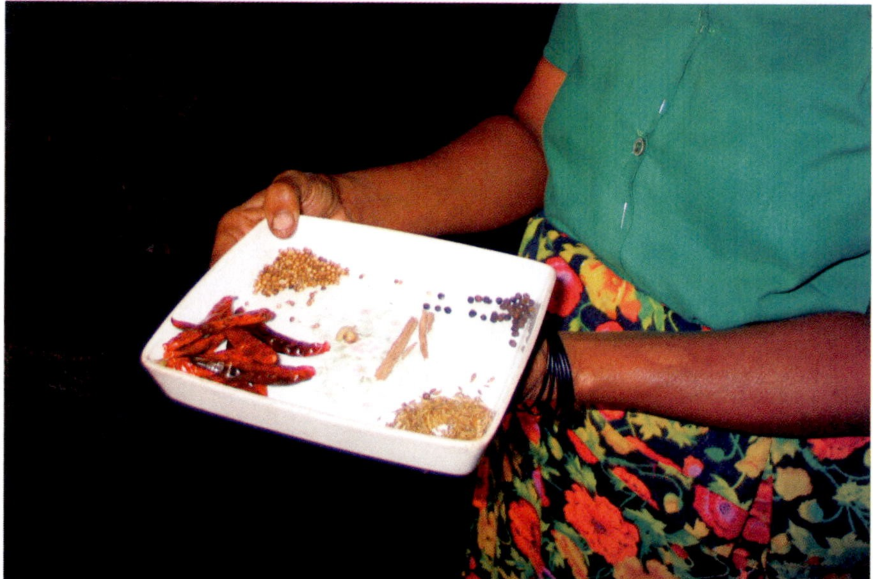

Figure C.125 Ingredients ready to be ground into garam masala for seasoning curry.

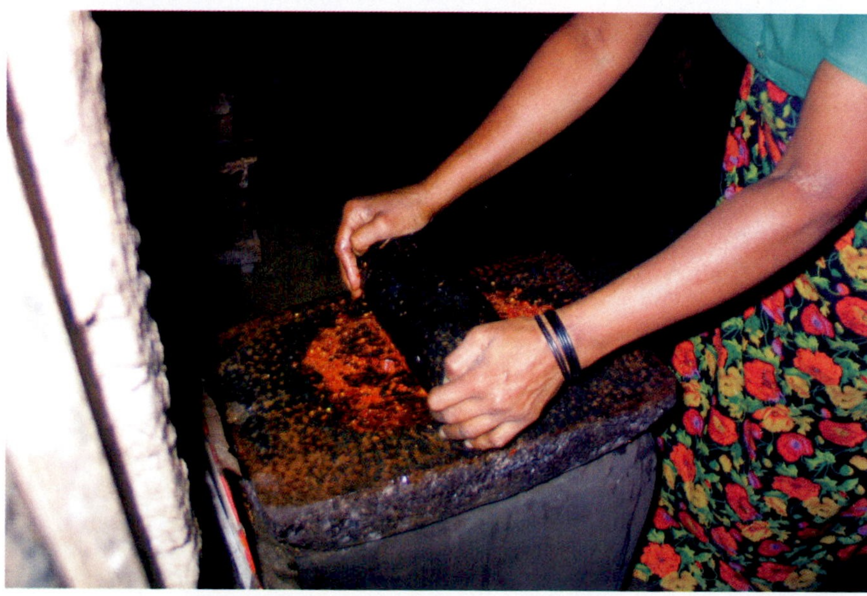

Figure C.126 Chilies and other spices are ground using a metate; hot water is added gradually to make a wet masala.

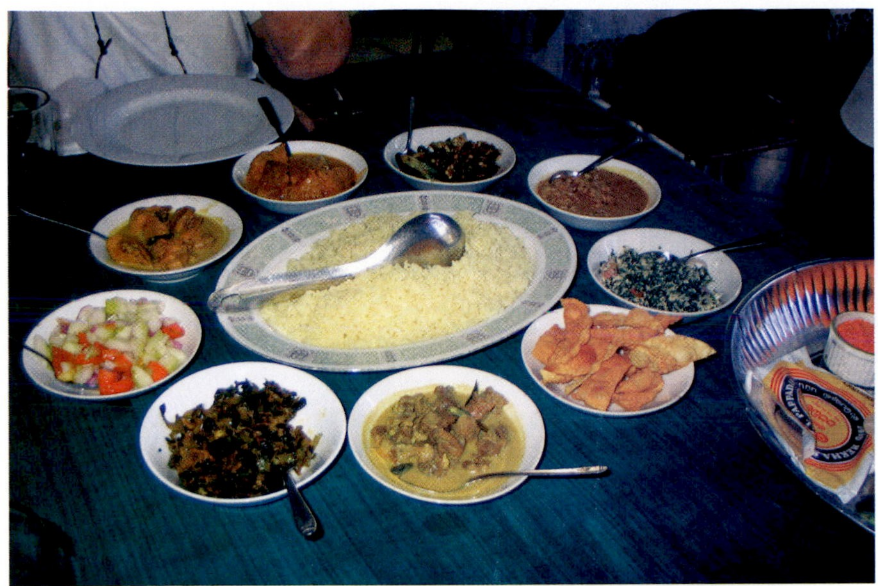

Figure C.127 Curry, the basic meal in Sri Lanka, always includes rice and several vegetable dishes, papandan, and dal; a chicken or meat curry may also be served.

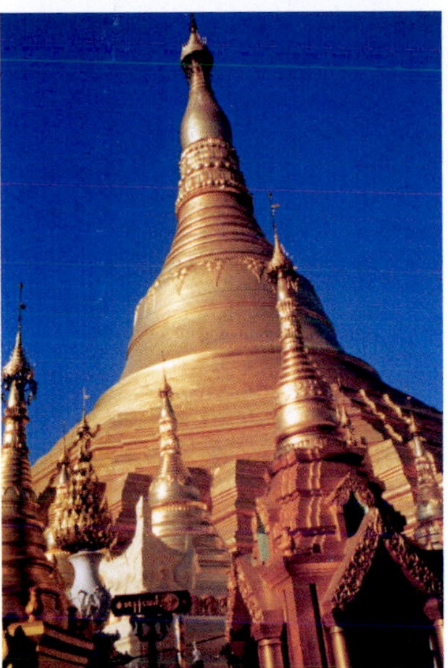

Figure C.128 Golden domes decorate Shwedagon Pagoda in Yangon, Myanmar (formerly Rangoon, Burma), and other pagodas around the nation.

Figure C.129 Two young brothers at the Shwedagon Pagoda are seriously pondering the responsibility of being young Buddhist monks, at least for a few days.

Figure C.130 A monk assigned to the day's kitchen duties in the monastery stirs huge pots of rice to feed the monks living in the very large Golden Palace Monastery in Mandalay, Myanmar.

Figure C.131 Fields along the Irrawaddy River, the watery lifeline of Myanmar, are used to grow seasonal crops after the annual floods of the shallow river.

Figure C.132 Many pagodas remaining from the 11th to 13th centuries add a haunting beauty to the scenes around Bagan, Myanmar.

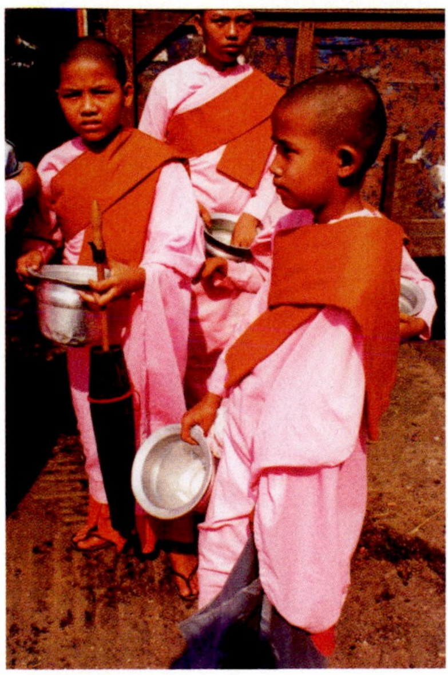

Figure C.133 Young Buddhist monks take their begging bowls with them around the market in Bagan in the morning to collect food for the rest of the day.

Figure C.134 Ancient pagodas in Bagan begin to assume an air of mystery in the dusty, golden haze of sunset.

Figure C.135 The Grand Palace in Bangkok, Thailand, is protected by this whimsically fearsome guard, just one of several amazing protectors of the fabled complex.

Figure C.136 Buddhists on their way to work in downtown Bangkok, Thailand, offer food and flowers at a shrine on a street corner.

Figure C.137 A delicious, colorful dinner of Thai chicken salad in a pineapple shell, chilled spring soup, noodles, and spring rolls ended with sweet glutinous rice cooked in coconut milk and sliced fresh mango.

Figure C.138 Durian (large fruit on left), mangoes, oranges, and bananas are for sale at this market stall in Chiang Mai, Thailand.

Figure C.139 Angkor Wat, a Hindu temple complex in northern Cambodia, was built in the 12th century by King Suryavarman and dedicated to the God, Vishnu and was later converted to a Buddhist temple.

Figure C.140 Numerous temples built by the Khmer kings dot the landscape around Angkor Thom and Angkor Wat near the modern town of Siem Reap, Cambodia.

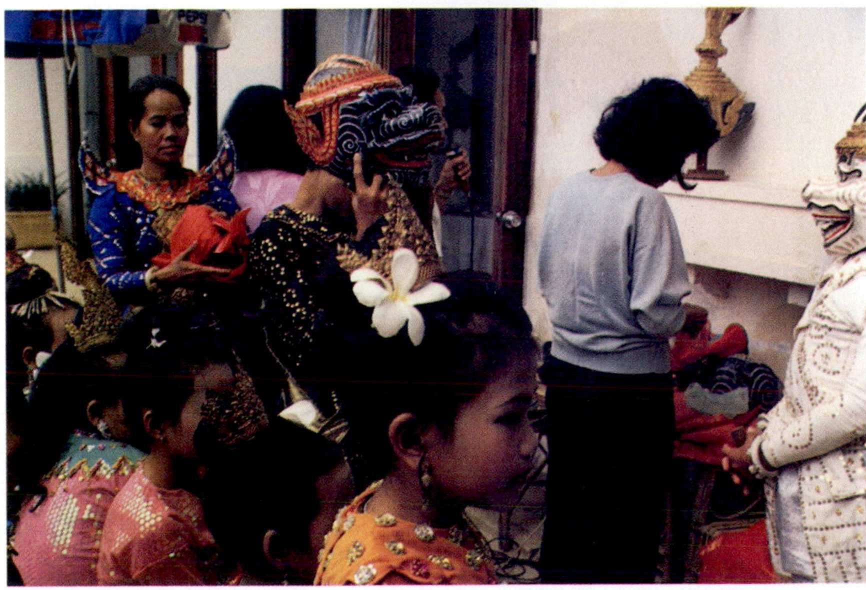

Figure C.141 A Cambodian dance group dons imaginative, colorful costumes and masks to present traditional dances of their culture.

Figure C.142 Chilies and passion fruit are just some of the local produce available in the street market in Siem Reap, Cambodia.

Figure C.143 Agricultural methods are often rather basic in rural areas, as can be seen at this family farm in northern Cambodia.

Figure C.144 Hot grilled chicken sold by this cheerful Cambodian vendor is an irresistible treat.

Figure 16.27 Crayfish are plentiful in the waters off Thailand, and they are a tasty seafood enjoyed in Southeast Asia. (Photo courtesy of Bill Malcolm.)

Coconut water—Liquid drained from fresh coconut by puncturing its eyes; used as beverage, but not as a cooking ingredient.

Poe (poi)—Starchy paste of boiled and pounded peeled taro root popular in Polynesia.

the eyes of the coconut is **coconut water,** which can be drunk but is not a cooking ingredient. Coconut milk or cream requires that the flesh of the coconut be pared to get rid of the brown skin; chunks of the white flesh are then put in a blender with an equal amount of hot water and blended for a minute on high. This purée has to be strained through cheesecloth, which then is squeezed to get the coconut milk to drip out. With less water, the coconut milk will be more creamy. Fortunately, canned coconut milk is available and saves considerable time.

Poe (spelled *poi* in Hawaii) is the starchy paste prepared by boiling and pounding peeled taro root to make a thick paste. Liquid can be added to achieve the desired consistency. Poe seems to be an acquired taste for some people, who describe it as a clone of library paste. However, Polynesians may flavor their poe with fresh fruits.

Ti leaves sometimes are used to wrap meat or fish before steaming it (Figure 16.28) to impart a bit of flavor. Banana leaves are also used in this way. Many different combinations of food can be wrapped and tied in banana, breadfruit, or ti leaves and then baked in the coals of an outdoor barbecue. This is a popular way of cooking food in a leisurely manner at a luau. These large leaves are even used to wrap food purchases at the markets in Polynesia.

Breadfruit almost seems to be a misnomer because its starchy character really suits it to serve as a replacement for potatoes. This large fruit can be prepared in virtually the same way that a potato would be. It plays a prominent role in the Polynesian diet, whether boiled, baked, or pounded to make a dish resembling poe. Polynesia also is home to another source of starch, arrowroot, which is generally used as a thickener by islanders.

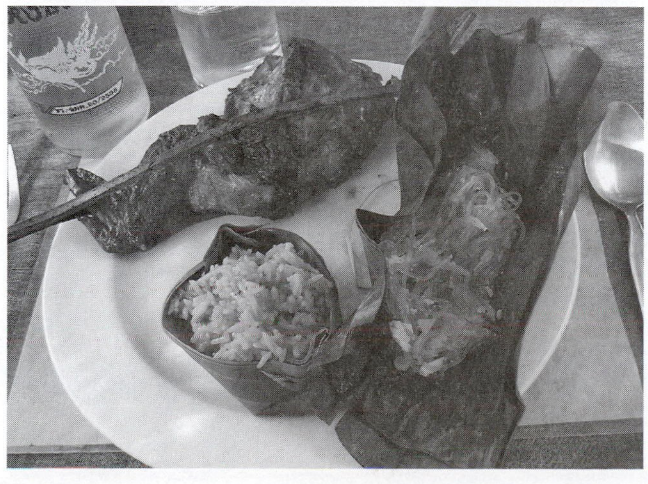

Figure 16.28 Ti leaves are used to hold rice and noodles that accompany the grilled chicken in this Thai meal. (Photo courtesy of Bill Malcolm.)

Recipes

Shrimp Curry (Myanmar) (Serves 4–6)

¾ lb shelled, deveined, raw shrimp
½ tsp turmeric
1¼ tsp paprika
1 tbsp shrimp sauce
1 tsp grated fresh ginger
2 garlic cloves, minced
3 medium onions, diced
¼ c peanut oil
1 c tomato paste
1 c water

1. Marinate shrimp for 1 hour in turmeric, paprika, and shrimp sauce mixture.
2. Saute ginger, garlic, and onions in oil gently for 2 minutes.
3. Add shrimp and stir-fry briefly until shrimp is beginning to turn pink.
4. Add tomato paste diluted with water and heat while stirring for 1 minute.
5. Serve with hot rice.

Beef Curry (Thailand) (Serves 4)

3 c coconut milk
1 tbsp red curry paste
2 tsp turmeric
1 lb beef (cubed)
1 star anise
½ cinnamon stick
3 bay leaves
1½ c cubed (1″) potatoes
3 onions, coarsely chopped

1. Bring 1 cup coconut milk, curry paste, and turmeric to a boil; stir while reducing to about ¼ cup.
2. Stir in remaining ingredients; cover and simmer for 45 minutes.
3. Serve with hot rice.

Fresh Coconut Milk (Makes 1 cup)

1 c chopped white coconut meat (from fresh coconut*)
1 c hot water

1. Poke holes in coconut eyes and drain the coconut water out.
2. Bake coconut at 375°F for 15 minutes.
3. Use hammer to tap shell open.
4. Remove coconut meat; pare the brown covering, leaving only white coconut meat.
5. Blend coconut meat and water until coconut is very fine.
6. Squeeze through layers of cheesecloth to strain out the coconut, leaving the milk, which will keep for 2 days in the refrigerator.

*Canned coconut milk can be purchased to save time.

Chicken Soup with Mint (Cambodia) (Makes 4 cups)

1 lb boneless, cubed chicken breast and/or thighs
3 tbsp rice
1 garlic clove, minced
2 tbsp thinly sliced green onions
Water to cover
1 tsp salt
½ tsp ground pepper
1¼ tsp sugar
¼ c lime juice
2 tbsp chopped mint leaves
Fish sauce

1. Put all ingredients except lime juice and mint in a large saucepan; cover with water.
2. Simmer, covered, for 30 minutes or until chicken is tender.
3. Add lime juice and heat briefly.
4. Add mint just before serving with a dash of fish sauce.

Pineapple Fried Rice (Thailand) (Serves 4)

2 small pineapples with tops
2 tbsp oil
½ lb pork, diced
2 green chilies, seeded and minced
1 onion, minced
3 c cooked rice
¼ lb cooked, shelled shrimp
2 tbsp fish sauce
4 tsp soy sauce
6 tbsp roasted cashews
2 scallions, chopped
1 green chili, seeded and sliced
2 red chilies, seeded and sliced
3 tbsp coarsely chopped mint leaves

1. Split pineapples (tops attached) in half; use sharp knife to cut out the pulp, discarding core and chopping the pulp into pieces.
2. Heat oil in a wok and stir-fry chilies, onion, and pork until pork is well browned on all sides.
3. Add rice, shrimp, pineapple pieces, sauces, cashews, and scallions. Heat while stirring to thoroughly mix and bring to serving temperature.
4. Place filling in pineapple shells and garnish with chilies and mint.

Fish Chowder (Serves 4–6)

½ c pureed pimiento
½ c chopped onion
1 garlic clove, minced
2 tbsp peanut oil
1 lb fish fillet, cubed
1 tsp salt
½ tsp pepper
4 c coconut milk
1½ c parboiled, cubed potatoes

1. Stir-fry pimiento, onion, and garlic in oil until onion softens (about 5 minutes).
2. Add fish and heat gently for 4 minutes.
3. Add salt, pepper, coconut milk, and potatoes.
4. Simmer 20 minutes before serving.

Shrimp-Pepper Curry (Malaysia) (Serves 4)

2 onions, chopped finely
2 hot chilies, seeded and finely chopped
1 green pepper, coarsely chopped
3 tbsp peanut oil
3 tomatoes, chopped
⅓ c slivered, blanched almonds
3 basil leaves, chopped
lemon grass, smashed (3″)
½ tsp thyme
1 tsp salt
1 zucchini, thinly sliced
½ lb fresh, cleaned shrimp
1 c coconut milk
2 tbsp flour

1. Saute onions and peppers in oil for 3 minutes.
2. Add all ingredients except flour and coconut milk, and simmer for 4 minutes.
3. Stir coconut milk gradually into flour until smooth, and then stir this slurry into the other ingredients.
4. Stir continuously while heating to thicken sauce.
5. Serve over hot rice.

Crab Rolls (Vietnam) (Serves 6–8)

Filling:
- 2 oz translucent mung bean threads (cellophane noodles)
- 5 dried Asian mushrooms (1″ diameter)
- 1 lb ground pork (lean)
- 1 onion, finely chopped
- ¾ lb cooked crab meat, minced
- 4 egg yolks, beaten
- ¾ tsp salt
- ¾ tsp pepper

Wrapping:
- 1 lb egg roll wrappers
- 1 egg, beaten
- Oil for deep-fat frying

1. Hydrate noodles in cold water and mushrooms in warm water for 30 minutes; drain and cut into 2″ lengths.
2. Stir pork and onions while frying in a skillet so that pork is in small pieces and shows no trace of pink.
3. Add all other filling ingredients and mix thoroughly.
4. Shape about 2 tablespoons of the mixture into a rod 4″ long and 1″ in diameter. Repeat until mixture is all shaped.
5. Wrap each rod by placing diagonally (between opposite tips) on a wrapper and folding over the tips; brush egg along borders, and then roll up the wrapper to firmly enclose the filling.
6. Deep-fat fry about four rolls at a time at 375°F until they are golden brown (about 4 minutes). Keep warm in 275°F oven and serve hot.

Ginger Beef with Coconut (Indonesia) (Serves 6)

2 c chopped onions
2 garlic cloves, minced
1 tbsp ground coriander
1 tsp freshly grated ginger root
¼ tsp turmeric
¼ tsp ground pepper
1¼ lb beef round steak in 1″ cubes
4 c coconut milk

1. Combine all ingredients in a Dutch oven.
2. Heat to a boil while stirring slowly.
3. Cover and bake in 375°F oven until beef is fork tender (about 2½ hours). Add water, if needed.
4. Serve with hot rice.

Fish Soup (Philippines) (Serves 6–8)

2 c canned tomatoes and juice
1½ c chopped onion
1 qt water
1½ tsp salt
1 lb firm white fish, cubed
1 c shredded cabbage
1 c peeled and cubed eggplant
1 c string beans (1¼″ pieces)
Juice of 1 lemon

1. Heat tomatoes, onion, water, salt, and fish to a boil and simmer for 10 minutes.
2. Add vegetables and simmer for 5 minutes more.
3. Stir in lemon juice.

Sweet Poe (Tahiti) (Serves 6–8)

1 large pineapple, pared and cored
2 mangoes, peeled and seeded
2 papayas (1 lb each), pared and seeded
3 bananas, peeled
6 tbsp arrowroot starch
1 c brown sugar
1 tsp vanilla extract
1 c coconut cream

1. Coarsely chop all of the fruits, place in a large mixing bowl, and sprinkle with arrowroot starch, brown sugar, and vanilla.
2. Gently mix together completely.
3. Transfer to buttered baking dish (14″ × 8″ × 2″) and bake in 375°F oven for about 1 hour (until top is golden).
4. Cool before chilling in refrigerator. Serve with chilled coconut cream.

Mango and Glutinous Rice (Thailand) (Serves 4–6)

1 c sticky rice (glutinous sweet)
¼ c sugar
½ c coconut milk
2 ripe mangoes (pared, seeded, sliced crosswise in ¼″ slices)
4 mint sprigs or leaves for garnish

1. Prepare rice according to package directions. Drain.
2. Dissolve sugar in coconut milk.
3. Stir coconut milk into rice and heat slowly until almost dry. Chill.
4. Place serving of rice on four dessert plates and arrange slices of mango alongside the rice. Garnish with mint,

Summary

Southeast Asia includes the countries of Myanmar (Burma), Thailand, Cambodia, Laos, Vietnam, and Malaysia on the Asian continent, and the island nations of Singapore, Indonesia, the Philippines, and Polynesia. Mountains dominate the northern portions of this section of the continent, and monsoons are responsible for the heavy rainfall that is so important to growing rice. This cereal is the foundation of the diets throughout the region.

The generally warm and very moist weather enables farmers to grow a variety of tropical and subtropical fruits and vegetables. Among the more common are coconuts, mangoes, papayas, citrus, bananas, greens of many types, chilies and other peppers, and tomatoes. Fish from the sea and from freshwater are good sources of protein. Augmenting the aquatic contributions are chickens, ducks, beef, and pork where religion does not prohibit certain flesh foods. Spices in abundance are grown in many parts of Southeast Asia.

The original inhabitants of this region were conquered by invaders from different directions throughout history; Kublai Khan came from the north in the 13th century, China from the east at various times, and Europeans and Arabs from the west before the 18th century. There also were numerous battles between the native groups, particularly between the Khmer, Thai, and Burmese. Thailand managed to remain independent of invaders from afar, but Burma and the peninsula of Indochina were ruled by foreign powers during the colonial era (notably by the French, British, and Dutch).

Religion plays a significant role in the countries throughout Southeast Asia. Buddhism is prominent, particularly in the nations on the continent. Hinduism is dominant on the Indonesian island of Bali and is practiced to a lesser extent in neighboring countries. Islam is the major religion in the Malay Peninsula and much of Indonesia as well as the southern island region of the Philippines. Catholicism dominates in most of the Philippines (heritage from the Spanish control) and is practiced by some minorities throughout the region. The art and dances of Southeast Asia frequently have religious inspiration. Intricate designs in handicrafts vary a bit from country to country, but clearly interconnect the various cultural groups. Bright colors and generous use of gold contribute to the dazzling impact of many buildings in the area as well as native costumes, carvings, and jewelry.

The traditional eating style of Southeast Asia is to eat with the fingers, although people living near China in Vietnam use chopsticks; however, many today choose silverware. Rice provides the backbone of the diets for people here. Wheat also is prominent in meals in the forms of noodles and breads. Chicken, duck, eggs, pork, fish, and soybean products (tofu and tempeh) are the sources of protein in diets, the specific choices being determined by religious dictates for some people. Tropical fruits and vegetables are used generously; often chilies and many indigenous spices and herbs are added to dishes to create unforgettable flavors (and heat). Sauces utilizing soy, coconut milk, or fish as principal ingredients form the basis for creating many of the recipes of the region.

Selected Sites

http://www-2.cs.cmu.edu/~mjw/recipes/ethnic/thai/—Carnegie Mellon Web site for ethnic recipes.

http://asiarecipe.com/burma.html—Information on culture and food in Myanmar and other countries in Southeast Asia.

http://fooddownunder.com/cgi-bin/search.cgi?q=philippines—Many recipes from the Philippines, Indonesia, Malaysia, Thailand, and Vietnam.

http://www.irri.org/—Information about the International Rice Research Institute.

http://www.fl-ag.com/tropical/—Pictures and information about some tropical fruits.

http://www.asiatour.com/thailand/e-02trav/et-tr155.htm—Information and pictures of some Thai fruits.

http://www.cuisinenet.com/digest/region/se_asia/index.shtml—Brief introduction to cuisines of various countries in Southeast Asia and information on some of the unique ingredients.

http://www.atasteofthai.com/—Thai recipes and slide shows of preparing them.

http://www.globalgourmet.com/destinations/thailand/—Information about Thai food and recipes.

http://www.globalgourmet.com/destinations/vietnam/—Information about Vietnamese food and recipes.

http://www.globalgourmet.com/destinations/indonesia/indowhat.html—Indonesian food and recipes.

Study Questions

1. Describe how the geography and climate influence the food patterns of people in Southeast Asia.
2. Where are the following countries and islands located: (a) Cambodia, (b) Myanmar, (c) Philippines, (d) Borneo, (e) Vietnam, (f) Thailand, and (g) Laos?
3. Trace the roles played by various European nations in Southeast Asia during the past 200 years.
4. Contrast the typical foods of Thailand with those of Polynesia.
5. Describe a dish that is typical of each of the following: (a) Thailand, (b) Myanmar, (c) Philippines, (d) Malaysia, (e) Laos, (f) Tahiti, and (g) Indonesia.
6. Plan a dinner menu for a Filipino family.
7. Plan a dinner that might be served in Indonesia.

Bibliography

Alejandro, R.G. and L.I. Tettoni. 2000. *Authentic Recipes from the Philippines.* Tuttle Publishing. North Clarendon, VT.

Barer-Stein, T. 1999. *You Eat What You Are.* 2nd ed. Firefly Books, Ltd. Ontario, Canada.

Basche, J. 1971. *Thailand: Land of the Free.* Taplinger Publishing. New York.

Claudio, V.S. 1994. *Filipino-American Food Practices, Customs, and Holidays.* American Dietetic Association. Chicago.

Cummings, J. 1998. *Laos.* 3rd ed. Lonely Planet. Oakland, CA.

Cummings, J. 2000. *World Food: Thailand.* Lonely Planet. Oakland, CA.

Dirige, O.V. 1995. Filipino-American diet and foods. *Asian American Business Journal 2/28/05:*11–17.

Forman, W., R. Mrazek, and B. Forman. 1983. *Bali: Split Gate to Heaven.* Orbis. London, England.

Gelle, E.M. 1998. *Filipino Cuisine: Recipes from the Islands.* Red Crane. Santa Fe, NM.

Hyman, G.L. 1993. *Cuisines of Southeast Asia: Culinary Journey through Thailand, Myanmar, Laos, Vietnam, Malaysia, Singapore, Indonesia, and the Philippines.* John Wiley and Sons. New York.

Layton, L. 1990. *Singapore.* Marshall Cavendish. New York.

Lwin, C.S. and C.S. Robert. 2000. *Food of Burma.* Tuttle Publishing. North Clarendon, VT.

Mansfield, S. 1997. *Guide to Philippines.* Globe Pequot Press. Old Saybrook, CT.

Munan, H. 1990. *Malaysia.* Marshall Cavendish. New York.

Pearcy, G.E. 1980. *The World Food Scene.* Plycon Press. Redondo Beach, CA.

Steinberg, R. 1970. *Pacific and Southeast Asian Cooking.* Time-Life Books. New York.

Taylor, C., T. Wheeler, and D. Robinson. 1996. *Cambodia.* 2nd ed. Lonely Planet. Oakland, CA.

Witton, P. 2002. *World Food: Indonesia.* Lonely Planet. Oakland, CA.

Xavavong, D. et al. 2000. *Taste of Laos: Lao/Thai Recipes from Dara Restaurant.* Snow Lion Graphics/SLG Books. Berkeley, CA..

Yin, S. M. 1990. *Burma.* Marshall Cavendish. New York.

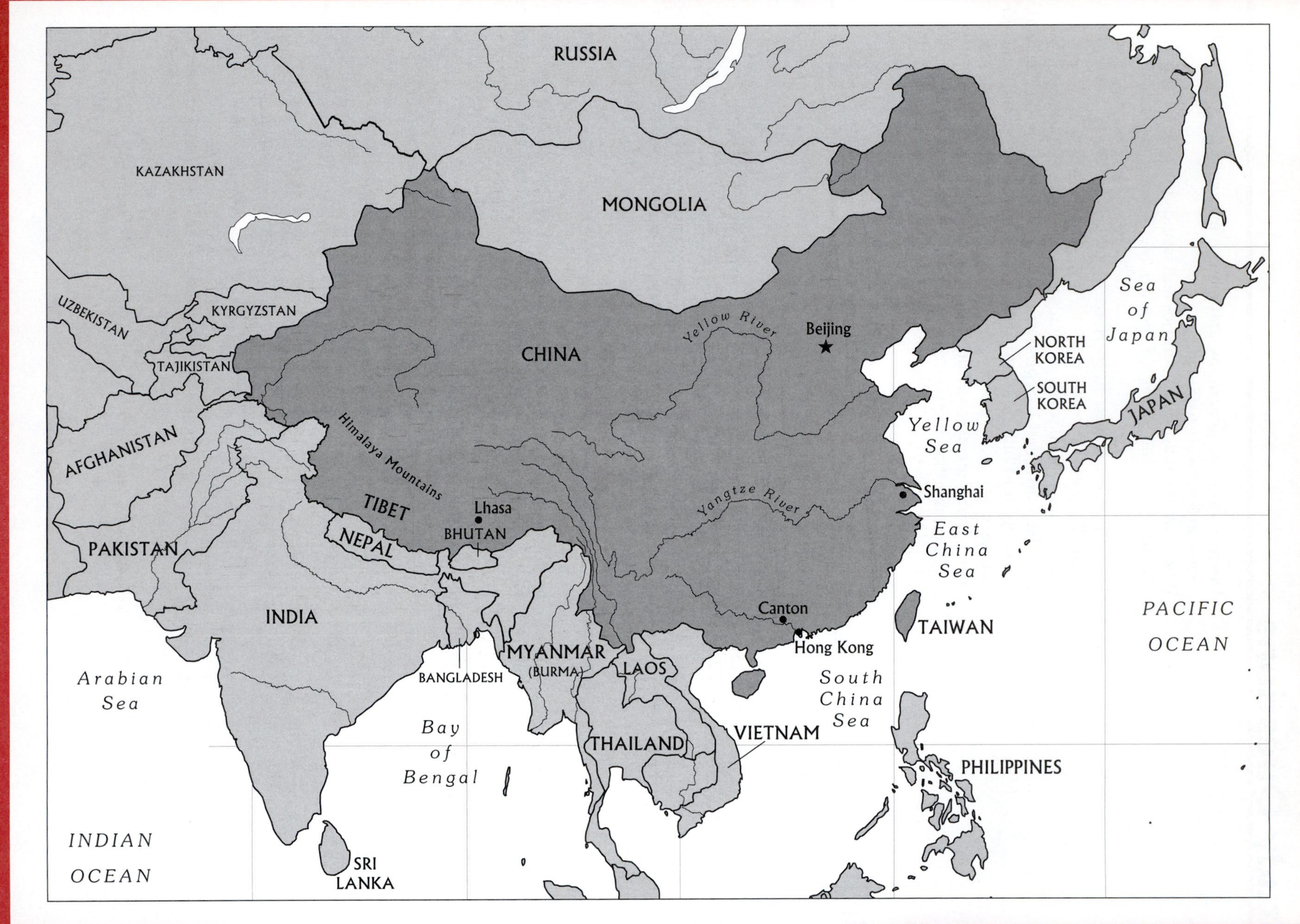
RUSSIA
KAZAKHSTAN
MONGOLIA
UZBEKISTAN
KYRGYZSTAN
TAJIKISTAN
CHINA
Yellow River
Beijing
NORTH KOREA
SOUTH KOREA
Sea of Japan
JAPAN
Yellow Sea
AFGHANISTAN
Himalaya Mountains
TIBET
Lhasa
BHUTAN
NEPAL
PAKISTAN
Yangtze River
Shanghai
East China Sea
Canton
Hong Kong
TAIWAN
PACIFIC OCEAN
INDIA
MYANMAR (BURMA)
LAOS
BANGLADESH
Arabian Sea
South China Sea
Bay of Bengal
THAILAND
VIETNAM
PHILIPPINES
INDIAN OCEAN
SRI LANKA

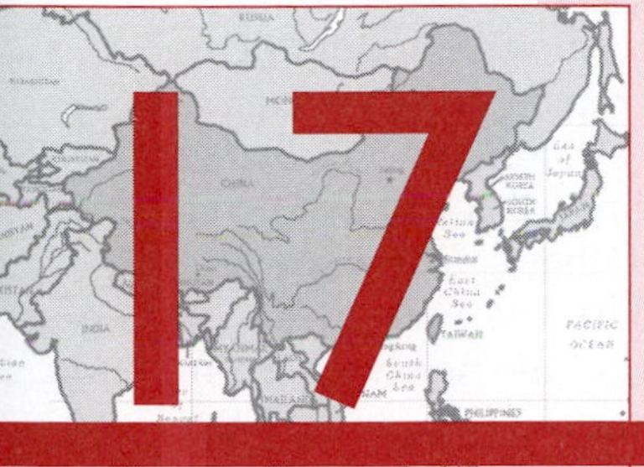

17 China

Geographic Overview

China, the most populous nation in the world, is a sprawling giant stretching across the equivalent of four time zones from the Yellow, East, and South China seas on its eastern shores to Afghanistan, Pakistan, and India on the west. Its long northern border abuts Russia, Mongolia, Kazakhstan, and Kyrgyzstan; southern neighbors include Vietnam, Laos, Myanmar, India, Bhutan, and Nepal. Although China's reach from east to west is even broader than the continental United States, all clocks are set to the time appropriate to Beijing, the capital. The result is that on a day when the sun rises at 6 A.M. in Beijing, it does not appear in Tibet until about 10 A.M. according to the clock.

Some of China's mountains form spectacular terrain, particularly in its Himalayan peaks along the southwestern borders, and include Tibet's Mt. Everest at more than 29,000 feet (the world's highest mountain). From this region of numerous peaks towering above 25,000 feet and Tibet's plateau that is more than 12,000 feet above sea level, China tends to slope downward toward the east, causing the Yangtze and other rivers to flow generally eastward to the sea. However, several other mountain ranges contribute to beautiful scenery in many parts of China. Another unique geographic feature of China is the Gobi Desert in the north.

The vastness of China and its mountains make it a land with diverse weather patterns: severe winters in the north and tropical conditions in the south. Rainfall tends to be heaviest in the summer in the south and diminishes as the storms move toward the northwest. In the winter and spring, a dry wind sweeps down from Mongolia and Siberia, bringing an abundance of dry desert sand from the Gobi Desert but almost no rain.

The combination of mountains, deserts, and high plateaus causes agriculture to be feasible on only a little more than 10 percent of the land. Added to this problem is the fact that the very large population needing to be fed is concentrated heavily along the east coast and is competing for space in areas well suited to agriculture. Another vexing problem involves the climatic variations that tend to swing between floods and droughts. Extensive irrigation and the massive Yangtze dam project are attempts to control the problems created by erratic rainfall. China's challenge to produce enough food for its people remains ongoing.

Farm productivity varies with the climatic conditions, with a single crop produced annually in the north and as many as three crops grown during the same period in the southern region. The principal cereal crop in the north is wheat, but rice is grown in abundance in the southern and eastern farming regions, where it is the mainstay of the diet (Figure 17.1.). Other cereals grown include corn, millet, a sorghum variety called **kaoliang,** and barley.

Kaoliang—Sorghum (grain) crop grown in northern China.

Soybeans, a particularly important food crop grown in the northeastern regions, are used for oil and many different food products throughout China. Other sources of oil are sesame seeds and rapeseed. Peanuts, sugar (from cane and sugarbeets), tea, apples, pears, grapes, and such semitropical fruits as citrus, bananas, and pineapple are produced commercially. Local farmers provide some vegetables, too.

Pigs are the animals raised most commonly, but cattle are also raised for meat. Sheep are raised for meat and wool. Horses are popular in the region of Inner Mongolia, where tribesmen are noted for their riding skills. In the desert regions of China, camels are raised for meat and other uses. Perhaps the most exotic animal involved in agriculture is the yak, which is used in Tibet to work fields as well as provide food and clothing. Silkworms are important because their cocoons are the source of fiber to make the famous silks of China. Both saltwater and freshwater fish are other sources of the protein supply.

History and Culture

The known history of Chinese civilization goes back more than 3,500 years, although evidence of earlier residents (Peking Man and others) dates back more than 600,000 years. More than 20 dynasties have ruled China since 1766 BCE. Qin Shihuang's dynasty, which began in 221 BCE, resulted in much progress in writing, education, business, and transportation networks despite being marked by gross human rights abuses. The discovery of the terracotta warriors buried near Xian has directed attention to this ancient ruler. He also is credited with efforts to

Figure 17.1 Rice is grown extensively in the region around Guilin along the Li River.

Figure 17.2 The Forbidden City in Beijing lies just beyond Tianamen Square, the gathering point for demonstrations and where Mao Tse Tung lies in state. (Photo courtesy of Eileen Welsh.)

unite many protective walls in the north to construct the Great Wall (Figure C.161, p. C54) that was vital in helping to block invasions from Mongolia.

The Han Dynasty followed Qin's death and lasted for more than 400 years, during which the development of foreign trade, notably the Silk Road, linked China and its exotic culture with Rome and other distant markets. Considerable turmoil followed the era of the Han rule. Eventually, the Tang Dynasty established control, and artistic and scholarly endeavors flourished. Several other dynasties reigned after the Tang period, including those of rulers from Mongolia. The Ming Dynasty was in power for almost 300 years, beginning in 1368 (Figure 17.2). This rather warlike period involved wars against the Japanese and the Mongols. Far-reaching sea voyages as distant as eastern Africa represent a hallmark of the Mings. Tourists are aware of this dynasty because of the Ming tombs outside Beijing (Figures 17.3 and C.157, p. C53). Artistic achievements also remain from this era.

Beginning with the Portuguese arrival in 1516, Europe spread its influence in trade with China. The most unsavory part of that phase of Chinese history was the British involvement in developing the opium trade during the Qing Dynasty in an attempt to expand its commercial rewards, which led to the **Opium War** in 1840. Out of this conquest, the British negotiated a treaty that gave them control of Hong Kong until nearly the end of the 20th century.

Opium War—War in 1840 caused by British involvement in the opium trade in China; resulted in the long-term lease of Hong Kong to Britain.

Boxer Rebellion—Violent uprising of a secret sect that trapped foreigners and missionaries in Peking for two months in 1900.

During the 19th century rule of the Qing Dynasty, China began to lose control of parts of its domain to other European powers and to Japan. France carved out the peninsula of French Indochina (Vietnam, Laos, and Cambodia), and Japan forced the Chinese to vacate Korea. Strong internal concerns about foreign influence in China culminated in the **Boxer Rebellion** in which foreigners and Chinese Christians were cornered in a fortified section of Peking in 1900 and fought

Figure 17.3 Large sculptures of animals adorn the roadway leading to the Ming tombs near Beijing.

off the Boxers, a secret sect, for almost two months until a force of foreign troops liberated the besieged.

Revolutionary foment against the Qing Dynasty in the very early part of the 20th century resulted in the overthrow of the dynasty and the establishment of the Republic of China with Sun Yatsen of the Kuomintang (Nationalist Party) serving as president until 1911. Quickly, Yuan Shikhai, the military head, forced Sun Yatsen's resignation and then named himself president for life when he was able to amend the constitution.

Following Yuan's death, diverse forces tangled until the People's Republic of China was established as a communist government in 1949. Chiang Kaishek played a significant role during this period, first leading military forces in an attempt to unify China, and subsequently pursuing an ongoing effort to eliminate the communists. In 1934 the communists, led by Mao Zedong and other future Chinese leaders, worked their way in what is now called the *Long March* to the north of China so that they could organize and mobilize peasant forces to drive out Chiang Kaishek and his Kuomintang associates.

During World War II, Chiang directed his attacks on the communists and left the fighting of the Japanese primarily to the United States. By the end of World War II, the Chinese communists were so well armed and organized that they ultimately claimed mainland China, leaving Chiang Kaishek to flee with his associates—and the entire national gold supply—to Taiwan.

Chairman Mao Zedong stated the communist doctrines that became the "Little Red Book," which served as the basis for educating all Chinese. Mao's programs led to serious hardships for the citizens, especially when crops failed, and his leadership came into question. To regain solid control, in 1966 Mao began the Cultural Revolution, a very repressive program that ended with his death 10 years later. Deng Xiaoping subsequently led the country into an era in which contact with foreign nations resumed. However, curbs on personal freedoms still exist in China. The tragic student demonstrations in Tiananmen Square in 1989 still linger in the minds of many.

The majority of Chinese are the Han, who originally were centered along the major rivers of central and eastern China. Among the minorities in China are the Zhuangs (in southwest China), the Huis (Muslims in northwest China), Manchus and Koreans (northeast China), Mongolians, and Tibetans (in the north and west, respectively). This diversity contributes to the dimensions of culture throughout the outlying regions. The nomadic Mongolians live in yurts (sturdy round tents with domed roofs) and are noted for their skill in riding and raising horses. Prayer wheels are part of the daily lives of most Tibetans, and sturdy, thick-walled, small houses protect them from the fierce winters of their lofty plateau. The Han and other dwellers in the lower lands live in more confined spaces, often with extended families nearby as the multitudinous population seek housing.

Religion plays a minor role in the lives of many contemporary Chinese, although Tibetans and some Buddhists in other regions devote their lives to their faith. Monks once again are allowed to live in their monasteries with little interference from Beijing (Figure 17.4). Followers of Islam are concentrated in the northwestern part of China. Christianity was brought to China rather aggressively by Protestant and Catholic missionaries in the 19th century and still is the faith of a small fraction of the population despite the suppression of religion during the Cultural Revolution. Prior to the Cultural Revolution, the majority of people were followers of a mixture of Buddhism, Taoism, and Confucianism. The government today does not encourage people to practice religion but does tolerate it.

Some mysticism surrounds various aspects of Chinese life. The traditional gods respected in China before the Communist era still are a part of life for many

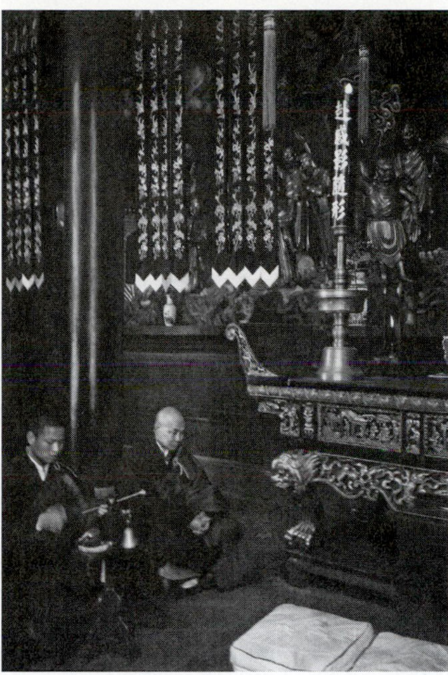

Figure 17.4 Buddhist monks worship in a Shanghai temple.

Kitchen god—Spirit of the hearth who determines wealth and longevity of people in the household; reports to Heaven annually regarding family's behavior.

Yin—Passive principle including female, moon, earth, water, darkness, evil, poverty, and sadness; complementary balance to yang.

Yang—Positive principle including male, sun, heaven, fire, brightness, good, wealth, and joy; complementary balance to yin.

Chinese today, whether they are living in China or overseas. Familiar examples are the **kitchen god,** door gods, the god of wealth, god of happiness, and spirits of the bedroom, to name a few. Importance is placed on living in harmony with nature, a value that is exemplified by feng shui, the art of placing buildings, rooms within buildings, and exterior landscaping to optimize the balance of energies for good health and fortune.

Traditional Chinese medicine also is related to the balance of **yin, yang,** and the five elements (water, fire, earth, metal, and wood) and is said to trace its origins to more than two millennia BCE. Extensive uses of herbs and exotic sources of medicine as well as reliance on needles of different metals in acupuncture are familiar aspects of medical treatment in China.

Art has long been a part of the Chinese culture. Even its form of writing emphasizes calligraphy and beauty of brush or pen strokes. Paintings often incorporate careful brush strokes that define the distinctive style of Chinese painters. Even very intricate silk embroidery on silk reflects the importance of line to convey an artistic message (Figure 17.5). Porcelain has been such a hallmark of this country that these dishes used throughout the world today are identified as *china,*

Figure 17.5 The fine art of embroidery is practiced in China, some of it being so intricate that a different picture is revealed on both sides of the fabric. (Photo courtesy of Eileen Welsh.)

a clear recognition of the outstanding development of this art form in China by the time of Marco Polo. The art of cloisonné (enamel painted into a wire network and fired on metal vases or plates) is prominent among China's contributions to decorative arts. Intricate papercuts are another form of Chinese art.

Opera is popular entertainment in China, but its performances and productions are quite different from western-style opera. The focus is a story, often with four performers; emphasis often is on vigorous dancing or action that may incorporate acrobatics. It is not unusual for music to be secondary in an opera, although some singing and musical instruments may be included. The musical instruments of Chinese origin that are particularly favored include the erhu, a two-stringed instrument made of wood and animal hide and played with a hair and bamboo bow. Children are taught to play this as well as the pipa (a lute), a zither called the *guzheng,* gongs (daluo), and western instruments such as the violin (Figure 17.6).

Physical fitness and achievement are important in China. Chinese acrobats perform not only at home, but also in many other countries. Many people in China practice martial arts daily. Tai chi is performed by many in public parks each morning and has become a form of exercise practiced by some in the United States.

The Chinese New Year is a time of great celebration and occurs on the first day of the Chinese calendar, which is based on 12 lunar months. Each of the years in a 12-year cycle is named for an animal that came to Buddha's deathbed: the rat, ox, tiger, rabbit, dragon, snake, horse, sheep, monkey, rooster, dog, and pig. Much importance is attached to the particular year in which a person is born. Celebration of the New Year can last for two weeks and end with the Festival of the Lanterns, but the festivities are concentrated in the first days, beginning with fireworks on New Year's Eve. Extensive housecleaning, new clothing, visits with family, and parades featuring the lion dance are all part of the holiday. Other traditional holidays celebrate various parts of the year, and political holidays honor important events, including the founding of the Communist Party of China, the birthday of the People's Liberation Army, and a national day honoring the government.

In China, flowers play a leading role in the celebration of the Lunar New Year. Peach blossoms, narcissus, peonies, and pussy willow are sold in the flower market as symbols of good luck and prosperity for the New Year. Other plants that bring good luck are the miniature orange and the kumquat.

Figure 17.6 At the Children's Palaces, children gain considerable skill in classes that range from math to the arts, including music.

Food Patterns

Schools

Southern (Cantonese) School Four rather distinctive styles of cooking, based largely on geography, characterize the cuisines found in China. The southern cuisine often is referred to as the **southern (Cantonese) school,** despite the change of the south's major city's name to Guangzhou. Traditional stories regarding this popular style of cooking suggest that the chefs who fled from the kitchens of the Ming Dynasty in Peking when the dynasty came to an end traveled south and gathered in Canton. There they incorporated local ingredients with their culinary skills and knowledge to bring Chinese food to new heights. Dishes were created using local vegetables and fruits with the available meats (Figure 17.7). Sweet and sour sauces are incorporated in some of the popular Cantonese dishes. Migration of people from Canton resulted in the establishment of many restaurants around the world featuring some of the highlights of Cantonese cuisine, such as **chow mein.**

Dim sum is a tradition of the Cantonese cuisine that has spread throughout much of China and to many Chinese restaurants around the world. Originally, this was the term for the steamed rolls or other small food items that accompanied tea when friends gathered at a teahouse to chat and relax after traveling or working. As sharing dim sum became a part of people's lifestyles, the menus expanded and began to include small servings of foods ranging from appetizers through sweets. **Char siu bao** and spring rolls are two items often served as part of dim sum. In restaurants, several dim sum carts are wheeled to diners so they can select items from the various dishes featured on the different carts. This amounts to a buffet service although the food comes to the diner rather than the diner going to the food.

Eastern (Shanghai) School The cuisine of eastern China relies heavily on foods from the sea. The large coastal city of Shanghai is identified with the **eastern (Shanghai) school** of Chinese cooking. Light broths, egg rolls, and paper-wrapped foods, such as **chi pao yu,** are prominent in this cuisine (Figure 17.8). Other specialties are soy sauces, rice wines, **red cooking,** stir-frying, and steaming to create dishes that are low in calories.

Northern (Peking) School The dish that seems to headline the **northern (Peking) school** of cuisine is **Peking duck,** which retains that name today despite

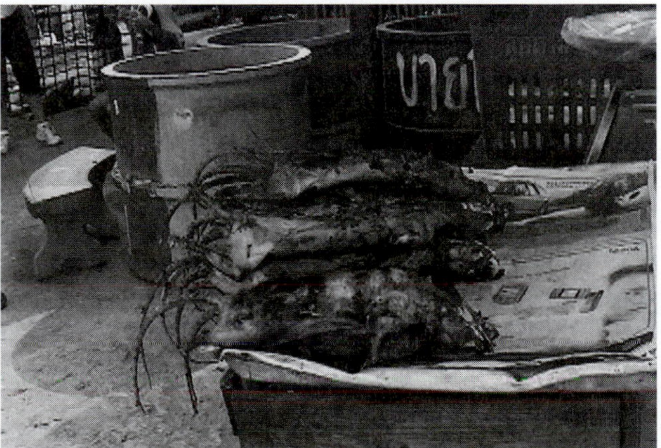

Figure 17.7 Occasionally meats other than traditional ones are on the menu; rats are considered to be a health food by some Chinese. (Photo courtesy of Bill Malcolm.)

Southern (Cantonese) school)—Designation of cuisine of the southern Chinese that features stir-frying, such dishes as egg rolls, dumplings (dim sum), and pork specialties, as well as generous use of vegetables, rice, and fruits.

Chow mein—Parboiled noodles fried briefly with other ingredients; a Cantonese stir-fry with noodles.

Dim sum—Small, steamed dumplings filled with any of a variety of meat or vegetable fillings and many other small servings of food ranging from appetizers to sweets.

Char siu bao—Steamed buns with a roast pork filling, a Cantonese specialty.

Eastern (Shanghai) school—Designation of cuisine of the eastern seaboard of China, notably of Shanghai; light broths, seafood, egg rolls, and paper-wrapped foods are characteristic.

Chi pao yu—Shanghai specialty; bits of seasoned raw fish wrapped in wax paper and fried in deep fat, then unwrapped, and eaten.

Red cooking—Braising meat mixtures in a sauce containing some soy sauce.

Northern (Peking) school—Designation of cuisine of the northern region of China that includes Mongolian fire pot and Peking duck as well as moo shu pork and other recipes that use wheat and wheat flour products.

Peking duck—Traditional dish of northern China, which involves special roasting of a duck until the skin is very crisp; skin, a bit of duck meat, and green onion are wrapped in a thin pancake liberally splashed with hoisin sauce. Plum sauce is also served.

Mongolian fire pot—Mongolian-designed unique chafing dish with a spot to burn charcoal, a chimney going up the center, and a surrounding round vessel where broth is kept hot enough for diners to cook their individual bites of meats and vegetables.

Moo shu pork—Slivered pieces of seasoned pork and bean paste or other ingredients wrapped in small, thin pancakes.

Pot stickers—Assorted fillings of shredded meats and/or chopped vegetables wrapped in a thin pancake, fried, and then simmered in chicken stock.

Western (Szechwan) school—Designation of cuisine developed in western China that is quite spicy and hot in character and uses considerable garlic, ginger, and oil.

Fan—Grain foods considered important as a balance (yin) with the ts'ai (other foods in the meal).

Ts'ai—Term designating the various other dishes that balance with the rice or fan (yin) in a meal; the yang part of the meal.

Sizzling rice soup—Rice that has formed a crust on the bottom of a wok before being deep-fat fried and then added to a hot broth, causing great sizzling sounds as it is stirred into the soup.

Wonton—Small pouches of food wrapped in thin wheat dough (wonton wrappers) and cooked in a broth or deep-fat fried.

Bitter melon—Vegetable resembling a cucumber with a wrinkled green skin and interior with red seeds.

Winter melon—Green, oblong melon similar in outward appearance to a watermelon, but with a white, pulpy interior and a seed-filled center.

Figure 17.8 Jumping shrimp soup derives its name from the fact that live shrimp are among the ingredients used to make it. (Photo courtesy of Bill Malcolm.)

the change of the city's name to Beijing. Sweet and sour recipes, generous use of garlic, scallions, and wheat products, including noodles, thin pancakes, and steamed breads, are typical of northern cuisine. **Mongolian fire pot** is a contribution of this cuisine. **Moo shu pork,** sweet and sour pork, **pot stickers,** and chicken with walnuts are popular menu items. Some emphasis is placed on elegant dishes appropriate to the status of Beijing as the political, artistic, and intellectual center of China.

Western (Szechwan) school **Szechwan** is the name usually given to the cuisine of western China. This designation conjures up images of burning sensations because of the abundant use of hot peppers. Ingredients in recipes often contribute a complex mixture of sweet, sour, and salty, with a fiery sensation superimposed from peppers and ginger. Many of the dishes are oily. Szechwan duck, stir-fried chicken with peanuts, and hot and sour soup are favorites of this region.

Cereals

Rice is a dominant part of most Chinese meals, even in the north of the country when it is affordable and available. A bowl of plain, boiled, long grain rice is served to each diner and is eaten as the **fan** (yin) part of the meal at the diner's pleasure. (The platters of food placed on the revolving center platform represent the **ts'ai,** or yang, of the meal.) Rice may also be incorporated into various dishes. **Sizzling rice soup** is perhaps the most dramatic rice dish; congee (a thick rice porridge) is frequently served, particularly for breakfast.

The other cereal widely utilized is wheat, which finds its way southward from the northern fields. It is used in the form of **wonton.** The *wonton* skins or wrappers encase many different types of fillings before being steamed, fried, or poached. The gluten in wheat enables wheat flour to be worked into dough for these wrappers. Noodles are another wheat product used in China.

Produce

Produce is prominent in Chinese meals, frequently in combination with bite-size pieces of various meats. **Bitter melon** is a popular, unique Chinese vegetable that resembles a pickling cucumber; the red seeds inside are removed before cooking. Its distinctly bitter flavor is due to the presence of quinine, which helps to explain why some people view it as a medicine. **Winter melon** is a large green melon re-

Bok choy—Vegetable that grows as a bunch with thick, white stalks and a top of several large, coarse green leaves.

Chinese cabbage—An elongated cabbage with crinkled green leaves extending from the long ribs; also called *napa cabbage*.

Daikon—Large, long white radish that has a delicate flavor and slight pungency.

Fungi—Designation for mushrooms in some Chinese recipes; may include shiitake, enoki, oyster, button, or other types of mushrooms, usually dried.

Water chestnut—Tuber that is sliced and used as a vegetable to add a crisp, distinctive texture; usually available canned.

Lotus root—Crunchy root of lotus (water lily) cut crosswise to use in stir-fries and soups, where its porous appearance due to many lengthwise cavities in the root adds visual interest.

Chinese parsley—Cilantro or coriander.

Snow peas—Flat, green peas in tender, crisp, edible pods.

Tofu (soybean curd)—Precipitate formed by adding calcium sulfate to a cooked soybean solution made from water and strained, ground soybeans; may be pressed to form firmer curd.

Black beans—Cooked and fermented soybeans preserved with ginger and salt.

Thousand-year eggs—Eggs (usually duck) preserved by packing them in a lime-clay mixture and storing for between 42 and 100 days, which transforms the white into a very dark, gelatinous material with a slightly fishy taste as the chemicals from the packing penetrate through the shells and throughout the egg.

Shark's fin—Usually transparent, yellowish, dried cartilage from the fin of a shark; requires rehydration when used in soup.

sembling watermelon until it is cut to reveal its white flesh and seeds. Slices of winter melon are used to make melon soup.

Bok choy is another popular Chinese vegetable. **Chinese cabbage** is a distinctive, elongated cabbage that is an ingredient in a variety of recipes or simply eaten as a vegetable. **Daikon,** a very large and long white radish, is another vegetable that may be used raw or cooked to add a rather delicate flavor as well as just a bit of pungency.

Fungi (mushrooms) of several types are included in many recipes, either dried or fresh. **Water chestnuts** and **lotus root** are two plant foods that add crisp texture to dishes. **Chinese parsley,** also called *coriander* or *cilantro,* is used to add a distinctive flavor as well as a bright green color. Another popular vegetable is the **snow pea,** which has such a tender, delicate pod that it is eaten with the tiny peas still enclosed inside. The delicate flavor, crisp texture, and green color are characteristics that make snow peas a frequent ingredient in stir-fry recipes.

Soy Products

Dairy products are not a part of the Chinese diet, but extensive use of various soy products and some vegetables augmented by the practice of eating the soft bones of fish helps to meet calcium needs. The creative ways the Chinese have found for using soybeans include soy milk, **tofu,** (soybean curd), **black beans** (preserved, fermented soybeans), fermented bean curd, sprouts, soy flour, and soy sauces (light, dark, and heavy). The excellent quantity and quality of soy protein adds important protein to the diet.

Protein Sources

Pork is the meat most commonly used, and it often is shredded or cut into small pieces as merely one ingredient in food mixtures. Poultry and eggs, lamb or mutton, and a little beef are other sources of protein. Among the less familiar sources of protein in Chinese diets are frog legs, camel, and shark fin. Religious dictates and the cost of pork and other meats limit the amount of meat consumed. Many Chinese are vegetarians. The availability of soy foods is of particular importance for them, and tofu often is an ingredient in stir-fry dishes and other food mixtures.

Thousand-year eggs are preserved eggs made by packing eggs in clay, lime, and ashes for at least six weeks or even 100 days. These conditions transform the interior to a dark, gelatinous mass that is considered to be a delicacy by some. Another delicacy is **shark fin** soup, which is made with dried shark fin as a key ingredient. Dried **seaweed** brings flavor overtones of the sea to numerous recipes, particularly soups.

Seasonings

Various spices and other ingredients are used to add distinctive touches to Chinese dishes. **Five-spice powder,** a blend of star anise, pepper, cinnamon, cloves, and fennel, is used frequently, particularly in Szechwan dishes. **Ginger root** is peeled and grated to add flavor and heat to some dishes.

Sauces often are flavoring components of dishes. **Hoisin sauce** is a dark, thick bean sauce containing garlic. **Oyster sauce** brings a distinct flavor of oysters to dishes containing this dark, salty soy-based sauce. **Plum sauce** provides quite a contrast to the soy sauces, for it introduces sweet and sour to heighten this plum and apricot chutney.

Seaweed—Various types of edible seaweeds and sea grass, as well as purple laver; usually used dried in soups.

Five-spice powder—Popular Chinese spice made by mixing star anise, Szechwan pepper, cinnamon, cloves, and fennel.

Ginger root—Gnarled root of ginger, which is usually peeled and grated; adds flavor as well as some heat to a recipe.

Hoisin sauce—Thick, dark, garlic-flavored bean sauce.

Oyster sauce—Salty, dark Chinese sauce made with soy sauce and the taste of oysters and other flavoring agents.

Plum sauce—Chutney made with plums, apricots, vinegar, chili, and sugar.

Bird's nest soup—Cornstarch-thickened soup made with the mucilaginous lining of the nests of the Asiatic swift, chicken broth, minced chicken, and egg white.

Wok—Round-bottomed, two-handled metal pan used for stir-frying or as the container for boiling water to steam food in bamboo steamer trays stacked on the wok.

Meals

Two important components of a typical meal are soup (eaten with a porcelain spoon) and a large fish cooked and presented whole to end the meal. **Bird's nest soup is** a unique soup favored by the Chinese. Sometimes more than one soup course is served.

Typically, serving bowls of the meal items are placed on a lazy susan in the center of the table. Each person places some of the closest item onto his or her plate, and then the platform is rotated until all items have reached all of the people at the table. This procedure is used for the soup and fish dishes as well as for the other platters. Diners eat with chop sticks and a porcelain, flat-bottomed soup spoon. Since almost all of the food is cut into bite-size or smaller pieces during preparation, chopsticks are effective tools for dining once the technique has been mastered.

A key tool for preparing Chinese recipes is a sturdy cleaver. This device can be used to smash garlic cloves by pressing the broad, flat side of the blade down hard on the clove. Obviously, the sharp blade is well suited to the considerable amount of chopping that must be done to get the numerous ingredients ready for cooking. Even the flat end of the round handle can be used to grind peppercorns.

A **wok** is a critical utensil because much stir-frying is done in this cuisine. A heavy frying pan is a bit less convenient to use, but it can serve as a substitute for a wok. A stack of bamboo steamer trays not only adds to the exotic feel of the kitchen, but also is very effective in allowing steam to permeate the food in the various layers in the stack placed above boiling water. A rice cooker is a convenient contemporary utensil that simplifies preparation of Chinese food, which tends to be labor intensive.

Recipes

Bean Curd Szechwan (Serves 4–6)

⅓ lb uncooked shrimp, shelled and deveined
2 tsp cornstarch
4 tbsp oil
2 cartons bean curd, drained and cut into 1″ cubes
1 tbsp sherry
1 tbsp soy sauce
½ c chicken broth
2 cloves garlic, minced
3 green onions, thinly sliced
2 tbsp cornstarch dispersed in 2 tbsp water
¾ tsp chili powder

1. Cut shrimp into eighths and dredge thoroughly in cornstarch, and then stir-fry in 2 tablespoons of oil until pink.
2. Heat 2 tablespoons of oil in wok, and then stir-fry bean curd gently to avoid breaking curd.
3. Return shrimp to wok, add all other ingredients, and stir while heating to thicken the sauce.

Beef with Oyster Sauce (Serves 4–6)

2 dried mushrooms
1 lb flank steak
1 tbsp cornstarch
1 egg white
2 tbsp oil
2 tsp minced ginger root
1 clove garlic, minced
2 tbsp oyster sauce
1 tbsp soy sauce
2 tsp sherry
½ tsp sugar
6 water chestnuts, sliced
2 green onions, chopped
2 tbsp beef broth
1 tsp cornstarch in 2 tsp water

1. Pour boiling water over mushrooms; soak, and then slice.
2. Cut beef in three lengthwise strips; cut strips crosswise in ⅛″ slices.
3. Dredge beef pieces in cornstarch, then coat with egg white.
4. Heat oil in wok with ginger and garlic; stir-fry beef.
5. Add remaining ingredients and stir while heating until the sauce is thickened.

Char Siu Bao (Makes 12)

Bun dough:
- 1 pkg quick-acting dry yeast
- ¼ c lukewarm water
- 1 tbsp sugar
- 3 c all-purpose flour
- 1 c lukewarm milk

Filling:
- ¼ lb cooked pork, finely chopped
- 1 tbsp chopped green onions
- ½ clove garlic, minced
- 1½ tbsp oyster sauce
- 1½ tbsp sugar
- 1 tbsp soy sauce
- 1½ tsp cornstarch
- ¼ c water

1. To make the bun dough, dissolve yeast in ¼ cup of lukewarm water; add sugar and let stand until it bubbles.
2. Place flour in mixing bowl; gradually stir in yeast mixture and then milk. Stir until well mixed, adding flour if dough is sticky.
3. Turn dough onto floured board and knead vigorously for 5 minutes, working in more flour if dough sticks.
4. Put dough in bowl, covered, and let stand until doubled (1 to 1½ hours).
5. Divide dough into 12 pieces and flatten each to ¼″ thickness.
6. To make the filling, combine all ingredients in a saucepan, and heat until thickened, stirring constantly. Cool slightly.
7. Fill each flattened dough with about 1 tablespoon filling; pleat sides and twist top of each bun.
8. Place each on a 3″ × 3″ square of wax paper and let rise until doubled.
9. Steam over rapidly boiling water for 10 minutes. Remove wax paper after steaming.

Walnut Chicken (Serves 4–6)

1 lb boneless, skinless chicken, cut into ½″ cubes
1 tbsp cornstarch
1 egg white
⅓ c broken walnuts
1 green pepper, cut into ½″ squares
1 sweet red pepper, cut into ½″ squares
1 tbsp brown bean sauce
1 tsp sugar
1 tbsp chicken stock

1. Dredge chicken in cornstarch and dip in egg white; stir-fry in oil. Remove from wok.
2. Stir-fry walnuts and set aside.
3. Stir-fry peppers for 1 minute. Remove from wok.
4. Heat bean sauce, sugar, and stock for 1 minute while stirring.
5. Add chicken and peppers to wok and heat while stirring until hot.
6. Garnish with walnuts.

Chinese Peas with Water Chestnuts (Serves 4)

1 tsp minced ginger root
2 tbsp oil
½ lb Chinese snow peas (tips cut off)
1 4-oz can drained, sliced water chestnuts
¼ tsp salt
1 tbsp cornstarch
¼ c water

1. Sauté ginger in oil in wok.
2. Add snow peas and stir-fry until bright green.
3. Add water chestnuts and salt.
4. Mix cornstarch with water and stir into vegetables.
5. Stir while heating until sauce thickens.

Chow Yung Cabbage (Serves 4)

1 bunch celery cabbage (Chinese cabbage)
2 tbsp oil
1 tsp grated ginger root
1 clove garlic, minced
¼ tsp salt
¼ c chicken broth
1 tsp sugar
1 tsp chili powder

1. Remove outer cabbage leaves; slice into diagonal slices ⅓″ thick. Set aside.
2. Heat oil, ginger, and garlic until wok is very hot.
3. Add cabbage and salt, and stir-fry for just under a minute.
4. Add broth and heat with a cover for 1½ minutes.
5. Uncover; add sugar and chili powder. Heat while stirring just to mix.

Egg Drop Soup (Serves 4–6)

3 c chicken stock
1 tbsp cornstarch
2 tbsp water
1 tsp salt
1 egg, slightly beaten
1 green onion and top, chopped

1. Heat stock to boiling.
2. Stir in slurry of cornstarch in water; add salt and continue heating while stirring until slightly thickened and clear.
3. Stir very slowly while slowly adding egg. Turn off heat.
4. Garnish with chopped green onion, and serve.

Hot and Sour Soup (Serves 4–6)

5 dried Chinese mushrooms
½ lb fresh bean curd (tofu)
⅓ c canned bamboo shoots
3 c chicken stock
¼ lb lean pork, slivered
½ tsp salt
¼ tsp pepper
1 tbsp rice vinegar
1 tbsp soy sauce
4 tsp cornstarch
2 tbsp cold water
1 egg, slightly beaten
1½ tsp sesame oil
2 green onions and tops, sliced

1. Soak mushrooms for 30 minutes in warm water. Drain. Cut in thin strips.
2. Shred drained bean curd and bamboo shoots. Set aside.
3. In a large saucepan, heat stock, mushrooms, pork, salt, pepper, bamboo shoots, vinegar, and soy sauce to a boil. Reduce heat, cover, and simmer for 4 minutes.
4. Add bean curd and cornstarch mixed with water and stir while heating until thickened.
5. Stir simmering soup while slowly adding egg and sesame oil.
6. Garnish with green onion, and serve.

Mongolian Lamb Fire Pot (Serves 6–8)

2 oz cellophane noodles
⅓ lb Chinese (celery) cabbage
¼ lb fresh spinach
¼ c soy sauce
1 tbsp sesame seed oil
1 tbsp sherry
1½ tsp brown sugar in 1½ tsp hot water
1 tbsp smooth peanut butter in 2 tbsp boiling water
⅛ tsp cayenne pepper
½ tbsp fermented red bean curd
5 c chicken stock
1 scallion, minced
1 garlic clove, minced
1½ tsp grated ginger root
2 tbsp Chinese parsley (cilantro)
1½ lb lean lamb in paper-thin slices 2″ × 3″ each

1. Soak noodles in 1 cup warm water for 30 minutes; then cut into noodles 6″ long.
2. Blanch 3″ pieces of cabbage for 3 minutes; drain and pat dry, and then arrange beside noodles on a platter.
3. Wash spinach thoroughly and remove stems; pat dry and add to platter.
4. Combine soy sauce, oil, wine, brown sugar mix, diluted peanut butter, pepper, and red bean curd in a bowl; place about a tablespoon of the mixture into each person's soup bowl. Put remainder in serving bowl.
5. Heat the stock to boiling; transfer to the hot fire pot at the dining table. Arrange an individual plate of lamb and a soup bowl at each plate.
6. Add scallions, garlic, ginger, and parsley to the stock; diners then drop in lamb pieces, which they remove when desired.
7. Ladle stock into soup bowls.
8. Heat vegetables and noodles for 1 to 2 minutes, then ladle with the last of the broth into the bowls.

Moo Goo Gai Pan (Serves 4–6)

4 dried Chinese black mushrooms
1 tbsp oil
¼ lb mushrooms, sliced
1 6-oz can water chestnuts, drained and sliced
¼ c water
1 c celery, sliced in 1″ diagonal pieces
¼ lb Chinese pea pods, ends trimmed
1 tsp salt
1 tsp sugar
1 lb boneless, skinless chicken breast in strips 2″ long
½ tsp grated ginger root
1 tsp soy sauce
1 tsp cornstarch in 2 tsp warm water

1. Soak Chinese mushrooms in water overnight; slice thinly.
2. Heat oil in wok; stir-fry both kinds of mushrooms and the water chestnuts.
3. Add water and steam, covered, for 2 minutes.
4. Add celery, pea pods, salt, and sugar; steam 2 minutes, and then remove all food from wok.
5. Stir-fry chicken for 4 to 5 minutes.
6. Add vegetables, ginger, soy sauce, and cornstarch slurry; stir while heating until sauce thickens.

Peking Shrimp (Serves 4–6)

¾ lb raw shrimp, shelled, deveined, and cut in half
1 tbsp cornstarch
2 tbsp oil
2 green onions, thinly sliced
1 c celery, thinly sliced
2 tsp grated ginger root
5 tbsp catsup
1 tsp chili powder
1 tbsp sugar
¼ c chicken broth
1 tbsp sherry

1. Dredge shrimp in cornstarch and stir-fry until they are pink. Remove from wok.
2. Saute onion and celery for 1 minute.
3. Add shrimp and rest of ingredients to wok and heat while stirring until mixture is bubbling hot.

Shrimp Dim Sum (Makes 16)

Dough:
- ¼ c boiling water
- 1¼ c all-purpose flour
- 1½ tsp oil
- 4½ tsp cold water

Filling:
- 1 tsp cornstarch
- ¼ tsp sesame oil
- 2 tsp soy sauce
- ½ tsp sherry
- ¼ lb shrimp, shelled, cleaned, and finely chopped
- 2½ tbsp bamboo shoots, finely chopped
- 1 tsp brown sugar

Optional garnishes: sliced red chili, soy sauce, green onion pompoms, shrimp crackers

1. To make the dough, stir boiling water into flour; add oil and cold water, and mix to form a ball.
2. Knead dough vigorously to create a smooth surface; cut into 16 pieces and flatten each into a circle.
3. To make the filling, stir together cornstarch, oil, soy sauce, and sherry.
4. Stir in shrimp, bamboo shoots, and sugar.
5. Place spoonful of filling on a circle; lift edges of dough and pinch to form a pouch.
6. Arrange pouches on damp towel in steamer and steam for 10 minutes.
7. Serve with garnishes or shrimp crackers, or both, if desired.

Sweet and Sour Pork (Serves 4–6)

1 lb lean pork in 1″ cubes
¼ c cornstarch
1 egg, slightly beaten
Oil for deep-fat frying
1 garlic clove, minced
1 green pepper (½″ squares)
1 carrot, thinly sliced
1 stalk celery, thinly sliced
1 c canned pineapple cubes, drained
½ c chicken stock
2 tbsp brown sugar
2 tbsp white sugar
¼ c red wine vinegar
1 tsp soy sauce
1 tbsp tomato paste
1 tbsp cornstarch in 2 tbsp cold water

1. Dredge pork in cornstarch, dip in egg, and then roll again in cornstarch.
2. Deep-fry pork in wok at 375°F, stirring to separate and brown all sides; remove to dish lined with paper towel and keep warm in 275°F oven.
3. Pour oil from wok, and then stir-fry garlic, green pepper, carrot, celery, and pineapple for 4 minutes or until tender.
4. Stir in remaining ingredients and heat, stirring until thickened.
5. Stir in pork. Serve.

Chengdu Chicken (Serves 4–6)

¾ lb boneless, skinless chicken cut into small cubes
2 tbsp cornstarch
1 egg white, slightly beaten
2 tbsp oil
1 green pepper in small cubes
2 red chilies, seeded and diced
2 green onions, chopped
½ tsp grated ginger root
1 tbsp hoisin sauce
1 tsp chili bean paste
1 tbsp rice wine
½ c salted, roasted cashews

1. Dredge chicken in cornstarch; dip in egg, and roll again in cornstarch.
2. Stir-fry chicken in oil, turning constantly to brown on all sides (1½ minutes). Remove to dish lined with paper towel and keep warm in 275°F oven.
3. Remove oil from wok and stir-fry green pepper, chilies, onions, and ginger for 1 minute.
4. Add chicken and remaining ingredients, except for cashews. Heat while stirring until hot.
5. Stir in cashews, heat very briefly, and serve.

Wonton Soup (Serves 4–6)

Wonton Filling:
- ¼ lb finely chopped, shelled shrimp
- ¼ lb ground pork
- 1 tsp grated ginger root
- 1 tsp sherry
- 8 water chestnuts, finely chopped
- 1 mushroom, finely chopped
- 1 tbsp chopped parsley
- 1 tbsp soy sauce
- 2 green onions, finely chopped
- 1 egg
- ½ pkg wonton skins

Soup:
- 4 c chicken broth
- 1 tbsp sherry
- 1 tbsp soy sauce
- ½ tsp sesame oil
- 1 bunch bok choy (1″ pieces)

1. To make wontons, gently combine above ingredients except wonton skins completely.
2. Place ½ teaspoon filling at center of a wonton skin and fold in half to make triangle; overlap lower two corners and seal together with drop of water (see note).
3. Add wontons to boiling water; when water returns to boil, lower heat and simmer for 5 minutes. Use colander to drain thoroughly.
4. To make soup, heat broth, sherry, soy sauce, and sesame oil to a boil, add wontons, and heat to a simmer.
5. Add bok choy and heat briefly before serving.

Note: Wontons can be deep-fat fried at 375°F to golden brown and served with soy or sweet and sour sauce as an appetizer.

Summary

A very densely populated nation in Asia, China extends across approximately one-sixth of the world from east to west. Geographically, it includes part of the Himalayas, other mountain ranges, the Gobi and other deserts, high plateaus, river valleys, and a long seacoast that reaches into tropical regions. The combination of many people to feed, much land unsuited to farming, and widely varying rainfall from year to year sometimes has led to serious food shortages even though the land can produce a wide variety of crops in good years.

The history of China goes back more than 600,000 years, with records available of events during the more than 20 dynasties that have ruled since 1766 BCE. Some of the more prominent dynasties have been the Qin Shihuang, Han, Tang, and Ming. European trade encounters by ship began with the Portuguese, who were followed by the French and British. The Opium War in 1840 and the Boxer Rebellion against foreigners in 1900 were the result of friction between these foreign influences and the native Chinese.

The formation of the Republic of China with Sun Yatsen as president occurred in 1911, marking the overthrow of the dynastic form of rule. Considerable internal problems developed subsequently, culminating in the Long March of the communists to northern China, followed by their ultimately forcing Chiang Kaishek's Kuomintang, or Nationalist Party, from the mainland to Taiwan and the establishment of separate rule there. Communist rule has been under the leadership of various people during the 20th century, including Mao Zedong and Deng Xiaoping. The Cultural Revolution began in 1966 and lasted for 10 disastrous years, from which the people and economy are still recovering.

The people in China are primarily Hans, but there are many other minority groups, such as those from Tibet and the Mongols. Many of Tibetan descent are Buddhists, as are some others throughout China. Muslims tend to be concentrated in the northwestern region. Christians (the result of a strong missionary movement from abroad earlier) are scattered in other regions, but definitely are the minority religion. Taoism, Confucian thought, and Buddhism are generally intermingled in eastern regions of China, but religions are still not prominent because of the actions during the Cultural Revolution designed to eliminate most religious worship. Nevertheless, many mystical traditions add richness to the culture as well as medical practices of China.

Art takes various forms, including calligraphy, painting, embroidery, cloisonné, papercuts, and fine porcelains. Opera is an important tradition, which relies heavily on acting and dancing with a bit of music. Music is valued and has developed along a form quite different from that of western cultures; it features unique instruments including the erhu and the guzheng. Physical fitness efforts include tai chi and martial arts.

Food patterns in China include four different schools of cooking: Cantonese (elegant dishes from southern China), Shanghai (eastern seafood and paper-wrapped foods), Peking (northern, featuring wheat noodles and Peking duck), and Szechwan (western dishes emphasizing hot spices and use of oil). Rice is the backbone of the Chinese diet. Pork is the most common meat, but beef, poultry, lamb, and some other types of meats and fish are used, although sparingly in small pieces combined with various other ingredients. Vegetables, some fruits, and seaweed appear frequently in Chinese meals. Soybeans in a wide array of forms are used extensively in Chinese cooking.

Chopping the many ingredients consumes most of the time required to prepare Chinese foods. Stir-frying and frying are common methods of cooking and require little time once the food is ready to be cooked. A wok, cleaver, and steamer are essential kitchen items.

Selected Sites

http://www.kitazawaseed.com/seeds.html—Description and pictures of many different Chinese vegetables.

http://lilt.ilstu.edu/rtdirks/EASTASIA.html—Bibliography of food habits in East Asia.

http://chinesefood.about.com/od/foodandchineseculture/—Discussions on food and culture in China, recipes, and menus.

http://www.travelchinaguide.com/intro/cuisine.htm—Covers various aspects of Chinese food.

http://chinesefood.about.com/library/blnoodlescook.htm—Description of different noodles and how to prepare them.

http://www.index-china-food.com/food-culture.htm—Several topics on food in China.

http://www.asian-nation.org/asian-food.shtml—Comparison of food preparation in different parts of Asia.

http://chinesefood.about.com/library/weekly/aa070700a.htm—Various topics regarding Chinese food.

http://www.travelchinaguide.com/map/china_map.htm—Maps, regional, and city information about China.

Study Questions

1. For each of three dynasties in China's history, (a) name it, (b) indicate the years it ruled, and (c) discuss its important contributions and achievements.

2. Why is wheat a more common cereal in the diet of people in northern China than in the southern region? Identify some dishes that include (a) wheat and (b) rice.
3. Name at least four food products made from soy, and identify recipes in which each can be used.
4. What meats are often found in Chinese menus? Discuss ways in which they are included. What factors limit the use of various meats?
5. What religions are of some importance in China today? What factors have contributed to their role in Chinese lives?
6. Select at least two examples of cultural contributions China has given to the world, and describe representative works.

Bibliography

Barer-Stein, T. 1999. *You Eat What You Are.* 2nd ed. Firefly Books, Ltd. Ontario, Canada.

Buckley, M. 1994. *China.* 4th ed. Lonely Planet. Oakland, CA.

Chang, K.C. 1981. *Food in Chinese Culture: Anthropological and Historical Perspective.* Yale University Press. New Haven, CT.

Ferroa, P. 1991. *China.* Marshall Cavendish. New York.

Fessler, L. 1963. *China.* Time, Inc. New York.

Fitzgerald, C.P. 1969. *The Horizon History of China.* American Heritage Publishing. New York.

Fu, C. 2005. *Origin of Chinese Food Culture.* Asiapac Books. Singapore.

Hahn, E. 1968. *Cooking of China.* Time-Life Books. New York.

Halsey, K. et al. 2004. *Food of China: Journey for Food Lovers.* Whitecap Books. Vancouver, CA.

Hong, Q.Y. 2003. *Origins of Chinese Food Culture.* Asiapac Books. Singapore.

Hsiung, D.T. and N. Simonds. 2001. *Food of China.* Whitecap Books. Vancouver, Canada

Kramer, M. 1988. *Illustrated Guide to Foreign and Fancy Food.* 2nd ed. Plycon Press. Redondo Beach, CA.

Lau, G. et al. 1998. *Chinese-American Food Practices, Customs, and Holidays: Ethnic and Regional Food Practices.* American Dietetic Assoc. Chicago.

Liang, L. 2002. *Chinese Regional Cooking.* Sterling Publishing. New York.

Newman, J. 2004. *Food Culture in China.* Greenwood Publishing Group. Westport, CT.

Newman, J.M. 1998. Chinese ingredients: Both usual and unusual. In J.M. Powers, ed. *From Cathay to Canada: Chinese Cuisine in Transition.* Ontario Historical Society. Willowdale, Canada.

Powers, J.M., ed. 1998. *From Cathay to Canada: Chinese Cuisine in Transition.* Ontario Historical Society. Willowdale, Canada.

Pearcy, G.E. 1980. *The World Food Scene.* Plycon Press. Redondo Beach, CA.

Petrov, V.P. 1976. *China: Emerging World Power.* 2nd ed. Van Nostrand. New York.

Simoons, F.J. and M.B. Cunha. 1990. *Food in China: Cultural and Historical Inquiry.* CRC Press. Boca Raton, FL.

Tan, A. 1991. *The Kitchen God's Wife.* Ballantine Books. New York.

Tannahill, R. 1995. *Food in History.* Three Rivers Press. New York.

Tom, K.S. 1989. *Echoes from Old China.* Hawaii Chinese History Center. Honolulu, HI.

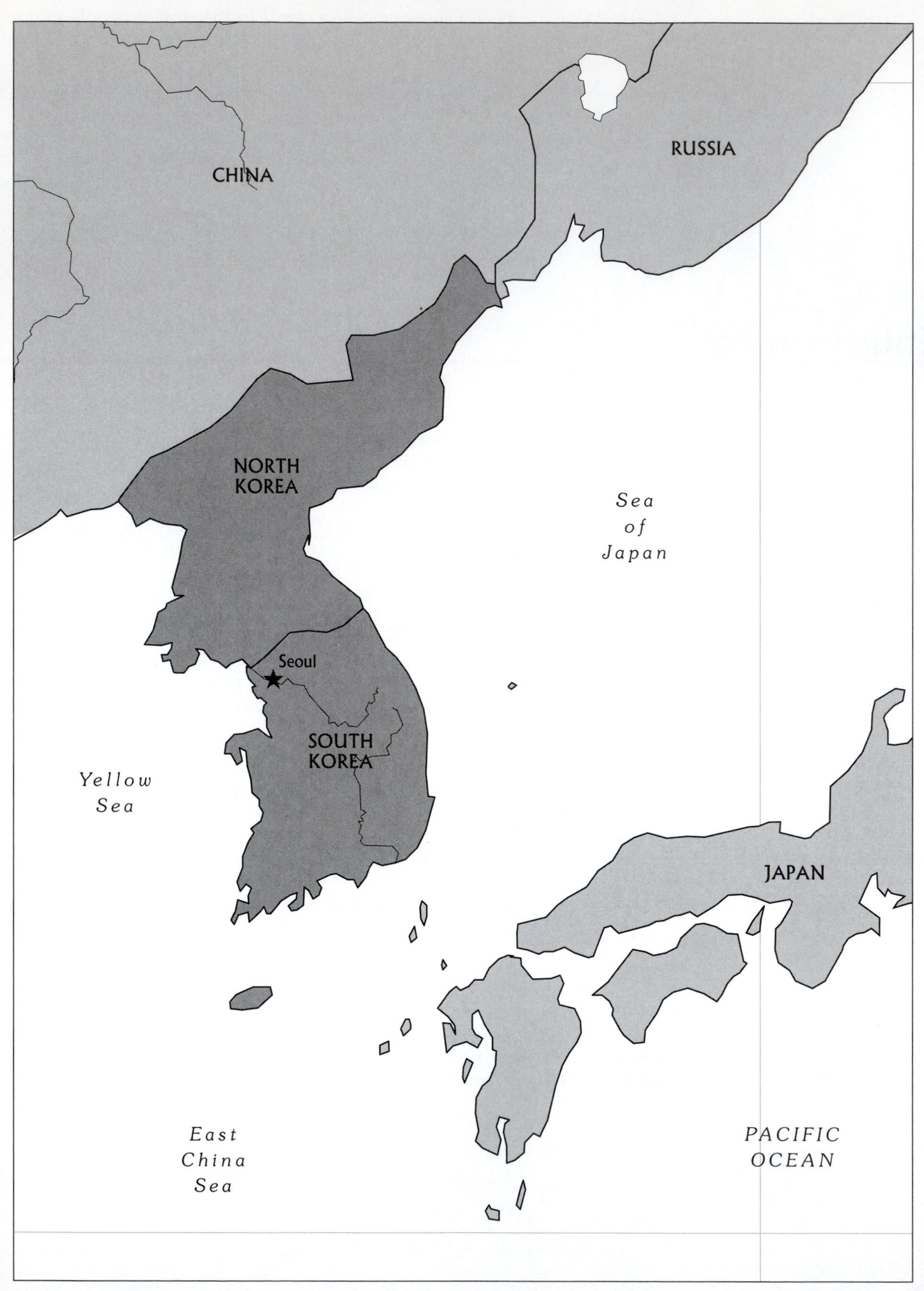
CHINA
RUSSIA
NORTH KOREA
Sea of Japan
Seoul
SOUTH KOREA
Yellow Sea
JAPAN
East China Sea
PACIFIC OCEAN

18 Korea

Geographic Overview

The Korean peninsula, which has been divided into the countries of North Korea and the Republic of Korea, or South Korea (south of the 38th parallel) since 1953, consists of mountains on the east dropping to coastal plains on the west. This peninsula, attached to the eastern edge of Asia, borders China on the north, with the Yellow Sea separating Korea's western shore from mainland China and the East Sea separating Korea from Japan's islands on the east. The whole peninsula is about 600 miles long and less than 150 miles wide.

The rugged terrain of much of Korea presents great challenges in food production to meet national needs. Much progress has been made agriculturally in South Korea since the Korean War ended in 1953. Although only a little more than 20 percent of the land is suitable for farming, the nation has constructed irrigation projects, mechanized much of the production, focused efforts on improving crop strains for better yields, and even built innumerable greenhouses to permit growth of crops that otherwise would not survive the harshness of the climate. With far fewer people actually farming, food production has nevertheless significantly increased as a result of the many technological efforts that have been directed toward agriculture.

As is true in other Asian nations, rice is the major grain crop in Korea. Barley and corn are other important grain crops. Soybeans play an essential role in the diet and are raised in great quantities. The climate of Korea is favorable for growing apples, peaches, persimmons, and grapes (Figure 18.1). Tangerines thrive in the very southern part of the country. Greenhouses are used extensively to raise vegetables.

Figure 18.1 Cherry blossoms in the spring herald the future crop of cherries from the trees in the mountains at Soraksan National Park in northeastern Korea.

As the South Korean economy improved following the Korean War, livestock production began to increase. Cattle (both for meat and dairy), pigs, goats, and rabbits are raised in numbers adequate to meet demand. Chickens are raised in huge numbers, too. In a slightly different vein, silkworms are produced for their fine strands needed in making silk cloth; they also are considered a delicacy to eat (Figure 18.2).

History and Culture

Early Kingdoms

Old Chosŏn is considered to be the earliest kingdom in Korea, holding the power for about 1,200 years beginning in the 24th century BCE. This was followed by splits that resulted in three tribal states in southern Korea and four in the north, which were considered a part of Han China.

The period of the Three Kingdoms was very significant in Korean history, lasting from 57 BCE to 668 CE. The Shilla Kingdom in the southeast was established in 57 BCE, the Koguryŏ Kingdom in the north in 37 BCE, and the Paekche Kingdom in the southwest in 18 BCE. Chinese influence was discarded; Buddhism was the religion of many. Shilla conquered Paekche and Koguryŏ in the 7th century, forming the Unified Shilla Kingdom with Kyŏngju as its capital. The golden age of Shilla rule lasted 250 years and resulted in many advancements in Korean culture and arts. The **Koryŏ** Dynasty that ruled from 918 to 1392 established Buddhism as the state religion. Korea derived its name from Koryo (Figure 18.3).

Koryŏ—Dynasty that ruled Korea from 918 to 1392 and subsequently was the source for the name Korea.

Figure 18.2 Silk worms (pan perched on the box) are just one of the delicacies offered for sale to visitors to a mountain shrine.

Figure 18.3 The Bulguska (temple) built in the 8th Century by Shilla rulers is restored now and listed as an international cultural site of UNESCO.

Han-gŭl—Phonetic Korean alphabet developed under the leadership of King Sejong in the 15th century.

Sejong the Great—Dynamic 15th-century Korean leader who sponsored development of han-gŭl, written music, movable type, astronomy, and a medical book.

The final dynasty in Korean history was the Chosŏn Dynasty, which ruled from 1392 until 1910 from Hanyang (now called *Seoul*). During this period, the Korean alphabet, called **han-gŭl,** was developed to greatly simplify reading based on phonics rather than on the thousands of Chinese characters. Confucian thought replaced Buddhism among the Chosŏn rulers. **King Sejong the Great,** who ruled from 1418 to 1450, sponsored many intellectual developments in music, science, medicine, and language. Tangible achievements under Sejong's rule included not only the development of han-gŭl, but also written notation of music, astronomical maps, a text on Chinese medicine, and developments in movable metal type.

Foreign Incursions

Korea's location between China and Japan has caused it to be the target of numerous foreign military efforts over the centuries. Near the end of the 16th century, Japan's General Hideyoshi invaded, but Korea's General Yi foiled the Japanese by using turtle-shaped iron-clad ships to defeat the Japanese navy support. Eventually, the Japanese persevered and forced many Korean artisans and scholars to go to Japan, where they influenced developments, particularly in the arts.

Manchu invaders from the north also conquered Korea, twice in the 17th century. Subsequently, Korean rulers focused on an internal view of their peninsula, only to be interrupted toward the end of the 19th century by western nations demanding trade opportunities. Japan also began to develop trade and ultimately took over the Korean peninsula in 1910 after several years of violence, as part of its move to conquer China. Considerable resistance to Japanese control developed over the decades, but liberation of Korea did not occur until the end of World War II.

Unfortunately, the decisions made after that war by the major winning powers (United States, Britain, Russia, and China) ultimately led to the Korean War in 1950 fought over the division of the two Koreas along the 38th parallel. More than 50 years after the start of that war, the two parts of Korea are still divided; the south is a highly developed nation, and the north is quite isolated and continually short on food and other needs for its people. Because of this isolation, the remainder of this chapter describes the Republic of Korea, often called simply *Korea* or *South Korea.*

Republic of Korea

Culture

Family Korea has changed dramatically, emerging as a high-tech nation in a period of about 50 years, but many aspects of its heritage are still cherished today. People usually have three names, with the surname usually being first (although the order is westernized by increasing numbers now). Among the surnames frequently seen in America are Lee, Kim, and Pak (often changed to Park), Cho, and Han.

Family is of great importance. Familial ties encompass relationships with extended parts of the clan and special appreciation for the elderly and the experiences they contribute to the family. The family fosters expectations of great personal effort by each person to develop physically and intellectually and to make the best contribution to the group and its nation.

The role of women has expanded in recent years, but for centuries, women were accorded a bit of freedom only if they were physicians, haenyo (divers), kisaeng (entertainers), or shamans (Figure 18.4). Today many women work in a wide range of jobs and are well educated. Nevertheless, a few women still dive for seafood off the shores of Cheju, the island off the southern tip of Korea.

Chogori—Short jacket tied off-center and worn with a chima to complete the traditional dress for Korean women.

Chima—Long, gathered skirt that is part of traditional dress for Korean women.

Most women in Korea wear western dress, although for special occasions they wear a hanbok, a two-piece dress consisting of a short jacket called a **chogori,** which is tied off-center with a bow, and a long, gathered skirt called a **chima** (Figure C.166, p. C56). Men rarely wear the traditional costume of bloomer trousers and a special coat (turumagi) over a vest.

For generations, hardy women living on Cheju island, just south of the Korean peninsula, have spent several hours daily diving in the cold waters along the shore to harvest various fish and other types of seafood. Their careers as divers extend well into their later years. Wet suits now make this a slightly more comfortable job than in years past, but these remarkably strong women still have one of the most challenging jobs on Cheju.

Sports Sports and games are important to Koreans throughout life. The parks and various playing fields for soccer, baseball, volleyball, and basketball attest to this interest, which was illustrated by Seoul's hosting of the 1988 Summer Olympiad. Intellectually challenging board games are played by people of all ages, as can be seen in city parks when the weather is favorable. Kite flying is another favorite activity.

The Arts Although Koreans have quite eclectic tastes in music today, there is great appreciation for traditional music, which is characterized by three beats in a measure—clearly different from the two beats used in both Japanese and Chinese compositions. The changgo, a drum with the shape of an hourglass, plays a key role in providing powerful and intricate rhythms for the dances that are part of the cultural heritage from the courts of earlier days and from the countryside. Flutes, zithers, and double-reed instruments (e.g., the oboe) add the melodies. Korea has also contributed world-class performers in classical western music.

Figure 18.4 Haenyo lady divers still dive off the shores of Cheju Island south of the Korean Peninsula.

Although the art of making pottery in Korea can be traced back to China, advancements were made by the Koryŏ Dynasty, which produced wonderful pieces of celadon (softly tinted bluish-green pottery) and by artisans during the Chosŏn period after 1392, who developed fine white porcelain. Paintings of the same period reflected the importance of Buddhism and Confucianism in people's lives. The fact that the Japanese conquerors took many artists and artisans back to Japan to add their influence to Japanese art is clear testimony to the achievements of Korean artists by the 16th century. Evidence of their work and of later artists can be found throughout Korea in temples, monasteries, public buildings, and museums.

Religion Religion can be practiced freely throughout Korea, a freedom that provides several choices. Buddhism and Confucianism have had very long histories in this country and are clearly in favor today (Figure 18.5). Added to these now is Christianity, which was brought by missionaries about 200 years ago, the Catholics first and the Protestants in 1885. Buddhism has the largest number of followers, with Protestantism ranking an unchallenging second place and Catholicism far behind. Islam has become a small part of the scene since the Korean War. Small indigenous religions also exist.

Holidays Many Koreans celebrate the new year twice: at the beginning of the calendar year in January and again at the first part of the first lunar month of the lunar year, which varies and may fall in February. The Lunar New Year is a special time to honor a family's deceased ancestors. The First Full Moon Day (**Daeborum**) in the middle of the first lunar month is important to farmers as a means of predicting the weather for the coming growing season.

Daeborum—Annual celebration of First Full Moon Day, which celebrates the first day of full moon in the first month of the Korean lunar calendar.

As is true in other Asian countries, Buddha's birthday is a cause for celebration on the eighth day of the fourth lunar month during the spring for all Buddhists. A lantern parade is a highlight of this day.

Children's Day is celebrated on May 5 in honor of all children, not just boys, who sometimes are viewed with special favor, especially during their first year of life. Special festivities are held publicly, and children are often dressed in special costumes for the parades and demonstrations of various martial arts. July 15 and August 18 are national holidays marking the constitution and liberation in 1948. October 3 marks Tangun Day, the legendary founding of Old Chosŏn in 2333 BCE.

Food Patterns

Preserved Vegetables The first word that leaps to mind when thinking about the foods of Korea is **kimchi** (pickled vegetables). This very traditional mainstay traces back centuries, during which time the pickling of vegetable crops and

Kimchi—Fermented, pickled vegetables (particularly cabbage).

Figure 18.5 Lovely sculptures and a Buddhist temple await worshipers who climb the steep mountainside to reach this religious spot.

storing in large crocks for use over the long winter and early growing season resulted in a variety of kimchi types (Figure 18.6). Pickling preserved vegetables so Koreans could have vegetables in their diets every day, despite the time of year. The huge crocks in which a family's kimchi supply was stored might be buried in the ground or placed outside in a cool spot where it would be easy to remove kimchi as needed for meals.

Production of the annual kimchi supply provided an opportunity for plenty of sociability while chopping the vast quantities of cabbage and other vegetables that were to be pickled. As much as 10 gallons of kimchi per person needed to be made prior to modern times, when canned and even some fresh produce became available to augment kimchi.

Cabbage (Chinese or round), cucumbers, and daikon (long, white variety of radish) are the most frequent components of kimchi and are augmented with generous quantities of salt, onions, hot red pepper, ginseng, garlic, scallions, ginger, and other seasonings, such as salted or dried shrimp. The preserving action in kimchi is the result of the large amount of salt and the fermentation period, which develops acidity. Kimchi is served at all Korean meals, sometimes as one of the main dishes and sometimes as an accompaniment.

Cereals Rice is another cornerstone of Korean meals. Its form may vary, but most commonly, it is boiled, short grain rice served in individual bowls. Rice flour made from sweet glutinous rice is used in making rice balls and rice cakes that sometimes are served as desserts. Rice porridge is a popular food, particularly at breakfast; sometimes it is mixed with red beans, bean sprouts, or other vegetables. Stir-fried dishes featuring rice are also popular. A traditional dish for New Year's is **tuk-kuk** (rice cake soup).

Tuk-kuk—Rice cake soup.

Noodles play a rather prominent role in the Korean diet. They may be made fresh in the home using wheat flour and egg to make a dough that subsequently is cut into noodles that are boiled in soups or used in other dishes. Wonton skins made with wheat flour are used to make dumplings. Buckwheat is also used to make noodles. Barley and corn (steamed ears) are other cereals in the Korean diet (Figure 18.7).

Soups Soups are served frequently at any or all of the usual three meals a day. The variety of soups can be quite wide, ranging from broth with only a few seasonings (often hot pepper and garlic or onion) to others that include slivers of meats or fish as well as vegetables. Individual bowls are used for serving soups, and these soups may be sipped from the bowl or eaten with a porcelain spoon when required for the vegetables or other ingredients.

Figure 18.6 Traditionally, kimchi (pickled cabbage and other vegetables) is stored in large earthenware crocks for use later in the year.

Figure 18.7 Corn is a staple cereal crop in the Korean diet.

Protein Foods Korea's geography readily explains the enthusiastic inclusion of fish in the diet, for the seas surrounding the peninsula provide generous bounty for the table (Figures C.169 and C.170, pp. C57). Crabs, shrimp, clams, oysters, bream, cod, and herring are just some of the seafood available in the shoreside markets in Pusan and other coastal cities.

Bulgogi—Grilled, marinated beef or other meat.

Beef, pork, chicken, and eggs are other sources of protein in Korean diets. Sometimes, recipes that are primarily meat dishes are prepared, typically as a barbecued meat (**bulgogi**). More commonly, meats are slivered or shredded to flavor and augment vegetables and soups that extend the meat to serve more people. Dairy products are not generally part of the Korean diet.

Roasted chestnuts are a favorite snack on cold days, and these may also be used in preparing mixed dishes (Figure 18.8). Two other nuts—pine and walnuts—are also incorporated in various dishes to add flavor, texture, and protein. Pine nuts are thought to help ensure a long life.

Seasonings Many Korean dishes are generously flavored with garlic, hot seasonings (ginger and red pepper, for example), and sesame seeds or oil. Although not all Korean dishes contain hot peppers to sear the mouth, this cuisine has a definite reputation for heat (although a bit less than may be found in Thailand).

Kochujang—Red pepper and bean paste used as a condiment and as an ingredient in Korean recipes.

Soy sauce is another dominant flavoring. Sauces containing soy sauce mixed with such ingredients as scallions, vinegar, garlic, red pepper powder, sesame oil, and sugar are served as accompaniments to a meal. **Kochujang** is a red pepper and bean paste that often is found as either a condiment or an ingredient in a meat or vegetable mixture.

Figure 18.8 Roasted chestnuts are a tempting snack on a cold morning in Seoul.

Laver—Edible seaweed popular in Korea.

Seaweed Seaweed of various types can be found dried or fresh at markets along the seaside. **Laver** (edible lettucelike seaweed) sometimes is brushed with sesame seed oil and toasted until crisp. Soy sauce may be used as a dip for seaweed. Some Korean soups feature seaweed as an ingredient.

Teas Teas of various types are popular beverages in Korea. Green tea is brewed from dried, unfermented tea leaves harvested from tea bushes in Korea or nearby countries. Ginseng may be brewed for its health benefits. Other herb teas featuring such flavors as ginger and cinnamon also are favored beverages that may be thought to have medicinal qualities. Fruit teas flavored with dried tangerine peel, pomegranate, citron, and other fruits are also popular.

Dining Patterns Koreans eat three meals daily, often including a hearty breakfast and a light lunch. Snacking is a very common part of eating patterns. However, overweight is not a problem for most Koreans.

Korean meals traditionally are served on long, low tables; diners sit shoeless on the floor, having already removed their shoes when entering the house (Figure 18.9). Each person is given chopsticks, a bowl of rice, and a bowl of soup. The other foods are placed in the middle of the table, and people serve themselves using chopsticks. Numerous dishes, including sauces and other condiments, typically are served at the beginning of the meal and replenished as needed during it. Eating generally assumes priority over conversation while people are dining.

Sang-chi-sam—Lettuce-wrapped meal containing many tidbits from numerous dishes selected by the diner.

Samgye t'ang—Whole small chicken stuffed with rice, ginseng, and chestnuts, covered in broth, and baked until meat almost falls from bones.

Shin sul ro—Korean hot pot.

Korean Specialties One particularly favorite meal features leaf lettuce brushed with a touch of sesame seed oil piled high on a platter (Figure 18.10). Holding a lettuce leaf, diners add various tidbits from the many dishes on the table and roll the lettuce leaf into a tight bundle to be eaten with enthusiasm (and perhaps some kochujang). This traditional meal is called **sang-chi-sam**.

Another specialty is **samgye t'ang**. This is a chicken about the size of a Cornish hen, which is stuffed with rice, ginseng, and chestnuts, placed in a large individual bowl, topped with broth, and then baked until the meat is ready to fall from the bones. Such an individual feast is not likely to happen often, but it is a favorite.

Korean hot pot (**shin sul ro**) is similar to the Mongolian fire pot of China. Many different versions of this dish are possible, but hot pot is always quite a heavy meal when prepared in Korea. Part of the appeal of Korean hot pot is that it is cooked at the table in the special fire pot and then ladled into soup bowls for all of the assembled diners.

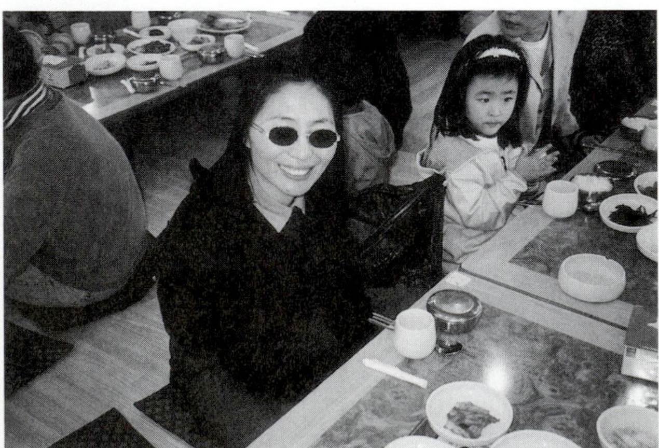

Figure 18.9 Diners in Korea traditionally eat while sitting on the floor at low tables, with shoes removed.

Figure 18.10 Lettuce leaves brushed with sesame seed oil are used to wrap several different vegetables and other fillings.

Recipes

Bulgogi (Korean Barbecued Beef) (Serves 2–4)

1 lb beef, sliced bacon thin
¼ c soy sauce
2 tbsp sugar
4 tbsp minced green onion
1 tbsp minced garlic
2 tbsp toasted sesame seeds
1 tbsp sesame oil
¼ tsp red pepper

1. Refrigerate beef in marinade (made by mixing all other ingredients together) for at least 4 hours.
2. Grill over charcoal or broil beef strips for 1 minute on each side.

Chap Chai (Glass Noodles) (Serves 4–6)

2 oz glass noodles (transparent bean threads)
¼ lb beef, sliced cross grain (bacon thin)
1 garlic clove, minced
3 tbsp soy sauce
1 egg
4 dried mushrooms (soaked 30 minutes, drained, sliced)
Cooking oil
1 onion, sliced vertically
2 carrots, julienne style
1 zucchini, julienne style
1 tbsp sugar
2 tsp sesame oil
¼ tsp red pepper
2 green onions, thinly sliced

1. Add noodles to 1 quart of boiling water and boil 3 minutes, stirring once.
2. Drain and cut into 6″ lengths. Marinate meat for 15 minutes in mixture of garlic and soy sauce.
3. Blend egg; cook in thin sheet in small skillet; then slice into ¼″ strips for garnish.
4. In sequence, sauté (adding oil to skillet as needed) mushrooms, onions, carrots, zucchini, meat until done, and then remove.
5. Combine noodles, vegetables, and meat with sugar, sesame oil, pepper, and any remaining marinade. Heat through, and then serve garnished with egg and green onions.

Chao-Mein (Fried Noodles) (Serves 4–6)

2 oz Chinese noodles
Oil for frying
½ onion, sliced vertically
½ carrot, julienne style
¼ lb shelled, chopped shrimp
2 dry mushrooms, soaked and sliced
2 oz bamboo shoots, rinsed and drained
¼ lb fresh bean sprouts
1 stalk celery, sliced
1 tsp cornstarch
1 tsp sugar
1 tsp salt

1. Boil noodles in 1 quart of water until tender (7 to 10 minutes), stirring every minute. Rinse in cold water; drain well.
2. Fry noodles in 2 tablespoons hot oil for about 2 minutes; set aside.
3. Stir-fry onion and carrot for 2 minutes in 3 tablespoons oil.
4. Add shrimp, remaining vegetables, and 3 tablespoons of water; cover and steam for 5 minutes.
5. Whisk together cornstarch, sugar, and salt with 1 tablespoon of water.
6. Pour over vegetables and heat while stirring to thicken the sauce.
7. Serve over fried noodles.

Clam Casserole (Serves 4–6)

20 clams
¼ lb beef, chopped
2 garlic cloves, minced
2 tbsp soy sauce
1 tsp red pepper powder
6 c boiling water
½ lb firm tofu, cubed
½ bunch watercress, cut in 2″ lengths
4 scallions, cut in 2″ lengths

1. Shuck and clean clams.
2. Mix beef thoroughly with garlic, soy sauce, and red pepper.
3. Add boiling water to beef in saucepan and simmer for 5 minutes.
4. Add clams and tofu, and simmer until clams are cooked.
5. Add watercress and scallions. Simmer for 1 minute, and then serve.

Egg Soup (Serves 4–6)

¼ lb beef, sliced thinly
1 garlic clove, minced
1 tsp sesame oil
2 tsp soy sauce
4 c boiling water
1 egg, slightly beaten
1 dried mushroom, soaked and sliced
½ tsp salt
¼ tsp pepper
1 green onion, chopped

1. Mix beef, garlic, sesame oil, and soy sauce well.
2. Brown meat, add water, and simmer for 20 minutes.
3. In small skillet, cook egg without stirring; slice in ¼″ strips for garnish.
4. Add mushrooms, seasonings, and green onion; garnish with egg.

Kimchi (Pickled Vegetables) (Serves 4–8)

4 c Chinese cabbage, cut in 1″ squares
¼ c salt
6 green onions and tops, chopped
2 garlic cloves, minced
2 tsp ginger root, grated
1 tsp sugar
1 tbsp chili powder

1. Sprinkle cabbage with salt and let stand 1 hour.
2. Rinse cabbage in three changes of water.
3. Mix cabbage with remaining ingredients.
4. Transfer to large jar; put weight on cabbage to hold it below water (adding water as needed to cover cabbage).
5. Cover and let stand at room temperature for 2 days, and then store in refrigerator for at least a week. (May be stored up to 1 month in refrigerator.)

Persimmon Punch (Serves 5–10)

2 oz ginger root, peeled and sliced
10 cinnamon sticks
10 c water
½ c sugar
5 dried persimmons
1 c water
1 tbsp pine nuts

1. Boil ginger and cinnamon sticks in water until liquid turns a pleasing red.
2. Remove ginger and cinnamon, add sugar, and cool.
3. Cut persimmons in half, removing core and seeds, and then soak in water for 1 hour. Discard water.
4. Add persimmons to red liquid an hour before serving.
5. Garnish with pine nuts, and serve.

Shrimp Soup (Serves 4–6)

5 c water
4 tbsp soy sauce
½ tsp salt
15 medium shrimp, shelled
½ bunch watercress, cut into 2″ lengths
2 scallions, cut into 2″ lengths
¼ tsp red pepper powder

1. Combine water, soy sauce, and salt; heat to boiling.
2. Add shrimp, watercress, scallions, and pepper; simmer for about 5 minutes until shrimp are done (turned pink).

Shin sul ro (Korean Hot Pot) (Serves 4–6)

6 c boiling water
½ daikon, cut into ½″ crosswise slices
½ lb beef, thinly sliced
Salt and pepper to taste
⅓ cake of tofu
1 tbsp minced garlic
¼ c flour
3 eggs, slightly beaten
3 tbsp oil
3 tbsp soy sauce
1 tbsp sugar
1 tbsp minced scallions
1 tsp sesame oil
½ tsp pepper
1 carrot, cut in ½″ by 2″ strips
5 pieces dried mushroom, cut in ½″ by 2″ strips
¼ lb white fish fillet
10 medium shrimp, peeled

1. Pour boiling water over daikon and half of the beef; simmer until daikon and beef are tender, and then remove them from the broth. Season broth with salt and pepper, and cool.
2. Combine cooked beef with bean curd, garlic, salt, and pepper, and form 20 meatballs. Dredge meatballs in flour, dip in egg, and fry to golden brown.
3. Shred remaining beef and mix with the soy sauce, sugar, scallions, sesame oil, and pepper.
4. Boil carrots; soak mushrooms.
5. Cut fish in thin slices 2″ long; dredge in flour, dip in egg, and fry until golden brown.
6. Cook remaining egg in thin sheet and slice in strips ¼″ × 2″.
7. In a hot pot, arrange a layer of daikon around the bottom, top with the shredded beef, then radially and artistically alternate rows of other ingredients, including shrimp, and finally add the beef broth.
8. Heat for at least 5 minutes so that everything is cooked.

Stir-Fried Rice (Serves 4–6)

¼ lb beef, shredded
2 tsp minced garlic
4 tsp sesame oil
¼ tsp red pepper powder
1 tbsp soy sauce
1½ c shredded carrots
4 c cooked rice
3 tbsp green peas
2 tbsp chopped scallions

1. Mix beef with garlic, sesame oil, pepper, and soy sauce.
2. Sauté carrots in oiled skillet, using medium heat, until tender.
3. Remove carrots, and then sauté beef mixture until beef is done.
4. Combine all ingredients in oiled skillet and stir-fry over medium heat for about 3 minutes or until hot and the raw vegetables are cooked a little.

Sweet Rice Chestnut Dessert (Rice Pudding with Chestnuts) (Serves 4–6)

3½ c sweet rice
¾ c brown sugar
2 tbsp sesame oil
4½ tsp soy sauce
1 c chestnuts, boiled and peeled
½ c chopped dates
½ tsp ground cinnamon
4 tsp pine nuts

1. Wash and soak sweet rice for 10 to 12 hours; drain.
2. Steam rice in covered steamer until tender.
3. Mix rice with remaining ingredients, reserving the pine nuts for garnish.
4. Heat mixture, covered, in a double boiler over gently boiling water or in a rice cooker for 20 minutes.
5. Garnish with pine nuts, and serve.

Tashima Daikon Soup (Serves 4–6)

½ lb daikon, thin slices, ½″ × 2″
2 oz beef, shredded
4 c water (total)
5 oz tashima (seaweed)
4½ tsp soy sauce
½ tsp sesame oil
1 tsp minced garlic
2 tsp sliced scallions
⅛ tsp red pepper powder

1. Gently boil daikon and beef in 1 cup of water for 3 minutes.
2. Add tashima and 3 cups of water; simmer until vegetables are tender.
3. Remove tashima; cut into ½″ × 2″ strips.
4. Add cut tashima and remaining ingredients to soup; cook 3 minutes. Serve hot.

Toasted Tashima (Seaweed) (Serves 4–6)

5 sheets tashima
1 tbsp sesame oil
½ tsp salt

1. Brush one side of seaweed with sesame oil and sprinkle with salt.
2. Place seaweed in single layer on cookie sheet and toast in 450°F oven briefly on both sides until color turns slightly green.
3. Use kitchen shears to cut into rectangles of desired size.

Vegetables and Rice (Serves 4–6)

2 c rice
4 c water
¼ lb chicken, chopped
¼ lb mushrooms, chopped
¾ c shredded carrots
½ c bean sprouts
¾ c green beans, julienne style
4 tsp soy sauce
½ tsp salt
⅛ tsp pepper
¼ c soy sauce
2 tsp sesame oil
1½ tsp red pepper powder
1 tsp sugar

1. Combine rice, water, chicken, vegetables, 4 teaspoons soy sauce, salt, and pepper in rice cooker or large saucepan.
2. Cook in rice cooker or boil gently in saucepan until rice is done.
3. Combine remaining ingredients to make sauce to serve with rice.

Summary

The Korean peninsula extends south from the eastern edge of Asia, bordered on land by China and on the sea by Japan. Limited farmland is available because of the mountainous terrain, but the Republic of Korea (South Korea) has effectively worked to raise rice, barley, corn, fruits and vegetables suited to the climate, and livestock (cattle, pigs, goats, rabbits) and poultry. Fishing in the seas surrounding the land adds significantly to the food supply, as does harvesting of seaweed.

Following the kingdom of Old Chosŏn for many centuries, the region eventually evolved into the Three Kingdoms shortly before the time of Christ. The Shilla Kingdom conquered both the Koguryŏ and Paekche kingdoms and established the Unified Shilla Kingdom, with Kyŏngju as its capital, in the 7th century. This was followed by the Chosŏn Dynasty (1392 to 1910), which ruled from the city that subsequently has been named Seoul. King Sejong made many contributions, including the development of han-gŭl in the 15th century.

Korea has been invaded by the Manchu from the north and by the Japanese from the east several times. Western nations also demanded trade with Korea in the 19th and 20th centuries. Ultimately, Korea was divided after World War II, leading to the Korean War and the isolation of North Korea in sharp contrast to the very rapid development of the Republic of Korea in the south.

Korean culture emphasizes the family and its expectations of individual members to reach their physical and intellectual potential for the family and for Korea. Consistent with this expectation are many public parks with sports facilities and the availability of opportunities to develop abilities in music, dance, and art. Freedom of religion has resulted in the presence of Buddhism, Confucianism (or a blend of these two), Christianity (Protestant followers outnumber Catholic, but both are active), and Islam. A few other religious groups have a few followers too.

Various holidays are tied to the lunar months (Lunar New Year, Moon Festival, and Buddha's birthday, for example). Others are specific dates, starting with New Year's Day on January 1. May 5 is Children's Day. National holidays are July 15 (celebrating the constitution) and August 18 (commemorating liberation in 1948).

Typically, Koreans eat a large breakfast and two other meals daily, plus several snacks. Kimchi, rice, soups, fish, kochujang (red pepper and bean paste), garlic, onions, daikon, lettuce, carrots, beans, seaweed, and red pepper powder are key foods in the diet. Meals usually are served at low tables, with diners sitting on mats in their stocking feet. Chopsticks and porcelain soup spoons are used for eating. Soup and rice are served in separate bowls to each diner. Other dishes are placed in the center for all diners to share. Desserts are served occasionally and often feature rice. Tea of various types may be the beverage.

Selected Sites

http://www.nationmaster.com/encyclopedia/Korean-cuisine—Descriptions of Korean cuisine, manners, and recipes; avoid using the links outside the main Web site.

http://www.pbs.org/hiddenkorea/food.htm—Brief introduction to Korean food by PBS.

http://www.lifeinkorea.com/culture/kimchi/kimchi.cfm—Pictures and information about Korea, including how kimchi is made and various aspects of Korean food and culture.

http://www.clickkorea.org/Food/foodView.asp?menubar=4&page=1&idx=24—Extensive list of recipes for Korean dishes.

http://www.asianinfo.org/asianinfo/korea/food.htm—Site with brief information about various aspects of Korean food.

http://www.clickasia.co.kr/about/h0115.htm—Information about the celebration of Daeborum (First Full Moon Day).

http://iml.jou.ufl.edu/projects/STUDENTS/Hwang/character1.htm—Aspects of Korean food and culture.

http://www.koreainfogate.com/taste/food/recipemain.asp—Recipes, pictures, background information, and description of kimchi and other Korean specialties.

Study Questions

1. How does the geography of Korea shape its food supply?
2. Trace the influence of other nations on the history of Korea.
3. Describe the food patterns of Korea, being sure to include a description of kimchi.
4. Identify at least four ways in which rice is used in Korean foods.
5. Define the following: (a) chogori, (b) chima, (c) han-gŭl, (d) shinsollo, and (e) tuk-kuk.
6. Plan a menu for a Korean dinner.

Bibliography

Barer-Stein, T. 1999. *You Eat What You Are.* 2nd ed. Firefly Books, Ltd. Ontario, Canada.

Chi, Y.S. 2001. *Korean Cuisine.* Wei-Chuan Publishing. Monterey Park, CA.

Chu, W.Y. 1985. *Traditional Korean Cuisine.* L. A. Korea Times. Los Angeles.

Chung, S.Y. 2001. *Korean Home Cooking.* Tuttle Publishing. Rutland, VT.

DeLand, A. and R. Miller. 1994. *Far East 94/95.* Fielding Worldwide. Redondo Beach, CA.

DuBois, J. 1994. *Korea.* Marshall Cavendish. New York.

Hepinstll, H.S.S. 2001. *Growing Up in a Korean Kitchen.* Ten Speed Press. Berkeley, CA.

Kim, H.E. 1985. *Facts about Korea.* 18th ed. Hollym Corp. Seoul, Korea.

Kim, Y.J. 1995. *Kyŏngju, Old Capital of Shilla Dynasty Enlivened with 2000-Year History.* Y.S. Kim. Seoul, Korea.

Lee, C.H.J. 2005. *Eating Korean: From Barbecue to Kimchi, Recipes from My Home.* Wiley. New York.

Marks, C. and M. Kim. 1993. *Korean Kitchen.* Chronicle. San Francisco.

Rutt, R. 1964. *Korean Works and Days.* Charles E. Tuttle. Rutland, VT.

RUSSIA
CHINA
NORTH KOREA
Seoul
SOUTH KOREA
Sea of Japan
Sapporo
HOKKAIDO
HONSHU
JAPAN
Tokyo
Hiroshima
Kyoto
Kobe
Osaka
SHIKOKU
KYUSHU
East China Sea
PACIFIC OCEAN

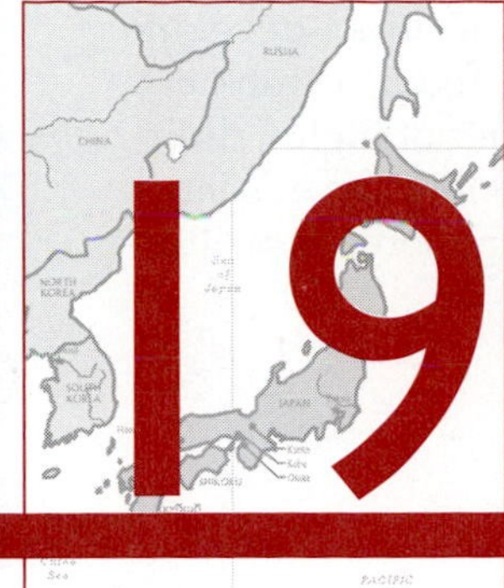

19 Japan

Geographic Overview

Honshu—Largest of the islands of Japan; Tokyo is on Honshu.

Japan, the island nation just east of the Asian continent, consists of four main islands (Hokkaido, **Honshu,** Shikoku, and Kyushu) stretching from latitudes equivalent to those of New England to Florida. The northernmost island is Hokkaido; Sapporo, its principal city, is familiar to many as the home of the 1972 Winter Olympics, a fact that attests to its cold and snowy winters and its mountainous terrain. A bit south and west of Hokkaido is the large main island of Honshu. Tokyo is located on its southern coast about where Honshu's shoreline turns west. Shikoku is a comparatively small island roughly paralleling the western peninsula of Honshu and just a bit south of it.

The fourth island, Kyushu, lies west and south from the tip of Honshu and Shikoku. Kyushu has quite a mild, rather subtropical climate due to its southern location. In fact, Kyushu is close enough to the Korean Peninsula that this island apparently was the route by which early people from the mainland entered the region that is now Japan. The Chinese referred to what is now Japan by the name *Jihpen,* Land of the Rising Sun, which indicated its location to the east of China.

Geographically, Japan experiences considerable shifting and earth movements, the result of its volcanic origins and the movement of tectonic plates. Mt. Fuji on the island of Honshu has its lovely, symmetrical volcanic peak rising more than 12,000 feet. It is but one of seemingly endless mountains that comprise about 85 percent of the surface of Japan.

Food Challenges

Only limited areas of relatively flat land are available throughout the country, and a huge population competes with farmers for this space. This competition for land has forced development of terracing and other efforts to expand the land that can be used for people and crops.

The Japanese are masters at maximizing crop yields from the land that is dedicated to agriculture. Fields generally are small, but intensively farmed, and almost no land goes to waste. Rice can be grown to produce two crops annually, and vegetables are planted and fertilized to achieve very high yields. Production of livestock is rather limited because of land constraints, but labor-intensive tending of cattle results in such high-quality meat as the world-famous Kobe beef.

The limited availability of suitable land for farming has fostered development of the fishing industry and the harvesting of seaweeds for food. Fortunately, Japan's seas surrounding its islands provide important quantities of highly desirable foods that are featured prominently in Japanese cuisine. In fact, Japan's large fishing fleets pursue their catches in waters very far from their shores as well as close to home.

History and Culture

Early Settlers

People made their way to the Japanese islands from China, Manchuria, and probably other parts of Southeast Asia before the end of the 3rd century CE. Unification of some of the groups began to occur in the 4th century, and Shinto began to emerge as a unifying religious tradition, which emphasized harmony and social unity. Then Buddhism was introduced from China in the 6th century and began to be interwoven with Shinto traditions. By the 8th century, the center of government was established at Nara on the major island of Honshu about 125 miles west of Tokyo (Figure 19.1).

Governance

Near the end of the 8th century, Kyoto became the center of government. The Heian period lasted from 794 to 1185. Although language and art showed strong Chinese influence, this period produced much literature and art that was distinctively Japanese. Governance also underwent changes, with the power gradually shifting from the emperor to very strong clans or families to military leaders (**shoguns**). The court of the emperor served a largely ceremonial role. The Fujiwara family gained control during the Heian period, only to be overshadowed by intensive power fights that resulted in Minamoto Yoritomo establishing his shogunate in Kamakura while the emperor's court remained in Kyoto. By 1333 the shogunate was moved back to Kyoto.

Shogun—Term for military rulers in Japan prior to 1867.

Numerous civil conflicts continued until Tokugawa Ieyasu became shogun. He moved his government to what is now Tokyo in 1600, although the emperor

Figure 19.1 This Buddhist shrine in Nara, Japan, attracts many Buddhists and other visitors.

was in Kyoto. It was during his reign that Portuguese Christian missionaries, who had arrived in the middle of the 16th century, were driven out of Japan. In fact, the only Europeans allowed to stay were some traders from Holland. Essentially, Japan sealed itself off from the West until 1853. A strong class system was established by the Tokugawa shoguns: samurai (warrior), farmer, artisan, and merchant (in descending order of prestige). Subsequently, the fact that merchants were the ones who gathered economic strength resulted in a shift in their status to a higher level.

Interactions with the West

Opening of contact with the West occurred as a result of Commodore Perry's visits, first in 1853 and again in 1854, to establish a treaty that opened two Japanese ports for limited trade with the United States. Other nations soon followed with their own trade treaties. Japan's isolation ended. Then the Meiji period unfolded with Emperor Meiji moving his government to Tokyo (called *Edo* at that time). Considerable development of the country took place internally, and Japan began to seek recognition in the world.

China and Russia were Japan's targets by 1912, when the Meiji era closed. The country's expansion continued under Emperor Hirohito. Military actions by Japan were conducted in Manchuria in 1931 and in China in 1937. The attack on Pearl Harbor in 1941 certainly was an event that stands out in U.S. history. Japan's defeat in 1945 left the nation in ruins. However, remarkable recovery and development from that time to the present have enabled Japan to emerge as a strong economic power in the world community (Figure 19.2).

Religion

Shinto—Early religion of Japan that focused on nature and considered the Emperor to be a descendant of the sun goddess.

Religion in Japan today is a somewhat nebulous aspect of the lives of people. **Shinto,** which is perhaps better described as a philosophical approach to life than as a discrete religion, plays a subtle role in Japanese traditions. Nature and harmony in life are values attributed to Shinto. Simple beauty provides harmony, as is evident in all aspects of Japanese art.

Buddhism is clearly evident in Japan, although it is not nearly as strong as in other neighboring countries in Southeast Asia. In Japan, there is a melding of philosophy and religion for many worshipers. People feel free to embrace aspects of Shinto and Buddhism to suit their own spiritual needs. Christianity also plays a role in the lives of some Japanese; missionaries began to return to bring their message to Japan after the country was again open to them during the Meiji rule.

Torii gate—Distinctive gateway to a Shinto shrine.

The combination of Shinto and Buddhist worship resulted in construction of lovely temples and shrines throughout Japan. The sacred ground of a Shinto shrine is carefully defined by rope, white gravel, and **torii gate** (distinctive arch or gate) to a Shinto shrine so that people considered to need purification will not

Figure 19.2 The streets of Tokyo, the present capital of Japan, are crowded near the entrance to this shrine within the city.

Figure 19.3 A large Buddhist shrine at Nikko consists of several buildings on the hillside.

enter until ritually purified. Various architectural styles of Shinto shrines can be found in Japan. A particularly large and impressive one is the Heian Jingu shrine in Kyoto. The Shinto shrine at Nikko is also often visited (Figure 19.3).

Buddhist temples or shrines may also be built in various styles and sometimes are built rather close to a Shinto shrine. Their architecture may be somewhat more intricate than the Shinto shrines and may feature a pagoda-type roof (Figure 19.4).

Traditions

The Japanese tea ceremony is an elaborate ritual that follows a lengthy, carefully choreographed program designed to emphasize beauty in all aspects of preparing, serving, and drinking tea artfully made using finely powdered tea leaves. Even the beauty of the cup is emphasized to enhance the interaction between the person preparing the beverage and the guest. Men traditionally performed the tea ceremony, although this ceremony is carefully taught to young Japanese women today.

Another tradition that can be traced to Shinto practices is the public bath. Public baths evolved as a social, carefully prescribed tradition in Japan. Bathers are expected to wash themselves with soap and to rinse thoroughly before entering the public bath. Actually, the communal bath is a place for soaking, relaxing, and chatting with family or friends. In some parts of Japan, natural hot springs conveniently provide the setting for public baths.

Figure 19.4 Pagodas in Japan feature intricate detail on the various roof levels.

The Arts

Two types of traditional Japanese entertainment have a long history of performances that are highly stylized presentations of very old folk stories. Noh dramas feature actors wearing wooden masks. Action is very slow, and performances are long. A shorter, lighter version is called kyögen. A particularly dramatic form of traditional Japanese entertainment is **kabuki,** which traditionally is danced by men wearing white face makeup, startling wigs, and very elaborate costumes. A performance might include sword fights, music, dancing, and even acrobatics.

Kabuki—Traditional, highly stylized drama performed by men in elaborate costumes and makeup, often featuring dancing and some music.

Bunraku—Puppet shows featuring large, complicated puppets very skillfully presented, often in traditional stories.

A related tradition is puppeteering, which is called **bunraku.** Large, elaborate puppets are crafted with amazing costumes for the various roles in a play. The puppeteers breathe life into these puppets as they maneuver their characters, giving them voice and emotion to bring complex stories to the audience.

Ceramics is a highly refined art in Japan. The simple designs and excellent glazes are recognized throughout the world. One of their finest examples is the instantly recognizable Imari porcelains from Kyushu, a type that traces its roots to the importation of Korean craftsmen in 1616 following the Japanese invasion.

Dance is an integral part of Japanese life for both spectators and participants. Originally, dances were performed to help ensure a good harvest or other need, such as successful fishing; other dances were to honor a god or a spirit. An example is the coal miner's dance (Tanko Bushi), which depicts the miners digging coal, pushing the filled carts, and carrying sacks of coal.

Japanese art reflects the pleasure conveyed by simplicity of line and subtlety or even absence of color. The calligraphy and brush art created by a combination of artistic strokes of varying widths of black on a simple white paper are representative of Japan. Scrolls painted with care and subtlety of color often depict nature at different seasons of the year. Wood blocks are used to create another distinctive Japanese art form, wood block prints. Although Japanese artists obviously had opportunities to become aware of the art of China and Korea, the style of art in Japan clearly is identifiable as its own. Origami, the art of paper folding, is another unique form of Japanese art.

Love of nature is reflected in the beauty created in Japanese gardens (Figure 19.5). Artful use of water, plants and trees of varying sizes and colors, and stones and gravel results in tranquil havens for quiet meditation and enjoyment. One of the features sometimes is an arched footbridge over a stream or pond. Artistically raked gravel provides harmony of line and peace in some gardens. Bonsai, the art of dwarfing a tree to create uniquely sculpted small trees, may be incorporated when designing a Japanese garden. A pot containing a small bonsai is likely to find its way into the home. If cut flowers are displayed, they will be arranged according to the rules of **ikebana** (flower arranging).

Ikebana—Japanese art of arranging cut flowers.

Japanese music is performed on traditional instruments and provides sounds very distinctive from western music. Stringed instruments with varying

Figure 19.5 A peaceful garden with flowers and artfully trimmed shrubbery and trees in front of this home in Kyoto exemplifies the Japanese love of nature.

numbers of strings, a range of sizes, and different shapes are often featured in Japanese musical performances. The samisen has three strings and resembles a banjo in shape. The koto is the Japanese version of a zither whose 13 strings made of silk provide a smooth sound when plucked. Another type of Japanese lute is the biwa, which has four strings and a short neck. The elegant style of music, called *gagaku,* dates from the Heian era and was centered at Nara. Big drums punctuate the music produced by playing flutes, stringed instruments, and other drums and reeds.

On quite a different note of culture are the geishas. These women are well schooled in the fine art of flower arranging, in the tea ceremony, and in musical performance. Japanese men have enjoyed the tradition of geishas for many centuries as entertainment away from home.

Entertainment

The Japanese love sports. Perhaps the most unique sport presented there is sumo wrestling. The stars of this sport are extremely heavy, often in excess of 350 pounds. They are an amazing sight as they enter the ring in their loin cloths and proceed to try to force the opponent to touch a part of the body to the floor or to exit the ring. This is a sport that is steeped in centuries of tradition. A far more recent passion is the sport of baseball, which was imported to Japan by Americans following World War II.

Holidays

In Japan, people love holidays and celebrate quite a few special ones, starting with New Year's Day on January 1. This may feature the wearing of kimonos and family celebrations. Boys are especially prized and honored on Children's Day, which is a national celebration held on May 5. The major holidays at vernal and autumnal equinoxes go back to the early eras when most people were farmers and therefore very attuned to agricultural seasons.

Food Patterns

Rice

Japanese food patterns prominently feature two crops: rice and soybeans. Rice may be prepared in different ways, most commonly today being cooked in a rice cooker and served either in a separate bowl or with other ingredients. A prized form of rice is **mochi,** a rice cake made especially for the New Year's celebration. Glutinous rice is first steamed until tender and then placed in extremely large wooden mortars where many people take turns pounding the rice with heavy wooden mallets to make a very sticky rice paste. This paste may be shaped into cakes that can be grilled or perhaps wrapped in seaweed and then dipped in soy sauce. Chunks of dry mochi can be deep-fat fried and eaten as a snack.

Mochi—Rice cake made by pounding cooked sweet glutinous rice; traditional for New Year's celebration.

Rice also appears on Japanese tables in the form of rice vinegar, **mirin** (sweet rice wine), and **sake,** the strong rice wine made by using Aspergillus oryzae for fermenting to an alcoholic content of 15 to 17 percent. Sake is served warm in special tiny cups.

Mirin—Sweet rice wine.

Sake—Strong rice wine, usually served warm.

Soy Products

Soybeans are found in many forms in the Japanese diet. Tofu has long played a significant role as a source of plant protein. Soy sauce, **miso** (fermented bean

Miso—Fermented soybean paste.

paste), and okara (powdered, dried pulp by-product of tofu production) are often used in Japanese cooking.

Food from the Sea

Sashimi—Very carefully cut and arranged slices of raw fish.

Sushi—Vinegared rice and small bits of other ingredients pressed into a mold or rolled tightly into a long log encased in a layer of nori and sliced vertically.

Nori—Dried seaweed available in thin, greenish-black sheets; used for wrapping sushi and other foods or as a garnish.

Wasabi— Finely grated, delicate green horseradish; also available as a powder.

Tempura—Batter-coated, deep-fried shrimp and thinly sliced vegetables.

Numerous kinds of fish and seaweeds are harvested from the seas around Japan. Not surprisingly, both of these foods are served in virtually all homes and restaurants. Sometimes, fish may be prepared with extreme care and served beautifully without any cooking—a dish called **sashimi.** Regardless of the type of fish being used for making sashimi, the key to success is great skill in cutting the fish correctly with exactly the right sharp knife. Of course, only the freshest fish can be used, and service should be prompt to ensure food safety.

Sushi preparation also is an art that involves careful selection of lovely and delicate ingredients (various seafood or vegetables, or both) to be arranged alongside vinegared rice (Figure 19.6). Sometimes, sushi is pressed into molds to form long fingers. A familiar style is made by arranging a layer of dried seaweed (**nori**) on a bamboo mat, and then artfully arranging the ingredients on the seaweed before rolling it carefully and tightly to enclose the filling as a long tube. Ultimately, the roll is sliced crosswise for lovely round slices with the seaweed serving as the outer covering. Vinegared ginger is usually served as an accompaniment for both sashimi and sushi. Another favorite, sinus-clearing condiment is **wasabi** (grated horseradish).

Tempura is quite a different, but extremely popular preparation of shrimp and vegetable slices. Surprisingly, this Japanese favorite food actually was brought to Japan by the Portuguese missionaries, and the tradition remained even though the missionaries were forced to leave. In fact, the name tempura is derived from the Latin "Quattuor Tempora," the designation the Catholic fathers gave to the four times a year they were required to eat seafood rather than meat. This special food was prepared by dipping shrimp in batter and deep-frying it. The Japanese were quick to adopt the dish (and to add thinly sliced vegetables to their tempura).

Soups

Dashi—Clear soup stock made with dried fillet of bonito and kelp.

Suimono—Clear Japanese soups.

Soups are a part of Japanese cuisine, and **dashi** is central to preparing some soups. It is a stock made with katsuo-bushi (dried fillet of bonito) and konbu (dried kelp). Fortunately, dashi is now available as an instant mix for use in making clear soups (**suimono**), which may be garnished with a small curl of lemon rind, a bit of shrimp, or other artistic touch. Suimono can be varied by including a slice of tofu, perhaps a bamboo shoot sliver, or a bite of fish fillet. Miso soups range from sweet

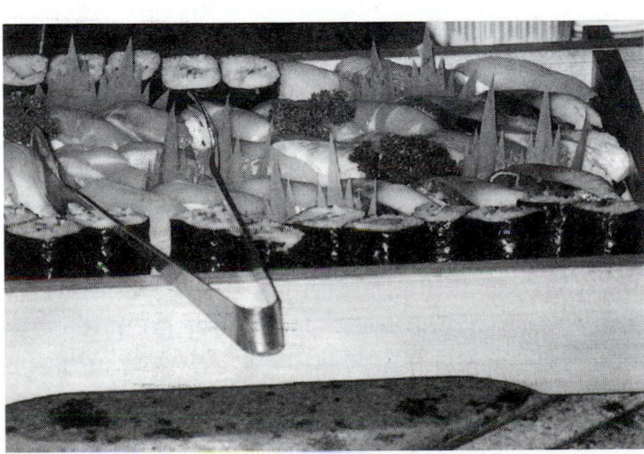

Figure 19.6 Sushi is skillfully prepared using the freshest ingredients and artfully arranged for service.

Figure 19.7 Fresh vegetables and thin cuts of meat are being grilled at the table in this Japanese restaurant.

to quite salty in taste. For breakfast, this traditional soup (made using fermented soybean paste) is augmented with a bowl of rice, pickles, and green tea.

Noodles

Soba—Noodles made from buckwheat flour from northern Japan.

Udon—Noodles made with wheat flour, typical of southern Japan.

Noodles represent another vital part of most Japanese diets. Ones made with buckwheat flour from the north of Japan are called **soba.** Noodles made using wheat flour are **udon** and are particularly popular in southern Japan. Soba noodles typically are a gray color and rather thin, while udon may be either flat or round and sometimes fairly wide and thick. The cooked noodles may be served with a dipping sauce or in a broth. In either case, they are politely sucked into the mouth, accompanied by an audible and appreciative slurping sound.

Vegetables

Tsukemono—Pickled vegetables.

Vegetables frequently are pickled (**tsukemono**) and served as accompaniments at meals. Mushrooms of various types (shiitake, for example) are used in their dried form in an array of recipes. Bamboo shoots and lotus root are important both for the texture they add and for their artistic appearance. Burdock (gobo), Japanese eggplant, kabocha (Japanese pumpkin squash), daikon (giant white radish), cucumbers, and spinach are among the vegetable ingredients in Japanese meals (Figure 19.7). Vinegared salads (**sunomono**) are served at many meals.

Sunomono—Vinegared salads.

Sukiyaki—Thinly sliced beef simmered with Japanese vegetables, soy sauce, mirin, and dashi in a pot at the table.

Sukiyaki is a well-known one-dish meal from Japan despite the fact that it was inspired in Japan in the mid-19th century when Westerners settling there brought their love of beef. Although Buddhism is a religion that values life, it allows eating meat. This dish featuring very thinly sliced beef and generous amounts of favorite Japanese vegetables cooked together quickly with soy sauce, dashi, and mirin for flavoring quickly became a favorite dish in Japan.

Dining

The presentation of food is an artistic statement as each dish is arranged for the table. A variety of small dishes suited for specific items is used to add the appropriate setting for the different menu items. Individual servings are small, and several dishes will be served at a meal, often accompanied with appropriate sauces to highlight the flavors. Chopsticks are used for dining, although broth of soup may be sipped from the diner's bowl. Meals are a time for experiencing the pleasure and beauty of food. Although dining at home is a regular practice, guests ordinarily are entertained at a restaurant. Families and individuals also dine out fairly often.

Recipes

Azuki and Mochi Gome (Red Beans and Rice) (Serves 4–6)

1¼ c azuki
1 qt water
2 c sweet rice (mochi gome)
2 tsp black sesame seeds (toasted)

1. Soak rinsed beans in cold water overnight. Heat to high simmer and simmer until tender (45 minutes). Drain beans, saving liquid for preparing the rice. Refrigerate beans.
2. Rinse rice in colander under running water until water runs clear. Soak rice at least 8 hours in bean liquid in refrigerator.
3. Drain rice (discarding liquid); add 1 cup cooked beans and steam for 45 minutes. Add salt if desired.
4. Serve with garnish of toasted black sesame seeds.

Deep-Fried Tofu (Serves 4–6)

12 oz tofu
Oil for deep-fat frying
½ daikon, grated
½ carrot, grated
⅔ c soy sauce
¼ c mirin (or sherry)
1 tsp grated ginger root

1. Drain tofu; place between paper towels and top with pie plate holding heavy can (for weight). Remove liquid every few minutes during 30-minute draining period. Discard all but the curd. Cut curd into bite-sized cubes.
2. Heat oil to 400°F, and then fry tofu for 4 minutes.
3. Garnish tofu with grated daikon and carrot. Serve with sauce of soy sauce, mirin, and ginger.

Oyako Domburi (Rice Topped with Chicken and Eggs) (Serves 4–6)

1 lb boneless, skinless chicken
1½ c chicken stock
⅓ c soy sauce
2 tbsp sugar
¼ c sake
3 dried mushrooms, soaked and sliced
¼ c bamboo shoots
½ onion, sliced
½ c peas
6 eggs, beaten
2 sheets nori (seaweed)
Hot cooked rice

1. Simmer chicken in stock until tender; shred.
2. Add soy sauce, sugar, sake, and vegetables. Simmer 5 minutes.
3. Heat to boiling and stir in eggs.
4. Serve immediately over hot, cooked rice in individual domburi bowls; garnish with toasted strips of nori.

Dashi (Soup Stock) (Serves 8)

2 qt water
3″ square sheet of dried kelp (konbu)
¾ c dried bonito

1. Heat water to boiling.
2. Add konbu, and then remove it as soon as water returns to a boil.
3. Immediately add dried fish and turn off heat. Let stand 2 minutes.
4. Strain through cheesecloth in a strainer to clarify stock. Serve as a soup with simple garnishes or use in other recipes.

Sweet Potato Sweet (Okashi) (Serves 6–8)

2 sweet potatoes, pared and cut in 1″ thick slices
1⅔ c sugar
2 c water
Pinch of salt
3 egg yolks

1. Boil sweet potatoes until tender. Remove from water to cool.
2. Heat sugar and water to boiling and boil for 3 minutes. Cool.
3. Mash potato before blending with salt, syrup, and yolks. Heat over very low heat, stirring constantly until thick and fluffy. Cool.
4. Form into balls 1½″ in diameter.
5. Shape each ball into a chestnutlike appearance by placing in a cloth and twisting to force out extra liquid.

Autumn Sweet (Ohagi) (Serves 4–6)

1 c short grain rice
1 c glutinous rice
2⅔ c chunky sweet red bean paste

1. Rinse rice until water is clear. Boil rice until tender in salted water.
2. Thoroughly mash rice after it has cooled for 10 minutes (use wooden spoon or Cuisinart).
3. Shape into spheres the size of golf balls. Coat some with a layer of red bean paste; make others with a center of red bean paste and an outer shell of rice.
4. Serve as dessert with green tea.

Chunky Sweet Red Bean Paste (Makes 3 cups)

1 c azuki (red beans)
3 c water
1 c sugar

1. Wash beans thoroughly, and then cover with water and bring to a boil.
2. Drain beans and simmer in 3 cups of water until beans are tender and water is almost gone.
3. Stir in sugar and salt to make chunky paste.

Shrimp and Melon Soup (Serves 6)

5 c dashi
2 tsp sake
1 tsp soy sauce
½ tsp salt
¼ honeydew melon, peeled and cut into 1″ cubes
6 cooked medium shrimp

1. Simmer dashi, sake, soy sauce, and salt with the melon cubes until melon is tender (10 to 15 minutes).
2. Remove melon and place 3 cubes in each soup bowl; add 1 shrimp to each bowl, and then gently pour the dashi into each bowl.

Sukiyaki (Serves 4–6)

1 lb sirloin, sliced very thin
1 8½-oz can bamboo shoots
1 8½-oz can yam threads (shirataki)
1 cake tofu, cut in bite-sized cubes
2 stalks celery, sliced diagonally
6 green onions, cut into 2″ lengths
1 bunch watercress, cut into 2″ lengths
1 gobo (burdock root), slivered
2 tsp oil
3 tbsp sugar
1 c sake
½ c soy sauce
2 c water (more as needed)

1. Arrange beef, bamboo shoots, yam threads, tofu, celery, onion, watercress, and gobo on platter for cooking at the table.
2. Preheat electric skillet, add oil, and cook the first ¼ of the beef quickly to light brown. Move cooked beef to side of skillet and keep adding beef until it is all cooked and moved to one side.
3. Add sugar, sake, soy sauce, and water, and heat to simmer; then add one ingredient at a time from the platter, cook each, and move aside for the next ingredient.
4. Diners serve their own plates while seated around the skillet at the table. Hot rice, perhaps a pickle, and green tea complete the meal.

Sushi (Vinegared Rice) (Serves 6–8)

2 c short grain rice
2½ c water
2″ square of dried kelp (konbu)
¼ c rice vinegar
2 tsp salt
2 tbsp mirin
3 tbsp sugar
Other suggested ingredients: Shrimp, crab, caviar, mushrooms, cucumber, spinach, dark tuna, various fish, nori, toasted sesame seeds, pickled ginger, soy sauce.

1. Wash rice thoroughly; combine with water and soak for 30 minutes.
2. Add konbu, cover, and heat to boil; reduce heat and simmer for 10 minutes until water is absorbed.
3. Turn heat to low for 5 minutes; remove from heat and let stand 5 more minutes. Discard konbu. Turn out rice to cool on large platter.
4. Meanwhile, heat rice vinegar, salt, mirin, and sugar to a boil and then cool it.
5. Thoroughly mix the vinegar sauce with the rice and cool to room temperature.
6. Sushi can be used by adding other tidbits of ingredients and squeezing them into small balls or by making a roll of nori enclosing carefully arranged sushi and such items as bits of fish and vegetables before slicing into rounds, or by encasing in a thin omelet in which similar ingredients are used to make an attractive packet.

Tempura (Serves 4–6)

1½–2 lb raw shrimp, shelled, butterflied
½ lb green beans, cut in half
½ lb Japanese eggplant, peeled and cut into ½″ thick slices
¼ lb snow peas
⅛ lb mushrooms, sliced
1 sweet potato, peeled and cut into ¼″ thick slices
Lotus root, bamboo shoots (optional)
¾ c dashi
¼ c soy sauce
¼ c mirin
Oil for deep-fat frying
1 egg
¾ c ice-cold water
½ c flour
¼ c cornstarch
½ tsp baking powder
⅓ c flour
¼ daikon, grated

1. Assemble shrimp and vegetables for dipping in batter.
2. Boil dashi, soy sauce, and mirin for sauce; cool.
3. While oil heats to 375°F, make batter: Beat egg and water, and then stir in sifted dry ingredients (flour, cornstarch, and baking powder) just enough to moisten the flour.
4. Dip shrimp and vegetables individually in flour and then in batter to coat completely. Fry only a few pieces at a time to keep oil at 375°F. Fry for 1 minute; then turn to fry the other side for 1 minute to light golden color. Drain on paper towels.
5. Keep warm in oven until frying is finished.
6. Serve with dipping sauce (dashi, soy sauce, and mirin, from Step 2) garnished with grated daikon.

Teriyaki (Serves 4)

½ c mirin
½ c soy sauce
1 tbsp sugar
½ c beef stock
2 tsp cornstarch
1 tbsp water
1 lb beef tenderloin, cut into ¼″ thick slices
1 tbsp powdered mustard mixed with hot water to form paste

1. Unless using bottled teriyaki sauce, briefly heat mirin in saucepan and ignite to burn off alcohol before adding soy sauce, sugar, and beef stock and bringing to a boil. Cool.
2. Make smooth slurry of cornstarch, water, and ¼ cup of teriyaki sauce (from step 1). Heat to boiling while stirring to make glaze.
3. Preheat hibachi or broiler.
4. Dip each slice of beef in teriyaki sauce (from Step 1) and broil 2 inches from heat for 1 minute on each side.
5. Serve on individual plates with a little glaze (from Step 2) spooned on the strips and a little mustard paste.

Udon and Chicken (Serves 4)

10 oz udon (uncooked wide noodles)
6 c water with 1 tsp salt
1 qt dashi
2 tsp soy sauce
1 tsp sugar
1½ tsp salt
⅓ lb boneless, skinless chicken breast, cut into thin strips
2 scallions, cut into 3″ strips

1. Boil noodles in salted water; turn off heat and let rest for 5 minutes. Place in colander and rinse in cold running water for 5 minutes.
2. Heat dashi to boiling, add soy sauce, sugar, and salt, and return to boil.
3. Add noodles and heat to boiling, and then remove them to four soup bowls. Add chicken and scallions to soup and boil for 2 more minutes.
4. Ladle broth, chicken, and scallions over noodles.

Umani (Vegetables with Chicken) (Serves 2–4)

2 shiitake mushrooms
1 gobo, pared and cut into 1″ pieces
½ lb boneless, skinless chicken breast, cut into slivers
1 tbsp oil
2 carrots, pared and cut into matchsticks
1 can bamboo shoots, sliced
1 c dashi
1½ tsp sugar
1 tsp soy sauce
1 tsp salt
½ c frozen peas

1. Soak mushrooms for 2 hours; discard water and stems, and slice caps in ½″ strips.
2. Boil pieces of gobo for 5 minutes and drain.
3. Stir-fry chicken in oil for 3 minutes, and then add vegetables (except peas), dashi, and sugar. Cover and simmer for 5 minutes.
4. Add mushrooms, soy sauce, and salt, and simmer for 10 minutes.
5. Add peas and simmer for 3 minutes.

Vinegared Shrimp and Cucumber (Serves 2–4)

1 c rice vinegar
1 c dashi
¼ c soy sauce
1½ tbsp sugar
2 cucumbers, peeled, seeded, cut into very thin slices
Salt
1 6-oz can small shrimp, drained

1. Heat vinegar, dashi, soy sauce, and sugar to simmering, and then cool.
2. On a cutting board, spread cucumber and sprinkle salt over all slices; knead 1 minute and put in a mixing bowl (without rinsing cucumber).
3. Pour about half of sauce over cucumbers and squeeze gently; drain and discard liquid.
4. Mix remaining sauce with the cucumbers.
5. Serve shrimp and cucumbers in small dishes to each person.

Yakitori (Serves 6)

Bamboo skewers
½ c sugar
½ c brown sugar
1 c soy sauce
¼ tsp grated fresh ginger root
1 clove garlic, minced
1 tbsp mirin
2 whole boneless, skinless chicken breasts cut into 1¼″ cubes
6 scallions, cut into 1¼″ lengths

1. Soak bamboo skewers in water.
2. Combine sugars and soy sauce, and heat until sugar dissolves.
3. Add ginger root, garlic, and mirin. Stir and set aside.
4. Alternate chicken and scallion on skewers.
5. Dip skewers to coat chicken and scallions with sauce, and then broil (hibachi or broiler) for about 3 minutes; dip in sauce again and broil second side for 3 more minutes.
6. Spoon a little sauce on skewers when served.

Summary

The nation of Japan has four major islands with rugged, volcanic terrain, limited tillable land, and restricted space for housing its population. Its proximity to Korea and China accounts for the migration of these people into Japan and the resultant cultural influences that are evident despite the unique interpretations in Japanese art and music.

Shintoism was the first religion, but Buddhism arrived from China in the 6th century and became intertwined with the earlier religion. Culture flourished during the Heian period (794 to 1185). The capital was moved from Nara to Kyoto, where the Emperor reigned. However, a powerful shogun, Minamoto Yoritomo, moved his center to Kamakura. A later shogun, Tokugawa Ieyasu, made his capital in Edo (now Tokyo) although the Emperor retained his court in Kyoto.

Portuguese missionaries brought the message of Christianity to Japan in the 16th century, and traders from Europe followed. All but a few Dutch traders were forced to leave Japan near the beginning of the 17th century, and the internally focused Japan developed a strong class-system society with the samurai at the top and merchants at the bottom. Commodore Perry opened Japan to trading with the United States in the 1850s, and other nations quickly followed during the reign of Emperor Meiji, a period when merchants gained considerable status. Meiji moved his capital to Tokyo and began Japanese aggression toward China and Russia. Emperor Hirohito continued expansionist efforts in Manchuria and China before his early conquests in the Pacific region and the attack on Pearl Harbor that directly brought the United States into World War II. Since the end of the war, Japan has rebuilt as an industrial nation.

Shinto and Buddhist shrines are representative of religion in Japan, where Christians and other sects are also found. Art and traditions have evolved along the Shinto traditions with emphasis on nature, beauty, simplicity, cleanliness, and adherence to ritual. These qualities are evidenced in the musical performances on unique Japanese instruments and in the dances performed by geishas and the people. Wood block prints, artfully painted scrolls, graceful calligraphy, origami, and artistically crafted ceramics are prized aspects of Japanese art. The tea ceremony, noh and kabuki performance, bunraku, and sumo wrestling are treasured traditions.

Beauty is also emphasized in the simple, elegant styling used in presenting foods in restaurants and homes. The cereal featured in the diet is rice in many different forms and types; sushi (vinegared rice), steamed rice alone or as part of a variety of dishes, mochi (pounded rice featured as a cake at New Year's), rice vinegar, mirin (sweet rice wine), and sake (strong rice wine) are familiar in Japanese diets. Soybeans also are seen in many different forms: soy sauce, miso (fermented soy bean paste), okara (powdered byproduct of tofu), and tofu.

Fish, whether raw (sashimi), batter-dipped and fried (tempura), or dried (bonito in dashi), are very prominent because of their variety and availability from the seas surrounding the islands. Seaweeds are also popular. Clear soups (suimono) and miso soups are found as part of most meals. Noodles from buckwheat flour (soba) and from wheat flour (udon) are eaten frequently, often with broth and other ingredients as accompaniments. Pickled vegetables, such as gobo and daikon, are frequent small dishes in a meal. Sukiyaki and yakitori are dishes featuring beef or chicken. Typically, these meals are served in many small dishes with sauces or accents such as wasabi. Chopsticks are used for cooking, serving, and eating solid food items, which probably explains the Japanese practice of preparing meats and vegetables in small pieces.

Selected Sites

http://www.japan-guide.com/e/e620.html—Addresses several topics about Japanese foods, recipes, and dining.

http://www.japaneselifestyle.com.au/food/food.html—Encyclopedia of Japanese food and information about Japanese dining and culture.

http://www.csuohio.edu/history/japan/japan11.html—Brief descriptions of many aspects of Japanese culture.

http://www.theblackmoon.com/Jfood/food1.html—Variety of recipes and discussions about Japanese food.

http://www.japaneselifestyle.com.au/culture/culture.html—Brief descriptions of the arts and interests that comprise Japanese culture.

Study Questions

1. Trace the interactions between Japan and other nations during the last 200 years.
2. Describe at least four traditions or art forms that are unique to Japan.
3. Define each of the following: (a) mochi, (b) mirin, (c) miso, (d) soy sauce, (e) tempura, and (f) dashi.
4. Explain why the sea is such a significant source of food for the Japanese, and identify some specific foods from the sea that are often eaten in Japan.
5. Identify and describe two types of Japanese noodles.
6. Plan a menu for a Japanese dinner.

Bibliography

Adler, S. and S. Wolf, 2000. *Fodor's Japan.* 15th ed. Fodor's Travel Publications. New York.

Ashkenazi, M. 2000. *Essence of Japanese Cuisine: Anthropological Essay into Food and Culture.* Routledge/Curzon. New York.

Barer-Stein, T. 1999. *You Eat What You Are.* 2nd ed. Firefly Books, Ltd. Ontario, Canada.

Bosrock, M.M. 1997. *Put Your Best Foot Forward: Asia.* International Education Systems. St. Paul, MN.

Busch, N.F. 1972. *Horizon Concise History of Japan.* American Heritage Publishing. New York.

Golden, A. 1997. *Memoirs of a Geisha.* Vintage Books. New York.

Hinnells, J.R., ed. 1997. *A New Handbook of Living Religions.* Penguin. London, England.

Hosking, R. 1996. *Dictionary of Japanese Food Ingredients and Culture.* Tuttle. Rutland, VT.

Ishige, N. 2001. *The History and Culture of Japanese Food.* Columbia University Press. New York.

Kasuko, E. 2001. *Japanese Food and Cooking: A Timeless Cuisine: Traditions, Techniques, Ingredients, and Recipes.* Lorenz Books. London, England.

Kinoshita, J. and N. Palevsky. 1990. *Gateway to Japan.* Kodansha International. Tokyo, Japan.

Kramer, M. 1988. *Illustrated Guide to Foreign and Fancy Food.* 2nd ed. Plycon Press. Redondo Beach, CA.

Pearcy, G.E. 1980. *The World Food Scene.* Plycon Press. Redondo Beach, CA.

Schinner, M.N. 1999. *Japanese Cooking—Contemporary and Traditional.* Book Publishing. Summerton, TN.

Seidensticker, E. 1965. *Japan.* Time, Inc. New York.

Steinberg, R. 1969. *Cooking of Japan.* Time-Life Books. New York.

Suchiyo, S. 1985. *Feast for the Eyes: Japanese Art of Food Arrangement.* Kodansha. Tokyo, Japan.

Tsuji, S. 1980. *Japanese Cooking: A Simple Art.* Kodansha International. Tokyo, Japan.

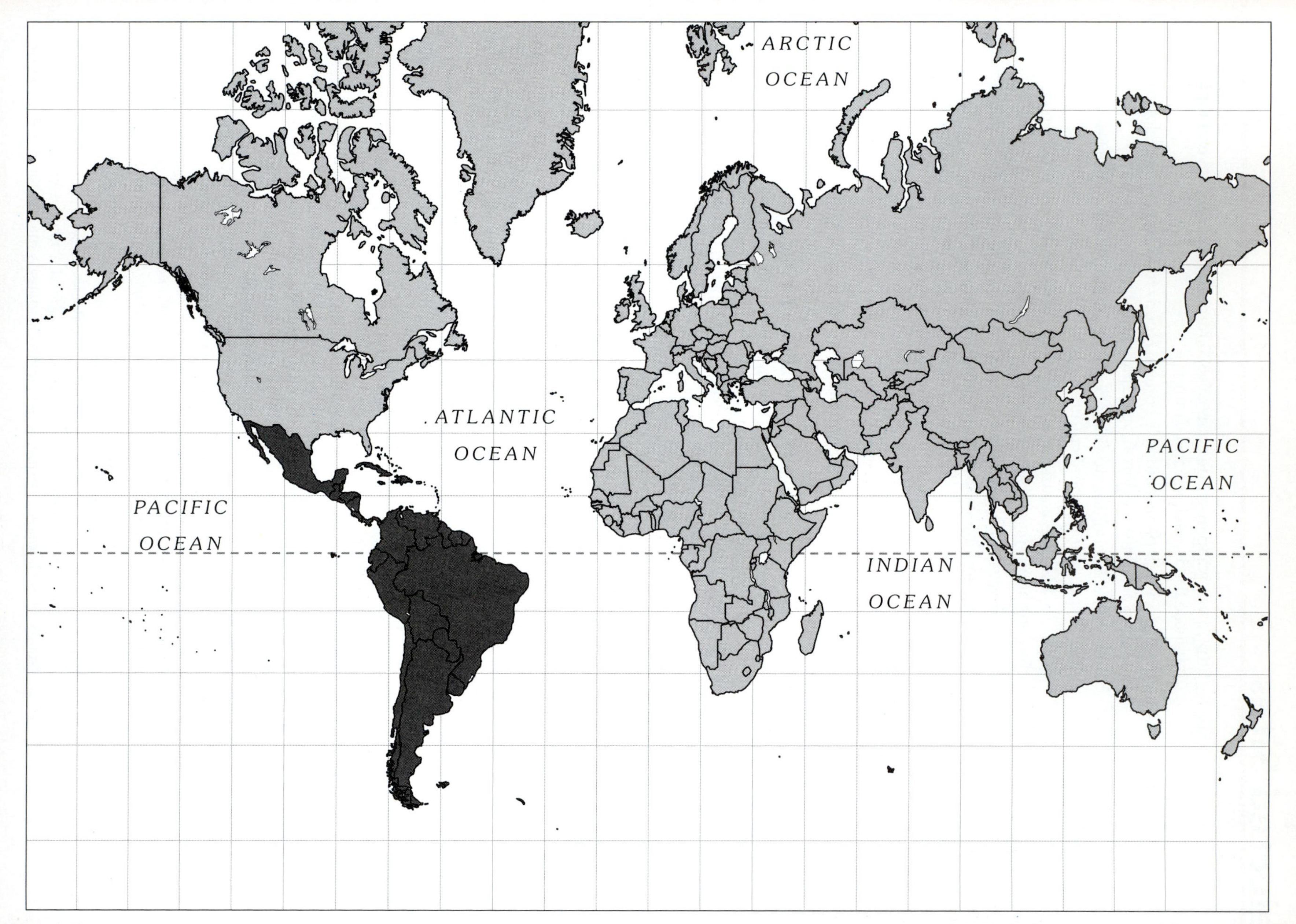
ARCTIC
OCEAN
ATLANTIC
OCEAN
PACIFIC
OCEAN
PACIFIC
OCEAN
INDIAN
OCEAN

Part VI Latin American Flavors

DOMINICAN REPUBLIC
CUBA
San Juan
JAMAICA
HAITI
Caribbean Sea
PANAMA
TRINIDAD
ATLANTIC OCEAN
VENEZUELA
COLOMBIA
Equator
ECUADOR
Amazon River
PERU
Andes Mountains
BRAZIL
BOLIVIA
PACIFIC OCEAN
PARAGUAY
Rio de Janeiro
URUGUAY
ARGENTINA
CHILE
ATLANTIC OCEAN

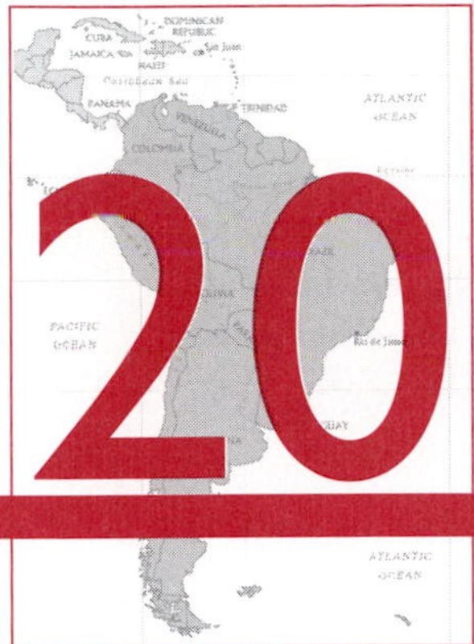

20 South America

Geographic Overview

South America is a continent with geographic features that include a very extended north–south range of mountains, the towering and rugged Andes. The rainforest of the Amazon River in the equatorial belt in the northeastern part of the continent is recognized as an invaluable resource for the world, which must be protected in the fight against global warming. Surprisingly, the driest desert in the world lies less than 400 miles to the west.

Agricultural Insights

The very heavy rainfall associated with rainforests makes agricultural development difficult in a large area of the Amazon basin. From an environmental perspective, allowing the forests to continue relatively undisturbed probably is by far the best use of the land. South America fortunately has much land that is well suited to raising livestock and crops. However, there are many arid regions in the interior of Argentina, Paraguay, and Bolivia where agriculture is barely possible.

Parts of Brazil and Argentina are well suited to agriculture of various types. The Argentine gauchos and their herds of cattle in the Pampas developed as a result of the European colonization of the region. The Incas and other Indians native to the continent were already growing potatoes, corn, and other crops on their high plateaus and in the valleys where they lived before the European conquests, and this land is still suited for farming today.

The northern part of South America actually lies north of the equator, and the equatorial heat plays a significant role in shaping the lifestyles and health of people throughout the region. Colombia lies adjacent to Panama and has coastline on both the Pacific and the Caribbean. Venezuela and its eastern neighbors of

Figure 20.1 The high Andes in Peru are covered in snow throughout the year, while lower valleys are suitable for some farming.

Guyana, Suriname, and French Guiana are along the northeastern shoulder of the continent facing the Atlantic. The highlands created by the northern end of the Andes in Colombia, Venezuela, and Ecuador provide somewhat temperate relief from the tropical heat along the Caribbean and Pacific shores of these countries and serve as the source of such important crops as potatoes, beans, sweet potatoes, manioc, cacao, peanuts, and pineapple. The benefits of living in higher elevations in the Andes were recognized by the Incans, who developed many centers along the Andes on southward to Peru.

The countries of Peru and Chile hug the western side of the Andes (Figure 20.1), reaching to the Pacific (Figure C.179, p. C60). This results in two very long and narrow countries that together stretch approximately two-thirds the length of the 7,000-mile long Andes Mountains. The very southerly location of Cape Horn and the southern port at Punta Arenas are famous for their cold and blustery weather conditions, a sharp contrast to the tropical challenges on the northern end of the continent. Santiago and Valparaiso, Chile's major cities, are located about midway from north to south and are in the region that is well suited to farming. The fact that the seasons are reversed in South America from those in North America has resulted in active international trading in fresh produce, notably fruits and flowers, to augment North American diets during the winter.

Chile's back-to-back neighbor is Argentina, which extends from the eastern side of the Andes peaks to the Atlantic Ocean until it forms a border with Bolivia on its northwest corner, Paraguay in the center, and Brazil and Uruguay for a dis-

Figure 20.2 The architecture of Buenos Aires clearly shows the effect of its European settlers.

tance along the northeastern edge. The Atlantic Ocean borders Argentina from Buenos Aires (Figure 20.2) all the way south to the tip of the continent. Only Bolivia and Paraguay lack a seacoast on the South American continent.

Brazil comprises much of the very large area bulging eastward from the Andes to the Atlantic. Both Argentina and Brazil have land well suited to raising wheat and livestock. Argentina in particular is noted for its beef production, much of which is exported. Brazil grows sugarcane in considerable quantities and (along with Colombia) is an important source of the world's favored coffees, which are grown at intermediate elevations in the mountains. Cacao is another export crop from Brazil.

History and Culture

Machu Picchu, also dubbed the "lost city of the Incas," sits atop a mountain in Peru overlooking a tropical river flowing far below. Flanked by neighboring mountains with a moderate climate, this city was the dramatic home of a large number of Incas when the Spaniards arrived in South America. After the Spanish conquest, this city faded into oblivion until it was discovered early in the 20th century and gradually opened as an important archeological site for tourists to visit.

Pre-Columbian

Prior to the arrival of the early Spaniards, the dominant culture in South America was that of the Incas, which dated from about 1100 CE. **Cuzco,** located in a valley of the Andes at an elevation of 11,000 feet, was the center of the Inca civilization (Figure 20.3). The Incas were a family-centered society that herded animals (llamas and alpacas) for their wool, thus providing clothing in addition to meat. They also produced crops. Their religion was based on the sun, and temples built to the sun were decorated with gold and silver as well as precious stones. The most important temple dedicated to the sun was in Cuzco. Tragically, the decorations were destroyed by the conquering Spaniards, who melted down the gold and silver into bars to ship back to Spain.

The Incas were noted for their roads and bridges that ran the length and width of their very large domain, providing effective links between even the outlying areas. The major sites included Ollantaytambo, Sacsayhuaman, Pisac, and Machu Picchu (Figures 20.4 and C.177, p. C59), which would have served as forts to protect Cuzco from invaders.

Cuzco—Center of the Incan civilization in a very high (11,000 feet) Andean valley in Peru.

Pizarro—Spanish conquistador who conquered the Incas in Peru and established Spanish dominance in Peru.

Spanish and Portuguese Conquests

Pizarro was the Spanish conquistador who led the expeditions southward from Panama beginning in 1524 after he had crossed Panama with Balboa. The conquest of the Incas was accomplished by a combination of bravery and fortitude in an arduous march to Atahualpo, chief of the Incas, and trickery that resulted in his capture. Spaniards began to occupy Peru, not only in the mountains at Cuzco, but also on the coast at Lima. Eventually, Pizarro was killed by some of his own men, but Spanish control of Peru continued for 300 years, marked by some of the

Figure 20.3 Sacsayhuaman is the amazingly crafted stone fortress near Cuzco, Peru, where the Spanish conquistadors defeated the Incas.

Figure 20.4 Machu Picchu, covered by jungle vegetation after Pizarro's conquest of 1532, has been excavated to reveal the amazing building skills of the Incas. (Photo courtesy of Bill Malcolm.)

horrors of the Inquisition and a Catholic legacy from the priests who continued to pursue their mission of saving souls in this foreign land.

Valdivia—Captain under Pizarro who led the Spanish expansion to Chile from Peru.

Valdivia, a captain under Pizarro, was the Spaniard who led the efforts to expand into and take over Chile after Peru had been secured. Unfortunately for Spain, Chile proved to be more of an expense than an asset, for the costs to the Spanish crown greatly exceeded any profits from goods shipped from Chile. The region was not only geographically inhospitable, but also was not rich in minerals. Interestingly, French ships traded in Chilean ports in the early 18th century and brought a distinctly French influence to Santiago and other Chilean towns despite the great distance from France.

Quesada—Spanish conquistador credited with conquering Colombia.

Quesada was the Spanish conquistador who led his men into the rugged terrain of Colombia, finally reaching the highlands and making contact with the natives of this region. He fought two other groups of Spaniards while attempting to establish control of the region, but his overall results were minimal.

Farther to the south, Buenos Aires actually was founded twice on the banks of the Plate River somewhat inland from the Atlantic. The first settlers migrated farther into the continent in search of a more favorable location and successfully established Asunción in what is now Paraguay. Finally, a successful settlement was established in Buenos Aires in 1580. The Spanish intermingled freely with the native women wherever they went in South America, resulting in a constantly growing mestizo population. This hardy population accounted for much of the population growth during the 300 years of Spanish colonialism and was particularly important in the early years. This accepted social pattern helped to reduce interracial tensions, an attitude that persists even now.

Cabral—Portuguese explorer who claimed Brazil for Portugal in 1500.

Cabral, a Portuguese captain, landed his ships in Brazil in 1500 and promptly claimed this big bulge of the continent for Portugal. Efforts to colonize were slow at first, but sugarcane was successfully introduced at Pernambuco in the north, and a few other settlements ranging to São Paulo in the south were able to grow; de Sousa was appointed governor-general of Brazil in 1549 by the King of Portugal, thus solidifying Portugal's domain amid the Spanish claims. The Portuguese men also mingled with the natives of their region, which added significantly to the population of the settlements.

Liberation

Simon Bolivar—Considered to be the liberator of South America from its European powers.

After 300 years of colonialism, South Americans evolved into revolutionaries. **Simon Bolivar** was the successful liberator of Venezuela and Colombia following several years of fighting and frustration. Considerable assistance from England and some help from the United States under President Monroe helped to eliminate Spanish shipping to South America and aided the revolutionaries. Unfortunately, the Spanish had carefully maintained a completely dominant governing role and had limited education for the colonial populations, which left South America ill-prepared for self-government.

In the other South American countries, different leaders led similar efforts for liberation from European conquerors. Mariano Moreno was the architect of Argentina's May Revolution in Buenos Aires in 1810 and inspired the revolutionists in that country until his death. Actual liberation from Spain occurred in 1816. San Martin played a very prominent role in the liberation of Chile and then Peru while Bolivar was fighting in the northern part of the continent. Eventually, Bolivar was in charge of the fight against the Spanish in Peru and Ecuador. At different times during the 19th century, the countries of South America finally threw off their bonds of colonialism. However, considerable internal political and military arguments persisted, leaving the vast majority of people living in a state of poverty and with very limited hope of a better life. The sharp economic division between the very wealthy upper class and the poor lower class remains even today.

Religion

Religion is largely Roman Catholic throughout South America, the result of the centuries of dominance by the various Catholic orders from the time of their arrival with the first conquistador (Figures 20.5 and C.178, p. C60). Although the Jesuits, Dominicans, and Franciscans established their missions independently in scattered parts of the continent, they all brought the message of the importance of believing in their God and worshiping in the churches they required their indigenous converts to build. The importance of a large place of worship with impressive gold and silver adornments was a clear priority, and the Catholic Church today still controls an amazing amount of wealth in South America despite the poverty level in which many of its believers still live. Although painting and other forms of art have developed rather minimally in South America, it is the Catholic Church that has served as the primary sponsor (Figure 20.6).

Figure 20.5 This rural church near Puerto Montt, Chile, presents a modest facade in contrast to the large cathedral in Santiago.

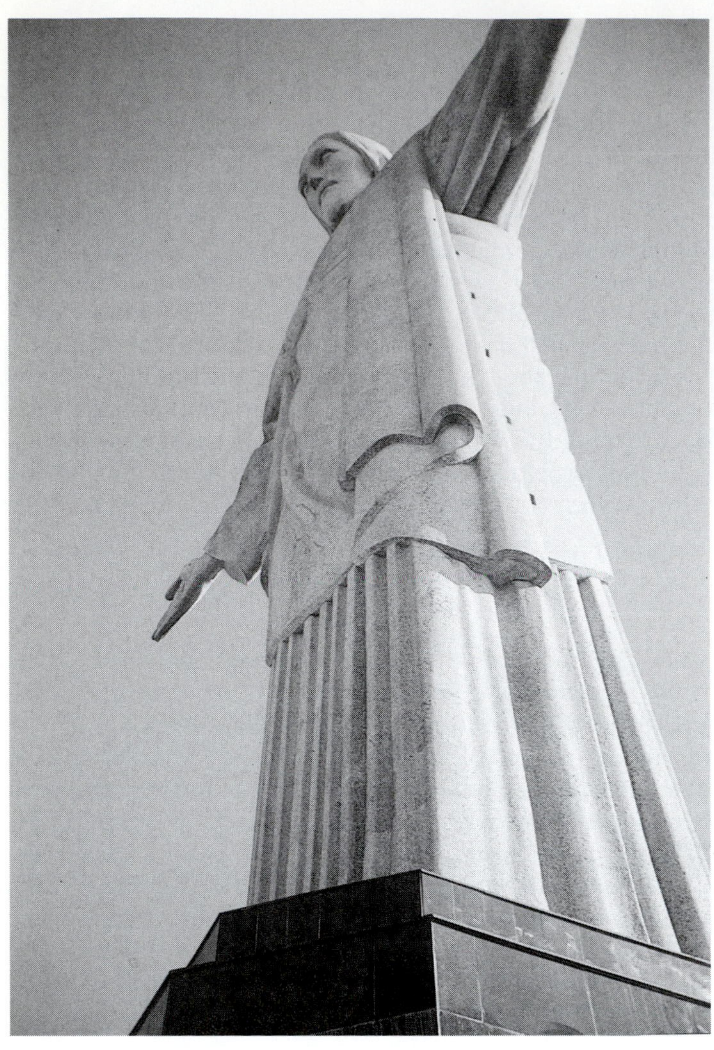

Figure 20.6 The statue of Christ the Redeemer on Corcovado, in Rio, is an amazing size: 130 feet tall.

The Arts

Music has been popular for centuries among the indigenous people of South America. The early instruments that they played included drums, rattles, and even crude trumpets made from shells, bone, or clay. Gourds were crafted for rhythmic sounds, and whistles were also carved. Such music still contributes to the culture today (Figure 20.7). In contrast to this type of native music, the music in the churches is basically European, reflecting the very strong influence of the Catholic missionaries.

Various folk dances exist. Perhaps the most familiar dance contributed by South America is the tango. This seductive dance has gained attention worldwide. Also, the exciting rhythms of South American music for dancing have made their way into contemporary music in other lands.

Not surprisingly, the culture of South America is varied, the result of (1) the influx of Europeans who superimposed their culture on the original peoples of the regions, (2) the importing of slaves from Africa (notably in Brazil), and (3) the geographic barriers separating countries. Certainly, it is not surprising that the various parts of South America have much that is unique in each country and sometimes only limited commonalities. Perhaps the most significant common factors are the dominance of the Catholic Church and the predominantly **mestizo** population, the result of extensive intermingling between peninsular men (from Spain and Portugal) with native women.

Mestizo—Person of mixed heritage of Spaniards and native Indian.

Figure 20.7 Folk music is popular in Argentina and throughout South America.

Food Patterns

Overview

Food patterns in South America vary a bit by country, but they all embrace some foods developed by the indigenous population and others from the European and African immigrants. Such staples as manioc, corn, potatoes, tomatoes, chilies, bananas, pumpkin, squash, and beans were well established before the Spanish arrived. Game occasionally was added to the meals of the Indians. The pigs, cattle, sheep, and poultry brought by the Spanish thrived and became a significant part of the diet (meat, milk, and cheese) in the temperate parts of South America where they were introduced and raised. Plant crops brought by the Spaniards included garlic, onions, coffee, sugarcane, wheat, and rice.

Colombia and Venezuela

Arepas—Corn flour–based small pancake that is baked or fried; eaten throughout the day in Colombia and Venezuela.

Hallacas—Colombian version of a tamale made by wrapping a layer of corn flour dough and a filling of meat or other ingredients in banana leaves and then steaming the packets.

Tostone—Twice-fried slices of plantain that are pounded thin before the second frying.

Yuca—Sweet cassava; root used as a starch in the tropical regions.

Café con leche—Coffee with warm milk, the style preferred in South America.

In the northern countries of Colombia and Venezuela, corn is dried and used as flour to make a dough with some water and perhaps egg yolks. The dough may be flattened or shaped into balls and then baked or fried into **arepas,** a favorite breadlike item similar to a small pancake that sometimes is split and filled. Kernels of fresh corn sometimes are the key ingredient of fritters and pancakes. Banana leaves are used as the wrappers to encase a layer of corn flour dough with a filling of meat before steaming the packets (Figure 20.8), which are called **hallacas** (the South American version of a tamale).

Plantains are another popular tropical food. They are quite versatile and may be fried (sometimes twice, as is done when fried slices are pounded thin and refried to make crisp **tostones**), boiled, or grilled. **Yuca** (sweet cassava) is another starchy food that is used extensively in the lowland areas of the tropics. Coconut and its milk are also important foods.

In Bogotá, Colombia (elevation about 8,500 feet), potatoes assume a significant role. Meats are also eaten more frequently if they can be afforded, but techniques such as stewing are essential to help tenderize them. Hearty soups containing meat are popular meal items (Figure 20.9). Coffee is popular, particularly for breakfast, when it usually is served **café con leche** (with warm milk). Breakfast typically is simply a bread and some coffee. The midday meal is more substantial and often followed by a siesta until the heat of the day has passed. South Americans follow the Spanish tradition of a late dinner (usually between 10 P.M. and midnight).

Figure 20.8 Fritanga, a plate composed of garlic sausage, ham, chunchullo (intestine), is accompanied by envueltos (Colombian type of tamale in corn husk) and potatoes as served in Colombia. (Photo courtesy of Carolina Vera.)

Manioc—Granular flour prepared by peeling and then grating bitter cassava roots and squeezing out absolutely all of the juice, which is poisonous until the juice is subsequently boiled. The dry grated material is broken to a powder by pounding.

Dendé—Yellow to reddish oil from a West African palm, which was introduced into Brazilian cooking by African slave women.

Feijoada completa—Celebrated Brazilian dish of several meats (including sausages and bacon), beans, rice, hot sauces, manioc meal, and sliced oranges.

Parrillada—Grilled mixture of meats, typical of Argentina.

Carbonada—Argentinian beef stew with rice, corn, potatoes, squash, sweet potatoes, and apples.

Brazil

Brazil is particularly noted for its food, and much of the credit for its cuisine goes to the African slave women who cooked at the plantations in Bahia and the surrounding northeastern region. These women integrated their African food traditions with the local foods when they arrived in their new land. They used the roots of bitter cassava that the native South American Indians grated, squeezed, and cooked to yield **manioc.** They relied heavily on **dendé,** the oil from a West African palm tree with a yellow to reddish color, to fry their foods and add a distinctive hue and flavor to their dishes. Beans (usually black beans) and rice were other staples of their cuisine, often seasoned with an unusually hot chili pepper (malagueta) that is hotter than tabasco.

Stews containing meats, poultry, or seafood sometimes have coconut milk as a subtle flavoring. **Feijoada completa** is a favorite dish for a Saturday or other time when a long siesta is possible after the meal. This dish includes smoked and other meats, including sausage and bacon, the traditional beans, rice, hot sauces, manioc meal, and oranges. The beans effectively bind the fat from the sausage and bacon, which accounts for the urge to take a long siesta after feasting on feijoada.

Argentina

Argentina's diet focuses on meat, which was the heritage from early gauchos (Figures 20.10 and 20.11). Grilled meats of various types are mixed to make **parrillada,** an Argentine favorite. Another favorite is **carbonada,** a stew of beef,

Figure 20.9 Ajiaco (soup made with chicken, three types of potatoes, corn on the cob and capers) is a typical lunch dish served with rice and avocado on the side and guanabana (a fruit drink) in this home in Bogota, Colombia. (Photo courtesy of Carolina Vera.)

Figure 20.10 Ranching and gauchos are the symbol of Argentina's pampas outside Buenos Aires.

Figure 20.11 Grilled sausages and chicken are just two of the entrees that are likely to be barbecued in Argentina, where meat is the main event.

Figure 20.12 Empanadas sometimes are served as appetizers and sometimes dessert, depending on the type of filling.

Empanadas—Fried or baked semicircular pastries filled with meat and raisins; prominent in Argentina, but also found in other South American countries.

Maté—Beverage brewed in a gourd by pouring hot water over crushed leaves of yerba maté, producing a caffeine-containing beverage that is sipped through a bombilla; pronounced ma-tay.

Bombilla—Fancy silver straw and filter used to sip maté from a gourd.

Sopa de pescado—Fish soup.

Ceviche—Raw fish marinated for 1 to 4 hours in lime juice and onion until flesh is opaque and the consistency of cooked fish; probably originated in Peru.

rice, potatoes, corn, squash, sweet potatoes, and even apples. **Empanadas,** meat-stuffed fried or baked semicircles of pastry, are popular (Figure 20.12). Italian immigrants added their touch to the food of Argentina with such universal dishes as spaghetti and lasagna (Figure 20.13).

Maté is a beverage found in many South American countries, but Argentina claims it as its own. Part of the pleasure of the drink, which actually is a tea brewed from chopped yerba maté leaves, is the sociability of passing the gourd containing the maté so that each person can sip some through the straw. The straw in the elaborately decorated gourd is called a **bombilla** and is made of silver with an enlarged filter at its base to strain out the leaves.

Chile

Chilean sea bass is so treasured in the United States that it comes as no surprise that the Pacific waters off Chile are the source of many favorite foods of Chileans (Figures 20.14 and 20.15). This has been true since colonial times and perhaps before. **Sopa de pescado,** or fish soup, curanto (thick fish stew with meats and potato), **ceviche** (traditionally raw fish marinated for 1 to 4 hours in lime juice with onion until flesh becomes white and somewhat shrunken, but which is safe when heated and then chilled), and grilled or steamed fish are regular dishes at lunch or dinner.

Chile has led in the development of the wine industry in South America. Its production today is sold widely in markets around the world. Now Argentina and its neighbor Uruguay are also developing their own wineries. Cabernet sauvignon, merlot, and chardonnay have been particularly successful Chilean wines. These and other wine varieties are popular in Chile, too.

Peru, Ecuador, and Bolivia

Aji—Very hot Andean chili pepper; pronounced ah-hee.

Malagueta—Another name for the extremely hot South American pepper, aji.

Peruvians, Ecuadorians, and Bolivians in the higher valleys and plateaus of the Andes rely on potatoes as the staple in their diets. **Aji** (also called **Malagueta**), a very hot Andean chili, is used to spice potatoes and other dishes, particularly in Peru. A sauce seasoned with aji and containing water or milk and some cheese is very common in this region.

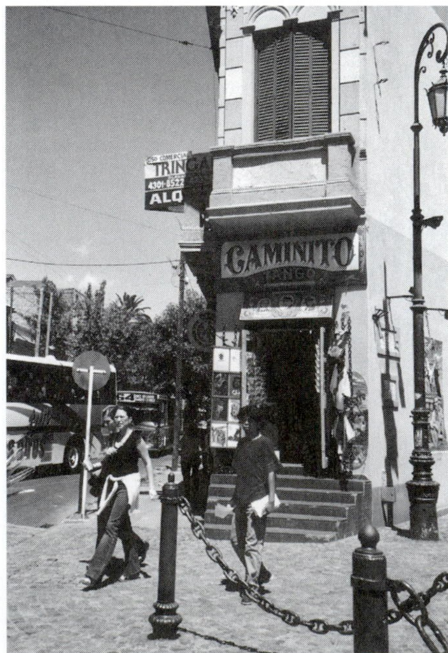

Figure 20.13 Italian immigrants settled in La Boca Barrio in Buenos Aires near the mouth of the La Plata River and created colorful buildings and entertainment (home of the tango), transforming the district into the most exciting part of the city.

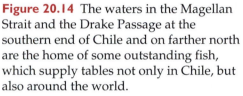

Figure 20.14 The waters in the Magellan Strait and the Drake Passage at the southern end of Chile and on farther north are the home of some outstanding fish, which supply tables not only in Chile, but also around the world.

Figure 20.15 Salmon farming in Chile starts with spawning and hatching in fresh mountain streams and then trucking the young salmon to pens like these next to the shore of the Pacific, where they grow to maturity.

Figure 20.16 This gigantic angel serves as the protector of Quito as it looks down from its Andean pedestal above Ecuador's capitol city.

Seafood is popular in Peru; in fact, ceviche may have originated there. Beef hearts in bite-sized pieces that are skewered and grilled are the traditional ingredient of anticuchos, although Peruvians often add other items, such as seafood. Causa a la limeña is an Indian-based dish of thick mashed potatoes, lemon juice, chopped onions, aji, and olive oil that may be served with hard-cooked eggs and shrimp.

Quinoa—Grain grown in the high Andes by Indians and eaten as a rich source of protein and starch in Peru and Chile; pronounced keen-wah.

Quinoa is a grain that has been grown in the high valleys of the Andes since before the Spaniards arrived. Its seeds are a useful starch and protein source, although wheat is needed in addition if quinoa flour is to be used in making breads.

Recipes

Arroz a la Peru (Serves 4–6)

½ lb veal, thinly sliced
½ lb pork, thinly sliced
2 tbsp flour
½ tsp salt
½ tsp pepper
2 tbsp oil
¼ c sherry
½ c water
¾ c rice
½ clove garlic, minced
½ onion, chopped
½ green pepper, chopped
½ red pepper, chopped
1 tbsp butter
1 hard-cooked egg, chopped
1 tbsp slivered almonds
1 tbsp raisins
1½ tsp cornstarch in 2 tbsp water
1 tbsp chopped parsley

1. Dredge meats in mixture of flour, salt, and pepper, and then brown in hot oil.
2. Add sherry and simmer for 5 minutes; add water and simmer until tender.
3. Meanwhile, boil rice according to package directions.
4. Sauté garlic, onion, and peppers in butter in a skillet just until tender.
5. Combine sautéed mixture with the rice, egg, nuts, and raisins, and keep warm.
6. Add cornstarch paste to the meat pan and heat to boiling while stirring until thickened.
7. Serve rice mixture topped with the sauce and garnished with parsley.

Carbonada Argentina (Serves 6–8)

1½ tsp crushed garlic
¾ c chopped onion
1 tbsp oil
1 lb beef loin, cut into 1″ cubes
½ c chopped green pepper
2 medium tomatoes, chopped
¾ tsp salt
½ tsp cracked pepper
2 c beef broth
¼ c sherry
4 dried peach halves, chopped
2 sweet potatoes, diced
2 potatoes, diced
1 c sweet corn kernels
1 medium pumpkin

1. Sauté garlic and onion in oil for 2 minutes, and then add beef, pepper, tomatoes, and seasoning.
2. Simmer, covered, for 20 minutes.
3. Add broth, sherry, peaches, sweet potatoes, potatoes, and corn; simmer for 45 minutes.
4. Meanwhile, cut a lid from the pumpkin and scrape out all seeds; butter and salt the interior.
5. Pour stew into pumpkin, top with lid, and bake in a shallow pan at 325°F for 30 minutes or until pumpkin is tender. Serve in pumpkin tureen.

Chicken Pie Venezuela (Serves 6–8)

½ c flour
2 c chicken broth
2 c canned tomatoes
3 c cubed, cooked chicken
¾ c chopped onions
2 tsp diced pimiento
½ c sliced black olives
2 tbsp capers
2 c flour
1 tsp salt
⅔ c shortening
⅓ c water

1. Make slurry of flour and broth, stir in tomatoes, and heat to boiling, stirring constantly.
2. Add chicken, onions, pimiento, olives, and capers, and heat to boiling. Let stand without heat while making crust.
3. Cut shortening into flour and salt until particles are size of rice grains.
4. Toss flour with fork while adding water in drops all around the bowl.
5. Press mixture with hands to form a ball firm enough to be divided in half and then rolled.
6. Roll both crusts into circles and fit one into a pie plate.
7. With slotted spoon, transfer filling into the bottom crust and pour in desired amount of sauce; add the top crust and pinch it closed all around the edge. Cut a 3″ slit in center of top crust.
8. Bake for 10 minutes in 425°F oven, then reduce heat to 325°F, and bake until top is golden and filling is bubbling.

Beef Empanadas (Serves 4–6)

½ tsp crushed garlic
¼ c chopped onion
¼ c red peppers, diced
¼ c green peppers, diced
1 tbsp oil
½ lb sirloin, finely chopped
½ c beef bouillon
¼ c raisins
½ tsp salt
½ tsp pepper
½ tsp chili powder
2 c flour
1 tsp salt
⅔ c shortening
⅓ c water

1. Sauté garlic, onion, and peppers in oil, and then sauté the meat; add bouillon, raisins, and seasonings, and simmer until meat is done, vegetables are soft, and the liquid is almost gone.
2. Cut shortening into flour and salt until particles are like rice grains.
3. Toss flour with fork while adding water by drops all around the bowl.
4. Press mixture with hands to form two balls.
5. Roll each ball ⅛″ thick; cut into circles 4″ in diameter.
6. Place 1 tablespoonful of filling on the center of each circle. Moisten edge of circle with water, then fold over and press edges together to make a semicircle with the filling sealed inside.
7. Bake in 400°F oven on baking sheet until browned (7 minutes), or fry in deep fat at 375°F.

Fruity Chopped Meat (Serves 4)

1 lb ground or chopped sirloin
1 tbsp olive oil
½ tsp salt
½ tsp black pepper
1 c minced onion
1 tsp crushed red chili peppers
½ tsp oregano
⅓ c orange juice
1 tsp orange zest
½ c raisins
½ c chili sauce

1. Sauté meat in oil, salt, and pepper, stirring to break up the meat into small pieces.
2. Add remaining ingredients and simmer, covered, for 30 minutes, adding liquid if necessary to keep from sticking.

Peruvian Sopa (Serves 4–6)

6 c water
½ lb beef bones with much meat
½ c chopped onion
2 carrots, sliced thinly
1½ c stewed tomatoes
2 tbsp chopped parsley
12 oz frozen lima beans
1 tsp salt
¼ tsp pepper
⅓ c cornstarch stirred into ⅓ c milk

1. In water to cover, simmer beef, onion, carrot, tomatoes, and parsley for 2 hours.
2. Remove meat, debone, and return to pot.
3. Add lima beans, salt, and pepper, and simmer for 20 minutes.
4. Stir cornstarch slurry into soup and stir while heating for 10 minutes to thicken and blend.

Roasted Chicken with Chestnuts (Serves 4–6)

1 roasting chicken
1 c Chablis
3 tbsp lemon juice
1 tsp crushed garlic
2 tsp chopped chives
2 tsp minced parsley
¼ tsp pepper
¼ tsp nutmeg
1 c pureed chestnuts
4 slices bacon

1. Refrigerate chicken in marinade of wine, lemon juice, garlic, chives, and parsley for 1 day.
2. Remove chicken from marinade and stuff with well-blended mixture of seasonings and chestnuts. Place on rack in shallow pan and arrange bacon over it.
3. Roast until breast registers 170°F.

Ceviche (Serves 6)

1½ lb bass or other firm, delicately flavored fish
¾ c lime juice
¾ c lemon juice
1½ red onions, thinly sliced in rings
1 red chili pepper, minced
½ green pepper, chopped
1 red sweet pepper, chopped
¼ tsp crushed garlic
½ c cooked corn kernels
½ green pepper, chopped

1. Arrange fish in single layer on a platter.
2. Prepare marinade of juices, onion, peppers, and garlic.
3. Pour marinade over fish, adding more juice if needed to cover all fillets.
4. Chill in refrigerator for at least 3 hours (fish will be opaque). Serve with garnish of cooked corn kernels and green pepper.

Sopaipillas a la Chile (Serves 4–6)

1 lb winter squash
1 stick cinnamon
1 c water
5 c flour
1 tsp salt
1 tbsp oil
Boiling water to moisten dough
Oil for deep-fat frying
1½ c brown sugar
¾ c water
1 tsp orange zest
1 stick cinnamon
¼ tsp ground cloves

1. Boil squash in cinnamon water until tender. Drain and remove cinnamon; peel and mash the squash.
2. Stir in flour and salt, and then add oil with kneading action to work mixture into a dough, adding a little boiling water while kneading. Add just enough water to make dough that does not stick to board.
3. While kneading dough, heat oil in deep-fat fryer to 375°F.
4. Roll dough into 2″ balls and fry three at a time for 3 minutes to golden brown. Drain on paper towels and keep warm in oven while frying rest of fritters and making syrup for dipping.
5. Boil remaining ingredients for about 4 minutes to make syrup. Dip fritters in hot syrup to serve.

Squash and Cheese (Serves 4)

1 lb winter squash, peeled, seeded, and sliced
½ tsp salt
Water to cover
¾ c cornmeal
1 tbsp sugar
1 tbsp butter
¼ lb grated cheddar cheese

1. Boil squash in salted water until tender, and then drain and mash.
2. Stir in cornmeal, sugar, and butter.
3. Stir while heating for 5 minutes over direct heat.
4. Place covered pan over simmering water and heat for 30 minutes.
5. Stir in cheese and continue heating just enough to melt cheese. Serve with a fish entrée.

Beef Pie (Serves 4–6)

¾ lb round steak, chopped
½ c chopped onion
1 tbsp oil
¾ c raisins
2 hard-cooked eggs, chopped
½ tsp salt
⅔ c grated cheddar cheese
1½ c mashed potatoes
¼ c buttered dried breadcrumbs

1. Brown meat and onions in oil.
2. Add raisins, eggs, salt, and half of the cheese; mix with beef; then transfer to casserole dish.
3. Top with mashed potatoes; garnish with remaining cheese and breadcrumbs.
4. Bake in 350°F oven until heated through and pleasingly browned (about 15 minutes).

Tomato Rice (Serves 4)

½ c chopped onion
1½ tbsp oil
1 c long grain rice
2 c chicken bouillon
1 tomato, chopped
¼ tsp salt

1. Sauté onion in oil for 2 minutes; stir in the rice to coat it with oil.
2. Add other ingredients and simmer for 20 minutes until all liquid is absorbed.

Summary

The lands of South America embrace sharp geographic contrasts, from the towering Andes to the Amazon River with its vast rainforests and to extremely arid deserts. This range of conditions explains the types of foods that were native to South America (potatoes, tomatoes, cacao, sweet potatoes, and peanuts, for example). These unique crops were transported to Europe by early explorers, and other European crops were introduced to South America, where they became crops (wheat, and sugarcane). The Europeans also introduced cattle.

Spain established a colonial empire in much of South America, beginning with Pizarro's conquest of the Incas and Peru. Valdivia was the Spanish captain who led the conquest of Chile. Quesada was credited with conquering Colombia, and the Spanish also settled and claimed Argentina. Cabral, the Portuguese captain, was responsible for Brazil becoming a Portuguese possession. Some other European presence, notably Dutch, German, Italian, and some French, also influenced the course of South America for 200 years. Bolivar spearheaded the 19th century liberation of the northern part of South America. San Martin and Moreno were important revolutionary figures to the south. Liberation was achieved in the 19th century, but stable governments have been difficult to establish.

The Catholic Church has played a very significant role in South America since the early days of the Spanish conquest. Priests came to establish missions and convert the Indians, a legacy that has continued to this day. Much of the population of South America is Catholic, and the Church has fostered the arts, as evidenced by the elaborate gold decorations and paintings in the churches.

Music in South America represents a blend of the Indian and European heritage and intermixing of these populations, plus the African heritage resulting from the slave trade during the colonial period, particularly in Brazil. Exciting rhythms and folk melodies are often performed with the help of drums, various rattles and percussive instruments, trumpets, and guitars. The tango is the most familiar of the dances that originated in South America.

Popular South American foods rely heavily on the use of corn, rice, potatoes, beans, pumpkins, squash, manioc, sweet potatoes, beef, pork, poultry, wheat, chilies, tomatoes, fish (in regions near the sea), and fruits ranging from tropical to apples and peaches of temperate climates. Much of the population has a rather limited diet because of lack of money, although some people are very rich and can afford to eat well. Breakfast usually is quite simple, the noon meal heavy, and the evening meal eaten very late (often 10 P.M. or later). Coffee is very popular as a beverage. Brazil's classic dish is feijoada completa, Argentina's is mixed grill, Chile's is seafood, and Peru may have created ceviche.

Selected Sites

http://www.pbs.org/conquistadors/—Description of the conquests of Pizarro and other conquistadors in Latin America.

http://www2.truman.edu/~marc/webpages/andean2k/conquest/—Discussions of various aspects of the Spanish conquests and subsequent developments in Latin America.

http://lilt.ilstu.edu/rtdirks/SOAMER.html—Bibliography on food habits in South America.

http://www.globalgourmet.com/destinations/brazil/—Various aspects of the food of Brazil.

http://www.marga.org/food/int/argentina/—Brief description of food in Argentina and a few recipes.

http://www.globalgourmet.com/destinations/argentina/—Overview of Argentine food and some recipes.

http://www.geocities.com/TheTropics/Cabana/6234/food.htm—Dictionary of Chilean dishes described in English.

http://www.journalnet.com/articles/2004/04/28/features/food01.txt—Article about Chilean food on Idaho State University Web site.

http://www.thewinedoctor.com/regionalguides/southamerica.shtml—Overview of wine production in South America.

Study Questions

1. Identify where each of the following is located and describe the geographic factors influencing the foods available in each: (a) Colombia, (b) Chile, (c) Paraguay, (d) Bolivia, (e) Argentina, (f) Brazil, and (g) Venezuela.
2. Select one of the early conquerors or explorers of South America and find additional information about him. How would you describe this individual and the influence he exerted on the region he conquered or explored?
3. What are four cereal grains that are grown in South America? Describe how each is prepared in South American kitchens.
4. Define (a) empanada, (b) manioc, (c) aji, (d) dendé, (e) maté, (f) mestizo, (g) quinoa, and (h) hallacas.
5. Name at least five fruits commonly used in South American meals.
6. Would the Incas have been eating pork prior to the Spanish conquest? Explain your answer.
7. Write a menu for dinner in (a) Rio, (b) Buenos Aires, and (c) Santiago, Chile.

Bibliography

Barer-Stein, T. 1999. *You Eat What You Are.* 2nd ed. Firefly Books, Ltd. Ontario, Canada.

Bernhardson, W. 1997. *Chile and Easter Island.* 4th ed. Lonely Planet. Oakland, CA.

Bernhardson, W. 1999. *Argentina, Uruguay, and Paraguay.* 3rd ed. Lonely Planet. Oakland, CA.

Coe S.D. 1994. *America's First Cuisines.* University of Texas Press. Austin, TX.

Crow, J.A. 1971. *The Epic of Latin America.* Rev. ed. Doubleday. Garden City, NY.

Foster, D. and R. Tripp. 2003. *Food and Drink in Argentina.* Aromas y Sabores. Buenos Aires Argentina.

Gade, D.W. 2000. South America. In K.F. Kiple and K.C. Ornelas, eds., *The Cambridge World History of Food.* Vol. 2. Cambridge University Press. Cambridge, England.

Kijac, M.B. 2003. *South American Table: Flavor and Soul of Authentic Home Cooking from Patagonia to Rio de Janeiro.* Harvard Common Press. Boston.

Leonard, J.N. 1968. *Latin American Cooking.* Time-Life Books. New York.

Lovera, J.R. 2005. *Food Culture in South America.* Greenwood Press. Westport, CT.

MacKenzie, R.A. et al. 2005. *Microbial Inactivation in Ceviche as a Function of Citrus Juice Treatment.* Institute of Food Technologists. Chicago.

Milton, J. 2005. *Food and Cooking of Mexico, South America, and the Caribbean.* Lorenz Books. London England.

Pearcy, G.E. 1980. *The World Food Scene.* Plycon Press. Redondo Beach, CA.

Peterson, J. and D. Peterson. 1995. *Eat Smart in Brazil.* Gingko. Madison, WI.

Rojas-Lombardi, F. 1991. *Art of South American Cooking.* Harper Collins. New York.

Winn, P. 1999. *Americas.* Updated ed. University of California Press. Berkeley, CA. 2001.

UNITED STATES
ATLANTIC OCEAN
Gulf of Mexico
THE BAHAMAS
CUBA
Greater Antilles
CAYMAN
MEXICO
BELIZE
JAMAICA
HAITI
DOMINICAN REPUBLIC
PUERTO RICO
BRITISH VIRGIN ISLANDS
U.S. VIRGIN ISLANDS
GUADELOUPE
DOMINICA
MARTINIQUE
ST. LUCIA
HONDURAS
GUATEMALA
EL SALVADOR
NICARAGUA
Caribbean Sea
ARUBA
CURACAO
BONAIRE
Lesser Antilles
GRENADA
TOBAGO
TRINIDAD
COSTA RICA
PACIFIC OCEAN
PANAMA
VENEZUELA
COLOMBIA
SURINAME
FRENCH GUIANA
GUYANA

21 The Caribbean

Geographic Overview

The Caribbean Sea, with its lengthy crescent of islands arcing from just 90 miles south of the tip of Florida to within sight of the northern coast of South America, greeted Columbus in 1492 and excited him with its beauty and bounty. The island of **Hispaniola** (now divided into Haiti on its western end and the Dominican Republic) served as the staging grounds for him and other Europeans who followed.

Hispaniola—Caribbean island where Columbus landed and that eventually became the countries of Haiti and the Dominican Republic.

The total landmass of the many islands that this archipelago comprises (collectively referred to as the *West Indies*) is only slightly larger than Oregon, but it is broken into around 7,000 islands. Cuba (the largest and closest to Florida), Jamaica just south of Cuba, Hispaniola, (now divided) and Puerto Rico stretch eastward in a somewhat linear grouping called the *Greater Antilles*. The remaining islands in the crescent extend in an arc southward from a bit east of Puerto Rico on southwest to Grenada and Trinidad and Tobago.

The many islands and various governments can seem rather confusing. Just east of Puerto Rico are the Virgin Islands. Then the island chain bends a bit toward the southeast in a grouping sometimes termed the *Leeward Islands* (including St. Kitts and Nevis). Continuing south and angling a bit west, this chain of islands is called the *Windward Islands* (Figure 21.1). Finally, the islands near Grenada are called the *Grenadines*. Collectively, these and more compose the lovely world of the Caribbean referred to as the **West Indies.**

West Indies—Islands of the Caribbean, ranging from near Florida to the northeast coast of South America.

All of this region is situated in the tropical zone, enabling crops suited to warm and humid climes to flourish much of the time. However, the islands face the natural hazards of volcanic eruptions, earthquakes, and hurricanes, all of which can wreak periodic havoc in a seeming paradise. The rugged Atlantic

Figure 21.1 St. Lucia is a volcanic island in the Windward Islands of the Caribbean.

Ocean washes the eastern shores, and the somewhat more tranquil Caribbean is the sea to the west.

The crops that thrive in much of the region include sugarcane, bananas, coconuts, pineapples, citrus, and peppers. Rice, breadfruit, cacao, mangoes, coffee, and various spices also proved to adapt well to the islands when people from Europe and Asia introduced them (Figure C.185, p. C.62). In short, plant foods of great variety generally were available to the early colonists and continue to be adequate for local use and even for export today.

History and Culture

Pre-Columbian

Arawaks—Peaceful Indians who greeted Columbus when he arrived on Hispaniola.

Carib—Fierce Indian tribe originating in South America that subsequently conquered the tribes in the Caribbean.

Prior to the arrival of Columbus, different Indian groups populated the Caribbean islands. Originally, the **Arawaks** inhabited many of the islands, usually peacefully. They were gentle and helpful when Columbus first arrived on Hispaniola, and this attitude tended to be the norm in the northern part of the Caribbean. Apparently, the Arawaks had been pushed gradually northward from the southern end of the Caribbean in earlier centuries as another tribe, the **Caribs,** pursued their warring ways northward from the South American mainland.

The Caribs, who may have been cannibals a long time ago, were able to claim any of the Arawak islands that they coveted. The Caribs presented the most warlike challenge to the various European expeditions seeking to establish their dominance over the Indians who were indigenous to the Caribbean.

European Impact

The arrival of Columbus in 1492 altered life in the Caribbean forever. His report upon returning to Spain quickly led Columbus to return there and beckoned other European explorers to visit there. Christopher Columbus's brother Bartolemé established Santo Domingo in 1496 on Hispaniola. Santo Domingo served as the launching point for Cortés, who first went to Cuba and then on to Mexico.

Ponce de León established a colony in Puerto Rico before proceeding to Florida via Cuba (Figure C.187, p. C63). Diego Valázquez de León is credited with establishing Santo Domingo in Cuba in 1514. Balboa and Pizarro journeyed to Panama and the Pacific Ocean from Santo Domingo, and Pizarro then proceeded southward for his conquest of the Incas and Peru.

The combination of the superior weaponry of the Europeans and the new health risks they brought to the Indians resulted in almost complete destruction of the Indian population. Only a very few Indians can be found today. Some descendants of the Indians have mixed blood, the contribution of their conquerors half a millennium ago. These people are the **mestizos.**

Mestizos—Descendants of Indians and the conquering Spaniards.

The riches that were extracted from Spanish conquests in the New World and shipped back to Spain caught the attention of other European nations. France, the Netherlands, and England became involved in attempting to claim various Caribbean islands as they scrambled to obtain some of the potential wealth from the region.

Some of the islands experienced numerous invasions as the competing powers attempted to gain permanent control. St. Lucia was variously in the hands of the British and the French at least a dozen times during the 16th and 17th centuries. The names of Soufriere (a town founded by the French) and Ft. Rodney (an English military fort) on St. Lucia subtly convey this tumultuous phase of its history. Many other islands in the Caribbean also exchanged hands more than once (Figure 21.2).

A treaty was the means by which Haiti, the western third of Spain's Hispaniola, was given to France. Somewhat later, Haiti conquered and then ruled Santo Domingo (the eastern two-thirds of Hispaniola) until the Santo Domingans rebelled successfully, only to again be annexed by Spain. Neighboring islands share similar histories.

Pirates

The rich shipments carried by Spanish galleons to Spain caught the attention of pirates as the ships traversed the Caribbean. Pirate attacks on shipping played a significant role in ending the Spanish dominance of the region. The competing European nations joined the fray as they attempted to gain control of the islands. Jamaica was the base for many pirate attacks. Among the most famous of the pirates were Henry Morgan and Blackbeard (actually named Edward Teach). Tales of their rich plunder have circulated in the intervening centuries.

Today Spanish wealth still is being found on the ocean floor, where the remains of wrecks shelter gold, silver, and jewels, but salvagers have replaced pirates in the recovery of these treasures. The *Nuestra,* a Spanish ship that sank near Key West in 1622, contained so much booty that a portion of the relics located to date has been valued at as much as $500 million.

Figure 21.2 A cannon still points seaward from Ft. Rodney on St. Lucia, a reminder of the British forces that once ruled the island.

Figure 21.3 Sugarcane, a very labor-intensive crop, spurred the market for slaves to tend the cane fields on the Caribbean islands in the 18th Century.

Colonialism

Settlements in the islands resulted in development of sugarcane plantations, a profitable but labor-intensive crop (Figure 21.3). Before long, the Indian labor supply proved inadequate, which led to importing slaves from Africa. In Jamaica and some of the other islands, slaves who escaped or who were freed by government decree or owners were called *Maroons*. People of European ancestry who were born in the Caribbean and who often had some African blood were called ***Creoles,*** and represent quite a large segment of the population in the Caribbean (Figure 21.4). After slavery was abolished in much of the region in the 19th century, workers were brought from India and China to augment the labor force, which also added to the cultural milieu.

Creoles—People born in the Caribbean of European ancestry, often mixed with African blood.

Governance

The United States was involved in Puerto Rico and Cuba as a participant in the Spanish-American War in 1898. The battleship *Maine* was destroyed in the harbor of Havana when it arrived to rescue Americans from the revolution in Cuba, an action that resulted in the United States declaring war. American forces invaded Puerto Rico that same summer, but the war was brief and ended with the signing of the Treaty of Paris with Spain at the end of 1898. Various governmental arrangements between Puerto Rico and the United States have been tested, and Puerto Rico is now an American commonwealth. Cuba, however, became a com-

Figure 21.4 A Creole woman holds her child at a street market on the island of Dominica.

munist state with Fidel Castro as its revolutionary leader and subsequently as president for more than four decades.

Many of the Caribbean islands have gained independence at various times in the 20th century. St. Kitts and Nevis were granted independence from the United Kingdom in 1983. Several other islands gained independence from the United Kingdom somewhat earlier: Jamaica in 1962, Barbados in 1966, the Bahamas in 1973, and Grenada in 1974, while St. Lucia chose in 1979 to stay in the British Commonwealth with independent status. The British influence clearly remains in these islands today.

France granted independence to Haiti in 1804, but Haiti did not give independence to the Dominican Republic on its island until 1844. This island of Hispaniola shows distinct French influences. The small islands that compose the Netherlands Antilles close to South America include Curacao, Bonaire, Saba, St. Eustatius, and St. Maarten. All are still Dutch possessions. The French still claim Martinique and Guadeloupe as their own.

Religion

The major religions in the various islands reflect the colonial history unique to each (Figure 21.5). Cuba and Puerto Rico were under Spanish rule for that extended period, and Catholicism was firmly entrenched, albeit somewhat influenced by animism. Islands controlled by the French also had a strong Catholic presence. The British brought the Anglican Church (Figure 21.6) and allowed other Protestant and Catholic churches.

However, many of the residents throughout the islands also integrated religious practices brought from Africa by the early slaves. For example, some Jamaicans participate in spirit cults and witchcraft, both of which may incorporate aspects of animism. **Rastafarianism,** which traces its teachings to the Old Testament, has three different groups in Jamaica. Members wore dreadlocks; reggae music has its roots in Rastafarianism. **Voodoo,** with its animism, spells, and hexes, is a strong influence in Haiti and to a limited extent in the Dominican Republic.

Rastafarianism—Jamaican religion traced to teachings in the Old Testament; members may have dreadlocks; reggae music originated in this group.

Voodoo—Type of worship found in Haiti based on spells, hexes, and animism traced to African roots.

The Arts

Music and dance are very much a part of Caribbean culture and have had a distinct impact on culture in the United States. Cuba's dances and the accompanying music include the rumba, congo, and mambo. Bomba and salsa music evolved in

Figure 21.5 The Catholic Church has a strong presence on many of the Caribbean islands, including Bequia in the Windward Islands.

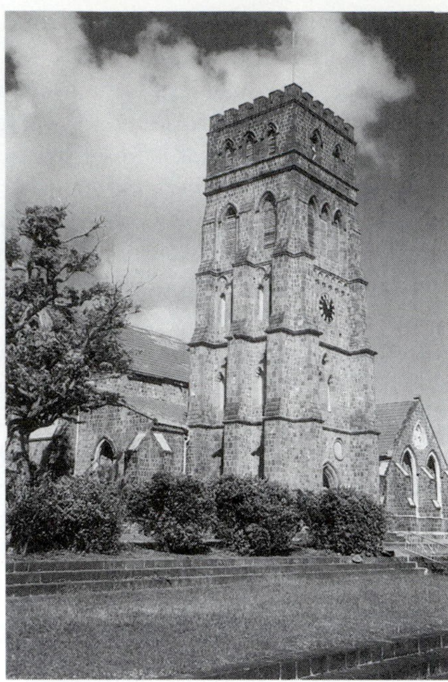

Figure 21.6 The British brought the Anglican Church to St. Kitts, where it still thrives today despite the island's independence from Britain.

The annual steel band competition that is held on one of the Caribbean islands generates stiff competition. Various steel bands compete on a makeshift stage, rolling their steel barrel drums onto the stage in a seemingly never-ending string of bands. The competition proceeds for several days until a winner finally is declared, giving it and its island bragging rights until the next competition.

Puerto Rico; reggae and calypso music and the limbo characterize Jamaican culture. The limping step of the merengue is a favorite in the Dominican Republic. These means of expression permeate various aspects of Caribbean life, ranging from generous use of music in religious services to much music and dancing in secular venues.

Various types of drums, including bongos, usually play a prominent role, while maracas (gourds with seeds or beans inside to rattle in rhythm), güiros (notched gourds that create percussive rhythm when a stick is stroked across the notches), and claves (two hollow sticks hit together) add to the rhythmic excitement of Caribbean music, which also often features guitars. Steel bands create exciting melodic and rhythmic music.

Literature has contributed to the culture of the Caribbean. Poetry has flourished on some of the islands, and novels and plays are also popular. Paintings by artists from the Caribbean often are very colorful and rather stylized with overtones of folk art. Folk art in such forms as masks, pottery, hammocks, leatherwork, and woodcarving also adds to the richness of the culture of the Caribbean.

Leisure

Leisure activities often feature sports, with baseball being a particular favorite. Cockfighting by gamecocks equipped with sharp spurs is a very bloody but popular activity in the islands. Other sports include golf, basketball, cricket, and water activities. Storytelling is another favorite pastime.

Many of the holidays are religious celebrations, with Easter and Christmas being of particular importance. Independence Day celebrations occur at various times on different islands.

Food Patterns

The food patterns of people living in the Caribbean reflect the various preferences of earlier immigrants from Europe, Africa, India, and China as well as the indigenous crops of the region. The climate on most of the islands makes it possible to grow good crops, even some that were originally imported from great distances.

Crops from Afar

Breadfruit, an important food in the diet today, was brought to the islands in the late 18th century from the South Pacific by the notorious Captain Bligh of *Mutiny on the Bounty* fame. Akee, a tropical tree fruit, arrived via slaves from Africa. Rice is now grown in the Caribbean as the result of the arrival of Chinese laborers. These crops and livestock are among the dietary additions resulting from immigration over the centuries and provide interesting variety to the indigenous fruits and vegetables.

Indigenous Foods

Coffee is a popular beverage in the region, particularly at breakfast when served with milk. Jamaica is a regional source of coffee beans. Sugarcane throughout the region (Figures C.183 and C.184, pp. C61 and C62) is the basis of the production of rum, the favored alcoholic product and one that is of economic importance at markets around the world. Fruit juices (Figure 21.7) are consumed generously to help fight the thirst resulting from the warm climate.

Favorite Dishes

Menus vary a little throughout the islands, with family income and the dominant immigrant influences on a specific island shaping what is served at lunch and dinner. The ready availability and comparatively low cost of plantains, bananas, mangoes, oranges, yams, pumpkins, squash, beans of various types, cassava, taro, and okra make these popular, frequently served vegetables and fruits (Figures 21.8 a and b). Available meats include chicken, beef, pork, goat, and lamb, but cost limits the frequency and quantity that families may consume. Seafood, including imported dried, salted cod, originally brought for feeding slaves, is popular today (Figures 21.9 and C.186, p. C62).

Cassava bread—Native, rather flat bread made with powdered roots of cassava.

Pepper pot—Long-lived stew common throughout the Caribbean, flavored with cassareep, containing meats and vegetables that are replenished from time to time as needed and available.

Cassava bread is a legacy of the indigenous island dwellers from pre-Columbian times. **Pepper pot** is another food tradition persisting from early times to today, especially in the southern islands of the Caribbean; it is a stew that is kept warm on the fire continuously for very extended periods, seemingly forever. New ingredients are added as needed and available, causing the flavors and textures constantly to evolve to provide a pleasing stew whenever a person is

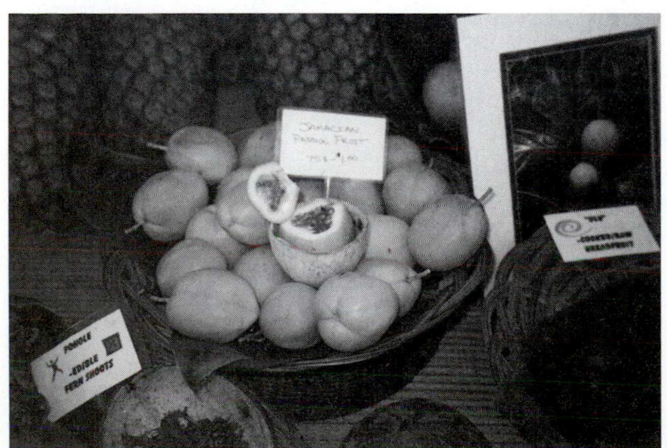

Figure 21.7 Passion fruit and pineapple are two of the fruits grown in the Caribbean that are often served as juice.

Figure 21.8a Various types of squash are key vegetables in the diet of the islanders of the Caribbean.

Figure 21.8b Taro, plantains, and lemons are among the choices for tonight's dinner on Dominica in the Windward Islands.

Figure 21.9 Fish fresh from the sea are important additions to the vegetables and fruits that can be grown on the islands in the Caribbean.

Cassareep—Bittersweet flavoring used in pepper pot, made from the boiled juice of the cassava root.

Callaloo—Spicy, thick, green soup containing spinach or other green plus okra, salt pork, coconut, and crabmeat.

Cocido—Hearty Caribbean stew containing beef, sausage, vegetables, and sofrito.

Sofrito—Hot, spicy sauce featuring chilies, tomatoes, garlic, ham or bacon, and coriander.

Sancocho—Stew popular in the Dominican Republic; contains plantain, chicken, cassava, vinegar, and pepper.

Mofongo—Puerto Rican specialty made with mashed plantains, pork cracklings, and garlic and either fried in balls or baked as a pancake.

Sopito—Fish chowder made with coconut milk in the Netherlands Antilles.

Coo-coo—Cornmeal pudding with okra, which is served either hot or cold.

Funchi—Cornmeal pudding prepared in the Caribbean.

Foo-foo—Mashed plantains with okra.

hungry. **Cassareep,** a bittersweet flavoring made from the juice of cassava root, gives its special touch to pepper pot.

Callaloo is a thick, spicy green soup, often made with taro leaves, but with various ingredients added to complete it, depending upon the island where it is made. Callaloo, the green vegetable similar to spinach, is used in the soup in Barbados, along with okra, salt pork, coconut milk, and sometimes crabmeat.

Cocido is a hearty stew featuring a variety of vegetables (potatoes, cabbage, green beans, and carrots), beef, and sausages, and flavored with **sofrito.** Sofrito is a hot, spicy sauce made of chilies, garlic, tomatoes, coriander, ham or bacon, and sometimes even more seasonings; this common sauce adds interest to many bland dishes.

Sancocho is a Dominican stew featuring plantain, chicken, cassava, and such flavorings as vinegar, coriander, and pepper. Plantain is also the base for a Puerto Rican dish called **mofongo,** which is a mixture of mashed, boiled plantain, pork cracklings, and garlic; the mixture is fried in balls or baked like a pancake. **Sopito** is a coconut milk fish chowder made in the Netherlands Antilles.

Okra is a common vegetable that sometimes is added to give a different twist to a very basic starchy dish. For example, **coo-coo** is made when okra is cooked with a simple cornmeal pudding called **funchi. Foo-foo** is a similar dish, introduced by African slaves, but okra is combined with mashed plantains.

Stamp and go is the intriguing name given to a Jamaican dish made with **bacalao** (salted, dried cod) in a heavy batter seasoned with onions, chilies, and annatto, and then fried. Spaniards brought **bacalao** (dried, salted cod) on their long ocean voyages to the New World and introduced this preserved food to the Caribbean. Chicharrones—pork cracklings—are eaten as a fried snack. A somewhat different treat is **escabeche,** cooked fish marinated in vinegar and spices that results in a product related to the ceviche (raw fish dish) in South America.

Moros y Cristiano, considered to be Cuba's national dish, is made by cooking black beans and rice with onions, green pepper, garlic, tomatoes, and various seasonings. Dominicans are fond of **pastelitos,** which are pastry turnovers with a spiced, minced, or ground meat filling. **Pasteles** are made in Puerto Rico by spreading a plantain leaf with mashed plantain or cornmeal paste, adding a filling of capers, meats, raisins, olives, and nuts then tying the leaf into a packet and steaming it like a tamale.

Keshy yena is a unique favorite in Curacao and the Netherlands Antilles; an edam cheese with the top sliced off and the center hollowed out serves as the

Figure 21.10 Ginger root (left) and nutmeg and mace (right) are spices grown on Grenada in the Windward Islands.

Stamp and go—Jamaican dish featuring salted, dried cod suspended in a heavy batter containing chilies, onions, and annatto and fried as a fritter.

Escabeche—Cooked fish marinated in vinegar and spices.

Moros y Cristianos—Cuban specialty containing black beans and rice cooked with garlic, onions, green peppers, tomatoes, and seasonings.

Pastelitos—Savory, small turnovers with meat filling made in the Dominican Republic.

Pasteles—Puerto Rican specialty made by spreading mashed plantain or cornmeal on a plantain leaf, adding a savory filling, wrapping, and steaming.

Keshy yena—Edam cheese stuffed with grated cheese, meat mixtures, and seasonings and then baked; from Netherlands Antilles.

Mace—Reddish coating on nutmeg, which is removed and dried for use as a spice.

Coui sauce—Popular Caribbean hot sauce made with cassava juice and hot peppers.

container for a filling of grated edam, meat mixtures, and seasonings, all of which is then baked in the oven.

Distinctive flavoring ingredients such as cloves and ginger are used (and many are grown locally) to heighten the appeal of some of the fundamentally bland foods of the Caribbean. Various chilies are used frequently. Allspice is from a pimento tree (not related to the pimiento of the Capsicum family). **Mace** (the reddish coating on ripe nutmeg) and nutmeg are grown in Grenada (Figure 21.10). Pepper is also raised in the Caribbean. Indian immigrants added curry and ghee to the richness of the flavors of the Caribbean. **Coui sauce,** a peppery mixture of hot peppers and cassava juice, is about as ubiquitous as cassareep, the other popular sauce based on cassava juice.

Recipes

Sofrito (Makes 3 cups)

⅛ lb salt pork, minced
1 tbsp minced garlic
1½ c chopped onions
1 chili pepper, roasted, seeded, and minced
2 green peppers, chopped
¼ lb ham, diced
3 tomatoes, seeded, peeled, and chopped
1½ tsp minced coriander
¾ tsp oregano
½ tsp salt
¼ tsp pepper

1. Fry salt pork until crispy brown; save fat and discard pork.
2. Sauté garlic, onions, and peppers until tender, stirring to avoid browning.
3. Add remaining ingredients and simmer, covered, for 30 minutes; stir occasionally.
4. Store in refrigerator.

Arroz con Pollo (Serves 4–6)

4 garlic cloves, minced
1 large red onion, chopped
2 tsp minced cilantro
1 tsp grated ginger root
1½ tsp sofrito
¾ tsp oregano
2 tsp black pepper
½ tsp salt
½ tsp saffron
½ tsp cumin
⅓ c lime juice
¼ c red wine vinegar
1½ lb boneless, skinless chicken pieces
¼ c olive oil
1½ c rice
3 c chicken broth
2 carrots, diced
1 bay leaf
½ c frozen peas
¼ c minced stuffed green olives

1. Grind garlic, onion, cilantro, ginger, sofrito, oregano, pepper, salt, saffron, and cumin and then combine with lime juice and vinegar.
2. Marinate chicken in mixture for at least 4 hours in refrigerator.
3. Slowly fry chicken in olive oil for 25 minutes, slowly adding marinade.
4. Meanwhile, boil the rice in broth with carrots and bay leaf for 20 minutes. Stir in peas.
5. Transfer rice to baking dish, scatter olives on rice, and place chicken on top, pouring juices over it.
6. Cover and heat for 15 minutes at 350°F.

Black Bean Soup (Serves 4–6)

1 lb dried black beans
Water to cover beans 2″
1 tbsp salt
4 c chicken broth
1 c minced onions
1½ tsp minced garlic
⅓ lb ham, diced
½ c tomato, seeded, peeled, and diced
2 tbsp malt vinegar
½ tsp cumin
Black pepper to taste

1. Rinse beans and place in saucepan; cover with salted water, heat to boiling, and simmer until tender (3 to 4 hours).
2. Remove from heat and puree 2 cups at a time in a blender, adding part of broth if needed.
3. Combine puree with the rest of the broth and other ingredients in pan, and simmer for 30 minutes, altering seasonings if needed.

Stamp and Go (Serves 4–6)

½ lb dried, salted cod
1 c minced onion
1½ tbsp oil
1 c flour
½ tsp salt
1 tsp baking powder
1 egg, well beaten
¾ c milk
1 tbsp melted butter
2 tsp minced chilies
Oil for frying

1. After soaking cod for at least 12 hours (changing the water every 3 hours), rinse well in cold running water, and then simmer it for 20 minutes in a pan of water deep enough to cover cod by an inch. Flake fish, removing bones and skin.
2. Sauté onion in oil until translucent.
3. Stir flour, salt, and baking powder together thoroughly in a mixing bowl.
4. In another bowl, mix the egg, milk, and butter.
5. Pour liquid ingredients into flour mixture and stir briefly; add onion, cod, and chilies. Stir to make smooth batter.
6. Heat ½″ of oil in a skillet to 375°F. Drop a tablespoonful of batter into hot fat and fry for about 4 minutes, turning with slotted spoon to brown both sides. Add other fritters to fry at the same time, but do only a few at any time to keep the fat hot.
7. Drain on paper towels.

Coo-Coo (Serves 4)

½ lb okra, cut into rounds ¼″ thick (stems cut off)
2 c water
¾ tsp salt
1 c cornmeal
1 tbsp butter

1. Boil okra in salted water and immediately reduce heat and simmer, covered, for about 10 minutes to tenderize okra.
2. Gradually stir in a thin stream of cornmeal and continue stirring constantly while heating until mixture becomes very thick.
3. Shape like a pancake on a serving plate; spread butter on the surface. Serve as a side dish with meat.

Keshy Yena (Serves 6–8)

1 ball edam cheese (2 lb), peeled
1 c minced onion
¼ tsp cayenne pepper
1 tomato, minced
½ lb bay shrimp
½ tsp salt
¼ tsp black pepper
¼ c fine dry bread crumbs
6 stuffed olives, minced
1 tbsp minced sweet pickle
1 egg, beaten

1. Slice 1″ lid across top of cheese and scrape out interior of ball, leaving a shell ½″ thick. Grate cheese removed from the ball. Soak lid and shell completely covered in cold water for 1 hour. Drain.
2. Sauté onion, and then add pepper and tomato. Stir in shrimp, salt, and pepper when vegetables are tender.
3. In a bowl, mix the shrimp mixture with the grated cheese, bread crumbs, olives, pickles, and egg.
4. Put cheese bowl in a greased baking dish that is snug enough to hold the cheese as the bowl softens in the oven. Fill the cheese bowl with the filling and cover with cheese lid.
5. Bake in preheated oven at 350°F for about 25 minutes until top is lightly browned. Serve in the baking dish.

Moros y Cristianos (Serves 4–6)

1 c dried black beans
6 c water
1½ tsp salt
3 strips bacon
1 garlic clove, minced
1 onion, minced
½ green pepper, diced
2 tomatoes, chopped
¾ c rice
1½ c water
Salt and pepper to taste

1. Rinse beans and cover with 6 cups of salted water in a saucepan; simmer for 3 to 4 hours until tender. Drain.
2. Fry bacon until crisp, and drain on paper towel. Crumble into bits.
3. Add garlic, onion, and green pepper to bacon drippings and sauté for 3 minutes; add tomato and sauté for 1 minute more.
4. Add bacon bits and sautéed mixture to beans, and mix well in saucepan.
5. Add rice and 1½ cups of water, and stir while heating to a boil; cover and simmer until rice is done and liquid is gone. Season to taste.

Callaloo (Serves 4)

1 onion, minced
2 garlic cloves, minced
1 hot chili, whole
2 tbsp oil
1 lb spinach or taro leaves, washed and sliced in strips
2 c chicken broth
1 c coconut milk
½ lb okra, chopped
1 tsp salt
2 tbsp chopped cilantro
4 green onions, chopped
2 sprigs thyme, chopped
Dash of hot sauce
½ lb cleaned crab

1. Sauté onion, garlic, and chili in oil until translucent.
2. Add greens and stir in other ingredients, except the crab, as the leaves wilt. Cover and simmer for 20 minutes, stirring occasionally.
3. Add crab and simmer for 5 minutes.
4. Remove chili before serving.

Pastelitos (Serves 4–6)

Filling:
- 1 lb ground chicken
- 2 oz ground ham
- ¼ tsp oregano
- ¼ tsp black pepper
- 1 garlic clove, minced
- 1 onion, minced
- 2 tsp vinegar
- 2 tbsp parsley
- 2 tbsp tomato paste
- ¼ c water
- 1 tsp capers
- 8 ripe olives, chopped
- 2 tbsp oil

Pastry:
- 2 c flour
- ¾ tsp salt
- ⅔ c shortening
- ⅓ c water

1. Thoroughly mix filling ingredients together and sauté slowly for 25 minutes, stirring occasionally.
2. Meanwhile, cut shortening into flour and salt to the size of rice grains.
3. Slowly sprinkle water on flour by drops while tossing flour with a fork. Press into a ball. Divide in half and roll each half ⅛″ thick. Cut in 2″ squares.
4. Place teaspoon of filling on half of the squares, and cover each with the other squares. Seal edges.
5. Deep-fat fry at 375°F to golden brown.

Pasteles (Serves 6–8)

4 garlic cloves, minced
½ tsp cayenne pepper
1 onion, minced
¼ c chopped chives
1 tsp thyme
1 lb ground beef
1 lb ground pork
4 tomatoes, diced
1½ tsp salt
1 tsp Worcestershire sauce
1 c diced black olives
¼ c capers
½ c raisins
4 c instant masa
4 c to 5½ c warm water
2 lb banana leaves (or aluminum foil) cut into 12″ squares

1. Sauté garlic, cayenne, onion, chives, and thyme for 5 minutes; add meats, tomato, and salt, and heat at medium for 30 minutes, and then stir in Worcestershire sauce, olives, capers, and raisins. Simmer for 15 minutes.
2. Meanwhile, put masa in bowl and quickly stir enough water into masa to make a dough that is smooth and not sticky.
3. Rub leaves with oil, and then put golf-ball-sized dough between two leaves and roll dough very thin.
4. Put 2 tablespoons of filling in center of dough, fold dough to cover filling, wrap dough parcel in leaf, and tie with a string.
5. Place all parcels on a rack in a steamer and steam for about 40 minutes to cook the masa.

Piononos (Stuffed Plantains) (Serves 6)

1 lb lean ground beef
¼ c cooked ham
1 garlic clove, minced
½ green pepper, chopped
1 long green chile, peeled, seeded, and chopped
1 onion, chopped
5 prunes, pitted
1 tsp oregano
1 tsp salt
1 tbsp malt vinegar
1 tbsp oil
1 tomato, seeded and chopped
1 tbsp raisins
2 tbsp chopped stuffed olives
½ c tomato sauce
3 ripe plantains
½ c lard
3 eggs, separated
¼ tsp cream of tartar
Oil for deep-fat frying

1. Grind together meats, garlic, green pepper, chile, onion, and prunes; blend in oregano, salt, and vinegar.
2. Sauté meat mixture in oil to brown, and then add tomato, raisins, olives, and tomato sauce.
3. Stir and simmer for 25 minutes.
4. Peel plantains and cut each into four strips lengthwise. Fry for 5 minutes on each side in hot lard.
5. Roll each plantain slice to make a ring 3" in diameter and fasten overlapping ends together with a toothpick.
6. Stuff each circle with meat mixture.
7. Beat egg whites until foamy, and then add cream of tartar; continue beating until stiff. Beat yolks and fold into whites.
8. Spoon egg mixture over all sides of each roll, and then fry in deep fat at 375°F for 3 minutes, turning to brown both sides.

Summary

The Caribbean islands stretch southward in an arc from just off the tip of Florida to almost the northeastern coast of South America. Of the more than 7,000 islands in the region, the four largest are in the north: Cuba, Jamaica, Hispaniola (divided into the countries of Haiti and the Dominican Republic), and Puerto Rico, which is a commonwealth of the United States. Their tropical climate occasionally is punctuated by hurricanes, and earthquakes and volcanic eruptions sporadically cause serious damage. Nevertheless, the islands are suitable for raising a wide range of crops that flourish in a tropical setting.

Peaceful Arawaks and other Indian tribes lived throughout the islands until they were driven northward by hostile Caribs coming from South America. Then the Spanish explorers, beginning with Columbus, arrived and began to exploit the region, shipping gold and other wealth through the Caribbean region back to Spain. The British, French, and Dutch followed as they struggled to gain control of various islands for their nations.

Settlements followed, and sugarcane plantations quickly expanded beyond the labor supply the Indians provided. Slaves from Africa were brought in large numbers and bought by the planters of the Caribbean, forever altering the racial mix and the culture of the region. Pirates added to the violence and struggles for the islands and their treasures in the 17th century.

The abolition of slavery during the 19th century led to the immigration of workers from India and China, as well as other countries, which further enriched the cultural mix. Independence has been acquired by many of the islands within the last century, but a few are still under foreign control.

The religion that predominates on each island usually reflects the beliefs of the country that has controlled it. Both Spain and France brought Catholicism to the islands, so there are many Catholics in the Caribbean, although the African slaves brought with them some of their traditions of animism and blended those with Catholic dogma. The Church of England and Protestant groups are dominant where England held sway. Haitians may practice voodoo, and some Jamaicans are Rastafarians. Religious holidays are celebrated in the various countries in colorful fashion. National holidays are also honored.

Music, dance, folk art, painting, and literature are very important and exciting aspects of Caribbean cultures. Rhythm is a key foundation to much of the music, and several types of drums and other percussive instruments originated in the region. Guitars add to the charm of their music and dances.

Food traditions show some overtones of the Europeans who conquered the islands, but the combination of the African slaves and their unique abilities to prepare tasty yet simple dishes using local foods really shaped the typical meals. Coffee and rum (made from the molasses derived from sugarcane) are the most popular beverages, although many excellent fruit juices are also consumed widely. Yams, sweet potatoes, breadfruit, taro, cassava, plantain, corn, rice, okra, squash, pumpkin, beans of many types, meats, seafood, and tropical fruits are all available in the region. Some of the favorite regional dishes and popular sauces include sofrito, callaloo, coo-coo, foo-foo, funchi, pastelitos, pasteles, coui sauce, and cassareep.

Selected Sites

http://www.jamaicans.com/cooking/foods/fruitglossary.shtml—Pictures and brief descriptions of some of the tropical fruits grown in Jamaica.

http://www.jamaicans.com/cooking/traditional/index.shtml—Many different Jamaican recipes.

http://welcome.topuertorico.org/culture/foodrink.shtml—Overview of Puerto Rican foods.

http://welcome.topuertorico.org/culture/—Overview of Puerto Rican culture.

http://www.travelgrenada.com/receipes.htm—Glossary of some foods and recipes of Grenada.

http://edis.ifas.ufl.edu/TOPIC_Cubas_Food_System—Information on various aspects of Cuba's food supply.

http://www.cs.yale.edu/homes/hupfer/global/regions/cam.html—Recipes and information about the food on many different Caribbean islands and Central American countries.

http://www.foodproductdesign.com/archive/2002/0602CC.html—Article about developing food products with Caribbean flavors.

http://www.foodproductdesign.com/archive/2002/0602CC.html—Story about banana farming on St. Lucia.

http://www.islandflave.com/recipes/islands.html—Recipes from Cuba, the Bahamas, Haiti, and other Caribbean islands.

http://www.siu.edu/~ebl/leaflets/taro.htm—Background information about taro and its cultivation.

Study Questions

1. Where are the following Caribbean islands located: (a) Hispaniola, (b) Curacao, (c) St. Kitts, (d) Grenada, (e) Cuba, (f) Puerto Rico, (g) Jamaica, and (h) Trinidad?
2. Why did pirates operate in the Caribbean, and what was the impact of their presence?
3. Why were African slaves brought to the Caribbean, and how did these immigrants influence the islands from their arrival through today?
4. Match the island with the nation that granted its independence or that still controls it today.

a. Haiti	1. United Kingdom
b. Curacao	2. France
c. Cuba	3. Netherlands
d. Jamaica	4. Spain
e. Martinique	5. Spain, and then the United States
f. Puerto Rico	
g. St. Kitts and Nevis	
h. Bahamas	
i. Barbados	

5. Define (a) Rastafarianism, (b) Creole, (c) bacalao, (d) cassareep, (e) sofrito, (f) pepper pot, and (g) mestizo.
6. Identify at least three dances and three musical instruments that are a cultural part of the Caribbean islands.
7. Plan a dinner menu that includes typical ingredients from the Caribbean.
8. Identify five food ingredients and/or products that are raised or produced in the Caribbean and then exported.

Bibliography

Barer-Stein, T. 1999. *You Eat What You Are.* 2nd ed. Firefly Books, Ltd. Ontario, Canada.

Clark, S. and M. Zellers. 1972. *All the Best in the Caribbean.* Dodd, Mead, and Co. New York.

Ferguson, J. 1999. *Traveler's History of the Caribbean.* Interlink Books. Brooklyn, NY.

Fleetwood, J. 2004. *Food and Cooking of the Caribbean, Central, and South America.* Lorenz Books. London, England.

Foley, E. 1995. *Dominican Republic.* Marshall Cavendish. New York.

Geddes, B. 2001. *Lonely Planet World Food: Caribbean.* Lonely Planet. Oakland, CA.

Gravette, A.G. 1990. *The French Antilles.* Hippocrene Books. New York.

Joy, M. 2002. Calypso cuisine: Cooking from the Caribbean. *Food Product Design.* 12(4): 6.

Houston, L.M. 2005. *Food Culture in the Caribbean.* Greenwood Press. Westport, CT.

Kramer, M. 1988. *Illustrated Guide to Foreign and Fancy Food.* 2nd ed. Plycon Press. Redondo Beach, CA.

Lalbachan, P. 1994. *Complete Caribbean Cookbook.* Tuttle. Rutland, VT.

Levy, P. 1995. *Puerto Rico.* Marshall Cavendish. New York.

McCullough, D. 1977. *Path Between the Seas.* Touchstone. New York.

Pearcy, G.E. 1980. *The World Food Scene.* Plycon Press. Redondo Beach, CA.

Porter, D. and D. Prince. 1998. *Frommer's 99 Caribbean.* Macmillan. New York.

Sheehan, S. 1994. *Jamaica.* Marshall Cavendish. New York.

Sheehan, S. 1995. *Cuba.* Marshall Cavendish. New York.

Tree, R. 1972. *A History of Barbados.* Random House. New York.

Van Aken, N. 2003. *New World Kitchen: Latin American and Caribbean Cuisine.* Ecco. St. Paul, MN.

Viard, M. 1995. *Fruits and Vegetables of the World.* Longmeadow Press. Ann Arbor, MI.

Winn, P. 1992. *Americas.* University of California Press. Berkeley, CA.

Wolfe, L. 1970. *Cooking of the Caribbean.* Time-Life Books. New York.

UNITED STATES
ATLANTIC OCEAN
THE BAHAMAS
Rio Grande River
BAJA
Western Sierra Madre Mountains
Eastern Sierra Madre Mountains
MEXICO
Gulf of Mexico
CUBA
Mexico City
YUCATAN
Acapulco
OAXACA
CHIAPAS
BELIZE
JAMAICA
HAITI
DOMINICAN REPUBLIC
HONDURAS
GUATEMALA
EL SALVADOR
NICARAGUA
Caribbean Sea
PACIFIC OCEAN
COSTA RICA
PANAMA
VENEZUELA
COLOMBIA

22 Central America and Mexico

Geographic Overview

The landmass encompassed by Central American nations and Mexico stretches in a generally southeastern direction from the United States to Colombia in South America. However, two places deviate from this pattern. The Yucatan is a peninsula jutting to the northeast from southeastern Mexico toward Cuba, delineating the Gulf of Mexico from the Caribbean.

Even more surprising is that Panama basically is aligned in an east-west orientation, with the Panama Canal tracing a north-south channel between the Caribbean and the Pacific (Figure 22.1). In Panama, the Caribbean beaches are the northern beaches, and the Pacific beaches are the southern ones, facts that tend to generate geographic whiplash.

Central America

The seven nations composing Central America are relatively small countries; together they are equivalent in area to only about 25 percent of Mexico, their northern neighbor. From north to south, they are as follows:

- Belize
- Guatemala (just south of Belize)
- El Salvador (south and east of Guatemala)
- Honduras (north of El Salvador)
- Nicaragua (south of Honduras)
- Costa Rica (south of Nicaragua)
- Panama (neighboring with Colombia in South America).

Figure 22.1 Although the Panama Canal cleaves Panama, it actually serves as a unifying force as it facilitates shipping food and other freight from ocean to ocean across the Isthmus of Panama.

Belize is only a little larger than El Salvador, which is the smallest country in Central America. The entire eastern boundary of Belize is lapped by the waters of the Caribbean. Guatemala, Belize's western neighbor, is almost four times larger than Belize; it is bordered on the northwest by Mexico and on the southeast by Honduras and El Salvador. Guatemala and El Salvador have Pacific beaches.

The total area of El Salvador, the smallest country, plus Nicaragua is equal to Costa Rica. Nicaragua, Costa Rica, and Panama extend across from the Caribbean to the Pacific and have long shorelines on both the Caribbean and the Pacific in comparison with the narrow width of their land, particularly in Costa Rica and Panama.

Panama is a mere 30 miles wide at its narrowest point, and the Panama Canal traverses only about 50 miles as it provides the essential link for ships to go between the Caribbean and the Pacific. Panama is the third largest country in Central America, and Costa Rica (Figure 22.2) is about half the physical size of Panama.

The countries with Caribbean shores (Belize, Honduras, Nicaragua, Costa Rica, and Panama) are subject to hurricanes and traditionally have heavy rainfall in the coastal areas. Rainfall in the interior and along the Pacific is lighter, particularly from June to November.

The low elevations in Central America are always hot and humid, which is not surprising in view of the tropical latitudes. The combination of heat and extensive swampy areas fosters health problems from insect vectors and microbiological sources; the name *Mosquito Coast* in Nicaragua and the notorious loss of life from malaria and other tropical illnesses during the construction of the

Figure 22.2 Costa Rica, a comparatively small country in Central America, has coastline on both the Caribbean and the Pacific.

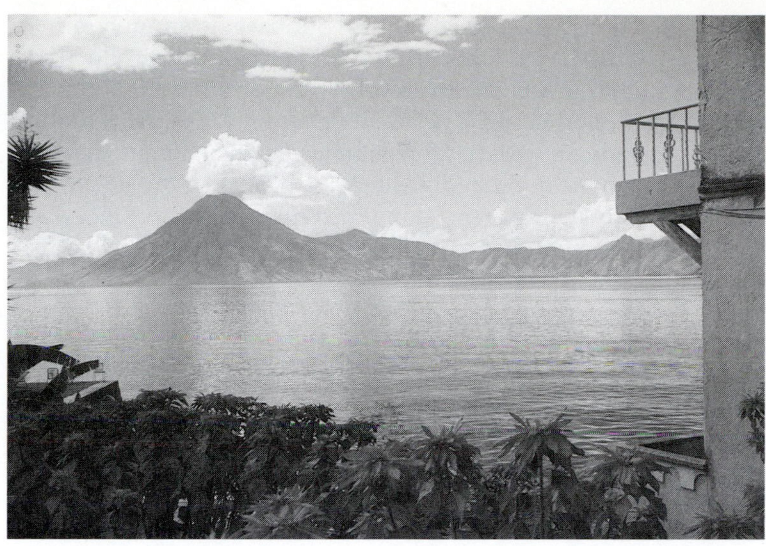

Figure 22.3 A volcano looms in back of Lake Atitlan in Guatemala.

Panama Canal are irrefutable evidence of such health hazards. The higher elevations in the inland regions reduce the difficulties a bit.

Geological factors add to potential problems in Central America, for two tectonic plates are the cause of very damaging earthquakes and volcanic eruptions (the Cocos Plate is slowly sliding under the Caribbean Plate). Among the active volcanoes in Central America are Poas in Costa Rica and Pacaya in Guatemala (Figure 22.3). Although many subsistence farmers in Central America till their small plots to raise beans, maize, fruits, and vegetables, the climate and soil allow some successful agricultural enterprises. Among the export crops are pineapple, citrus, bananas, and coffee.

Mexico

Mexico is the giant northern neighbor of Central America. From north to south, Mexico stretches more than 2,000 miles, and its shared border with the United States is almost 2,200 miles long. Mountains in the vicinity of Mexico City include Popocatepetl (a volcano 17,288 feet high). The Gulf of Mexico extends along the eastern edge of Mexico until the Caribbean commences on the eastern side of the Yucatan Peninsula. Baja, California (largely desert), reaches more than 800 miles southward from the northern border, forming a western peninsula separated by the Sea of Cortez and with the Pacific on its western edge (Figure 22.4).

Figure 22.4 The tip of Baja California ends in dramatic rocks in the sea at Cabo San Lucas, Mexico.

Between arid conditions (only 12 percent of the country gets enough rain for crops) and challenging terrain, Mexico has had limited agricultural productivity. Many of the farmers operate at a subsistence level, with corn, beans, and some rice or wheat being their common crops. The high elevation (7,500 feet) around Mexico City is suited for growing a variety of vegetables (such as tomatoes, potatoes, squash, and chilies) and wheat. Some livestock are raised in the north, and sugarcane is grown successfully in low areas along the Gulf of Mexico. Chocolate, vanilla, avocados, papayas, and guavas are available from the tropical lowlands.

History and Culture

Early Civilizations

Humans have lived in various parts of Central America and Mexico for more than 10,000 years, but archaeologists have found very limited evidence of early people. Apparently, some crops were grown in Panama at least a millennium before the birth of Christ. With the exception of some interaction with the Incas to the south, little development occurred in the region of present-day Costa Rica and Panama until the arrival of the Spaniards.

Olmecs However, several Indian cultural groups existed in Mesoamerica, the region defined by archaeologists as reaching from the desert barrier of northern Mexico to as far south as parts of El Salvador and Honduras. The Olmecs, who lived along the coast of the Gulf of Mexico, left huge basalt carvings depicting human heads as evidence of the level of achievement during their era from 1200 BCE to 400 BCE. Apparently, the abundant rainfall and good soil allowed them not only to raise the food they needed, but also to develop an organized society that constructed towns and conducted trade with other Indian societies throughout Mesoamerica. Shamanism and human sacrifices, as well as the slightly more friendly sport of playing ball, were parts of the Olmec culture that have been found in subsequent cultures of the region.

Mayans—Indians living in Guatemala, Belize, and southern Mexico from 600 BCE to 1200 CE.

Mayans The **Mayans** developed their amazing culture in the tropical rainforests and jungles of Guatemala, Belize, and southern Mexico from about 600 BCE to 1200 CE. Their achievements included planned cities, construction of pyramids (Figures 22.5 and C.191, p. C64), a system of writing and recorded texts, and an

Figure 22.5 Mayans built impressive pyramids and buildings that were overgrown by jungle but are now being restored in Tikal, Guatemala.

accurate solar calendar that was superior to the calendar used in Europe at the time.

Zapotecs—Indians who developed the city of Monte Alban near Oaxaca in Mexico around 500 BCE.

Aztecs—Indians in power in Mexico City region from the 14th century until Cortés conquered them in 1521.

The Zapotecs developed systems of writing and a calendar. The ruins of Monte Alban near Oaxaca in southern Mexico add further evidence of the level of development of this group. Their skills in ceramics have been passed down over the ages and can be seen today in the region.

Zapotecs and Toltecs Concurrently with the Mayan developments along the coast, the **Zapotecs** were creating their center at Monte Alban near Oaxaca in the interior of Mexico (Figure 22.6). During their time of influence (500 BCE to 700 CE), the Zapotecs had considerable contact with the Toltecs living to the north at Teotihuacan, where the Pyramid of the Sun and the Pyramid of the Moon still stand only 30 miles from Mexico City. Although Teotihuacan dates from about 150 BCE to 750 CE (somewhat later than the founding of Monte Alban), its claim to being the home of the gods and evidence of physical dominance suggests that contact between the two groups may have been more brutal than friendly.

Mixtecs and Aztecs The Mixtecs eventually established their dominance around Monte Alban and Oaxaca, and the **Aztecs** took over the region around Mexico City in the 1300s and ruled from Teochtitlan until the Spanish arrival and conquest in 1521.

European Influences

Conquistadors Spanish influence in Panama and Costa Rica began to be felt in the early 16th century; an attempt at establishing a settlement in Panama dates from 1510. The importance of this region was viewed by the Spanish to be primarily as a means of accessing wealth from elsewhere. Panama provided a route to bring out the valuables taken from the Incas in the Andes.

Somewhat later, Spain used the overland route across the isthmus to transport goods offloaded from ships in the Pacific onto ships in the Caribbean waiting to load precious cargo to carry to Spain. In fact, this means of avoiding having to sail around Cape Horn was used (in spite of Henry Morgan and his pirates' attacks) until the British seized Portobela on the Caribbean side in 1739.

Although a successful Spanish settlement was created later in Costa Rica, the lack of local gold or silver caused the Spanish to basically ignore exploitation of the natives as they made their way northward to Nicaragua. The Spanish, traveling from their base in Panama, in 1519 established settlements in Nicaragua near the Pacific, including one on Lake Managua and one on Lago de Nicaragua. The latter had the trading advantage of a navigable river (Rio San Juan) to the Caribbean. Spanish forces from the north fought their counterparts from the south there. However, the English and pirates of European heritage claimed the eastern Caribbean shoreline of Nicaragua.

Figure 22.6 Monte Alban, built by the Zapotecs near Oaxaca, Mexico, featured a ball court, as well as many buildings.

Under orders from Cortés, Cristobal de Olid conquered Honduras. Guatemala came under Spanish control when Alvarado, another soldier sent by Cortés to extend their conquests, seized much of both Guatemala and El Salvador with the help of Aztecs in 1524. Guatemala was ruled by Spain as a large region, which included the area from Guatemala south to Panama. Its capital was moved twice before being established in 1543 at what is now Antigua (Figure 22.7). The terrible earthquake of 1773 caused so much damage that the final move was made to Guatemala City.

Many stories swirl around the events that took place in Mexico when Cortés was seeking to capture Montezuma and finally subjugating the Aztecs in the Mexico City area in 1521. The loss of life and dignity the Indians suffered are changes that permanently altered the face of Mexico. Spanish soldiers were granted land in very large parcels, along with Indian servants to work them.

The Catholic Church The authority of the Catholic Church to convert the natives was granted to three mendicant orders: Franciscan, Dominican, and Augustinian. The Franciscans arrived in 1524 and busily began their work in converting the Indians to Christianity and then having them build religious structures and housing for the friars. Some of the friars recorded history of times past, as told to them by the Indians, a legacy that has proven to be valuable to learning the background of the area.

The Spanish occupation and the Catholic friars created a culture that encompassed some of the Indian heritage but added a greatly altered lifestyle that is still very much in evidence today. The principal language is Spanish (although some Indian languages can be found), the Catholic Church dominates the religious scene, and a strong class division (with the majority being required to labor hard for very little financial benefit) remains.

Few pure Spanish are found in Mexico today because of considerable intermarriage among the Spaniards, Indians, and Africans throughout the Spanish occupation, and most people of mixed racial heritage had little opportunity to escape their servitude and poverty.

The French French influence came into Mexico indirectly when the French Bourbons maneuvered Philip V onto the Spanish throne. Governmental changes effected by the French in Mexico (actually then called *New Spain*) resulted in considerably increased revenues from the colony and somewhat improved income for the Mexicans. Despite this, there was a growing desire among the population

Figure 22.7 Antigua was the early capital of Guatemala, but the severe destruction from an earthquake in 1773 caused the seat of the government to be moved to Guatemala City.

throughout Central America and Mexico to become independent from Spain. Napoleon deposed the Bourbons in the rule of Spain and its colonies.

Mexican Independence

Upheavals in Europe paved the way for upheavals in the Spanish possessions toward the west. Among the names prominent in the efforts to obtain freedom are Miguel Hidalgo, who is celebrated on September 16 in recognition of his impassioned plea to the people to rise up in 1810; Morelos, a mestizo priest whose leadership was another vital part of the effort to become independent; and Iturbide, Guadalupe Victoria, and Vicente Guerrero, who were united in their final efforts to gain independence, which was proclaimed in Mexico City on September 27, 1821.

Instability characterized the Mexican government following its achievement of independence. Iturbide became Emperor Agustín I for a period of about a year, but Santa Anna gained control and drew up a constitution in 1824; Guadalupe Victoria (actually, Felix Fernandez) became the first president. Vicente Guerrero, with the help of Santa Anna, became president in 1828, and Santa Anna was made president in 1833 (actually, he held that position 11 different times as the position ricocheted to different aspirants).

Santa Anna's defeat is credited with the U.S. acquisition of Texas, New Mexico, Arizona, and California from Mexico. This phase of Mexican history traces back to the Bourbon decision in the early 1700s to attract settlers to occupy Texas and acquire land grants from Mexico in the hope of creating loyal settlers to keep out the United States. This merely drew Americans, including Stephen Austin, who led the settlers against Santa Anna's army, leading to the siege of the Alamo by Santa Anna and his later defeat by Sam Houston's forces.

The treaty signed in 1836 created Texas as an independent republic with the Rio Grande (known in Mexico as the *Rio Bravo*) separating Texas from Mexico. Texas remained independent until 1845, when it became a state in the United States. Furthermore, its claim of a very large amount of land as far west as western New Mexico and northward into parts of Colorado and Utah threatened considerable loss of territory that Mexico had claimed to possess.

When the Mexican army attacked General Zachary Taylor's troops at Brownsville, Texas, President Polk had Congress declare war, and the Mexican-American War began. American generals moved successfully across what is now New Mexico and Arizona to California and southward into Mexico, where they were confronted by Santa Anna briefly at Buena Vista. Surprisingly, Santa Anna left the battle scene; General Scott landed at Veracruz and fought his way to Mexico City, with the final assault at Chapultepec Castle on September 13, 1847.

The desert southwest became part of the United States. The sale of the Gadsden Purchase in 1853 by Santa Anna to the United States defined the border between Mexico and the United States. Problems continued for Mexico, with deep divisions growing between factions. Finally, Benito Juárez was installed as the first Indian president in 1860. Combined forces of Spain, France, and England blockaded the port of Veracruz because of debts owed them from Mexico.

While the United States was busy fighting its own Civil War, the French decided to invade Mexico. Heavy fighting occurred at Puebla, and finally the French captured Mexico City. Maximilian, an Austrian archduke, and his wife Carlotta were sent to rule Mexico, which they did from 1864 to 1867 (Figure 22.8). Then Juárez forced them out and had Maximillian executed. Juárez served as president from 1867 until he died in 1872, a time when the country became considerably more stable.

The dictatorship of Porfirio Díaz followed for 34 years. He did much to modernize Mexico, but discontent erupted into Civil War in 1910, fueled by such fighters as Pancho Villa, Pascual Orozco, Jr., and Emiliano Zapata. Frightful fighting

Figure 22.8 Dishes used by Maximilian and Carlotta during their brief tenure in Mexico reveal how little they understood the Mexican culture.

and hardships on the citizenry marked the decade of the Civil War. Olvaro Obregón became president in 1920, followed by President P. E. Calles. The period since then has had various crises, but democracy has been maintained, and economic development has been moving ahead.

Religion

The major religion throughout Central America and Mexico is Catholic, the result of the extensive conversion efforts initiated by the Spanish friars of the colonial era (Figure 22.9). The Catholic Church has a powerful economic base throughout the region and is the center of many festivals and celebrations. The strong emphasis on the importance of family and extended family found throughout these countries has been fostered over the centuries by the teachings of the Catholic friars.

Machismo and male authority within the family and the role of women as mothers and caretakers of the home are a firmly established pattern. Morality among women is expected and carefully guarded. Despite the dominance of the Catholic Church, religious freedom is respected.

Figure 22.9 The cathedral at Chichicastenango, Guatemala, is a place of great activity on market day in the village.

Holidays

Las Posadas—Procession of Mary and Joseph's search for lodging reenacted from December 16 until Christmas Eve as part of Christmas festivities.

Cinco de Mayo—Celebration on May 5 honoring Mexican defeat of the French at Puebla in 1862.

Christmas is a time for special celebrations and features the **Posadas** in Mexico, which is marked every night from December 16 through Christmas Eve by a procession featuring Mary and Joseph knocking on doors and seeking lodging for the night until they are welcomed into a house and the party begins. A piñata, usually in the shape of an animal or a star and made of papier-mâché or clay and loaded with treats, is the feature attraction, and it is broken by someone swinging a broom handle while blindfolded; the swinging continues until the treats are broken out of the piñata. Epiphany, the day (January 6) when the three kings are thought to have arrived, is the traditional time for Mexicans to exchange gifts. Various other religious and national holidays are also celebrated. **Cinco de Mayo** (May 5) celebrates the 1862 defeat of the French at Puebla.

Similar celebrations are held in the countries of Central America. An interesting addition to the religious holidays in Guatemala at Easter is the making of alfombras (a carpet made outdoors using flower petals and sawdust to make lovely and colorful patterns). All Saints' (Todos Santos) and All Souls' days (November 1 and 2, respectively) also are celebrated throughout the region. Candlelight vigils are held, and breads and other foods shaped to resemble skeletons and skulls are prepared for the honored memory of departed family members. Pilgrimages to special religious shrines also are a part of the culture. People from all over Central America gather at Esquipulas in Guatemala on January 15 to light a candle before a statue of a black Christ, the site of a miraculous cure in 1737.

Food Patterns

The foods commonly eaten in Mexico and Central America are a flavorful blend of the native plants and fish eaten by the Indians mingled with pork, spices, and other European ingredients brought by the Spanish invaders. Although there are some differences in various regions of Mexico and its neighbors to the south, most people today eat a diet that strongly reflects the heritage of the Indian ancestors (Figure 22.10). Corn, the hardy cereal crop that formed the foundation of the diet prior to the arrival of the Spanish, still is the dominant staple, augmented by wheat and rice brought by the Spaniards. Beans of various types, chilies, and tomatoes eaten by early Indians are today likely to be flavored with lard, onions, and garlic, the contributions of their conquerors.

Figure 22.10 Corn tortillas are the base for this plate of nachos, which is served with garnishes of peppers, tomatoes, and onions plus a generous scoop of guacamole.

Cereal Uses

Tortillas Corn is featured on the menu all day long throughout this entire region. **Tortillas** appear at all meals. Their preparation often is done in factories today, but they frequently are made at home. Preparation of tortillas requires **masa harina,** the flour made in earlier days by grinding hull-less, lime-soaked corn (**nixtamal**) with a hand-shaped stone (mano) on a flat stone (**metate**). After masa harina is worked into a dough with added water, balls of dough are patted or pressed into flat circles about one-eighth inch thick and usually 6 to 8 inches in diameter. These flat disks of dough are baked on a flat, cast-iron griddle (**comal**) and served immediately, or the baked tortillas may be reheated (often by frying) when used later.

Wheat is used to make flour tortillas; its gluten particularly makes the tortilla dough easier to manipulate than the dough made with corn. This characteristic is evident in the large disks commonly made when preparing flour tortillas. The sturdy, rather flexible texture of flour tortillas is illustrated effectively in **burritos,** the Mexican-American dish featuring a hearty filling such as beans or meat (or both) and other ingredients wrapped in a large flour tortilla and often garnished with salsa (sauce of chopped tomatoes or other ingredients and seasoned with chilies and various spices).

Several recipes use corn tortillas as their base. Corn tortillas are thicker and less malleable than flour tortillas because of the lack of gluten. However, they can be folded or rolled to make various popular dishes. **Tacos** are made with corn tortillas (either fried to make a crisp shell or left soft) folded in half to hold the desired filling made with any combination of beans, slivered meats, chopped tomatoes and lettuce, salsa, grated cheese, and sour cream. **Enchiladas** are also made with corn tortillas, but they are rolled with a filling and covered with a sauce and grated cheese and then baked.

Quesadillas are made by placing grated cheese alone or with other fillings over half of a flour tortilla and then folding the other half over before it is heated in the oven or sometimes fried. Often a **tostada** is made by frying a corn tortilla to make it crisp and then generously topping it with layers of refried beans, slivered meats, chopped tomatoes, onions, cilantro, grated cheese, guacamole, and **salsa** (Figure 22.11). Another tostada version is made with a flour tortilla fried in the shape of a bowl; this crisp, edible bowl is filled with layers of refried beans and the other ingredients used in making a tostada with a corn tortilla.

Figure 22.11 Flour tortillas are baked using dough with enough gluten so they can be folded or rolled, as is demonstrated in these quesadillas accompanied by salsa and guacamole for added flavor excitement.

Tortilla—Dough of masa harina (or flour) and water, which is pressed into thin disks and baked.

Masa harina—Cornmeal made by grinding corn kernels that have been soaked in lime (calcium oxide); the corn flour used to make tamales.

Nixtamal—Hull-less, lime-soaked corn.

Metate—Stone on which nixtamal is ground to masa harina.

Comal—Flat, cast iron griddle used to bake tortillas.

Burrito—Wheat flour tortilla wrapped around bean or meat filling.

Taco—Crisply fried or soft tortilla folded in half over a filling of beans, meats, and other ingredients.

Enchilada—Corn tortillas rolled around a filling and covered with a sauce before baking.

Quesadilla—Flour tortilla folded over a layer of grated cheese and heated.

Tostada—Fried corn tortilla topped with beans, shredded meat, chopped vegetables, guacamole, grated cheese, and sour cream; sometimes a flour tortilla is fried in the shape of a bowl that is filled with the same ingredients.

Salsa—Sauce containing finely chopped vegetables and seasonings used to add flavor excitement to many Mexican and Central American dishes.

Flautas—Tightly rolled corn tortillas containing a small amount of filling that are fried until crisp.

Guacamole—Mashed avocado, chilies, tomatoes, cilantro, and lemon juice; served as an accompaniment or a garnish.

Chalupas—Fried tortillas topped with refried beans, slivered meat, chopped tomatoes and onions, and grated cheese.

Chilaquiles—Shredded, fried tortillas baked with chili sauce.

Gordita—Thick, small tortilla fried and slit to form a pocket that is stuffed with meats or seafood, lettuce, and cheese; served topped with salsa, shredded lettuce, chopped tomatoes, and grated cheese,

Tamale—Masa harina spread on cornhusks and wrapped around a filling of meat or other ingredients, and then steamed until done.

Masa—Cornmeal dough made by mixing masa harina and water; main ingredient of tamales.

Frijoles refritos—Cooked beans mashed and fried in lard to create a somewhat lumpy texture.

Flautas are made by putting a small amount of filling very tightly into a corn tortilla, rolling it into a pencil shape and then frying it until crisp. **Guacamole** (a favorite accompaniment of mashed avocado accented with chilies, chopped tomatoes, cilantro, and lemon juice) is often served as a dip with flautas, tortilla chips, or other finger foods, in salads, and as a topping with many other dishes.

Other dishes featuring corn tortillas are **chalupas** (fried tortillas topped with ingredients similar to those used in a tostada), **chilaquiles** (shredded tortillas, fried before baking with chili sauce), and **gorditas** (thick, small tortillas fried and slit to form a pocket, and then stuffed with meats or seafood, beans, lettuce, and cheese).

Tamales **Tamales** with a variety of fillings are popular throughout this region. Their place in the menu may be as the main part of a meal, or as a dessert if sweet. Basically, tamales are made from masa harina and water and mixed into a dough ***(masa).*** Masa is spread on dried cornhusks and a filling is added before the filled tamale is wrapped snugly in its cornhusk wrapper (or banana leaves, in tropical regions), placed in a large steamer, and steamed until the dough is done and the filling is cooked. The wrapping is then discarded, and the tamales are devoured with enthusiasm.

Rice

Rice cannot be made into tortillas because it does not have textural properties that are well suited to making a dough (Figure 22.12). However, rice is served at most meals except breakfast. It may be boiled and served plain, although it often is served as Spanish rice (rice sautéed and steamed with onions, garlic, and tomatoes and seasoned with cilantro and sometimes cumin).

Other Foods

Beans Beans are a staple item in diets throughout Mexico and Central America. Frequently, they are fried with lard and sometimes cheese, a dish called **frijoles refrito** (refried beans) or simply *refritos.* Sometimes, beans are served after they have been simmered until soft but without adding lard or other fat. The protein content of beans is augmented when they are served with rice. These two protein sources complement each other to provide the equivalent of a complete protein. This is of particular importance for people who may not be eating meat on a daily basis.

Chilies Many different types of chilies are grown in Mexico and Central America and are used as flavoring or even as a main ingredient, as in chiles rellenos. Anaheim (or California) long green chilies are used in making chiles rellenos, and

Figure 22.12 Enchiladas at the upper left on this sampler plate, quesadillas at the extreme left, chiles rellenos in the middle, rice, guacamole with corn tortilla chips, and refried beans complete this selection.

Table 22.1 Selected Chilies of Mexico and Central America

Chili	*Color*	*Size and Shape*	*Comments*
Anaheim (California)	Green	6 to 9 inches long, 1½ inches wide at stem	Peel and seed fresh chile to reduce bite; available canned
Ancho	Dark green, bright red when ripe	8 inches long, 1½ inches wide at stem	Mild to moderately hot; milder as it ripens
Chile roja	Red	Varies with type	General term for any red chile
Chile verde	Green	Varies with type	General term for any green chile
Chipotle	Red	2½ inches long, 1 inch wide at stem	Hot, mature jalapeño pepper that has been smoked; available canned
Jalapeño	Dark green	2½ inches long, 1 inch wide at stem	Very hot; available fresh and canned, pickled or plain
Pasilla	Dark green (immature, dark brown (ripe); chocolate colored (dried)	8 to 11 inches long, 1½ inches wide at stem	Ranges from mild to hot; available fresh or canned
Poblano	Dark green		Mild
Yellow	Yellow	Varies with type	Very hot, varies with type

various other dishes utilize them or other chilies (Table 22.1). Poblano is another variety that commonly is stuffed or used in recipes needing a comparatively mild chili.

Considerable care is required when working with chilies to avoid burning hands, mouth, and eyes with the juices and fumes that come from them while removing the seeds and interior veins, which are the extremely hot parts of the chilies. Chilies for chiles rellenos are singed over a gas flame or in the oven to blacken and crisp the skin for easy removal; the cleaned chile is filled with grated cheese and dipped in a frothy egg batter and then deep-fried in lard or oil.

Lard Lard is a traditional ingredient in many recipes to contribute its distinctive flavor overtone in this cuisine. When the Spaniards brought pigs to the New World, they introduced not only a new type of meat, but also lard. The cuisine now has evolved to one encompassing many fried foods and generous use of lard in recipes, although butter and oil (corn and some olive) also are used.

Dairy Milk and dairy products are somewhat limited, although fresh cheeses are available. Canned and sweetened condensed milk are the preferred sources of milk, a pattern that developed because these products do not require refrigeration until opened, and refrigeration is of limited availability to many. Milk may be used in cooking and is sometimes consumed as a beverage.

Specialties Some unique items in the Mexican and Central American diets are **nopales** (leaves of prickly pear cactus, usually pickled or fried), **tajaditas** (fried banana chips), **jícama** (root vegetable with a crisp texture, often sprinkled with chili powder and lemon and eaten raw), and fruit of the prickly pear cactus (often used as juice and jelly).

Nopales—Leaves of prickly pear cactus.

Tajaditas—Fried banana chips.

Jícama—Brown root vegetable with crisp white interior, often served in raw slices with chili powder sprinkled on them.

Atole—Gruel-like, thick beverage with a cornmeal base.

Agave—Century plant; source of the sap used to make tequila and pulque.

Beverages

Beverages include two that are often made with milk: **atole** (a thick, cornmeal-based drink) and hot chocolate (often flavored with cinnamon and beaten with a carved wooden beater). Tequila is a twice-distilled alcoholic beverage prepared from sap of the **agave** or century plant, that traditionally is served with salt and

Desayuno—Breakfast (usually coffee and pastry) eaten early in the morning in Mexico and Central America.

Almuerzo—Late-morning, light meal (usually tortilla-based dish and a beverage) often eaten in Mexico and Central America.

La Comida—Heaviest meal of the day, eaten in midafternoon, in Mexico and Central America; includes soup, main dish, beans, rice, tortillas, dessert, and a beverage.

Flan—Baked custard dessert.

Merienda—Late-afternoon light refreshment eaten in Mexico and Central America.

Cena—Supper meal (light menu) served in Mexico and Central America in the evening.

lime), and pulque is a mildly alcoholic beverage that also is made from agave sap. Coffee, usually served con leche (with milk), is another very popular beverage.

Meal Patterns

Meal patterns are influenced by economic factors and rural or urban locations of families. Breakfast (**desayuno**) may be as simple as café con leche and a bread, pastry, or tamale before city people leave for work, or more substantial for rural workers who may do chores before eating a meal that adds beans and tortillas. To help hungry workers survive until the typically late lunch, **almuerzo**, (usually a tortilla-based dish and a beverage) is served shortly before noon.

The main meal is **la comida,** which is eaten in midafternoon and followed by a siesta. The menu for this meal is large, often beginning with soup and continuing with beans, rice, and tortillas or a hearty main dish, a dessert (perhaps **flan** or fruit), and a beverage.

A very late afternoon refreshment is the **merienda,** a time for enjoying a sweet pastry or roll, such as buñuelos, and a beverage (perhaps atole, hot chocolate, or coffee). Finally, supper (**cena**) may be served sometime between 8 P.M. and midnight in the city. This may be as simple as leftovers from comida. Snacking often also adds to the food intake of most people.

Recipes

Arroz con Pollo (Serves 4–6)

2 lb chicken pieces
2 tbsp oil
1 green pepper, chopped
1 large onion, coarsely chopped
2 garlic cloves, minced
6 stuffed olives, chopped
2 tomatoes, chopped
2 tomatillos, peeled and chopped
1 tsp capers
¼ tsp oregano
½ tsp salt
Pepper
2½ c water
1 c rice

1. Brown chicken in oil in deep skillet or Dutch oven.
2. Add vegetables, seasonings, and water; cover and simmer for 45 minutes.
3. Add rice and simmer, covered, until rice is done (about 20 minutes).

Atole de Leche (Serves 4–6)

3 c water
½ c masa harina
1 cinnamon stick
3 c milk
1 c sugar (or to taste)

1. In a pan, stir water into masa harina; add cinnamon and heat while stirring until thickened.
2. Add milk and sugar; stir slowly while heating to a simmer.
3. Remove cinnamon and serve hot in mugs or cups as a beverage.

Buñuelos (Serves 12–16)

2 eggs, well beaten
¼ c milk
2 tbsp melted butter
2 c all-purpose flour
½ tsp salt
1½ tsp sugar
Oil for frying
2 tsp cinnamon
2 tbsp sugar

1. Combine eggs, milk, and butter in a mixing bowl.
2. Sift flour, salt, and sugar together, and then add to liquid ingredients and stir well to make a dough.
3. Form dough into 1″ balls.
4. On a floured board, press each ball into a very thin disk.
5. Deep-fat fry each disk in 375°F oil to a golden brown. Blot on paper towels.
6. Sprinkle with cinnamon and sugar mix.

Burritos (Serves 4–6)

1½ lb beef stew meat
2 onions, chopped
3 oz canned diced green chiles
1½ tsp salt
6 flour tortillas

1. Combine beef, onions, chiles, and salt in a casserole; cover and bake at 225°F for 8 hours.
2. Shred beef after it is cooled.
3. Place about ½ cup of meat filling on a tortilla, fold right and left sides in about 1″ over the filling; roll loosely, starting at the bottom so that the filling is encased in the wrap.

Chicken Enchiladas (Serves 4–8)

2½ lb chicken pieces
Water to cover
Salt and pepper to taste
1½ onions, chopped
8 corn tortillas
1 10-oz can enchilada sauce
1 c grated cheddar cheese

1. Cover chicken with water and simmer, covered, until very tender. Remove and discard skin and bones; shred chicken meat. Salt and pepper to taste.
2. Sauté onions and chicken in oil until golden. Remove from skillet.
3. Fry each tortilla separately to soften.
4. Place about ½ cup chicken mixture on each tortilla, pour some sauce over each filling, and then sprinkle with cheese.
5. Fold both edges loosely over the filling and invert when arranging enchilada in an oblong baking dish.
6. Sprinkle remaining cheese and sauce over the pan of enchiladas, and then bake for 15 minutes at 350°F.

Chiles Rellenos (Serves 6)

6 long green chiles (or canned whole green chiles)
6 cubes of Monterey Jack cheese (1″ × 1″ × ½″)
6 eggs, separated
¼ tsp cream of tartar
1 c salsa or enchilada sauce

1. Blister chile skins under broiler or over gas flame; cool and peel, and then core and remove seeds; put a piece of cheese inside each chile.
2. Make six rings about 5″ in diameter using folded aluminum foil and arrange on jelly roll pan.
3. Beat egg yolks until thick and lemon-colored; beat whites until foamy, add cream of tartar, and continue beating until peaks form.
4. Fold the yolks into the whites, gently but completely.
5. Spoon a large spoonful of egg batter into each ring of foil, and then arrange the stuffed chiles in the rings.
6. Spoon remaining egg batter over the chiles and bake at 350°F for 20 to 30 minutes until golden brown. Serve with salsa or enchilada sauce.

Salsa (Makes 2 cups)

3 tomatoes, peeled and diced
1 3½-oz can chopped green chiles
1 large onion, finely chopped
¼ c finely chopped cilantro
1 garlic clove, minced
1 tsp salt
Black pepper to taste
Juice of 1 lemon or 2 limes
1 tbsp salad oil

1. Combine all ingredients.
2. Store covered in refrigerator for up to 4 days.

Guacamole (Makes 1½–2 cups)

2 ripe avocados
1 tbsp lemon juice
½ onion, minced
1 tomato, peeled, seeded, and finely chopped
3 tbsp canned diced green chile
1 tbsp minced cilantro
1 tsp salt
¼ tsp white pepper

1. Peel avocados, discard seeds, and mash flesh with fork until smooth.
2. Stir in lemon juice thoroughly.
3. Add remaining ingredients. Stir to mix; then cover with plastic wrap and refrigerate for no longer than a day. Serve as a dip or garnish.

Gazpacho (Serves 2–4)

1 garlic clove, minced
3 tomatoes, seeded, peeled, and diced
1 cucumber, seeded and diced
1 green pepper, seeded and diced
2 stalks celery, minced
1 onion, minced
2 c V-8 juice
⅓ c lemon juice
Tabasco sauce and pepper to taste

1. Combine all ingredients, cover, and chill thoroughly in refrigerator.
2. Serve very cold in chilled bowls.

Nopalito Salad (Serves 4)

8 medium nopales (cactus leaves)
4 green onions, minced
1 tbsp chopped cilantro
2 tomatoes, diced
3½ oz canned diced green chiles
1 tbsp salad oil
2 tbsp vinegar
Salt and pepper to taste
¼ c grated cheddar cheese

1. Clean, remove stickers, and slice nopales in ⅛″ × 1″ strips.
2. Boil nopale strips for 15 minutes until tender but crisp. Drain and cool.
3. Combine all ingredients except the cheese.
4. Garnish with grated cheese.

Jicama Salad (Serves 4–6)

2 c peeled, diced jícama
1 green pepper, seeded and diced
1 medium onion, thinly sliced
1 cucumber, seeded and diced
3 tbsp canned diced green chiles
1 tbsp salad oil
2 tbsp lemon juice
¼ tsp oregano
Pinch of cumin
½ tsp salt
Pepper to taste

1. Combine all ingredients and mix lightly.

Tamales (Makes 6 dozen)

2 lb beef chuck roast
2 lb fresh pork shoulder
1 tbsp salt
4 garlic cloves, pressed
Water to cover meat
2 pkg dried cornhusks
½ lb dried pasilla chiles
1 lb lard
¼ c ground cumin
2 garlic cloves, minced
1 tsp salt
¾ c shortening (yellow)
½ c chili powder
5 lb fresh masa (or add stock to masa harina to hydrate)

1. Stew meat, salt, and garlic in simmering water until fork tender (about 3 hours). Save stock; sliver and finely chop the meat.
2. Remove silks and any dirt from cornhusks; cover completely with very hot water and soak for at least 2 hours (or overnight).
3. Remove seeds and stems of chiles and simmer in at least 2 cups of water until soft and skin starts to peel. Mash through a colander, discarding the skins and saving the pulp.
4. Melt ½ pound of lard; add cumin, garlic, salt, and chiles, simmer for 3 minutes, and then add meat. Add a little of the stock if necessary to create a spreading consistency. Simmer until needed.
5. Melt ½ pound of lard and ¾ cup shortening, and heat stock separately.
6. Work the fat mixture and chili powder into the masa harina and then gradually add enough stock to work the dough to a spreadable mass.
7. Spread individual cornhusks thinly with the masa, covering the left two-thirds of the husk, leaving the right edge bare. Place a long strip of meat filling down the middle of the masa.
8. Fold the left side of cornhusk over to the right edge of the masa; fold the right edge over to the fold on the left side of the tamale. Tie both ends with a strip of husk, or fold up one end to close the tamale; place vertically (closed end at bottom) on a rack in a Dutch oven.
9. Add 2 to 3 cups stock and continue arranging tamales in a circular pattern until all tamales are filled and the pan is full.
10. Cover tamales with cornhusks, and then steam in covered Dutch oven heated at simmering for 2½ hours until masa is firm in a center tamale.

Note: This recipe can feed a crowd. Preparation usually is a family project and serves as part of the entertainment for a family gathering. Tamales can be frozen for reheating in the microwave oven at a future date.

Frijoles Refritos (Serves 4–6)

1 lb pinto beans
Water to cover
½ c to 1 c lard
Salt and pepper to taste
¼ c diced Monterey Jack cheese (optional)

1. Wash and pick over beans to remove pebbles; cover with water in a saucepan, heat to boil, and turn off heat. Let stand for 1 hour. Bring to boil again and simmer until tender, adding water if needed.
2. Drain cooked beans and mash with potato masher.
3. Heat ½ cup lard in a skillet; stir in beans. Heat, stirring constantly, and add more lard if beans are dry. Add salt and pepper to taste.
4. Turn off heat; add cheese (if desired) and let it melt. Serve immediately.

Yam Fritters (Serves 4–6)

½ lb ground pork
1 tomato, chopped
1 onion, chopped
1 tbsp oil
½ tsp oregano
½ tsp salt
¼ tsp pepper
½ tsp cayenne
2 tsp chopped parsley
1 egg, hard cooked and chopped
2 lb cooked, mashed yams
1 egg, beaten
Oil for frying

1. Fry pork, tomato, and onion in oil until no pink remains in meat. Turn off heat and mix in seasonings, parsley, and chopped egg. Set aside.
2. Knead yams and beaten egg into a dough.
3. Pat 3 tablespoons of yams into a flat disk, place 1 teaspoon of meat in the center, and bring up dough edges to cover the filling in a football shape.
4. Fry balls at 375°F in deep fat for 4 to 5 minutes. Serve hot.

Mole de Olla (Serves 4)

4 boneless, skinless chicken breast halves
½ lb dried pasilla chiles
¼ lb dried California chiles
Boiling water to cover
⅓ c slivered almonds
3 garlic cloves, minced
½ onion, chopped
1 corn tortilla in small pieces
2 tbsp oil
4 whole cloves
1 stick cinnamon
6 peppercorns
2 tomatoes, seeded and peeled
1 c chicken bouillon
1 square unsweetened chocolate

1. Roast chicken uncovered at 400°F for 25 minutes.
2. Soak chiles covered with boiling water until soft. Drain, remove stems and seeds, and scrape pulp from peel.
3. Fry almonds, garlic, onion, and tortilla pieces in oil to golden brown. Drain.
4. Blend almond mixture, chiles, cloves, cinnamon, peppercorns, and tomato in blender, adding enough chicken bouillon to blend to a slightly thick, smooth consistency.
5. Simmer for 20 minutes, add chocolate, and heat just long enough to melt the chocolate.
6. Add chicken to the mole sauce and simmer for 5 minutes, stirring constantly until chicken is heated through.

Sopaipillas (Makes 30)

2 c all-purpose flour
1 tbsp baking powder
1 tsp salt
2 tbsp lard
¾ c water
Oil for frying
Honey

1. Combine flour, baking powder, and salt, and then cut into lard to the size of rice grains.
2. Stir the water all at once into the flour mixture to make dough.
3. On a lightly floured board, knead the entire ball of dough until smooth.
4. Lightly flour the board and rolling pin; roll dough to a 15″ × 18″ rectangle. Cut into 30 3″ × 3″ squares.
5. Fry a few at a time in hot oil (375°F), turning with a slotted spoon as they brown and rise so that both sides are golden brown.
6. Drain puffs on paper towels. Serve hot, with honey available to drip into the hollow after a corner has been bitten off.

Mexican Rice (Serves 4)

1 c long grain rice
2 tbsp oil
½ onion, chopped
½ garlic clove, minced
½ tsp salt
2 c chicken broth
4 oz canned tomato sauce

1. Soak rice in hot water for 15 minutes, rub with hands, drain, and rinse. Repeat with cold water until water is clear. Spread drained rice on clean towel to dry.
2. Briefly sauté rice in oil in a skillet, then add onion, garlic, and salt, and sauté until tender.
3. Add broth and tomato sauce; cover and simmer until liquid is absorbed and rice is tender and fluffy (30 to 40 minutes).

Capirotada (Bread Pudding) (Serves 8–10)

3 c water
2 sticks cinnamon
1 c raisins
11 pieces panocha (Mexican cone-shaped sugar pieces)
5 tbsp butter
1 loaf French bread, cut in 1″ thick slices
3 oz slivered almonds
2½ c grated cheddar cheese

1. Boil water, cinnamon, raisins, and panocha for 5 minutes. Remove cinnamon and let mixture cool.
2. Melt butter in skillet and fry six slices of bread on one side to a golden brown. Set aside.
3. Toast both sides of remaining bread slices in oven at 350°F.
4. Cover the bottom of a greased 9″ × 13″ × 2″ baking pan with the toasted slices.
5. Spoon half the raisin mixture and scatter half the almonds and cheese over the toasted slices.
6. Make a top layer of the butter-fried slices and top with remaining ingredients.
7. Bake in 350°F oven for 30 minutes to melt cheese.

Summary

Mexico and its Central American neighbors (Belize, Guatemala, El Salvador, Honduras, Nicaragua, Costa Rica, and Panama) stretch between the United States in the north and Colombia in the south to connect the two continents of the Americas. The terrain ranges from mountains to coastal lands, deserts to tropical jungles. Olmecs, Mayans, Zapotecs, and Toltecs were among the early dominant Indians; the Aztecs were in control of the large area centering around Mexico City when Cortés arrived from Spain in 1521 and conquered them. Other Europeans intervening included the French, Spanish, and English invasion of Mexico as well as the brief reign of Maximillian and Carlotta from 1864 to 1867.

The major religion of the region is Roman Catholic, and many of the holidays are religious celebrations. The culture emphasizes the importance of families, with women being the mothers and caretakers and men being the authority figures in families.

Corn, beans, wheat, and rice are key ingredients of the diet throughout the region. Tortillas made from corn or wheat flour are universally popular and eaten at most meals. Lard is the preferred fat. Pork, poultry, and beef are also eaten, the amount influenced significantly by the income level of the family. Other ingredients include tomatoes, chilies, cilantro, nopales, avocados, jicama, cumin, onions, garlic, and chocolate. Beverages include hot chocolate, atole, pulque, and tequila (the latter two from the agave or century plant).

Selected Sites

http://www.bbc.co.uk/history/discovery/exploration/conquistadors_01.shtml—Overview of the conquistadors in Central America and Mexico.

http://www.mexonline.com/mexfood.htm—Various topics such as Spanish/English vocabulary of food, Mexican culture, food, and history.

http://www.mexico-info.com/food.htm—Guide to some sources about Mexican food; sponsored by the Mexican Institute of Greater Houston.

http://www.sallys-place.com/food/ethnic_cusine/mexico.htm—Description of the history and cuisine of Mexico.

http://costa-rica-guide.com/Introduction/Recipes.htm—Recipes for favorite Costa Rican foods.

http://cp.settlement.org/english/honduras/eating.html—Brief description of food in Honduras.

http://www.belizeanjourneys.com/features/bzefood/newsletter.html—Illustrated comments by a student from Belize about how and what people there eat.

http://www.knowledgehound.com/topics/central_american_recipes.htm—Compilation of recipes from various Central American countries.

http://members.tripod.com/foro_emaus/BanPlantsCA.htm—Information about banana plantations in Central America.

http://www.foodsubs.com/Chilefre.html—Pictures and descriptions of several kinds of chilies.

Study Questions

1. Where is each of the following located: (a) Panama, (b) Mexico, (c) Yucatan Peninsula, (d) Nicaragua, (e) El Salvador, (f) Guatemala, (g) Costa Rica, (h) Honduras, and (i) Baja California?
2. Locate the region in which each of the following lived and indicate the approximate time when they were in power: (a) Zapotecs, (b) Aztecs, (c) Mixtecs, (d) Olmecs, and (e) Mayans.
3. Define (a) tortilla, (b) jícama, (c) nopales, (d) masa harina, (e) tamale, (f) enchilada, and (g) tostada.
4. Identify and describe at least three types of chilies.
5. Describe a typical schedule of meals in Central America and identify the types of food that might be included in the menus.

Bibliography

Algert, S.J., E. Brzezinski, and T.H. Ellison. 1998. Mexican American food practices, customs, and holidays. In *Ethnic and Regional Food Practices.* American Dietetic Association/American Diabetes Association. Chicago.

Barer-Stein, T. 1999. *You Eat What You Are.* 2nd ed. Firefly Books, Ltd. Ontario, Canada.

Bayless, R. and D.G. Bayless. 1987. *Authentic Mexican.* Morrow Cookbooks. New York.

Buckley, K. 1991. *Panama: The Whole Story.* Simon and Schuster. New York.

Cameron, S. and B. Box. 1999. *Mexico and Central America Handbook.* 10th ed. Passport Books. Chicago.

Cipriani, C. 1998. *Fodor's Belize and Guatemala.* Fodor's Travel Publications. New York.

Faneklli-Kuczmarski, M. et al. 1995. Food usage among Mexican-American, Cuban, and Puerto Rican adults. *Nutr. Today 30:* 30–37.

Foster, L.V. 1997. *Brief History of Mexico.* Facts on File. New York.

Leonard, J.N. 1968. *Latin American Cooking.* Time-Life Books. New York.

McGaffey, L. 1999. *Honduras.* Marshall Cavendish. New York.

Noble, J.W. et al. 1998. *Mexico.* 6th ed. Lonely Planet. Oakland, CA.

Palazuelos, S. 1991. *Mexico: The Beautiful Cookbook.* Harper Collins. New York.

Pearcy, G.E. 1980. *The World Food Scene.* Plycon Press. Redondo Beach, CA.

Reilly, M.J. 1991. *Mexico.* Marshall Cavendish. New York.

Rockwood, C.M. 1999. *Costa Rica.* Fodor's Travel Publications. New York.

Sanjur, D. 1995. *Hispanic Foodways, Nutrition, and Health.* Allyn and Bacon. Boston.

Sheehan, S. 1998. *Guatemala.* Marshall Cavendish. New York.

Winn, P. 1992. *Americas.* University of California Press. Berkeley, CA.

Zingarett, D. et al. 2001. *Central America on a Shoestring.* 4th ed. Lonely Planet. Oakland, CA.

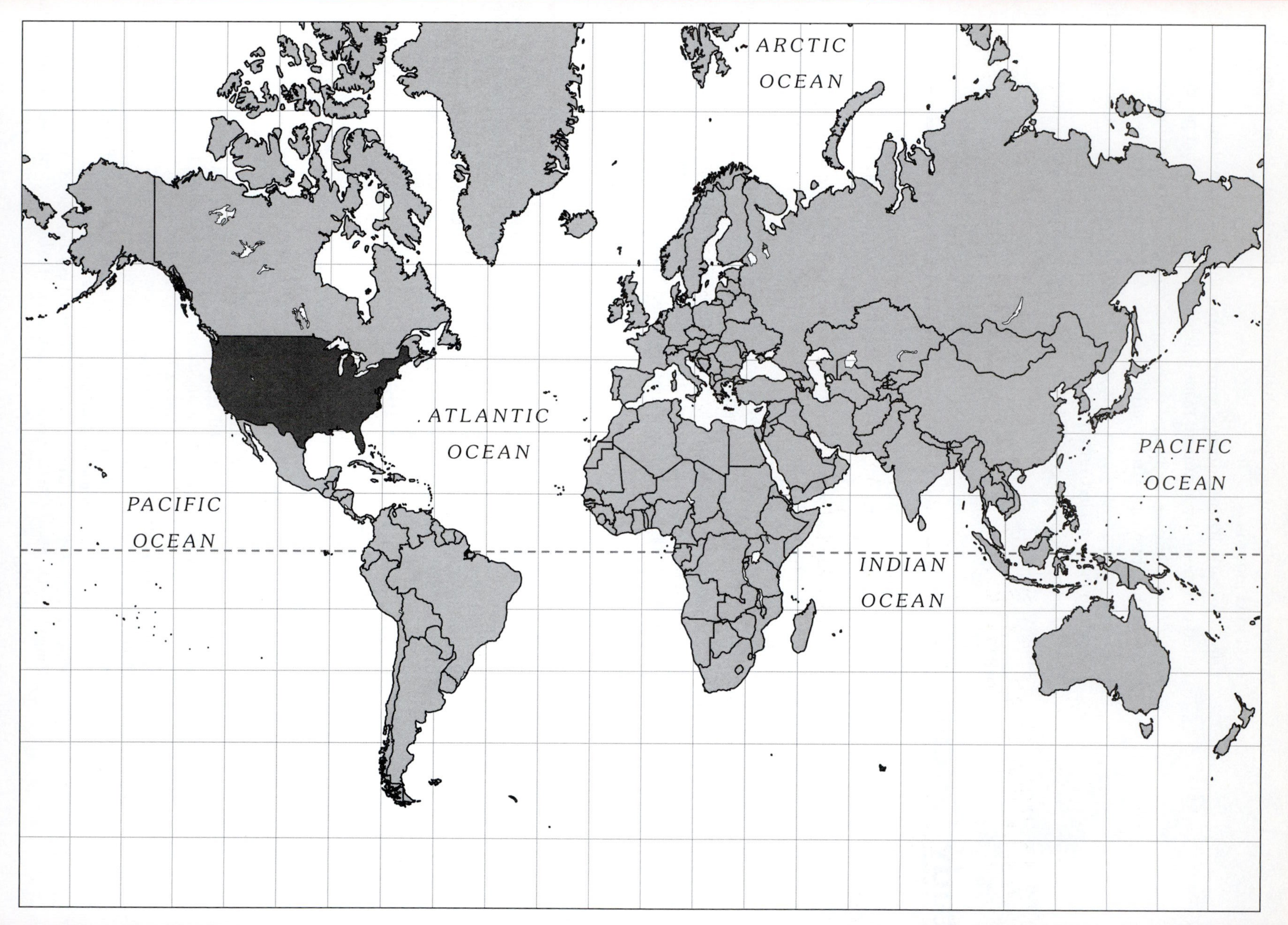
ARCTIC OCEAN
ATLANTIC OCEAN
PACIFIC OCEAN
PACIFIC OCEAN
INDIAN OCEAN

Part VII

America's Food Scene Today

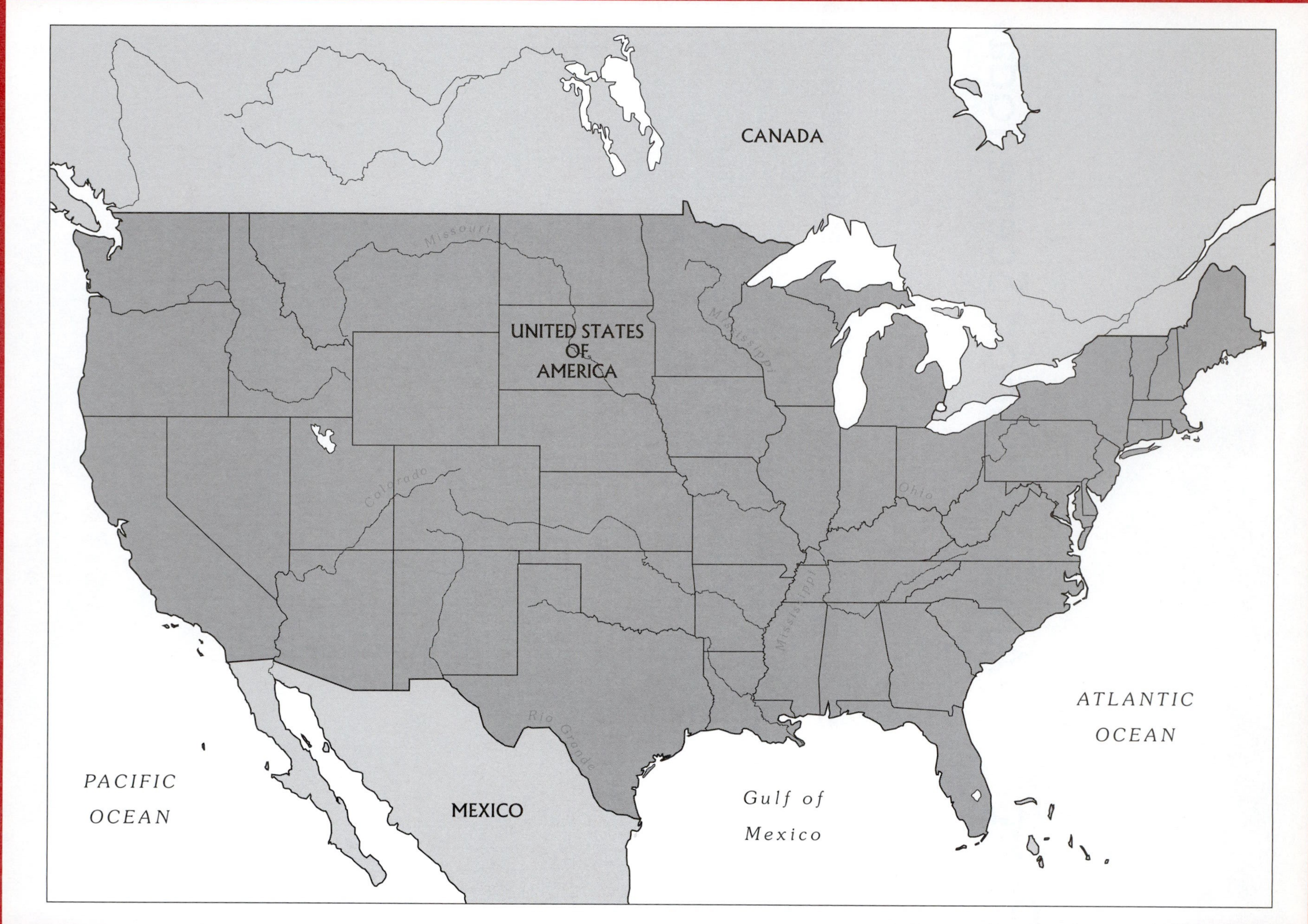
CANADA
UNITED STATES OF AMERICA
Missouri
Mississippi
Colorado
Ohio
Mississippi
Rio Grande
PACIFIC OCEAN
MEXICO
Gulf of Mexico
ATLANTIC OCEAN

23 United States

Traditional Regional Foods

Around the United States, food specialties have helped to define the food patterns of different regions. Probably the first area that comes to mind is the Northeast because that is where American History as a subject in school usually begins. Other major regions in terms of food patterns are the South, the Midwest, the Southwest, and the West.

The foods that characterize each region reflect the heritage of the people who established it. The food traditions that have been studied in previous chapters often contributed to the foods that developed into a cuisine characterizing each region, depending on the local traditions or the country of origin of the immigrants.

Northeastern Traditions

Native American Indians contributed to the dietary practices that the Pilgrims and other early settlers brought to the Northeast. Indians added wild turkey to the menus as well as corn, cranberries, and maple syrup. In addition, lobsters and clams were available. These early settlers cooked meats and vegetables in plain dishes typical of English cuisine. Special dishes that reflect the Northeast are Indian pudding, Boston brown bread, and Boston clam chowder.

Southern Cuisine

Settlers arrived from England along the Atlantic coast, but other significant groups shaping food in the South came from Africa (usually as slaves), France via Canada and the Caribbean, and Spain (via the Caribbean). Southern cooks combined familiar cultural dishes with such available foods as okra, greens, pork, and cornmeal. The result was that Southern cooking traditionally produced such specialties as deep-fat fried chicken, ham and red-eye gravy, biscuits, bacon, salt pork and beans, greens, and Hoppin' John (rice and black-eyed peas).

In southern Louisiana, two distinctive styles of cooking developed in the late 18th century as a result of immigrant groups arriving in that area. The Acadian French came from Nova Scotia and settled in the bayous and rural areas where they established **Cajun** cooking. This style can be described as simple cooking usually done in a single pot and often laced with fiery pepper. Examples of Cajun dishes that are famous include gumbo and jambalaya.

Cajun—Style of one-pot cooking developed in southern Louisiana based on combining fish or meat, local vegetables, and rice.

Creole—Flavorful cuisine of New Orleans and southern Louisiana that integrates spices from the Caribbean with cuisines brought by French, Spanish, and African immigrants.

Creole is the other unique cuisine; it developed in New Orleans and other urban centers in southern Louisiana. Wonderful spices brought by immigrants from the Caribbean blended with the French, African, and Spanish cuisines of other immigrants over two centuries ago to create Creole dishes, such as shrimp Creole.

Midwest Fare

British, Scandinavian, German, and some Italian immigrants frequently settled in the Midwest as the country was developing, and typical meals reflect their ethic of hard work and plenty of good, simple food. Chicken that is usually fried in some butter, mashed potatoes and gravy, corn on the cob, and apple pie immediately come to mind when one thinks about traditional foods in the Midwest. Excellent cheeses, sausages, and beers are available, due particularly to the Scandinavian and German settlers. Italians added pizza and some of their sauces and pastas to the mix.

Southwestern Food

In terms of real time, the Southwest cuisine developed before that in the Northeast because of the push of the Spaniards northward through Mexico. Some Spanish influences on Mexican food are seen in Southwestern foods (e.g., enchiladas, burritos, tacos). Beef in the form of steaks or shredded is used in traditional Southwest dishes, which is not surprising in view of the ranching that is typical in this part of the country. Guacamole, salsa (ranging from mild to killing hot), pinto beans, and tortillas are very much part of the food scene.

Western Dishes

Fusion is a word that may best embody the range of dishes typical of the West. This descriptor fits because cuisines from all around the world have migrated to this part of the nation. That cultural input has been combined with the wide array of produce that can be grown in California and some other parts of the West. The result is that no single picture emerges. The Chinese influenced food when they were brought to the area to help build the railroads. Although Mexican and Spanish influences were already defining the cuisine, Chinese ingredients began to be used in some dishes. Subsequently, many immigrants brought aspects of such unique cuisines as those from India and Vietnam. Creative cooks have blurred many of the lines between these cuisines to the point where *fusion* indeed describes food in the West.

Special foods in the West include Dungeness crab, clams, calamari, and many other ocean fish. The Northwest is known not only for its salmon, but also its excellent raspberries, other berries, and apples. California grows a wide range of produce, particularly strawberries, avocadoes, broccoli, artichokes, asparagus, and tree fruits. Nuts and rice are other foods grown in significant quantities for use in the West and the rest of the nation, too.

Recipes

Boston Clam Chowder (Northeastern) (Serves 4)

1 strip bacon, chopped
1 large onion, chopped
1 stalk celery, diced
1 garlic clove, minced
1 tbsp butter
½ tsp dried thyme
½ tsp dried basil
1½ tbsp flour
½ tsp salt
1 c bottled clam juice
1¼ c milk
2 medium Red Triumph potatoes, boiled and diced
1 6½-oz can clams

1. Sauté bacon, onion, celery, and garlic in butter over low heat, but avoid browning.
2. Stir in spices and flour; stir in clam juice gradually to make a smooth slurry before finally stirring in the milk.
3. Heat to boiling while stirring continuously to avoid lumps.
4. Add potatoes and clams (including their juice), and stir before simmering covered for 5 to 10 minutes.

Hoppin' John (Southern) (Serves 3)

1 onion, chopped
2 tsp bacon drippings
¾ c cooked ham, chopped
1 can (about 16 oz) black-eyed peas
¼ tsp cayenne pepper
2 c cooked rice

1. Sauté onion in bacon drippings.
2. Add the ham, black-eyed peas, and cayenne; stir before covering and simmering 5 to 10 minutes.
3. Add the rice and stir while heating to serving temperature.

Fried Chicken (Midwestern) (Serves 4)

1 frying chicken or 4 pieces chicken parts
½ c milk
1 c butter
½ c flour
1 tsp season salt
½ tsp ground pepper

1. Soak chicken in milk while preheating oven to 400°F.
2. Put butter in a baking dish that will hold chicken pieces in a single layer; place in oven to heat and melt the butter.
3. Put flour and seasonings in a 1-quart plastic bag and mix before adding chicken pieces and coating each with the mixture.
4. Remove baking dish from oven, and arrange chicken pieces with the skin side down in the butter.
5. Bake for 20 minutes; turn each piece over and return to the oven to bake 20 more minutes.

Sopaipillas (Southwestern) (Serves 6)

2 c flour
1½ tsp baking powder
½ tsp salt
2 tbsp shortening
¾ c water
Oil for deep-fat frying

1. Stir the flour, baking powder, and salt together.
2. Add the shortening and cut it in with a pastry blender until the size of rice grains.
3. Add water and stir with a fork until the dough is all moistened and holds together.
4. Turn out onto a floured bread board, flour fingers, and knead the dough by folding over, rotating, and pressing lightly with the fingertips; continue folding, rotating, and pressing about 9 times or until the dough is cohesive. Wrap in plastic wrap and refrigerate at least 30 minutes.
5. Preheat oil to 375°F, starting heating after dough has been chilling 20 minutes.
6. Divide the dough into 2 pieces. Add flour to the board and then roll one of the pieces into a thin rectangle. Cut into 3″ squares. Repeat with the second piece of dough.
7. Carefully place squares in the hot oil, frying very few at a time so the oil stays hot enough. Use tongs to turn them over once so that both sides brown nicely.
8. Remove from oil with tongs and drain on paper toweling.
9. Serve hot with honey available to drizzle into the center after diners bite off a corner and reveal the cavity in the middle.

California Salad Toss (Western) (Serves 4)

1 head Bibb lettuce, torn into pieces
8 leaves red leaf lettuce, torn into pieces
8 arugula leaves
2 green onions, thinly sliced
4 radishes, sliced
1 carrot, sliced
1 stalk celery, diced
1 small jar marinated artichoke hearts
½ c alfalfa sprouts
½ c Chinese snow pea pods
2 tbsp diced red pepper
⅓ c crumbled feta cheese
Salt
Coarsely ground black pepper
3 tbsp olive oil
1 tbsp balsamic vinegar

1. Spin the washed lettuce pieces in a salad spinner; place all ingredients except the oil and vinegar in a large salad bowl.
2. When ready to serve, toss the salad with the oil and vinegar. (NOTE: The oil and vinegar cruets can be placed on the table for each person to add to the salad, as desired.)

The Changing Scene

Just as the immigrants shaped the traditional foods in various parts of the United States in earlier times, the influx of immigrants today is altering the types of food eaten in different regions of the country. Many large U.S. cities today have enclaves of the various ethnic groups that compose our rich cultural mix. The foods in the markets and the dishes that are prepared most frequently reflect the cultural heritage and dietary patterns of specific cultural groups rather than simply the region of the country where the people live.

Due to increased mobility of the population and the diverse, large numbers of immigrants, regional food patterns are much less clear than they once were. Instead, the palate of food choices is broadening in many markets, particularly in urban settings, because of the increasing cultural milieu. Food traditions brought by immigrants when they came to this country provide comfort and pleasure in their new lives. They also have broadened the dining experiences of many others.

Evolving Demographics

Changes in population size and demographics are discussed in this section to highlight the reasons why our menus are increasingly reflecting of the way people choose to eat all around the world.

European Immigration

The United States is a nation that has always admitted immigrants from other parts of the world to start new lives here. Dreams of better lives as a result of increased riches, freedom, and escape from political risks are just some of the many factors that have motivated people to immigrate to America. Many immigrants in the 19th century were from Europe (Table 23.1), with Great Britain, Ireland, and Germany contributing a little less than half a million people to the American influx between 1830 and 1860, according to Rischin 1989.

These three countries plus Scandinavia were the source of about 10 million more new arrivals in the second wave of immigration that occurred between 1860 and 1890 (Figure 23.1). The third wave (between 1890 and 1930) brought a different mixture of Europeans from Greece, Austria-Hungary, Italy, Poland, Russia, Portugal, and Spain. The numbers during this third European immigrant wave totaled another 22 million. These waves of emigration from Europe resulted in a population that was predominantly white, and had some commonalities as well as many differences. The focus for these immigrants was on fitting in by learning English and working to support their families.

African Immigrants

This European heritage presents only part of the picture, for workers from other parts of the world became part of the nation's population as this fledgling country developed agriculturally and industrially in the 18th and 19th centuries. African slaves were reluctant immigrants exploited by southern plantation owners to develop their lands and fortunes. This chapter in American history remains a legacy still being resolved as African-Americans seek better lives for themselves and their families today.

Asian Immigrants

Asians also entered this country as strong workers to aid in building railroads and performing other work required to develop the American West in the 19th century. The majority of these workers came from China (Figure 23.2), and many stayed in this country after their original tasks were finished. Subse-

Table 23.1 Origins of U.S. Legal Immigrants from 1820 to 1976

Region of Origin	*Approximate Percent of Total Immigrants*					
	1820–60	*1861–1900*	*1901–30*	*1931–60*	*1961–70*	*1971–76*
Northern and western Europe	95	68	23	41	17	7
Canada	3	7	11	21	12	4
Southern and eastern Europe	—	22	58	17	15	13
Asia	—	2	3	5	13	32
Latin America	—	—	5	15	39	41
Other	2	1	—	1	3	3

Adapted from data from Population Reference Bureau.

Figure 23.1 This church on Cape Cod in Massachusetts is representative of the religion familiar to Americans whose heritage was often rooted in Protestant parts of Europe.

quently, wars at various places around the world have triggered immigration from Asia and other regions. The influx of Vietnamese resulting from American involvement in the Vietnam War created a significant presence that is evident today (approximately 225,000 people from there as of 2002). Political ties with the Philippines created the opportunity for many Filipinos to immigrate into the United States.

Current Immigrants

Economic opportunity clearly is a strong factor motivating immigration to the United States, even in the face of legal limits on the numbers admitted annually. Illegal border crossings and smuggling via land, sea, and air currently are taxing

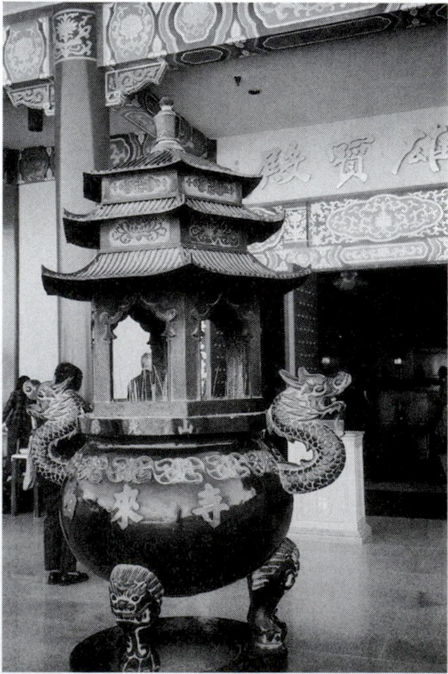

Figure 23.2 Buddhism was brought to the United States by early Chinese immigrants and then expanded as other immigrants from Asian countries followed.

Table 23.2 Immigration Trends in the United States from 1981–2002*

Country of Origin	*Total, 1981–1990*	*Total, 1991–2000*	*2002*†
Europe	705,600	1,311,400	174,200
Mexico	1,653,300	2,251,400	219,380
India	261,900	383,300	71,105
China	388,800	424,600	61,282
Philippines	495,300	505,600	51,308
Vietnam	401,400	421,100	33,627
El Salvador	214,600	217,400	31,168
Cuba	159,200	180,900	28,272
Bosnia/Herzogovina	Not available	39,100	25,373

*Data from U.S. Census, 2000.
†The figures are for one year only; other columns are for 10 years.

U.S. Immigration and Naturalization Service—Federal agency responsible for enforcing immigration and naturalization regulations and laws.

the **U.S. Immigration and Naturalization Service**'s resources as an attempt is made to control immigration.

The trends in sources of immigrants over the years are presented in Table 23.2. Clearly, the demographics in the United States are changing significantly as a result of the decline in immigration from Europe and the dramatic increases from Asia and Latin America (Figure 23.3). These data reflect legal immigration and ignore the significant numbers who enter unauthorized (Table 23.3), particularly along the southwestern border that stretches from Texas to California. Of the total unauthorized immigrants in 2000, 68.7 percent were from Mexico and the next most numerous were from El Salvador (2.7 percent).

Figures on immigration changes represent only a partial picture because births and deaths in the resident population also contribute to demographic changes. Data from the U.S. Bureau of the Census (Table 23.4) indicate the changes in the racial mix. A significant increase in the percentage of Hispanics is occurring and is predicted to continue, while the percentage of Caucasians is decreasing. Other minorities are also increasing, but at a significantly slower rate than Hispanics.

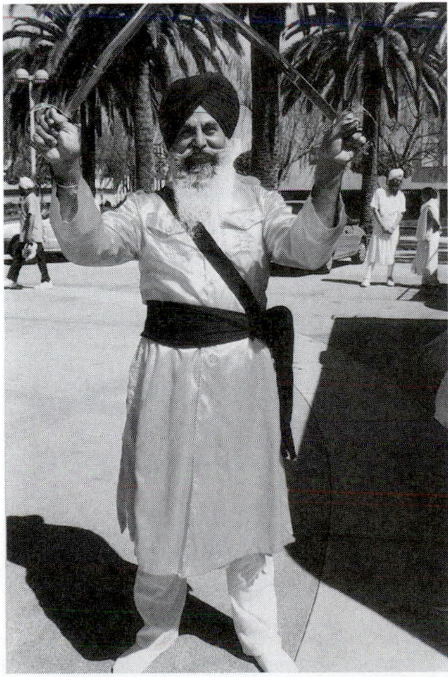

Figure 23.3 Sikhs, many of whom are immigrants from India, celebrate their religion in Los Angeles on a day of worship and a parade for Sikhs from as far away as San Francisco.

Table 23.3 Unauthorized immigration estimates*

State	*1990*	*2000*	*Percent in 2000*†	*2004*‡
Total United States	3,500,000	7,000,000	2.5	10,300,000
California	1,476,000	2,209,000	6.5	2,400,000
Texas	438,000	1,041,000	5.0	1,4000,00
New York	357,000	489,000	2.6	650,000
Illinois	194,000	432,000	3.5	400,000
Florida	239,000	337,000	2.1	850,000
Arizona	88,000	283,000	5.5	200,000–250,000
Georgia	34,000	228,000	2.8	500,000
North Carolina	26,000	206,000	2.6	300,000
Colorado	31,000	144,000	3.3	200,000–250,000

* Data from U.S. Immigration and Naturalization Service.
† Percentage of total population living in the state in 2000.
‡ Adapted from Passell, J.S. 2005. *Unauthorized Migrants: Numbers and Characteristics.* Pew Hispanic Center. Washington, D.C.

The overall changes are occurring somewhat differently within the various states (Tables 23.5 and 23.6). In 2002, California was the state receiving the most legal immigrants (Figure 23.3), followed by New York, Florida, Texas, Illinois, and Georgia, in descending order. The influx of undocumented immigrants (Table 23.3) adds to the impact of immigration on many of the same states. The striking increases in the Latino and Asian populations in California are partially the result of geography (a long border with Mexico and a logical entry point for arriving Asian immigrants).

Nationwide, the numbers of Asians and Latinos have increased significantly, although African-Americans remain the largest minority group. The figures are quite remarkable and clearly indicate that the United States is undergoing significant demographic changes that are creating an evolving pattern affecting almost all aspects of people's lives, including their diets and the foods available to them. Although these states are encountering the changes accompanying increased cultural diversity significantly now, most states are noticing similar, but smaller, shifts in demographics.

Immigrant Adjustments

"Little Saigon" is the local designation for part of Westminster, Orange County, in southern California (Figure 23.4). This name is a proud indication that the area is the focal point for the largest Vietnamese American community in the United States (approximately 200,000 in southern California). Vietnamese political refugees arriving at the peak of migration in 1975, when Saigon fell, were distributed quite broadly around the nation.

The cultural isolation this approach to resettlement created was too painful for many of the new immigrants. They moved a second time to cluster in cultural

Table 23.4 Racial Mix of U.S. Population*

Race	*Percent in 2000*	*Percent in 2003*	*Percent predicted in 2050*
White alone	75.1	66.8	50
Black alone	12.3	12.8	15
Hispanic	12.5	13.7	24
Asian	3.6	4.1	8
American Indian	0.9	1.0	2

* From U.S. Bureau of the Census figures (exceeds 100 percent) due to rounding of figures.

Table 23.5 Racial Distribution in the United States in 2000*

Foreign Born (percent)	*States*
>15	California, Florida, Hawaii, Nevada, New York
10–14.9	Arizona, Connecticut, Illinois, Massachusetts, Rhode Island, Texas
5–9.9	Alabama, Alaska, Colorado, Idaho, Kansas, Michigan, Minnesota, New Mexico, North Carolina, Oregon, Utah, West Virginia
<5	Arkansas, Georgia, Indiana, Iowa, Kentucky, Louisiana, Maine, Missouri, Montana, Nebraska, New Hampshire, North Dakota, Ohio, Oklahoma, Pennsylvania, South Carolina, Tennessee, Vermont, West Virginia, Wisconsin

*U.S. Census 2000.

enclaves along the eastern seaboard from Boston to Washington, the Gulf Coast from Texas to Mississippi, the Pacific Northwest, San Jose and the Silicon Valley in California's Bay Area, and southern California's Orange and San Diego counties.

The consequence of such population movements has been a growing appreciation of the culture, including the cuisine, of the Vietnamese, as they have brought demand for the unique food ingredients that help to define Vietnamese food and have held their festivals and celebrations, not only for themselves, but also for their new neighbors in their new land.

This broadening of cultural awareness and understanding of new food patterns is occurring in many parts of the country and for other immigrant ethnic groups, as well as for the Vietnamese. The specific cultural and ethnic groups differ with the particular region or location within the country, but tremendous opportunities for becoming acquainted with new foods and other cultural components are widely available and continue to increase as more immigrants arrive and are assimilated (Figure 23.5).

Restaurants and ethnic markets are wonderful places to gain knowledge and to experience foods that may be quite new to you. The potential may be more varied in an urban rather than a rural setting. For instance, among the ethnic neighborhoods scattered around the Los Angeles area now are German, Chinese, Latino, Korean, African-American, East Indian, Vietnamese, Japanese, and Thai. This list does not include the many other small spots where special ethnic markets and restaurants are clustered and shoppers can experience foods from the Middle East, Greece, Italy, and just about any other place you wish to name.

Table 23.6 Legal Immigration in United States and Selected States in 2002 (U.S. Census data, 2004)

Country	*U.S.*	*California*	*New York*	*Florida*	*Texas*	*Illinois*	*New Jersey*
Total	1,063,733	291,216	114,827	90,819	88,365	47,235	57,721
Mexico	219,380	105,699	2,250	3,822	44,694	11,461	1,209
India	71,105	18,265	4,728	1,652	4,294	5,197	9,683
China	61,282	19,494	9,872	1,022	2,561	2,768	2,966
Philippines	51,308	21,971	2,319	1,897	2,258	2,451	3,111
Vietnam	33,627	13,126	760	887	3,704	594	557
El Salvador	31,168	13,497	5,123	665	3,289	266	933
Cuba	28,272	548	449	22,262	87	128	1,274
Bosnia/Herzegovina	25,373	901	2,074	1,926	293	1,483	211

Figure 23.4 This large shopping mall in Westminster ("Little Saigon") attracts Vietnamese immigrants from all of Southern California; it provides wonderful flavors of their original country.

Ethnic Celebrations

Special holiday celebrations (Figure 23.6) of ethnic groups also draw attention to the increasing cultural richness in America. Iranians now living in Southern California (estimated to be about 600,000 in the region in 2000) mark their new year (coincident with the beginning of spring, the vernal equinox) with a 13-day celebration that includes prayer, purification and rejuvenation of the spirit, gift giving, and feasting, and culminates in a huge gathering at a public park to mark the end of the celebration.

Kwanzaa—African-American holiday lasting a week at the end of the year to celebrate African-American heritage.

Cinco de Mayo—Celebration on May 5 honoring Mexican defeat of the French in 1862 at Puebla; celebrations in the United States also recognize the Mexican Americans living in this country.

Kwanzaa is an African-American holiday (December 26 to January 1) celebrated in Los Angeles since 1966, an event that was inspired by Maulana Ron Karenga, who was at that time chair of the Black Studies Department at California State University, Long Beach. This celebration of African-American heritage has spread to various points in the United States and abroad to include parts of West Africa. It is estimated that 20 million people enjoy this tradition annually, despite its recent founding.

Cinco de Mayo, which is celebrated on May 5 in many locales with a significant presence of Mexican Americans, is yet another highly visible holiday celebration that emphasizes the importance of our nation's ever-broadening cultural heritage.

Figure 23.5 This beautiful Hindu temple in Southern California is a place of worship and comfort for many Hindus from India now living in the United States.

Figure C.145 A pagoda and temples with intricate designs decorating their walls are the site of worship for Buddhists in Luang Prabang, the old capital in northern Laos.

Figure C.146 A setting sun is a prelude to a tranquil evening on the shore of the Mekong River at Luang Prabang, Laos.

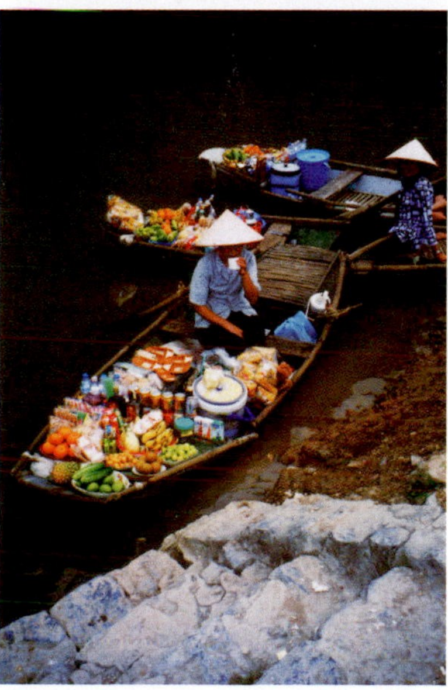

Figure C.147 Women vendors tout their wares from their boats near Hanoi, Vietnam.

Figure C.148 The street market in Hanoi, the capital of Vietnam, is alive with various prospective ingredients for tonight's dinner.

Figure C.149 Shoppers can purchase somewhat more convenient ingredients at the street markets in Hanoi, Vietnam.

Figure C.150 In the rural areas near Ho Chi Minh City (formerly Saigon) in Vietnam, countless rice paper wrappers for spring rolls dry in the sun on bamboo racks.

Figure C.151 Local farmers fence off small fish farms along the channels in the meandering Mekong Delta in southern Vietnam.

Figure C.152 This parade celebrates a Hindu festival in Bali; the predominant religion on other Indonesian islands is Muslim.

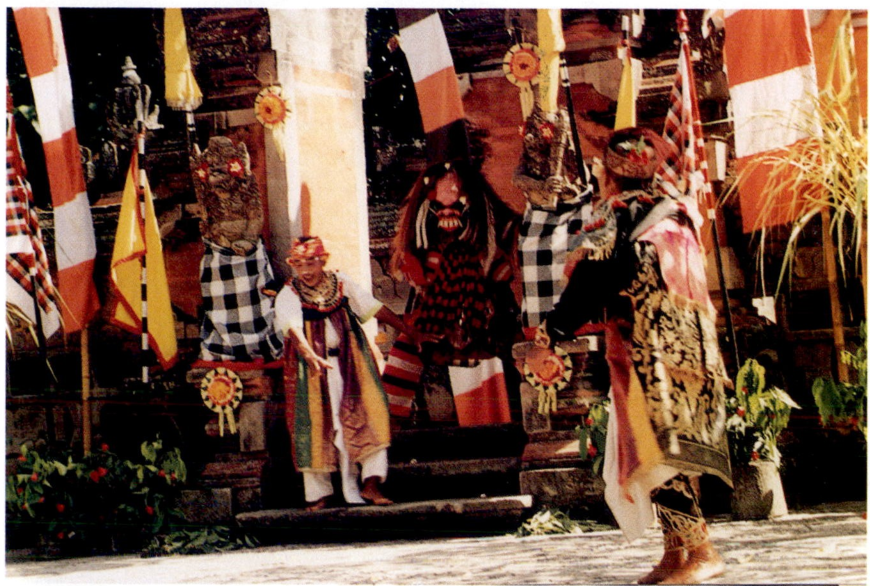

Figure C.153 Colorful costumes and frightening masks enable dancers to bring alive traditional folklore on Bali, one of the islands that compose Indonesia.

Figure C.154 Her lovely Polynesian smile complements the beauty of tempting fruits marketed in Papeete on the island of Tahiti, one of the Society Islands in the South Pacific.

Figure C.155 The starch-rich root of taro (looking somewhat like a bulb) emerges from the ground that is shaded by the plant's large leaves.

Figure C.156 Coconut palm trees and land crabs add to the available foods on Bora Bora in French Polynesia in the South Pacific.

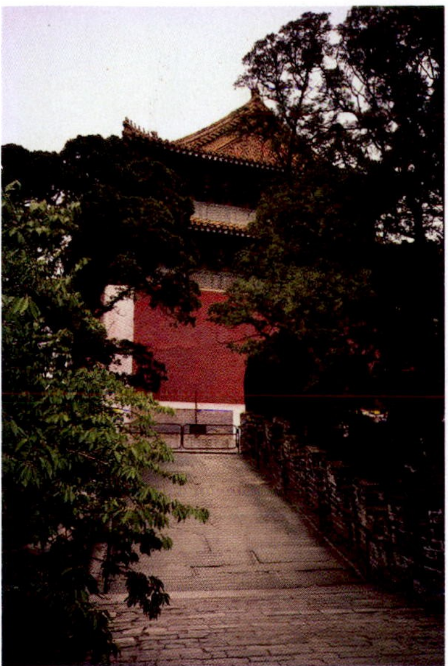

Figure C.157 Tombs of the Emperors from the Ming Dynasty (13th to 17th centuries) are located a short distance outside Beijing, China.

Figure C.158 Buddhist monks perform rituals and chant their prayers in this temple in Shanghai, China.

Figure C.159 Chinese architectural designs stress harmony with nature, as can be seen in the complex where Du Fu, a Chinese poet from Chengdu, lived during the 8th century.

Figure C.160 Oranges are a special treat in Chengdu, China, and may be served on a lazy Susan at dinner.

Figure C.161 The Great Wall of China was ordered built by the first Emperor of China more than 2000 years ago to hold back the Mongol hordes, but today tourists besiege it.

Figure C.162 This market boasts a wide selection of different varieties of rice for its customers.

Figure C.163 Birdcages on sale in a market in Xian are evidence of the popularity of birds as pets in China.

Figure C.164 Dried foods, including fish and mushrooms of various types, are sold alongside dried legumes and spices in this market in Beijing, China.

Figure C.165 Tai Chi is performed faithfully in groups in public parks in China every morning.

Figure C.166 Traditional dress for Korean women includes a long, gathered skirt (chima) and a short jacket tied off-center with a bow (chogori).

Figure C.167 One of four very fierce guards at the entrance to a Buddhist temple in South Korea.

Figure C.168 A young Buddhist monk worships at a Buddhist temple in the northeastern mountains of South Korea.

Figure C.169 Eager vendors in Pusan, Korea, market their fish that is barely out of the sea.

Figure C.170 Mollusks and crustaceans are part of the ocean catch sold dockside at the outdoor fish market in Pusan, Korea.

Figure C.171 Koreans eagerly eat their meal of smgye t'ang (rice-stuffed small hen baked in broth) and kimchi.

Figure C.172 The original Golden Pavilion was built in Kyoto, Japan, to be the home of shogun Ashika Yoshimitsu, but became a Zen temple when the shogun died in 1408. The present building, a precise reconstruction, was built in 1955 after the original was destroyed by fire.

Figure C.173 The Great Buddha of Kamakura, (cast in bronze in 1252 and still the second largest in Japan) has been exposed to the elements since a tsunami in the 15th century washed away its protecting temple.

Figure C.174 This Shinto shrine is tucked into a small corner of a neighborhood in Kyoto, Japan.

Figure C.175 Baked sweet potatoes are available to ward off the chill on a cold day at the deer park and temple in Nara, Japan.

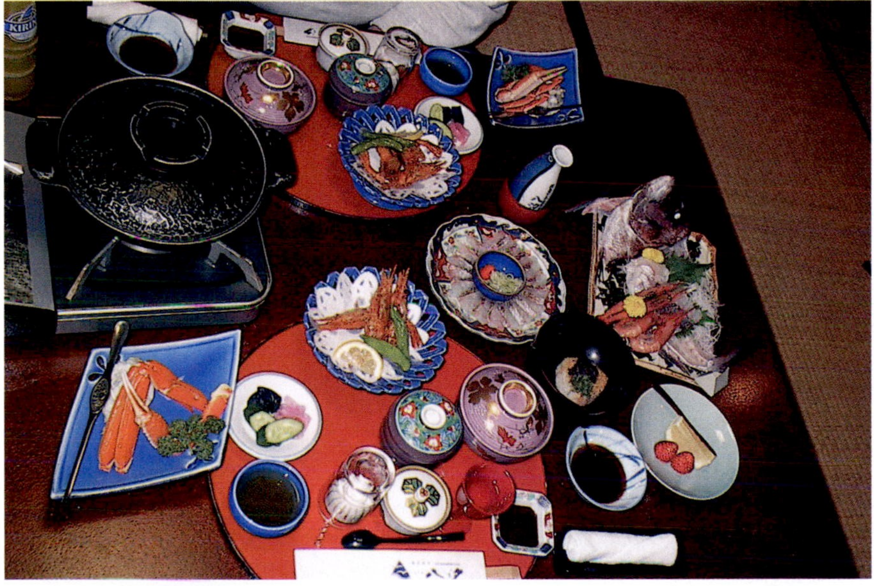

Figure C.176 The importance of art to the Japanese is evident in the beautifully designed dishes and artistic display of food at this festive meal. (Photo courtesy of Madoka Watabe-Betzel.)

Figure C.177 Machu Picchu, the remote city of the Incas hidden in the Andes in Peru, was at its zenith before Pizarro's men conquered the Incas in the early 16th century. Today's visitors see a partial reconstruction. (Photo courtesy of Bill Malcolm.)

Figure C.178 The principal cathedral of Santiago, Chile, in the Plaza de Armas still reflects the heritage begun by de Valdivia, the city's Spanish founder, even though this fourth structure was rebuilt in the mid-18th century after earthquakes had destroyed the previous three.

Figure C.179 The turbulent geologic history of South America is revealed in Chile, where Osorno (volcano near Puerto Montt) and the Andes Mountains shape life today.

Figure C.180 Chilean wines produced from their local vineyards are exported around the world; Chilean fruits are shipped during summers there to northern markets that are experiencing winter's chill.

Figure C.181 This food stall in Montivideo, Uruguay, features a sizzling barbecue on which various sausages, chicken, beef steaks, kebabs, and large red peppers are grilled to perfection to satisfy the hearty appetites of local diners.

Figure C.182 Rio de Janeiro's fabled beaches, as seen along the Atlantic shore from atop Sugar Loaf Mountain, are a highlight of this major city in Brazil, which was formerly a possession of Portugal.

Figure C.183 Sugarcane, a major crop on Caribbean islands, is the source of two major export items, sugar and rum.

Figure C.184 The crumbling remains of a sugar factory and its chimney provide a haunting reminder of the long-ago days of sugarcane plantations and slavery in the Caribbean islands.

Figure C.185 The yellow pod from the Theobroma cacao tree contains chocolate nibs, clusters of red cashew apples are on the branch, and the curved nuts that grow in their separate shell are in the bowl.

Figure C.186 A fisherman on Union Island in the Windward Islands painstakingly mends his fishing net before testing his luck in the warm Caribbean waters.

Figure C.187 From the old Spanish fort in San Juan, Puerto Rico, the modern city can be seen, its shoreline being swept by waves from the Atlantic Ocean.

Figure C.188 The Panama Canal traverses the Isthmus of Panama north to south, providing the essential shipping link between the Caribbean and Pacific Oceans.

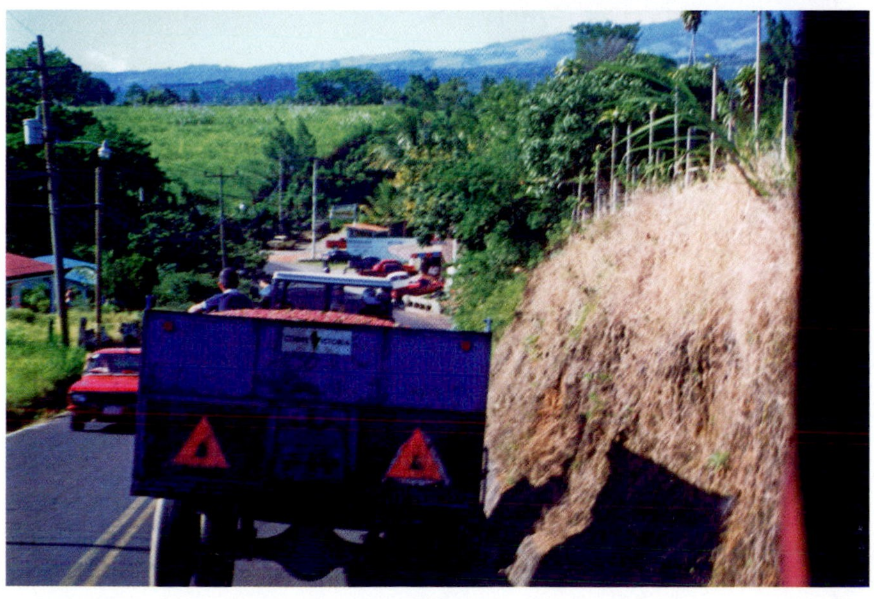

Figure C.189 Coffee cherries grown in the lush highlands of Costa Rica are transported in this truck to the roasting facility.

Figure C.190 Squash of various types, taro, garlic, and bananas are among the common vegetables and fruits used in Central American kitchens.

Figure C.191 Mayan pyramids, such as this one in Chichen Itza on the Yucatan Peninsula, continue to document the rich cultural heritage of Mexico and other nations in Central America. (Photo courtesy of Paul Peterson.)

Figure C.192 Tortilla chips and salsa accompany this traditional Mexican meal of chile rellenos, enchilada, guacamole, rice, and beans.

Figure 23.6 Float in a holiday parade commemorates the vision of Our Lady of Guadeloupe, an important celebration for Hispanic Catholics in East Los Angeles.

Immigrants from around the world have brought their religions with them, resulting in construction of places of worship quite different from the traditional churches and synagogues that dominated much of the United States until just the past few years. Religious structures in the United States now include Hindu shrines, Buddhist temples, and mosques, as well as Christian and Jewish places of worship. In 2000, Ramadan, Christmas, and Hanukkah happened to fall at approximately the same time. Public displays celebrating these three major religious events (Figures 23.7, 23.8, and 23.9) occurred together at a major intersection in Mission Viejo, California, clearly showing the evolving demographic shifts occurring in the United States today.

Religion

Religion is another increasingly diverse part of the nation's rich mixture of beliefs, traditions, and cultures. Christianity has been a prominent religion in the United States since its founding as colonies. Various Protestant faiths and Catholicism continue to draw large numbers of followers throughout the nation. Other faiths that have been practiced here for many years include Seventh Day Adventists and Jesus Christ of Latter Day Saints.

Eastern religions are becoming increasingly prominent in various communities around the United States today. Islamic mosques, Buddhist shrines and Hindu temples, now are available to worshipers, with the temples being considerably more numerous than the shrines.

Jewish synagogues and temples are concentrated in New York, Los Angeles, Miami, Ft. Lauderdale, and Chicago (in descending number of worshipers). Surprisingly, the Jewish population in the United States in 1997 exceeded that in Israel.

Smaller groups also add to the religious scene; for example, the Ethiopian Christian Church. Eastern Orthodox churches also often add their celebrations to the cultural mix.

Muslim presence in America can be seen anywhere from the mosque on a Navajo Indian reservation in New Mexico to those in cities. Worshipers originate from many parts of the globe (particularly from Southeast Asia) and various races (African-Americans, represent more than 40 percent of this presence).

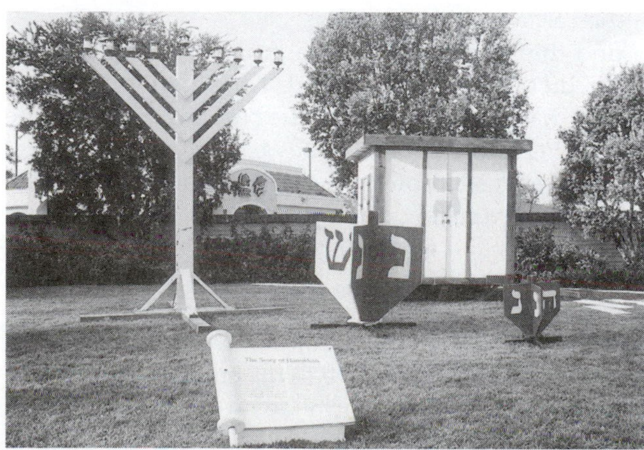

Figure 23.7 Jewish street corner display in celebration of Hanukkah in Mission Viejo, California.

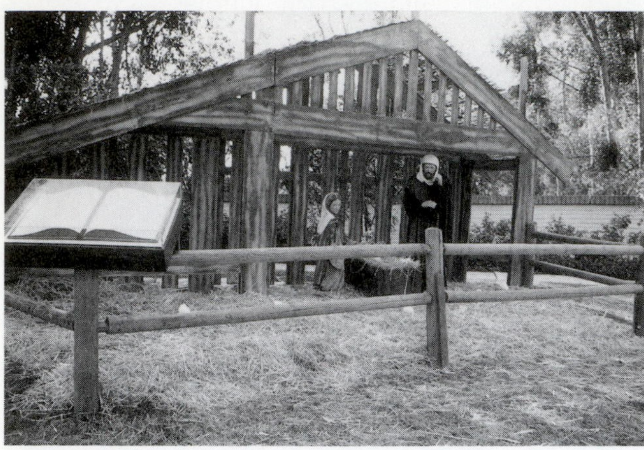

Figure 23.8 Manger scene is displayed at Christmas in Mission Viejo, California.

The First House of Worship on Earth
Season's Greetings
The Islamic Community in Mission Viejo

Figure 23.9 Giant photograph of a mosque is displayed in Mission Viejo, California, to celebrate the Muslim observance of Ramadan.

New Foods in the Marketplace

Depending on where you live, you may find some unfamiliar food items in your local markets and restaurants. Their presence is a clear indication of the evolving cultural blend in your neighborhood. A spirit of adventure will be helpful as you reach out for new food experiences. A basic ingredient guide may help you translate and enjoy your cultural food experiments. The listings in Tables 23.7 through 23.15 indicate the familiar food categories into which different ethnic foods fit (breads and cereals, vegetables and fruits, meats and related protein foods, dairy, and fats and oils, and others, such as sweets and sauces).

Recent immigrants can find this new country a daunting place to find the familiar foods that formed their diets in their homeland. Labels are difficult or impossible for them to read if they have not yet learned the basics of English. The feeling of helplessness that shopping can create becomes easy to understand if you venture into an ethnic market and attempt to figure out what some of the foods are and how to prepare them. Fortunately, the large wave of immigrants in the last few years has created such demand for their basic food commodities in some communities that enterprising merchants are importing and stocking a wide assortment of the foods so important to immigrants (and to others who seek knowledge and experience in the foods of other cultures).

Most cities have some ethnic markets appropriate to the cultural diversity of the specific locale. Lingering visits at such markets provide an invaluable look at the most important ingredients needed to prepare the dishes of that specific cuisine. You will learn even more if you purchase some items and prepare them

Table 23.7 Selected African Foods Categorized by Food Groups

Breads and Cereals	*Produce*		*Meats and Proteins*	*Dairy*	*Fats and Oils*	*Other*
	Vegetables	*Fruits*				
Corn	Amaranth leaves	Akee	Acacia seeds	Camel milk	Dendé oil	Cacao seeds
Fonio	Baobab pulp	Cape gooseberry	Agobono seeds		Palm oil	Coffee
Guinea Corn	Cassava	Cashew apple	Alligator			
Hungary rice	Chilies	Citrus	Antelope			
Kaffir corn	Fufu	Mango	Barracuda			
Millet	Gari	Melon	Bat			
Sorghum	Greens	Monkey bread pulp	Beef			
Tef	Iyan	Papaya	Bonito			
Wheat	Karkadeh flower pods and leaves	Roseapple	Bream			
	Manioc		Caterpillars			
	Peppers		Cod (dried, salted)			
	Plantain		Crickets			
	Potato		Crocodile			
	Sweet potato leaves		Dorado			
	Taro		Goat			
	Yam		Grasshoppers			
			Groundnuts			
			Grubs			
			Kaffir pea			
			Lamb			
			Legumes			
			Tilapia			

Table 23.8 Selected Asian Foods Categorized by Food Groups

Breads and Cereals	*Produce*		*Meats and Proteins*	*Dairy*	*Fats and Oils*	*Other*
	Vegetables	*Fruits*				
Acorn noodles	Amaranth leaves	Durian	Azuki beans	Donkey milk	Pork fat	Barley tea
Bao	Bamboo shoots	Fuzzy melon	Barracuda	Yak milk	Sesame oil	Bird's nest
Buckwheat	Bok choy	Japanese plum	Bat			Boxthorn tea
Congee	Bottle gourd	Kumquat	Beans			Five spice powder
Millet	Bracken fern	Loquat	Blowfish			Ginseng tea
Mochi	Chinese cabbage	Lychee	Bonito			Rice vinegar
Rice noodles, sticky sweet flour	Chinese kale	Persimmon	Caterpillars			Rice wine
Soba	Chinese mustard greens		Chicken			Sake
Sorghum	Chinese spinach		Crab			Soy sauce
Udon	Cloud ears		Dog			
Wheat	Daikon		Dried beans			
Wonton	Eggplant		Duck			
	Garlic		Eel			
	Ginger root		Eggs (fermented, preserved, quail, turtle)			
	Gobo		Fugu			
	Hairy cucumber		Miso			
	Kelp		Mung beans, curd			
	Kimchee (cabbage, cucumber, radish)		Pigeon			
	Laver		Pork			
	Lotus root		Roe			
	Mushrooms		Sea cucumber			
	Nori		Sea urchin			
	Peppers		Shark fin			
	Purslane		Shrimp			
	Seaweeds		Silkworm pupa			
	Snow peas		Snail Snake			
	Taro		Soy products			
	Wasabi		Tofu			
	Water chestnut		Yellowtail			
	Winter melon					

Table 23.9 Selected Indian (Asian) Foods Categorized by Food Groups

Breads and Cereals	*Produce* *Vegetables*	*Fruits*	*Meats and Proteins*	*Dairy*	*Fats and Oils*	*Other*
Barley	Agathi leaves	Bananas	Almonds	Buttermilk	Ghee	Chutney
Chapati	Amaranth leaves	Cape gooseberries	Bengal gram dal	Milk	Peanut oil	Curry
Chickpea flour	Bottle gourd	Cashew apple	Black gram dal	Yogurt	Rapeseed oil	Garam masala
Corn flour	Breadfruit	Coconut	Bombay duck		Sesame seed oil	Saffron
Millet	Lily root	Durian	Bush beans			Sugarcane
Oats	Okra	Jackfruit	Cashew nuts			
Paratha	Onion	Loquats	Chana dal			
Puri	Plantain	Lychee	Chicken			
Rice	Purslane	Roseapple	Chickpeas			
Roti	Spinach		Conger eel			
Wheat	Tampala		Crocodile			
			Fish			
			Goat			
			Green gram dal			
			Jujube			
			Kidney beans			
			Lentils			
			Mung beans, dal			
			Peanuts			
			Pigeon peas			
			Red gram dal			
			Squab			
			Turtle eggs			

yourself. Each cuisine around the world has the potential to broaden your eating excitement. If you have a chance to visit a range of ethnic markets, your experiences with food can be broadened still more.

Ethnic restaurants offer another way of experiencing food from other cultures. The variety available in many U.S. cities today is amazing. Try eating at an ethnic restaurant that features a cuisine you have never tried before. Read the entire menu and notice the items that are new to you. If you cannot read the menu, ask your server to explain each of the dishes so that you will know just what is available.

The server's specific recommendations may help you figure out what you want to order so that you get a good introduction to the cuisine. Look around to see what diners from the culture of the restaurant are eating. Their choices can give excellent clues to finding favorites of that cuisine. You may want to make some notes about the foods you eat at your first meal and jot down the names of dishes to order next time. Try other cultural restaurants too. Ask friends and acquaintances from other cultures where they like to eat and what they think are some of the best dishes to order.

World cuisines have developed in extremely varied settings over many centuries. However, foods sold in the United States are required to meet the legal standards established governing food safety in this country. In some instances, long-standing traditions of preparation of certain foreign foods may not meet legal requirements.

An illustration of such problems occurred in Los Angeles in the 1980s when the county's health department moved against a local producer of Peking duck because the steps in the production of this classical dish did not meet the temperature control standards for food handling in the city. Although no evidence was presented that Peking duck caused food-borne illnesses, action was initiated to

Table 23.10 Selected Caribbean Islander Foods Categorized by Food Groups

Breads and Cereals	*Produce* *Vegetables*	*Fruits*	*Meats and Proteins*	*Dairy*	*Fats and Oils*	*Other*
Barley	Amaranth leaves	Acerola	Bacaloa	Milk	Palm oil	Cocoa
Cornmeal	Beans	Akee	Barracuda	Yogurt	Pork fatback	Coffee
Rice	Breadfruit	Avocado	Beef			Rum
Rye	Calabaza (pumpkin)	Banana	Blood sausage			Sugarcane molasses
Wheat	Callaloo	Barbados cherries	Chicharrones			
	Carrot	Caimito	Chicken			
	Cassava	Cashew apple	Cod (dried, salted)			
	Celery root	Citrus	Dorado			
	Chayote squash	Coconut	Dried beans			
	Chichi	Cocoplum	Eggs (iguana, turtle)			
	Christophene	Mamey apple	Fish			
	Cocoyam	Mango	Goat			
	Corn	Naseberry	Iguana			
	Dasheen	Pineapple	Lamb			
	Eddo	Roseapple	Mackerel			
	Malanaga	Sapodilla	Marlin			
	Manioc	Soursop	Pigeon			
	Name	Star apple	Pigeon peas			
	Okra		Pork			
	Onion		Turtle, green			
	Palm hearts					
	Peppers					
	Plantain					
	Potatoes					
	Pumpkin leaves					
	Squash					
	Swamp potato					
	Tanier					
	Taro					
	Tomato					
	West Indian pumpkin					
	White sweet potato					
	Yam					
	Yautia					
	Yuca					

halt its production. Finally, a truce was negotiated that included some modification of the original procedure.

In 2000, some Vietnamese and Korean rice specialties that were being marketed as ready-to-eat delicatessen items failed to meet required refrigerated storage conditions for selling them in California. Similar dishes sold in Vietnam and Korea are not refrigerated in those countries even during long, hot days. Clearly, such discrepancies cause hardships and misunderstandings for new immigrants, but cooperative efforts are now being made to help draft acceptable, safe methods and standards that will ensure safety without seriously altering palatability.

Shifting Food Patterns

No sudden transformation in food habits will occur the minute immigrants arrive in the United States, just as you probably are going to take a little time to accept some of the food specialties from their cuisines. However, changes in the habits

Table 23.11 Selected European Foods Categorized by Food Groups

Breads and Cereals	*Produce*		*Meats and Proteins*	*Dairy*	*Fats and Oils*	*Other*
	Vegetables	*Fruits*				
Barley	Beans	Apples	Bacalhau	Cheeses	Butter	Coffee
Buckwheat and kasha	Beets	Cherries	Baccala	Clotted cream	Olive oil	Beers
Millet	Bracken fern	Grapes	Bacon	Cornish cream		Brandies
Oats	Cabbage	Plums	Beef	Crème fraiche		Liquers
Pasta	Cardoon	Olives	Black pudding	Devonshire cream		Sauerkraut
Rice	Carrots	Lingonberries	Blood sausage	Ice cream		Tea
Rye	Chickweed leaf	Pears	Bush beans	Milk		Vinegars
Wheat	Cucumber		Caribou	Sour cream		Wines
	Dock		Caviar			
	Laver		Chickpeas			
	Leeks		Cod (dried, salted)			
	Mushroom		Conger eel			
	Onion		Eggs			
	Peas		Fish			
	Potato		Goat			
	Sweet peppers		Ham			
	Tomato		Horse			
	Truffles		Lamb			
			Mutton			
			Pork			
			Reindeer			
			Sausage			
			Squab			
			Veal			

Table 23.12 Selected Mexican and Central American Foods Categorized by Food Groups

Breads and Cereals	*Produce*		*Meats and Proteins*	*Dairy*	*Fats and Oils*	*Other*
	Vegetables	*Fruits*				
Amaranth grain	Amaranth leaves	Avocado	Bonito	Cheese	Lard	Atole
Cornmeal	Breadfruit	Banana	Chicharrones	Milk		Chocolate
Fideo	Calabacitas (summer squash)	Citrus	Chorizo			Coffee
Masa	Cassava	Guava	Cod (dried, salted)			Pulque
Pan dulce	Chiles	Nance	Dorado			Sugarcane
Polvillo	Chilies	Naranjilla	Frijoles			Tequila
Quinoa	Jicama	Papaya	Garbanzo beans			Vanilla
Rice	Nopales	Pineapple	Goat			
Sopaipilla	Palm hearts	Sapodilla	Legumes			
Thin spaghetti	Plantain	Sapote	Marlin			
Tortillas	Purslane	Soursop				
	Squash	Starapple				
	Squash blossoms	Strawberry pear				
	Taro	Tree melon				
	Tomatillos					
	Tomato					

Table 23.13 Selected Middle Eastern and North African Foods Categorized by Food Groups

Breads and Cereals	*Produce*		*Meats and Proteins*	*Dairy*	*Fats and Oils*	*Other*
	Vegetables	*Fruits*				
Bulgur	Amaranth leaves	Banana	Antelope	Camel milk	Olive oil	Coffee
Couscous	Cauliflower	Citrus	Bream	Donkey milk	Sesame oil	Grape leaves
Millet	Eggplant	Dates	Bush beans	Ewe milk		Mint tea
Pasta	Garlic	Figs	Camel	Feta cheese		Ouzo
Rice	Okra	Grapes	Caviar	Goat milk		Raki
Wheat	Onion	Loquat	Chicken	Yogurt		Retsina
	Parsley	Olive	Chickpeas			Tahini
	Potato	Papaya	Donkey			
	Spinach	Pomegranate	Lamb			
	Tomato		Legumes			
			Mutton			
			Nuts			

and food choices occur over time with repeated contact and immersion in aspects of new food choices. Among the factors influencing changes in eating patterns among immigrant populations are the generation (whether a first-generation new arrival, a second-, or third-generation immigrant), age of the individual, children in families, income level, occupation of workers, educational level (particularly of the food preparer), and living environment (rural or urban, isolated or in an ethnic community). These factors play roles of somewhat varying degrees of significance, depending on the individual and the unique cultural gap. For those with language differences, the transition has an added impediment. Children often pick up language skills rather quickly and can play a key role in helping parents learn about foods in the markets.

The first generation of immigrants (particularly if they are older when they arrive) is more resistant to giving up their original food patterns than is the

Table 23.14 Selected South American Foods Categorized by Food Groups

Breads and Cereals	*Produce*		*Meats and Proteins*	*Dairy*	*Fats and Oils*	*Other*
	Vegetables	*Fruits*				
Cornmeal	Amaranth leaves	Avocado	Bacon	Cheese	Dendé oil	Coffee
Quinoa	Apio	Banana	Barracuda	Milk	Palm oil	Sugarcane
Rice	Arracacha	Cashew apple	Beef			
Wheat	Breadfruit	Citrus	Bonito			
	Cassava	Coconut	Chicken			
	Chayote squash	Cocoplum	Cod (dried, salted)			
	Chocho	Jaboticaba	Dorado			
	Chuno	Mamey apple	Egg			
	Garlic	Melonpear	Fish			
	Manioc	Nance	Goat			
	Onion	Naranjilla	Guinea pig			
	Palm hearts	Papaya	Horse			
	Peppers	Pepino	Iguana			
	Plantain	Sapodilla	Lamb			
	Potato	Soursop	Legumes			
	Pumpkin	Starapple	Mutton			
	Taro	Tree melon	Pork			
	Tomato		Sausage			
	Yuca					

Table 23.15 Selected Southeast Asian and Pacific Islander Foods Categorized by Food Groups

Breads and Cereals	*Produce*		*Meats and Proteins*	*Dairy*	*Fats and Oils*	*Other*
	Vegetables	*Fruits*				
Mochiko (rice flour)	Amaranth leaves	Avocado	Aku	Carabao (water buffalo) milk	Palm oil	Bagoong (fermented fish)
Noodles	Bean sprouts	Banana	Bat	Milk	Sesame oil	Fish sauce
Rice	Breadfruit	Carambola	Bonito			Lemon grass
Wheat	Cassava	Cashew apple	Chicken			Sugarcane
Wonton	Chilies	Coconut	Dilir (fried fish)			
	Kelp	Durian	Dog			
	Laver	Fuzzy melon	Dolphin-fish			
	Manioc	Guava	Dried beans			
	Palm hearts	Jackfruit	Duck			
	Palmetto cabbage	Java plum	Egg			
	Plantain	Mango	Fish			
	Squash	Orange	Goat			
	Sweet potato	Papaya	Mahi-mahi			
	Taro	Pawpaw	Marlin			
	Tomato	Pineapple	Mung beans			
	Yam	Pomelo	Pork			
		Roseapple	Sea cucumber			
		Sapodilla	Seafood			
		Tamarind	Snake			
			Squab			
			Tempeh			
			Tofu			

second generation, according to Kalcik. Second-generation food preparers are likely to retain part of their original food preferences but often make adjustments in the techniques used to prepare them as a means of saving valuable time. This generation may even give up most of its food traditions, leaving revival of their heritage to the eager third generation. The meal that is most likely to retain many of the cultural foods is dinner, for this is a time when the family is most likely to be together and to have a bit more time available. Breakfast and lunch patterns from the country of origin may give way fairly quickly to U.S. patterns, particularly if these meals are eaten away from home.

The shift toward more U.S. dietary patterns certainly is not necessarily a shift toward improved nutrition, for clearly Americans as a group are rapidly becoming an overweight population with eating habits that are not noted for being healthful. The desirable transition obviously is for new immigrants to pick up new habits that improve their nutritional status rather than cause new health problems.

Romero-Gwynn et al. found that second-generation Mexican American immigrants reported some healthful dietary changes, including decreased consumption of lard, cream, and chorizo (Mexican pork sausage). Offsetting these improvements, however, were decreased consumption of such healthful foods as atole, fruit juices, and pasta dishes with vegetables.

Increased intakes of soda, mayonnaise, sour cream, white bread, and expensive ready-to-eat cereals are detrimental dietary changes. Increased consumption of flour tortillas rather than corn tortillas, although seemingly not a change, actually is a shift for many immigrants from southern areas of Mexico where corn tortillas are the norm. Unfortunately, flour tortillas contain as much as 4 grams of fat in comparison with the usual 0.5 gram in a corn tortilla. Substitution of lard with oil is a healthful change that many are making, although the amounts used may still be too high. Also, powdered, instant fruit drinks heavily sweetened with sugar are often an empty calorie replacement for the healthful fruit juices that were part of the diet in Mexico.

Satia et al. studied the dietary practices of 30 Chinese American women living in the Seattle area. They reported a shift to a U.S.-style breakfast but the retention of the Chinese-style lunch by the majority and the consumption of a Chinese dinner by all. Only some of the women still observed the importance of balancing yin and yang in food selections. Reasons cited for food selections included convenience of U.S. foods, better quality of U.S. beef, milk, and tofu (but poorer quality chicken and fish), and cost.

These examples illustrate possible shifts in dietary patterns that immigrants may make as they become assimilated into U.S. society. Individuals obviously will make their own adjustments to their personal needs and living situations. Dishes from the various cultures may be altered as they are integrated into the American scene. These changes may be due to the need to use somewhat different ingredients as substitutions when the original ones are not available. Restaurants and other food producers may alter some dishes a bit to attract Americans to their cultural dishes.

Interestingly, immigrants are not the only ones making changes in the food patterns of their heritage. Many Americans are learning more and more about foods from many points around the world. Even the fast-food industry reflects this development, as evidenced by the growth of Mexican American items on their menus. Food courts and restaurants abound in Chinese foods, Greek dishes, Thai menus, and Vietnamese items, for example. Obviously, U.S. tastes are changing and expanding.

Summary

Food patterns in the United States developed in different regions of the country because of the cultural background of the immigrants and the foods that were available in the new land. Indians in the Northeast added to the familiar foods of the English and other European settlers who came to that region. Early immigrants to this region were primarily European, particularly British, Irish, and German at first, followed by Scandinavians and later waves from Greece, Austria-Hungary, Italy, Poland, Russia, Portugal, and Spain.

In the South, African slaves significantly influenced the cuisine, bringing their traditional dishes and adding seasonings from home to the food they cooked in their new land. French, French Acadians, and Spanish brought their distinctive cuisines to southern Louisiana.

Immigrants from Germany and other northern European countries helped shape the food patterns in the Midwest. The Southwest was influenced very early not only by Native American Indians, but also Spanish and Mexican residents who had well-established food patterns very different from the other parts of the United States. Chinese came as workers in the western part of the country in the 19th century. Added to these earlier waves of immigrants today are political refugees from Vietnam and other countries, as well as people from Mexico, Central and South America, the Caribbean, the Middle East, and Asian countries seeking improved economic opportunities. The West developed a food pattern that today is best described as "fusion" because of the wide diversity of its immigrants.

These immigrants have brought along their cultural heritage, which includes their cuisines, religions, and holidays. This diversity has created many ethnic markets and restaurants as well as new food items available in regular grocery stores. Many Americans embrace the increasing dining choices that result from the growing diversity of cultures in this country. Immigrants also are adopting many of the foods and dietary practices of their new country. Sometimes these changes are nutritionally helpful, but others may be detrimental.

Selected Sites

http://www.infoplease.com/ipa/A0762156.html—Racial census data for the U.S. in 2003.

http://www.trinity.edu/~mkearl/race.html—Discussion and numerous references on the sociology of race and ethnicity.

http://food.oregonstate.edu/prodev/demos99.html—Discussion and related Web sites for studying demographic trends and food resources.

http://lilt.ilstu.edu/rtdirks/NOAMERIND.html—Bibliography on Indian food patterns.

http://www.keyingredients.org/—Information about food throughout the United States; on-line companion to Smithsonian's *Key Ingredients: America by Food.*

http://www.agmrc.org/agmrc/markets/Food/food+ethnic.htm—Bibliography of some ethnic food trends.

http://www.nal.usda.gov/fnic/pubs/bibs/gen/ethnic.html—Resource list of materials on food and ethnicity in the United States.

http://www.recipelink.com/rcpusa.html—Information on regional cooking.

http://lilt.ilstu.edu/rtdirks/SEASIA.html—Bibliography of Asian ethnic foods.

Study Questions

1. Describe traditional food patterns in these parts of the United States: (a) the Northeast, (b) South, (c) Midwest (d) Southwest, and (e) West.
2. What ethnic and cultural groups live in your area? For each group, describe the food markets, unique food ingredients, and special menu items in their restaurants.
3. Visit an ethnic market and read the labels on five items for ingredient and nutrition information. Describe any problems you have in reading and understanding the labels.
4. What are the racial demographics of your school? Does the campus food service include food items that reflect this population? If so, identify the foods and, if possible, their frequency of service.
5. During the past week, have you eaten any foods that are considered to be part of any cuisine different from your heritage? If so, indicate each item and the typical frequency with which you eat it, and briefly describe what you like about it.
6. Which meal of the day is likely to be the first one that an immigrant alters to the U.S. style? Which meal is the last to be changed? Why do you think these changes occur in the order you indicated?
7. Why are some prepared cultural foods encountering problems in relation to U.S. laws covering food in the marketplace?

Bibliography

Acevedo, M.C. 2000. Role of acculturation in explaining ethnic differences in pre-natal health-risk behaviors, mental health, and parenting beliefs of Mexican-American and European American at risk women. *Child Abuse and Neglect 24:* 111–127.

Adrogue, H.J. and D.E. Wesson. 1996. Role of dietary factors in hypertension of African Americans. *Seminar in Nephrology 16:* 94–101.

Algert, S.J., E. Brzezinski, and T.H. Ellison. 1998. Mexican American food practices, customs, and holidays. In *Ethnic and Regional Food Practices.* American Dietetic Association/American Diabetes Association. Chicago.

Altschiller, D. 1995. Turkish Americans. In R.J. Vecoli et al., eds. *Gale Encyclopedia of Multicultural America.* Gale Research. New York.

Bachman-Carter, K., R.M. Duncan and S. Pelican. 1998. *Navajo Food Practices, Customs, and Holidays.* American Dietetic Association/American Diabetes Association. Chicago.

Bouvier, L. F. 1977. International migration: Yesterday, today, and tomorrow. *Population Bull. 34*(1): 6.

Bradley, B. 2000. *Journey from Here.* Artisan. Victoria, Australia.

Brown, L.K. and K. Mussell, eds. 1984. *Ethnic and Regional Foodways in the United States.* University of Tennessee Press. Knoxville, TN.

Burke, C.B. and S.P. Raia. 1995. *Soul and Traditional Southern Food Practices, Customs, and Holidays.* American Dietetics Association/American Diabetes Association. Chicago.

Byars, D. 1996. Traditional African foods and African Americans. *Agriculture and Human Values 13:* 74–78.

Camarota, S.A. 2002. *Immigrants in the United States—2002: Snapshot of America's Foreign-Born Population.* Center for Immigration Studies. Washington, DC.

Claudio, V.S. 1994. *Filipino-American Food Practices, Customs, and Holidays.* American Dietetic Association. Chicago.

Dirige, O.V. 1995. Filipino-American diet and foods. *Asian American Business Journal 2/28/05:* 11–17.

Faneklli-Kuczmarski, M., R.J. Kuzmarski, and M. Naijar. 1995. Food usage among Mexican Americans, Cuban, and Puerto Rican adults. *Nutr. Today 30:* 30–37.

Gutierrez, C.P. 1992. *Cajun Foodways.* University of Mississippi Press. Oxford, MS.

Ikeda, J.P. 1999. *Hmong American Food Practices, Customs, and Holidays.* American Dietetic Association/American Diabetes Association. Chicago.

Kalčik, S. 1984. Ethnic foodways in America and the performance of identity. In L.K. Brown and K. Mussel, eds. *Ethnic and Regional Foodways in the United States.* University of Tennessee Press. Knoxville, TN.

Lee, H.G. 1992. *Taste of the States: A Food History of America.* Howell. Charlottesville, VA.

Lee, S.K., J. Sobal, and E.A. Frongillo. 1999. Acculturation and dietary practices among Korean Americans. *J. Am. Dietet. Assoc. 99(9):* 1084.

Leistner, C.G. 1996. *Cajun and Creole Food Practices, Customs, and Holidays.* American Dietetic Association/American Diabetes Association. Chicago.

Levenstein, H. 2003. *Paradox of Plenty: Social History of Eating in Modern America.* Rev. ed. University of California Press. Berkeley, CA.

Mandel, A. 1996. *Celebrating the Midwestern Table.* Doubleday. New York.

McIntosh, E.N. 1995. *American Food Habits in Historical Perspective.* Praeger. Westport, CT.

Norris, R.E., and L.L. Haring. 1980. *Political Geography.* Charles F. Merrill Publishing. Columbus, OH.

Pan, Y. L. et al. 1999. Asian students change their eating practices after living in the United States. *J. Am. Dietet. Assoc. 99(1):* 54.

Raj, S., P. Ganganna, and J. Bowering. 1999. Dietary habits of Asian Indians in relation to length of residence in the United States. *J. Am. Dietet. Assoc. 99*(9): 1106.

Rischin, M. 1989. Immigration. In *World Book Encyclopedia 10:* 82. World Book. Chicago.

Romero-Gwynn, E. et al. 1993. Dietary acculturation among Latinos of Mexican descent. *Nutr. Today 28*(4): 6.

Satia, J.A. et al. 2000. Use of qualitative methods to study diet, acculturation, and health in Chinese-American women. *J. Am. Dietet. Assoc. 100*(8): 885.

Shortridge, B.G. and J.R. Shortridge. 1998. *Taste of American Place.* Rowman and Littlefield. Lanham, MD.

Stoddard, R.H. et al. 1986. *Human Geography: People, Places, and Cultures.* Prentice-Hall. Englewood Cliffs, NJ.

Weaver, T., N. Kanelklos and C. Esteva-Fabregal, eds. 1993. *Handbook of Hispanic Culture in the United States: Anthropology.* Arte Publico Press. Houston.

Wilson, D.S. and A.K. Gillespie, ed. 1999. *Rooted in America: Food Lore of Popular Fruits and Vegetables.* University of Tennessee Press. Knoxville, TN.

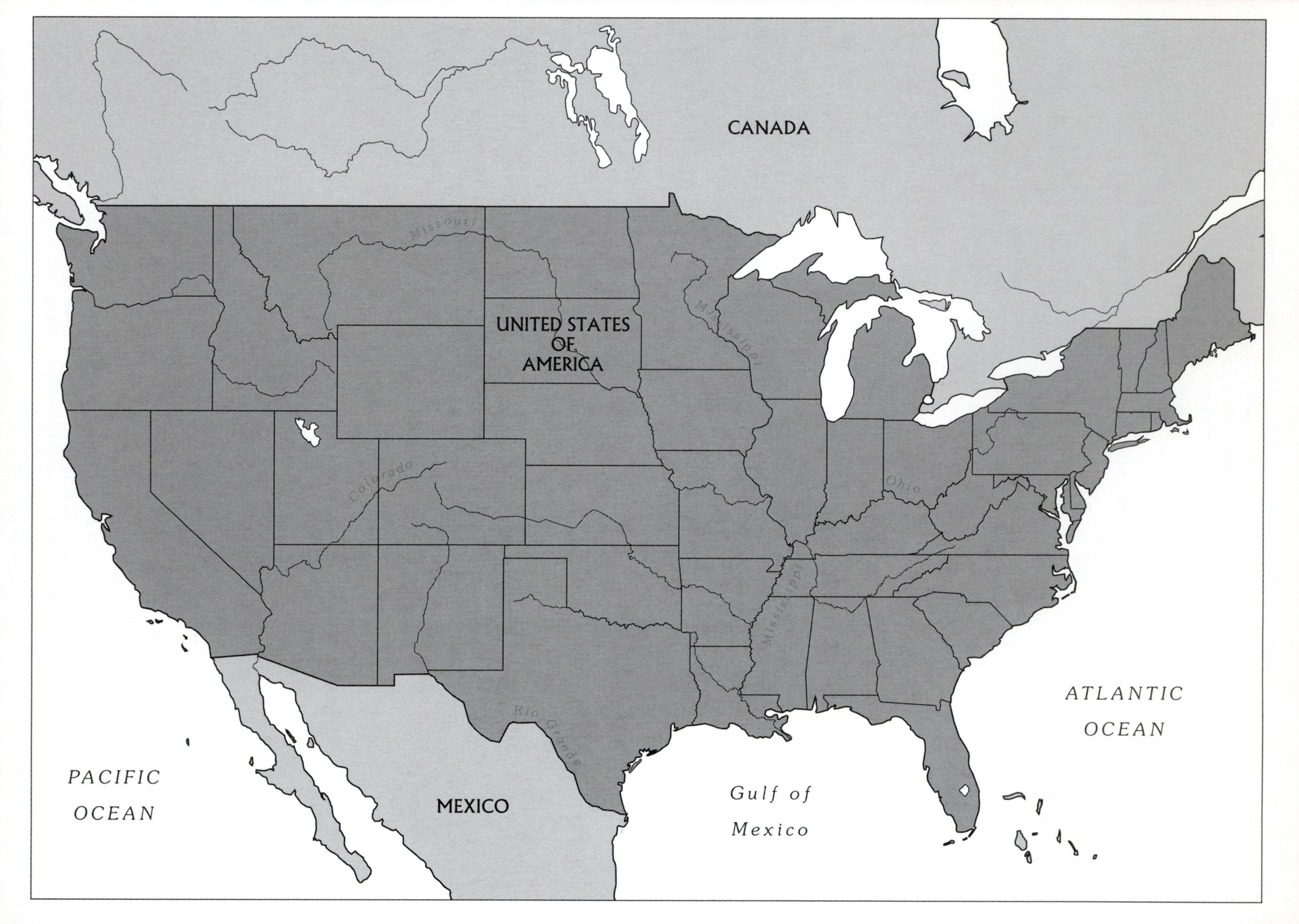

CANADA
UNITED STATES OF AMERICA
Missouri
Mississippi
Colorado
Ohio
Rio Grande
PACIFIC OCEAN
MEXICO
Gulf of Mexico
ATLANTIC OCEAN

24 Diet Counseling in our Cultural Milieu

The rapidly expanding cultural milieu in the United States is presenting significant challenges to dietitians and others who are involved in communicating messages of good nutrition. For meaningful communication to take place between a client and a health professional, a mutual understanding needs to be developed. For this to happen, you, as the health professional, need to approach the counseling session with an understanding of the actual situation in which the client lives and a familiarity with the diet patterns that probably form the basis for the foods that will be accepted and consumed.

Familiarity with the culture and the foods associated with it is essential for people to accept suggestions about eating and diets. Obviously, there will be individual differences about the foods that immigrants from a particular country select as their favorites, but the general preferences within a country serve as a reasonable starting point for communication. This book gives you considerable information that will help you understand the culture and foods pertinent to individual clients. This chapter presents graphic nutritional guides that have been developed in some countries; these may be useful in counseling individuals or talking to groups.

The way in which you conduct each counseling session needs to be compatible with your client's culture, for one country's view of good manners often is significantly different from that of another country. Awareness of some of the possible pitfalls in communication is essential to effective counseling. This important topic is discussed in this chapter to provide a basic background in intercultural communication.

Figure 24.1 MyPyramid, the graphic developed by the U.S. Department of Agriculture, replaced the Food Guide Pyramid in 2005 as the tool for eating for good health in the United States.

Food Guide Pyramid and MyPyramid

Food Guide Pyramid—Educational tool used in the United States to guide people in making healthy food choices.

MyPyramid—Graphic guide to good nutrition introduced in 2005 to replace the Food Guide Pyramid as an instructional tool for nutrition education.

Graphics have been developed consistent with the food preferences of people living in some countries; these can be useful in presenting dietary suggestions to individuals or to groups. For example, the **Food Guide Pyramid** was used in the United States as a graphic to help transmit information on healthy eating to Americans for several years. It resulted in various proposals by professionals in other countries to adapt the concept to match the dietary preferences and available foods in their own countries or locales. In 2005, the Food Guide Pyramid was revised and replaced by the new U.S. graphic **MyPyramid** (Figure 24.1).

Other Food Guides

Some graphics developed for diet counseling in other countries are presented here.

The Filipino Pyramid Food Guide

Filipino Pyramid Food Guide—Food guide developed in the Philippines to guide people in making healthy food choices using the local foods.

The **Filipino Pyramid Food Guide** (Figure 24.2) was presented in the Philippines in 1996 as a visual means of teaching good dietary practices to help avoid overweight and obesity while eating for good health. This guide consists of five groups. The foods in the first group, rice, root crops, corn, noodles, breads, and cereals, are pictured and named as the base of the pyramid, with the advice to "eat most." The other groups are as follows:

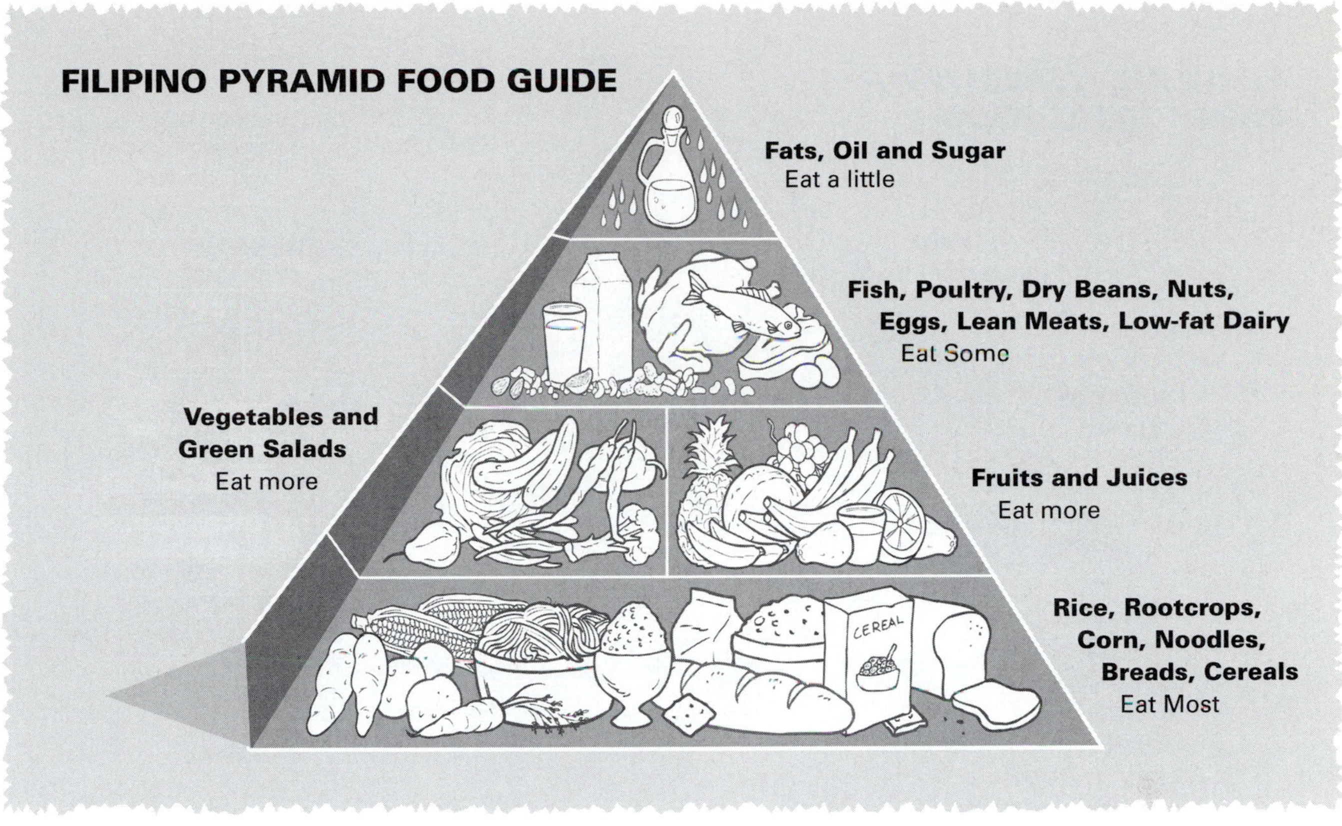

FILIPINO PYRAMID FOOD GUIDE

Fats, Oil and Sugar
Eat a little

Fish, Poultry, Dry Beans, Nuts, Eggs, Lean Meats, Low-fat Dairy
Eat Some

Vegetables and Green Salads
Eat more

Fruits and Juices
Eat more

Rice, Rootcrops, Corn, Noodles, Breads, Cereals
Eat Most

Figure 24.2 The Filipino Pyramid Food Guide. Developed by Sanirose S. Orbeta, M.S., R.D., and the Food and Nutrition Research Institute and endorsed by the Philippine Association for the Study of Overweight and Obesity. 1996.

- Two groups are included on the second level: Vegetables are pictured on the left half, fruits are on the right half, and captioned to "eat more."
- The third layer from the bottom is one group (fish, poultry, dry beans, nuts, eggs, lean meats, and low-fat dairy) and is captioned to "eat some."
- The apex of the pyramid includes fats, oils, and sugar, with the admonition to "eat a little."

An obvious departure in the Filipino guide from the pyramid developed by the United States is the elimination of the milk, yogurt, and cheese group, a move that was taken because of the paucity of dairy foods in the typical Filipino's diet. The lack of emphasis on dairy may result in a somewhat low intake of calcium. The other key difference is the use of action words rather than specific recommendations on numbers of servings and serving sizes. Proponents of this guide find this is a useful device for promoting interest in eating more of the lower two levels of the pyramid and less of the upper two levels.

Piramide Alimentaria para Puerto Rico

Viandas—Generic word used in the Piramide Alimentaria para Puerto Rico to include bland foods high in starch.

A Piramide Alimentaria para Puerto Rico (Macpherson-Sanchez, 1998) was developed in Puerto Rico (Figure 24.3) using the U.S. pyramid as its launching point, but adapting it to the unique requirements engendered by the tropical setting. To highlight the importance of adequate water intake to Puerto Ricans, a stylized triangle that looks like the pyramid's shadow appears at the base and reminds people to drink six to eight glasses of water daily. The foundation block of the pyramid is identified as cereales y viandas (7 to 12 portions) and includes pictures of some foods in this group. **Viandas** are defined as bland plant foods high

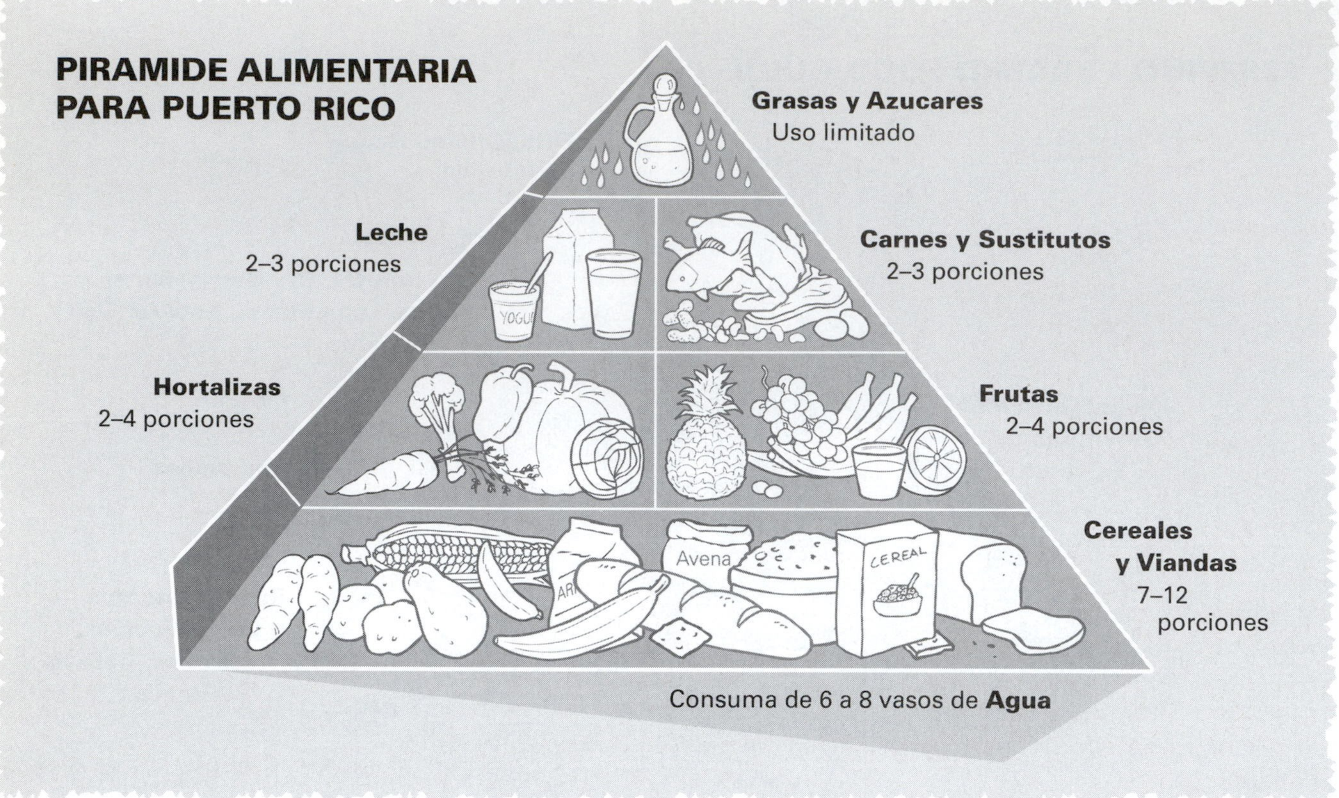

Figure 24.3 Piramide Alimentaria para Puertio Rico. Developed by the University of Puerto Rico with the U.S. Department of Agriculture. 2nd ed. 1995.

in starch, such as green bananas, yuca, breadfruit and its seeds, plantains, sweet potatoes, potatoes, white yams, yautia, and malanga. Cereals include rice, oats, wheat, barley, and corn (kernels as well as the dried, granular meal).

The second level is divided in half, with hortalizas (nonstarchy vegetables) on the left and frutas on the right (with the suggestion to eat two to four servings of each group). The next level also is divided in half: leche (milk and dairy) on the left and carnes y sustitutos (including legumes, nuts, and eggs in addition to meat and poultry with the suggestion for two to three servings for each group) on the right. The peak has grasas y azucares (fats and sugars, to be in limited use). Minor variations in recommended servings are the result of shifting starchy plant foods such as potatoes into the bottom category (cereales y viandas) rather than counting them as vegetables in this pyramid.

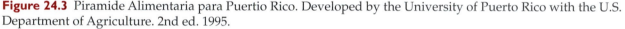

Chinese Food Guide Pagoda

Chinese Food Guide Pagoda—Educational tool developed in China to guide people in making healthy food selections.

The Chinese version of a guide for daily eating is a five-tiered pagoda (Figure 24.4). At the base of the **Chinese Food Guide Pagoda** are cereals (300 to 500 grams) such as rice, wheat and breads baked from wheat, noodles, and corn. The second tier has vegetables (400 to 500 grams) and fruits (100 to 200 grams). The third or middle tier specifies three different types of protein-rich foods daily: meat and poultry (50 to 100 grams), fish and shrimp (50 grams), and eggs (25 to 50 grams). The fourth tier has two categories: milk and milk products (100 grams), and beans and bean products (50 grams). The top tier is fats and oils (25 grams). No mention is made of sugars because they are not likely to be consumed in very large quantities in the typical Chinese diet. The pagoda reflects the limited intake of milk and dairy products that may be needed to accommodate those who are

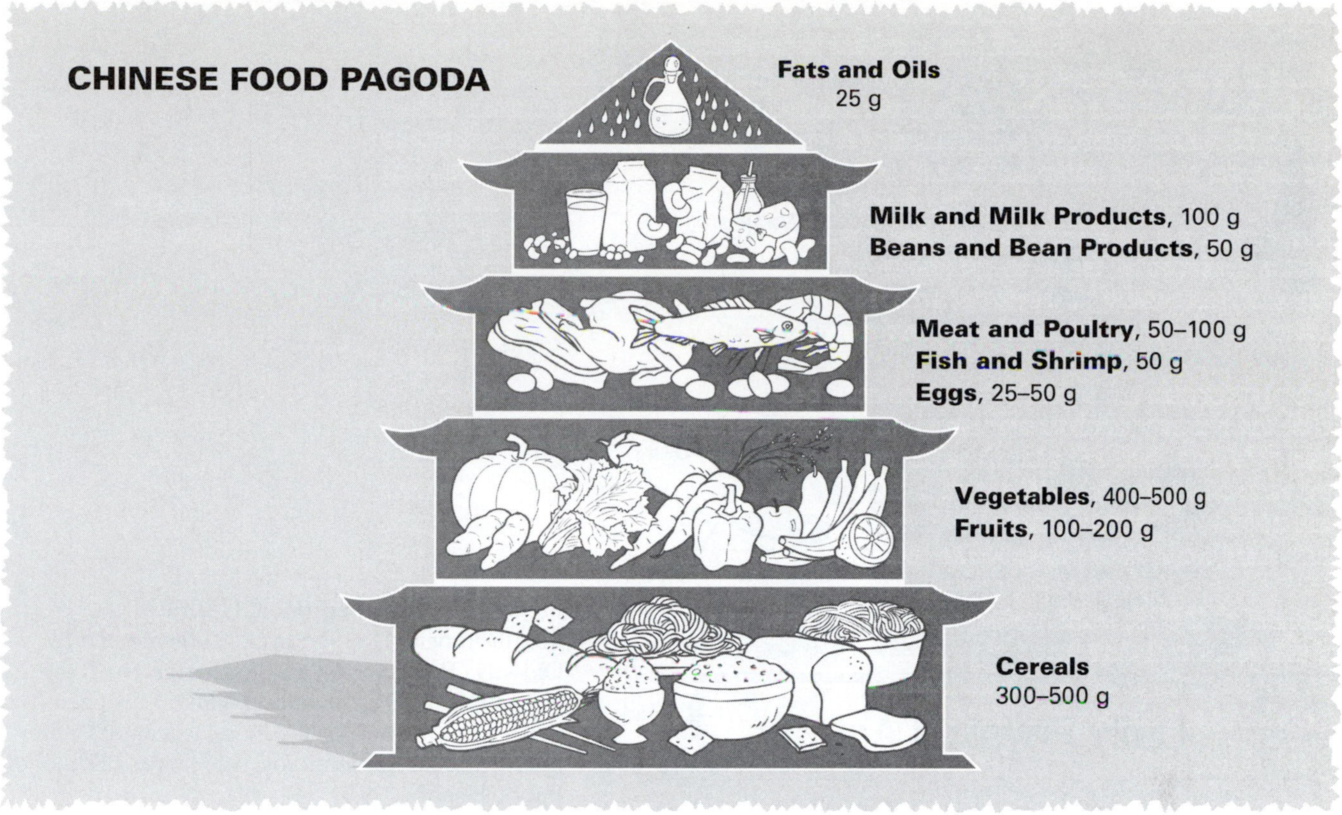

Figure 24.4 Food Guide Pagoda for Chinese Residents. Developed by the Chinese Nutrition Society. 1999.

lactose intolerant; inclusion of tofu or other bean products in the fourth tier encourages calcium intake from this supplemental source. Use of the pagoda for the graphic provides a clear message that this guide is specifically for Asians.

Mediterranean Diet Pyramid

Traditional Healthy Mediterranean Diet Pyramid—Food pyramid designed to incorporate the foods common to the Mediterranean in a pattern that has 11 categories.

The **Traditional Healthy Mediterranean Diet Pyramid** (Figure 24.5) presents the classic shape of a pyramid, but several modifications have created one that encompasses 11 categories and two additional suggestions that accompany this pyramid. Because of this detail, the pyramid must be read carefully. The base of the Mediterranean Diet Pyramid is composed of cereals (breads, pasta, rice, couscous, polenta, bulgur, other grains, and potatoes). As is basically true for the entire pyramid, the base does not indicate the number of servings, although foods from this foundation category are to be eaten daily. The next level, which is also to be eaten daily, places fruits on the left, covering about 40 percent of the space; beans and other legumes and nuts occupy about the middle 10 percent of this level; and vegetables compose the right half. Olive oil in variable amounts, but daily, is the thin block above the fruits and vegetables. Cheese and yogurt, to be eaten daily, represent the next thin layer. Fairly thin layers then rise above the dotted line. The proviso is given that these items (in ascending order on the pyramid) should be eaten a few times per week: fish, poultry, eggs (a very thin layer), and sweets. The tip of the pyramid is labeled red meat, with the recommendation that this should be eaten only a few times per month. To the left of the pyramid is the suggestion that individuals should have regular physical activity, and to the right is the suggestion to use wine in moderation. This guide reflects the basic diet from the Mediterranean region, but is somewhat challenging to remember.

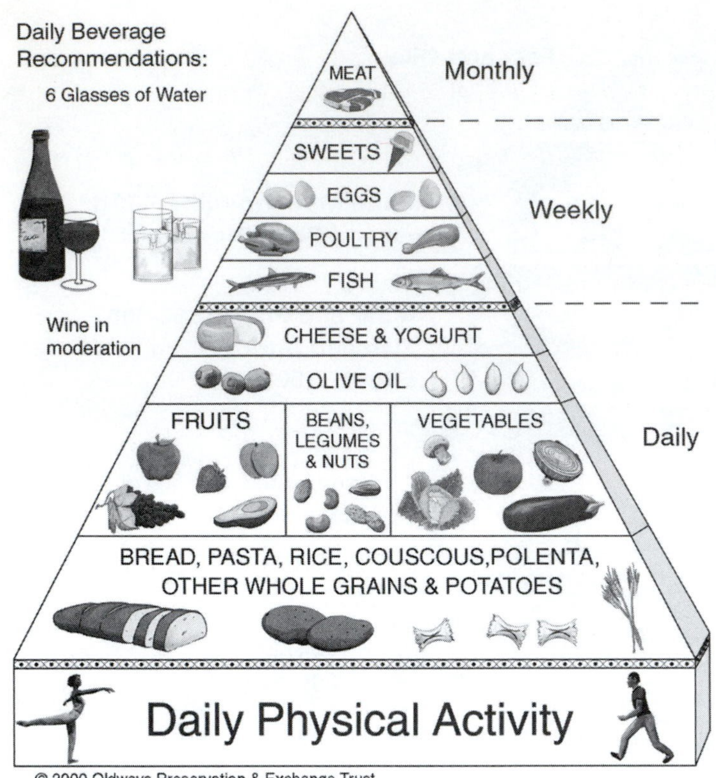

Figure 24.5 The Traditional Healthy Mediterranean Diet Pyramid. Codeveloped by Oldways Preservation and Exchange Trust, the World Health Organization (WHO) European Office, and the WHO/FAO Collaboration Center in Nutritional Epidemiology at Harvard School of Public Health. 1994.

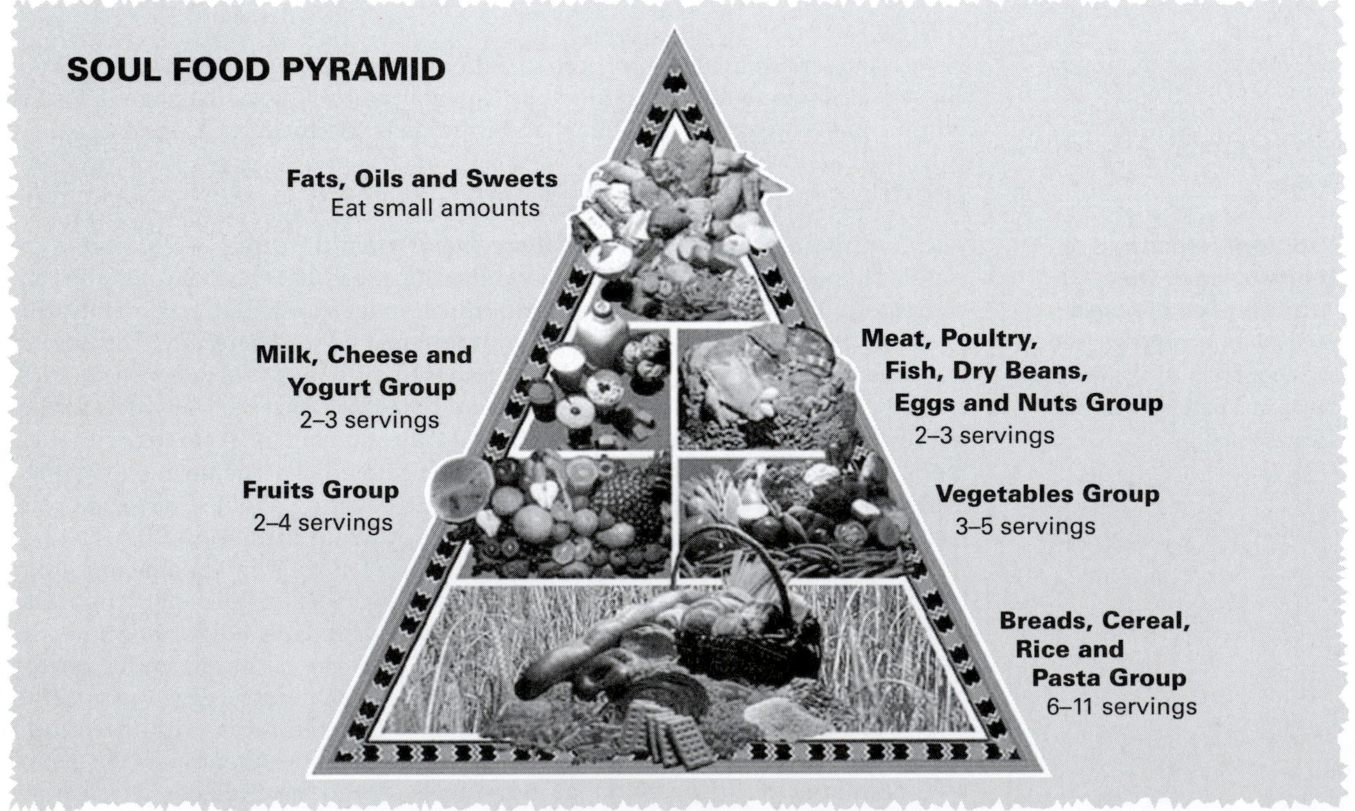

Figure 24.6 Soul Food Pyramid. Hebni Nutrition Consultants Inc., 4630 S. Kirkman Road, #201, Orlando, FL 32819. Web site: www.soulfoodpyramid.org.

Soul Food Pyramid

Soul Food Pyramid—Healthy food guide for persons who are lactose intolerant and need to limit fat intake to control weight.

Dietary suggestions for people wishing to follow a "soul food" diet are depicted in yet another pyramid, the **Soul Food Pyramid** (Figure 24.6). Lactose-reduced milk, yogurt (low fat or fat free), and reduced fat cheeses are excellent choices for reducing discomfort for those with lactose intolerance and keeping calories low if weight is a concern. To avoid high fat intake when selecting within the meat group, the pyramid suggests avoiding such high-fat items as chitterlings (chitlins), fatback, pig's feet, hog jowls, sausage, and pork neck bones. Keeping snack foods and sweets to a minimum also is emphasized.

Canada's Food Guide to Healthy Eating

Canada's Food Guide to Healthy Eating—Rainbow graphic used to teach good food patterns to Canadians.

Our neighbor to the north uses **Canada's Food Guide to Healthy Eating,** a rainbow graphic, to explain its dietary recommendations (Figure 24.7). The outer yellow band is grain products, the next green band is for vegetables and fruits, the blue band is for milk products, and the red innermost band is for meat and alternatives. The fact that the outer band encompasses the largest total space and each successive inner band is progressively smaller visually reinforces the quantities that are recommended for each category. The color designations subtly suggest the types of foods in the bands.

When counseling patients who are likely eating a diet that could be somewhat similar to one of these adaptions of the U.S. Food Guide Pyramid, you may

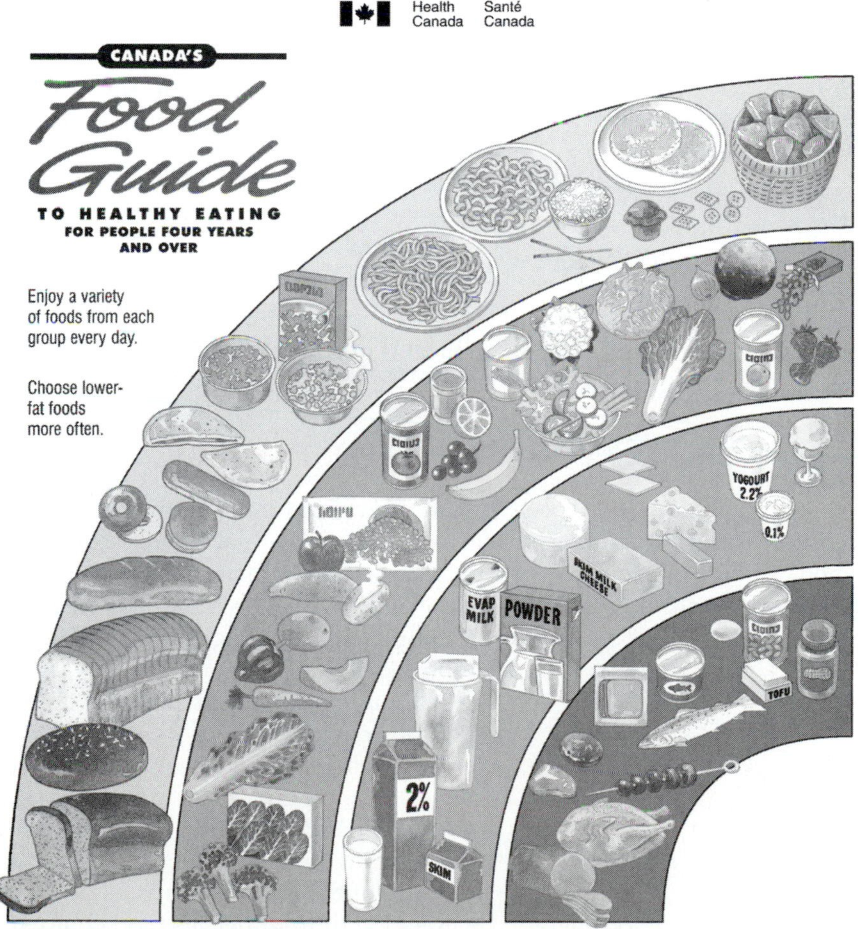

Figure 24.7 Canada's Food Guide to Healthy Eating.

find that the appropriate version is helpful in exploring food patterns and preferences. Then you might shape your suggestions to take advantage of this visual. The picture will help to convey the message even when your words may be a little difficult for your client to understand.

Intercultural Communication

Even when two people speak the same language but come from different countries, communication may be somewhat confused because of idioms, different definitions of the same word, or accents. When little or no knowledge of each other's language is added, communication can be very limited or nonexistent.

Unfortunately, the very different cultural backgrounds that the client and the health professional can have could magnify the problem because what the client may understand could be something other than what the health professional is saying even if an interpreter is helping with the session.

The challenges of effective communication with your clients are apparent. For success in helping your clients, you will need to be familiar with their general cultural traditions. Added to this knowledge is the need to establish the rapport with each client that will facilitate your understanding of the aspects of culture the client practices and considers important. Careful listening, including watching your client's body language, is a key to establishing good rapport and achieving effective counseling.

Body Language

Body language—Movements made that communicate attitude or feelings to another person.

Body language is an aspect of communication that needs to be considered. Body language is subtle, yet has a strong impact. The various movements you might make as a normal part of your style of interacting with another person happen automatically unless you make a conscious effort to control a behavior that may be misinterpreted in the culture of your client.

Possible problems related to body language include space you maintain between you and your client, whether any handshake or other physical contact is made, whether or not eye contact is acceptable or expected, and hand motion, particularly the manner of pointing. Even your feet could be conveying messages contrary to your client's culture.

Cultural Parameters

Customs—Traditions that are common to a cultural group, such as shaking hands or bowing.

Your recommendations to your clients need to be made in the context of the beliefs and **customs** of each individual. For example, you should be aware that some foods simply are not allowed by religious beliefs. Others may be totally outside the culture's typical diet. Special qualities could be attributed to some foods in a culture, thus giving them unique importance at special times, such as at childbirth.

Although each client presents a somewhat different communication challenge, consideration of the following points regarding cultural expectations will help you in establishing an appropriate context for your meeting.

- Language (English first or second, or none; other)
- Body language (personal space, greeting, eye contact, hands)
- Foods of the culture (kinds, beliefs, preparation, traditions)
- Religion (if it influences food choices)
- Values regarding time

An idea that you might find helpful in refining your counseling skills is to arrange for several friends to join you in videotaping a mock counseling session. One of the friends can be your client, and the other can videotape the session. You may be uncomfortable at first, but you probably will be able to relax enough to provide a good sample of your counseling techniques. You can review the tape privately if you prefer, or you can critique it with your friends to develop ideas that could be effective for you to use in actual counseling sessions. The chance to actually view yourself, as the client sees you, can be invaluable in improving counseling skills.

Obviously, the ability to speak in your client's language is extremely helpful, but often may not be possible. If your client has limited knowledge of English, you may need to speak slowly and in short sentences, using as simple a vocabulary as possible. Be sure to speak clearly, leaving a bit of space between words.

Watch the eyes (unless the client's culture does not permit) to help determine whether you are being understood. It could be necessary to say the same thing in more than one way to get your message across. If you and your client have no language in common, you will need to have an interpreter assist you in your meeting. Having appropriate visual materials and brochures written in the client's language also may be helpful.

If at all possible, counsel in a conversational format in which you provide a small amount of information and draw your client into the conversation, perhaps with a simple question that will help you know whether you have been understood before moving to the next point. This type of dialogue may take time to establish, but it is helpful in determining that your information is being understood correctly.

Avoid asking questions that can be answered with a simple yes or no. Many people of other cultures wish to avoid embarrassing you or themselves in giving an answer. For example, if you ask a client if he or she understands what has just been said, the answer will almost certainly be yes or a positive nod of the head, even if the client did not understand.

Food Attitudes and Traditions

Questioning your client regarding any special foods enjoyed by the family, particularly those served for holidays, can help strengthen the understanding between you and the client and aid you in creating dietary strategies that will be helpful to and used by the client. The insights you gain from such conversations may be of value in working with others from a similar background.

Also, exploring whether your clients avoid some foods will help you to create realistic dietary suggestions that accommodate religious dictates or health beliefs regarding foods. Because health beliefs regarding such implied attributes as hot and cold (yin and yang) foods and their balancing in the diet vary even among people of the same country, individual client input is essential if you are to proceed appropriately in diet counseling.

Try to create an ever-expanding knowledge base about the cultures and the food patterns of your clients. Your work will not only be more interesting, but also will become increasingly effective. In addition to using knowledge gained from interviews with clients, read books and articles about the their countries of origin, and eat at ethnic restaurants to expand your personal food experience and gain appreciation of the types of food that are familiar to them.

Cultural Differences

Many cultural differences—far more than can be included here—can be found around the world. However, the following discussion will help identify some of the distinctive ones that you may need to recognize. Although many people in a particular culture may fit the descriptions, keep in mind that you are working with individuals, and each one could have quite different beliefs and practices than those presented here. The key words to remember in your counseling are *listen, observe,* and *think about* your client as a unique individual, even though he or she is likely to follow certain cultural patterns.

Attitude toward Time Cultural attitudes toward time are highly variable and tend to linger long after immigrants have settled in the United States. The typical

U.S. system that requires one eye to be on the clock at all times simply refuses to mesh with the more leisurely attitudes of people from countries where personal interactions take priority over punctuality. To establish rapport with some of your clients, you may have to take a few deep breaths to shift gears into a more relaxed and friendly style. Your warm, welcoming smile will not only relax your client, but also be surprisingly helpful in easing your frustration regarding the wasted time. Try it.

Far East Cultural Insights

Space and Greeting Customs and behaviors in the Far East vary a bit from country to country, but are generally somewhat restrained. The Japanese have a particular appreciation for private space. A bow serves as the greeting, with the depth of the bow reflecting the importance and/or age of the person being greeted. If there is a handshake, Japanese usually prefer a weak grip. Men from South Korea may bow slightly and shake hands, sometimes with both hands, but women do not ordinarily shake hands. Touching is uncommon among Chinese.

Business cards are very important when meeting people of Far Eastern background, who read them carefully to appreciate the title of the person on the card. Exchange of business cards is usually done in a formal manner that honors the donor of each card.

Body Language Body language also is important in the Far East; for example, avoid any prolonged eye contact, do not expose the sole of your shoe, keep the palm of your hand downward when pointing or beckoning, and avoid showing your mouth open (Japanese and Koreans often cover their mouths when smiling or laughing).

Names and Family Names may be confusing because the family name is often the first name in the sequence followed by the given name. Among key values is the importance of the family (superseding one's personal needs), respect for the elderly, and paternalistic and rigid hierarchy in family organization.

Other Values The people of the Far East appreciate formality and rules as well as indirect and circuitous dialogues; they dislike confrontation and disagreements. Beliefs and superstitions (for example, these regarding hot and cold foods) are important. Personal questions may not be welcome. Beauty and style are particularly important to people from a Japanese background.

India and Southeast Asia

Greeting In India and Southeast Asia, greetings vary a bit from those of the Far East, although there are certainly many similarities because of the numerous interactions over the centuries. Indonesians and Filipinos shake hands. Malaysians may extend their palms outward and touch fingers in greeting, while Thai, Balinese, Indian women, and some other Hindus greet people with their hands together in a prayerlike manner and sometimes with a slight bow. Indian men shake hands.

Middle Easterners

Family Values The customs of the Middle East often reflect its religious heritage. For Muslims, women are important within their families and may be quite protected from the rest of the world, which is evidenced in their wearing of the chador (or similar enveloping outer garment). The family and its honor are at the center of values; males are clearly recognized as the leaders of their families, and male children are especially cherished.

Interactions Men may embrace each other in greeting, may touch, and may stand quite close to others while talking. Punctuality is not a value in this part of the world, but warm hospitality is important. Expressing interest in the family's well-being precedes any business. Generosity often is so great that Middle Easterners may give you an item that you admired. Friday is the Islamic religious day, and no business is to be conducted.

Eating Traditions Women and children may eat separately, after the men, but the foods served both sexes usually follow Muslim laws: no alcohol or pork, goat, dog, crabs, lobsters, or products containing them. Fasting is required during Ramadan.

Jewish Practices

Judaism is prominent in Israel, which means that the religious day is Saturday. The food laws differ from those of Muslims: pork and shellfish are prohibited; Orthodox Jews require that their food be kosher (see Chapter 3) and that dairy and meat products be kept separate.

Hispanic Values

In the western hemisphere, Hispanics are characterized as a family-oriented, paternalistic society, which places the family (and extended family) as its dominant value. Typically, women are expected to take care of the children and home while men make the important decisions.

When talking with others, sharing news of family takes priority over proceeding with the business at hand. Sociability is valued more than punctuality. Conversation and greetings often involve touching and standing close. However, South Americans often greet each other with a handshake rather than an embrace.

Summary

Health professionals today counsel many clients with cultural backgrounds quite different from their own heritage. Successful communication requires an understanding of the food patterns and cultural practices commonly followed in the client's culture. The Food Guide Pyramid has been adapted to some other parts of the world and can provide a basis for dietary counseling. In the United States, MyPyramid replaced the Food Guide Pyramid as the tool for nutrition education in 2005. The food guides presently available in various countries include the Filipino Pyramid Food Guide, the Piramide Alimentaria para Puerto Rico, the Chinese Food Guide Pagoda, the Mediterranean Diet Pyramid, the Soul Food Pyramid, and Canada's Food Guide to Healthy Eating.

When counseling clients from other cultural backgrounds, professionals should consider many dimensions in addition to actual dietary information if communication is to be effective. Among these dimensions are language, body language, food appropriate to the culture, religion, and values (particularly about time). Some of the basic considerations for counseling Asians, Middle Easterners, and Hispanics are mentioned in this chapter.

Selected Sites

http://www.nal.usda.gov/fnic/etext/000039.html—Information on nutritional guidelines for various nations.

http://www.mypyramid.gov/global_nav/media.html—Information on the revised pyramid.

www.**mypyramid**.gov/—Discussion of dietary recommendations for individual Americans.

http://www.hc-sc.gc.ca/fri-an/food-guide-aliment/index_e.html—Canada's Food Guide to Healthy Eating information.

http://www.cyborlink.com—Background information on culture and traditions in many different countries; designed for business and professional interactions.

Study Questions

1. What food and cultural practices need to be considered before beginning to counsel a recent immigrant from the Middle East?
2. What food and cultural practices need to be considered before beginning to counsel a recent immigrant from China?
3. What food and cultural practices need to be considered before beginning to counsel a recent immigrant from Mexico?
4. Are there habits in your style of talking with another person that might need to be altered when you are working with clients from different backgrounds? If so, what are they, and how do you plan to make these changes?

Bibliography

Axtell, R.E. 1990. *Do's and Taboos of Hosting International Visitors.* John Wiley and Sons. New York.

Baldridge, L. 1985. *Complete Guide to Executive Manners.* Rawson Assoc. New York.

Basaran, P. 1999. Traditional foods of the Middle East. *Food Technol. 53*(6): 60.

Chinese Nutrition Society. 2000. Dietary guidelines and the Food Guide Pyramid. *J. Am. Dietet. Assoc. 99*(2): 886.

Curry, K.R. 2000. Multicultural competence in dietetics and nutrition. *J. Am. Dietet. Assoc. 100*(10): 1142.

Devine, E. and N.L. Braganti. 1995. *Traveler's Guide to Customs and Manners.* St. Martin's Press. New York.

Dresser, N. 1996. *Multicultural Manners.* John Wiley and Sons. New York.

Elkort, M. 1991. *The Secret Life of Food.* St. Martin's Press. New York.

Ge, K. and K. McNutt. 1999. Publication of the Chinese Guidelines and Pagoda: How it happened. *Nutr. Today 34*(3): 104.

Gordon, B.H.J. et al. 2000. Dietary habits and health beliefs of Korean-Americans in the San Francisco Bay Area. *J. Am. Dietet. Assoc. 100*(10): 1198.

Hampden-Turner, C.M. and F. Trompenaars. 1997. *Riding the Waves of Culture: Understanding Diversity in Global Business.* McGraw-Hill. New York.

Hampden-Turner, C.M. et al. 2000. *Building Cross-Cultural Competence: How to Create Wealth from Conflicting Values.* Yale University Press. New Haven, CT.

Harris, P.R. and R.T. Moran. 1987. *Managing Cultural Differences.* 3rd ed. Gulf Publishing. Houston, TX.

Harris-Davis, E. and B. Haughton. 2000. Model for multicultural nutrition counseling competencies. *J. Am. Dietet. Assoc. 100*(10): 1178.

Kleiner, S.M. 1999. Water: Essential but overlooked nutrient. *J. Am. Dietet. Assoc. 99*(2): 200.

Lukins, S. 1994. *All Around the World.* Workman Publishing. New York.

Macpherson, A.E. 1998. Food Guide Pyramid for Puerto Rico. *Nutr. Today 33*(5): 198.

Orbeta, S. 1998. Filipino Pyramid Food Guide: Perfect match for the Philippines. *Nutr. Today 33*(5): 210.

Packard, D. and M. McWilliams. 1993. Cultural foods heritage of Middle Eastern immigrants. *Nutr. Today 28*(3): 6.

Painter, J., J. Rah, and Y. Lee. 2002. Comparison of international food guide pictorial representations. *J. Am. Dietet. Assoc. 102*(4): 483.

Peterson, B. 2004. *Cultural Intelligence: Guide to Working with People from Other Cultures.* Intercultural Press. Yarmouth, ME

Sonnenfeld, A. 1996. *Food: Culinary History from Antiquity to Present.* Columbia University Press. New York.

Storti, C. 2001. *Art of Crossing Cultures.* Nicholas Brealey Publishing. London, England.

Glossary

Achaemenid Empire: Empire that extended from the eastern end of the Mediterranean eastward to central Asia, and then southward to northern India and the Persian Gulf (also called the *Persian Empire*); conquered in 331 BCE by Alexander the Great (Ch. 1).

Adobo: Filipino stew using meats marinated in vinegar seasoned with bagoong before being fried with onions and garlic, and then stewed (Ch. 16).

Aebleskiver: Small Danish doughnuts prepared in a special pan (Ch. 5).

Afrikaans: Language spoken by Afrikaners (South African farmers of Dutch heritage); one of the official languages of South Africa (Ch. 14).

Agave: Century plant; source of the sap used to make tequila and pulque (Ch. 22).

Aji: Very hot Andean chili pepper; pronounced ah-hee (Ch. 20).

Aksum: Early, well-developed settlement in the highlands of Ethiopia of importance in the 4th and 5th centuries CE (Ch. 14).

Almuerzo: Typical late-morning light meal (usually tortilla-based dish and a beverage) in Mexico and Central America (Ch. 22).

Alsace-Lorraine: Eastern region of France bordering Germany (Ch. 9).

Angkor Wat: Very large temple complex built by the Khmers in northwest Cambodia (Ch. 2).

Antipasto: "Before the pasta" (hors d'oeuvre); wide variety of tidbits or appetizers, often olives, bread sticks, pickled vegetables, or other simple items (Ch. 8).

Apfel strudel: Austrian pastry made with extremely thin dough spread with melted butter and an apple filling, then rolled into a log, sliced into 3-inch lengths, and baked (Ch. 6).

Appelflappen: Fried, batter-dipped slices of apple sprinkled with confectioner's sugar (Ch. 6).

Aquavit (akvavit): Aged whiskey made in Scandinavian liquor distilled from potato mash and flavored with caraway; considered possibly to be the national Scandinavian drink (Ch. 5).

Arawaks: Peaceful Indians who greeted Columbus when he arrived on Hispaniola (Ch. 21).

Ardennes: Region north of Paris to the English Channel (Ch. 9).

Arepas: Corn flour–based small pancake that is baked or fried; eaten throughout the day in Colombia and Venezuela (Ch. 20).

Atole: Gruel-like, thick beverage with a cornmeal base (Ch. 22).

Avatar: Person who is so saintly that he is thought to be an incarnation of a deity (Ch. 3).

Aztec Empire: Empire extending to both coasts of central Mexico south to Guatemala that was controlled by Aztecs from 1345 to 1519 CE (Ch. 1).

Aztecs: Indians in power in Mexico City region from the 14th century until Cortés conquered them in 1521 (Ch. 22).

Bacalao: Dried, salted cod (Ch. 21).

Bachalhau: Salted, dried cod (Ch. 10).

Bagoong: Filipino fermented, salted shrimp paste (Ch. 16).

Baklava: Baked dessert made of multiple layers of phyllo brushed with butter and with honey or rosewater (or both) plus chopped nuts (Ch. 11).

Balsamic vinegar: Special herb-flavored vinegar made by aging a thick syrup boiled from sweet white wine grapes acidified with the addition of some aged balsamic vinegar; the best is made in the vicinity of Modena in northern Italy (Ch. 8).

Bannock: Pancake made with oat instead of wheat flour (Ch. 4).

Bantus: Very large group of Africans originally from west and central regions of Africa who spread east and south prior to colonial days (Ch. 14).

Barley: Cereal grain suitable for human and animal diets (Ch. 1).

Bar mitzvah: Celebration of maturity at which a boy reads from the Torah in the synogogue at age 13 (Ch. 3).

Bartolonneu Diaz: See Diaz, Bartolomew.

Bastilla: Flaky-crusted pigeon pie flavored with ginger, cumin, cayenne, saffron, and cinnamon and dusted with confectioner's sugar; Moroccan specialty (Ch. 12).

Basques: Group living in the Pyrenees Mountains near the Bay of Biscay in northeastern Spain; some are seeking independence from Spain (Ch. 10).

Bat mitzvah: Celebration of a girl reaching maturity (age 12) (Ch. 3).

Béarnaise sauce: Sauce similar to hollandaise but with vinegar, shallots, and seasoning used instead of lemon juice (Ch. 9).

Béchamel sauce: Basic white sauce made with cream or milk and thickened with flour (Ch. 9).

Belgian endive: Oblong, small head vegetable consisting of very pale leaves around a central core; grown in the dark to prevent greening and displayed in light only when being sold in the market (Ch. 6).

Belgian waffle: Oblong, crisp waffle with deep indentations (Ch. 6).

Berbers: Early inhabitants of much of Libya and the Maghreb; noted as fierce fighters (Ch. 12).

Berlin Conference of 1884–85: Meeting at which European colonial powers divided the African continent without including Africans in their decisions (Ch. 13).

Bet tai: Disc-shaped, yeast-leavened wheat flour Arab bread, usually about 14 inches in diameter (Ch. 12).

Betel nut: Nut from a climbing pepper that is chewed for its digestive qualities; it has a deep red juice (Ch. 15).

Bird's nest soup: Cornstarch-thickened soup made with the mucilaginous lining of the nests of the Asiatic swiftlet, chicken broth, minced chicken, and egg white (Ch. 17).

Biscuit: Flat cracker or cookie (Ch. 4).

Bitter melon: Vegetable resembling a cucumber with a wrinkled green skin and interior red seeds (Ch. 17).

Black beans: Cooked and fermented soybeans preserved with ginger and salt (Ch. 17).

Bliny: Small, thin Russian pancake (Ch. 7).

Blood (Black) Pudding: Sausages made of toasted oatmeal, blood, onions, and seasonings (Ch. 4).

Bocaloa al Pil-Pil: Basque dish made with salted cod served in a garlic sauce (Ch. 10).

Bodhisattva: Semidivine, mystical being incorporated in Mahayana form of Buddhism (Ch. 3).

Body language: Movements that communicate attitude or feelings to another person (Ch. 24).

Boer: South African of Dutch descent (Ch. 14).

Boeuf bourguignon: French beef stew with vegetables and red wine (Ch. 9).

Bok choy: Vegetable that grows as a bunch with thick, white stalks and a top of several large, coarse green leaves (Ch. 17).

Bolivar, Simon: Considered to be the liberator of South America from its European powers (Ch. 20).

Bolshoi Ballet: World renowned Russian ballet ensemble (Ch. 2).

Bombilla: Fancy silver straw and filter used to sip maté from a gourd (Ch. 20).

Bordeaux: Western region of France that is home to some outstanding wines, including cognac (Ch. 9).

Bordelaise: Dark sauce made with meat juices, bone marrow, tarragon, shallots, and red wine of Bordeaux (Ch. 9).

Borrel: Dutch gin (Ch. 6).

Borsch: Russian soup featuring beets and cabbage and topped with sour cream. (Ch. 7).

Bosporus: Narrow channel that separates Europe from Asia between the Sea of Marmara and the Black Sea (Ch. 11).

Bouillabaisse: Soup made with many types of sea food; created originally in Marsailles (Ch. 9).

Boulangerie: French bakery (Ch. 9).

Boxer Rebellion: Violent uprising of a secret sect that trapped foreigners and missionaries in Peking for two months in 1900 (Ch. 17).

Braaivleis: Barbecues in the southern countries of Africa (Ch. 14).

Brahma: Creator god in Hindu religion (Ch. 3).

Brahmans: Highest caste in Hinduism; priests and teachers (Ch. 3).

Brillat-Savarin: Author of *The Physiology of Taste* (Ch. 9).

Brioche: Rich, uniquely shaped bread that highlights the special butter of Normandy (Ch. 9).

Brittany: Peninsula jutting from the northwest corner of France (Ch. 9).

Bruschetta: Italian bread brushed with olive oil, garlic, and sometimes tomato, and then broiled (Ch. 8).

Bubble and squeak: Dish of leftover beef, potatoes, and vegetables that makes these noises while being fried together (Ch. 4).

Bulgogi: Grilled, marinated beef or other meat (Ch. 18).

Bulgur: Partially cooked and dried cracked wheat (Ch. 11).

Bunraku: Puppet shows featuring large, complicated puppets very skillfully presented, often in traditional stories (Ch. 19).

Burghul: Granular cereal product made by boiling and drying cracked wheat; also called *bulgar* (Ch. 12).

Burgundy: Region on the eastern side of France north of the Rhone Valley and southeast of Paris; wine is produced in the region (Ch. 9).

Burnoose: Dark, capelike, hooded garment worn by Arab men, particularly in Morocco (Ch. 12).

Burrito: Wheat flour tortilla wrapped around bean or meat filling (Ch. 22).

Byzantine Empire: Eastern part of the former Roman Empire; was powerful for almost a millennium (129 BCE to 1071 CE) (Ch. 11).

Byzantium: Early name for the city once called Constantinople but now called *Istanbul* (Ch. 11).

Cabral: Portuguese explorer who claimed Brazil for Portugal in 1500 (Ch. 20).

Café au lait: Coffee with milk, the most common breakfast beverage (Ch. 9).

Café con leche: Coffee with warm milk, the style preferred in South America (Ch. 20).

Caffe latte: Coffee with a generous amount of milk added (Ch. 8).

Cajun: Style of one-pot cooking developed in southern Louisiana based on combining fish or meat, local vegetables, and rice (Ch. 23).

Calabash: Dried hard shell of a gourd suitable for holding liquids and foods (Ch. 14).

Callaloo: Spicy, thick, green soup containing spinach or other green plus okra, salt pork, coconut, and crabmeat (Ch. 21).

Calvados: Apple brandy from Normandy (Ch. 9).

Camembert: Ripened dessert cheese originating from Camembert in Normandy (Ch. 9).

Canada's Food Guide to Healthy Living: Rainbow graphic used to teach good food patterns to Canadians (Ch. 24).

Cannelloni: Ridged tubes of pasta that are designed to be filled with various stuffings for entrées or desserts (Ch. 8).

Cape of Good Hope: Region at the southern tip of the African continent where the Atlantic Ocean meets the Indian Ocean (Ch. 14).

Capellini: Angel hair (very thin, spaghetti-like pasta) (Ch. 8).

Cappuccino: Espresso topped with frothy white milk (Ch. 8).

Carbonada: Argentinian beef stew with rice, corn, potatoes, squash, sweet potatoes, and apples (Ch. 20).

Caravels: Sturdy vessels with lateen sails (triangular sails extended on a spar and flying from a rather low mast) (Ch. 10).

Carcassonne: Walled city founded by Visigoths that served as a fortress in southwest France during the Middle Ages (Ch. 9).

Carib: Fierce Indian tribe originating in South America that subsequently conquered the tribes in the Caribbean (Ch. 21).

Carthage: Important trading city on the Mediterranean shore of Tunisia (Ch. 1).

Casbah: Walled part of Arab city in North Africa (Ch. 12).

Cassareep: Bittersweet flavoring used in pepper pot; made from the boiled juice of the cassava root (Ch. 21).

Cassava: Tropical plant that is harvested for the starch abundant in the roots (Ch. 23).

Cassava bread: Native, rather flat bread made with powdered roots of cassava (Ch. 21).

Cassoulet: Meat and bean casserole from Toulouse in Languedoc-Roussillon (Southwestern France) (Ch. 9).

Cawl: Welsh name for soup or one-dish meal, usually containing cabbage, leeks, and bacon, as well as other ingredients that may be available (Ch. 4).

Cena: Supper meal (light menu) served in Mexico and Central America in the evening (Ch. 22).

Ceviche: Raw fish marinated for 1 to 4 hours in lime juice and onion until flesh is opaque and the consistency of cooked fish; probably originated in Peru (Ch. 20).

Ch'a-shao-pao: Cantonese dish of steamed buns filled with roast pork (Ch. 17).

Chalupas: Fried tortillas topped with refried beans, slivered meat, chopped tomatoes and onions, and grated cheese (Ch. 22).

Champagne: Region east of Paris where sparkling wine is produced (Ch. 9).

Chapati: Pancake-like grilled whole wheat bread popular in India (Ch. 15).

Char siu bao: Steamed buns with a roast pork filling, a Cantonese specialty (Ch. 17).

Chicharrones: Fried snack of pork cracklings (Ch. 21, 22).

Chilaquiles: Shredded fried tortillas baked with chili sauce (Ch. 22).

Chima: Long, gathered skirt that is part of traditional dress for Korean women (Ch. 18).

Chinese cabbage: An elongated cabbage with crinkled green leaves extending from the long ribs; also called *napa cabbage* (Ch. 17).

Chinese Food Guide Pagoda: Educational tool developed in China to guide people in making healthy food selections (Ch. 24).

Chinese parsley: Cilantro or coriander (Ch. 17).

Chi pao yu: Shanghai specialty; bits of seasoned raw fish wrapped in wax paper and fried in deep fat, then unwrapped, and eaten (Ch. 17).

Chogori: Short jacket tied off-center and worn with chima to complete the traditional dress for Korean women (Ch. 18).

Chorizo: Sausage flavored with paprikas and chilies that may be seasoned to be picante (hot) or dulce (sweet) (Ch. 10).

Choucroute garnie: Casserole of sauerkraut, sausage, and pork that is popular in Alsace (Ch. 9).

Chorten: Tibetan religious (Buddhist) monument, often with some gold or silver gilding (Ch. 3).

Chow mein: Parboiled noodles fried briefly with other ingredients; a Cantonese stir-fry with noodles (Ch. 17).

Churro: Spiral-shaped fried quick bread similar to a doughnut but extruded into a fluted, thick stick before frying. (Ch. 10).

Chutney: Chunky and flavorful sauce often served as an accompaniment to curry (Ch. 15).

Cinco de Mayo: Celebration on May 5 honoring Mexican defeat of the French in 1862 at Puebla; celebrations in the United States also recognize the Mexican Americans living in this country (Ch. 22, 23).

Circumambulate: Process of prostrating and prayings repeatedly while encircling a Buddhist temple once or many times (Ch. 3).

Cloudberries: Orange-yellow, plump berries that are similar in shape to blackberries; primarily available briefly from the far north of Scandinavia in summer (Ch. 5).

Cocido: Spanish meal consisting of three traditional courses (soup, cooked vegetables, and boiled meats) with specific ingredients varying. (Ch. 10); hearty Filipino stew containing a variety of meats, Spanish sausage, chickpeas, saba (sweet cooking bananas), tomato sauce, and lard (Ch. 16); hearty Caribbean stew containing beef, sausage, vegetables, and sofrito (Ch. 21).

Cockaleekie soup: Hearty soup containing chicken, barley, and leeks (Ch. 4).

Coconut cream: Pureed and strained creamy liquid prepared from freshly grated white meat of mature pared coconut and hot water (Ch. 16).

Coconut milk: Coconut liquid similar to coconut cream but with more liquid (Ch. 16).

Coconut water: Liquid drained from fresh coconut by puncturing its eyes; used as beverage, but not as a cooking ingredient (Ch. 16).

Colcannon: Scottish recipe for boiled potatoes, cabbage, turnips, and onions that are sautéed in butter (Ch. 4).

Comal: Flat, cast iron griddle used to bake tortillas (Ch. 22).

Comida: Heaviest meal of the day, eaten in midafternoon, in Mexico and Central America; includes soup, main dish, beans, rice, tortillas, dessert, and a beverage (Ch. 22).

Congee: Rice gruel often served at breakfast in southeast Asia (Ch. 16); in China, flavoring, meat, or fish are sometimes added (Ch. 17).

Coo-coo: Cornmeal pudding with okra, which is served either hot or cold (Ch. 21).

Coq au Riesling: Chicken cooked in Riesling, a white wine (Ch. 9).

Coq au vin: Chicken cooked with red wine (Ch. 9).

Coquilles St. Jacques: Dish made by poaching scallops before serving in white wine sauce (Ch. 9).

Corned beef and cabbage: Cured (corned) beef simmered about 3 hours before cabbage wedges are added and cooked with the meat for about 20 minutes (Ch. 4).

Cornish pasties: Turnovers filled with meat and vegetables; pronounced pas tē (rhymes with nasty) (Ch. 4).

Cortés: Spanish explorer in Central America, particularly Mexico, in the 16th century (Ch. 10).

Coui sauce: Popular Caribbean hot sauce made with cassava juice and hot peppers (Ch. 21).

Couscous: Cereal product made by drizzling water on wheat flour and rolling it into small pellets, which are then steamed until fluffy (Ch. 12).

Crayfish: Freshwater crustacean; apparently introduced to Scandinavia via ships from Britain (Ch. 5).

Creole: Flavorful cuisine of New Orleans and southern Louisiana that integrates spices from the Caribbean with cuisines brought by French, Spanish, and African immigrants (Ch. 23).

Creoles: People born in the Caribbean of European ancestry, often mixed with Negro blood (Ch. 21).

Crêpe: Thin French pancake served with a variety of fillings and sauces (Ch. 9).

Crumpet: Similar to an English muffin, but somewhat thinner and more springy (Ch. 4).

Culture: Way of life of a group of people (what they create, do, and think) (Ch. 2).

Curry: Hearty and well-seasoned stewlike dish featuring meat or legumes and served with several accompaniments (Ch. 15).

Customs: Traditions that are common to a cultural group, such as shaking hands or bowing (Ch. 24).

Cuzco: Center of the Incan civilization in a very high (11,000 feet) Andean valley in Peru (Ch. 20).

Cyrillic alphabet: Alphabet developed by Cyril and Methodius, Byzantine monks who lived in the 9th century; used in Russia and many Slavic regions (Ch. 7).

Daeborum: Annual celebration of First Full Moon Day, which celebrates the first day of full moon in the first month of the Korean lunar calendar (Ch. 18).

da Gama, Vasco: Portuguese navigator who opened trade routes to India in 1498 and 1502 (Ch. 10).

Daikon: Large, long Asian radish that has a delicate flavor and slight pungency (Ch. 17, 23).

Dal: Puree of lentils or other legumes, usually rather blandly seasoned (Ch. 15).

Dashi: Clear soup stock made with dried fillet of bonito and kelp (Ch. 19).

Dendé: Yellow to reddish oil from a West African palm, which was introduced into Brazilian cooking by African slave women (Ch. 20).

Desayuno: Breakfast (usually coffee and pastry) eaten early in the morning in Mexico and Central America (Ch. 22).

Devi: Hindu goddess, the wife of Shiva (Ch. 3).

Diaspora: Settling of Jews outside Palestine (Ch. 3).

Diaz, Bartolomeu: Portuguese navigator who sailed around the Cape of Good Hope (southern tip of Africa) in 1488 (Ch. 10).

Dim sum: Small, steamed dumplings filled with any of a variety of meat or vegetable fillings and many other small servings of food ranging from appetizers to sweets. (Ch. 17).

Dolmas: Stuffed grape leaves usually containing rice and often other ingredients; may be served hot or cold (Ch. 11).

Dravidians: Early people of southern India (Ch. 15).

Dulceata: Romanian dish of simmered fruits in very heavy syrup (Ch. 7).

Durian: Large Asian fruit with bumpy skin and extremely strong smell (Ch. 23).

Dutch East India Company: Trading company that established Cape Town as a post to restock its ships plying between the East Indies and Holland (Ch. 14).

Eastern (Shanghai) school: Designation of cuisine of the eastern seaboard of China, notably of Shanghai; light broths, seafood, egg rolls, and paper-wrapped foods are characteristic (Ch. 17).

Einkhorn: A type of wheat grown in Syria around 9000 BCE (Ch. 1).

Eintopf: Hearty German stew of meat, vegetables, and a cereal or dumplings (Ch. 6).

El Cid: Spanish military hero who fought many battles for both the Moors and the Catholics, and freed Valencia from the Moors in 1094 (Ch. 10).

Emmer: An early form of wheat farmed in Palestine by 10,000 BCE (Ch. 1).

Empañadas: Fried or baked semicircular pastries filled with meat and raisins; prominent in Argentina, but also found in other South American countries (Ch. 20).

Empire of Ghana: Dominant power in West Africa from 5th to 11th centuries (Ch. 13).

Empire of Mali: Empire dominating trade from Senegal to Egypt from the 13th to the 15th centuries (Ch. 13).

Empire of Songhai: Dominant empire in West Africa (including Timbuktu) after splitting from Mali in the 14th century and into the 16th century (Ch. 13).

Enchiladas: Corn tortillas rolled around a filling and covered with a sauce before baking (Ch. 22).

Escabeche: Cooked fish marinated in vinegar and spices (Ch. 21).

Escargot: Snails, usually served with butter or other sauce in Burgundy (Ch. 9).

Escoffier: Chef considered to be the definitive writer about French cuisine (1846–1935) (Ch. 9).

Espresso: Very strong Italian coffee made by brewing dark-roast, finely ground coffee with steam (Ch. 8).

Ethnicity: Affiliation with a race, people, or social group (Ch. 2).

Etruscan: Group who settled in Tuscany and moved south, ultimately taking over Rome and contributing their alphabet, speech, and ability to wage war (Ch. 8).

Fado: Distinctive sad musical form of the blues sung to a guitar accompaniment (Ch. 10).

Falafel: Dish made by creating a paste of soaked chickpeas and seasonings, shaping into balls or other forms, and frying in deep fat (Ch. 11).

Fan: Grain foods considered to be important as a balance (yin) with the ts'ai (other foods in the meal) (Ch. 17).

Färikäl: Thick lamb stew with cabbage; popular in Norway (Ch. 5).

Feijoada completa: Celebrated Brazilian dish of several meats (including sausages and bacon), beans, rice, hot sauces, manioc meal, and sliced oranges (Ch. 20).

Feta: Soft cheese made from ewe's milk (Ch. 11).

Filipino Pyramid Food Guide: Food guide developed in the Philippines to guide people in making healthy food choices using the local foods (Ch. 24).

Finnan haddie: Smoked haddock poached in milk on a bed of onions (Ch. 4).

Fish and chips: Batter-dipped pieces of cod or other fish that are deep-fat fried; served with deep-fat fried thick strips of potato (Ch. 4).

Fiskebeller: Norwegian fishballs (Ch. 5).

Five Pillars of Islam: Requirements of Islam: Shahada (creed), Salat (prayers), Saum (fasting), Zukat (purifying tax), and Hajj (pilgrimage to Mecca) (Ch. 3).

Five-spice powder: Popular Chinese spice made by mixing star anise, Szechwan pepper, cinnamon, cloves, and fennel (Ch. 17).

Fjord: Narrow, steep-sided inlet from the sea (Ch. 5).

Flan: Baked custard dessert, usually containing caramel; served in Spain, Portugal, Central America, and Mexico (Ch. 10, 22).

Flautas: Tightly rolled corn tortillas containing a small amount of filling that are fried until crisp (Ch. 22).

Flying buttress: External architectural feature to support the relatively thin, windowed walls of Gothic cathedrals (Ch. 9).

Fondue: Swiss dish prepared by melting cheese with wine in a chafing dish and using long-handled forks to dip cubes of bread into the cheese mixture (Ch. 6).

Fontina: Cheese well suited for making fondue; originally from Valle d'Aosta in northern Italy near Great St. Bernard Pass (Ch. 8).

Food Guide Pyramid: Educational tool used in the United States to guide people in making healthy food choices (Ch. 24).

Foo-foo: Mashed plantains with okra (Ch. 21).

Fool: Sweetened fruit puree blended with custard or cream; served cold (Ch. 4).

Forbidden City: Walled area in Beijing built by Chinese emperors as the seat of government and power (Ch. 2).

Foul: Mixture of cooked chickpeas and black or broad beans that have been soaked together for at least two days before being cooked; served with topping of garlic, olive oil, lemon, tomato, and cilantro (Ch. 11).

Franco: Spanish dictator for about 40 years in the 20th century (Ch. 10).

Frijoles refritos: Cooked beans mashed and fried with lard to create a somewhat bumpy texture (Ch. 22).

Frikadeller: Danish meatballs (Ch. 5).

Fruit soup: Dessert soup popular in Scandinavia; often made with various dried fruits that are readily available through long winters (Ch. 5).

Fufu: Starchy paste produced by pounding and boiling manioc or other rich source of starch and then dipping each bite in a spicy sauce; popular in West Africa (Ch. 13); starchy paste or dough made of cassava; popular specifically in Kenya (Ch. 14).

Funchi: Cornmeal pudding prepared in the Caribbean (Ch. 21).

Fungi: Designation for mushrooms in some Chinese recipes; may include shiitake, enoki, oyster, button, or other types, usually dried (Ch. 17).

Fusilli: Wavy, spaghetti-like pasta (Ch. 8).

Garam masala: Basic mixture of spices usually prepared in quantity and used as desired to season many different dishes in India (Ch. 15).

Gari foto: Stew of hard-cooked eggs, onions, and tomatoes (Ch. 13).

Gazpacho: Chilled soup made with many chopped vegetables of Spain plus beef or chicken stock, red wine vinegar, and olive oil (Ch. 10).

Gelato: Italian ice cream (Ch. 8).

Ghandi, Mahatma: Famous pacifist in India who led a 200-mile march to the sea in 1930 to protest the salt tax (Ch. 2).

Ghee: Clarified butter made by boiling to evaporate the water and precipate the milk solids before filtering to clarify it; clarified butter that has been cooked down a little to add flavor; expensive, but preferred fat for cooking in India (Ch. 15).

Ghiveciu: Romanian casserole consisting of browned chunks of pork or veal and vegetables combined with tomato paste, red wine, and green grapes (Ch. 7).

Gibanica: Yugoslavian layered cheese pie (Ch. 7).

Ginger root: Gnarled root of ginger, which usually is peeled and grated; adds flavor as well as some heat to a recipe (Ch. 17).

Gnocchi: Yugoslavian small dumplings of wheat or cornmeal, or both (Ch. 7, 8).

Gorditas: Thick, small tortilla fried and slit to form a pocket that is stuffed with meats or seafood (or both), lettuce, and cheese served topped with salsa, shredded lettuce, chopped tomatoes and grated cheese (Ch. 22).

Goree: Island just off the coast of Dakar, Senegal, from which vast numbers of slaves were shipped to the Americas and Caribbean islands (Ch. 13).

Gorgonzola: Blue-veined cheese that originated in Gorgonzola near Milan in northern Italy and is now produced in the Po Valley (Ch. 8).

Gothic: Style of cathedral featuring pointed arches, high and thin walls containing stained glass, and strengthened by flying buttresses on the exterior (Ch. 9).

Gravet: Smoked salmon, a Norwegian delicacy (Ch. 5).

Great Rift Valley: Vast depression in the earth extending from Jordan south and west to Mozambique (Ch. 14).

Great Zimbabwe: Settlement in Zimbabwe featuring the Great Enclosure built of stone in the 14th century (Ch. 14).

Guacamole: Mashed avocado, chilies, tomatoes, cilantro, and lemon juice; served as an accompaniment or a garnish (Ch. 22).

Gulyás: Hungarian stew made with chunks of braised meat, seasoned with onion and paprika, and cooked with varying amounts of liquid (Ch. 7).

Haggis: Scottish traditional pudding of oatmeal, variety meats, suet, onions, and seasonings boiled in a sheep's stomach; often served at dinners honoring Robert Burns, Scotland's famous poet (Ch. 4).

Hajj: Pilgrimage to Mecca; one of Five Pillars (Ch. 3).

Hallacas: Colombian version of a tamale made by wrapping a layer of corn flour dough and a filling of meat or other ingredients in banana leaves and then steaming the packets (Ch. 20).

Han-gŭl: Phonetic Korean alphabet developed under the leadership of King Sejong in the 15th century (Ch. 18).

Hapsburg: Family that ruled Austria and its neighbors for about seven centuries until World War I (Ch. 6).

Harira: Hearty soup containing legumes, meat, and vegetables and seasoned with spices and lemon; important for suppers during Ramadan (Ch. 12).

Hellenistic Greece: Ancient Greek civilization that reached its peak of political dominance and cultural influence from about 323 BCE to 27 BCE (Ch. 1).

Hispaniola: Caribbean island where Columbus landed and that eventually became the countries of Haiti and the Dominican Republic (Ch. 21).

Hittites: Civilization occupying parts of Turkey to Syria and Mesopotamia for more than four centuries, ending in about 1200 BCE (Ch. 11).

Hmongs: People native to the northern hill regions of Laos (Ch. 16).

Hohenzollern: Family that ruled Prussia and neighboring regions for three centuries, ending with the end of World War I (Ch. 6).

Hoisin sauce: Thick, dark, garlic-flavored bean sauce (Ch. 17).

Hollandaise sauce: Sauce made of an emulsion of butter, egg yolks, lemon juice, and seasoning (Ch. 9).

Honshu: Largest of the islands of Japan; Tokyo is on Honshu (Ch. 19).

Hot cross buns: Easter yeast buns containing cinnamon, allspice, and raisins, and topped with a cross of candied orange peel or a strip of dough to represent the cross of Christ (Ch. 4).

Hummus: Dip made with pureed, cooked chickpeas, tahini, lemon juice, garlic, and olive oil (Ch. 11).

Hutspot: Hearty stewlike dish made in the Netherlands by simmering a large cut of meat with vegetables and then mashing the cooked vegetables before serving them with the sliced meat (Ch. 6).

Iberian Peninsula: Peninsula composed of Spain and Portugal forming the western part of Europe (Ch. 10).

Ibrik: Turkish coffee maker designed with a long handle and a narrow neck (Ch. 11).

Id al-Fitr: Three-day holiday celebrating the end of the Ramadan, the month of fasting (Ch. 3).

Idlis: Rice cakes (Ch. 15).

Ikebana: Japanese art of arranging cut flowers (Ch. 19).

Ile de France: Region within a 50-mile circle of Paris (Ch. 9).

Illyrians: Group of people settling the Balkans prior to the Romans (Ch. 7).

Imam: Person who leads Muslims in their daily prayers (Ch. 3).

Incan Empire: Region of Andes in Peru controlled by Incas from about 1300 CE until Pizarro conquered it after his arrival in 1533 CE (Ch. 1).

Inquisition: Period when Spain required non-Catholics to convert or leave the country; torture sometimes was part of the imprisonment process in Spain, Peru, and Portugal (Ch. 10).

Irish soda bread: Round loaf of bread leavened by carbon dioxide produced from buttermilk and soda, ingredients in the dough (Ch. 4).

Irish stew: Stew featuring lamb cubes or other meat, potatoes, onions, leeks, cabbage, and/or other vegetables; frequently served with red cabbage in Ireland (Ch. 4).

Jenné-Jeno: Very early town (before 500 CE) in Mali (Ch. 13).

Jicama: Brown root vegetable with crisp white interior, often served in raw slices with chili powder sprinkled on them (Ch. 22).

Jollof rice: Dish composed of layers of meat, tomatoes and other vegetables, and steamed rice (Ch. 13).

Jugged: Slow, moist-heat cooking of meat in a covered clay pot (Ch. 4).

Ka'ba: Black stone cube with a meteorite in its wall; shrine in the center of Mecca that pilgrions circumambulate as part of the Hajj (Ch. 3).

Kabob (kebab): Meat grilled, sometimes with other items, on a skewer (Ch. 11).

Kabuki: Traditional, highly stylized drama performed by men in elaborate costumes and makeup, often featuring dancing and some music (Ch. 19).

Kacca: Hindu term for level of food just below pakka, but made without ghee (Ch. 3)

Kama: Hindu god of love (Ch. 3).

Kami: The supernatural form of a deceased ancestor (Ch. 3).

Kaoliang: Sorghum (grain) crop grown in northern China (Ch. 17).

Kapi: Thai salty, dried shrimp paste (Ch. 16).

Karma: Force generated by actions in a Hindu's life that will determine what the next life will be Ch. 3).

Kasha: Buckwheat groats (or sometimes other cereals) boiled in liquid until light and fluffy; popular in Russia and its environs (Ch. 7).

Kashruth: Requirements outlining the preparation and types of food that Orthodox and other Jews may eat (Ch. 3).

Keshy yena: Edam cheese stuffed with grated cheese, meat mixtures, and seasonings and then baked; from Netherlands Antilles (Ch. 21).

Khatib: Person who reads the Friday sermon (Ch. 3).

Khmers: People native to Cambodia (Ch. 16).

Kibbeh: Deep-fat fried, egg-shaped shell of finely minced lamb and cracked wheat paste encasing a filling of another meat (Ch. 11).

Kielbasa: Polish sausage made of ground beef and pork, well seasoned with garlic (Ch. 7).

Kimchi: Fermented, pickled vegetables (particularly cabbage) (Ch. 18).

Kippers: Herring prepared in the traditional Scottish way of splitting them and then salting, drying, and smoking to preserve them (Ch. 4).

Kitchen god: Spirit of the hearth who determines wealth and longevity of people in the household; reports to Heaven annually regarding family's behavior (Ch. 17).

Knedliky: Flat, circular potato or bread dumplings popular in the Czech Republic and Slovakia (Ch. 7).

Kochujang: Red pepper and bean paste used as a condiment and as an ingredient in Korean recipes (Ch. 18).

Koldt bord: Literally, cold table; bread, butter, and cold dishes that are the beginning part of a smørgasbørd (Ch. 5).

Koran: Writings from Allah given to Muhammad by Angel Gabriel to define the spiritual life of Muslims (Ch. 3).

Koryŏ: Dynasty that ruled Korea from 918 to 1392 and subsequently was the source for the name Korea (Ch. 18).

Kringle: Nut-filled coffee cake from Denmark (Ch. 5).

Krishna: Hindu god celebrated as the eighth incarnation of Vishnu (Ch. 3).

Kshatriyas: Second caste in Hinduism; warriors and rulers (Ch. 3).

Ku lao jou: Dish containing starch-coated fried cubes of pork, stir-fried green peppers, various vegetables, and pineapple cubes in a thickened sweet-sour tomato sauce (Ch. 17).

Kulich: Russian traditional yeast-leavened Easter bread containing candied and dried fruits, nuts, and liqueur (Ch. 7).

Kutho: Kind or generous act that brings merit to help strive toward Nirvana (Ch. 3).

Kwanzaa: African-American holiday lasting a week at the end of the year to celebrate African-American heritage (Ch. 23).

Languedoc-Roussillon: Region in southern France that includes the marshy delta of the Rhone River (Ch. 9).

L'apéritif: Cocktail hour preceding dinner in France (Ch. 9).

Lapin: Rabbit, a popular meat in Belgium (Ch. 6).

Lapskaus: Chunky and thick meat and potato stew (Ch. 5).

Lasagne: Broad, ribbonlike pasta used in casserole dishes (Ch. 8).

Lascaux: Area in southern France where cave paintings from prehistoric people have been found (Ch. 9).

Laver: Edible seaweed popular in Korea (Ch. 18).

Laverbread: Jellylike mass resulting from boiling a special seaweed harvested along the coast of Wales (Ch. 4).

Lavosh: Armenian cracker bread; basically a very thin version of pita without a pocket (Ch. 11).

Lebkuchen: German gingerbread cookies baked in picture molds (Ch. 6).

Lebneh: Soft cheese made by draining whey from yogurt (Ch. 11).

Lefse: Norwegian flatbread (Ch. 5).

Le goûter: Afternoon snack (Ch. 9).

Lemon curd: Egg yolk-thickened sweet filling flavored with lemon juice and rind; often used as filling for tarts and pies (Ch. 4).

Le petit déjeuner: French breakfast (typically a croissant and coffee) (Ch. 9).

Levant: Land at the eastern end of the Mediterranean Sea (Ch. 11).

Lingonberries: Mountain cranberrylike fruit particularly popular in Sweden (Ch. 5).

Longyi: Long, saronglike cloth worn in Burma, tucked in at the waist; can be hiked up in the very hot weather (Ch. 16).

Lotus root: Crunchy root of lotus (water lily) cut crosswise to use in stir-fries and soups, where its porous appearance due to many lengthwise cavities in the root adds visual interest (Ch. 17).

Lumache: Large, conch shell–shaped pasta suitable for stuffing (Ch. 8).

Lutefisk: Cod soaked in lime until very soft (about 3 days) before being rinsed in running water for 2 days and subsequently poached or boiled (Ch. 5).

Mace: Reddish coating on nutmeg, which is removed and dried for use as a spice (Ch. 21).

Madeira wine: Sweet, fruity wine produced on Madeira, the Portuguese island in the North Atlantic Ocean (Ch. 10).

Magellan: Portuguese navigator who led the first circumnavigation of the world from 1519 to 1522 but died in the Philippines during the trip (Ch. 10).

Maghreb: Countries in the northwestern part of Africa: Morocco, Algeria, and Tunisia (Ch. 12).

Magyars: Ancestors of today's Hungarians (Ch. 7).

Mahayana: Mystical form of Buddhism practiced in Tibet, Mongolia, and the Himalayas (Ch. 3).

Malagueta: Extremely hot South American pepper, also called *aji* (Ch. 20).

Mamaliga: Romanian cornmeal mush similar to Italian polenta (Ch. 7).

Manicotti: Long, plain tube of pasta appropriate for stuffing (Ch. 8).

Manioc (cassava): Inclusive name for group of related tropical plants native to the western hemisphere that had fleshy roots rich in starch (Ch. 1); granular flour prepared by peeling and then grating bitter cassava roots and squeezing out absolutely all of the juice, which is poisonous until the juice is subsequently boiled. The dry grated material is broken to a powder by pounding (Ch. 20).

Mantra: Hindu incantation (Ch. 3).

Manu: Source of Hindu laws on living, and ancestor of Hindus, progenitor of human race and source of Vedas (Ch. 3).

Marmitako: Basque stew made with tuna and potatoes (Ch. 10).

Masa: Cornmeal dough made by mixing masa harina and water; main ingredient of tamales (Ch. 22).

Masa harina: Ground corn that has been soaked in lime (Ch. 22).

Mascarpone: Unripened Italian dessert cheese made from fresh cream; may be flavored with honey, liqueurs, or candied fruit (Ch. 8).

Maté: Beverage brewed in a gourd by pouring hot water over crushed leaves of yerba maté, producing a caffeine-containing beverage that is sipped through a bombilla; pronounced ma-tay (Ch. 20).

Mayan Empire: Region including the Yucatan Peninsula and Guatemala controlled by Mayans from 300 BCE to about 1200 CE (Ch. 1).

Mayans: Indians living in Guatemala, Belize, and southern Mexico from 600 BCE to 1200 BCE (Ch. 22).

Mealie meal: South African name for cornmeal (*mealie* means *corn*) (Ch. 14).

Medici: Powerful Florentine banking family; Cosimo, Lorenzo, and Caterina (who carried the excellence of Florentine cuisine to France when she married future King Henri II) are credited with influencing the artistic and culinary renaissance particularly in the 15th and 16th centuries, (Ch. 8).

Medina: Old native quarter of a North African city (Ch. 12).

Mediterranean Diet Pyramid: Food pyramid designed to incorporate the foods common to the Mediterranean in a pattern that has 11 categories (Ch. 24).

Menorah: Jewish candelabra designed to hold four candles in a row on each side of a central holder slightly higher than the eight holders; one additional candle is lighted each day of the eight days of Chunukah (Ch. 3).

Merienda: Late afternoon light refreshment eaten in Mexico and Central America (Ch. 22).

Meseta: High central plain in Spain (Ch. 10).

Mestizo: Person of mixed heritage of Spainards and native Indians (Ch. 20, 21).

Metate: Stone quern used for grinding nixtamal to masa harina (Ch. 22).

Mihrab: Niche in an interior wall of a mosque indicating the direction of Mecca for worshipers during Salat (Ch. 3).

Minaret: Tower of a mosque from which people are called to prayer (Ch. 3).

Minbar: Staircase topped with a pulpit in a mosque (Ch. 3).

Minoans: Mediterranean people who developed a prosperous, artistic civilization on Crete that was ended by a tidal wave in 1625 BCE (Ch. 1).

Mirin: Sweet rice wine (Ch. 19).

Miso: Fermented soybean paste (Ch. 19).

Mochi: Rice cake made by pounding cooked sweet glutinous rice; traditional for New Year's celebration (Ch. 19).

Mofongo: Puerto Rican specialty made with mashed plantains, pork cracklings, and garlic and either fried in balls or baked as a pancake (Ch. 21).

Mongol Empire: Barbaric, short-lived empire ranging southward from central Asia and westward to threaten even Vienna in Europe. (Ch. 1)

Mongolian fire pot: Mongolian-designed unique chafing dish with a spot to burn charcoal, a chimney going up the center, and a surrounding round vessel where broth is kept hot enough for diners to cook their individual bites of meats and vegetables (Ch. 17).

Mons: People native to Burma (Ch. 16).

Moors: Islamic inhabitants of northwestern Africa (mixture of Arabs and Berbers) from Morocco who invaded Spain in the 8th century (Ch. 10, 12).

Moo shu pork: Slivered pieces of seasoned pork and bean paste or other ingredients wrapped in small, thin pancakes (Ch. 17).

Moros y Cristianos: Cuban specialty containing black beans and rice cooked with garlic, onions, green peppers, tomatoes, and seasonings (Ch. 21).

Mosque: Place of worship for Muslims; contains a mihrab pointing to Mecca, a minbar atop a staircase for delivering the Friday sermon and daily prayers, and at least one minaret (Ch. 3).

Moussaka: Eggplant casserole usually containing lamb, onions, tomato sauce, and eggplant slices (Ch. 11).

Mozzarella: Cheese used on pizzas, originally made from buffalo milk, but now often made from cow's milk (Ch. 8).

Muesli: Breakfast cereal of toasted oats, nuts, and dried apples developed by a Swiss doctor (Ch. 6).

Muezzin: Person who calls Muslims to prayer five times a day (Ch. 3).

Muhammad: *See* Prophet Muhammad.

Mulligatawny: Curry-flavored rich soup made with a chicken or lamb base; reflecting British period in India (Ch. 4).

Myceneans: Civilization centered on the Greek Peloponnesus that controlled Crete and other Mediterranean islands (Ch. 1).

MyPyramid: Graphic guide to food nutrition introduced in 2005 to replace the Food Guide Pyramid as an instructional tool for nutrition education (Ch. 24).

Naan: Oval-shaped whole wheat bread baked by sticking it to the wall of a tandoor (Ch. 15).

Nam pla: Fermented fish sauce popular in Thailand (Ch. 16).

Niger River: One of the longest rivers of the world traverses much of West Africa, running north before turning east and south; has an interior delta and one at the coast (Ch. 13).

Nixtamal: Hull-less, lime-soaked corn (Ch. 22).

Nopales: Leaves of prickly pear cactus (Ch. 22).

Nori: Dried seaweed available in thin, greenish-black sheets; used for wrapping sushi and other foods or as a garnish (Ch. 19).

Normandy: Northern region of France just east of Brittany that lies along the coast of the English Channel (Ch. 9).

Northern (Peking) school: Designation of cuisine of the northern region of China that includes Mongolian fire pot, and Peking duck as well as moo shu pork and other recipes that use wheat and wheat flour products (Ch. 17).

Nuoc cham: Vietnamese condiment made with chili peppers, citrus juice, garlic, onions, and vinegar (Ch. 16).

Nuoc mam: Fermented, salted fish sauce popular in Vietnam (Ch. 16).

Olmecs: Dominant cultural group in Central America from 1200 to 150 BCE; settled predominantly on the coast of the

Gulf of Mexico along the Bay of Campeche west of the Yucatan Peninsula (Ch. 1).

Om: Sound chant repeated by Hindus for long periods to generate religious energy (Ch. 3).

Opium War: War in 1840 caused by British involvement in the opium trade in China; resulted in the long-term lease of Hong Kong to Britain (Ch. 17).

Osso buco: Braised veal shanks simmered with herbs and wine until very tender (Ch. 8).

Ottoman Empire: Large empire centered in Turkey that ruled for more than 600 years, ending after World War I. (Ch. 11).

Ouzo: Greece's distilled alcoholic drink from grape skins that are cooked with star anise and a variety of other herbs prior to distillation (Ch. 11).

Oyster sauce: Salty, dark Chinese sauce made with soy sauce and the taste of oysters and other flavoring agents (Ch. 17).

Paella: Traditional rice dish colored and flavored by saffron and topped with cooked vegetables and meats (Ch. 10).

Pagoda: Shrine of several stories where Buddhists worship (Ch. 3).

Pakka: Hindu word for food containing ghee; offered to gods and then high-ranking guests (Ch. 3).

Pannetone: Coarse, sweet yeast bread containing raisins and candied fruit (Ch. 8).

Paratha: Whole wheat bread circles about 7 inches in diameter, made with ghee in the dough and fried in ghee on the griddle (Ch. 15).

Parmesan: Hard cheese often aged for more than two years; frequently grated over Italian dishes (Ch. 8).

Parrillada: Grilled mixture of meats, typical of Argentina (Ch. 20).

Parthenon: Classical Greek structure dominating the Acropolis in Athens (Ch. 2).

Paskha: Pyramid-shaped Russian Easter cake (Ch. 7).

Pasteles: Puerto Rican specialty made by spreading mashed plantain or cornmeal on a plantain leaf, adding a savory filling, wrapping, and steaming (Ch. 21).

Pastelitos: Savory, small turnovers with meat filling made in the Dominican Republic (Ch. 21).

Patis: Fermented, salty fish sauce popular in the Philippines (Ch. 16).

Peking duck: Traditional dish of northern China, which involves special roasting of a duck until the skin is very crisp; skin, a bit of duck meat, and green onion are wrapped in a thin pancake liberally splashed with hoisin sauce. Plum sauce is also served (Ch. 17).

Peloponnesus: Peninsula extending off the southwestern region of Greece (Ch. 11).

Penne: Tubular pasta cut diagonally into pieces about an inch long (Ch. 8).

Pepper pot: Long-lived stew common throughout the Caribbean, flavored with cassareep, containing meats and vegetables that are replenished from time to time as needed and available (Ch. 21).

Perigord: Area north of the Pyrenees where truffles are found (Ch. 9).

Pesto: Flavorful thick sauce made by pulverizing fresh basil and adding such ingredients as piñon nuts, parmesan cheese, garlic, and olive oil (Ch. 8).

Phoenicians: People living in Lebanon who sailed extensively to trade with many other regions by 1000 BCE (Ch. 1).

Phyllo: Extremely thin dough that is formed into large sheets and serves as the main ingredient for desserts and some main dishes (Ch. 11).

Pierogi: Polish dish consisting of small pockets of dough containing a filling (vegetable or sweet) (Ch. 7).

Pikelet: Small pancake served at tea in Wales and Scotland (Ch. 4).

Pirozhki: Small Russian pastry filled with meat (Ch. 7).

Pita: Pocket bread that is common throughout the Middle East (Ch. 11).

Pizarro: Spanish explorer who conquered the Incas in Peru in the 16th century and established Spanish dominance there (Ch. 10, 20).

Plantain: Very starchy banana, which is cooked before serving (Ch. 23).

Plum sauce: Chutney made with plums, apricots, vinegar, chili, and sugar (Ch. 17).

Plum pudding: Dense, steamed pudding containing some suet and a generous amount of dried and candied fruits that is served warm, usually with hard sauce and often flamed with brandy (Ch. 4).

Poe (poi): Starchy paste of boiled and pounded peeled taro root popular in Polynesia (Ch. 16).

Polenta: Traditional northern Italian dish; cornmeal cooked in milk or other liquid with frequent stirring until it forms a mushy, soft paste, at which time butter and sometimes other ingredients are added (Ch. 8).

Pombe: Kenyan beer (Ch. 14).

Porchetta: Whole, suckling pig flavored with fennel, peppercorns, and garlic and roasted; popular entrée in Tuscany (Ch. 8).

Porrusalda: Basque soup that features potatoes and leeks. (Ch. 10).

Posados: Procession of Mary and Joseph's search for lodging reenacted from December 16 until Christmas Eve as part of Christmas festivities (Ch. 22).

Potala: Seat of Tibetan Buddhism and the former home of the Dalai Lama (Ch. 15).

Pot stickers: Assorted fillings of shredded meats and/or chopped vegetables wrapped in a thin pancake, fried, and then simmered in chicken stock (Ch. 17).

Prester John: Mythical Christian leader of a domain originally rumored to be in India and then reported to be deep in Africa (Ch. 14).

Prince Henry the Navigator: Portuguese leader who sponsored voyages of exploration aboard caravels to very distant places (Ch. 10).

Prophet Muhammad: Arab man who founded Islam in the 7th century (Ch. 3).

Prosciutto: Thinly sliced, well-cured Parma ham (Ch. 8).

Provence: Region in southern France adjacent to the French Riviera (Ch. 9).

Puja: Hindu worship ritual that begins with seating, cleansing, and dressing a deity. Food is offered to the god and then some is eaten by the worshiper (Ch. 3).

Pumpernickel: German dark, coarse bread made with unsifted rye flour (Ch. 6).

Punic Wars: Three wars fought between Carthage and Rome between 264 and 146 BCE (Ch. 1).

Puri: Deep-fat fried rounds of whole wheat bread that are puffed in the middle during frying (Ch. 15).

Quesada: Spanish conquistador credited with conquering Colombia (Ch. 20).

Quesadilla: Flour tortilla folded over a layer of grated cheese and heated (Ch. 22).

Quiche Lorraine: Tart featuring a bacon and custard filling originally made in Lorraine region of France (Ch. 9).

Quinoa: Grain grown in the high Andes by Indians and eaten as a rich source of protein and starch in Peru and Chile; pronounced keen-wah (Ch. 20).

Raclette: Swiss favorite consisting of melted cheese served with a sliced, boiled potato, sweet gherkin, and pickled pearl onions (Ch. 6).

Raki: Distilled Turkish alcoholic beverage made from grape residue and with anise for added flavor; turns milky if water is added. (Ch. 11).

Ramadan: One-month period of fasting from sunrise to sunset each year; one of the Pillars of Islam (Ch. 3).

Rastafarianism: Jamaican religion traced to teachings in the Old Testament; members may have dreadlocks; reggae music originated in this group (Ch. 21).

Ratatouille: Highly flavorful medley of vegetables and herbs from Provence (Ch. 9).

Ravioli: Rectangular pasta pouches stuffed with ground meat or cheese (Ch. 8).

Red cooking: Braising meat mixtures in a sauce containing some soy sauce (Ch. 17).

Retsina: Greek rosé or white wine flavored with pine resin (Ch. 11).

Rijsttafel: Rice table originating in Indonesia; brought to the Netherlands by the Dutch East Indies Company; consists of some highly spiced dishes and many other somewhat bland dishes, which are prepared at the table (usually in restaurants) (Ch. 6).

Risotto: Rice dish from northern Italy made by sautéing Arborio or other short-grain rice before slowly adding a bit of white wine and other liquid while cooking and stirring until grains are tender and the texture is creamy (Ch. 8).

Roma: Nomadic group originating from India but particularly numerous in Romania that has spread into most parts of Europe (Ch. 7).

Roman Empire: Vast empire based in Rome that gradually was formed to cover much of the areas along the Mediterranean coast into Turkey, France, and England. (Ch. 1)

Romano: Sharp, aged sheep's milk cheese; very hard cheese, ideal for grating (Ch. 8).

Rømmegrøt: Norwegian porridge of milk and sour cream thickened with flour and flavored with cinnamon and coarse sugar granules (Ch. 5).

Rösti: Swiss dish of parboiled, grated potatoes sautéed in sizzling butter to make a pancake-like disk that is browned well on both sides (Ch. 6).

Roti: Indian word for bread (Ch. 15).

Sachertorte: Austrian dessert; layered chocolate cake spread with apricot jam and topped with a chocolate glaze (Ch. 6).

Sacred cow: Wandering cow where Hindus live; protected from harm because of respect for life (Ch. 3).

Sadza: Zimbabwean name for a stiff cornmeal porridge (Ch. 14).

Saffron: Orange to yellow spice; the stigma of purple crocus; adds color and flavor to dishes (Ch. 10).

Safsari: Robes worn by women in North Africa to cover their bodies, including a headpiece with a veil to cover their face except the eyes. (Ch. 12).

Sahel: Broad band of land across West Africa between the Sahara and the lush vegetation along the southern coast (Ch. 13).

Sake: Strong rice wine, usually served warm (Ch. 19).

Salat: Muslim daily prayer according to the Five Pillars (Ch. 3).

Sally Lunn: Light yeast bread baked in a tubular pan, sliced in half, and then topped with whipped cream or melted butter; originated in Bath, England (Ch. 4).

Salsa: Sauce containing finely chopped vegetables and seasonings used to add flavor excitement to many Mexican and Central American dishes (Ch. 22).

Sambar: Spicy purée of lentils, which often is served with idlis (Ch. 15).

Samgye t'yang: Whole small chicken stuffed with rice, ginseng, and chestnuts, covered in broth, and baked until meat almost falls from bones (Ch. 18).

Sami: Nomadic reindeer herders (Lapplanders) living in the arctic reaches of Scandinavia; shorter stature and darker coloring than the Scandinavians from the lower parts of this region (Ch. 5).

Samosa: Fried pastry enclosing a filling (Ch. 15).

Samovar: Elaborate Russian device equipped with a chimney, a teapot for the essence of the tea, and a large area where the water is boiled for dispensing from the spigot (Ch. 7).

Sancocho: Stew popular in the Dominican Republic; contains plantain, chicken, cassava, vinegar, and pepper (Ch. 21).

Sang-chi-sam: Lettuce-wrapped meal containing many tidbits from numerous dishes selected by the diner (Ch. 18).

Sangria: Red wine blended with fruit juices (Ch. 10).

Sashimi: Very carefully cut and arranged slices of raw fish (Ch. 19).

Sauerbraten: German dish; roast marinated in vinegar and wine and simmered with seasonings until very tender, and then served with a gingersnap-containing gravy and red cabbage cooked with tart apples (Ch. 6).

Sauerkraut: Pickled shredded cabbage, a German specialty (Ch. 6).

Saum: Ritual of fasting (Ch. 3).

Schnitzel: German term for thin cutlet of veal or other meat that is dipped in a batter prior to cooking (Ch. 6).

Scone: Quick bread made from a dough that is rolled and cut into triangles or circles, and then baked in a very hot oven; popular for teatime (Ch. 4).

Scotch Broth: Thick soup made of vegetables and a meat broth (Ch. 4).

Seaweed: Various types of edible seaweeds and sea grass, as well as purple laver; usually used dried in soups (Ch. 17).

Sejong the Great: Dynamic 15th-century Korean leader who sponsored development of han-gŭl, written music, movable type, astronomy, and a medical book (Ch. 18).

Shahada: One of the Five Pillars; chanting of creed, "There is no god but God; Muhammad is the Messenger of God" (Ch. 3).

Shark's fin: Usually transparent, yellowish, dried cartilage from the fin of a shark; requires rehydration when used in soup (Ch. 17).

Shashlyk: Russian version of shish kebabs (Ch. 7).

Shawarma: Thinly sliced chicken as lamb layered tightly with fat and formed into a solid that is grilled vertically on a rotisserie and sliced off in very thin, long slices while still on the skewer (Ch. 11).

Shchi: Cabbage-containing soup made in Russia (Ch. 7).

Shepherd's pie: Deep-dish meat pie made with cooked meat and onions, and topped with a crust of mashed potatoes before baking (Ch. 4).

Shiite: Branch of Islam practiced by those who follow Ali, the prophet's son-in-law (Ch. 12).

Shin sul ro: Korean hot pot (Ch. 18).

Shinto: Early religion of Japan that focused on nature and considered the Emperor to be a descendant of the sun goddess (Ch. 19).

Shiva: Destructive Hindu god, also called *Siva* (Ch. 3).

Shofar: Hollowed out ram's horn blown in the synagogue during Rosh Hashanah to call man to be aware of his shortcomings and to emphasize that God is the divine king (Ch. 3).

Shogun: Term for military rulers in Japan prior to 1867 (Ch. 19).

Shortbread: Very rich, buttery cookie (biscuit) rolled into a circle and cut into wedges before baking (Ch. 4).

Sibelius: Composer from Finland who lived from 1865 to 1957; his most famous orchestral work is *Finlandia* (Ch. 2)

Simon Bolivar. *See* Bolivar, Simon.

Sinhalese: Descendants of Aryans living in Sri Lanka (Ch. 15).

Sinterklaas: Name for Saint Nicholas in the Netherlands (Ch. 6).

Sizzling rice soup: Rice that has formed a crust on the bottom of a wok before being deep-fat fried and then added to a hot broth, causing great sizzling sounds as it is stirred into the soup (Ch. 17).

Slatko: Sweet Serbian dish made of fruit simmered with blossoms in a thick sweet sugar syrup (Ch. 7).

Slivova: Bulgarian plum brandy (Ch. 7).

Slivovitz: Plum brandy liqueur drunk by Czechs and Slovaks (Ch. 7).

Smørgasbørd: Very elaborate Scandinavian buffet with ample arrays of cold foods and hot dishes, as well as dessert choices (Ch. 5).

Smørrebrød: Scandinavian open-faced sandwiches, usually with a base of rye bread and butter and artfully arranged toppings (Ch. 5).

Snow peas: Flat, green peas in tender, crisp, edible pods (Ch. 17).

Soba: Noodles made from buckwheat flour from northern Japan (Ch. 19).

Sofrito: Hot, spicy sauce featuring chilies, tomatoes, garlic, ham or bacon, and coriander (Ch. 21).

Sopa de ajo: Garlic soup popular in Spain (Ch. 10).

Sopa de pescado: Fish soup (Ch. 20).

Sopito: Fish chowder made with coconut milk in the Netherlands Antilles (Ch. 21).

Sosaties: Barbecued pieces of meat on a stick (Ch. 14).

Soufflé: Baked foam of egg whites combined with a yolk and chocolate (or cheese or other flavoring ingredient) sauce (Ch. 9).

Souk: Arab marketplace featuring specific types of shops that sell items such as spices and gold (Ch. 12).

Soul Food Pyramid: Healthy food guide for persons who are lactose intolerant and need to limit fat intake to control weight (Ch. 24).

Southern (Cantonese) school: Designation of cuisine of the southern Chinese that features stir-frying, such dishes as egg rolls, dumplings (dim sum), and pork specialties, as well as generous use of vegetables, rice, and fruits (Ch. 17).

Spanakopite: Main dish consisting of many layers of phyllo, spinach, and various other ingredients according to taste (Ch. 11).

Springerle: Anise-flavored German picture cookie popular at Christmas (Ch. 6).

Spritsar: Swedish ring-shaped cookie often made at Christmastime (Ch. 5).

St. Peter's Basilica: Very large cathedral in the Vatican in Rome (Ch. 8).

Stamp and go: Jamaican dish featuring salted, dried cod suspended in a heavy batter containing chilies, onions, and annatto and fried as a fritter (Ch. 21).

Steak-and-kidney pie: Hearty, savory pie containing pieces of beef steak and kidneys in the filling (Ch. 4).

Stoemp: Mashed potatoes made with plenty of butter, cream, and seasonings in Belgium (Ch. 6).

Stupa: Covered mound, often containing a relic of significance for Buddhists (Ch. 15).

Sudras: Lowest Hindu caste; menial workers (Ch. 3).

Suimono: Clear Japanese soups (Ch. 19).

Sukiyaki: Thinly sliced beef simmered with Japanese vegetables, soy sauce, mirin, and dashi in a pot at the table (Ch. 19).

Sunni: Branch of Islam practiced by those who follow the descendants of the fifth caliph (Ch. 12).

Sunomono: Vinegared salads (Ch. 19).

Sushi: Vinegared rice and small bits of other ingredients pressed into a mold or rolled tightly into a long log encased in a layer of nori and sliced vertically (Ch. 19).

Sukkot: Nine-day Festival of Tabernacles; celebrated five days after Yom Kippur (Ch. 3).

Tabouli: Salad containing soaked bulgur, minced parsley and mint, diced tomatoes, olive oil, and lemon juice (Ch. 11).

Taco: Crisply fried or soft tortilla folded in half over a filling of beans, meats, and other ingredients (Ch. 22).

Tagine: Stew prepared in a round pottery bowl topped with a conical lid (bowl and conical lid also called *tagine*), a unique product of Morocco (Ch. 12).

Tahini: Paste of finely ground sesame seeds, sesame oil, and lemon juice (Ch. 11).

Taj Mahal: Mausoleum built by Shah Jahan in Agra, India, to honor the memory of his favorite wife, Mumtaz (Ch. 2, 15).

Tajaditas: Fried banana chips (Ch. 22).

Tak paesuk: Whole small chicken stuffed with rice, covered in broth, and baked until meat almost falls from bones (Ch. 18).

Talik: The colored mark (often red) that many Hindus wear on the forehead between the eyebrows. (Ch. 3).

Talmud: Authoritative body of Jewish tradition (Ch. 3).

Tamale: Masa harina spread on cornhusk and wrapped around a filling of meat or other ingredients, and then steamed until done (Ch. 22).

Tamils: Descendants of early invaders of Sri Lanka (Ch. 15).

Tandoor: Thick-walled, deep jar-shaped clay oven used for roasting meats and baking naan (Ch. 15).

Tapa: Small plate of tidbits of food designed for nibbling while having a drink in the late afternoon or early evening (Ch. 10).

Taro: Starchy root vegetable that thrives in tropical climates (Ch. 1).

Tarte tatin: Apple tart made by arranging apples neatly in a tart pan and covering with a pastry; tart is inverted after baking (Ch. 9).

Tatars: Mongol invaders who originally gathered military might under Genghis Khan and who conquered Russia under his grandson's leadership (Ch. 7).

Tempura: Batter-coated, deep-fried shrimp and thinly sliced vegetables (Ch. 19).

Theravada: Buddhist sect practiced in Southeast Asia in which monks carry begging bowls in the mornings. (Ch. 3).

Thousand-year egg: Egg (usually duck) preserved by packing them in a lime-clay mixture and storing for between 6 weeks and 100 days, which transforms the white into a very dark, gelatinous material with a slightly fishy taste as the chemicals from the packing penetrate through the shell and throughout the egg (Ch. 17).

Toad-in-the hole: Sausages cooked in a quick-bread batter (Ch. 4).

Tofu (soybean curd): Precipitate formed by adding calcium sulfate to a cooked soybean solution made from water and strained, ground soybeans; may be pressed to form firmer curd (Ch. 17).

Torah: First five books of the Old Testament that are the foundation for Judaism (Ch. 3).

Torii gate: Distinctive gateway to a Shinto shrine (Ch. 19).

Tortiglioni: Spiral-shaped pasta (Ch. 8).

Tortilla: Dough of masa harina (or flour) and water, which is pressed into thin disks and baked (Ch. 22).

Tostada: Fried tortilla filled with beans, meat, chopped vegetables, guacamole, grated cheese, and sour cream; sometimes flour tortilla is fried in the shape of a bowl and filled with the same ingredients (Ch. 22).

Tostone: Twice-fried slice of plantain pounded to be thin before the second frying (Ch. 20).

Transylvania: Region in western Romania bounded by the Carpathian Mountains (Ch. 7).

Treacle: Very thick, sweet molasses (Ch. 4).

Trekboer: Boer who made the Great Trek to settle the interior of South Africa (Ch. 14).

Trifle: Elaborate dessert made in a pretty glass bowl, which has been lined with lady fingers or slices of pound cake and then filled with layers of stirred custard, whipped cream, slivered almonds, and raspberries and generously laced with sherry (Ch. 4).

Truffle: Dark, subterranean fruity body of a fungi; especially rare and flavorful ingredient prized in French recipes (Ch. 9).

Ts'ai: Term designating the various other dishes in a meal that balance the meal with the rice or fan (yin) in the meal; the yang part of the meal (Ch. 17).

Tsetse fly: Vector for sleeping sickness, a very serious disease in parts of West Africa (Ch. 13).

Tsukemono: Pickled vegetables (Ch. 19).

Tuk-kuk: Rice cake soup (Ch. 18).

U.S. Immigration and Naturalization Service: Federal agency responsible for enforcing immigration and naturalization regulations and laws (Ch. 23).

Udon: Noodles made with wheat flour, typical of southern Japan (Ch. 19).

Ugali: Kenyan name for stiff cornmeal porridge (Ch. 14).

Untouchables: Person unworthy of belonging to a caste (Ch. 3).

Vaisyas: Third level Hindu caste; farmers and businesspeople (Ch. 3).

Valdivia: Captain under Pizarro who led the Spanish expansion to Chile from Peru (Ch. 20).

Vasco da Gama: *See* da Gama, Vasco.

Vassilopita: Rich sweet bread containing a good-luck coin to celebrate the New Year (Ch. 11).

Vedas: Four volumes of the collective wisdom on how Hindus must live (Ch. 3).

Velouté: Basic flour-thickened sauce made with a fish or chicken stock (Ch. 9).

Viandas: Generic word used in the Piramide Alimentaria para Puerto Rico to include bland foods high in starch (Ch. 24).

Vishnu: Preserver god of Hindu religion (Ch. 3).

Voodoo: Type of worship found in Haiti based on spells, hexes, and animism traced to African roots (Ch. 21).

Voortrekker: Boer who used oxen and covered wagons to make the Great Trek between 1835 and 1839; also called *trekboer* (Ch. 14).

Wasabi: Finely grated, delicate green horseradish; also available as a powder (Ch. 19).

Wassail: Traditional spiced wine or ale drink served at Christmas in the United Kingdom (Ch. 4).

Water chestnut: Tuber that is sliced and used as a vegetable to add a crisp, distinctive texture; usually available canned (Ch. 17).

Waterzooi: Belgian fish stew (Ch. 6).

Welsh rarebit: Sauce usually made of cheddar cheese and beer that is served over toast or other bread as a main dish (Ch. 4).

Western (Szechwan) school: Designation of cuisine developed in western China, that is quite spicy and hot in character and uses considerable garlic, ginger, and oil (Ch. 17).

West Indies: Islands of the Caribbean, ranging from near Florida to the northeast coast of South America (Ch. 21).

Weiner schnitzel: Traditional Viennese dish consisting of thin veal cutlets dipped in flour, egg, and bread crumbs before being fried in butter (Ch. 6).

Winter melon: Green, oblong melon similar in outward appearance to a watermelon, but with a white, pulpy interior and a seed-filled center (Ch. 17).

Wok: Round-bottomed, two-handled metal pan used for stir-frying or as the container for boiling water to steam food in bamboo steamer trays stacked on the wok (Ch. 17).

Wonton: Small pouch of food wrapped in thin wheat dough (wonton wrapper) and cooked in a broth or deep-fat fried (Ch. 17).

Worcestershire sauce: Pungent sauce made of soy sauce, vinegar, and garlic and used quite universally at British tables; originated in Worcestershire, England pronounced wüs-ta-shir (Ch. 4).

Yang: Positive principle including male, sun, heaven, fire, brightness, good, wealth, and joy; complementary balance to yin (Ch. 17).

Yarmulke: Skullcap worn by Jewish men (Ch. 3).

Yassa: Dish made with lemon-marinated chicken or meat (Ch. 13).

Yin: Passive principle including female, moon, earth, water, darkness, evil, poverty, and sadness; complementary balance to yang (Ch. 17).

Yom Kippur: Day of Atonement; celebration 10 days after Rosh Hashanah (Ch. 3).

Yorkshire pudding: Puffy, crusty pudding baked on meat drippings in a very hot oven; batter is thin egg–milk–flour mixture similar to popover batter (Ch. 4).

Yuca: Sweet cassava; root used as a starch in the tropical regions (Ch. 20).

Zapotec: Indians who developed the city of Monte Alban near Oaxaca in Mexico around 500 BCE (Ch. 22).

Zeljanica: Yugoslavian cheese and spinach pie (Ch. 7).

Zukat: Purifying tax; one of the Five Pillars (Ch. 3).

Recipe Index

Iberian Peninsula

Greece, Turkey, and the Levant

North Africa

West Africa

East and South Africa

India and Its Neighbors

Southeast Asia and Its Islands

China

Korea

Japan

South America

The Caribbean

Central America and Mexico

United States

Subject Index

A

B

D

G

J

K

L

M

N

O

P

T

Y

Z